D1469692

third edition

READINGS IN COST ACCOUNTING BUDGETING AND CONTROL

WILLIAM E. THOMAS, JR., Ph.D.
Professor of Accountancy
College of Commerce and Business Administration
University of Illinois

Published by **SOUTH-WESTERN PUBLISHING COMPANY**

Cincinnati • Chicago • Burlingame, Calif. • Dallas • New Rochelle, N. Y.

A95

PREFACE

Upon consideration of the needs of teachers of cost accounting and budgeting, the Executive Committee of the American Accounting Association concluded that a collection of readings in the field would be extremely helpful. Such a collection could be used to supplement the textbooks by presenting the various, and sometimes contradictory, views of leading practitioners and teachers, and to provide an intellectual challenge to the student. Teachers well know the practical difficulties of assembling and maintaining sufficient copies of periodicals in the library to provide students with an extended series of readings. The assembly of articles in textbook form was thought to be the solution to this problem.

The result of that decision was the publication of the first edition of this textbook in 1955, followed by a revision in 1960. The judgment of the Executive Committee was confirmed by the success of the publication. Since the publication of this textbook is no longer considered a high-risk venture, the American Accounting Association has withdrawn its sponsorship in order to support other endeavors having academic implications.

The basic structure of this edition consists of articles to provide basic background and theory in the areas of planning, control, and income determination, followed by articles treating specific problems arising from the application of the theory to business situations. In the latter group are sections dealing with accounting for product and period costs, organizing the planning and control functions, problems of planning, problems of control, and reports for management.

Inevitably, some of the articles range over more than one of the classifications, and it has been necessary to be quite arbitrary in placing them in the book. Certainly, some of the articles dealing primarily with a problem area contain excellent expositions of theory in the general field of managerial accounting. Frequently articles which deal with planning and control also contain a treatment of reporting for managerial control. However, if the reader is appreciative of these difficulties, it is believed that he will find the general organization of the material a helpful orientation to this large and growing field of managerial accounting.

The criteria for selection of articles were quality and coverage. In every case, the editor looked for a high quality of thought and expression and sought those articles which were intellectually challenging. Coverage was also an important criterion. On the one hand, the editor tried to cover the field of cost accounting, budgeting, and control without making the textbook unduly long. On the other hand, in view of the fact that this textbook is to be used as a supplement to existing texts, a deliberate attempt was made to omit topics which are usually treated at length in the standard texts on cost accounting and budgeting. If the reader keeps in mind the objectives of the textbook, he will not be concerned about what otherwise might be considered "gaps" in the book. Unfortunately, some topics could not be included in the collection because acceptable articles could not be found.

The editor wishes to express appreciation to the many teachers and practitioners who answered questionnaires and letters with suggestions on the organization and content of the textbook. This was of great help in designing a textbook which will be of maximum usefulness to the students and teachers. Special thanks for assistance and encouragement go to Professor Frank P. Smith, President of the American Accounting Association at the time the first edition of this work was begun; Professors C. J. Gaa, Paul Garner, and Wayne Shroyer, who were members of the Executive Committee; and to Mr. Ray Marple, who was Research Director of the National Association of Cost Accountants.

The copyright owners and authors of the articles were most generous in allowing their materials to be reproduced here. Every request to use material was granted.

Since this textbook is intended to convey the views of many authors, it has seemed proper that the editor should not interlace the series of articles with his own interpretative comments. One of the prime functions of the textbook is not only to present stimulating ideas, but also to encourage the reader to make his own interpretation and appraisal of those ideas.

WILLIAM E. THOMAS

CONTENTS

• v •

ARTICLE   PAGE

PART I

BACKGROUND AND THEORY OF ACCOUNTING AND BUDGETING AS MANAGERIAL TOOLS FOR PLANNING AND CONTROL

Cost accounting and budgeting are tools used for planning and controlling the operations of economic enterprises. It is apparent that these tools must be designed for use by managers in performing their tasks of planning and control. It is in this use that the specifications of the tools are found.

Part I comprises readings which were selected to provide a groundwork in the function of management as it relates to the subject at hand.

Planning is essentially the process of arriving at and making decisions. The articles in Section A relate this process to systems and to accounting and then examine decision making in some depth. The integration of cost concepts with the decision process is made and then the idea of the control of planning and, finally, planning by the use of simulation is introduced.

Control is the process of acting in such a way that desired conditions or goal states may be attained and maintained. Articles in Section B of this Part are concerned with the principles of management control. The goals must be set as in a charter of accountability, measurement must be made of performance in relation to accountability, and a system must be established for the feedback of appropriate information to control centers. The information feedback should be of a nature to facilitate planning and decision making which are an inherent part of the control process.

The readings in Part I are to provide a basic framework within which planning and control can be studied more effectively. There is a multitude of problems in implementing these basic concepts. Many are presented in the readings of Section B.

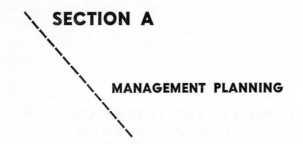

SECTION A

MANAGEMENT PLANNING

Planning involves the selection of a goal or goals and the means of attaining them. When applied to the business firm a problem arises in relating the goals of the firm to the goals of the individual members of the firm. Various theories of the firm bearing upon this critical problem are reviewed and critiqued in the first article. The second article investigates the integral relationship between planning and control and between budgeting and accounting.

One whose task is to facilitate planning by providing relevant information must understand the basic process of decision making. Often more than a one-time choice of an alternative, a decision may be one of a sequence or of several sequences. Decision tree techniques are useful in dealing with such decision problems.

The understanding of decision making leads to an extended but basic consideration of cost concepts for planning purposes. Since project or product planning may be complex and lengthy it may be necessary to devise a system for controlling the planning process.

The last article deals with the need to manipulate easily the elements in plans to test various hypotheses. This may be done by budget modeling and simulation.

I. SOME THOUGHTS ON INTERNAL CONTROL SYSTEMS OF THE FIRM *

Zenon S. Zannetos †

If we were to capture in a few words the changes that have occurred and will occur over the years in the notions of management

* From *The Accounting Review* (October, 1964). Reprinted by permission of the American Accounting Association.

† Zenon S. Zannetos, Associate Professor of Industrial Management, Alfred P. Sloan School of Management, Massachusetts Institute of Technology.

control, we could say, at the danger of oversimplification, that all the progress is embodied in the change from deterministic to probabilistic systems. The elements that we witness today in the organizational and control structures of the firm are neither as haphazard as these may appear to be, nor do these completely defy the rigor of analysis.[1] It may be that some of the changes were employed unconsciously under the pressure of necessity or alternatively instigated deliberately through the power of successful imitation. In either case, however, we can at least arrive at some rational justification of such changes even though *ex post facto*.

As a preparatory step toward the substantiation of the aforementioned assertions, let us first review the two most important deterministic models that purport to describe behavior of productive factors, show their inadequacies, introduce an alternative model of the firm, and then embark into the discussion of the essential elements of control systems. The two models that will be discussed are the economic model of rational action (entrepreneurial theory of the firm), which is underlying the equilibrium of production and exchange,[2] and Taylor's model of rationalization of operations.[3]

CLASSICAL THEORY OF THE FIRM

In classical microeconomic theory (under the entrepreneurial model of the firm), because the factors of production are *in the end result* considered as lacking "will," issues of control and organizational nature do not arise. Not wishing to mislead those who are not familiar with the literature in this field, we hasten to provide here a clarification. We must stress that actually microeconomic theory assumes that people *are fully willful*, rational, and independent agents, all through the process of entering the markets, seeking

---

[1] The analytical aspects of organization structures have been the subject of another paper by the same author entitled "On the Theory of Divisional Structures: Some Aspects of Centralization and Decentralization of Control and Decision Making," *Some Thoughts on the Firm, Its Objectives, Control Process, and Organization Structure*.

[2] The principles underlying the economic model of rational action may be found in any one of many books dealing with the theory of the firm. For example, J. M. Henderson and R. E. Quant, *Microeconomic Theory* (New York: McGraw-Hill Book Co., Inc., 1958); J. R. Hicks, *Value and Capital* (London: Oxford University Press, 1953), Part II; R. G. D. Allen, *Mathematical Economics* (London: Macmillan & Co., Ltd., 1957), Chapter 10.

[3] The main works of Frederick W. Taylor are: *The Principles of Scientific Management* (New York: Harper & Brothers, 1911); *Shop Management* (New York: Harper & Brothers, 1919), and *Scientific Management* (New York: Harper & Brothers, 1947).

appropriate employment, and discharging the responsibilities "demanded by their chosen field of endeavor." In the end result, however, given any type of employment, it would have made no difference at all what *any one* particular individual willed or wanted to achieve. At equilibrium, all are paid the value of their physical productivity, no more and no less, and this value is determined by market forces. Consequently, people are forced to conform by an *external* self-regulating mechanism.

There is also a qualification that must be made concerning the notion of independence. While it is true that all participants in any one market are interdependent, yet to the extent that each agent is so small and there are so many, the behavior of *any pair* of these agents appears to be unrelated. It is only through the impersonal interactions of the markets and within such markets that the agents are "unconsciously" influenced. In other words, while each productive agent appears to be fully willful and pursuing "relatively independent" goals, yet he can exert no perceptible influence by himself. In fact, because of the interactions in the various markets, he is *unconsciously forced* to channel his energies in the best or optimizing manner. Consequently in the end result, at equilibrium, the productive agents appear *to be without any will,* because while being rational they have unconsciously accepted as guiding factors for their behavior the standards imposed upon them by external forces. It is in this sense that rationality becomes objective. If by any chance an individual does not perform according to the established standards, then he is forced out of that particular market and into one where his best performance conforms with expected behavior. This dynamic market mechanism, of course, operates both in cases of relative efficiencies or inefficiencies, and results in *uniformity* at equilibrium.

Under a system of perfect competition, as a result, issues of internal control do not arise. The "price," as determined by the market forces, serves as a perfect informational device and as a feedback control mechanism, to guarantee perfect allocation of resources in a "take it or leave it" situation. This applies not only to final products and services, but also to intermediate factors of production. Consequently, the only control mechanism that one observes in the case of the perfectly competitive equilibrium is purely *external* and not internal.[4]

---

[4] See also our arguments under "Morality, Social Welfare and the Objectives of the Firm," *Some Thoughts on the Firm, Its Objectives, Control Process, and Organization Structure.*

Scientific Management and Comparison with Classical Equilibrium

Taylor's scientific management, if we are to put it harshly, purposefully *attempts to eliminate will* by converting individuals into special purpose machines. Through a study of operations and motions a standard is established, reflecting "the most efficient method performed by the most efficient worker" and made part of the worker's routine. Thus, by surpressing judgment and substituting habit for it, or what is now called programmed behavior, Taylor's theory bases the allocation of human resources on the physiological rather than the cognitive (rationality) limitations of the individual.[5] Consequently, by fitting individuals to tasks (and machines), all the necessary control ingredients are made part of the definition of the task and are carried out automatically. The individuals under such a scheme are "paced by machines," for tasks that they cannot define or change. Consequently, operationally, the people assigned to such tasks *lack will,* and any deviations that occur are assumed to be of purely physiological origin. As a result, control systems for influencing *behavior* are completely unnecessary, because under Taylor's model, multidirectional purposeful behavior is presumed to be absent.

Of course, one can readily see one of the limitations of Taylor's theory in that it is applicable only in the case of programmable tasks, where the physiological inputs are the critical factors for effective performance. Any value judgments and planning under this model are expressed and executed by a master planner.

We therefore see that, although starting from different sets of premises, both classical microeconomic theory and Taylor's scientific management are in the end result alike. Because of the assumptions underlying both of these models, the individual *cannot effectively exercise his will, thus obviating the necessity for internal controls.* In each case, efficiency and deterministic solutions are in the end achieved because of regimentation. This is another illustration of cases where measurement takes place on a circular rather than a linear scale. The two extremes in the end are similar, even though emanating from "diametrically" opposite philosophical arguments.

Another similarity that is worth mentioning between the two models that we briefly analyzed lies in the method by means of which decision making and planning is carried out. In both cases decisions

---

[5] Taylor's experiments included an extensive study of muscle fatigue and of the conditions under which restoration of *total* muscle power is achieved.

and plans are made by a single individual, the entrepreneur or master planner.[6] As a result, *issues of rationality are transformed into special cases of consistency.*

In discussing microeconomic theory of rational action and Taylor's scientific management model, we paid considerable attention to the issue of willfulness. This, of course, was intentional, in order to serve as a point of departure and set the stage for an alternative formulation, which we believe is more in line with present day business realities.

MODERN THEORY OF THE FIRM

The modern theory of the firm, in contrast to the above, emphasizes in its various forms conscious and purposeful cooperative behavior. The latter in some models is depicted as rational, or, as in the case that we will adapt for our purposes here, partly rational.[7] There is one characteristic that all *comprehensive* models have in common, and that is the assumption or necessity for coordinative controls.

We must admit that the necessity for internal control systems of the firm is a highly controversial issue that has been generally contested by people in the human-industrial relations areas. However, a lot of the arguments advanced against controls lie in the sphere of judgmental hypothesis and personal philosophy, and contain little or no analytical foundation. Any empirical evidence that is presented mostly points out the evils of misguided use of the output of control systems, but in no way discredits the notion of managerial controls, in our estimation. Later on in the course of our discussion, we will present some theoretical justifications for internal controls, and also expound in more detail the opposing arguments.

The firm, according to an influential school of organization theorists, is defined as "a group of consciously coordinated activities for the accomplishment of common objectives." [8] Thus, neither the people

---

[6] It may be observed in this context that the critical factor is not so much the monistic (single person) character of the decision, but the conditions that guarantee monolithic decisions and plans. So in effect group decision making is not precluded, unless it leads to nondeterministic decisional situations. Of course, under such circumstances the complete identity group action will often prove to be redundant, and that is why it is assumed to be absent.

[7] For an exposition on this subject, see Chester I. Barnard, *The Functions of the Executive* (Cambridge, Mass.: Harvard University Press, 1938); Herbert A. Simon, *Administrative Behavior* (New York: The Macmillan Co., 1957); and James G. March and Herbert A. Simon, *Organizations* (New York: John Wiley & Sons, Inc., 1958).

[8] Andreas G. Papandreou, "Some Basic Problems in the Theory of the Firm," *A Survey of Contemporary Economics*, ed. B. F. Haley (Homewood, Ill.: Richard D. Irwin, Inc., 1952), Vol. II, pp. 183-219.

that work for a firm nor their actions constitute the organizational entity. The latter is merely the group of activities, and it utilizes, in a consciously coordinated manner, people as phases of conscious cooperation.

With the above definition in mind, we will now proceed to examine its implications, and also its consequences, for the control process of the firm—and all this, in order to assess eventually the requirements imposed upon the "accounting," control systems.

Group Action

Starting with the word "group," we notice that it implies the *necessity* for interaction of more than one activity and individual. Such an interaction, of course, is only necessary because of the inherent definitional assumption that resources, operations, and knowledge are *complementary*, in "the accomplishment of common objectives." But then, what is the meaning of such complementarity and what are its implications? As we will soon appreciate, this notion is a fundamental cornerstone upon which modern organization theory builds, and does indeed have far-reaching implications.

Complementarity. Two or more operations, resources or individual activities are defined as complementary, in the process of pursuing a well-defined goal, or goals, if their combined effort, entering at the right time and in the proper proportions, contributes more to the end result, than the sum of contributions of comparable efforts on an individual and independent basis. Realizing the complexity of this definition, especially for people who never encountered this notion before, we will attempt to illustrate it by using an example that has become over the years a stable item in the repertoire of economists.

We all know of people who drink their coffee with both sugar and cream. If we exclude those aspects of the initial quality of the inputs, that admittedly are very important for a connoisseur, we find that each one of these individuals mixes the given inputs, in the right proportions, in order to achieve what he considers the essence of good coffee. To him, although an avid coffee drinker, a cup of coffee, without the right proportions of sugar and cream, may not be of any greater value than no coffee at all. Next assume that we gave an individual the proper proportions of coffee, cream, and sugar, but instead of mixing them together we asked him to take them separately, one at a time. More often than not, we will find that, for our hypothetical individual, the sum value of the three inputs taken separately, is much less than the value of all three *mutually inter-*

acting and taken together. This is in effect the result of what we call complementarity of resources.

There is another point that is related to the issue of complementarity, however, and which is very important for our later discussion, that needs stressing. Often we find that overutilization of economic resources does not only result in the loss of the extra dose of an input, but also results in disutility. In terms of our coffee-cream-sugar example, if we put more sugar or cream than the prescribed proportions, not only do we waste the extra resource, but also we do not derive as much pleasure as we would have experienced without it. Consequently, cases of extreme complementarity of resources may harbor in them aspects of destructibility.

Specialization. Inherent in the necessity for group action and the complementarity of resources is the issue of specialization, and/or limitation of human capacities. It is obvious that if resources both human and material were of multipurpose nature and there were no capacity limitations, especially with respect to human beings, there would be no necessity for multiresource interaction. Such, however, is not the case. All of us know from empirical observations that resources are complex, and that it is impossible for any one individual to know, both in depth as well as in breadth, all there is to know. Consequently, there arises the need for learning and specialization, and with it emerge interdependencies for the accomplishment of unified goals.

The generation of the proper environment for achieving these advantages of specialization, transmitting information on the results so achieved, and reconciling interdependencies, are part of the requirements of the organizational and control structure of the firm.

Purposeful Behavior

The arguments that we have just presented, relating to the notion of specialization and concerning the limitations of human capacities, must not be confused with issues of *limited rationality* that emanate from purposeful behavior, and to which issues we will now turn.

Modern organization theory assumes that the various individuals, as phases of cooperation, are willful and purposeful participants within, of course, their capabilities. Such an assumption, however, implies also that all the particularities of the various individuals are undoubtedly reflected in their behavior. As a result, disagreements, open conflict, and incompatibilities may arise in an organization, pointing out the necessity for a system that will encourage people to reconcile their differences, give them guides toward such reconciliation, and coordinate their activities for the accomplishment of the goals of the organization.[9] In fact if it were not for these elements that create stabilities in expectations and behavior, there would be no organization at all.

In order that we may be able to appreciate the significance of the requirements that the above mentioned individual characteristics impose upon the control system of an organization, let us briefly examine the type and manifestations of such particularities. Discussions such as this usually appear under the title of limited rationality,[10] and as we have just pointed out, they are the consequence of assumptions of purposeful behavior. Although the various issues that will be taken up separately are in our estimation aspects of the same central notion, yet they harbor particularities that merit individual emphasis. Consequently, the expositional separation should not be taken to imply mutual exclusiveness or independence.

Cognitive Limitations of Individuals. This aspect of limited rationality is based on the biological characteristics of the individual. While no one can claim that all individuals are the same, yet from empirical observations we can also conclude that no one has unlimited capacity. With the complexity of the present day technology of the firm and the extensive economies of specialization (through learning), people are forced, in various degrees, to trade off between depth and breadth. Consequently, at any moment of time, the individual cannot possibly know of all the feasible alternatives in their details, and as a result his decisions cannot be universally-monolithically fully rational as assumed under the classical theory of the firm.[11] That is why deterministic solutions of universal applicability must give way to alternatives of particular probabilistic validity, under environmental constraints.

Differences among Personal Goals. Another consequence of the assumption of purposeful behavior is the possibility of substitution of personal goals for those of the organization as a determinant of

---

[9] We will not be concerned here with the details of such esoteric issues as, for example, how motivation is promulgated and conflict resolved, although it is realized that these issues have a considerable impact on the design of information and control systems. Those interested in the topics of motivation and conflict resolution may wish to consult some of the references given in "On the Theory of Divisional Structures: Some Aspects of Centralization and Decentralization of Control and Decision Making" Footnotes 7 through 11. Also March and Simon, *op. cit.,* Chapters 3, 4, and 5.

[10] March and Simon, *op. cit.,* Chapters 6 and 7.

[11] It is already obvious that although the notion of limited rationality may be universally applicable, yet its manifestation is relative to the environment.

motivation. This substitution, of course, can be either unintentional, because of the lack of proper information as to what the individuals are expected to do and on how their activities contribute toward the overall goals of the organization, or else intentional. The information and control systems of the firm have a vital role to play in both cases, although the nature and difficulty of this role are different, depending on the conditions that necessitate it. If we assume, however, that human nature is inherently good and it is only through ignorance or corruptive influence by the operational environment that misdirection occurs, then the two cases merge essentially into one, and result in unified information-control system requirements. And thus, because preventive, guiding as well as corrective characteristics are the essential elements of any managerial control system.[12]

In cases where honest differences of opinion arise, then we revert to issues of conflict resolution, that obviously cannot be *completely* handled as part of the existing continuous information and control system. The latter can only judge rationality on the basis of consistency with the objectives of the firm. Its premises can be challenged, however, by the conflict, and changes may result as a consequence of such challenge in an adaptive manner.

Out of our discussion emerges an awareness that merits emphasis, and it concerns the *relativity of the notion of rationality*. Once we deviate from the deterministic setting of the perfectly competitive equilibrium, we can no longer claim the existence of monolithic standards of rationality. Everything is relative to the specific situation, and can only be judged in terms of its probabilistic impact on the overall objectives of the firm and the behavior that is postulated for the successful pursuit of such objectives. This awareness foretells the changes through which the control systems of the firm must undergo in order to become of real aid to management in decision making and measurements.

Satisfactory versus Optimal Alternatives. Although this discussion may be considered as a part of the issue of "cognitive limitations," yet we choose to treat it separately in order to stress certain aspects of the overall topic of boundaries to rationality.

A consequence of the assumption of cognitive and capacity limitations is the compartmentalization of tasks in order to simplify them and make them manageable. Because of this presumed preference toward simplification of problems, people may stop once they find an

---

[12] Our use of the term control system is much more comprehensive than usual. It includes planning, information dissemination, and feedback control.

acceptable alternative rather than continue searching for an optimum. This is what March and Simon call satisficing behavior.[13]

Challenging Simon's claims, Charnes and Cooper [14] considered the extent of search as an investment decision. Consequently, under their assumptions and formulation, an individual does not stop searching because he satisfices (does not have the courage to optimize), but because the expected cost of such search is greater than the expected returns. Thus they converted satisficing into an optimizing behavior.

The above arguments were presented just for background and not because they bear different implications on control systems. It is obvious that both the satisficing as well as the search-optimizing model depend on subjective elements that are not amenable to deterministic quantitative generalizations for evaluating behavior. These particular elements are, in the satisficing model, the capacity of the individual to deal with complex situations and, in the other, the subjective probabilistic distributions that determine the particular marginal considerations. For information-control system design, however, as we previously stressed, the cases merge. We are interested in providing as much information for estimation as the expected benefit can justify. Consequently, whether this will result in a better solution because of optimal search effort allocation, or because of simplification of the problem setting, is rather immaterial. There is one thing that we must emphasize, however, that given any situation demanding resolution, the "feasible" alternatives as a result of the aforementioned assumptions multiply extensively, and so do the demands on the information-control systems of the firm.

Time, Uncertainty, and Sequential Decisions. Another consequence of purposeful behavior, closely related to the three that we have already mentioned, emanates from the introduction of the time element. The latter, of course, in turn introduces more indeterminism and uncertainty, characteristics of any realistic theory of the firm.[15]

Over time people learn, thus increasing their capacity to deal with more complex situations, but also discover alternatives of whose existence they were not aware before. Consequently, sequential decision making is encouraged—for partial elimination of uncertainty—and adaptive behavior results, complicating the process of evaluation

[13] *Organizations, op. cit.*, p. 169; also Herbert A. Simon, *Administrative Behavior, op. cit.*, pp. 61-109.

[14] A. Charnes and W. W. Cooper, "The Theory of Search: Optimum Distribution of Search Effort," *Management Science*, Vol. 5, No. 1 (October, 1958).

[15] For a challenging presentation on the impact of time on economic measurements, see: G. L. S. Shackle, *Time in Economics* (Amsterdam: North-Holland Publishing Company, 1958).

of the efficiency of decisions on an *a priori* basis. Even a realistic
ex post evaluation is in many cases impossible, because there is no
way of storing all the feasible alternatives and tracing their consequences in parallel for eventual comparisons. This does not necessarily imply, however, that a good start may not be had by designing a
system capable of tracing the probabilistic consequences of *some*
alternatives, together with the projections of the environment that
governs their success and failure.

Conscious Coordination

It is for all the above reasons, that is to say the consequences of
the necessity for group action and the assumptions of purposeful
behavior, that conscious coordination is indispensable.

Even in the case of material resources—which are lacking will—
however, there is a necessity for a coordinative control system. For
as we have previously mentioned,[16] in order to realize the potentials
of complementary resources, a firm must use these resources in the
right proportions. Furthermore, economies of scale, through specialization and fixities in material resources, introduce complementarities
and interdependencies *over time*,[17] further pointing out the necessity
for conscious coordination.[18]

In brief then, coordination and control are necessary for two
general reasons: first of all because of the limited capacities and
bounded rationality of human beings; and second because of the complementarity of specialized resources that complicated technological
requirements dictate.

Common Objectives

It is usually assumed by social psychologists that the individual
is motivated by self-interest. If that is the case, then empirical evidence implies that there are enough similarities between the drives
of each and every individual and the firm for the establishment of

---

[16] See the arguments presented under "Group Action," "Complementarity,"
and "Specialization."

[17] One of the two main reasons behind the economies of scale is the natural
efficiency of size. For discussion see E. H. Chamberlin, "Proportionality, Divisa-
bility, and Economies of Scale," *Quarterly Journal of Economics* (February,
1948), pp. 229-62. Also on other aspects of the same problems, especially the
interdependencies that are introduced over time, see J. M. Clark, *Studies in the
Economics of Overhead Costs* (Chicago: The University of Chicago Press, 1923)
and E. A. G. Robinson, *The Structure of Competitive Industry* (Cambridge:
Nisbet and Co., Ltd., 1953).

[18] It is interesting to note here the elements of conflict in designing the
organizational structure of the firm. We readily see that the complementarity of
specialized resources requires centralization while the *process* of specialization
and learning requires decentralization. For more on this see "On the Theory
of Divisional Structures, etc."

a common ground. For if not, then the individual will be unable to identify his egotistic objectives with those of other individuals and the firm, and therefore there can be no effective coordination.[19]

Again in the area of individual commitment to the goals of the firm, the organization and control structures of the firm play a very important role. For it is through these systems that tasks are defined, their value judgment content placed in the proper perspective, and information on such communicated to the various individuals entrusted with the accomplishment of the various tasks. Since a greater range of *relative rationality* is required at high hierarchical levels, a matching process of tasks and people must take place. The amount of value judgment that an individual is allowed to exercise in the process of performing his activities must be a function of:

1. The range of an individual's mental capacities.
2. The degree of identification between his personal motives and goals of an organization.
3. The capabilities of a person to conceive and perceive relations between environmental factors affecting his task setting and the task itself.
4. The individual's projective insights and adaptability to the uncertainties of the planning horizon that is an integral part of task characteristics.

We have implied in the above discussion that the organization structure of the firm and the control system must impose *relative* limitations (ranges) on the freedom of the individual. This we know will be seriously challenged by human relations experts who advocate self-control and self-direction, and who, more often than not, do not qualify such statements and thus present them as universally applicable.

The questions that remain unsatisfactorily unanswered by many advocates of universal self-control, and which need to be answered before one can accept these propositions, and become a convert, include the following:

1. How are the objectives defined and how are these broken up into subobjectives?
2. Who defines what?
3. How do people know what they are supposed to do? Are they *assigned* tasks, or do they define their task independently of anything else? How is coordination achieved?
4. What is the role of the organizational structure of the firm and what are the determinants of divisionalization?

---

[19] See also the discussion on "Morality, Social Welfare and the Objectives of the Firm," *op. cit. Some Thoughts.* . . .

5. How does a firm solve the problem of differences in the mental capacities of individuals?

6. How does a firm take advantage of the complementarities of resources, and the economies of scale and specialization through learning?

It appears to us that the validity of the claims made by the students of human relations *is limited to marginal considerations in well-defined situations;* that is to say, the statements should imply that given a task and other things equal, *relative* self-control is desirable. The important thing, of course, is not to criticize, but to understand why the situation became what it was, always knowing when motivated by sentiment and when by objectivity. Alternatively, the statements made by these people may refer to a bygone era of an enterpreneurial economy, under which the owner made all the decisions and took the initiative, while his employees performed purely repetitive and independent tasks. But is this realistic in view of the extensive group decision making, technical and technological processes, interrelationships, and uncertainty that govern present day operations? Or is this another case of the "fallacy of composition" where partial observations have no transfer validity for the total firm?

In our estimation, to stress it again, the necessity for control systems can be proved on the basis of the notions and various dimensions of limited rationality and economies of scale-complementarity of resources. Such a justification we have attempted to provide in our previous arguments, and hopefully have made some progress in this direction.

SUMMARY

To summarize, we have initially examined the implications and shortcomings of two important deterministic models, that of the classical theory of the firm and Taylor's model of rationalization of operations. We have shown that under their assumptions, neither one necessitates any internal control systems, because the individuals are unconsciously influenced to allocate their efforts optimally. Then we have examined an alternative model that emphasizes conscious coordination of activities for the accomplishment of common objectives. The firm according to this model is viewed as a group of resources (people usually) that are brought together for the accomplishment of a common goal or an array of goals. These people are considered as willful agents with different degrees of rationality and capable of making value judgments. Consequently one cannot automatically assume that their behavior is "optimizing," but must find ways of guaranteeing that the behavior of each and everyone of these willful agents is consistent with the overall objective or objectives. That is one important place where the necessity of conscious coordination and control of activities enters. If people are left alone they will attempt to maximize what they perceive to be in their own best interest. If this happens to coincide with the interests of the firm well and good, otherwise the objectives of the firm are superseded by the interests of the individuals which may in themselves be conflicting.

No one can honestly claim that a firm will succeed in enforcing an absolute identity between its goals and those of its employees. This problem is not unlike the one that has been plaguing the economists in their efforts toward maximizing social welfare. There is no doubt, however, that the firm can influence the direction as well as the magnitude of its employee's efforts. It would be quite disappointing, not only to managers but also to us as educators of managers, if we were to find out that managerial skills as well as complicated control systems can do nothing to change the particular behavior and range of rationality of an individual.

As a consequence of the assumption that the output of the firm is the result of consciously coordinated activities, motivation, information, learning, and remedial action are among the critical inputs at the disposal of the firm. Organizational structures can facilitate or inhibit the effective utilization of the aforementioned inputs. Accounting control can perform the very vital and sensitive task of communicating information on the objectives to be accomplished, providing a standard for motivating efficient behavior and finally providing means for the evaluation of performance, learning, and instigation of remedial action. Evaluation is important not so much for rewarding or penalizing individuals and operations, but for *a posteriori* learning, with the aim toward more efficient decisions.

Since we have assumed that proper "control" aims at communicating information, evaluating performance, and motivating efficient behavior, then we must devise a system such that the information communicated is the most relevant to the task to be performed, and that the performance we are evaluating is the result of the person being evaluated. Only then can we hope to motivate efficient behavior. Realizing, however, the nondeterministic nature of managerial activities, and aware of the existence of excessive complementaries among skills and operations, both at any moment of time and over time, we are convinced that future control systems will be probabilistic, providing explicitly for both environmental factors and patterns of interactions among resources, be these material or human.

2. THE FUNCTIONAL CYCLES OF ACCOUNTING AND MANAGEMENT *

Chester F. Lay †

Mankind's need for independent inspection and frank criticism of prevailing current viewpoints and human activities has been provided over the centuries by institutions for the moment deemed to be free from influences upon which judgment was to be passed. Perhaps today in the practical matters involving business activities, the profession of accountancy may perform this necessary function of independent inspection for our economy through the exercise of competence, integrity, and frankness.

It is increasingly recognized that public accountancy is largely independent professionally and that in every individual enterprise there is an important place and work for accountancy apart from the production, commercial, or even financial activities of operating management.

Yet there is a still more important matter, to which this article addresses itself. Accountancy, like management, achieved its standing as our economic world became more and more complex. What is the *relationship* between the two fields and the personnel which man them? Staff and advisory workers are of the analytic and planning type whether working on legal problems, industrial relations, or accounting work. But the typical line management executive tends toward the extrovert, for the self-conscious essence of management is "getting things done." Is accounting separate from management, a critical outsider? Is it within management, a subordinate service? Is it within management but not of it, a paralleling intelligence considering results and prospects with a lesser degree of impulse and a greater degree of reserve and calculation than those who must act can properly do?

The writer believes that each of these three alternatives is suggestive of a portion of the truth but that none of them is wholly

* From *N.A.C.A. Bulletin* (June 15, 1949). Reprinted by permission of the National Association of Cost Accountants.

† Chester F. Lay, Professor of Accounting and Management, Southern Methodist University, Dallas, Texas.

accurate. At the very least, operating management is heavily dependent on accountancy—more so than it is generally aware of—for operating facts and a steadying hand. I believe that if we streamline management to its essentials and do the same for accounting, it will be seen that accounting functions or activities actually parallel the prime functions of management.

THE CYCLE OF MANAGEMENT

In demonstrating this parallelism, which may turn out to make it clear that management and accounting are alter egos of somewhat different but balancing mental attitudes and temperaments, it will help to devote attention first to the management function. The soundest managers realize that whoever performs the unique work of guidance is in fact a manager. Administration is the task of guiding group action to single objectives.

The managerial activity as a whole includes five phases, or "life processes." First, logically, is the determination of policies, the purposes or goals of the joint efforts of all participants in the enterprise and the principal methods to be followed in their achievement. Second comes the breakdown of the activities or operations necessary to put the policies into effect. This is the process of organization for operation, including the selection of personnel. The third phase comprises the issuance of directions or instructions to the personnel to put the business in motion toward its goals. Fourth, there is the necessary supervision over those who have been given directions, in order to inspect results while action is taking place or immediately afterward. The last process is the judging or appraising of accomplishments, including a sort of judicial review of the four preceding management activities themselves so that, if the policies laid down for the operating cycle have not proved to be wise, they can be corrected or discarded in the *next* cycle of operations. Likewise the organization structure and organization principles followed may need revision, the directions may need to be made more clear, and the methods of supervising workers may need improvements.

These five managerial tasks must *all* be done and sound reasoning requires that for best results they be done in the order stated. Policy must precede and make possible organization, after which directions can be issued, making possible in turn the supervision of the operations through which the policy objectives are realized. These are followed finally by careful study and review of the complete operating

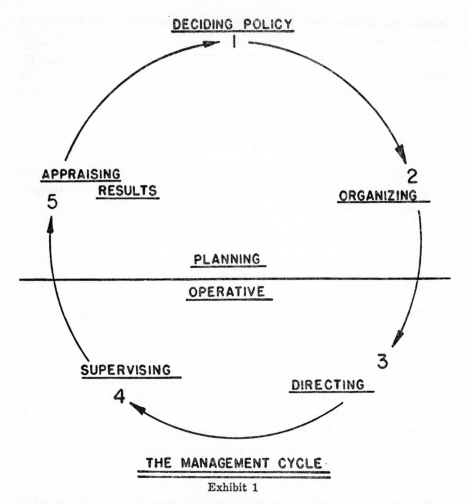

THE MANAGEMENT CYCLE

Exhibit 1

cycle as an appraisal of success or failure. Then the cycle repeats, beginning again with policy formation. Possibly a wheel chart, Exhibit 1, can best show this graphically. If three dimensions could be used, a spiral would do even better and would suggest improvement in management technique, with each full cycle. Of course all analysis, and especially graphic analysis, tends to oversimplify any complex matter. Nevertheless, this representation of the elements of management or guidance, however static or simplified, contains the truth on which we need to keep our attention focussed as we approach an analysis of the accounting function.

But, first, how does the concept of levels in management correlate with the policy, organization, direction, supervision, and appraisal cycle?

Actually managers on each level are likely to engage to some extent in every phase of management from time to time. Also some problems faced by management may involve two or more phases simultaneously. It should likewise be kept in mind that there are levels within each of the five cycle phases of management. For example, the president's decisions upon matters of organization will usually be wider in scope, number of personnel involved, and permanence of the decision than will the organization decisions by the superintendent of the power plant. Again, before proceeding to the nature of accounting, attention is drawn to the horizontal line on Exhibit 1 separating the active and less active elements of the cycle. Management includes both advance planning and operative execution of plans and—as we shall see—so does accounting.

THE CYCLE OF ACCOUNTING

The description and analysis given of the work of managers may not seem at first thought to tend toward the case here being made or even to involve any close cooperation with accounting or accountants. Actually, however, the relationship is very close. Condensing the multifarious activities of accounting into essential types, we have the same number, five, as in management. Arranged in time sequence of their performance, they are, simply stated:

1. The design of accounting systems for recording and reporting business operations, properties, and obligations. Without this, the organization remains, so to phrase it, speechless.

2. Recording within this deliberately created accounting system the physical and financial costs and other facts needful for operation and management of the enterprise including the obligation to inform investors and others. Here the accountant himself is directing a necessary portion of operations.

3. Auditing, both internal and external, the true inspection function, which may be especially effective within the enterprise itself when done close to the point and time of the operations being checked but including also verification of the financial reports. Without this medium of control all phases of *supervising* may be substantially inoperative.

4. Analyzing and interpreting cost and financial statements to the executives and others concerned, including recommendations and advisory services. In this lies the material of appraisal.

5. Budgeting and standard cost work are often centered in the chief accounting officer. In relation to management, budgeting work of the accountant typically includes the basic assembly of facts for virtually all policy decisions which management makes.

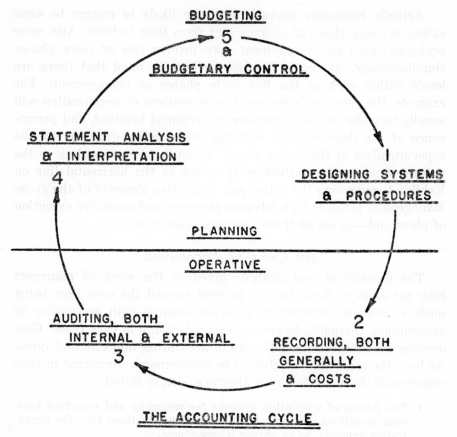

THE ACCOUNTING CYCLE

Exhibit 2

Exhibit 2 does for these elements of corporation accounting activity what Exhibit 1 does for the elements of management proper. Exhibit 2 shows the cycle of accounting, beginning with system design which makes possible recordative accounting (including cost records and summaries) and which enables auditing to be performed. These three elements are then followed by statement analysis and finally by budgeting work, completing the first cycle and leading to the next. That these five types of accounting work are in fact essentially as different as they are in turn dependent on each other is indicated by the emphasis of budgeting and system design upon the future, record keeping upon the present, and of auditing and statement analysis upon the past. Again as in the analysis of the management cycle, the horizontal line on Exhibit 2, dividing the more active from the less active elements, may be noted.

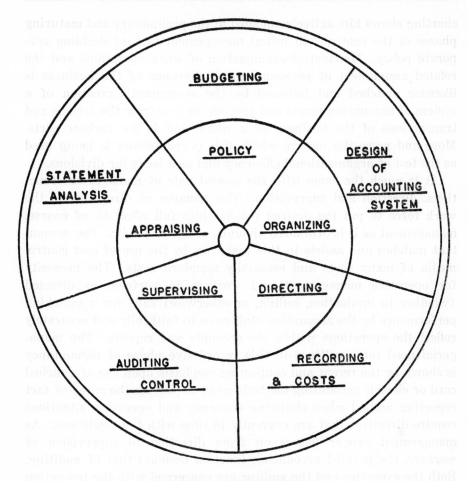

SUGGESTED INTEGRATION
OF
MANAGEMENT CYCLE & ACCOUNTING CYCLE

Exhibit 3

CORRELATION OF ACCOUNTING AND MANAGEMENT ACTIVITIES

The effect of the representation in Exhibit 3 is to put together and in relationship the accounting functions shown in Exhibit 2 and the management functions shown in Exhibit 1. The first two elements of management have been identified as policy determination and organization. The manager's beginning task of policy determination is matched by the accountant's task in the formulation of budgets and in assisting at budget policy councils for as James O. McKinsey has insisted, the budget is in fact only policy expressed in figures. Certainly the accountant's use of flexible budgeting and break-even charting shows him actively engaged in the preliminary and maturing phases of the central and initial management task of deciding corporate policy. Managerial organization of work operations and the related assignment of personnel to all divisions of the business is likewise matched and followed by the accountant's creation of a system of accounting forms and procedures to mirror the actions and transactions of the business as a whole and in its various parts. More and more the picture which this mirror shows is being used as the test of organizational efficiency and as a basis for divisions.

It is much the same with the second pair of management functions, direction and supervision. The issuance of directions to the work force to put the desired policies into full effect is, of course, management as it is ordinarily thought of by the public. The accountant matches and assists in this task, too, by the use of cost control media of many sorts and especially standard costs. The necessity for operative management and workers to perform as directed (whether in production, selling, or otherwise) calls for a matching performance by the accounting staff so as to faithfully and accurately reflect the operations within the accounts and reports. The managerial need for excellence in this recordative phase of accountancy is shown by the recent and continuing emphasis upon use of punched card or electric accounting methods so as to provide the speed of fact reporting needed when changing economic and operating situations require directives that are currently in tune with the conditions. As management proper passes on from direction to supervision of workers, the parallel accounting function becomes that of auditing. Both the executive and the auditor are concerned with the inspection function in its purest aspect and with the fact of performance or nonperformance under controls.

There remains of the management tasks the one we have designated as appraising results. All operative and management activities must be brought into review and judgment must be reached as to their effectiveness or failure and the consequent health and strength of the enterprise. In this field, the accountant has developed perhaps even further than the manager. Certainly accounting statement analysis of balance sheet, profit or loss, and related reports, are almost universally in use by top management and boards of directors and are perhaps the principal medium of review. The mutuality of interest in this final work of accountants and corporation management is highlighted by the current vigorous debate as to whether profits of American corporations have been overstated for 1948 because of accounting failure to enter in the reports an adjustment for the shrinking value of the dollar. Certainly corporate policy on such matters as expansion, dividends, and wage increases requires the use of all analysis and appraisal techniques available and currently depends on those of the accountant.

Accounting Is Part and Parcel of Management

Accounting has made its greatest contribution by helping executives of business corporations set our civilization on a high economic level by maintaining control over multifarious and complex activities, often widely separated geographically, which otherwise might well have been torn apart by centrifugal forces. There is justification for pride by both in the high accomplishments of "our business civilization" under their guidance.

As we have seen, this is true not simply by way of generalities, nor is accounting, although a service function, at the elbow of management in the role of servitor. The role is rather that of alter ego. Through the processes and techniques of accounting properly applied, management is not merely informed. Its thinking is provided with standards of reference, vehicles of judgment, and forms in which to express these judgments and to effect changes. The accountant is an integral part of the personality of management.

3. THE DECISION PROCESS
IN ADMINISTRATION *
Robert D. Calkins †

STEPS IN DECISION MAKING

The businessman seldom knows how he makes decisions any more than the golfer knows how he makes a good drive. A query by *Fortune* sometime ago brought forth responses ranging from "I don't know" to "Every time I stop to think I make a mistake." We all know that countless decisions are made by time and neglect. I recall the advice of a college dean some years ago: "Don't be concerned about it; if it's important enough, someone will do something about it."

Some decisions are made by custom and tradition. Others are made in response to pressures, or to escape other current difficulties, or to emulate others—or for less certain reasons, both relevant and irrelevant. Many decisions are essentially negotiated. They involve so many people, agencies, and points of view that the process of getting assent to a course of action almost defies description, and the reasons are too hidden and complex to be traced. But in spite of much bad and much complex decision making, it can be demonstrated that in many affairs, and especially in industry, we have moved a long way toward a more conscious deliberative appraisal of problems in an effort to improve results. It is this process that I wish to consider in some detail.

However much they may be obscured or circumvented in practice, there are five general steps inherent in the process of rational decision making. They are (1) to identify the problem and understand it; (2) to define or clarify the goals sought; (3) to pose alternatives for the attainment of those goals; (4) to analyze the anticipated consequences of each major alternative; and (5) to appraise the alternatives and choose. Let me elaborate.

* From *Business Horizons* (Fall, 1959). Reprinted by permission of the Foundation for Economic and Business Studies, Indiana University.

† Robert D. Calkins, President of the Brookings Institution, Washington, D. C.

Identify the Problem

Identifying the problem sounds like a simple task and sometimes it is; but most problems have to be discovered as well as defined. A plant breakdown presents a problem, but to anticipate and forestall a breakdown of operations calls for warning systems that notify in time to identify the problem and to take action. In business, elaborate reporting systems are established so that current activities may be compared with standards of satisfactory performance. Note that I say standards of *satisfactory* performance—for the criterion is not a maximum performance, as the economist assumes, but something less than that, which is more readily attainable and acceptable to the participants.

In the flow of events, the administrator has to be alert to know whether a problem is developing. An event occurs, perhaps outside the enterprise. Until its meaning is known, its import to the management cannot be diagnosed. Management must have an elaborate system of communications to detect and interpret such developments.

The interpretation of events is one of the major tasks in the application of knowledge. Its importance was suggested by Lincoln in his "House Divided" speech, when he said, "If we could first know where we are, and whither we are tending, we could better judge what to do, and how to do it." As those who try to interpret day-to-day developments in business know, the import of a present situation is rarely easy to detect.

When we ask for the meaning of some event, the scholar is disposed to explain it by showing how it arose, what caused it, and why. But for the practical man this is the smaller share of what he needs to know. He must know the future potentialities of the event, what it is likely to lead to. Since that usually cannot be forecast reliably, he wants to know the event's capabilities, what it *could* lead to and *how*, under *what* conditions. Thus, he wants past experience distilled to yield not just broad universal generalization but also a great many special conclusions about how and why things behave as they do in different specified conditions. This will be of practical use to him. In biology, we have classified and systematized such knowledge far better than we have even tried to do in the social sciences. Vast amounts of information can be found about the behavior under different conditions of nearly every known form of life. Little such systematized knowledge exists in the social sciences.

For many years, the prevailing view in management was that if we got the facts, the solution would be indicated. It was supposed that if the facts were obtained and analyzed, the cause of a problem would become evident; and by treating the cause, we would solve the problem. But few problems are resolved so simply.

In the first place, getting the facts is often a large investigation in itself. What are the facts and the dimensions of the problem of waste in a plant, or in a university, or in our foreign aid program? To discover this calls for a major investigation. When the facts are known, the causes of the difficulty are usually not apparent and must be discovered, often by testing hypotheses and experimentation. And when the causes are found, the question still remains: Are they the strategic factors through the control of which, or modification of which, a more favorable set of conditions can be created that will yield the results desired?

Thus, the cause of a problem may be morale of staff, and the remedy may be a wholly different system of mechanization. My chief point, however, is that detecting, analyzing, and understanding problems represents an elaborate and diverse process about which we know relatively little. We probably do it badly, but no one knows.

Define Goals

It is necessary next to define and clarify goals. The administered organization ordinarily has fairly clear continuing purposes and goals. Yet these are never wholly given; they are administratively set and then are reaffirmed or neglected as time passes. The top administrators in charge inevitably give import to this system of goals and values, emphasizing some and deemphasizing others. Any change in leadership is watched for its effect on that vague but well-sensed system of purposes, goals, and values by which the participants are expected to operate. One of the complaints in the early Eisenhower subcabinet was that no one ever told the members what the administration was *for* or what its operating philosophy was to be. That they had to discover from experience.

Within an organization, however, problems seldom come with solutions or clear goals attached. The decision maker must define the specific objective that will yield the larger goals of the enterprise without excessive cost or other disadvantages. Such goals are not final; they are instrumental. From above they are seen as but means to an end; from below they are purposes to be achieved. The structuring of instrumental goals is inherent in all administration.

Here the social scientist has let the man of affairs down badly. For the scholar has abjured the study of goals as beyond the range of scientific purity. All but a few of the most general goals that the administrator sets are instrumental goals to some more ultimate purpose. His task is therefore that of choosing systems of intermediate ends and means that meet acceptable standards of efficiency. Though the administrator does exercise value judgments in affirming or reshaping the purposes of the organization and the standards it will follow, a great deal of this so-called goal-setting is basically an economic problem of finding and choosing the most economical course of action for the attainment of desired ends.

One is inclined to suspect that the social scientist shies away from many of these tasks not because they require value judgments but because they involve judgment and responsibilities for choice under highly uncertain conditions. It may be that a mistaken judgment arising from uncertainty, more than a mistaken choice of values, is what the social scientist fears. In any event, this whole area is an unexplored wilderness at the heart of every center of economic life. We have not yet learned how to think about goals, or how we structure them, or how ends and ancillary values become the criteria for appraising and judging alternative courses of action. No area of social science related to administration is in quite so primitive a state as this area of how to think about goals and how to organize them.

Discuss Alternatives

The posing of alternative courses of action for consideration is perhaps the most creative aspect of decision making. But we must not overestimate the creativity actually shown. More ideas are in fact copied from other known experience than are generated *de novo*. A common practice is to discover what others do in similar situations and then do likewise or adapt such practices. Much effort is often expended on surveys to find out what practices are followed, while too little effort is ordinarily expended to discover which practices yield the best results; the latter involves the adoption of a standard, appraisal, and judgment. Simon has pointed out that alternatives are not given, they must be sought; and no administrator explores all alternatives, he explores at best only a few.[1]

Now we may ask how the administrator decides to rule out some practices and to consider others. With an objective defined and

---

[1] Herbert A. Simon, *Administrative Behavior* (2d ed.; New York: The Macmillan Co., 1957), pp. 67, 81; and Richard M. Cyert, Herbert A. Simon, and Donald B. Trow, "Observation of a Business Decision," *The Journal of Business*, XXIX (October, 1956), p. 237.

various standards of ethical conduct established as policy, a quick appraisal will show that some alternatives will not serve the combination of ends desired. Others will be found to violate ethical or other policy criteria and hence are ruled out. Still others are too uncertain and undependable to warrant adoption. Some will seem promising; but to be effective, they would require other changes that are undesirable. After considering a number of alternatives in a preliminary way, several may survive for more careful analysis and appraisal—or better proposals must be thought of that deserve serious consideration.

Analyze Consequences

The fourth step is to analyze the consequences of each of the principal alternatives. At this point, the social scientist is inclined to revive his interest, for he believes that his science can predict consequences—at least under specified conditions. The task soon proves formidable, however, for the social scientist cannot foretell the actual conditions that will prevail in the future. He finds it risky to assume them. Moreover, he finds that the administrator's problem is to foresee consequences under any of several possible conditions that may prevail. Here the social scientist is likely to retreat, insisting that since he cannot predict future conditions, he cannot reliably predict consequences. He cites an established dogma to this effect, and he believes it. He therefore insists that he should leave the whole matter to the administrator who, in his sloppy way, is expected to operate in the loose and unscientific manner required.

But I wonder if social scientists have really given this process the attention it deserves. The literature claims predictive powers for social science but none for social scientists in the real world. I wonder if the problem of prediction is properly represented? As I have observed, administrators do not *predict* the future; they postulate it, and ask how a given course of action will work and what results it will have under those postulated conditions. For example, by projection or extrapolation, they postulate a continuation of business about as it has been, using this or last year as a model for the future, or they assume a rate of growth or a recession in line with recent experience. But prudent administrators seldom risk a major decision on the basis of results expected under only one set of postulates. They also ask how this course of action will work if we have a war, or a depression, or a boom. They postulate a number of contingencies and consider the consequences under each. They may, and sometimes do, fail to postulate the most likely future or the future that is later realized, but their several efforts are intended to come fairly close to any set of conditions that may emerge.

On this basis, the social scientist could be more effective in exercising his abilities in tracing out consequences under alternative models of prospective conditions. Strangely, he has seemed reluctant to do this. One difficulty, I suspect, is his preconception that he must come up with a judgment for one course of action as superior to all others, when in fact there may be no such clear preference as between several alternatives serving slightly different objectives in contingent futures.

Some will argue that there remain for the social scientist, even under a postulated future, insurmountable uncertainties rendering any statment of consequences too tentative for reliable choice. This indeed is a problem, and yet the administrator has ways of dealing with uncertainties. He does not insist on the impossible. He is accustomed to dealing with crude information having a wide margin of error. He is even accustomed to acting without information, if act he must. But he has devices of protection. He adopts measures that permit adjustment to change on what is now called the feedback principle. He operates with some slack that allows him flexibility for adjustment to unforeseen developments. He allows a margin of safety in his profit objectives; he keeps personnel for possible future use even when he may not need it currently; he builds up a cash account for uncertainties, reserves of space, personnel, sources of raw material, and a host of arrangements that permit adjustments on short notice. He asks his lawyer to keep him out of commitments that in possible contingencies could be costly. He keeps his policies flexible and adjustable. The administrator spends a good deal of his time reviewing contingencies and building precautions against them into his commitments and his operating system. I suggest that social scientists have made the problem seem more unmanageable than in fact it is, and I suspect that this derives from our failure to look at the process carefully.

To return to the analysis of consequences for a moment, we may ask how the analyst applies scientific knowledge. He uses the concepts, skills, and techniques of the scientist, of course. He may use scientific generalizations or established knowledge of relationships as major premises for deducing *a priori* conclusions. More often, I suspect, he employs such general knowledge of experience to suggest hypotheses to be checked for consistency against other knowledge.

But precisely how he uses the body of scientific knowledge available to him is again an unexplored region.

In spite of all that is assumed about the uses and applications of formal scientific knowledge (and here I refer mainly to the social sciences), the literature is strangely devoid of explanation of just what is meant by application and how it is done. We all apply such knowledge; but I suspect that if we examined how we do it, we would be astonished at how different the process is from what we assume it to be. And most of us would be surprised at how flimsy and inadequate our methods are. Our confidence in the results would surely be shaken. But I know of no way to improve this process until we understand what is done and wherein the defects are serious.

Appraisal and Choice

The appraisal of alternatives is the fifth stage in the process of decision making that requires scrutiny. The several alternatives chosen for consideration are presumably selected because of their capacity to yield the results desired. But there are always incidental and secondary consequences to consider and, moreover, some courses of action ordinarily yield the desired results more effectively than others. Hence, the several alternatives must be appraised.

The more promising alternatives at this stage have usually passed the test of scientific validity. On the basis of known causal relationships, they are expected to yield the results intended. They have also, as a rule, passed the test of ethical principle and established policy. They are acceptable on ethical and policy grounds. The final choice depends, then, on how well the alternatives serve the objectives of the enterprise or agency with regard to benefits and costs.

The consequences of several alternatives are accordingly compared with the results desired or considered acceptable. These results and requirements become the criteria, or norms, against which comparisons are made. At times, modifications will be made in the proposed courses of action to yield better results and to avoid undesired consequences. The case for and against each alternative may finally be summarized in pros and cons. But it should be noted that pros are consequences regarded as beneficial, and cons are consequences judged to be unfavorable. Moreover, the pros and cons for no one alternative alone afford a basis for choice, for the relevant choice is not to accept or reject a given alternative; it is to accept the most favorable alternative among those available. Thus, it is important to be reasonably sure that the most promising alternatives are considered and appraised.

The choice itself is an act of judgment; it amounts to a commitment if the decision is final, and it is therefore a judgment of high importance. But wherein does judgment enter?

In the earlier consideration of alternatives, a judgment is made that each alternative chosen for study will yield reasonably well the primary results desired, and each alternative is judged acceptable by the ethical and policy standards of the enterprise as administered. A judgment is also made as to the consequences to be expected from each chosen course of action under postulated conditions. In the final appraisal, a judgment is made as to how well the consequences approximate the desired objectives and which alternative offers the most favorable combination of results. Some of these judgments are reasonably objective; others are influenced more by personal value systems.

The choice of a course of action often is not final, but must be approved by others—by higher officials, by a board of directors, by other parties, and so on. Here an explanation of the action proposed and the reasons for it are required, and often a defense of such proposals may be necessary. In my experience the most effective presentations to boards of directors come from officers who explain the problem, review the several actions that might be taken, offer a definite proposal, and explain what results are expected from it and why it is a more prudent course to pursue than the others. The function of the board is not just to approve; it is also to test the analysis by inquiring about contingencies and consequences that may have been overlooked or improperly appraised. In the end, the board may approve the recommendation or modify it to achieve the overall purposes more effectively.

Conclusions

Let me review some of the major tasks in decision making that deserve more study by social scientists.

A very great effort must go into the gathering and interpretation of information. This covers not only regular reporting but also special investigation of expected problems to find out what the facts are, what the situation means, what its import for the future is, and what the nature of the problem is in fact. A large share of the policy-planning work of government and of business is of this sort.

The setting of goals and the clarification of objectives, as I have suggested, are often tasks of posing alternative ends-means systems in which the ends are intermediate or instrumental to some more general purpose. No aspect of the decision making process is less studied and less understood. The choice of instrumental goals that economically achieve a larger purpose is not the sort of value judgment that social scientists may justifiably rule out as beyond their province. Certainly, the expert can often indicate which ends-means systems are most economical on reasonably objective grounds.

The posing of alternatives often leads to more fact-gathering, for it often calls for studies of what others have done in similar situations and what results were obtained. While the posing of alternatives affords opportunity for creativeness and social inventiveness, it also permits emulation and even slavish following of custom.

It is in the analysis of the consequences of one course of action or another that the social scientist has his greatest opportunity to draw on the body of scientific knowledge and skills in his field. But it would be an exaggeration to say that the art at this stage has reached a very high level of development. The naïve views of social scientists on the necessity of forecasting rather than of postulating is testimony of this.

The task of comparing alternatives and their consequences against some set of norms and requirements is often done in a slipshod way. Even the methods by which proper comparisons should be made for reliable results remain a subject about which little is known and less has been written.

In these areas are countless problems for research. The social sciences, especially economics, have important contributions to make if they will direct their attention to the neglected aspects of the decision making process. But there is also an approach to problem analysis that needs development. Too often the social scientist seeks to play advocate rather than adviser, and this has added to his confusion about value judgments.

I can illustrate this point best perhaps by considering the role of the economic adviser. His task is not to decide for the administrator or the public what final action shall be taken. His primary task is to lay before the administrator the best alternatives open—to show him their consequences, how well they will attain the stated or assumed objectives—and leave the matter for the administrator to resolve. If the adviser's recommendations are desired, they may be requested; and he should make clear the basis on which they are reached. It is not the function of the adviser to decide, so much as it is to lay a sound foundation for decision by others.

In these areas there is ample room for systematic study of how we apply knowledge and how we can better use it.

4. DECISION TREES FOR DECISION MAKING *

John F. Magee †

The management of a company that I shall call Stygian Chemical Industries, Ltd., must decide whether to build a small plant or a large one to manufacture a new product with an expected market life of ten years. The decision hinges on what size the market for the product will be.

Possibly demand will be high during the initial two years but, if many initial users find the product unsatisfactory, will fall to a low level thereafter. Or high initial demand might indicate the possibility of a sustained high volume market. If demand is high and the company does not expand within the first two years, competitive products will surely be introduced.

If the company builds a big plant, it must live with it whatever the size of market demand. If it builds a small plant, management has the option of expanding the plant in two years in the event that demand is high during the introductory period; while in the event that demand is low during the introductory period, the company will maintain operations in the small plant and make a tidy profit on the low volume.

Management is uncertain what to do. The company grew rapidly during the 1950's; it kept pace with the chemical industry generally. The new product, if the market turns out to be large, offers the present management a chance to push the company into a new period of profitable growth. The development department, particularly the development project engineer, is pushing to build the large-scale plant to exploit the first major product development the department has produced in some years.

The chairman, a principal stockholder, is wary of the possibility of large unneeded plant capacity. He favors a smaller plant commitment, but recognizes that later expansion to meet high volume demand would require more investment and be less efficient to operate. The

* From the *Harvard Business Review* (July-August, 1964). Reprinted by permission of the President and Fellows of Harvard College.

† John F. Magee, Vice President, Management Services Division, Arthur D. Little, Inc.

chairman also recognizes that unless the company moves promptly to fill the demand which develops, competitors will be tempted to move in with equivalent products.

The Stygian Chemical problem, oversimplified as it is, illustrates the uncertainties and issues that business management must resolve in making investment decisions. (I use the term "investment" in a broad sense, referring to outlays not only for new plants and equipment but also for large, risky orders, special marketing facilities, research programs, and other purposes.) These decisions are growing more important at the same time that they are increasing in complexity. Countless executives want to make them better—but how?

Exhibit I. Decision Tree for Cocktail Party

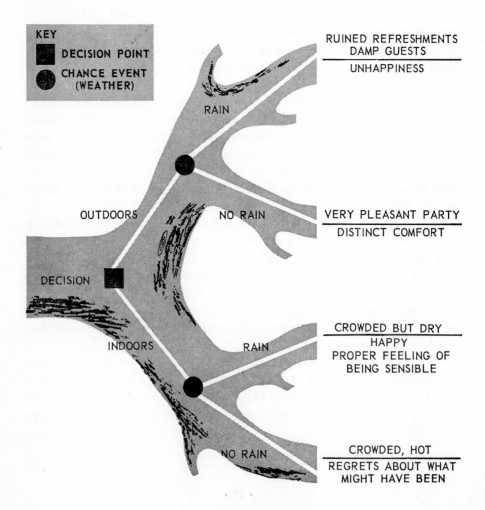

In this article I shall present one recently developed concept called the "decision tree," which has tremendous potential as a decision making tool. The decision tree can clarify for management, as can no other analytical tool that I know of, the choices, risks, objectives, monetary gains, and information needs involved in an investment problem. We shall be hearing a great deal about decision trees in the years ahead. Although a novelty to most businessmen today, they will surely be in common management parlance before many more years have passed.

Later in this article we shall return to the problem facing Stygian Chemical and see how management can proceed to solve it by using decision trees. First, however, a simpler example will illustrate some characteristics of the decision tree approach.

Displaying Alternatives

Let us suppose it is a rather overcast Saturday morning, and you have 75 people coming for cocktails in the afternoon. You have a pleasant garden and your house is not too large; so if the weather permits, you would like to set up the refreshments in the garden and have the party there. It would be more pleasant, and your guests would be more comfortable. On the other hand, if you set up the party for the garden and after all the guests are assembled it begins to rain, the refreshments will be ruined, your guests will get damp, and you will heartily wish you had decided to have the party in the house. (We could complicate this problem by considering the possibility of a partial commitment to one course or another and opportunities to adjust estimates of the weather as the day goes on, but the simple problem is all we need.)

This particular decision can be represented in the form of a "payoff" table:

Events and Results

Choices	Rain	No Rain
Outdoors	Disaster	Real comfort
Indoors	Mild discomfort, but happy	Mild discomfort, but regrets

Much more complex decision questions can be portrayed in payoff table form. However, particularly for complex investment decisions, a different representation of the information pertinent to the problem —the decision tree—is useful to show the routes by which the various possible outcomes are achieved. Pierre Massé, Commissioner General of the National Agency for Productivity and Equipment Planning in France, notes:

> The decision problem is not posed in terms of an isolated decision (because today's decision depends on the one we shall make tomorrow) nor yet in terms of a sequence of decisions (under uncertainty, decisions taken in the future will be influenced by what we have learned in the meanwhile). The problem is posed in terms of a tree of decisions.[1]

Exhibit 1 illustrates a decision tree for the cocktail party problem. This tree is a different way of displaying the same information shown in the payoff table. However, as later examples will show, in complex decisions the decision tree is frequently a much more lucid means of presenting the relevant information than is a payoff table.

The tree is made up of a series of nodes and branches. At the first node on the left, the host has the choice of having the party inside or outside. Each branch represents an alternative course of action or decision. At the end of each branch or alternative course is another node representing a chance event—whether or not it will rain. Each subsequent alternative course to the right represents an alternative outcome of this chance event. Associated with each complete alternative course through the tree is a payoff, shown at the end of the rightmost or terminal branch of the course.

When I am drawing decision trees, I like to indicate the action or decision forks with square nodes and the chance event forks with round ones. Other symbols may be used instead, such as single-line and double-line branches, special letters, or colors. It does not matter so much which method of distinguishing you use so long as you do employ one or another. A decision tree of any size will always combine (a) *action* choices with (b) different possible *events* or *results* of action which are partially affected by chance or other uncontrollable circumstances.

Decision-Event Chains

The previous example, though involving only a single stage of decision, illustrates the elementary principles on which larger, more complex decision trees are built. Let us take a slightly more complicated situation:

You are trying to decide whether to approve a development budget for an improved product. You are urged to do so on the grounds that

---

[1] *Optimal Investment Decisions: Rules for Action and Criteria for Choice* (Englewood Cliffs, N. J.: Prentice-Hall, Inc., 1962), p. 250.

Exhibit II. Decision Tree with Chains of Actions and Events

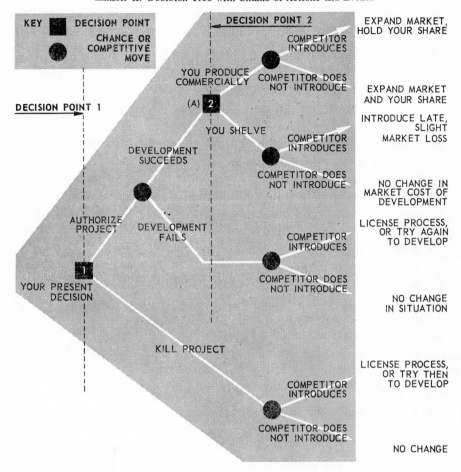

KEY █ DECISION POINT
● CHANCE OR COMPETITIVE MOVE

DECISION POINT 2

DECISION POINT 1

COMPETITOR INTRODUCES — EXPAND MARKET, HOLD YOUR SHARE

YOU PRODUCE COMMERCIALLY

COMPETITOR DOES NOT INTRODUCE — EXPAND MARKET AND YOUR SHARE

(A) 2

COMPETITOR INTRODUCES — INTRODUCE LATE, SLIGHT MARKET LOSS

YOU SHELVE

COMPETITOR DOES NOT INTRODUCE — NO CHANGE IN MARKET COST OF DEVELOPMENT

DEVELOPMENT SUCCEEDS

AUTHORIZE PROJECT

DEVELOPMENT FAILS

COMPETITOR INTRODUCES — LICENSE PROCESS, OR TRY AGAIN TO DEVELOP

COMPETITOR DOES NOT INTRODUCE — NO CHANGE IN SITUATION

1
YOUR PRESENT DECISION

KILL PROJECT

COMPETITOR INTRODUCES — LICENSE PROCESS, OR TRY THEN TO DEVELOP

COMPETITOR DOES NOT INTRODUCE — NO CHANGE

the development, if successful, will give you a competitive edge, but if you do not develop the product, your competitor may—and may seriously damage your market share. You sketch out a decision tree that looks something like the one in Exhibit II.

Your initial decision is shown at the left. Following a decision to proceed with the project, if development is successful, is a second stage of decision at Point A. Assuming no important change in the situation between now and the time of Point A, you decide now what alternatives will be important to you at that time. At the right of the tree are the outcomes of different sequences of decisions and events. These outcomes, too, are based on your present information. In effect you say, "If what I know now is true then, this is what will happen."

Of course, you do not try to identify all the events that can happen or all the decisions you will have to make on a subject under analysis. In the decision tree you lay out only those decisions and events or results that are important to you and have consequences you wish to compare. (For more illustrations, see the Appendix on page 47.)

ADDING FINANCIAL DATA

Now we can return to the problems faced by the Stygian Chemical management. A decision tree characterizing the investment problem as outlined in the introduction is shown in Exhibit III (page 39). At Decision 1 the company must decide between a large and a small plant. This is all that must be decided *now*. But if the company chooses to build a small plant and then finds demand high during the initial period, it can in two years—at Decision 2—choose to expand its plant.

But let us go beyond a bare outline of alternatives. In making decisions, executives must take account of the probabilities, costs, and returns which appear likely. On the basis of the data now available to them, and assuming no important change in the company's situation, they reason as follows:

Marketing esitimates indicate a 60 percent chance of a large market in the long run and a 40 percent chance of a low demand, developing initially as follows:

Initially high demand, sustained high:	60%
Initially high demand, long-term low:	10% ⎫
Initially low and continuing low:	30% ⎬ Low = 40%
Initially low and subsequently high:	0% ⎭

Therefore, the chance that demand initially will be high is 70 percent (60 + 10). *If* demand is high initially, the company estimates that the chance it will continue at a high level is 86 percent (60 ÷ 70). Comparing 86 percent to 60 percent, it is apparent that a high initial level of sales changes the estimated chance of high sales in the subsequent periods. Similarly, if sales in the initial period are low, the chances are 100 percent (30 ÷ 30) that sales in the subsequent periods will be low. Thus the level of sales in the initial period is expected to be a rather accurate indicator of the level of sales in the subsequent periods.

Estimates of annual income are made under the assumption of each alternative outcome:

1. A large plant with high volume would yield $1,000,000 annually in cash flow.

2. A large plant with low volume would yield only $100,000 because of high fixed costs and inefficiencies.

3. A small plant with low demand would be economical and would yield annual cash income of $400,000.

4. A small plant, during an initial period of high demand, would yield $450,000 per year, but this would drop to $300,000 yearly in the long run because of competition. (The market would be larger than under Alternative 3, but would be divided among more competitors.)

5. If the small plant were expanded to meet sustained high demand, it would yield $700,000 cash flow annually, and so would be less efficient than a large plant built initially.

6. If the small plant were expanded but high demand were not sustained, estimated annual cash flow would be $50,000.

Exhibit III. Decisions and Events for Stygian Chemical Industries, Ltd.

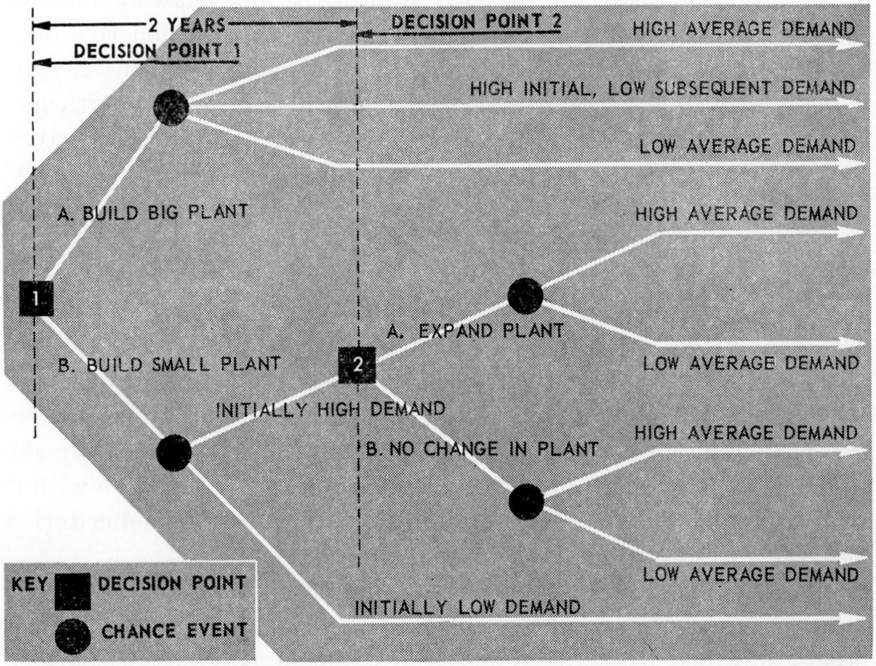

It is estimated further that a large plant would cost $3 million to put into operation, a small plant would cost $1.3 million, and the expansion of the small plant would cost an additional $2.2 million.

When the foregoing data are incorporated, we have the decision tree shown in Exhibit IV. Bear in mind that nothing is shown here which Stygian Chemical's executives did not know before; no numbers have been pulled out of hats. However, we are beginning to see dramatic evidence of the value of decision trees in *laying out* what management knows in a way that enables more systematic analysis and leads to better decisions. To sum up the requirements of making a decision tree, management must:

1. Identify the points of decision and alternatives available at each point.

2. Identify the points of uncertainty and the type or range of alternative outcomes at each point.

3. Estimate the values needed to make the analysis, especially the probabilities of different events or results of action and the costs and gains of various events and actions.

4. Analyze the alternative values to choose a course.

CHOOSING COURSE OF ACTION

We are now ready for the next step in the analysis—to compare the consequences of different courses of action. A decision tree does not give management the answer to an investment problem; rather, it helps management determine which alternative at any particular choice point will yield the greatest expected monetary gain, given the information and alternatives pertinent to the decision.

Of course, the gains must be viewed with the risks. At Stygian Chemical, as at many corporations, managers have different points of view toward risk; hence they will draw different conclusions in the circumstances described by the decision tree shown in Exhibit IV. The many people participating in a decision—those supplying capital, ideas, data, or decisions, and having different values at risk—will see the uncertainty surrounding the decision in different ways. Unless these differences are recognized and dealt with, those who must make the decision, pay for it, supply data and analyses to it, and live with it will judge the issue, relevance of data, need for analysis, and criterion of success in different and conflicting ways.

For example, company stockholders may treat a particular investment as one of a series of possibilities, some of which will work out, others of which will fail. A major investment may pose risks to a middle manager—to his job and career—no matter what decision is made. Another participant may have a lot to gain from success, but little to lose from failure of the project. The nature of the risk—as each individual sees it—will affect not only the assumptions he is willing to make but also the strategy he will follow in dealing with the risk.

The existence of multiple, unstated, and conflicting objectives will certainly contribute to the "politics" of Stygian Chemical's decision, and one can be certain that the political element exists whenever the lives and ambitions of people are affected. Here, as in similar cases. it is not a bad exercise to think through who the parties to an investment decision are and to try to make these assessments:

What is at risk? Is it profit or equity value, survival of the business, maintenance of a job, opportunity for a major career?

Exhibit IV. Decision Tree with Financial Data

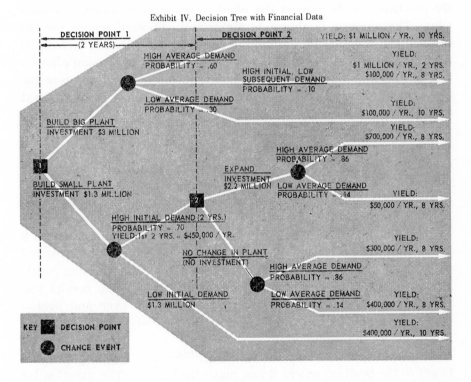

Who is bearing the risk? The stockholder is usually bearing risk in one form. Management, employees, the community—all may be bearing different risks.

What is the character of the risk that each person bears? Is it, *in his terms,* unique, once-in-a-lifetime, sequential, insurable? Does it affect the economy, the industry, the company, or a portion of the company?

Considerations such as the foregoing will surely enter into top management's thinking, and the decision tree in Exhibit IV will not eliminate them. But the tree will show management what decision today will contribute most to its long-term goals. The tool for this next step in the analysis is the concept of "roll-back"

"Roll-Back" Concept

Here is how roll-back works in the situation described. At the time of making Decision 1 (see Exhibit IV), management does not have to make Decision 2 and does not even know if it will have the occasion to do so. But if it *were* to have the option at Decision 2, the company would expand the plant, in view of its current knowledge. The analysis is shown in Exhibit V. (I shall ignore for the moment the question of discounting future profits; that is introduced later.) We see that the total expected value of the expansion alternative is $160,000 greater than the no-expansion alternative, over the eight-year life remaining. Hence that is the alternative management would choose if faced with Decision 2 with its existing information (and thinking only of monetary gain as a standard of choice).

Readers may wonder why we started with Decision 2 when today's problem is Decision 1. The reason is the following: We need to be able to put a monetary value on Decision 2 in order to "roll back" to Decision 1 and compare the gain from taking the lower branch ("Build Small Plant") with the gain from taking the upper branch ("Build Big Plant"). Let us call that monetary value for Decision 2 its *position value*. The position value of a decision is the expected value of the preferred branch (in this case, the plant-expansion fork). The expected value is simply a kind of average of the results you would expect if you were to repeat the situation over and over— getting a $5,600,000 yield 86 percent of the time and a $400,000 yield 14 percent of the time.

Stated in another way, it is worth $2,672,000 to Stygian Chemical to get to the position where it can make Decision 2. The question is: Given this value and the other data shown in Exhibit IV, what now appears to be the best action at Decision 1?

Turn now to Exhibit VI. At the right of the branches in the top half we see the yields for various events if a big plant is built (these are simply the figures in Exhibit IV multiplied out). In the bottom half we see the small plant figures, including Decision 2 position value plus the yield for the two years prior to Decision 2. Reducing all these yields by their probabilities, we get this comparison:

Build big plant: ($10 × .60) + ($2.8 × .10) +
        ($1 × .30) − $3 = $3,600,000
Build small plant: ($3.6 × .70) + ($4 × .30) −
        $1.3 = $2,400,000

Exhibit V. Analysis of Possible Decision No. 2
(*Using maximum expected total cash flow as criterion*)

Choice	Chance Event	Probability (1)	Total Yield, 8 Years (Thousands of Dollars) (2)	Expected Value (Thousands of Dollars) (1) × (2)
Expansion	High average demand	.86	$5,600	$4,816
	Low average demand	.14	400	56
			Total	$4,872
			Less investment	2,200
			Net	$2,672
No Expansion	High average demand	.86	$2,400	$2,064
	Low average demand	.14	3,200	448
			Total	$2,512
			Less investment	0
			Net	$2,512

The choice which maximizes expected total cash yield at Decision 1, therefore, is to build the big plant initially.

ACCOUNTING FOR TIME

What about taking differences in the *time* of future earnings into account? The time between successive decision stages on a decision tree may be substantial. At any stage, we may have to weigh differences in immediate cost or revenue against differences in value at the next stage. Whatever standard of choice is applied, we can put the two alternatives on a comparable basis if we discount the value assigned to the next stage by an appropriate percentage. The discount percentage is, in effect, an allowance for the cost of capital and is similar to the use of a discount rate in the present value or discounted cash flow techniques already well known to businessmen.

Exhibit VI. Cash Flow Analysis for Decision #1

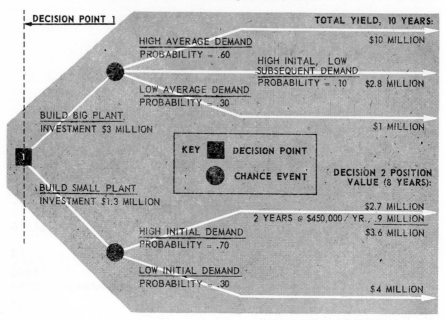

When decision trees are used, the discounting procedure can be applied one stage at a time. Both cash flows and position value are discounted.

For simplicity, let us assume that a discount rate of 10 percent per year for all stages is decided on by Stygian Chemical's management. Applying the roll-back principle, we again begin with Decision 2. Taking the same figures used in previous exhibits and discounting the cash flows at 10 percent, we get the data shown in Part A of Exhibit VII. Note particularly that these are the present values *as of the time Decision 2 is made.*

Now we want to go through the same procedure used in Exhibit V when we obtained expected values, only this time using the discounted yield figures and obtaining a discounted expected value. The results are shown in Part B of Exhibit VII. Since the discounted expected value of the no-expansion alternative is higher, *that* figure becomes the position value of Decision 2 this time.

Having done this, we go back to work through Decision 1 again, repeating the same analytical procedure as before only with discounting. The calculations are shown in Exhibit VIII. Note that the Decision 2 position value is treated at the time of Decision 1 as if it were a lump sum received at the end of the two years.

The large-plant alternative is again the preferred one on the basis of discounted expected cash flow. But the margin of difference over the small-plant alternative ($290,000) is smaller than it was without discounting.

Exhibit VII. Analysis of Decision No. 2 with Discounting

A. Present Values of Cash Flows

Choice — Outcome	Yield	Present Value (in Thousands)
Expand — high demand	$700,000/year, 8 years	$4,100
Expand — low demand	50,000/year, 8 years	300
No change — high demand	300,000/year, 8 years	1,800
No change — low demand	400,000/year, 8 years	2,300

B. Obtaining Discounted Expected Values

Choice	Chance Event	Probability (1)	Present Value Yield (in Thousands) (2)	Discounted Expected Value (in Thousands) (1) × (2)
Expansion	High average demand	.86	$4,100	$3,526
	Low average demand	.14	300	42
			Total	$3,568
			Less investment	2,200
			Net	$1,368
No expansion	High average demand	.86	$1,800	$1,548
	Low average demand	.14	2,300	322
			Total	$1,870
			Less investment	0
			Net	$1,870

NOTE: For simplicity, the first year cash flow is not discounted, the second year cash flow is discounted one year, and so on.

UNCERTAINTY ALTERNATIVES

In illustrating the decision tree concept, I have treated uncertainty alternatives as if they were discrete, well-defined possibilities. For my examples I have made use of uncertain situations depending basically on a single variable, such as the level of demand or the success or failure of a development project. I have sought to avoid

Exhibit VIII. Analysis of Decision No. 1

Choice	Chance Event	Proba-bility (1)	Yield (in Thousands)	Discounted Value of Yield (in Thousands) (2)	Discounted Expected Yield (in Thousands) (1) × (2)
Build big plant	High average demand	.60	$1,000/year, 10 years	$6,700	$4,020
	High initial, low average demand	.10	1,000/year, 2 years 100/year, 8 years	2,400	240
	Low average demand	.30	100/year, 10 years	700	210
				Total	$4,470
				Less investment	3,000
				Net	$1,470
Build small plant	High initial demand	.70	$ 450/year, 2 years	$ 860	$ 600
			Decision No. 2 value, $1,870 at end of 2 years	1,530	1,070
	Low initial demand	.30	$ 400/year, 10 years	2,690	810
				Total	$2,480
				Less investment	1,300
				Net	$1,180

unnecessary complication while putting emphasis on the key inter-relationships among the present decision, future choices, and the intervening uncertainties.

In many cases, the uncertain elements do take the form of discrete, single-variable alternatives. In others, however, the possibilities for cash flow during a stage may range through a whole spectrum and may depend on a number of independent or partially related variables subject to chance influences—cost, demand, yield, economic climate, and so forth. In these cases, we have found that the range of varia-bility or the likelihood of the cash flow falling in a given range during a stage can be calculated readily from knowledge of the key variables and the uncertainties surrounding them. Then the range of cash-flow possibilities during the stage can be broken down into two, three, or more "subsets," which can be used as discrete chance alternatives.

CONCLUSION

Peter F. Drucker has succinctly expressed the relation between present planning and future events: "Long-range planning does not deal with future decisions. It deals with the futurity of present decisions." [2] Today's decision should be made in light of the antici-

---

[2] "Long-Range Planning," *Management Science* (April, 1959), p. 239.

pated effect it and the outcome of uncertain events will have on future values and decisions. Since today's decision sets the stage for tomorrow's decision, today's decision must balance economy with flexibility; it must balance the need to capitalize on profit opportunities that may exist with the capacity to react to future circumstances and needs.

The unique feature of the decision tree is that it allows management to combine analytical techniques such as discounted cash flow and present value methods with a clear portrayal of the impact of future decision alternatives and events. Using the decision tree, management can consider various courses of action with greater ease and clarity. The interactions between present decision alternatives, uncertain events, and future choices and their results become more visible.

Of course, there are many practical aspects of decision trees in addition to those that could be covered in the space of just one article.

Surely the decision-tree concept does not offer final answers to managements making investment decisions in the face of uncertainty. We have not reached that stage, and perhaps we never will. Nevertheless, the concept is valuable for illustrating the structure of investment decisions, and it can likewise provide excellent help in the evaluation of capital investment *opportunities*.

APPENDIX

For readers interested in further examples of decision tree structure, I shall describe in this appendix two representative situations with which I am familiar and show the trees that might be drawn to analyze management's decision making alternatives. We shall not concern ourselves here with costs, yields, probabilities, or expected values.

New Facility

The choice of alternatives in building a plant depends upon market forecasts. The alternative chosen will, in turn, affect the market outcome. For example, the military products division of a diversified firm, after some period of low profits due to intense competition, has won a contract to produce a new type of military engine suitable for Army transport vehicles. The division has a contract to build productive capacity and to produce at a specified contract level over a period of three years.

Figure A illustrates the situation. The dotted line shows the contract rate. The solid line shows the proposed buildup of produc-

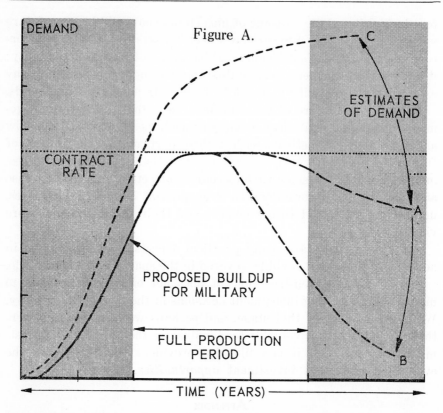

Figure A.

DEMAND

ESTIMATES
OF DEMAND

CONTRACT
RATE

PROPOSED BUILDUP
FOR MILITARY

FULL PRODUCTION
PERIOD

TIME (YEARS)

tion for the military. Some other possibilities are portrayed by dashed lines. The company is not sure whether the contract will be continued at a relatively high rate after the third year, as shown by Line A, or whether the military will turn to another newer development, as indicated by Line B. The company has no guarantee of compensation after the third year. There is also the possibility, indicated by Line C, of a large additional commercial market for the product, this possibility being somewhat dependent on the cost at which the product can be made and sold.

If this commercial market could be tapped, it would represent a major new business for the company and a substantial improvement in the profitability of the division and its importance to the company.

Management wants to explore three ways of producing the product as follows:

1. It might subcontract all fabrication and set up a simple assembly with limited need for investment in plant and equipment; the costs would tend to be relatively high and the company's investment and profit opportunity would be limited, but the company assets which are at risk would also be limited.

2. It might undertake the major part of the fabrication itself but use general-purpose machine tools in a plant of general-purpose construction. The division would have a chance to retain more of the most profitable operations itself, exploiting some technical developments it has made (on the basis of which it got the contract). While the cost of production would still be relatively high, the nature of the investment in plant and equipment would be such that it could probably be turned to other uses or liquidated if the business disappeared.
3. The company could build a highly mechanized plant with specialized fabrication and assembly equipment, entailing the largest investment but yielding a substantially lower unit manufacturing cost if manufacturing volume were adequate. Following this plan would improve the chances for a continuation of the military contract and penetration into the commercial market and would improve the profitability of whatever business might be obtained in these markets. Failure to sustain either the military or the commercial market, however, would cause substantial financial loss.

Either of the first two alternatives would be better adapted to low volume production than would be the third.

Some major uncertainties are: the cost-volume relationships under the alternative manufacturing methods; the size and structure of the future market—this depends in part on cost, but the degree and extent of dependence are unknown; and the possibilities of competitive developments which would render the product competitively or technologically obsolete.

How would this situation be shown in decision tree form? (Before going further you might want to draw a tree for the problem yourself.) Figure B shows my version of a tree. Note that in this case the chance alternatives are somewhat influenced by the decision made. A decision, for example, to build a more efficient plant will open possibilities for an expanded market.

Plant Modernization

A company management is faced with a decision on a proposal by its engineering staff which, after three years of study, wants to install a computer-based control system in the company's major plant. The expected cost of the control system is some $30 million. The claimed advantages of the system will be a reduction in labor cost and an improved product yield. These benefits depend on the level of product throughout, which is likely to rise over the next decade. It is thought that the installation program will take about two years and will cost a substantial amount over and above the cost of equipment. The engineers calculate that the automation project will yield a 20 percent return on investment, after taxes; the projection is

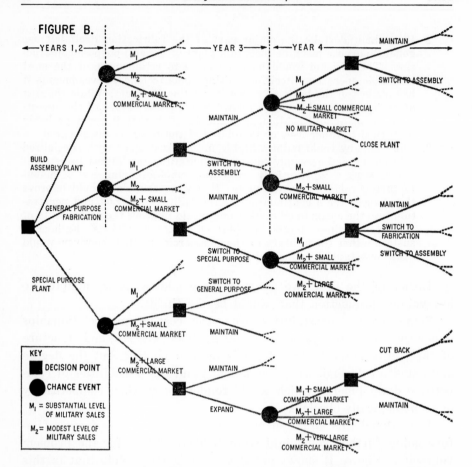

FIGURE B.

based on a ten-year forecast of product demand by the market research department, and an assumption of an eight-year life for the process control system.

What would this investment yield? Will actual product sales be higher or lower than forecast? Will the process work? Will it achieve the economies expected? Will competitors follow if the company is successful? Are they going to mechanize anyway? Will new products or processes make the basic plant obsolete before the investment can be recovered? Will the controls last eight years? Will something better come along sooner?

The initial decision alternatives are (a) to install the proposed control system, (b) postpone action until trends in the market and/or competition become clearer, or (c) initiate more investigation or an independent evaluation. Each alternative will be followed by resolution of some uncertain aspect, in part dependent on the action taken. This resolution will lead in turn to a new decision. The dotted lines

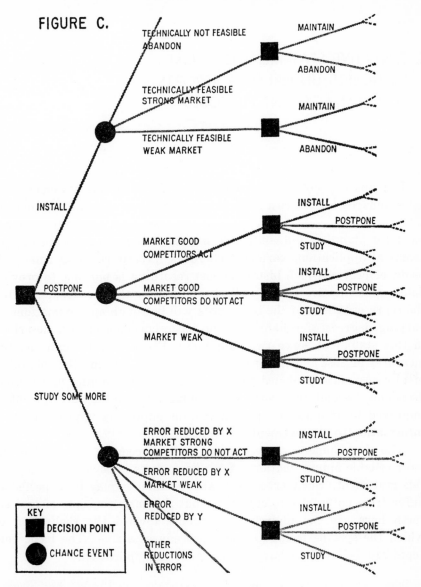

FIGURE C.

TECHNICALLY NOT FEASIBLE
ABANDON

MAINTAIN

ABANDON

TECHNICALLY FEASIBLE
STRONG MARKET

MAINTAIN

TECHNICALLY FEASIBLE
WEAK MARKET

ABANDON

INSTALL

INSTALL

POSTPONE

MARKET GOOD
COMPETITORS ACT

STUDY

INSTALL

POSTPONE

MARKET GOOD
COMPETITORS DO NOT ACT

STUDY

MARKET WEAK

INSTALL

POSTPONE

STUDY

STUDY SOME MORE

ERROR REDUCED BY X
MARKET STRONG
COMPETITORS DO NOT ACT

INSTALL

POSTPONE

ERROR REDUCED BY X
MARKET WEAK

STUDY

ERROR
REDUCED BY Y

INSTALL

POSTPONE

OTHER
REDUCTIONS
IN ERROR

STUDY

KEY

■ DECISION POINT

● CHANCE EVENT

at the right of Figure C indicate that the decision tree continues indefinitely, though the decision alternatives do tend to become repetitive. In the case of postponement or further study, the decisions are to install, postpone, or restudy; in the case of installation, the decisions are to continue operation or abandon.

An immediate decision is often one of a sequence. It may be one of a number of sequences. The impact of the present decision in narrowing down future alternatives and the effect of future alternatives in affecting the value of the present choice must both be considered.

5. TENTATIVE STATEMENT OF COST CONCEPTS UNDERLYING REPORTS FOR MANAGEMENT PURPOSES *

Committee on Cost Concepts and Standards †

Explanatory note: The concepts set forth in this statement are not standards for the cost accounting procedures of recording historical cost. They represent concepts of the costs most useful to management for planning and control decisions. It is to be expected that in practical application, various techniques, procedures, and rules will be developed, of which historical cost recording is but one, to provide data representative of the costs suggested by these concepts. Often the representations of the basic costs will be rough approximations of varying degrees of reliability. The basic concepts of cost described in this statement serve two functions: First, they indicate desired measures of cost and thus serve as a basis for judging the reliability of any cost data provided to management for planning and control decisions. Second, they serve as an inducement to the development of improved techniques and procedures for supplying appropriate cost information to management.

The development of techniques and procedures to provide the most reliable approximations of the basic costs is beyond the scope of this statement. Such procedures and techniques may be expected to differ from enterprise to enterprise but the basic concepts of cost set forth here are the underlying concepts toward the realization of which the specific techniques and procedures strive. The basic concepts are believed to have rather general application.

PREFATORY NOTE

In June, 1936, the Executive Committee of the American Accounting Association issued a tentative statement of accounting principles

* From *The Accounting Review* (April, 1956). Reprinted by permission of the American Accounting Association.

† Members of the Committee were as follows: Robert N. Anthony, Harvard University; James S. Schindler, Washington University; Edward L. Wallace, University of Chicago; Glenn A. Welsch, University of Texas; and Norton M. Bedford, Chairman, University of Illinois.

underlying corporate financial statements. That statement and subsequent revisions suggested concepts and standards underlying the preparation of accounting reports on financial position and income. While reports of income and financial position are used by managements in reaching certain broad decisions, a far greater proportion of managerial decisions and actions are based upon other reports. This suggests the need for a statement of the concepts underlying these other reports.

For several years, work has been proceeding toward the development of a statement of cost concepts useful in the preparation of reports for management. Progress in this area has now reached a point where it seems desirable to issue a tentative statement of such cost concepts. This statement seems advisable to advance the following objectives:

1. To stimulate further study and discussion of the accounting information needed by management.
2. To suggest cost data which are pertinent to various types of management problems.
3. To call attention to the broad and indefinite nature of cost as a general term and to reveal how appropriate costs depend upon the purpose for which they are to be used.
4. To describe a portion of the field of accounting within a framework sufficiently broad to provide an insight into the problem of providing accounting information for management purposes.

The concepts set forth here represent a broad approach to the problem of business cost. As such they include concepts generally not appropriate for the determination of income and include costs which may not be a part of the basic accounting records. Essentially they suggest the most appropriate cost data for management uses. In this report attention is directed toward the development of underlying concepts. These concepts, in turn, may require further development of procedures and working approximations to effect their application in any given business situations.

The Nature of Business Cost

For business purposes, cost is a general term for a measured amount of value purposefully released or to be released in the acquisition or creation of economic resources, either tangible or intangible. Normally it is measured in terms of a monetary sacrifice involved. There is, however, nothing to prevent its measurement in other terms nor to prevent the adjustment of monetary sacrifices to common units of purchasing power. Conceptually, cost excludes distribution of capital and income as well as certain unexpected value releases.

Basic Framework

An understanding of the nature of cost requires comprehension of (a) the purposeful aspect of the term "cost," (b) the relationship of business risk to cost, and (c) methods of measuring value releases.

(a) To qualify as cost, the value release must be for the purpose of furthering a managerial objective. There are two aspects to this concept. First, only the value releases necessary for the acquisition or creation of economic resources to carry out a managerial objective are costs. Second, the amount released will depend upon the use to be made by management of the computed costs. Thus the cost of acquiring or creating economic resources for a managerial objective should include only those value releases necessary to carry out the specific objective. But, because the purpose in measuring the value releases may be to aid management in varying levels of planning and control decisions, the amount of value release will depend upon the use to be made of the computed costs. In somewhat comprehensive terms, the purposeful aspect of cost means that because managerial objectives vary both in scope of activity (ranging from overall activities to a multitude of minor activities) and in the nature of the management function being performed (ranging from planning to control), the value releases to be included in any cost report will vary with the situation of the firm as well as with the specific objective of management. In a broad sense, this recognizes that the cost of anything will depend upon the purpose for determining cost.

(b) Business operations necessarily involve risk. In some instances these risks are transferred to an insuror. In others, though not transferred, they are measured and allowed for as an element of cost. In still others, they cannot be foreseen or, if foreseen, are so uncertain that estimation is impractical. Value releases occasioned by the transfer of risk to an insuror, or by uninsured risk which lend themselves to measurement, are costs. Value releases occasioned by unforeseen, or highly uncertain, risks are not costs but should be considered in evaluating the risk of the operation. If incurred they are, of course, considered as losses in determining income.

(c) Normally, value releases due to operations are measured in monetary terms. The measurement of the monetary sacrifice involved in the acquisition or creation of economic resources is simplest when the value release is an outflow of cash. Adjustment for the timing of cash outflow is sometimes necessary and can be accomplished by discounting or advancing outflows at an appropriate rate of interest. Similarly, adjustment for changes in the purchasing power of money can be made by the use of appropriate price indexes. The needs of management for a report on monetary sacrifice, however, often require the measurement of noncash outflows. Most often such outflows result from the release of economic resources now on hand. It is in the measurement of these latter outflows that special difficulties arise.

Cost Classifications

Cost is classified normally in terms of a managerial objective. Its presentation normally requires subclassification. Such subclassification may be according to functional lines, areas of responsibility, the nature of the cost elements, or some other useful breakdown. The appropriate subclassification depends upon the uses to be made of the cost report.

Uses of Business Cost Reports

Within the foregoing framework of the nature of cost, various concepts may be developed that are appropriate in the preparation of cost reports useful for business decisions.

Managerial functions may be grouped into the areas of (1) planning and (2) control. Cost concepts appropriate for each of these two areas are developed in this statement. In general, the cost concepts useful for planning are those relevant to a managerial decision on future action; whereas the cost concepts useful for control are those which aid in carrying out adopted plans. In addition, because the costs in accounting records are used by management as a basis for planning and control, it is advisable to set forth certain concepts which underlie these accounting costs. Accordingly, this statement deals with cost concepts appropriate for planning and for control, and with historical cost reports to management. The concepts set forth are somewhat ideal. Approximations of these basic concepts often must be used in business situations.

Costs for Planning

Depending upon the purpose for which it is undertaken, all business planning may be classified as (1) project planning or (2) period planning. Project planning is the process whereby management, confronted by a specific problem, evaluates each alternative in order to arrive at a decision as to the course of future action.[1] Period plan-

---

[1] In a broad sense project planning may be defined as the process of reaching a decision on future action. It may range from the least important decision of the least important worker to the broadest of decisions by the board of directors. As a process it may be described as (a) recognizing several possible courses of future action, (b) evaluating each alternative (in both monetary and nonmonetary

ning is the process whereby management systematically develops an acceptable set of plans for the total future activities of the enterprise, or some functional subdivision thereof, for a specified period of time.

The two types of planning can and often do occur simultaneously. While some of the more important problems requiring project planning are apt to occur sporadically and involve alternatives of long and varying time periods, others follow the fixed time pattern of period planning. The second situation exists because management is able to control the length of time for which alternative commitments may be made, and chooses to employ the period planning cycle as that length of time. For this reason many activities entailed in the process of period planning are actually project planning. Whereever a selection between alternatives is necessary, project planning is involved.

COSTS FOR PROJECT PLANNING

Costs for project planning are estimates of future value releases anticipated as a result of adopting any one of the alternative courses of future action considered by the company. Such costs are future costs which may be expressed as differential costs because evaluation is a comparative process requiring the determination of how total costs (and revenues) are likely to vary under different sets of future conditions.[2]

In estimating future differential costs of each of a given set of alternatives, it is necessary to recognize one alternative as the standard. Often this standard is the alternative which envisages mere continuation of the current plan. All services [3] required by each of the other alternatives which differ as to type, quantity, or time of release from those required by the standard, must be determined and their future costs estimated.

---

terms), and (c) expressing a decision to adopt one of the alternatives as the course of future action. Planning costs are concerned primarily with the evaluation process.

[2] Any alternative may be analyzed by determining the total expected value release occasioned by all future activities of which it is but a part and comparing this cost with the total costs of other alternatives, determined in the same manner. Since many costs are common to every alternative, the comparison actually rests on the differences in total costs of the alternatives. In this "Tentative Statement of Cost Concepts" the more direct procedure is stressed. Only differential costs of the alternatives are to be measured and compared. The difference between the two methods is procedural, but care must be taken in the direct approach to ensure that important differences are not overlooked. There is less chance of making this kind of an error if the total cost procedure is used.

[3] The term "services" is sometimes used in a more narrow sense to refer to personal services but there seems no sound reason to restrict the term when it is evident that the purchase of either labor or physical assets is for the purpose of acquiring the services in these resources.

In order to measure the future costs of these differential services, a distinction should be made between differential services on hand, or for which the company is irrevocably committed, at the beginning of the planning period, and those to be acquired within that period; between those expected to be entirely consumed within that period and those of which a residual is expected to remain at the end of the period; and between those which management considers replacing and those which it does not.

Furthermore, when the project planning period is long, it is necessary to adjust all differential costs in order to take account of significant time and risk variations. The most satisfactory method for doing this is by means of the discounting procedure.

Differential Services to Be Acquired and Fully Consumed

The basis for estimating future costs of differential services to be acquired and fully consumed within the planning period is the expected future outlay of cash, or its equivalent, required for their acquisition.

1. When the cash outlay is expected to coincide with service acquisition and both will take place over a period of time, the proper measure of cost is the sum of the discounted amounts of (a) the initial outlay, (b) the complementary outlays required for realization of the initial outlay, and (c) any further outlay required to dispose of the acquisition.

2. Often the outlay will be in the form of a promise to pay cash, or its equivalent, at a time subsequent to the service acquisition date. In this situation the value release as of the date of expected service acquisition should be measured by discounting the expected cash outlay to the date of service acquisition. A rate of interest equivalent to that required for borrowing money may be used for the discounting process. The resulting amount should be treated as in 1 above.

3. At times the outlay will be in the form of services other than cash, or promises to pay cash. If replacement of such services is considered, the cash equivalent is measured by their estimated replacement cost, at the time of expected replacement discounted to the date of acquisitions. If replacement is not considered, cash equivalent is measured by the estimated net proceeds foregone (i.e., net selling price adjusted for estimated selling costs) because of the exchange.[4] The resulting amount should be treated as in 1 above.

---

[4] The concept employed here is frequently called value in best alternative use. Where replacement is considered, the value in best alternative use is presumed to be a substitute for the cost of replacement. If the time period between the date of exchange and the date of expected replacement is long and storage costs are important, replacement cost at the time of expected replacement should be ad-

Different Services to Be Acquired and Partially Consumed

The basis for estimating future costs of differential services to be acquired and partially consumed during the project planning period is the future outlay of cash, or its equivalent, required for their acquisition, less the estimated cash equivalent valuation of services remaining at the end of the period.

1. The measure of the cash, or its equivalent, for the acquisition of these services is the same as that used in measuring differential services acquired and fully consumed.
2. If replacement of the remaining services is considered by management, their valuation can be measured by estimated replacement cost, at the time of expected replacement, discounted to the end of the period.
3. If replacement of these residual services is not a present consideration, their valuation may be measured by estimated net proceeds as of the end of the period.

Differential Services on Hand and Fully Consumed

The basis for estimating future costs of differential services on hand, or for which the company is irrevocably committed, at the beginning of the period which are expected to be fully consumed within that period is their cash equivalent valuation at the time of utilization.

1. If replacement of such services is considered by management, their valuation is estimated replacement cost at the time of utilization.
2. If replacement of such services is not a consideration of management, their valuation is estimated net proceeds foregone at the time of utilization.

Differential Services on Hand and Partially Consumed

The basis for estimating future costs of differential services on hand, or for which the firm is irrevocably committed, at the beginning of the period which are expected to be partially consumed within that period is their cash equivalent valuation at the time of utilization.

If replacement of such services is considered, their valuation is estimated replacement cost, at the date of expected replacement, discounted to the time of utilization.

---

justed by the estimated differential storage costs saved through the proposed exchange.

If replacement is not considered, net proceeds are the higher of the remaining alternatives of (1) sale as is, or (2) use in some other production or distribution activity. In the latter case, the value cannot exceed replacement cost.

Throughout this entire section, it is presumed that management's consideration of replacement reflects the fact that it is the best alternative; that is, it considers replacement only where the discounted replacement cost is in excess of net proceeds. If this assumption were dropped, the proper measure of cost would be discounted replacement cost or net proceeds whichever is the higher.

Time, Risk, and Uncertainty Adjustments

The future differential costs associated with each alternative must be adjusted for time, risk of loss, and uncertainty of risk before evaluation is possible. Discounting each anticipated future cost to some common point in time is usually the most satisfactory method of adjustment for time and risk factors. The rate(s) of discount used for these purposes should reflect management's appraisal of the risk entailed by each prospective undertaking.

If the time periods of two or more of the alternatives are significantly different, these differences must be taken into account in any calculation. One method of doing so is to compare the two alternatives on the basis of the rates of return implied by their respective investments and future net proceeds.

Another method is to select a common time period, preferably the shortest period, to which the firm would be committed by the adoption of any one of the alternatives. Each of the longer alternatives can then be fitted to the shortest period by estimating the cash equivalent valuation of the residual services as of the end of the common time period.

The degree of uncertainty attending each of the estimates of future differential cost for each of the various alternatives may be taken into account by employing different rates of discount, or setting forth a range for each set of estimates. Full disclosure of the bases for the estimates should be made to assist in its evaluation.

Pricing

A special area of planning which warrants separate attention is pricing. Cost is one element in the determination of price, but it must be considered in concert with numerous other factors embodied in the total concept of demand.

In nonrepetitive sales, the future differential cost of making and selling the product, measured from the costs of not making and selling the product, ordinarily establishes a lower limit for price. This limit may be ignored by management for short periods because of certain nonmonetary factors, but the monetary sacrifice entailed in so doing is measured by the difference between price and future differential cost. It is management's responsibility to determine subjectively whether or not this sacrifice is warranted by nonmonetary considerations.

In repetitive selling, many nonmonetary factors such as competitive reactions, legal requirements, or ultimate needs for replacement, usually dictate a higher minimum than that embodied in any short period planning cost. Conceptually, the planning costs for pricing goods which are sold repetitively should take into account the discounted total future gains and losses occasioned by the adoption of any one price or price structure rather than another. Since most of these future gains and losses defy satisfactory expression in monetary terms, the selection of the margin of price over future differential costs is a direct responsibility of management.

Costs for Period Planning

The principal objective of period planning is the development of various sets of plans and their conversion into a single overall plan in order to direct and coordinate each of the separate activities and to assure that their summation is an acceptable whole. The period adopted usually is one year. The adopted plan is the basis for communication and includes cost data useful for control of subsequent operations.

Period planning usually results in an overall budget. Such planning ordinarily is carried on within the framework of anticipated costs and revenues for income determination purposes or other rather complete accumulations of costs rather than differential cost constructions. In this respect period planning represents a potential area of conflict between planning and income determination costs. For those activities whose future service requirements within the budget period will be consumed during the same period, the period planning employs essentially the same cost concepts as project planning. One difference is that for convenience project plans are often measured in terms of differential costs, whereas period plans are stated in terms of rather complete accumulations of cost. In those activities for which services are on hand at the beginning or end of the planning period, the results of the two also may differ because period planning uses the booked cost valuations for income determination as opposed to the cost concepts appropriate for project planning purposes.

In many instances project planning is carried out as a part of period planning. In other instances, it is not feasible to subject all areas of the business at short intervals to a review and replanning of past adopted plans or to undergo project planning for all items. These latter items then enter into the planning process directly via period planning.

Normally, the process of period planning involves a buildup of estimated future costs by areas of responsibility and functions which must be performed if major policies and previously adopted plans are to be followed. Typically, the estimating procedure utilizes historical costs. The concept of variable cost is a useful device for such planning purposes, but it can be easily misinterpreted. Because it normally reflects the relationship of only one variable (volume) to the behavior of total costs, this concept is often inadequate, since expected changes in factors other than volume (e.g., price, efficiency, or management attitude) will have a significant effect upon future outlays. Variable cost may be used as a first approximation of future cost. Adjustments can be made to take account of expected changes in the other variable before final estimates are determined.

Period planning provides for an overall evaluation by top level management of a master plan prepared in accordance with major policies and restrictions previously imposed by it. It is constructed as a reviewing device rather than as a means of providing the basis for the preparation of another master plan or revision of the plan under consideration. Changes in planned combinations of activities, induced by apparently unsatisfactory total results presented in period planning, should be reexamined in the light of the proper concepts of project planning cost before they are effected.

The communication of adopted period plans normally envisions their construction in such a manner as to coordinate and control the activities of the firm. This involves the assignment of these period plans to areas of responsibility.

COSTS FOR CONTROL

Cost data are useful in the control of current operations. The selection of cost concepts for such purposes is a matter of personal discretion depending upon the cost construction which in the given situation is believed to be best able to accomplish the objectives. Therefore, such costs may be historical costs, standard costs, planning costs, or even constructions which merely simulate costs. They are useful for three main purposes:

1. Costs are useful, along with other devices, as a means of communicating information about approved plans.
2. Costs may be constructed and used in a way that will motivate individuals within the organization to take action most likely to further the interests of the firm.
3. Costs are useful as a means of reporting actual performance and the

differences between actual performance and the performance that should have been attained under the circumstances. These reports may provide a useful tool for improving performance in future periods.

Costs as a Communication Device

Cost data help to convey information about the objectives that management wishes to achieve, the methods to be used to achieve these objectives, and the limitations to which the organization is expected to adhere. These objectives, methods, and limitations are the result of decisions reached in the planning process. Cost data, therefore, are devices by means of which management can direct individuals within the organization to carry out plans. In this use, costs may be classified in terms of activity, personal responsibility, or types of services to be used in carrying out the adopted plans. While the budget is one form of communicating information of this type, it is, of course, not the sole means and rarely is it as important as other communication devices, particularly oral instructions.

The measurable concepts of cost appropriate for the communication function require a mutual understanding by management and individuals of the bases upon which the costs are calculated.

Costs as a Device for Motivation

Cost data, if properly constructed and if accompanied by proper management action and attitude, can be an important factor in motivating the organization, for they may serve as an incentive for accomplishing the planned objectives. Some concepts useful in developing cost data that help to motivate individuals within the organization may be suggested.

1. A basic concept of motivation is that it is best accomplished when costs are related to personal responsibility, but this does not mean that individuals should be charged only with costs for which they are completely responsible. There are few, if any, elements of cost that are the sole responsibility of one person. Some guides in deciding the appropriate costs to be charged to a person (responsibility center) are as follows:

   a. If the person has authority over both the acquisition and the use of the services, he should be charged with the cost of such services.

   b. If the person can significantly influence the amount of cost through his own action, he may be charged with such costs.

   c. Even if the person cannot significantly influence the amount of cost through his own direct action, he may be charged with those elements with which the management desires him to be concerned so that he will help to influence those who are responsible.

2. A method of motivation that may be useful is the designation of a cost limit to serve as a restriction on service acquisition or utilization for a specified activity. This approach is especially useful in areas where costs cannot be related to specific performance, such as research personnel and other staff functions.

   a. The limitation may represent an inviolate ceiling or merely a statement of expectations around which a certain amount of latitude is permitted.
   b. The limitation may be expressed as a single amount or it may be broken down into detailed service categories depending upon the type of control that management wishes to exercise.

3. The basis of measurement used in providing cost data for control is often a matter of management discretion and an important consideration in motivation. Different bases may significantly affect the way in which different individuals are motivated. For this reason, the bases of measurement selected should be consistent with the type of motivation desired. For example, different types of motivation may result when maintenance costs are charged to a responsibility center on the bases of: (1) a rate per maintenance labor hour, (2) a rate per job, or (3) a single amount per month.

4. Reporting with respect to costs for which any person is held responsible should be consistent both as to basis for measuring any given cost factor and the type of cost factors included in such reports. This implies that if a budget includes labor costs measured on a standard basis, performance costs being compared with the budget should be measured according to the same standard. Likewise, a person should not be held responsible for a cost factor in one report, and be freed from responsibility for the same factor in another report.

Costs as an Appraisal Device

Costs for control purposes are prepared (1) before the fact (in the form of standard, or budgets) and (2) after the fact (in the form of performance reports). Actually, control can be achieved only before the fact. Nothing that happens after the fact can in any way alter or undo what has already been done. The appraisal process that is based on performance reports is useful only insofar as it leads to better performance in the future, by instigating a study to avoid repeating previous mistakes. In addition, knowledge of the fact that an appraisal is to be made can be an important stimulus to good performance on the part of the person being judged. The performance reports used in the appraisal process are both a device for motivating individuals and a means of conveying information to management useful in starting a new planning cycle.

Some concepts underlying the construction of a cost reporting system are:

1. The concept of a standard. Costs can be set forth as a standard against which actual performance is to be measured. A standard cost is a statement of expected costs, or what costs should be under an assumed set of conditions. There are various types of standards. Normally they are predetermined costs and serve both the communication and motivation control functions. They may be expressed as average product costs and as functional or area of responsibility costs in such form as "normal capacity" costs, "ideal" costs, "current attainable" costs, and "budgeted" costs. When the standard is in terms of specific responsibilities within the firm, it may be classified in varying degrees of detail depending upon the degree of control management desires to exercise. For close control a detailed classification is appropriate so that variations of all types are reportable to management. If close control is not desired, in order to encourage employee initiative, or if not possible, because of the nature of the activity, a broad classification of standards covering longer periods of time or broader area of activity is appropriate.

2. The equity concept. The person being appraised should understand the basis on which performance is being judged and accept it as an equitable base.

3. The exception concept. Effective reports ordinarily are designed so that attention is focused on areas where performance costs differ significantly from standards.

4. The frequency with which costs are reported depends on the time interval within which significant departures from standards may occur, the cost of reporting, and on the time required to take corrective action.

While the foregoing comments are primarily applicable to subdivisions of the enterprise, there is a quantitative measure especially useful in appraising overall performance of the organization. This measure is the rate of return on investment. The standard against which the return may be compared is the rate of return which might have been earned if the investment were in another enterprise of comparable risk. This is often approximated by the return earned by other companies in the same industry or by other divisions in the same company.

From the foregoing, it should be apparent that no objective, universal definitions can be made for costs used for control. Since costs are constructed in accordance with the motivation desired, they are necessarily subjective, and it follows that "objective truth" has no relevance as a concept in the area of control. This does not imply intentional dishonesty or trickery, any more than do the principles of semantics. It does mean that there cannot be a single, objective definition of costs for control purposes.

HISTORICAL COST REPORTS FOR PLANNING AND CONTROL

The previous sections on planning and control have set forth basic concepts appropriate for cost reports for management. The implementation of these concepts in cost reports rests on varying degrees of reliability. As a result, many firms use the data available in the conventional accounting system as a basis for planning and control decisions. It is appropriate therefore that a statement be prepared indicative of the concepts underlying such cost reports for planning and control. It must be recognized that these concepts are approximations of the more basic concepts previously set forth. In this statement, only those concepts at variance with or supplementary to the concepts underlying corporate reports to stockholders are presented.

1. Assets, exclusive of cash and direct claims to cash, are bundles of services and cost accounting is concerned with the acquisition, utilization, and disposition of services.

2. Acquisition cost is the cash or cash equivalent released, on the acquisition date, to acquire services but there is no reason to assume that every service has an acquisition cost attached to it.

   a. Normally, interest is not recorded as a cost of nonmonetary services acquired but is treated separately as a cost of money. This should not preclude the treatment of minor elements of interest as cost when its separation is difficult and involved.

   b. For some purposes (such as a status report on firm investments as an aid in future planning) recognition in memorandum accounts may be granted services to be acquired on the date the order is placed. For most purposes, however, recognition in accounting records may be delayed until the acquisition of the services.

   c. Services acquired should be classified in a manner which facilitates their tracing on subsequent use. Because management normally plans in terms of types of physical units and changes these plans frequently, the most useful basic classification is in accordance with the form containing the services. Other classifications may supplement this basic classification to reveal intended use and assigned responsibility.

3. Utilization cost is a measure of the cost of the services used in a specific period of time. There are two aspects of this problem: (1) measuring the services used, and (2) assigning a cost to the services used.

   a. In measuring services used, this classification is often helpful:
      (1) The services expiring due to the passage of time alone.
      (2) The services which would have been consumed by the passage of time, but were in fact used in the operation process.
      (3) The services used solely because of the operation process.
      (4) The services which preclude reasonable determination of the time of their use and must be treated conventionally, such as types of advertising.

    b. The services used in any period of time should be measured first in terms of a portion of the acquisition cost (according to some assumed flow) to the firm. Ideally, such a measure should reflect the intent of management. For example, if a higher price were paid for some of the services in an asset (as might be the case in the first year's services of a machine or building), the measures of the services used should reflect such managerial intent. If specific intent is not known either by management or the accountant, it seems desirable to reflect the typical use of asset services and measure them in the following manner:

    (1) Services used as acquired (such as labor and utilities) but paid for at regular intervals may be costed as though every service had the same cost within the pay period. This should not, however, preclude the more accurate procedure of costing according to individual measures of services used when the amount involved is important or significant and the information is available, as in the case of labor under piece rate pay.

    (2) Services which attach to physical units and flow with them (such as materials and supplies) may be costed at the average cost of each unit in individual bundle purchases or at the average cost of each unit for all bundle purchases in a period of time. When a different average is computed for each bundle purchase, any flow of sequence in which the bundles are used may be assumed. Consistent use of one adopted flow becomes important if management is to understand resulting reports.

    (3) Services which flow from physical units without any flow of physical units (such as depreciation) may be costed on the assumption that services flow with output and cost assigned as an equal amount per unit of output. Or, the assumption may be made that services flow with the passage of time and services used may then be costed to periods of time either in equal amounts per unit of time or according to some other method of apportionment.

    (4) Services whose time of utilization is difficult to determine, such as advertising and administrative salaries, ideally should be set up as assets acquired and treated as utilization cost on some reasonable basis representative of the effort applied through the use of such services. This basic conception, however, should not preclude the general view that such services are used as acquired provided there is no basis for the more satisfactory treatment.

    c. In addition to the measurement of services used in terms of acquisition cost, it is sometimes helpful to measure the use of these services in terms of replacement cost [5] so as to provide a separation of the gain or loss due to nonoperational factors from the operating gain or loss.

---

    [5] Replacement cost is used here as the cash or cash equivalent currently required to replace the services used, not necessarily the physical unit. Also it is conceived in terms of the normal method of purchasing, which involves bundle purchases of services. Replacement cost is thus a share of the cost of replacing the bundle of services which normally will be purchased. The allocable share should be measured in a manner similar to that used in determining the share of acquisition cost used.

(1) It may be useful to separate general price level gains or losses from specific price level gains or losses.

(2) As services acquired at no cost or at significantly less than fair market value are used they may be measured in terms of replacement cost and the resulting gain separated from other gains.

4. Activity cost is a measure of the cost of the services used in performing some function, such as creating a product or some activity in the process of doing so. Any allocation of costs involves approximations. When allocations are to be made, such as for product costing, they may be measured in terms of utilization costs and may be separated between those due exclusively to the operating process and those which would have been consumed with the passage of time if not used. In some cases it may be possible to allocate services used in a period of time according to one overall basis. In other cases each element of cost may be assigned according to some physical unit representative of the flow of the services. In still other cases where there is no feasible way of allocating costs according to the flow of services, any reasonable basis of allocation may be used.[6]

5. Disposition costs are a measure of the services disposed of during a period of time and are useful in income reports to management. Frequently it is desirable to separate such costs between those whose services were originally used solely because of the operating activity from those whose services were related to the passage of time. Normally they are measured in terms of acquisition costs, but it is sometimes desirable to separate acquisition costs into the two elements of utilization costs and variations of utilization costs from acquisition costs.

a. The cost of services traced to units of products should not be considered disposed of until the product is sold or otherwise relinquished.

b. Services used in operations but not assigned to products should be separately classified in income reports unless there are reasons to defer them. Such reasons relate to the intent of management at the time of their use and the extent to which they are expected to aid in providing revenue in subsequent periods.

COSTS FOR EXTERNAL PURPOSES

Financial Statements

Costs are, of course, an important consideration in the measurement of income and in the valuation of assets for purposes of financial statements prepared for stockholders and other outside parties. Cost concepts relevant for these purposes are included in the statements on "Concepts and Standards Underlying Corporate Financial State-

---

[6] There should be no assumption that only manufacturing overhead should be assigned as a cost of product.

ments" prepared by the Committee on Accounting Concepts and Standards of the American Accounting Association, and therefore are outside the scope of the work of the present committee.

Cost Type Contracts

Many contractual agreements specify that payment be made on the basis of cost or of cost plus an allowance for profit. In view of the fact that no generally agreed upon definition of "costs" exists, it is important that the parties to the contract define in considerable detail what they mean by "cost" in the particular situation to which the contract applies.

Even though care is taken in framing this definition, it is unlikely that all problems that will arise can be foreseen. Most of these problems pertain to the treatment of "common costs"; that is, costs that relate partly to the work being done under the contract in question and partly to other work done by the enterprise. A case in point is the occupancy costs of a building in which both work under the contract and other work are being performed during the same time period. When the contract itself does not specify how these costs are to be divided, the division should be made in terms of conventionally accepted accounting procedures. To the extent that conventionally accepted accounting procedures do not provide a solution, the appropriate allocation may be made by references to arbitration or to courts of law.

There seems to be a belief in some quarters that there is, or should be, some scientifically correct way of dividing these costs. This belief is incorrect. Although there are generally recognized customs or conventions that may be helpful in certain areas, none of these has, or can have, the status of scientifically valid rules since common costs are, by definition, not precisely identifiable with one specific contract or project.

6. THE PAST IS HISTORY . . .
. . . THE FUTURE IS PLANNING * E. B. Rickard †

If a management control system is to operate effectively, it must be placed in the hands of imaginative, creative people with sound business judgment who, in fact, have the capacity to develop far-sighted solutions to the problems, risks, and changing environment that confront the particular enterprise. How to recognize such people in the first place, and assure their promotion in the business organization in the second place, is a subject of the greatest importance—but it is not a subject with which we shall be concerned here.

A second essential ingredient in an effective management control system is the existence of a set of organizational responsibilities which have been defined with reasonable clarity and which allow individual members of the organization to define with reasonable precision the contribution they are expected to make to the welfare of the enterprise and the manner in which their contribution relates to, or is affected by, other individuals who are working toward the common goal of the enterprise.

There is a third essential aspect of a management control system—the one we will discuss in this article. It relates to this question: *Given an able, imaginative and farsighted management group possessed of good business judgment and with clearly defined responsibilities, what can be done to harness and direct the energies of that group to achieve the optimum results for the business enterprise?*

It is obvious that some companies should rank higher than others in managerial effectiveness, based on historical results. Organizations such as General Motors, du Pont, and Standard Oil of New Jersey have shown an extraordinary ability to achieve excellent results in spite of complete changes in their executive roster over a period of years.

On the other hand, we are all acquainted with companies which have been organized around the business genius of one man—or which

* From *The Controller* (October, 1962). Reprinted by permission of the Financial Executives Institute.

† E. B. Rickard, General Parts and Service Manager, Ford Division, Ford Motor Company, Dearborn, Michigan.

have been organized to exploit the advantages that have accrued from a particular invention or a particular technological development unique to that company—or which have been favored with some fortunate accident of locational advantage that has conferred on the company a competitive headstart. However, the advantages enjoyed by these latter companies are transient and temporary. In time the genius passes on, the invention becomes obsolete, or locational advantages give way to less favorable developments or new competitors.

What we should be seeking in our quest for the essential ingredients of an effective management system are those elements which tend to assure perennial success for a business enterprise in the face of technological changes, in spite of changes in management personnel, and regardless of the elimination of some temporary advantages which the company may have enjoyed.

If you read the literature of business management, you find countless discussions of the individual tools of the control technician, such as budgeting, forecasting, profit planning, cash management, performance reporting, and so on. However, you do not find these separate tools exposited as part of an integrated general management philosophy which lends itself to application in different companies in different industries with different kinds of business problems. Too often the discussion describes how a particular company in a particular situation dealt with a particular control problem.

The recent past has seen, however, a considerable amount of introspection on this subject. As competition becomes keener, as decisions become more complex, and as the problem of survival becomes more acute, the premium placed on effective management action becomes increasingly high. The cost-price squeeze in which industry has found itself in the past few years and the increasing competition from foreign sources have made it mandatory for businessmen to seek more effective means of organizing and directing the collective efforts of the individuals who contribute to the business process.

There was a time when we could excel foreign competitors in the automotive industry because of superior production methods. While we paid higher wage rates in this country, we overcame that disadvantage with superior productivity. However, such advantages are rapidly disappearing and our reliance in the future will have to be placed increasingly on superior and more responsive management controls.

Electronic data processing has been touted as a part of the answer to this fundamental problem. Others have emphasized the contributions to be made through the mathematical techniques of operations research. In the curricula of the business schools of the country, you find increasing attention being given to a subject described as "Managerial Accounting." All these different approaches profess to improve a manager's ability to deal more effectively with his complicated environment. They all are provincial in their approach, however, and tend to deal in the language of technicians—a language that does not lend itself to general management consumption nor motivation.

This article will discuss some concepts which appear to have validity in the area of managerial effectiveness. To some extent these views have been formed as a result of participation in the research project of Financial Executives Research Foundation on the subject of management planning and control. They have also been influenced by my intimate association with the financial control system of the Ford Motor Company.

MANAGEMENT'S RESPONSIBILITIES

Before we can talk about management controls we must define management's job more precisely. Unless we can agree on the essential responsibilities of management, it is obviously impossible to agree on the systems, methods, procedures, or approaches by which management shall discharge its responsibilities.

We probably would all agree that managerial responsibility is epitomized by decision making—that is, choosing among a number of alternative courses of action. The alternatives may involve such fundamental considerations as basic corporate policies, future product or facility programs, or other major plans or proposals that will have an important long-run influence on the future profits and asset requirements of the enterprise. In addition, management must make decisions relative to the near-term or shorter-run operating problems of the enterprise, and must devise the plans or programs which should be adopted within the confines of the fundamental policies and programs which have been adopted. Moreover, management must determine whether or not the performance of the several operating segments of the business is satisfactory, and what shall be done in those instances where performance is not satisfactory.

THE DECISION MAKER

The role of decision maker, which is the essential role of management, is obviously a complicated one. Management is seldom asked to choose between two alternatives of which only one is acceptable. On the contrary, an endless and overwhelming array of alternatives usually exists. The number of alternatives is limited only by the imagination and creativeness which management can bring to bear on its problems. In addition, the degree of risk that each alternative entails may vary as greatly as the potential rewards.

It is not enough to recognize that decision making is the essence of management's task. We must also agree on the criteria which management should use in reaching its decisions. *What are the standards that should govern when one alternative is selected in preference to another?*

There are only two criteria that should guide management: The first of these criteria is that management should seek to maximize its profits in the long run with the resources and assets that are at its disposal; and second, management should seek opportunities for the employment of additional capital or additional resources on which it can earn a satisfactory rate of return.

There really is no other course of action open to management in the long run. You may find a business enterprise that is sufficiently well off and so strong financially that it can enjoy the luxury of making decisions on a basis that is not profit-oriented. This, however, cannot be a constant way of life in a competitive business situation. If management pursues such an approach to decision making, it sooner or later will find itself compelled either to retrace its steps and begin making decisions on a sound profit basis, or it will be forced out of business by its competitors.

You will note that I have not suggested that management attempt to maximize profits in the *short run*. Short-run profits can be realized by disregarding high-quality standards, price-gouging, or other practices which will, in time, alienate the customer by giving him less for his money. The only way to maximize profits *in the long run* is to adopt a consumer-oriented approach to your business. You must cultivate your customers with care and supply value with quality, or they will spend their money elsewhere. The ability to please the public, while earning over a long period of time a rate of return as good as, or better than, your competitors, is the only hallmark of a successful company. It should also be noted that giving more people improved products at lower cost is the essence of social responsibility and Christian endeavor.

LOOK AHEAD—NOT BACK

If you accept the premise that management, in its decision making role, must be primarily concerned with profit maximization, there are some important corollary propositions that follow.

One of these corollaries is that management is, or at least should be, primarily interested in the future not in the past. That, perhaps, is a trite statement. Yet it appears not to be trite to many people, including controllers, academicians, and members of the accounting fraternity. There is a considerable feeling afoot that historical accounting information is a pretty useful tool, along with historical production, sales, and operating statistics, if you have to make an important decision.

I couldn't disagree more fully. Such data are helpful in deciding what your problems are, but they don't help a bit in choosing among alternative ways of solving those problems. They form a basis upon which you can erect the data or the analyses which you need if you are to make a decision. However, taken alone, accounting information relates to the past and there isn't a confounded thing you can do about the past. The accounting data are historical and they are recorded. But they are also irrevocable. Management must seek to order the corporate affairs of the months and years ahead so that the profit-and-loss statement and the balance sheet will be pleasing to look at in the future. It cannot do that by paying attention primarily to historical information.

Obviously, it is necessary for a business management to know the current and past levels of profits, or the quality of historic cost or sales performance, so that it can be aware of its present position and can determine better the magnitude and priority of the tasks that lie ahead of it. But management's decisions relate to the months and years ahead for which no financial statement, budget performance reports, and sales statistics are yet available.

Looking back over my experience in Ford Motor Company, I cannot think of any significant management decision which relied on historical accounting data in choosing among alternative courses of action. Such data are simply not responsive to the needs of the situation. I do not mean to suggest that accountants do not render an important service in corporate affairs. We would not employ as many as we do in industry if that were so. It does seem clear, however, that the historical reporting function is slanted in directions which are not related to the main stream of management responsibility.

There are some additional corollaries which follow if you accept the premise that management's basic responsibility is to maximize profits in the long run. Rather than deal with these corollaries as abstract philosphical concepts, it may be more useful to develop their nature and meaning by using selected aspects of the financial control system of the Ford Division to illustrate the points I have in mind.

While I shall use the Ford Division as a vehicle to illustrate an approach to the development of a management control system, the basic propositions which we shall be discussing are not only applicable to the automotive industry but, in may opinion, are generally applicable to other companies in other industries, whether they be manufacturers of plastic products, retailers of soft goods, or sellers of a service.

ELEMENTS OF PLANNING AND CONTROL

Our discussion of the elements of an effective management planning and control system can be divided into three broad sections:

1. The decision making process;
2. The manner in which a business enterprise accumulates the effect of operating decisions to form a total operating plan; and
3. The methods or techniques used in evaluating the effectiveness with which individuals execute the plans and programs of the enterprise.

In dealing with the first area, the decision making process, I would like to discuss the method by which decisions are reached in an area which is of major importance to an automotive manufacturer, that is, an annual model change program.

For many companies one of the most difficult, complex, and risk-laden areas of decision making relates to the introduction of new products or services. In this area the automobile industry not only faces the unique problem of attempting to determine whether a proposed product will meet the demands of the public three to five years in the future, but it also must recognize that any such decision will be a major determinant of our future profits, first because of the large investment required by new product programs, and also because of the heavy financial penalties which result if the product does not appeal to the public when it is introduced.

Before describing this aspect of our control system, it might be useful to review the timing and planning strategy required to bring a new product to the market.

EXHIBIT I

PRODUCT PLANNING CYCLE OF THE 1964 GALAXIE

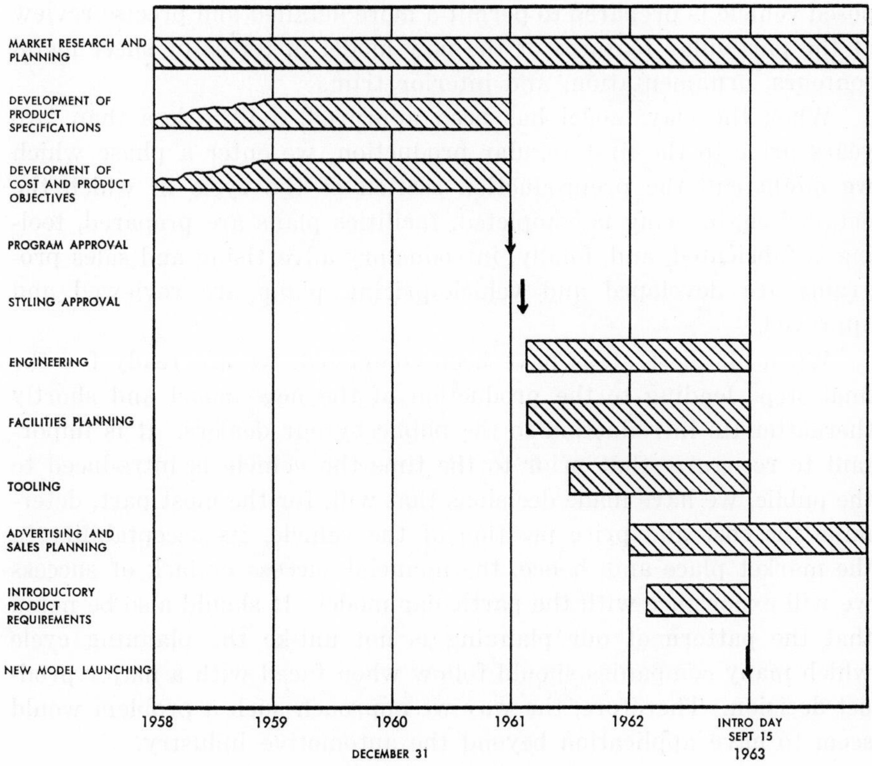

PRODUCT PLANNING CYCLE

Exhibit 1 traces the product planning cycle of a typical model change which we shall assume is the 1964 Ford Galaxie.

The first several years of the cycle are basically a conceptual period that ends with the approval of the product program. This phase would include the market research and planning which may begin three to five years before the eventual introduction of the product. The product decision we make will be shaped, to an important degree, by the results of this research as to probable future automotive demand and, particularly, the anticipated wishes of the public.

The next two steps will be the development of alternative product specifications and cost and product objectives.

After evaluation of alternative plans, a specific program for the 1964 Ford car is recommended, usually about two and a half years prior to the scheduled production of the particular model. Following this "paper" program proposal, a full-sized clay version of the proposed vehicle is prepared to permit a more detailed and precise review of the particular features of the new model in terms of sheet metal contours, ornamentation, and interior trim.

When the clay model has been approved, a little less than two years prior to the first regular production, we enter a phase which we might call the preproduction section of the cycle in which the detailed engineering is completed, facilities plans are prepared, tooling is fabricated, and, finally, introductory advertising and sales programs are developed and vehicle-pricing plans are reviewed and approved.

When all these steps have been completed, we are ready for the final steps leading to the production of the new model and shortly thereafter its introduction to the public by our dealers. It is important to recognize that prior to the time the vehicle is introduced to the public, we have made decisions that will, for the most part, determine the cost and price position of the vehicle, its acceptability in the market place and, hence, the financial success or lack of success we will experience with the particular model. It should also be noted that the pattern of our planning is not unlike the planning cycle which many companies should follow when faced with a major product decision. Therefore, the way we approach such a problem would seem to have application beyond the automotive industry.

Control System

We shall now describe the way in which our control system operates to assist the planning and execution of this typical product program from its inception to the introduction of the model to the public, and the way in which we attempt to assure that our plans and programs will be financially sound.

When management reviews the 1964 Galaxie product program, it is given first a full statement of the product and merchandising considerations that have dictated the design recommendations on which that program is based. As an integral part of such a review, a summary of product and financial objectives is presented.

Figure 1 shows an example of the product and financial objectives that might be presented in connection with the review of the Division's plans for the 1964 Galaxie. All the data are hypothetical and are only illustrative. The product objectives established for the 1964

FIGURE 1

1964 GALAXIE
REVIEW OF A PROPOSED PRODUCT CHANGE

	1964 Galaxie	Comparative Data		
	Original Objective	1960 Falcon	1962 Galaxie	1962 Competitor A
Package Size				
Weight	3670	2387	3771	3702
Length overall	209.9	181.2	209.3	209.6
Wheelbase	119.0	109.5	119.0	119.0
H∶ight	55.0	54.5	54.8	55.0
Headroom—front	39.0	38.8	38.1	37.9
Legroom—front	44.1	43.0	44.1	43.4
Performance				
Acceleration (Feet travelled in 10 seconds)	452	387	443	429
Passing time at 50 M.P.H. (Sec.)	10.4	14.2	11.2	11.0
Average miles per gallon	15.3	24.0	14.9	14.9
Volumes and Timing				
Initial production date	9-1-63	9-1-59	9-1-61	
Planning volume (units)	700,000	500,000	700,000	
Maximum capacity (units)	1,200,000	750,000	1,200,000	
Variable Costs				
Material	$1420	$1163	$1424	
Labor and overhead	151	146	155	
Total Variable Costs	$1571	$1309	$1579	
Fixed Expenditures (Millions)				
Styling	$ 2.3	$ 1.9	$ 2.1	
Engineering	10.9	9.6	11.2	
Tooling	55.4	44.2	36.0	
Launching	11.7	9.8	8.7	
Facilities	8.9	6.9	6.2	
Total Fixed Expenditures	$ 89.2	$ 72.4	$ 64.2	
Ford Division Profits (At financial planning volume)				
Profits—economic—per unit	XXX	XXX	XXX	
—accounted—per unit	XXX	XXX	XXX	
—accounted—millions	73.8	XXX	XXX	
Return on assets (after taxes)	XX.X%	XX.X%	XX.X%	

car will include details of the vehicle's physical characteristics, specific performance goals, including acceleration, passing performance and a specific gasoline economy objective. These product objectives are developed in recognition of the characteristics of prior model Ford cars, competitive products, and whatever our marketing research studies have told us about probable future consumers' desires,

In addition to detailed product objectives on package size and performance, the product presentation includes the product's related volume characteristics, including planning volume and maximum capacity, as well as the initial production date.

Next, the variable costs of the new model are compared with the costs of prior models and other car lines. In addition to the variable cost objectives, the major fixed expenditures that are directly associated with the program are shown. These include the expenditures that will be required for styling, engineering, tooling, launching, and facilities.

In addition to detailed product and cost objectives, the presentation includes detailed profit objectives. You will note that the Ford Division profit objectives have been stated at a so-called "financial planning volume." It is necessary to take a moment to discuss the volume concept that we use in developing our future financial projections in an industry beset by wide swings in consumer demand.

Obviously, vehicle sales volumes can and do vary greatly from year to year. We have no way of determining the probable level of industry volume in each of the next three or four years, nor can we be sure of the share of industry volume which will be secured by the Galaxie. To solve this volume problem, we attempt to estimate the probable average annual sales volume of the Galaxie and all Ford cars over the next five years and use that vehicle volume as the basis for our planning. Under this approach we are willing to accept the penalty of low volume and low profits in certain years in the expectation that it will be offset by higher profits in those years when sales volume is about average. We call this assumed volume "financial planning volume." The use of financial planning volume as a planning base provides an essential continuity to our pricing, product planning, and cost planning. We do not expect to raise our prices or cheapen our products in years when volumes are below average and, conversely, we do not cut our prices or increase our product costs when volumes are above average. As we look further into our system of financial planning and control, you will see that financial planning volume is the basis on which we make all our financial projections.

The financial summary of program objectives, shown at the bottom of *Figure 1*, includes the estimated Ford Division profits both before and after the assignment of fixed costs are shown on a per unit basis and in total millions of dollars. We use the term "economic profit" to refer to profits excluding fixed expenses, while the term "accounted profits" includes all costs that are properly assignable to the Galaxie in 1964. We also determine the assets properly assignable to the Galaxie product line and establish a return on assets objective.

The cost, profit, and expenditure information shown in *Figure 1* does not represent a set of financial projections which have been developed in the Controller's Office of the Division; rather, each operating activity which is affected by the future program (especially manufacturing, purchasing, and engineering) is furnished with a detailed description of the product program so that it is in a position to evaluate the probable effect of the program on its operations and enters into a commitment to the effect that it will be able to carry out its share of such a program for the amount shown as its responsibility.

Each of the financial figures is backed up in considerable detail. One of the lessons you learn rather early in the game when you are involved in controlling the results of future programs is that you can not control in any greater detail than the detail with which you developed your initial plan.

If you plan on spending $10 million (with no detail) for tooling, and actual expenditures turn out to be $11 million, you have no means of determining what went wrong or why the $1 million overrun occurred. You can only determine the reason for the overrun and take appropriate corrective action if you have developed your initial estimates in sufficient detail so that you can isolate the specific tools that have caused the overrun and can determine why the initial estimate was less than the actual cost. Only then can you truly understand the overrun. The same is true of other expenditure figures as well as the profit estimates.

An effective control system must begin with the development of objectives in detail rather than in aggregates. If you don't plan in detail, you can't control in detail. If you don't control in detail, you don't control effectively. How much detail is required is, of course, a matter of judgment which must be determined in the light of the specific problems which face the company and the seriousness or urgency with which those problems are viewed.

Profit Picture in Advance

Returning to our hypothetical 1964 Galaxie program, it is quite possible that when the initial analysis is completed, we may find that the planned program is not a particularly attractive venture. It may involve cost increases or asset investments which cannot be contained within our established objectives. If this is the case, the product assumptions are changed or other modifications are made to be sure that the plan, in its initial conception, is a financially attractive venture. The key point is that management is told precisely what the expenditures and profits are going to be before they are asked to make a decision. Stated differently, our objective is to have management aware of the full financial impact of future programs before a decision is made, not after.

In presenting the 1964 Galaxie proposal, we also summarize the effect of the decision on the profit position of the Galaxie, the Ford Division, and the company. *Figure 2* shows how we would describe the effect of a product decision on company profits. We have shown at the top an estimate of profits, assets, and returns for the model years 1962 through 1965. We have then shown the effect on profits, assets, and returns of the 1964 Galaxie program decision. In the years 1962 and 1963, the program will reduce profits $2.4 million and $3.0 million respectively. However, in 1964 and 1965, the program will improve profits $10.0 million and $20.0 million. In the bottom section we have shown the current estimate of profits, assets, and returns, assuming the proposed 1964 Galaxie program is approved.

As indicated before, this kind of summary is shown for the individual product line, for the Ford Division, and for the total company, and permits the management of the Division and the company to see their overall profit position at the time a major product decision is made and to examine this information *before* a decision is made.

FIGURE 2

EFFECT OF 1964 GALAXIE PROGRAM
GALAXIE PROFITS, ASSETS AND RETURNS
(At Financial Planning Volume)

	Model Years			
Prior Estimate	1962	1963	1964	1965
Profits before taxes (millions)	$ 71.0	$ 63.0	$ 63.8	$ 66.8
Assets (millions)	XXX.X	XXX.X	XXX.X	XXX.X
Return after taxes (per cent)	XX.X%	XX.X%	XX.X%	XX.X%
Effect of Proposed Program				
Profits before taxes (millions)	$ (2.4)	$ (3.0)	$ 10.0	$ 20.0
Assets (millions)	(0.5)	(5.0)	(20.0)	(10.0)
Return after taxes (per cent)	(0.4)%	(0.9)%	0.6%	2.9%
Current Estimate				
Profits before taxes (millions)	$ 68.6	$ 60.0	$ 73.8	$ 86.8
Assets (millions)	XXX.X	XXX.X	XXX.X	XXX.X
Return after taxes (per cent)	XX.X%	XX.X%	XX.X%	XX.X%

The objective of our control system as it relates to decision making is to determine the profit effect and the degree of financial risk involved, evaluate the attractiveness of available alternatives, assure that all the reasonable alternatives have been explored, that the representations made by the supporting offices are appropriate, attainable, and are recorded as commitments which those offices will be expected to achieve. Such detailed analyses are not only undertaken in the product area but are a part of every significant decision which management makes. Such matters as major facility changes, sales contests, major changes in advertising and sales promotion programs, quality programs, pricing actions, cost reduction programs, reliability and durability programs, and so forth, are ordinarily subjected to a careful financial evaluation as part of the management approval process.

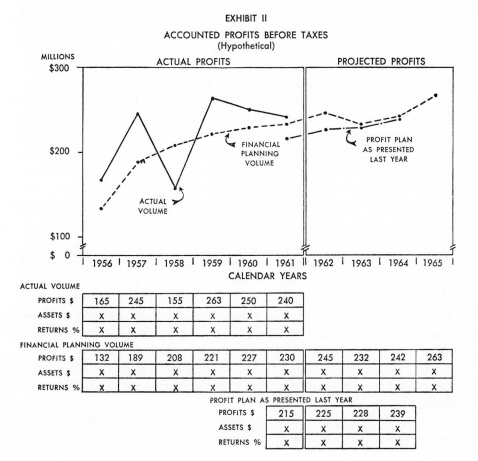

EXHIBIT II

ACCOUNTED PROFITS BEFORE TAXES
(Hypothetical)

ACTUAL VOLUME									
PROFITS $	165	245	155	263	250	240			
ASSETS $	X	X	X	X	X	X			
RETURNS %	X	X	X	X	X	X			

FINANCIAL PLANNING VOLUME									
PROFITS $	132	189	208	221	227	230	245	232	242	263
ASSETS $	X	X	X	X	X	X	X	X	X	X
RETURNS %	X	X	X	X	X	X	X	X	X	X

PROFIT PLAN AS PRESENTED LAST YEAR			
PROFITS $	215	225	228	239
ASSETS $	X	X	X	X
RETURNS %	X	X	X	X

Periodic Evaluations

Thus far we have indicated that an effective control system must provide management with evaluations and analyses that assist in decision making. However, it must also provide management with periodic summaries or evaluations of the total profit and investment position of the business. In other words, we must synthesize the total effect of the operating plans and programs that have been approved into a consistent and coordinated control program for the entire business. The vehicle through which this synthesis is accomplished at Ford is the profit plan or profit budget. The profit plan is not a financial forecast but is a synthesis of the collective effect on profits of all the approved plans and programs of operating activities of the business. We take the same decisions we've just been talking about plus those that can be reasonably foreseen at that point in time, bundle them up and take a financial reading, crosscut, through all of them, and produce a statement of the profits, assets and returns that will be realized in future years if everyone meets his commitments. We try to be realistic in the sense that if somebody will obviously fail to meet his commitments and management has in effect agreed that the deviation is unavoidable, we modify our plans accordingly. However, we try to assure that the decision to depart from the plan gets proper review and approval. We don't cavalierly disregard the commitments that people have made. We try to hold their feet to the fire if it appears at all reasonable.

Future Profits

Exhibit II shows a chart from the annual presentation of our profit plan to corporate management. In the course of this review we discuss historical profits but the major emphasis is on our profit plans for the future. As shown by the two lines, profits are stated on two bases: first, at actual volume which varies with industry volume changes and Ford market penetration; and second, at the Division's financial planning volume which is a constant volume. Future profits are shown only at financial planning volume. We also show, in this presentation, the profit projection which was included in last year's review. This provides management with an opportunity to review the organization's total profit performance versus the commitments we made a year ago.

It should be emphasized again that the projections for future years in our profit plan are not mere forecasts of profit results. They are the cumulative result of specific detailed commitments which have been received from each operating activity in the Division. Consequently, our projections represent a financial expression of the specific contributions each office has agreed to make to the profits of the Division in future years.

The remainder of the profit plan presentation to corporate management describes in some detail these future operating plans both in financial and nonfinancial terms.

The question which frequently arises in this connection is how far the profit plans of an enterprise should be carried into the future. *Should we seek to project profits for one year, five years, or some other period of time?* It seems apparent that the answer to this question will vary among companies—there is no simple pat answer that can be given. A company should extend its planning far enough into the future to be able to anticipate and adapt itself to developments that may have a potential effect on its future operations. The objective of a control system is to avoid the possibility of the company being suddenly confronted with adverse developments which have not been foreseen and for which no provision has been made in the operating plans and programs of the enterprise. It would appear that most companies should be developing their future plans in detail for at least four or five years in the future, while in some instances, five to ten years might not be an unreasonable period.

MEASURING EFFECTIVENESS

The third and final element in the Ford Division's control system is the measurement of how effectively individuals and the total Division execute the plans and programs in line with the objectives which have been established. The essential characteristic of this aspect of our control system is that we compare actual or anticipated performance with planned performance. We isolate the variances that have arisen, determine the cause, and take whatever action we can to correct the situations that appear to be unsatisfactory. Some of our performance reports, however, have a unique flavor which deserves special mention. This is illustrated in *Figure 3* which is taken from a monthly report we provide for the general management of the Division. It describes the status of each forward product program.

As shown at the top of the report, the objective (referred to as the "Product Planning Committee Objective") is the same objective approved by management for the original program. This is the base with which the current position is compared. All product changes, revisions in cost estimates, and projected expenditure overruns or underruns are summarized monthly and presented to management with concise explanations as to why the program is ahead or behind objective.

If this report were to indicate, for example, that the program was lagging behind its financial objectives, management attention would be directed to the unfavorable areas and attempts would be made to correct the specific problem that caused the overrun. Failing this, all aspects of the program would be subjected to an intensive review to offset the unfavorable variance by taking action in other areas of the program.

The point that warrants emphasis in connection with this discussion of performance reporting is that we seek to determine far enough in advance what our performance will be so that we can

FIGURE 3

STATUS OF 1964 GALAXIE PROGRAM
CURRENT ESTIMATE VERSUS
PRODUCT PLANNING COMMITTEE OBJECTIVE

	Profits Per Unit	*Assets Per Unit*	*Return After Taxes*	*Fixed Expenditures (Millions)*
Product Planning Committee Objective	$XXX	$XXX	X.X%	$89.2
Current Estimate	XXX	XXX	X.X	88.3
Current Estimate Fav./(Unfav.) versus P.P.C. Objective	$ 5	$ 2	0.5%	$ 0.9
Explanation of Variance				
Design Changes:				
Improved hood release mechanism	$(1)			
Added floor pan reinforcement	(2)			
Seat belt attaching hardware to all models	(1)			
Tooling:				
Reduced cost of rear doors due to styling change	1	1		0.4
Projected reduction in tooling cost due to change in vendor	1	1		0.5
Freight:				
Increased usage of multilevel rail cars	5			(0.1)
Launching and Overhead Costs:				
Closing of Chester Assembly Plant	1			0.3
Added cost of redesigning front suspension				(0.2)
Final estimate of the effect on labor costs of the U.A.W. contract	1			
Total Variance	$ 5	$ 2	0.5%	$ 0.9

change our thinking if we do not like what we see. If a program has been reviewed and approved, we do not necessarily wait until that approval has been translated into actual profits or actual costs and is, therefore, beyond repair.

MANAGEMENT CONTROL PATTERN

In addition to reports for each product line, we also prepare a monthly financial summary that brings together the effect of all future product programs and all other operating programs. We compare this to our position as planned in the annal operating plan discussed earlier.

In *Exhibit III* I have attempted to portray graphically the cyclical or circular pattern of an effective management control system. Each step bears a direct relationship to the next succeeding step. We have placed "Performance Evaluations" at the top of the circle. These evaluations, when combined with the impact of competitive, economic, technological, social, and political developments, lead management to

EXHIBIT III

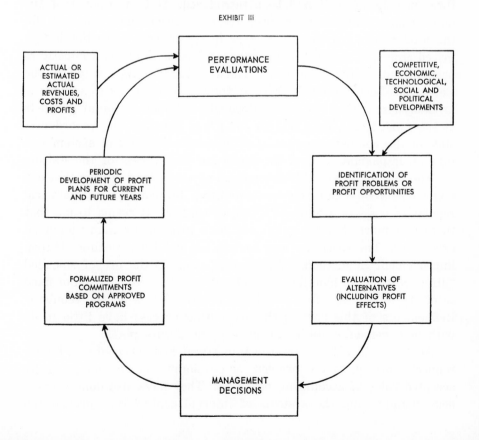

the identification of profit problems or profit opportunities which confront the business. In turn, the identification of such problems or opportunities requires that management evaluate the acceptability of alternative courses of action for dealing with each such situation. Out of such deliberations flow specific management decisions.

The profit commitments which are implicit in those decisions must be formalized and recorded. They must also periodically be accumulated into a profit plan, or financial plan, that summarizes the profit effect in current and future years of the approved plans and programs of the enterprise. These profit plans or profit budgets, when compared with actual or estimated actual revenues, costs and profits, represent the basic tool of performance evaluation. Thus, we return to the beginning of the cycle we have been describing.

Proof of the Pudding

One of the notable successes in the automobile business in recent years is the Ford Falcon, which outsold all other compact cars within three months after it had been introduced. It is a product of the management control system we have been discussing. Not only did the Falcon turn out to be a success in the market place but it was priced from $70 to $90 below comparable vehicles of our competitors brought out at the same time. Notwithstanding its low price, the Falcon has been a financial success for the company as well. This is probably less true of our competitors who introduced similar products at the same time. They had to cut prices substantially in order to stay in the competitive race. Our management control system can take an important part of the credit for the success of the Falcon.

You will note from this description of our control system that our management does not rely on accounting information or historical reports of costs or profits as a tool of control. It seems to me that there is a moral here that has not been grasped by many financial executives. The success of our system has not been contingent upon improvement in methods of allocating costs or the use of so-called "direct costing" in handling fixed charges, or the reevaluation of fixed assets to reflect the effect of changing price levels on the economy. Refinements of this sort in the accounting process have little to do with management's ability to make sound future plans.

Accountants, after a great deal of study, have arrived at a highly refined approach to the problem of developing sound and generally accepted rules of accounting practices. They have also done a great deal in improving the systems of internal control that protect the

presently owned assets of the company. Financial executives have
not always shown a similar zeal for protecting the future financial
position of the company through a system of forward-looking controls.

There is little solace in the knowledge that we have accurately
recorded all the events that have pushed a company into bankruptcy.
It is much more useful and satisfying to devote our energies to the
development of a system of controls which prevents bankruptcy.

Summary

Further refinements in the accounting process are not necessary
to meet management's need for useful control tools. Historical accounting information is one subject management should not pay attention to in decision making. What management *should* pay attention
to—and this cannot be overemphasized—is the development of a control system which has three essential characteristics:

1. The system must provide management with adequate information on
   the probable financial consequences of a decision *before* the decision
   is made—not after.

2. The financial results on which a decision is based must be analyzed
   in enough detail so that the responsible persons in the organization
   can be assigned a clearly defined financial task in carrying out the
   decision. Only by so doing can we accept and meet the financial
   commitments which are implicit in the particular decision.

3. A system must exist under which you know well in advance whether
   each operating activity will meet its commitments so that appropriate
   and *timely* action may be taken if it appears that a particular program
   is not on target.

If we compare these criteria with the usual published description
of the type of information that management should receive from a
controller's office, it is apparent that they have very little in common.
It is easy to place too much emphasis on the value to management
of budget performance reports, comparative cost reports, and similar
analyses of past performance. It is true that financial data have to
be the universal language of business management, since they are
the only common denominator which allows management to deal with
such unrelated factors as units of output, square feet of floor space,
quality of production, number of hourly employes, and so on. While
you must control a business enterprise in terms of revenues, costs,
and profits, it is essential to recognize that an effective control system
must be able to determine the factors that will affect costs and profits
in the years ahead rather than analyze the factors that have influenced costs and profits in the months or years that have gone by.

7. BUDGETING MODELS AND SYSTEM SIMULATION *

Richard V. Mattessich †

Exposition of the Problem

Periodic budgeting, as practiced in industry and taught in the accounting curriculum, combines estimates by individual departments in a process of coordinative aggregation. The purpose is to supply management with a financial plan for future operations.

Frequently, budgeting is charged with the more ambitious task of "finding the most profitable course" [1] for an enterprise. If this means selecting a combination of managerial policies which *optimizes* the long-term profit of the enterprise, the above definition of the purpose of this discipline seems to overstate the potential of traditional budgeting activity. It makes the layman believe that this area of accounting is in a position to determine *optimal solutions*. Undoubtedly, this is not the case since budgeting traditionally neither applies any algorism to optimize the long-term profit function nor provides any means for determining and comparing *all* the alternatives resulting from the *innumerable* factor and policy combinations feasible for an enterprise. If it means, however, finding a policy that yields a prospective profit considered to be *satisfactory*, the above definition is acceptable (provided the term "satisfactory" is interpreted in the Simonian meaning of the best acceptable solution within a limited range of alternatives. Herbert Simon calls such a procedure "satisficing" as opposed to the more demanding operation of "optimizing" [2]).

* From *The Accounting Review* (July, 1961). Reprinted by permission of the American Accounting Association.

† Richard V. Mattessich, Associate Professor, University of California, Berkeley, California.

The author wishes to acknowledge gratefully (1) the financial support of the Management Science Group—Berkeley (Ford Foundation funds) during the summer of 1960 to this project, (2) the stimulating discussions under the eminent leadership of Professor C. West Churchman, and (3) the advice and comments he has received from Professors C. Devine, M. Moonitz, and J. Wheeler.

[1] J. B. Heckert and J. D. Wilson, *Business Budgeting and Control* (2d ed.), p. 14.

[2] Herbert A. Simon, "Theories of Decision Making in Economics and Behavioral Science," *American Economic Review* (June, 1959), 49, p. 264. See

With the application of mathematical-scientific approaches to management problems and the progressive use of automatic data processing, the question arises: In what way can future periodic budgeting be improved? Before a quest for reform can be considered it is necessary to make a distinction between the immediate future and the long run. There is no doubt that *ultimately* it will be desirable to "optimize" within our budgeting models, but only as long as the mechanism for optimization does not restrict the budgeting procedures in other directions or impose upon them other over-simplifications. The optimization model which has been proposed in the award-winning dissertation by Stedry [3] is a meritorious attempt to find a starting point for the development of managerial models in budgeting; it is a pioneering effort which, considering the lack of "operational research" procedures in accounting, cannot be praised highly enough, though there is still much room for improvement. On the other hand, we must not overrate the immediate *practical* usefulness of this approach on a large scale (for further details see Footnotes 13 and 15); like most managerial optimization models it suffers under the serious handicap of being restricted to a single department or limited area of operations, thus enabling us only to *suboptimize* without any hope for *"overall-optimization"* of the whole enterprise. It, therefore, seems opportune to develop a less ambitious approach which, however, has the advantage of applying to the *whole* enterprise and which eventually may be utilized in combining sub-optimization models for individual departments. One purpose of this paper is to stimulate experimentation and simulation with "aggregation models." The concrete example presented in the third section is a first attempt at formalizing such a model and, therefore, constitutes an illustration rather than an ultimate solution; hence suggestions for further improvement are invited.

As established before, traditional budgeting already offers a primitive procedure of "satisficing" a goal function. It suffers, however, from the shortcoming of including too small a number of possible alternatives from which to choose in determining the "most satisfactory" solution. Besides, we all recognize that the traditional budget, even if it is a flexible budget, is very difficult to adjust to suddenly changing conditions; it is at best "flexible" only with regard to a changing sales or production volume. Our present proposal,

also J. G. March and H. A. Simon, *Organizations* (New York: John Wiley & Sons, Inc., 1958), pp. 140-41, 169.

[3] Andrew C. Stedry, *Budget Control and Cost Behavior* (Englewood Cliffs, N. J.: Prentice-Hall, Inc., 1960), pp. 113-43.

therefore, rests on the simple assumption that a model which permits the calculation of a larger number of alternatives, based on more numerous "flexible" variables and eventually changing parameters, would yield a better approximation to the ideal but unattainable optimum solution. This could be made possible by means of electronic computers and system simulation (discussed in the next section). To construct a model for such a task requires the translation of a traditional budgeting system into algebraic terms. This has not been done before, since accountants are accustomed to present their knowledge through particular examples and individual illustrations, a practice that explains the overemphasis on technicalities and the abounding use of illustrative tables with long figure columns in textbooks of accounting and related fields. The "general" formulations of the accountant rest mainly on verbal descriptions, and past attempts to break this habit were not successful largely because of the conservative attitude of accountants. The present situation appears more promising as more and more accountants realize that soon they will be working in a highly mathematical atmosphere whether they desire it or not. It also must be borne in mind that a few decades ago modern algebraic notations (e.g., sigma and matrix notations) were not applied at all, at least not in the economic sciences. It is due to these notational devices that a concise and yet general presentation is made possible.

To some operations analysts the mere translation of accounting models into mathematical terminology, without a calculus for determining an optimum, might appear to be a rather pedestrian task. We are convinced, however, that as long as accounting methods are acceptable to the industry the mere change to a mathematical formulation will be advantageous for several reasons: (1) it can be considered a prerequisite for applying electronic data processing to certain accounting problems,[4] (2) it articulates the structure of the accounting models and illuminates accounting methods from a new point of view, revealing many facets so far neglected or unobserved;

---

[4] For those who appeal to G. Clarkson and H. Simon's statement that "we are beginning to learn that models do not have to be stated in mathematical or numerical form to permit us to simulate their behavior with electronic computers,": "Simulation and Group Behavior," *American Economic Review* (December, 1960), p. 923 (cf. Herbert A. Simon, *The New Science of Management Decision* [New York: Harper & Brothers, 1960], pp. 22, 24-25), we may reply that even if mathematics in the narrow sense of the word can be relinquished, symbolic logic will have to be substituted for it. Therefore, if we promote the acquisition of mathematical knowledge by accountants we refer to it in the broadest sense of the term and include the achievements of modern logic as well.

(3) it enables a *general* and hence more scientific presentation of many accounting methods; (4) it facilitates the exploration of new areas, thereby accelerating the advancement of accounting. The example chosen for this paper shall particularly emphasize this point; and finally (5) it leads to more sophisticated methods and might help to lay the foundation for close cooperation of accounting with other areas of management science. Therefore, we will attempt to develop a concise but fairly general frame for traditional budgeting and explore the possibility of extending or modifying such a model for the purpose of determining "satisfactory" if not "optimal" managerial plans.

Such an approach has the advantage of using traditional budgeting as a basis for developing a more refined and perhaps a more scientific treatment of the problem.

The Meaning of Simulation

Whether accounting is considered to be a part of management science will depend to a great extent on the effort accountants make in absorbing tools and techniques of management science and in incorporating them into their own conceptual apparatus. So far, in spite of recognizable endeavors, the vocabulary of management science still constitutes a "foreign" language to many accountants, and before embarking upon construction of a budgeting model for *simulation* purpose it becomes advisable to subject the concept of "system simulation," and its use by management scientists, to some investigation.

For a long time social scientists have envied physicists and chemists their vast opportunity of experimentation. This, it is true, has not been their only object of envy, but considering the broad experimental basis on which the achievements of the natural sciences rest, it is still a major target of envy. Everyday life, no doubt, supplied social scientists with *surrogate* experimental material, the cognitive value of which shall by no means be underrated; [5] but it usually forces relinquishment of the most important features of the experiment: control of certain variables and arbitrary repetition, a limitation which holds in particular for economics and business administration. In practice, neither the whole economy nor an individual firm lends itself to experimentation in the true sense of the word.

---

[5] Joseph A. Schumpeter, *History of Economic Analysis* (New York: Oxford University Press, 1954), p. 16 (*vide* his citation of Leon Walras).

The advent of electronic data processing systems, however, seems to have opened the door to experimental ventures—and adventures— for the economic sciences mainly through the channel of "system simulation." Such experiments are of course of a different nature than those of the physicist as they do not deal with the medium of reality itself but only with its mathematical structure; they do enable, however, the mental reproduction of a large number of alternative situations and thus help to determine *satisfactory* if not approximately optimal solutions. As Malcolm says, "System Simulation has the most useful property of permitting the researcher and management to experiment with and test policy, procedure, and organization changes in much the same way as the aeronautical engineer tests his design ideas in the laboratory or in the 'wind tunnel.' Thus we might think of System Simulation as a sort of 'management Wind Tunnel' which is used to pretest many suggested changes and eliminate much needless 'experimentation' with the 'real' people, machines, and facilities." [6]

In contrast to the "wind tunnel," the simulation models of the management scientist are analytical or analog models which frequently incorporate probability concepts. Where the latter holds— particularly in cases which hinge on a statistical distribution whose structure is not exactly known—a special simulation approach has been developed under the name of *Monte Carlo method*.[7] The frequently encountered identification of the term "simulation method" with the expression "Monte Carlo method" does not seem justified however, since the former implies a much more comprehensive concept than the latter. Not every simulation model relies on a "simulated probability distribution"; the following example of a budgeting system for simulation purposes may be taken as a case in point. For problems which cannot be forced into the straitjacket of an optimization model, or for optimization problems of a forbiddingly complex mathematical structure, *approximate solutions* may be found by simulation; that is, by determining and scanning an array of alternative combinations and selecting that with the most favorable outcome. This, of course, is a fairly crude approach since "the result of a simulation is always the answer to a specific numerical problem with-

---

[6] D. C. Malcolm, Forward to *Report of System Simulation Symposium* (New York: John Wiley & Sons, Inc., 1959), p. v.
[7] D. W. Miller and M. K. Starr, *Executive Decisions and Operations Research* (Englewood Cliffs, N. J.: Prentice-Hall, Inc., 1960), pp. 152-55.

out any insight into why that is the answer or how the answer would be influenced by a change in any of the data." [8]

Nevertheless simulation may have some appeal to accountants, and indeed the traditional approach to periodic budgeting can, with some imagination, be regarded as a simulation model. It is true that this model so far has not appeared in mathematical attire, just as it is undeniable that the array of alternatives calculated is usually restricted to a small number only. The test for the existence of a simulation approach, however, is the selection of a satisfactory solution from alternatives, even if it is reflected in the preparatory work to the budget rather than in the coordinative level of the budgeting model itself. On this coordinative level the "flexible" budget could be interpreted as a series of alternatives; here the purpose of calculating conditions under various output levels serves primarily to adjust the budget for suddenly changing output conditions, while changes in the product mix, in wage rates, material prices, and other costs are rarely given consideration. By simulating the firm through a budgeting model it should be feasible to extend the flexibility into these other directions. Therefore, a major purpose of the proposed project is to provide for a *multidimensional variability or flexibility* of the budget. According to the needs, certain alternatives could be printed out at the beginning of the budgeting period while other alternatives would be quickly available through a stored computer program into which data for the changed variables or parameters could be inserted.[9]

TRADITIONAL BUDGETING AS A MATHEMATICAL MODEL

Budgeting, as traditionally practiced, is frequently regarded as "accounting for the future." Even if thereby no individual double entries are recorded, the coordination of financial flows is carried out with reference to the classificational device of accounts. Sometime ago we hinted at the possibility and eventual usefulness of presenting accounting in form of a system of simultaneous definitional

---

[8] Robert Dorfman, "Operations Research," *American Economic Review* (September, 1960), 50, p. 604.

[9] For the reader who wants to inform himself in greater detail about many facets of system simulation we recommend "Simulation: A Symposium" (three articles by G. H. Orcutt, M. Shubik, G. Clarkson, and H. Simon) *American Economic Review* (December, 1960), pp. 893-932; and the *reports* of the first and second *System Simulation Symposium* (sponsored by the American Institute of Industrial Engineers, The Institute of Management Science, and the Operations Research Society of America, New York, 1958 and 1960).

equations.[10] This is what Dorfman [11] calls the "first" or "straight-forward descriptive aspect" of model building; although it is an indispensable step, it no doubt results in "an essentially tautological and sterile description of the problem." In budgeting, however, the second aspect, the state of "creative hypothesizing" is, at least in principle, also materialized—though it may be a matter of controversy whether the hypotheses of customary budgeting constitute a satisfactory and creative achievement. Yet, the question arises whether budgeting may not be the most fertile soil of accounting for planting meaningful mathematical models. It is, therefore, not surprising that the problem of budgeting (in the broadest sense of the word) has been attacked *mathematically* from various points of view. The oldest, occasionally encountered, and most elaborate approach is the construction of "flow models" for the whole firm. It is true that the hypotheses used in some of these models might be considered as being less crude than those of traditional budgeting; but apart from the fact that their aim might be considered as going beyond the task of a purely financial plan, it is, from the viewpoint of actual practice, not too successful an approach and for the time being has been restricted to business games. It may well be the most promising method of the future, but in spite of intensive experimentation by many research groups so far the immense number of variables and the magnitude of the task of determining a host of unwieldy parameters have prevented results which give hope to any *wide* and immediate application in the area of industrial budgeting.[12] The second approach can be called a "behavioral model" and is restricted to the control task of budgeting. It is contained in the first part of Stedry's thesis [13] and its originality may warrant further study by the reader.

Stedry makes a rigorous distinction between budgeting for control purposes and budgeting for planning purposes. Out of this distinction

[10] Richard V. Mattessich, "Towards an Axiomatization of Accountancy, with an Introduction to the Matrix Formulation of Accounting Systems," *Accounting Research* (October, 1957), pp. 328-55, and "Mathematical Models in Business Accounting," *Accounting Review* (July, 1958), pp. 472-81.

[11] Robert Dorfman, "Operations Research," *American Economic Review* (September, 1960), 50, p. 604.

[12] However, a project of such a "flow model" or "management control system" has been undertaken on a large scale by the Systems Development Corporation (Santa Monica). So far only one aspect of management control has been investigated—the effect of using particular decision rules—through a mathematical model constituting a huge queuing network. Theoretically, this is a fascinating approach and no doubt will bear fruit in the *long run*. *Vide:* J. B. Heyne, "Planning for Research in Management Control Systems," *Technical Memorandum—546*, SDC (October, 1960), p. 30.

[13] Andrew C. Stedry, *Budget Control and Cost Behavior* (Englewood Cliffs, N. J.: Prentice-Hall, Inc., 1960), pp. 17-42.

follows the third approach (also developed by Stedry and mentioned previously) which consists of a linear programming model for maximizing the profit function of an individual department. Such "planning" models might be incorporated into the aggregation model suggested below but are not by necessity an integral part of it; it is conceivable that budgeting on the departmental level may continue in the traditional way while only the budgeting activity on the coordinative level uses a mathematical model. Even then a multitude of alternatives is feasible.

Fundamentally there is no difference between the following budgeting model and other simulation models of management science. The main criticism against such an approach, therefore, cannot be found on the methodological plane but must be sought on the level of hypotheses formulation. It is as easy for accountants to demonstrate that their traditional approach is nothing but the application of various models (translatable into mathematical terms) as it is difficult for them to refute the reproach that their models are too simple and their hypotheses too crude. The main weapon in their defense, of course, lies in the counter-argument that "too simple" and "too crude" are very relative concepts; and what may appear to the theoretician crude might be considered by the man in practice, who has to weigh costs against benefits, as fairly satisfactory. Therefore, this challenge becomes critical only in the moment when the hypothesis becomes so crude and the model so full of "gaps" that it must be considered meaningless. In the following model we have used those hypotheses generally accepted in budgeting textbooks as well as in actual practice. Our answer is therefore highly pragmatic, if we justify our approach with the evidence that these hypotheses are used in thousands of enterprises all over the world. Their present acceptance is certainly enough justification for using them as a *starting point* for the construction of a framework which, due to its general formulation, should be flexible enough to be adaptable to more refined hypotheses.

This model, fully spelled out, consists of several hundred simultaneous equations and is intended for experimental use in various enterprises. To avoid overburdening this paper with so many equations we present here only the most important equations, primarily those which represent in a *succinct* way the tables occasionally encountered in textbooks of budgeting [14] in a fairly general form.

---

[14] Glen A. Welsch, *Budgeting: Profit-Planning and Control* (Englewood Cliffs, N. J.: Prentice-Hall, Inc., 1957).

We may point out that in order to understand the presentation of the budgeting model in symbolic form no knowledge of higher mathematics is required; some familiarity with algebra and the handling of the sigma notation should prove sufficient. The sigma notation is shortly explained in the following and can easily be mastered by practicing the writing of summations in the new, but perhaps unaccustomed, way. Thereby it is well to remember that the various sub- or superscripts refer to different "dimensions" and that we are here concerned with four dimensions, the product, the cost item, the department, and the time. Only the very last part in which we have tried to connect our model with Stedry's departmental optimization approach requires some familiarity with maximization under constraints. In order to make the explanation to these equations as concise as possible, a key of symbols with short explanations precedes the equations. It should be mentioned that the list of all variables is actually much longer but is abbreviated through a device explained as follows:

Assume in a factory producing furniture the subscript i refers to the product "chairs No. 3487," the subscript j to the labor of "carpenters at the wage rate of \$2 per hour," the subscript d to the department "polishing." Furthermore, assume that the symbol L represents the total labor hours in the factory (during the period anticipated), then L_i represents the labor hours to be devoted to product i—in this case to chairs No. 3487—and L_j expresses the "carpenter" labor hours to be required, and L_d the labor hours expected in department "polishing." It is important to recognize that, first, these subscripts can be generalized (e.g., $i = 1, \ldots, n; j = 1, \ldots, r;$ and $d = 1, \ldots, u$), which means they do not anymore refer to a certain product, cost item, or department respectively, but to *any* of the n products, the r cost items, or the u departments respectively; and, second, that various combinations of these subscripts are possible like L_{ij} (labor hours of work j for product i), or L_{jd} (labor hours of work j in department d), or L_{ijd} (labor hours of work j in department d required for product i), or L_{id} (labor hours in department d required for product i), etc. Hence, the reader must be aware that L_i and L_{ij} or L_d are *different variables*. Consequently, the following formulation:

$$L = \sum_i L_i = \sum_i \sum_j L_{ij} \sum_i \sum_j \sum_d L_{ijd}$$

$$= \sum_i \sum_d L_{id} = \sum_d L_d = \sum_j L_j$$

expresses the fact that the total of the labor hours (anticipated in the budgeting period) is equal to the sum of all subtotals of labor hours required for the various products $(i = 1, \ldots, u)$; is also equal to the sum total of all labor hours required for the individual products specified according to the various cost items $(j = 1, \ldots, r)$; is furthermore equal to the sum total of all labor hours required for the individual products specified according to both cost items and departments; etc.

The sigma notation as used here is one of the most valuable tools of modern algebra and very easy to learn; it may be unfamiliar at first but after a little practice it proves to be a very *simple* tool but highly useful, especially in accounting where summations or aggregations occur continuously.

The reader will notice that to our three *dimensions*—product item $(i = 1, \ldots, n)$, cost items $(j = 1, \ldots, r)$ and department $(d = 1, \ldots, u$ for producing departments and $h = 1, \ldots,$ e for service departments)—time is added as a fourth dimension (using the superscript t for various budgeting periods—omitted when misunderstandings are not likely—or τ for subperiods like *months* as used in the present model).

Some Explanations to the Symbolic Presentation

The following does not identify each individual symbol but gives a general notion of the basic symbols to which, according to the specification desired, the following subscripts and superscripts will have to be added. If in a formula no sub- or superscript is attached to a symbol, the pertinent variable or parameter refers to the entire production or sales activity of the enterprise and the whole budgeting period.

Subscripts

i indicates the kind of product $(i = 1, \ldots, n)$
j indicates the kind of cost item $(j = 1, \ldots, r)$
d indicates the kind of producing department $(d = 1, \ldots, u)$
h indicates the kind of service department $(h = 1, \ldots, e)$
d and h are mutually exclusive and refer to the same dimension.

Superscripts

t indicates the budgeting period. In cases where no doubt can arise the omission of the superscript t means that the pertinent symbol *refers to the whole budgeting period* in case the symbol represents a flow concept, or it *refers to the end of the budgeting period* in case the symbol represents a stock concept. Accordingly, t—1 *refers to the whole period preceding* the budget period in case of a flow concept; and the end of the preceding period (= *the beginning of the budgeting period*) in case of a stock concept.

τ refers to a whole subperiod of the budgeting period (usually a certain month, $\tau = 1, \ldots, 12$) in case of a flow concept, or to the end of this subperiod in case of a stock concept. Accordingly, τ — 1 refers to the subperiod preceding, in case of a flow concept, or the beginning of τ (= the end of τ — 1) in case of a stock concept.

It should be noted that an increasing number of subscripts of a basic symbol indicates a decreasing degree of aggregation and vice versa.

A sub- or superscript below a $\sum$-sign indicates the summation over the whole range of the pertinent script.

It may also be pointed out that in general we have tried to adhere to the following scheme: Upper case letters refer to variables whose units are other than $\$$; lower case letters refer to variables expressed in $\$$; Greek letters are used for denoting parameters. Since the border between exogenous variables and parameters is occasionally vague, the latter distinction cannot always be relied upon. Finally, it is important not to confuse basic symbols with subscripts; this danger could not be avoided since the limited number of letters requires the use occasionally of one and the same letter for a symbol as well as for a subscript.

Key to Symbols

F quantitative performance in units (hours, etc., depending on the basis of factory overhead costs) of producing departments

G quantitative performance in units (hours, etc., depending on the basis of overhead costs) of service departments

I finished goods inventory (including partly finished goods inventory in equivalent units)

J raw material inventory (in t, lbs., m^3, etc.)

L labor hours

M raw material purchases (in t, lbs., m^3, etc.)

N raw material consumption (in t, lbs., m^3, etc.)

P production (in equivalent units)

S sales (in units)

a addition in capital budget (cost value of added fixed assets)

b bad debt reserve (addition during period)

c cost or expense item (not mutually exclusive with e, f, l, m, etc.)

d depreciation charge (not mutually exclusive with e, f, l, m, etc.)

e operating expenses (administrative and selling expenses)

f factory overhead expenses of producing departments *after prorating* service departments

f^* factory overhead expenses of producing departments *before prorating* service departments

g factory overhead expenses of service departments

h cash holding

i cost of finished goods inventory

j cost of raw material inventory

k fixed asset (average)

l labor cost

m cost of raw material purchases

n cost of raw material consumption

o owners' equity increase through additional investment in cash

p cost of production

q collection of accounts receivable

r accounts receivable (balance)

s sales revenues (net)

t income tax cash payments

u repayment of debt capital

v variable operating expenses

w variable factory overhead cost of producing departments after prorating service departments

w^* variable factory overhead cost of producing departments before prorating service departments

x cash expenditures

y owners' equity decrease (dividends, etc.)

z liquid funds to be procured during period

α coefficient (parameter) expressing the sales (in units) as a percentage of sales of the previous period

β coefficient expressing the sales (in units) of a subperiod as a percentage of the corresponding sales for the whole budgeting period

γ coefficient expressing the quantity of raw material required ($=$ to be consumed in production process) in a subperiod as a percentage of the quantity of the raw material requirement for the budgeting period

δ coefficient expressing the purchases of raw material in a subperiod as a percentage of the corresponding concept for the budgeting period

ϵ fixed cost portion of operating expenses

ζ unit cost of finished goods inventory

η coefficient expressing the production performance during a subperiod as a percentage of the corresponding concept for the budgeting period

θ coefficient expressing the production activity in units of the basis on which factory overhead costs are calculated

ι fixed portion of factory overhead costs of service departments

κ standard rate of labor (in hours per equivalent product unit)

λ wage rate (in $ per labor hour)

μ unit cost of raw material

ν coefficient prorating variable factory overhead costs of service departments to producing departments

ξ variable rate of factory overhead costs of producing departments after prorating service departments

ξ^{*} variable rate of factory overhead costs of producing department before prorating service departments

π unit cost of production

ρ raw material requirement (in material units) per product unit

σ sales price per unit of finished product (average)

τ coefficient of capital (asset) addition distribution during budgeting period

υ depreciation rate

ϕ fixed portion of factory overhead cost of producing departments after prorating service departments

ϕ^{*} fixed portion of factory overhead cost of producing departments before prorating service departments

χ variable rate of factory overhead costs of service departments

Ψ variable overhead rate of operating departments (after prorating service departments)

ω coefficient prorating fixed factory overhead costs of service departments to producing departments

Γ applied factory overhead rate

Φ function (or parameter) expressing accounts receivable solicitation in terms of sales or accounts receivables

Ω function (or parameter) expressing expenditures as a function of costs

MODEL OF A GENERALIZED PERIODIC BUDGETING SYSTEM

Sales budget:

$$s = \sum_{i} s_i = \sum_{i} \sigma_i S_i = \sum_{i} \sum_{r} \sigma_i \beta_i^r S_i^r$$

$$s = \sum_{i} \sigma_i \alpha_i S_i^{t-1}$$

Production budget:

$$S_i = I_i^{t-1} + \sum_{r} P_i^r - I_i$$

$$P = \sum_i P_i = \sum_i \sum_r P_i^r$$

$$\pi_i = \frac{\sum_r \pi_i^r}{12}$$

$$p = \sum_i \sum_r \pi_i^r P_i = \sum_i \left(\pi_i^r \sum_r n_i^r P_i \right)$$

Raw material and purchasing budget:

$$M_j^r = J_j^{r-1} + \sum_i \delta_{ij}^r N_{ij} - J_j^r = \gamma_j^r M_j$$

$$m = \sum_j \mu_j \left(J_j^{t-1} + \sum_i \sum_r \delta_{ij}^r N_{ij} - J_j \right)$$

$$m = \sum_j \left(j_j^{t-i} + \sum_i n_{ij} - j_j \right)$$

Direct labor budget:

$$l^r = \sum_i \sum_j \sum_d \kappa_{ijd} \lambda_j \eta_{ijd}^r P_{ijd}$$

$$l = \sum_j \sum_d \lambda_j L_{jd}$$

Factory overhead cost budget, producing departments and service departments:

$$f = \sum_j \sum_d (\phi_{jd} + w_{jd})$$

$$= \sum_j \sum_d \sum_r \left(\frac{\phi_{jd}}{12} + w_{jd}^r \right)$$

$$f_d^r = \sum_j \frac{\phi_{jd}}{12} + \xi_d^r F_d^r$$

$$\Gamma_d = \frac{f_d}{F_d} = \xi_d + \frac{\sum_j \phi_{jd}}{F_d}$$

$$\zeta_d = \frac{\sum_r \zeta_d^r}{12} = \frac{w_d}{F_d}$$

$$f_d = \phi_d{}^* + \sum_h \omega_{dh}\iota_h + w_d{}^* + \sum_h \nu_{dh}\chi_h G_h$$

$$g_h = \iota_h + \chi_h G_h$$

Operating expense budget:

$$e_j^r = \frac{\varepsilon_j}{12} + \psi_j \sum_i s_i^r$$

$$e_j = \varepsilon_j + v_j$$

Capital additions budget and depreciation schedule:

$$a = \sum_j a_j = \sum_j \sum_r r_j^r a_j = \sum_j \sum_r a_j^r$$

$$d = \sum_j d_j = \sum_j k_j v_j = \sum_j \sum_r d_j^r = \sum_j k_j \frac{v_j}{12}$$

The expense items e, f, l, and m are mutually exclusive among themselves, but are not mutually exclusive with the expense items b, c. d.

Accounts receivable collection budget:

$$q = \sum_i q_i = \Phi_i^{t-1}(r_i^{t-1} - b_i^{t-1}) + \sum_r \Phi_i^r s_i^r$$

Cash budget:

$$x_j = {}_e c_j + {}_p c_j - {}_b c_j$$

$$x = \sum_j x_j = \sum_j \Omega_j c_j = \sum_j ({}_e c_j + {}_p c_j - {}_b c_j)$$

$$h^{t-1} + q^1 - u^1 + o^1 - x^1 - y^1 - t^1 + z^1 = h^1$$
$$h^1 \;\; + q^2 - u^2 + o^2 - x^2 - y^2 - t^2 + z^2 = h^2$$
$$\vdots \qquad\qquad\qquad\qquad\qquad\qquad \vdots$$
$$h^{11} + q^{12} - u^{12} + o^{12} - x^{12} - y^{12} - t^{12} + z^{12} = h^{12} = h$$

The symbol c_j $(j = 1, \ldots, r)$ may represent any cost or expense item. That means it may stand for n_1 or l_3 or f_5 or g_6 or e_7, etc.

The prescripts b, p, e of the symbol c indicate beginning balance, purchases, and ending balance respectively (beginning and ending balances, of course, refer to deferred or accrued items in the broadest sense of the word).

In a similar way (i.e., by further use of nonmutually exclusive variables) a projected balance sheet and income statement may be constructed. Both statements can be developed from the previous equations by mere accounting identities without the use of further behavioral parameters. (It is, however, possible to include parameters in the form of liquidity coefficients and other statement ratios if one insists on a certain statement structure—obviously the best way to achieve this is to impose certain constraints on the model.) Another aspect is the possibility of combining Stedry's limited substitution maximization model with the above aggregation system.

Within this framework such a maximization problem would assume the following form if our interpretation of Stedry's model is correct:[15]

---

[15] In comparing Stedry's model (see below) the reader will notice that the maximization model has not only been translated into our symbolism but also had to be adjusted somewhat to make it conform to the structure of our aggregation model.

Maximize:

$$\sum_{i}^{m} \left(c_i y_i - \sum_{j \in q_i} \sum_{k=1}^{nj} c_{ijk} x_{ijk} \right)$$

subject to:

$$\sum_{k=1}^{nj} x_{ijk} - y_i = 0 \qquad i = 1, \ldots, m \; j \in q_i$$

$$\sum_{i=1}^{m} b_{ijk} x_{ijk} \leqq b_{jk} \qquad k = 1, \ldots, n_j \; j \in q_i$$

$$y_i \leqq U_i$$

$$-y_i \leqq -L_i$$

For the sake of comparison we have stated here the original model *without*, however, listing the pertinent *key* of symbols. For the latter see *Budget Control and Cost Behavior*, p. 120. Note that in contrast to Stedry, we assume above that the limitations set by machine (and buildings) capacity are incorporated in the constraints set by $N_{jd}{}^{r\max}$ and $L_{jd}{}^{r\max}$, hence, do not need separate consideration.

Maximize:

$$\sum_i \left[\Delta_{id}^r P_{id}^r - \sum_j \left(\mu_j \frac{N_{ijd}^r}{\rho_{ijd}^r} + \lambda_j \frac{L_{ijd}^r}{\kappa_{ijd}^r} \right) \right]$$

subject to the following constraints:

$$\sum_j (N_{ijd}^r + L_{ijd}^r - \rho_{ijd}^r \kappa_{ijd}^r P_{ijd}^r) = 0$$

$$\sum_j \rho_{ijd}^r P_{ijd}^r \leq N_{jd}^r \max$$

$$\sum_j \kappa_{ijd}^r P_{ijd}^r \leq L_{jd}^r \max$$

$$*I_i^r \max \geq *I_i^{r-1} + *P_i^r - S_i^r \geq *I_i^r \min$$

At this point a new symbol and three superscripts have to be explained:

Δ_i^r ... the contribution per unit of the ith item to profit and costs (for subperiod τ); the superscript "max" refers to the *maximum* (capacity) of a certain material or labor factor (in a certain department) or of an inventory level permissible for a certain raw material; corresponding to the latter the superscript "min" refers to the *minimum* inventory level. The *asterisks* in the last equation merely indicate that I and P refer to *completely* finished goods and are not (as previously, cf. key to symbols) determined on an equivalent unit basis.

The reader will have noticed that the concept Δ_i^r (or in Stedry's notation c_i) is a contribution margin, which however is not identical to the contribution margin of direct costing. By employing such a concept Stedry circumvents the difficulty of incorporating some overhead costs in his model. This, of course, does not solve the overhead cost problem but only shifts it to another level (a level outside the maximization model). It should be added that Stedry offers concrete suggestions for computing his maximization model by means of a linear programming approach with "diadic" arrangement.[16]

---

[16] A. Charnes, W. W. Cooper, and M. H. Miller, "Dyadic Problems and Sub-Dual Methods" (mimeo) Carnegie Institute of Technology (cited from Stedry, *idem.*)

In this connection we ought to draw the reader's attention to another proposal made by K. J. Arrow,[17] who also emphasizes departmental profit maximization. Arrow shows under which circumstances suboptimization can lead to overall optimization and presents concrete suggestions for using interdepartmental *shadow prices* for the attainment of this goal. He furthermore recommends for the purpose of determining the profit maximum step-by-step approximations —eventually by means of computing machines—but does not rely, as Stedry does, on linear programming methods. Arrow's paper pivots around the question whether and when decentralization within a firm is possible and thus illuminates the problem from an entirely different point of view. Some of the results of this study, however, seem to be relevant to our problem and shall shortly be summarized.

Under perfect competition and absence of purely "internal goods" (those not available in the market) the optimum policy for the firm is simply to instruct each process manager independently to maximize profits, computed at market prices. "There may indeed be problems of control to insure that maximization does take place and it is clear that such problems present a challenge to the accounting procedures as well as incentive schemes." [18] If, however, internal goods that are not traded in the market are admitted, we can again have decentralization by instructing the manager to maximize a *shadow profit,* that is, the profit computed by valuing the commodities at their market price and the internal good at its shadow price which can be found through a process of successive approximations. "Let some central agency within the firm announce a tentative shadow price for the good which is used only internally. Then let the manager of each process maximize his shadow profit, as given by Formula 8 (here not reprinted). As a result, it will be found in general that the total amount demanded of Good 3 (the internal good) within the firm is greater or less than the amount available. These demands and supplies are forwarded by the process managers to the central office. If the demand in total exceeds the supply, the shadow price is raised for the next period; otherwise it is lowered. This provides a new shadow price, on the basis of which the process managers again optimize. It can be shown, under certain conditions, that if this

---

[17] Kenneth J. Arrow, "Optimization, Decentralization, and Internal Pricing in Business Firms," *Contributions to Scientific Research in Management* Proceedings of the Scientific Program following the dedication of the Western Data Processing Center, Graduate School of Business Administration, University of California, Los Angeles, 1959, pp. 9-18.
[18] *Ibid.* p. 12.

process is continued long enough, the operations of the firm will gradually converge to a position of maximum total profitability." [19] Under imperfect competition complete decentralization is not possible, since there has to be some single agency to supply the marginal revenues which are affected by the actions of the process managers. "It would not be correct to allow each process manager to maximize his profits taking account of the effect of his output on his own prices but not taking into consideration the effect of his output on the prices received by the other process manager." [20]

Practical Application and Conclusion

At this stage the reader who is not familiar with the application of mathematical models for practical purposes and with computer simulation may ask: How can the budgeting model, presented in this paper, serve a particular purpose in actual practice? We will try to answer this question by indicating the various steps necessary for the implementation of such a simulation system.

1. The existing budgeting system will have to be examined and translated into mathematical terms, step by step, each subbudget for itself as shown in the previous model. One must not forget that our model is only an illustration, and the idiosyncracies of each individual budgeting system have to be reflected through appropriate choice of variables, parameters, and model structure. If desired, one might, at this point, consider certain changes that improve upon the structure of the previously available budgeting system. It also must be taken into consideration that in our presentation we received the benefit afforded by the application of *general* sub- and superscripts like i $(i = 1, \ldots, n)$, j $(j = 1, \ldots, r)$, etc. For practical purposes, however, each sub- or superscript must be spelled out; this increases immensely the number of variables, parameters, and equations. Finally, it must be borne in mind that in our exposition we have selected only a few equations—namely, the more interesting and significant ones—out of a whole system of simultaneous equations. Such a system must be tested for determinacy (ordinarily the number of independent equations must be equal to the number of endogenous variables).

2. The complete model now has to be translated into machine language, conveniently by way of an automatic coding system and the necessary flow diagrams (beware that not all coding systems are suitable for our model: e.g., the most frequently applied IBM-FORTRAN language cannot be used without difficulties since it permits only three dimensions while our model uses four). In writing the computer program, attention has also to be paid to some of the items listed below.

---

[19] *Ibid.* p. 13.
[20] *Ibid.* p. 15.

3. Values must be assigned to the exogenous variables and to the parameters, based on the data, estimates, forecasts, and past experience of the enterprise. In this connection it has to be decided which of the alternative business situations shall be computed; that means which exogenous variables (and perhaps even parameters, although in this case the distinction between exogenous variable and parameter might become vague) shall be varied and within which ranges shall that be done. This, of course, involves the decision which exogenous variables shall be varied with each other; that is to say, one has to decide how many *combinations* of "basic alternatives" shall be computed. Hence, in many cases a whole set of values will have to be assigned to a single exogenous variable.

4. After this preparatory work the computation in the electronic data processing system can be carried out and the output should yield the budgeting data of the firm simulated under a large number of different conditions. These conditions may partly depend on the entrepreneurial policy, or on external, and in many cases uncontrollable, conditions. The computer output can be arranged in such a way as to *print* a sales budget, a production budget, etc., and finally a cash budget as well as projected position and income statements each of them with all desired alternatives. The selection of that alternative which appears to be most satisfactory (with regard to the controllable exogenous variables) can be done by visual inspection and comparison of the various alternatives. In case of too large a number of alternatives (especially where one cannot rely on a limited number of key figures as, for example, net profit, sales volume, asset and capital structure, liquidity ratio, etc., for selection of the most satisfactory alternative) it should be feasible to complement the program with satisficing criteria such that the comptuer selects automatically the most "satisfactory" choice or a more limited number of "best" alternatives from which the top executives can make their own selection.

5. Finally, in case of internal or external changes of data during the business year a recomputation with the newly assigned values (of exogenous variables or parameters)—but the original computer program—can be carried out. In this way a revised budget can be calculated rapidly; furthermore, one can afford to compute revisions more frequently than this is possible under present circumstances.

Using electronic computers, the calculation of even a large number of alternatives should not be very time consuming and the suggested method is by no means restricted to firms in possession of an EDP system. Computations outside the enterprise, at statistical service or consulting firms, should be within the range of feasible expenses and will facilitate the general application of the proposed approach. Obviously the models presented here are designed for use in connection with a *digital* computer; however, the application of *analog* computers to budgetary and related managerial planning might offer decisive advantages (less expensive, handier, more compact and concise data, etc.) and deserves serious consideration. Since the output of analog computers can best be arranged in the form of a graph, it is conceivable to arrange this output in the form of a *multidimensional* break-even chart. Thus, with the help of a somewhat modified model and the necessary input data, the analog computer would be in a position to supply a set of diagrams containing whole families of cost, revenue, and profit curves, offering information of different alternatives for one and the same purpose as well as for different managerial goals. Proposals for improving and expanding the application of break-even charts as made by Dean,[21] Eiteman,[22] Barber,[23] and others may in this way approach a fuller realization. Dean's assertion that "break-even analysis has not measured up to its potential usefulness, but it can if it embodies these kinds of cost forecasting and thus becomes a versatile device for flexible comparison of conjectural income statements under a variety of projected conditions," [24] still holds.

So far we have assumed that most of the data are being supplied by the individual departments without worrying about the way in which these data were created—that means we have gone only as far as textbook budgeting reaches. If, however, the budgeting activity on the departmental level shall be incorporated into the simulation approach it will be necessary to develop a model, perhaps even a maximization model à la Stedry, for each department. Thus many of our previous exogenous variables will have to be converted into endogenous variables and a long array of new exogenous variables will emerge; needless to say, this increases considerably the number of simultaneous equations and complicates the program. If departmental optimization models shall be used it may be advantageous to compute these departmental optima independently from, and prior to, the overall budget model. This *independent* treatment, however, is probably not feasible if an *overall* optimization by way of interdepartmental prices and shadow prices à la Arrow is intended. This second or extended stage of budgeting simulation will have to be experimented with at some length before detailed recommendations can be made. In the long run, this second stage will, however, become

[21] Joel Dean, "Methods and Potentialities of Break-Even Analysis," *The Australian Accountant* (October-November, 1951). Reprinted in *Studies in Cost Accounting*, ed. David Solomons (London: Sweet & Maxwell, Ltd., 1952), pp. 227-66.

[22] Wilford J. Eiteman, "Application of Break-Even Charts to Cash Situations," *The Controller* (June, 1951). Reprinted in *Readings in Cost Accounting, Budgeting and Control*, ed. W. E. Thomas (2d ed.; Cincinnati: South-Western Publishing Co., 1960), pp. 472-75.

[23] Raymond J. Barber, Jr., "When Does Part of a Business Break Even?," *N.A.C.A. Bulletin* (May, 1951). Reprinted in *Readings in Cost Accounting, Budgeting and Control*, ed. W. E. Thomas (2d ed.; Cincinnati: South-Western Publishing Co., 1960), pp. 463-71.

[24] Joel Dean, "Methods and Potentialities of Break-Even Analysis," *The Australian Accountant* (October-November, 1951). Reprinted in *Studies in Cost Accounting*, ed. David Solomons (London: Sweet & Maxwell, Ltd., 1952), pp. 227-66.

as important as is the first. Finally, it is hoped that in time the two extreme approaches of simulating the firm, the "flow model" on one side and the budgeting model on the other, will move towards each other. Then we may hope for the day when it is possible to fuse them to such a degree that an economic model of the firm emerges which corresponds to the needs and facilities of a particular enterprise without being unsound from the viewpoint of hypothesis formulation. This no doubt is a dream at present, but where would we stand today had our ancestors failed to indulge in their own dreams?

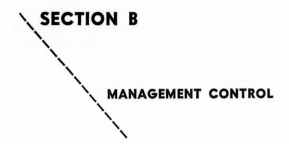

SECTION B

MANAGEMENT CONTROL

Accounting and budgetary controls are an integral part of management controls. A good understanding of management controls is necessary for the theoretical development of accounting and budgeting as control tools.

This section begins with a formulation of the principles of management control. But management can control operations only if goals or objectives have been set. Their nature and development are in the "Charter of Accountability for Executives." The performance of individuals must be measured, related to the goals, and fed back to the manager exercising control. A classic example of this in accounting is responsibility accounting which has gained widespread attention in the past 15 years.

Responsibility accounting as a concept is clear but in its application can be quite difficult. One of the reasons is the rapid development of control subsystems, for example, inventory control. They not only provide information but also provide programmed decisions, whether by individuals or the computer. These subsystems are designed by staff or consultants. This may require responsibility distinctions between those who authorize, design, monitor, and/or operate the system.

Finally, to complete the cycle of control, the information feedback should be of such nature that the manager can more easily make the routine and recurring decisions necessary to keep operations in conformity with objectives set.

8. MANAGEMENT CONTROL: A SUGGESTED FORMULATION OF PRINCIPLES *

Harold Koontz †

Although the need for improving management in all kinds of enterprises is widely recognized, and although much inquiry into management and the training of managers is being undertaken, there is serious question that enough attention is being given to formulating a conceptual framework from which to approach these important tasks. Much of both research in management and training of managers seems to have been proceeding from the questionable premise that exchange of experience and emphasis on technique are adequate to meet the widely recognized need for improving the quality of management.

One cannot deny the importance of analyzing experience through case study or research, or of giving managers lessons in "how-to-do-it" as indicated by experience. But particular techniques of dealing with problems must be passed on with care since these are not always transplantable from one manager to another or from one enterprise to another. What can be transferred, however, are the generalizations that can be distilled from specific situations. Generalizations—or principles—which can be applied in certain areas and which have a predictive value in guiding thought and action in these areas can be a practical means of understanding and improving management. And if these principles can be arranged logically in a conceptual scheme, they can furnish the elements of a useful theory of management.

Control is one of the most widely discussed and studied areas of management. Yet it is a functional area in which little attempt has been made to formulate principles that might be useful to practicing managers, helpful in training them, and suitable for guiding research. Considerable attention has been given to organization principles, and

* From the *California Management Review*, Vol. I, No. 2 (Winter, 1959). Reprinted by permission of the Regents of the University of California.

† Harold Koontz, Professor of Business Policy and Transportation, University of California at Los Angeles.

the basics of formal organization have been so well recognized and explained that most research and practice in organization show a clear awareness of theoretical implications, an awareness which may account for the relative effectiveness of most managers in organizational matters. Some attention has been given to the codification of principles of planning.[1] But rather little has been given to formulating and codifying principles of control, staffing, or direction.

This is not to say that principles of control cannot be found. A number of profound inquiries have been made in this area, many basic truths have been highlighted, and great contributions made, but they lack the refinement, completeness, and codification found in organization. In other words, while many individual principles of control have been recognized by such scholars as Frederick Taylor, Henri Fayol, Chester Barnard, Billy Goetz, Lyndall Urwick, and Joel Dean, as well as by many practicing business managers, the entire area has been inadequately reviewed and summarized.

The development of such activities as medicine, dentistry, engineering, music, and agriculture has characteristically been towards the evolution of a science, a systematized body of knowledge dealing with a given area and formulated with reference to principles and laws. A mature field of management cannot be developed without a scientific foundation, and a framework of principles appears to be a proper starting place. As Talcott Parsons, himself a scholar in another "young" science, put its:

> It is scarcely too much to say that the most important index of the state of maturity of a science is the state of its systematic theory. This includes the character of the general conceptual scheme in use in the field, the kinds and degrees of logical integration of the different elements which make it up, and the ways in which it is actually used in empirical research.[2]

In the rapidly evolving programs of management research and training, there is often so much recounting of experience—without reflecting on what is fundamental in the job of management and without expressing this experience in these terms—that findings tend

---

[1] See, for example, the author's "A Preliminary Statement of Principles of Planning and Control," *Journal of the Academy of Management*, I, 1 (April, 1958). In this paper, originally given before the Academy of Management in 1956, only four principles of control were identified and it was felt that the managerial function of control was largely a technical matter about which few generalizations could be made. Further study and reflection have indicated that this position was incorrect.

[2] *Essays in Sociological Theory, Pure and Applied* (Glencoe, Ill.: Free Press, 1949), p. 17.

to contribute only a hodgepodge of structureless facts. If research efforts were realigned to broaden knowledge of principles and to interpret this research in the light of principles, more progress could surely be made towards the development of scientific foundations for management.

Apart from its necessity as a guide for research and for the development of scientific management, a framework of principles is important in training managers. Principles describe the nature of the managerial job, crystallize the purpose of management, and act as a kind of checklist for the manager to follow in practicing the art of management. In doing so, they furnish the basis for seeing the manager's job as a whole and become the cornerstone upon which the training of managers can be undertaken.

Early students of management—eminently practical scholars such as Henri Fayol, Chester Barnard, Lyndall Urwick, and Alvin Brown— felt strongly the need for a body of theory in the teaching of management. For example, in his great classic published originally in 1916, Fayol bemoaned the absence of management teaching in the vocational schools and ascribed it to the lack of theory since, as he said, "Without theory no teaching is possible." [3] Similar observations have been made by those now teaching management.[4]

Principles, or theory, and art are not, of course, mutually exclusive. As principles are formulated, verified, and applied in solving problems, they become the working rules of an art. While management will always be an art and perhaps will depend largely on know-how, improvements in the art of management, as in the art of bridge building or missile design, can come from an understanding of principles.

As the working rules of an art, principles can, then, increase managerial efficiency. Probably no task is more complex or has a greater number of variables than that of the manager. The application of principles to this job should facilitate reasoned decisions, might make unnecessary much laborious research and trial-and-error operation, and could show the way to understanding many of the complexities of the task. But unless these principles are clearly related to the job of management and logically organized, their usefulness to the manager and to the researcher will be limited.

---

[3] *General and Industrial Management* (New York: Pitman Publishing Corp., 1949), pp. 14-15.
[4] Leon C. Megginson, "The Pressure for Principles: A Challenge to Management Professors," *Journal of the Academy of Management*, I, 2 (August, 1958), pp. 7-12.

CONTROL AS A FUNCTION

In order to see the managerial function of control in proper perspective, it must be regarded in the light of the other functions of the manager. In my opinion, control is one of five major functions of the manager at any level of an enterprise—whether president or foreman—and in every organized enterprise—whether business, government, education, church, or other kind. These functions, all of which are necessary to the job of getting things done through people and all of which differ from those of the engineer, accountant, machinist, or personnel expert, may be summarized as follows:

1. *Planning*—the selection from among alternatives of enterprise objectives, policies, procedures, and programs.
2. *Organizing*—the grouping of activities necessary for accomplishing enterprise objectives and the assignment of these groupings to a manager with the necessary authority for undertaking them and with provision for vertical and horizontal coordination of the authority relationships.
3. *Staffing*—the selection and training of subordinates.
4. *Directing*—the guidance and overseeing of subordinates.
5. *Controlling*—the measurement and correction of activities of subordinates to make sure that plans are transformed into action.

It will be readily seen that all of the functions of the manager are so closely interrelated that it is difficult in practice to ascertain where one function ends and another begins. Indeed, in practice these functions tend to coalesce because the operating manager performs all of them virtually at the same time. Planning and control are particularly closely related since the purpose of control is to make sure that plans are accomplished. Any attempt to control without planning would be meaningless since no one can tell whether his subordinates are doing what he wishes them to do unless he first knows what his wishes are. As Goetz has put it, "Managerial planning seeks consistent, integrated and articulated programs," while "management control seeks to compel events to conform to plans." [5] Plans thus furnish the criteria for control.

Similarly, since the manager accomplishes enterprise or department goals through people and since events can only be made to happen by people, control and organization are closely intertwined. For, just as planning furnishes the criteria for control, so organiza-

---

[5] *Management Planning and Control* (New York: McGraw-Hill Book Co., Inc., 1949), p. 2.

tion defines who must be controlled. Without the assurance that subordinates who are expected to accomplish tasks hold the necessary and coordinated authority, no manager can properly carry out the function of control.

Given the prerequisites of integrated and clear plans and sound organization, the control process is the same wherever it is applied. Whether the manager wishes to assure quality of product, availability of necessary cash, orderly production, a desired level of inventories, or any other planning goal, the control process involves three steps: (1) the establishment of standards; (2) the appraisal of performance against these standards; and (3) the correction of deviations.

It should be noted that the third control step overlaps other managerial functions. Deviations from plans may, of course, be corrected through additional planning, through better direction, through selecting someone else to do it, through a program of subordinate training, or through reorganization.

CLASSIFICATION OF PRINCIPLES

One of the major purposes of a theory is to explain the nature of a subject by presenting a clear and systematic view of it. With this in mind, it appears that managerial control can be analyzed by placing the basic principles of control into the categories of (1) those dealing with the nature and purpose of control, (2) those having to do with the structure of control, and (3) those explaining the process of control.[6] (The same classification of principles could, no doubt, be used for the managerial functions of organizing and planning, and perhaps also for staffing and direction.)

In placing the principles which I believe to be basic to managerial control within this framework, I must emphasize that this classification is tentative. The classification does appear to have the merit of being widely applicable to all functions of management, and it does appear to deal with those facets of management important to the practicing manager. Disagreement as to the classification is expected [7]

---

[6] The author used a similar classification in his suggested principles of planning. See "A Preliminary Statement of Principles of Planning and Control" (Footnote 1).

[7] For example, Urwick, who has perhaps done more than anyone else to develop a systematic theory of management, has classified principles of control (as other principles of management) in a logical scheme based upon the premise that every problem area or subject has an underlying principle, which in turn has a process, and an effect. In turn, each of these has its principle, process, and effect. See Lyndall F. Urwick, *The Pattern of Management* (Minneapolis: University of Minnesota Press, 1956), Chapter 5. As Urwick has often pointed

and it is probable that others would identify principles other than those stated in each classification.

Most of these principles are not, of course, original. As will be noted, many of them have been referred to in almost the same language by others who have attempted to dissect the job of the manager.

Nature and Purpose of Control

The nature and purpose of managerial control seem to be reflected in five principles, which may be summarized as follows:

1. *Principle of Assurance of Objective.* Controls must contribute to the accomplishment of group objectives by detecting deviations from plans in time and in a manner to make corrective action possible.

It is obvious that the purpose of all organized enterprise is the accomplishment of group objectives, ends which cannot be accomplished by individuals acting alone. This essential fact has been recognized in many analyses of management.[8]

For example, a company's objective in instituting a new product program may be to maximize return on investment; but if, as the program proceeds, a forecast of revenues and expenses indicates that the program (perhaps because of a competitor's action) will yield a negative or a negligible return, control should make it possible to reconsider the original decision and modify or replace the program before it is too late. If a control were designed to show only the state of progress in the development of the product itself, the company might find itself with a fully developed but relatively unprofitable new product which had already absorbed its resources.

Therefore, controls must have as their essential reason the attainment of objectives or goals, just as the other functions of the manager must have as their *raison d'etre* the accomplishment of objective. In the case of control, this purpose can be accomplished only if the techniques used make it possible to detect failure in plans. This is a simple truth, but one which often is overlooked by the practicing manager.

---

out, this logical scheme was borrowed from Mooney and Reilly, who, in turn, borrowed it from the German logician, Louis F. Anderson. While this system, which leads to neat groups of nine principles, has a certain graphical charm, it does not appear to be as useful or understandable as the one adopted here.

[8] As Barnard, in his *The Functions of the Executive* (Cambridge, Mass.: Harvard University Press, 1938) pointed out (p. 23), "Cooperation justifies itself, then, as a means of overcoming the limitations restricting what individuals can do" and (p. 82), "An organization comes into being when (1) there are persons able to communicate with each other (2) who are willing to contribute action (3) to accomplish a common purpose."

2. *Principle of Efficiency of Control.* Controls are efficient if they effectively detect deviations from plans and make possible corrective action with the minimum of unsought consequences.

Chester Barnard has very clearly pointed out the applicability of the scientific concepts of effectiveness and efficiency to systems of human cooperation.[9] A control may be effective in the sense that it does assure the attainment of objectives, but it is inefficient if it does so at unnecessarily high cost in dollars, hours, lost morale, or individual dissatisfaction.

Techniques of control have a way of becoming costly, complex, and burdensome. It is entirely possible for a manager to spend considerably more than it is worth to detect deviations from plans. And such costs go beyond dollars. For example, a control technique so vigorous and thorough that it negates authority delegations or seriously impairs the morale of those who must execute plans can easily result in costs beyond any possible value it might have. Among the countless instances of costly controls found in practice are complex engineering procedures and controls which hamstring creativeness and human efficiency, detailed budget controls which place a straitjacket on the manager, and purchasing controls which not only delay deliveries but involve costs beyond the value of the items purchased.

3. *Principles of Control Responsibility.* Control can be exercised only by the manager responsible for the execution of plans.

The principle follows logically from the two preceding it. If the organization structure, through its delegation of authority and assignment of tasks, gives a manager responsibility for the accomplishment of certain plans or portions of plans, this responsibility cannot be waived without changing the organization. It is logically and practically inconsistent to expect a manager to make and accomplish plans and not to expect him to exercise control to make sure that these plans are being accomplished. Yet this principle is sometimes misunderstood in practice. Some managers expect control to be exerted only from some top point in an enterprise, or they wait to be told from above what controls to exercise and when.

The principle of control responsibility also appears to clarify the often misinterpreted role of controllers and centralized control units. Although these agencies may, in a staff or service capacity, assist the manager by furnishing him information needed to control his de-

---

[9] Barnard, p. 19.

partment, they cannot assume the part of actually exercising these controls without destroying the unity and meaning of the manager's job.

    4. *Principle of Future Controls.* Effective control should be aimed at preventing present and future deviations from plans.

It has sometimes been said that planning is looking ahead and control is looking back. This seems to be a distorted view of control. Just as planning must be forward looking, so must control. Since the manager cannot possibly control the past, and too seldom can move fast enough to detect and correct current deviations from plans, his controls should be aimed at the future.

The tendency to regard control as looking back has arisen largely because managerial control has been so dependent upon accounting and statistical data instead of forecasts and predictions. In the absence of any means to look forward, reference to history, on the assumption that what is past is prologue, is admittedly better than not looking at all. But this principle does point to the need for more control information based on forecasts.

One can hardly deny that the alert manager would prefer a forecast of what *will* happen in the execution of a given plan, even though this projection has a margin of error in it, to a decimately accurate report of the past, about which he can do nothing. Of course, what a manager would probably like best of all is a system of control that would operate with instantaneous feedback, like the servosystem of an automated machine tool, so that deviations might be corrected before they occur by means of correcting tendencies to stray from desired performance.

That managers are increasingly looking ahead for purposes of control is apparent from the greater attention being given to expense and revenue projections and the forecasting of cash. Well-managed companies always forecast cash requirements carefully for periods varying from four to 24 months in advance. By seeing their cash needs well ahead of time, they are usually able through careful planning to provide for them *before* cash stringencies occur. On the other hand, many companies have found themselves in desperate circumstances by suddenly awakening to the fact that they do not have the cash to meet commitments. And it is almost a tradition that cash is difficult to get in emergencies, but easy to obtain if arranged for well ahead of needs.

    5. *Principle of Direct Control.* The most effective technique of control in an enterprise is to assure the quality of subordinate managers.

Most controls used by managers are actually indirect controls because they are based on the need to keep subordinates, particularly managerial subordinates, from making mistakes. Unquestionably, the best and most direct kind of control is to assure the best possible quality of managers. Able and well-trained managers plan well and thoroughly, delegate authority, assign tasks, and do the most effective job of selecting, training, and directing subordinates. They make fewer mistakes and require fewer indirect controls.

The Structure of Control

A second group of three principles is significant for the structure of control techniques, particularly in their relation to plans, organization, and the managerial incumbent.

> 6. *Principle of Reflection of Plans.* Controls must be designed so as to reflect the character and structure of plans.

This principle underlines the fact that controls must be tailored to individual plans. Thus, if the control of costs is the aim, the control technique used must be based on planned costs of a definite and specific type. If one would control inventory, clearly the controls must take into account and follow those plans which influence inventory; and true inventory control must be based upon the entire program of production planning and scheduling, purchasing, shipping, warehousing, sales, and finance. Too often, in these and similar cases, the manager deceives himself by thinking he is controlling an aspect of operation when his control technique is not designed to reflect the pertinent plans involved.

> 7. *Principle of Organizational Suitability.* Controls must be designed to reflect organization structure.

Since managers and their subordinates are the means through which the events of planning must be accomplished, it follows that effective controls must be applicable to a manager's authority area and must, therefore, reflect the organization structure. Consequently, any device of control must be tailored to the manager and his position in the organization, and information to appraise performance against plans must be suitable to the manager who is to use it. Urwick has expressed this as the principle of uniformity and has emphasized that "all figures and reports used for purposes of control must be in terms of the organization structure." [10]

---

[10] Lyndall F. Urwick, *Elements of Administration* (New York: Harper & Brothers, 1943), p. 107.

As can be readily seen, this principle is similar to the principle of control responsibility outlined above. The principle of control responsibility, however, emphasizes that countrol of events can be exercised only through people, with the manager the focal point of control. But control techniques must be structured so that a certain manager can be held responsible. This can be done only by making the controls consistent with organization structure. It does no good to hold a manager responsible for costs, for example, if the cost reports do not pinpoint which manager in an organization position is responsible. In other words, one principle has to do with the personal responsibility for control, the other with the orientation of control information to the organization structure.

8. *Principle of Individuality of Controls.* Controls must be designed to meet the personal needs of the individual manager.

An important factor in any system of control is the fact that people do vary in terms of personal biases, training, and ability to comprehend information. No matter how much a statistician, mathematician, or accountant might like to mold a manager into his own image, it is a fact of life that what a manager cannot understand or will not understand cannot be useful to him for control. What might be a delight to the figure-minded treasurer might be abhorrent to the plant superintendent. What might be meaningful to the chief engineer might be incomprehensible to the sales manager. Some managers may like reports, others tables, some charts, and still others mathematical formulae or curves. Control devices and information are important enough that they should be tailored to these needs.

The Process of Control

In the operation of controls, there appear to be six principles which point to the most effective possible techniques of control. To be sure, control, being so much a technique, rests heavily on the art of management, on "know-how" in a given instance. But experience in control yields certain benchmarks which no manager should overlook in practice.

9. *Principle of Standards.* Effective and efficient control requires objective, accurate, and suitable standards.

Standards are authoritative criteria by which performance can be measured. The principle of standards implies that every plan must have measures of effectiveness which are as specific and simple as possible and which accurately measure whether a planned program is being accomplished.

Not only are such standards highly desirable from the standpoint of giving the manager a precise measurement of operations in relation to plans, but they are desirable because events are controlled through people. Actual performance is sometimes camouflaged from the manager by a subordinate's sparkling or dull personality or by his ability to "sell" a deficient performance. Thus measurements of performance that are not objective can often be wrong. Moreover, good standards objectively applied as a measure of a subordinate's performance are most likely to be accepted by the subordinate as fair and reasonable.

   10. *Principle of Strategic Point Control.* Effective and efficient control requires that attention be given to those factors which are strategic to the appraisal of performance.

It is ordinarily wasteful and unnecessary for a manager to follow every detail of the execution of plans. What he must know is that plans are being executed in such a manner that their goals can be accomplished. He should, therefore, concentrate his attention on selected parts of performance which will indicate whether significant deviations in the total plan are occurring or will occur.

There are no easy guidelines which might be applied by a practicing manager to determine the strategic points he should watch, since the selection of these is predominantly a matter of the managerial art. Perhaps the manager can reach his own solution to the problem by asking himself what things in *his* operations will show *him* best whether the plans for which he is responsible are being accomplished.

   11. *The Exception Principle.* Efficiency in control requires that attention of the manager be given primarily to significant exceptions.

This principle, which was pointed out many years ago by Frederick Taylor,[11] is sometimes confused with the principle of strategic point control. But they are essentially different concepts even though both have to do with the utilization of standards. Strategic point control refers to the selection of certain key factors which determine whether performance conforms with plans, while the exception principle has to do with watching for (and taking action with respect to) significant deviations at these points.

The difference between the exception principle and the principle of strategic point control can be illustrated by the techniques a sales

---

[11] *Shop Management* (New York: Harper & Brothers, 1919), pp. 126-27.

manager might employ to control field sales. He might select as critical points to watch such items as sales per salesman, sales by products and by territories, or gross profits from sales by product. However, in watching these critical points, he would see no need for action unless he detected deviations beyond limits which he regarded as normal, that is, deviations which constitute noteworthy exceptions.

The exception principle is often quoted as an essential requirement of managerial control efficiency. However, the manager who first chooses the fewest practicable strategic points to watch and then concentrates on exceptions increases his efficiency markedly. The necessary number of strategic points to be watched will depend upon the importance of the plan and the extent to which strategic points showing progress under the plan can be found or devised. This difference might be illustrated by practices in quality control. It may be important to test carefully every part of a missile guidance and control system and hold each part to close performance tolerances; but in the missile fuselage shell there might be only few points to be checked, and the allowable tolerances might be relatively broad.

12. *The Principle of Flexibility of Controls.* Controls should incorporate sufficient flexibility to remain effective despite the failure of plans.

Stated negatively, this principle, first given clear form by Goetz,[12] means that controls should not be so inextricably bound into a particular plan that, should unforeseen events or shifts in goals make the plan unworkable, all control is lost. This principle is best illustrated by the considerations which led to the flexible, or variable, budget. Such budgeting, which provides for budgets to be changed quickly and virtually automatically if the business outlook changes, arose from fears that under fixed budgets control might be lost through continuation of managerial authority to spend at a level determined by previous sales forecasts but not justified by actual sales volume.

While this principle is difficult to implement in practice, the manager should be aware of the desirability of such flexibility. Otherwise, the manager may go along blithely thinking that he has proper control of the execution of a plan, only to find that the situation for which the plan was tailored has been changed. Many managers tend to lose control over the costs of new product programs when the unforseen difficulties of such ventures cause costs to mount—while the elusive rabbit of completion seems to be around one more corner.

---

[12] Billy E. Goetz, *Management Planning and Control* (New York: McGraw-Hill Book Co., Inc., 1949), p. 229.

13. *Principle of Review.* The control system should be reviewed periodically.

Because of the dynamics of enterprise and the environment in
which it operates, not only should controls be kept flexible but the
system and techniques of controls should periodically be reviewed.
Controls, like plans, are never final. Just as the manager should
continually reevaluate his plans and take navigational readings to see
if he is on course, so should he periodically and systematically review
his controls to make certain that the standards used, the strategic
points selected, and the tolerances permitted are consistent with his
plans and goals.

14. *Principle of Action.* Control is only justified if measures are undertaken to correct indicated or experienced deviations from plans
through appropriate planning, organizing, staffing, and directing.

Control is meaningless and wasteful and the application of the
principles above a fruitless exercise unless action is taken to correct
deficiencies detected. These corrections may be in the form of revised
or new plans, new or different delegations of authority and assignments of tasks, better training or selection of subordinates, or a better
order of counseling and guidance by the manager.

This principle not only underscores the action aspect of control
but also the fact that control tends to coalesce with the other functions of the manager. It emphasizes the basic unity of management
and the essential fact that control functions cannot be delegated,
cannot be centralized in a staff or department which does not have
the authority to execute a plan, and cannot be taken away from the
manager without destroying managership itself.

9. CHARTER OF ACCOUNTABILITY
FOR EXECUTIVES *

Phil N. Scheid †

FUNDAMENTAL PROBLEM

Once there was a first-line supervisor who worked for the Enterprise Corporation. His name was Axel McTurner, and he was a responsible supervisor. His boss knew this because responsibility was very important in the selection of all Enterprise supervisors. McTurner's associates knew this because he was one of them, and they too were responsible supervisors. The employees also knew that Axel was a responsible supervisor because, after all, he was a supervisor and, like all other supervisors, he must be responsible or he would not be a supervisor. All the supervisors of Enterprise Corporation were proud of their responsibility, for it set them apart from the nonsupervisors.

Business was good, and the Enterprise Corporation grew larger. With its growth came more complex problems which had to be solved. Axel McTurner was promoted. He became a responsible manager. He discovered there were varieties of managers—all were equally responsible, but they were not the same kind of responsible manager as he. Some, he learned, were called staff managers. Axel became confused. Now he was no longer certain of his responsibility, because these staff managers acted as if they too were responsible—many times for the same assignments Axel thought he was responsible for.

Widespread Puzzlement

Soon it became apparent that the confusion Axel felt about his responsibility was widespread throughout the Enterprise Corporation. Axel found that his fellow line managers were equally puzzled. He saw that the staff managers were not so confident as they pretended to be. The confusion was so prevalent that all the managers grew angry. They said unkind things about one another. (Sometimes

* From the *Harvard Business Review* (July-August, 1965). Reprinted by permission of the President and Fellows of Harvard College.
† Phil N. Scheid, Management Operations Manager, Ground Systems Group, Hughes Aircraft Company, Fullerton, California.

they even forgot just what they were angry about.) Angry thoughts led to evil deeds. The managers fashioned crude weapons for unkind purposes. They fought with carbon copies, squeaky wheels, arm-waving, and other power tactics.[1] They organized empires, demanded tribute, and negotiated feudal alliances.

The Executive Manager sensed he had a problem. To make his managers friendly again, he called his advisers together and said, "Our managers are growing restless. What can we do?" All the advisers were eager to demonstrate to the Executive Manager how sound their advice was. In fact, they were so eager that they paid little attention to the advice of the other advisers, for each adviser thought he alone "had the responsibility." As the Executive Manager listened, he began to understand why all the managers were becoming restless, for he saw the same dissension among his advisers.

Solution Attempt

He decided to start solving this problem with a management development program. He gave this responsibility to the People Adviser, saying that he wanted all the line and staff managers to learn about their different types of responsibility. Further, he stated that he wanted the managers to work together like a team of players, working hard to win for the Enterprise Corporation. He closed the meeting and went on about his business of executive managing.

Although none of the advisers or the line or staff managers said so, no one seemed to like the idea of management development. They didn't like it because none of them had thought of this solution, and besides they felt that it would not solve what each referred to as the "fundamental problem." Thus:

The Money Manager thought that the fundamental problem could be solved if the other managers would stop spending so much money.

The Selling Manager judged that it could be solved if the other managers would think and act like salesmen.

The Buying Manager felt that it could be solved if the other managers would stop trying to buy things and let him do it.

The Think-It-Up Manager believed that it could be solved if the other managers would go away and quit bothering him.

The Get-It-Done Manager reasoned that the fundamental problem could be solved if the other managers would stop talking and get to work.

---

[1] Norman H. Martin and John Howard Sims, "Power Tactics" (Thinking Ahead), *Harvard Business Review* (November-December, 1956), p. 25.

Despite these divergent viewpoints, the management development program was started. All the managers went back to school. Although Axel McTurner, as all the others, did not like the management development idea, he did go to some of the meetings—especially to those he knew the Executive Manager was going to attend.

The development of Axel McTurner, responsible manager, began with an explanation of the principles of management. He learned about "span of management" control. He listened to discussions on planning, organizing, staffing, directing. He heard about the advantages and disadvantages of centralization versus decentralization. He became interested in the delegation of responsibility and authority, and was heartened when he learned that there can be only one boss in an efficiently run organization (but he, of course, did not need to go to school to learn this).

Axel found that these management subjects had been thought out years ago in a period known as the scientific management era. He became familiar with the works of Taylor [2] and others, and learned that these early pioneers had done much to develop organization structures and management measurement techniques—concepts which had contributed to the evolution of the business system.

He next learned about employee perceptions, the benefits and pitfalls of improved employee communications, and the trends toward participative management. He thus saw that the line manager had to be familiar with human relations,[3] and had to recognize the real and imaginary grievances of his employees. He was told that he needed to be more skilled in counseling and in learning how to listen. He was informed that each employee should be treated as an individual because each had his own unique reasons and needs for working.

Abject Misfire

At this point, Axel became aware that the management development program had done little to allay his concern about his degree of responsibility. It now seemed to him that in addition to being a responsible line manager, he also had to be something of a psychologist, a sociologist, and perhaps even a cultural anthropologist. It became increasingly difficult for Axel McTurner to concentrate on his managerial responsibility, for now he realized that his job was

---

[2] Frederick Winslow Taylor, *Scientific Management* (Hanover, N. H.: Dartmouth College, 1912).

[3] Elton Mayo, *The Human Problems of an Industrial Civilization* (Boston: Division of Research, Harvard Business School, 1933).

not at all as he had envisioned it in the initial days of his management career.

The confused situation throughout the Enterprise Corporation about the division of responsibility didn't get any better. The managers were now quick to quote their favorite scientific and behavioral management spokesmen in defense of their schemes. Axel earnestly longed for the simpler days before he became a responsible manager. Now that he saw all the additional problems he was expected to solve while defending himself against the onslaughts of the staff "advisers," he was not so sure that he was in the right situation at all. He wondered if there wasn't an easier way to make a living. He felt more like a differential than an Axel.

RESPONSIBILITY AND AUTHORITY

There are many Axel McTurners in our society today, each striving diligently to do his best for what he perceives to be the purpose and objectives of his respective company. Each is faced with enough frustration and confusion brought on by the increased pace of change and technology without being burdened with ambiguity in words and concepts. Now, for most of the McTurners, the previously solid concept, "responsibility with commensurate authority," has failed.

Semantic Confusion

Because of its injudicious and widespread use, the term "responsibility" has become more symbolic than substantive in its value and meaning. At best, responsibility is a vague concept that sometimes implies a task; other times, a condition of being; and, in still other instances, an objective to be attained. To add further confusion, responsibility is delegated, accepted, rejected, retracted, modified, or evaluated. The very proliferation of the use of responsibility in indiscriminate and inept applications has tended to eliminate it as a practical, useful concept.

Unfortunately, we continue to manage our enterprises on this shifting foundation. Often a middle manager is not aware of his so-called responsibility until he finds himself in trouble. Moreover, there is evidence that some middle managers purposely practice managerial brinkmanship in order to determine the precise parameters of their responsibilities because definitive direction from top management is lacking.

Most experienced business managers will concede that responsibility for enterprise success or failure rests with the highest ranking executive within the organization. Salary structures support this assumption in that executives are traditionally compensated in an ascending order relative to their proximity to the top of the organization. It follows that a chief executive may appear to be delegating responsibility, but in practice may not be, because in the final analysis he knows that he alone must answer for all successes and failures incurred. This fact is borne out repeatedly when we hear of managers defecting from their responsibilities by a series of machinations that range from buck-passing to formal resignation.

Conflicting Philosophies

The confused state of mind of Axel McTurner is typical of many middle managers in business and industry today. Conventional management education programs have done little to illuminate the practical differentiations between responsibility and authority, and between responsibility and accountability. It should come as no surprise that McTurner wonders if perhaps there is a better way to earn a living. Figuratively speaking, he has become the focal point of a confrontation of at least two seemingly conflicting management philosophies. Within his lifetime he has been exposed to the advantages and disadvantages of both the scientific and behavioral management methodologies. It is difficult for him to "unlearn" many of the implied principles of scientific management in order to accept the suggestions of the industrial behaviorists. He immediately sees a conflict of interest between these two philosophies, and has a tendency to build defensive bulwarks against the invasion of his management domain by change or the unfamiliar.

Well he might wonder just what degree of responsibility has been delegated to him, for he sees his responsibility diluted by an ever-increasing number of functional and staff counterparts. Among corporations there is a tendency to superimpose project management assignments on existing organizational formats. This is particularly true in technologically oriented industrial areas. The net effect on organizational sophistication is an obscuring of the relationship between the roles of executive management and the functions of middle managers. One might well raise the question, "Can ultimate responsibility for corporate success or failure truly be delegated?"

ACCOUNTABILITY CONCEPT

Recognizing the confusion surrounding responsibility as a management concept, the term *accountability* is suggested in order to specify a more definitive delegation of assignment. Admittedly, by dictionary definition there is little distinction between the two terms. However, in application there is a surprising difference in the way the Axel McTurners react to the delegation of accountability versus responsibility. It is this attitudinal difference that makes it possible to effect some improvements in the division and performance of work.

Distinct Segments

If we accept, for the moment, the premise that accountability can be delegated more precisely than responsibility, it follows that accountability can be more easily subdivided into operational or functional segments—lower orders of accountability—which more closely parallel the conventional divisions of work found in a typical business organization.

Since accountability, by our definition, more accurately represents the various parts of an executive's job, the role and mission of Axel McTurner as the manager of an operational or functional segment of the Enterprise Corporation can be reduced to a descriptive document—a Charter of Accountability—which will be discussed shortly.

Accountability requires a clarification of the functional relationship between individuals—in our case, McTurner and his boss—by stating operational objectives, goals, and criteria against which performance may be evaluated on a predetermined reporting timetable.

This concept actually provides for an effective division of the supervisory and staff labor resources of an organization. Each functional area, or division of activity, becomes subdivided and resubdivided throughout the organizational hierarchy into the functional task elements, but always within a particular and well-defined organizational relationship anchored to the company's purpose and objectives. In practice, accountability says that people are held accountable *to* someone *by* someone for doing specific things, according to specific plans, and against certain timetables to accomplish tangible performance results.

Such an accountable condition is easily identifiable, understandable, and directly related to the various other activities and functional areas within the total organization. Functional accountability, therefore, promotes efficiency and effectivity by providing specific managerial direction and measurably improved visibility. In essence, the manifestation of the concept can produce a uniquely profitable coalition of strategic and tactical decision making effort.

Management Theories

However, before attempting to formalize such a condition, it appears appropriate at this point to review briefly the prevailing schools of management philosophy which have contributed to the development of the accountability system. Listed below are the four theories and concepts, compounded of experience and concern for continued improvement, which have provided the intellectual resource and theoretical base for the development of the accountability concept:

1. From the scientific management school we took the idea that accountability for functional performance can be delegated. However, this applies only in those circumstances where such delegation is accompanied by direct authorization to perform or to obtain the wherewithal for performance. The scientific managers tell us that functional performance for which an individual may be held accountable can also be isolated and measured, and that these measurements may be used to evaluate the individual manager's performance. (The reader should note that we speak of the delegation of an accountability. Responsibility, as we have rationalized, cannot be delegated.)

2. The behavioral scientists contributed to our idea of accountability with their concept that individual managers in performing particular tasks have a tendency to impose on themselves more difficult functional goals than those that might be set by their supervisors; and, further, that individuals respond more appropriately and willingly to objective evaluation of their performance than to subjective trait appraisal. The latter situation, they argue, is a possible source of resentment for an individual who may otherwise respect the judgmental capability of his superior.

3. From the revisionists, who attempted an amalgam of the previous two general categories of thought,[4] we found that operating managers are best equipped to establish appropriate performance criteria which describe a job well done and provide the opportunity for self-evaluation of progress. Further, task performers resolve functional problems much more effectively and constructively when they accept performance criteria as valid indicators of their functional performance.

4. Finally, from the management scientists we adopted the idea that a systematic management approach is possible that does not sacrifice the sanctity of the individual or violate the social contract of Rousseau.[5] Even more important, we discovered that resources and capabilities can be organized in such a way as to be self-improving in actual operation.

These assumptions are representative of most of our experiences, and they are not confusing or contradictory to one another. They are

---

    [4] Warren G. Bennis, "Revisionist Theory of Leadership" (Keeping Informed), *Harvard Business Review* (January-February, 1961), p. 26.
    [5] Jean Jacques Rousseau, *The Social Contract*, translated by Charles Frankel (New York: Hafner Publishing Co., 1949).

complementary assumptions and can be welded into a coherent body. It is from this welding together that the concept of accountability has evolved.[6]

CHARTER OF ACCOUNTABILITY

Although the concept of accountability provides a channel for the confluence of the scientific, behavioral, revisionist, and management science approaches to management, it does not in itself bring improved results. A formalized program or implementing vehicle is required both for the Axel McTurners who make the wheels of the company go and for the executive managers who plot the course and require a more responsive helm.

The concept of accountability stipulates a condition of mutual and strictly objective understanding between two individuals—again, in our case, Axel McTurner and his boss. This condition is formalized in a physical Charter of Accountability document for the immediate activity Axel supervises. Such a charter provides a vehicle for executive management to establish clearly the organization's purpose and objectives. It also provides a method by which middle managers, such as Axel, can isolate the functional accountabilities of their assignments.

Establishing Guidelines

It is essential that each Charter of Accountability be developed by a select group of supervisors or managers who are intimately involved with the day-by-day operations of each major division, provided a clear statement of the overall company purpose and objectives is defined and communicated by executive management. Such a group or study team is best equipped to define necessary functional accountabilities (which may or may not represent the existing organizational chart). The team can also define the specific subtasks which, in total, comprise a major functional accountability, as well as the accomplishment goals isolated to represent successful performance attainment. More importantly, the group can specify the significant and highly peculiar criteria which are to be used to motivate positive managerial performance, improve operating visibility, and facilitate information processing.

Once these data have been developed a Charter of Accountability can be drafted which contains the following information.

---

[6] O. A. Ohmann, "Search for a Managerial Philosophy," *Harvard Business Review* (September-October, 1957), p. 41.

1. A statement of purpose.

2. A listing of important objectives.

3. A breakdown of the functional accountabilities necessary to accomplish the objectives.

4. A subseries of performance tasks which provide middle managers with definitive targets toward which to orient their specialized efforts.

When the charter is approved by all parties concerned, including the chief executive, it provides a set of guidelines for the administration of the organization's total effort. A large company may have as many charters as are necessary to represent the major divisions within in the total enterprise. But all such charters have the common benefit of orienting functional endeavor toward the successful accomplishment of the company's communicated purpose and objectives.

Separate Aspects

In implementation, the Charter of Accountability serves two distinct but compatible ends:

1. It provides a participative development program leading toward a descriptive document for each operating unit of the organization. The charter clearly defines the purpose and nature, operating characteristics, and organizational relationships of each company unit.

2. It provides a functional system which not only serves managers *at all levels* as a tool to control their individual operations, but also provides top management with an instrument for continuous review and evaluation of each manager's functional performance.

In these respects, the charter is not an abstraction, but a concrete document, and this should be clearly understood at the start of the program. It is in this way that the accountability program differs quite significantly from traditional efforts which have neither provision for, nor expectation of, tangible evidence of improved organizational performance.

The charter management system starts with the formulating of the local purpose and objectives for each company unit as they have evolved in the development phase of the program. From this charter, operational plans are established. These include requirement analyses, allocation of resources, design of implementation procedures, execution of plans, and the measurement and reporting of the progress and performance toward operational objectives. Next, provision is made for performance review and evaluation. Finally, the charter system enables top management to take appropriate corrective action to achieve the established plans, purpose, and objectives of the organization.

A Hypothetical Case

Now let's assume that Axel McTurner's executive superior is impressed with the concept of accountability and is eager to launch an implementing charter program. How would such a plan affect Axel McTurner? In this situation, let's also assume that Axel McTurner is Manager of the Widget Division of the Enterprise Corporation, with four or five departmental supervisors reporting to him.

In the first place, Axel must be convinced that the charter program is worth the time and attention he should personally devote to its application within his division. He must perceive the benefits accruing to himself, as well as the larger benefits to the corporation. Secondly, for the concept to be operationally effective, Axel (with the go-ahead from his boss) must accept specific accountability for the installation and implementation of the new management system. This will require time and conditioning. He must be shown that the accountability concept establishes a means by which his previous, and perhaps conflicting, management concepts can be brought together and applied where most appropriate. (A hypothetical Charter of Accountability for Axel McTurner's Widget Division of the Enterprise Corporation is given in the Appendix on page 138 for the reader who would like a more detailed breakdown of a typical charter.)

Procedural Stages

Once Axel is genuinely convinced that there are certain values to be gained from the introduction of the accountability concept, he should then proceed with the following eight steps to develop a specific Charter of Accountability for the Widget Division.

1. He requests and receives a clear statement of the purpose and objectives of the Enterprise Corporation from his immediate superior. (This may take a little time, for it is possible that Axel's boss may not have the answers readily available.)

2. Axel convenes a meeting of his division's departmental supervisors to explain the Charter of Accountability system and his commitment to its installation, and to appoint his charter development team.

3. The Widget Division's charter development group, composed of key operating personalities within the division, is now asked to assemble

regularly on a convenient schedule. At these sessions, the team will analyze and commit to writing succinct statements of functional accountabilities performed within the division. Normally, this will represent the existing formal organization format. However, in some situations it may be determined that existing functional parts of an organization no longer serve to enhance the division's reason for existence (purpose) and direction (objectives) as established at the outset. In such cases, the team may decide to recommend that these assumed functional operations be deleted in the interest of economical and functional scope.

4. Once the functional divisions of labor are clearly redefined and committed to the charter document draft, the group develops detailed task statements. These represent subdivisions of the previously established functional accountabilities. Each task identifies one or more specific goals representing desirable performance targets. With each goal should be associated one or more unique and *operationally recognizable criteria*. Each criterion serves as a monitor or indicator of performance measured against the task goal. Herein lies the heart of the Charter of Accountability—the evolution of unique criteria which can be used for the operational evaluation of task performance. For example:

   Cost criteria in Axel McTurner's division might turn out to be something totally different from the traditional rates or ratios applied by the Money Manager. Therefore, Axel and his subordinates are best equipped to determine criteria which can be used as a management motivational tool—criteria which are more meaningful at the effort and expenditure level—and which are oriented toward the ultimate realization of the Enterprise Corporation purpose.

5. Axel's charter team also reviews and digests the wealth of the existing documentation available within the Enterprise Corporation which purports to describe the affairs of the Widget Division. Examples of such sources include appropriate job descriptions of Axel and his supervisors; company policy and procedural statements; financial, sales, and contractual directives; pertinent interoffice memos; and the implied or inferred relationship between Axel and his executive superior.

   As a by-product, the charter of the Widget Division serves to assimilate much of these data and brings their import to bear on the activities of the Widget Division. This, in turn, provides a comprehensive and realistic description of Axel McTurner's managerial position in terms directly related to his anticipated performance—a condition which is not apparent in a review of traditional job description statements.

6. At the completion of this effort, Axel's team submits for his review a draft Charter of Accountability for the Widget Division. The draft, which represents the total effort to be performed in order to accomplish the division's goals and objectives, is subdivided into the following sectional treatments:

   a. Statement of Widget Division purpose.
   b. Objectives of the division.

    c. Scope and domain of division activity.

    d. Essential functional accountabilities to be performed by the division.

    e. Specific task efforts which comprise each functional accountability.

    f. Goals that represent successful task realization.

    g. Unique and operationally meaningful criteria against which task progress is to be evaluated.

7. Axel reviews and modifies the draft until he is satisfied that it represents the basis on which he, as Widget Division Manager, is willing to be judged. When Axel is satisfied with his division's Charter of Accountability, he then approaches the Executive Manager of the Enterprise Corporation for official sanction to operate within the parameters established in the charter. Assuming there is no conflict of understanding, the Executive Manager approves Axel's charter and authorizes its application by affixing his signature approval.

8. Axel now has a combined instrument in the charter which serves both as a definition of the operational scope of his divisional effort and as a system for visibility and control. Task performance, reported to him in a variety of media, can now be related to the specific goals and unique criteria established. Since his supervisors have actively participated in the evolution of these realization indicators, they, in turn, will be motivated to demonstrate effective individual performance.

Resulting Efficiency

The net result should be a more efficiently managed division which will constantly relate its effort to the primary purpose and objectives of the Enterprise Corporation. Axel McTurner, accountable manager, now performs in a supportive leadership role. He has established a planning mechanism; he has permitted his supervisors to apply their ingenuity in accomplishing mutually important goals and objectives; and he is now able to function in a management-by-exception basis— applying his time and talent to assist those supervisors who express some difficulty in achieving their targets.

He has decentralized, in effect, his surveillance of the division, but with the assurance that his supervisors know what is expected of them and how they must perform in order to be evaluated as effective supervisors. Axel also recognizes that the total performance of his division will represent his own efforts, for better or worse, in managing a segment of the Enterprise Corporation in concert with the overall purpose and objectives of the organization.

McTurner now begins to feel and act more like a governor than an Axel.

RESPONSIBILITY AND ACCOUNTABILITY

Unfortunately, as we noted earlier, it is not possible to redefine accurately the word responsibility since it has become generic in any number of instances and applications. It is possible, however, to define a word or a concept precisely for a specific application or instance. Such an attempt will be made here.

Responsibility in this connotation is construed as a personal characteristic, an element in the condition of being, either inherent or acquired, dealing with an individual's personal standards of integrity and the manner in which he applies himself and his resources to whatever task is set before him (and, by the same token, the manner in which he operates in his various business and social environments). The quality of responsibility, then, becomes that attribute which an individual imparts to his organization or work assignment —not something which can be legislated, imposed, delegated, or otherwise established arbitrarily.

Hopefully, through judicious communication it will be possible to establish a new and more precise concept of responsibility. This will remove one of the confusion factors that exists to hinder the effort of establishing a smooth and effective operating organization. It does not, however, provide a useful substitute or replacement for those things which have to be done in the company's operation. Hence, the need for the concept of accountability.

Vital Ingredient

However, this concept, and its peculiar characteristic of being subject to delegation, cannot be translated into an effective system if accountability is delegated to an individual manager, supervisor, or staff assignee who does not possess the personal quality we have defined as responsibility. Without a high level of personal responsibility, it is doubtful that any system of management operation would be effective.

Many attempts have been made over the years to develop effective organizational systems, ostensibly to arrive at some indication of an individual's managerial value. And most of these approaches have been relatively unsuccessful. This failure has been due primarily to an insignificant correlation between subjective determinations of potential and objective analyses of results.

An accountable and responsible manager welcomes the opportunity to be evaluated and compensated on the same basis—or, in other words, to be compensated in terms of his actual performance on the job that he is qualified for and assigned to.

CONCLUSION

By and large, due partially to the experience, clairvoyance, and general direction of experienced middle managers, our traditional management systems have had a relative degree of success. If, in some instances, these managers have been found deficient, let us assume that their perception was faulty—perhaps indicating a lack of responsibility on the part of executive management in providing them with appropriate direction for the profitable application of their talents.

Regardless of where the failure lies, top management has the means available today if it wishes to capitalize on the recent findings and experimentations in the art and science of management. The Charter of Accountability system provides a philosophy and vehicle for accomplishing this end, and offers the following significant advantages over prior management systems designed for similar purposes:

1. Greater managerial incentive toward attainment of the total company purpose and objectives.

2. Better information essential to effective top-management decision making and control on an exception basis.

3. Clearer channels of communication not only for those directly involved, but also for associated company units concerned with the scope and range of functional jurisdiction.

4. More accurate results oriented evaluation—based on actual subordinate performance accomplishment.

5. Quicker identification of individuals with future executive potential, which, in turn, offers ample opportunity for recognition, development, and compensation for effective performance.

Perhaps most significant, the Concept of Accountability provides supervisors and managers with an immediate and comprehensible index of their own managerial effectiveness. Functional managers are (as they should be) the first to know and evaluate operational status in order to take near real time, appropriate action.

Since the Charter of Accountability approach serves to bring about an equitable conciliation between apparently divergent management philosophies, it would seem to provide an effective method for administering and managing modern day complex organizational structures within business and industry. Further, the concept seems to provide for the appropriate blend of executive leadership required to maintain and improve the American business system and the largely untapped reservoir of latent creative energy within each staff or line supervisor and manager who is eager for the opportunity to demonstrate his total capability.[7]

APPENDIX: HYPOTHETICAL CHARTER OF ACCOUNTABILITY

WIDGET DIVISION, ENTERPRISE CORPORATION

I. *Introduction*—This Charter of Accountability is established to:

A. Delineate the cognizant functional, administrative, and financial parameters of the Division.

B. Establish management visibility for the objective evaluation of Division performance.

C. Specify management positions and incumbents accountable for performance realization.

II. *Purpose*—The Division purpose is:

To provide a competitive capability in the field of advanced widget technology which will enhance the growth of the Division and complement the goals and objectives of the Enterprise Corporation.

III. *Objectives*—The Division objectives are:

A. Long-Range
1. Establish and maintain the Division as both preeminent and competitive in the marketplace.
2. Return a reasonable profit on resources employed.
3. Fulfill the contractual commitments.

B. Short-Range or Annual
1. Increase annual sales.
2. Improve net profits.
3. Realize all terms and conditions of the Division Charter of Accountability.

IV. *Scope of Accountability*—The Executive Manager has designated the Division as a major product line division of the Enterprise Corporation and will expect the Division Manager to pursue his functional, administrative, and financial accountabilities in accordance with the following precepts:

A. Functional Accountabilities—Perform the following exclusive *assignments* for Enterprise Corporation:
1. Sponsor and conduct research and engineering development in advanced widget technology.
2. Market the widget product line.

---

[7] Edward C. Schleh, "Make Your Staff Pay Its Way," *Harvard Business Review* (March-April, 1957), p. 115.

3. Manufacture widgets for inventory and customer commitments.

4. Support other divisions requiring widget capability.

5. Service widgets in the field.

B. Administrative Accountabilities—Manage the following *processes* in accordance with the Enterprise Corporation policy and procedure:

1. Establish and implement the Division Charter of Accountability.

2. Prepare and submit annual Division plans for review and approval.

3. Organize the Division to effectively administer the approved plans.

4. Attract and develop qualified administrative, technical, and production personnel.

5. Motivate personnel and direct the affairs of the Division.

6. Monitor and control Division performance.

7. Maintain mutually beneficial relationships with the managers and staff directors of other Divisions.

8. Establish industry, educational, association, and community liaison contacts compatible with Division affairs.

9. Serve on the Advisory Committee of Enterprise Corporation.

C. Financial Accountabilities—Monitor and control the *schedules, costs, expenses,* and *profits* of the Division in accordance with the following financial and budgetary requirement standards:

1. Annual sales by item.

2. Delivery commitments.

3. Material costs and expense.

4. Inventory status and turnover.

6. Total labor requirement.

7. Overhead expense rate.

8. Total cost of sales

9. Net return on sales and invested capital.

10. Gross and net profit.

V. *Performance Tasks, Goals, and Criteria*—Successful Division performance requires the isolation of specific subaccountabilities or performance tasks with associated goals and progress criteria. Positive performance realization on all the following performance tasks constitutes total effective Division annual performance.

(Tasks illustrated in the following three examples are representative only. Normally, in a typical charter for a major organization, there would be 20 or more such performance tasks.)

PERFORMANCE TASK (Example A)

TASK No. 100   Functional performance

TASK STATEMENT: Realize annual and backlog sales projection.

ACCOUNTABILITY: Division Manager (Axel McTurner)

                              Marketing Manager (Bill Beaver)

GOALS: 1. Annual Sales—$2,250,000.

    2. Diversify customer mix.

    3. Committed sales backlog—$800,000.

CRITERIA: 1. Plan a 7 percent annual sales increase.

    2. Plan a 5 percent change in customer mix.

    3. Plan a 33 percent annual backlog residual.

REPORTING   1. Weekly Sales Report.

MEDIA: 2. Monthly Marketing Review sessions.

PERFORMANCE   First Quarter—Behind plan.

STATUS: Second Quarter—Trends look promising.

    Third Quarter—Customer mix slipping.

    Fourth Quarter—Incomplete.

PERFORMANCE TASK (Example B)

TASK No. 200   Administrative performance

TASK STATEMENT: Select, develop, and upgrade personnel required to realize Division plans.

ACCOUNTABILITY: Division Manager (Axel McTurner)

    All Department Heads

GOALS: 1. 150-employee year-end manpower force.

    2. Develop four departmental understudies.

    3. Encourage eight engineers to enroll in refresher courses.

    4. Reduce departmental turnover.

CRITERIA: 1. Plan a 30 percent manpower increase by year-end.

    2. Plan for one understudy program per calendar quarter.

    3. Plan for two enrollments per academic quarter.

    4. Plan for a maximum average monthly turnover of 0.5 percent.

REPORTING   1. Monthly Departmental Status Reports.

MEDIA: 2. Quarterly Performance Review sessions.

PERFORMANCE   First Quarter—Slow on No. 1, OK on Nos. 2, 3, and 4.

STATUS: Second Quarter—All criteria in "go" condition.

    Third Quarter—Need more employment assistance.

    Fourth Quarter—Incomplete.

PERFORMANCE TASK (Example C)

TASK No. 300	Financial Performance
TASK STATEMENT:	Reduce Division's incurred manufacturing cost of sales.
ACCOUNTABILITY:	Division Manager (Axel McTurner)
	Production Manager (Hank MacHinery)
GOALS:	1. Reduce material costs.
	2. Reduce direct labor costs.
	3. Reduce overhead costs.
	4. Automate selected manufacturing operations.
CRITERIA:	1. Plan for a 23 percent direct material cost.
	2. Plan for a 26 percent direct labor cost.
	3. Plan for a 12 percent indirect labor cost.
	4. Plan for a 21 percent annual cost reduction due to the introduction of automated equipment.
REPORTING MEDIA:	1. Monthly P & L Statement.
	2. Weekly Manpower Reports.
	3. Weekly Material Reports.
	4. Special Summary Reports.
PERFORMANCE STATUS:	First Quarter—Criteria No. 1 OK; no progress on Nos. 2, 3, and 4.
	Second Quarter—On target on all but No. 4 —needs help.
	Third Quarter—No. 4 poor—need staff specialist.
	Fourth Quarter—Incomplete.

VI. *Delegated Management Authority*—In order to effectively implement this Division Charter of Accountability, the Executive Manager of the Enterprise Corporation delegates to the Division Manager the following Approval Authority:

A. Sales Contracts—to and including dollar values of $100,000.

B. Purchases—to and including item values of $5,000.

C. Personnel—to and including annual salary rates of $10,000.

D. Capital Investment—to and includoing commitments of $5,000.

VII. *Charter Summary*—The preceding purpose, objectives, scope of accountability, performance tasks, criteria, and authority comprise the Charter of Accountability for the Widget Division of the Enterprise Corporation.

The Executive Manager expects that the Division Manager will assume a large measure of self-direction in managing the affairs of the Division under the terms and conditions of this Charter. The Executive Manager does *not* intend to:

A. Manage the internal activities of the Division.

B. Resolve, at executive level, problems generated by faulty, inadequate, or untimely information or intelligence.

C. Indefinitely support poorly performing operations.

The Executive Manager *does* intend to:

A. Periodically review the performance of the Division based on the progressive realization of the accountabilities set forth herein.

B. Review Division plans and recommendations.

C. Provide advice, counsel, and supportive leadership to assist the Division Manager in the positive realization of this Charter of Accountability.

D. Review, modify, and approve specific performance tasks, goals, and criteria.

These Charter conditions are mutually acceptable to the undersigned.

Submitted by: _____
Manager, Widget Division

Approved by: _____
Executive Manager,
Enterprise Corporation

Date: _____

10. MEASUREMENT—PLUS PLANNING:

REMARKS ON A CONTROL SYSTEM * Raymond Villers †

After years of uncertainty with regard to what is meant by control system, a trend is now developing that is characterized by two essential points: (1) the need for diversified standards of measurement and (2) the need for a control function as part of the organization structure.

THE NEED FOR DIVERSIFIED STANDARDS OF MEASUREMENT

Profit making at a rate that provides an adequate return on investment is the ultimate goal of the business enterprise. It is therefore beyond question that the accounting figures provide the standard of measurement of the performance of the company as a whole. The problem is how to relate profit making to the performance of each of the executives and supervisors to whom authority and responsibility have been delegated: the vice president-manufacturing, the director of research, the chief accountant, the plant manager and each foreman.

The efforts made to solve this problem can be classified as three major steps taken during the last 60 years:

Step 1 started with Frederick W. Taylor's work—the determination of work measurement standards. This has proved to be a very useful step that provided the basis for cost accounting. The same approach is now being used in various fields, including office work, applying such statistical concepts as the work sampling method.

Step 2 has been the use of budgets that makes it possible to control expenses on the basis of foresight rather than on the basis of wisdom of hindsight. In the late 1940's budgeting was still considered a nonpractical approach in most companies. During the last decade, industry has taken this Step 2. Budgeting is now the rule rather than the

---

* From *The Controller* (October, 1960). Reprinted by permission of the Financial Executives Institute.

† Raymond Villers, Consultant on Industrial Management, Rautenstrauch and Villers, New York City.

exception, as indicated by the recent survey conducted under the sponsorship of Controllers Institute Research Foundation.

Step 3 is the recent trend which is essentially the subject of this paper. Work measurement standards and expense budgets—Steps 1 and 2—tell you whether or not the money spent was the amount that could be reasonably expected for what was accomplished. They provide a useful expense control. But expense control is only one aspect of profit making. The other aspect involves what has been accomplished and also what should have been done and has not been done. Step 3 is the development of a control system that provides a measurement of this other aspect of profit making: what has been obtained as a result of the money that was spent.

Considering the organization as a whole, the answer is clear-cut and accounting data provide this answer. The sales income is what has been obtained as a result of the expense. The difference between the two is the profit that measures the performance of the whole organization. But the question is:

How can the head of the organization measure the performance of his subordinates at the various levels of management with regard to what they have accomplished for the money they spent?

A useful approach is divisionalization. The manager of a division has to show a profit for his division. This approach provides such a clear-cut answer that it has been widely practiced. There is room for argument as to how far to go in the direction of divisionalization and this has been widely discussed. But there is no room for argument that, regardless of the size of the division, divisionalization in modern industry will always end with a functional organization because, on its own, the division is a functional organization.

No profit can be made by the organization unless the various functions contribute effectively, but no function makes a profit on its own. Attempts have sometimes been made to create profit centers within the functional organization, which amounts to semidivisionalization, but this procedure is rather exceptional. The question then is:

How to measure the performance of a manager in the functional organization?

For many years the answer has essentially been of a qualitative nature: the opinion of one or several executives. A report by the president to the board of directors could emphasize the "splendid accomplishment" of the marketing people; the plant manager could ask for an increase in salary of this foreman, because of his "excellent job," or could decide to fire that foreman because he is "no good." Obviously this approach leads to abuses, misunderstandings, and misjudgments.

With a quantitative measurement of actual performance, these problems can be solved and the management of the functional organization can become much more efficient, making it possible to operate on the basis of functional decentralization.

In recent years, increasing attention has been given to the need for standards of performance. As stated by W. Benton Harrison, senior vice president-administration of Sylvania Electric Products:

> *What can be quantified?* There is no question that businessmen have learned to measure and apply mathematical techniques to new facets of business activities during the past decades. Relatively little progress, however, has been made in applying these quantitative methods to management. I can think of nothing needed more than a method for measuring the effectiveness of a manager.

To serve this purpose, the activities of the manager have to be analyzed and his performances related to certain key centers of the business, i.e., the centers of activities that deserve special attention because of the conditions of operation.

To select the key factors, not too many and enough of them; to select an adequate unit of measurement: sales volume, sales mixture, rate of rejects, absenteeism, turnover, among many other units; to prepare reports that do not require too much paperwork and at the same time provide all the information needed by each executive or supervisor who has to know how his subordinates have performed— this is the problem.

THE NEED FOR A CONTROL FUNCTION AS PART OF THE ORGANIZATIONAL STRUCTURE

As is always the case in a new field, there is room for uncertainty and disagreement. This is the case with this new control function, specifically with regard to four fundamental questions:

Question I

What will be the field of activities of this function? I suggest that it will include planning and budgeting as well as control, because in many cases the adopted plan of action provides the standard of measurement of the actual performance.

I also suggest that it should include the responsibility for data processing. Recent and expected new developments in the field, including electronic computers and telecontrol, the new production control equipment, clearly indicate that integrated data processing is part of a well-managed control system.

Question 2

What are the responsibility and the authority of this function?

I think that it should be clearly established that this function acts as a service department for the benefit of management, with no authority to give orders but with the responsibility of offering assignments as part of planning, which assignments have to be accepted by the operating people, with no authority to investigate what has already been done, but with the responsibility of providing an adequate control system. This stimulates the effective concept of functional decentralization.

If properly organized, managerial control is an objective method of effective management that is essentially based on (a) the determination of a standard of performance (call it S); (b) the recording of the actual performance (call it A); (c) the computation and eventual analysis of the variance ($V = S - A$); and the proper managerial action.

The decision to act depends upon the information provided. The actual performance A and the predetermined standards may draw attention to significant problems and the need for change in the conditions of operation, or to significant opportunities that should be taken advantage of. The variance $V = S - A$, if adequately measured and analyzed, indicates whether or not the operations are conducted as expected. The action suggested by V may be a reward or a rebuke, a change in procedure of any other action. The decision may even be *not* to act, either because V is a variance that is within expected or acceptable limits, or because it is recognized that for the time being nothing can be done about it.

The problem that has to be solved is to determine what information should reach this or that manager, how standards of measurement can be detemined, how the actual data are recorded, how detailed they have to be, how accurate they can be, and how the analysis of the variance $V = S - A$ can be made and presented.

This is the responsibility of the control function.

Question 3

Who will take over this new control function?

The nature of this problem is best illustrated by the article recently published in the *Journal of Industrial Engineering* by E. B. Cochran, who thinks that this new function will be part of the controller's office. His article is preceded by a note of the editors who indicate their opinion that the industrial engineer should be considered. In a following issue of the *Journal of Industrial Engineering*, the author of the article answered the editors' note. Illustrative of the transition period we are going through is also the fact that exactly a year ago—it was in May, 1959—I myself was given the opportunity of addressing the national convention of the American Institute of Industrial Engineers and of presenting a paper also related to the control function.

Question 4

Last but certainly not least—*How to organize the control system?*

What is needed is an *integrated system*. This point has been very clearly indicated in recent years in various studies, including the research work sponsored by Controllers Institute Research Foundation and several papers presented before the American Management Association.

An integrated system is best provided by the operations control book system.

An operations control book is a set of reports made available to each manager or supervisor and intended to give him the information he needs to evaluate his own performance and to know to what extent he can rely upon the subordinates to whom he has delegated some of his responsibilities.

Too much information results in reports too extensive or too intricate which may either remain unread or be misunderstood. Too little information may leave gaps in the texture of managerial controls and defeat their own purpose. A solution of this dilemma is to provide at top management level a synthesis of information and a very analytic information at the lower levels and to relate them to each other through progressively less synthetic and more analytic but closely interrelated information from top to bottom. This means a complete departure from the frequent practice of issuing one report, copy of which goes to all levels of management, thus saving a great amount of paperwork but wasting a great amount of managerial effort and even taking the risk that the information will be misunderstood or will not receive the attention it deserves.

To illustrate the approach of issuing a synthetic related to analytic reports, let us take a hypothetical case. In a given business, the president receives synthetic reports that summarize the main activities of the business. The vice president-manufacturing, the shop superintendent, and the foremen receive reports related to their own problems in an increasingly analytic manner from top to bottom.

During a given period, the scrap of material in one department has reached a very unusual level. The report received by the president reveals that the actual cost of production is far above standard. The report received by the vice president-manufacturing does not give the final answer to the question asked by the president with regard to this variance, but it shows that the variance has occurred in the shop, not in the assembly department. The shop superintendent's report includes the item "scrap" which reveals that this particular element of cost is the one out of line. But it gives only a total value of the scrap expense. A breakdown of this expense by type of material is available in the more detailed reports sent to the foremen. The foreman's report discloses which material is responsible for the unidentified variance shown in the report to the president between actual and standard cost of manufacturing. This provides the information the president needed to take action. He immediately calls the vice president who supervises the purchasing agent and tells him to find out why this material that does not meet the specifications was ever purchased by his subordinate.

The needs and conditions of operations of each organization vary so much that the key centers—that is, for practical purpose, the listing of all subjects to be included in the operations control books— will vary greatly from company to company.

The following five steps have been found useful in introducing and operating the operations control book system:

Step 1. Determine what reports are needed by top management and how often they are needed, so as to serve two essential purposes:

1. Provide an overall picture of the company's situation for which top management is responsible.

2. Throw light on mistakes made or troubles encountered at lower levels of management, to whom responsibility and authority have been delegated. This has to be done early enough so that action can be taken before excessive damage has resulted.

Among the reports that are used in practically every company are the reports on sales, cost and profit, compared to forecasts and budgets; the timing of deliveries to customers compared to promised dates; the complaints from customers; the efficiency of plant operations; and the employes' morale and attitude.

Step 2. Determine the key centers at the next level of management, by analyzing the key centers at top level. For instance, the actual total sales vs. the forecast is the report that reaches the president; the actual sales, district by district vs. the forecast by district, is the report that reaches the director of marketing.

Step 3. Proceed in the same manner, until the lowest level of management is reached: the report of actual sales for each salesman vs. his sales quota is what reaches the district sales manager.

A practical approach when starting at top management level is to review the reports that are now received. In many cases, it will be found that the number of reports received is beyond reason, that quite a few duplicate each other, and that many of them include so much data that the executive involved cannot be expected to read them.

Step 4. Organize the preparation and distribution of operations control books. The data are collected either by the control function (whether it is part of the controller's office or of a planning and control department) or by the function involved: safety, dispatching, scheduling, marketing, etc. In the latter case, however, the reports are sent to the control function and not directly to the executives or supervisors who will ultimately receive them.

The control function studies the reports, eventually summarizes them, or presents them as graphs, or analyzes the variances and makes comments. These reports are then incorporated in the operations control book, a set of reports that is permanently on the desk of each executive or supervisor, and in which all reports are classified according to a permanent arrangement recorded in a table of contents.

The operations control books are kept up to date by periodic replacement of the reports. The issuance of the new reports by the control function may be on a quarterly, monthly, weekly, or even daily basis, depending upon the report and the purpose it is intended to serve.

The size of each operations control book is kept at a minimum. It should include preferably less than 15 or at most 20 pages. Each page should be a report on its own, using tables, graphs, and eventually adding a few comments. What makes it realistic to reduce to such a small quantity the number of reports that reach a manager is the interrelationship between the synthetic presentation at top level and the more and more analytic presentations at each level of management, from top to bottom.

Step 5. Use effectively the operations control books. Essentially the two purposes of the operations control book are to inform the one who receives it and to facilitate communications between him and his subordinates so that effective decisions can be made. These two purposes are best served by organizing methodical periodic reviews of the operations control books. The frequency of such reviews varies not only with the company but with the levels of management and the reports involved. To go to an extreme, the general foreman may meet once a day with his foremen to review the rate of rejects. What is desirable is to establish a pattern that facilitates communications from bottom up. A typical approach is to have a monthly meeting of the president with the three vice presidents in charge of marketing, manufacturing, and administration, at which the president reviews his own operations control book, page by page, and asks questions whenever he feels that some variances or some performances require explanations. The procedure should be that each vice president had a similar meeting with his own subordinates a few days before, who, in turn, had previously met with their own subordinates, and so on down the line.

If the president asks a pertinent question related to the data shown on his operations control book, the question should have been anticipated by the vice president because the latter's own operations control book also shows the situation that requires attention and in fact shows even more details. The same is done at all levels of management. This means that, although the question is likely to come from the top, the initiative to consider the problem most of the time will have to come from the bottom, because each subordinate has anticipated that the question would be asked.

To summarize and analyze the recent trends in the organization of control, the following can be said:

1. From a technical point of view, recent developments in data collecting and data processing have greatly increased the possibility of operating an efficient system of operations control.

2. From the point of view of the enterprise, an adequate system of control makes it possible to detect mistakes early enough and select the best opportunity at the time of decision making.

3. From the point of view of human relations, an effective control system not only does *not* affect the individuals adversely, but it greatly stimulates the revival of the entrepreneur spirit about which we speak so much but which is so difficult to practice in modern industry unless we reconcile the need for coordinated effort with the need for each individual to act freely on his own. The control function can organize the system that provides the framework that supports the coordinated effort needed by the organization and within which the operating people at all levels of management and supervision can act freely on their own initiative.

    As stated by Rensis Likert, director of the Institute for Social Research, University of Michigan:

    People seem most willing and emotionally able to accept, and to examine in a nondefensive manner, information about themselves and their behavior, including their inadequacies, when it is in the form of *objective* evidence.

4. Last but not least the development of the control function will eliminate the duplication of reports, reduce the paperwork involved and make it possible for the executives and supervisors to manage much more effectively.

The big challenge we now face is to have these facts fully understood and to stimulate our research work in the direction of an effective organization of the control function, the management of which requires an executive who has been well trained in accounting, finance, production control data analysis, data processing, planning methods, and who fully understands all the problems of general management.

11. RESPONSIBILITY ACCOUNTING—
A BASIC CONTROL CONCEPT *

William L. Ferrara †

Responsibility accounting requires a specific and precise recognition of the individual areas of responsibility specified by the firm's organization structure. Areas of responsibility are the organizational units within a firm which are subject to the direction of an individual (sometimes a committee) who has been assigned the responsibility and delegated the authority to accomplish an objective(s). The ultimate refinement in responsibility areas is the individual worker or, in some instances, a group of workers within a work center.

The essence of responsibility accounting is the accumulation of costs and revenues according to areas of responsibility in order that deviations from standard costs and budgets can be identified with the person or group responsible. Reports prepared along responsibility lines are in effect "report cards" which inform the head of each area of responsibility and his superior how well he has performed in terms of costs and profits. The objective is not to find fault. To be effective, control must be conceived as a means of locating those activities and people in the organization in need of help so that assistance can be rendered and the scarce resources of the firm more effectively utilized.

CONTROL IN MANUFACTURING ACTIVITIES

Useful Cost Classifications

Within the manufacturing framework the basic control problem relates to the control of costs, since revenues are not normally influenced by manufacturing personnel. Thus, control in manufacturing is essentially cost control.

Implicit in the concepts of responsibility accounting and cost control is the idea that it is appropriate to charge to an area of respon-

* From the *N.A.A. Bulletin* (September, 1964). Reprinted by permission of the National Association of Accountants.

† William L. Ferrara, Associate Professor of Accounting at the Pennsylvania State University, University Park, Pennsylvania.

sibility only those costs which are subject to the control of the person in charge of each area of responsibility. The costs which are not controllable by one individual or group are always controllable by another individual or group. There is no place in the framework of responsibility accounting for the idea of a "noncontrollable cost." All costs are controllable at some point in time by some person or group. Within an individual firm there is a responsibility "slot" for each and every cost element. This is a point which should not be forgotten. Thus, if there is any cost distinction useful in responsibility accounting, it is the distinction between costs controllable by me (or us) and costs controllable by others, and not the erroneous distinction between controllable and noncontrollable costs. In some instances, particularly at lower levels of an organization, there is substantial agreement between the segregation into the fixed and variable costs and the distinction between costs controllable by me (or us) and costs controllable by others. In another sense, it might be useful to keep in mind (perhaps to use as subcategories) the distinction between fixed and variable costs, as the control procedures for fixed and variable costs differ significantly. Variable cost deviations are controlled by way of their elimination, that is, by making sure that variances do not occur or are minimized. Fixed costs, on the other hand, are subject to control in terms of whether or not commitments are made or allowed to continue at the point where changes in commitments can be made.

A Reporting Framework

Within a manufacturing plant there appear to be at least three levels of responsibility reporting: the worker level, the department level, and the total plant level. For each of these levels, the problem is simply a matter of tracing the costs to the individuals in charge of each level.

Due to the cost of responsibility reporting, it may not be worthwhile to deal with many small responsibility areas. A series of smaller areas can be combined into a larger responsibility area such as a work group, work center or department. With smaller areas of responsibility, such as the individual worker, formal reporting may be foregone in favor of an informal process such as observation by a foreman or supervisor. In many instances, however, some formal reporting may be retained at the worker level—the usual case in point being a direct labor performance report covering individual workers.

When the costs controllable by individual workers are added up they form a total which is the department head's or foreman's responsibility, with one exception, that is, the costs applicable to the foreman's function. These costs applicable to the foreman's function do not pertain to any individual worker; they pertain only to the foreman's direct responsibilities which he cannot or does not delegate to the individual workers under his jurisdiction. Thus, the costs included within the foreman's responsibility are those costs controllable directly by him and those controllable indirectly by him through his subordinates. This same analogy can be used when referring to the sum total of costs controllable by all formen to which must be added the cost of the plant superintendent's office in order to obtain the sum total of the costs applicable to the plant superintendent's responsibility area. This analogy can also be applied to costs subject to the control of the vice president in charge of all production activities.

All of the above points can be summarized diagrammatically as shown in Exhibit 1. In addition, Exhibit 1 can be readily quantified as shown in Exhibit 2. One should make a special note of two items in Exhibit 2:

1. The lines and arrows which direct attention to costs of smaller areas of responsibility being included in larger areas of responsibility.

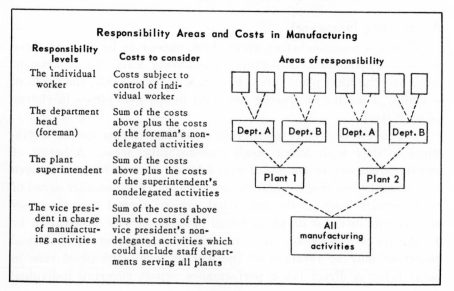

EXHIBIT 1

2. The budget columns which should point out more clearly than ever that plans in the form of budgets or other standards of performance are essential to control.

Cost Controllable by Others

As mentioned previously, a person should be charged only with those cost factors he can control for responsibility accounting purposes. However, there are some people who would prefer to also include the costs controllable by others. Thus, in the case of a fore-

Responsibility Reports for Manufacturing
Report to Department Head – Preforming
(Thousands of Dollars)

	Budget		Over or (under) budget	
	Current month	Year to date	Current month	Year to date
Direct materials	322.9	1411.0	(5.5)	(8.6)
Direct labor	153.6	693.8	8.1	5.4
Factory overhead - dept. head responsibility				
Indirect labor	88.6	364.6	(5.3)	(5.2)
Idle time	19.6	79.4	(.8)	(1.1)
Fuel	16.7	71.6	3.3	1.9
Utilities	15.4	62.3	(1.1)	(.8)
Sundry supplies	61.4	210.6	(4.3)	(4.9)
Stationery	4.6	16.3	.2	.4
Total - dept. head's responsibility	628.8	2909.6	(5.4)	(12.9)

Report to Plant Superintendent – Plant I
(Thousands of Dollars)

	Budget		Over or (under) budget	
	Current month	Year to date	Current month	Year to date
Plant superintendent's office	6.5	24.1	(.1)	.2
Preforming	682.8	2909.6	(5.4)	(12.9)
Molding	491.9	2215.8	(3.2)	(5.7)
Inspection	53.6	198.6	.8	1.2
Finishing	128.7	549.6	(2.1)	(2.4)
Maintenance	47.5	173.6	(3.4)	(2.3)
Receiving and shipping	28.1	73.4	.6	1.2
Mold and tool making	69.2	249.6	.7	(.7)
Total - supt's responsibility	1508.3	6394.6	(12.1)	(21.4)

Report to Vice-President – Production
(Thousands of Dollars)

	Budget		Over or (under) budget	
	Current month	Year to date	Current month	Year to date
Vice-president's office	8.4	31.5	.2	.8
Plant I	1508.3	6394.6	(12.1)	(21.4)
Plant II	1057.7	4378.3	(1.7)	3.9
Plant III	931.3	3857.2	(4.6)	(12.2)
Personnel	6.8	24.3	(.3)	(1.1)
Engineering	27.1	93.2	(.2)	2.1
Total v-p's responsibility	3539.6	14779.1	(18.7)	(27.9)

EXHIBIT 2

man, he would be charged with both the costs which he could and the costs which he could not control. This may seem to be diametrically opposed to the concept of responsibility accounting, but it need not be. In fact, charging a person for costs that he cannot influence could be a useful adjunct to responsibility accounting.

For example, consider Exhibit 3. All costs incurred in the department, including those the foreman is responsible for and those "others" are responsible for, are a part of the report. But in order to make the report useful for responsibility accounting, a distinction is drawn in the report between the costs subject to the foreman's influence and the costs subject to the influence of others.

Now we must come to grips with why both groups of costs might be included in the report.

In general we can support the inclusion of both groups of costs on the basis that the foreman will be informed of two useful facts:

1. His own cost performance in terms of costs he is responsible for.
2. The costs which the company must incur in order to support the foreman's activities even though the foreman is not responsible for such costs.

Departmental Cost Report Covering All Departmental Costs and Including Cost Distinctions Necessary for Control

Department A

	Budget	Actual	Variance
Direct materials	$10,500	$10,200	$(300)
Direct labor	18,400	18,800	400
Factory overhead - foreman's responsibility			
Indirect labor	2,800	2,900	100
Idle time	500	550	50
Supplies	340	325	(15)
Stationery	110	106	(4)
Salaries — staff	800	750	(50)
Depreciation — equipment	4,800	4,800	—
Total foreman's responsibility	$38,250	$38,431	$ 181
Factory overhead other responsibilities			
Salaries — department head	1,200	1,200	—
Depreciation — building	2,200	2,200	—
Payroll taxes	810	870	60
Insurance	220	220	—
Total departmental costs	$42,680	$42,921	$ 241

EXHIBIT 3

Report to Sales Manager – District A

Actual and Budgeted District Report
(All Figures in Thousands)

April, 19___

	Actual				Budget			
	Product Y	Product X	Total $	%	Product Y	Product X	Total $	%
Units sold	3149.0	410.0			3137.5	605.0		
Sales	$1578.5	$549.6	$2128.1	100.0	$1560.0	$818.5	$2378.5	100.0
Standard cost of goods sold	1198.0	344.5	1542.5	72.5	1181.0	468.1	1649.1	69.3
Gross profit	$ 380.5	$205.1	$ 585.6	27.5	$ 379.0	$350.4	$ 729.4	39.7
District selling expenses –								
Sales manager's responsibility								
Bonus			$ 1.1	.1			$ 1.3	.1
Commissions			34.3	1.6			43.2	1.8
Travel – salesmen			13.1	.6			10.1	.4
Travel – general			1.3	.1			1.1	.1
Stationery			.6	.0			.7	.0
Postage			.5	.0			.5	.0
Telephone			2.2	.1			1.6	.1
Sales manager's profit contribution			$ 532.5	25.0			$ 670.9	28.2
District selling expenses –								
Other responsibilities –								
Salaries			$ 4.2	.2			$ 4.2	.2
Employee benefit programs			1.3	.1			1.5	.1
Depreciation			5.6	.3			5.6	.2
Taxes			1.2	.1			1.4	.1
Insurance			.3	.0			.3	.0
Advertising			10.5	.5			8.0	.3
District profit contribution (before taxes)			$ 509.4	23.8			$ 649.9	27.3

EXHIBIT 4

Obviously, the cost report to a foreman should include the costs he is responsible for. If the costs he is not responsible for are included in the report, they must be separated from the costs he is responsible for. However, the reason for including costs the foreman is not responsible for must be understood in its proper light. Without the inclusion of these other costs in his report, the foreman will perhaps not realize the size and extent of the useful and necessary organization behind him which is costly to operate. It is this point which is the major argument for including (but distinguishing) costs a foreman is not responsible for in the report covering the foreman's cost responsibility.

CONTROL IN DISTRIBUTION ACTIVITIES

A Comparison with Manufacturing Activities

The major difference in responsibility accounting as it relates to manufacturing and distribution activities is the fact that under the distribution function revenues as well as costs must be considered. This inclusion of revenues gives rise to a "profit" calculation for areas of responsibility in distribution.

The areas of responsibility, the revenues, and costs in the distribution function can be summarized diagrammatically in essentially the same manner as the manufacturing function (Exhibit 1).

Exhibit 4 is a report covering the activities of a sales manager who is in charge of a group of salesmen. Note that the report shows two profit figures, that is, the sales manager's profit contribution and the district profit contribution. Included in the sales manager's profit contribution are sales, standard cost of sales, and district expenses subject to the control by the sales manager. This profit figure shows the contribution of his efforts (including the efforts of salesmen subject to him) to costs controllable by others plus profits.

The district profit contribution involves the deduction of district selling expenses for which others are responsible from the sales manager's profit contribution. The inclusion of these costs in the report brings into the picture all costs which can be associated with district activities.

Some Problems Related to Distribution Activities

There are at least three potential problem areas in responsibility accounting for the distribution function. These are:

1. Difficulties in establishing standards.

2. Use of cost of goods sold in the construction of distribution responsibility reports.

3. Constructing responsibility reports for salesmen.

One should never forget the differences in establishing standards in the manufacturing and distribution functions. In manufacturing a great deal can be done in establishing fairly exacting standards or relationships between costs incurred and results accomplished. But in the distribution area there are many difficulties involved in trying to establish these relationships, especially in the areas of sales promotion and field sales effort. Results are more often than not the product of a salesman's skill and judgment and the creative ability of sales promotion personnel. Thus, one has to be more careful in his evaluation of cost and profit reports in the distribution area.

In Exhibit 4, standard cost of goods sold appears as an element in the determination of a sales manager's profit contribution. The inclusion of actual cost of goods sold would be inadequate in the sense it would introduce factory efficiencies and inefficiencies into the responsibility reports covering the distribution function. If cost of goods sold is to be included, it must be a standard cost of goods sold.

However, since the sales division does not normally have any influence over the cost of goods sold, there is legitimacy in the question of whether or not cost of goods sold is properly included in the report. The only sound basis for including it is to draw the attention of sales personnel to the profits derived from sales so that they realize that they should concentrate their efforts on profitability of sales and not sales volume as such. In many instances this point is brought home by basing commissions on gross profits or profit contributions rather than on sales volume.

Our final problem is the construction of a report similar to Exhibit 4 for individual salesmen. Such a report is not very difficult to construct, but there is one feature which could render it virtually useless. To illustrate, imagine for a moment that Exhibit 4 covers the activities of an individual salesman. Then relate the percentage of commissions earned (1.6 percent and 1.8 percent) to the profit contribution percentages (25.0 percent and 23.8 percent). There is no doubt that many salesmen who are confronted with such data might get the impression they are grossly underpaid—and to convince them otherwise might be quite difficult if not impossible. In this case a report similar to Exhibit 2 may not be useful. We should rather consider a report covering sales volume and costs subject to the salesman's influence. The salesman can be forced to concentrate on high margin items through the payment of higher commissions (as a percentage of sales price) on higher margin items.

The Problem of Dual Responsibility

The moment one begins to consider those costs which can be influenced by an individual or group, even though such costs are traceable to another responsibility area, difficulties begin to arise. The problem here is one of dual responsibility for costs. Service department costs, for instance, can be influenced both by service department personnel and the personnel of the serviced departments. Another case would be capital expenditures which can be influenced by those who propose capital expenditures and also by those who approve them.

Without doubt there are many who regard the problem of dual responsibility as a typical cost allocation problem. This, however, is not an accurate interpretation of dual responsibility for costs since there is always a primary area of responsibility to which the entire cost can be properly charged. For example, the maintenance department can be charged with all costs subject to the influence of the maintenance department foreman, and the committee or person that approves capital expenditures can be charged with all costs related to approved capital expenditures. Our problem is with the secondary areas of responsibility which may influence the costs of the primary areas of responsibility. In order to complete the structure of responsibility accounting, an attempt must be made to measure the extent of this influence and charge each secondary area of responsibility with its measured influence.

Generally speaking, primary and secondary areas of responsibility seem to fall into two broad categories:

1. Expenditure approving and expenditure proposing groups (individuals).
2. Service departments and service consuming departments.

As for the expenditure approving and expenditure proposing groups there is no denying that both of them should be held responsible for the approved expenditures. This seems like double counting but a justifiable double counting since both the proposing authority and the approving authority relate to the total approved costs.

In order to delineate more precisely what is meant by expenditure approving and expenditure proposing authorities, it is useful to distinguish between capital expenditures for buildings, machinery and equipment, research expenditures, and expenditures for sales promotion and advertising campaigns. In this light it is easier to see that an area head should be charged for depreciation and salaries if he has authority to propose equipment expenditures and salary changes. We can also see why the person or groups which approve equipment expenditures and salary changes must also be charged with responsibility for the same expenditures.

In the case of service and service consuming departments we should draw a distinction between two classes of service departments:

1. Those which facilitate the operations of other departments but provide little or no opportunity to objectively measure service rendered.

2. Those which also provide for an objective measure of service rendered.

In the first group are central office staff departments and even the general administrative division, while the inspection and maintenance departments in a manufacturing organization belong to the second group. The key to solving the problem of dual responsibility in this second type of service departments is the ability to measure service rendered which gives rise to an opportunity to charge the service consuming departments (i.e., the secondary areas of responsibility) with the costs they can influence. These costs can be stated in physical terms, such as the number of each class of maintenance hour and the number of units inspected and rejected, or in dollar terms, when a price per unit of service is established. However, since there is normally no attempt to turn the service department into a profit center, the price per unit of service would be established on the basis of a total standard unit cost.

Thus, dual responsibility is nothing to be afraid of—it can be dealt with. In the case of expenditure approval authority and expenditure proposal authority, dual responsibility is handled by charging both groups. There is no allocation problem here simply because each group's responsibility covers the total expenditure.

In the case of service and service consuming departments, dual responsibility can be handled via an objective measure of service rendered if it can be established. Many times all that is required to establish an objective measure of service rendered is an intensive reconsideration of the services offered and a bit of imagination and/or ingenuity. Where objectivity is considered impossible, it is recommended that no charge be made to the service consuming department, since any charge made would most likely be arbitrary and arbitrariness is the antithesis of responsibility accounting.

Some might, however, consider the use of a measure of service consumption as the basis of an allocation. Our preference here is not to consider this to be an allocation scheme. It is based on objectively verifiable data, while cost allocation, as the term is used today, has an aura of arbitrariness attached to it and, therefore, is inappropriate in the context of responsibility accounting.

The Dollar Measuring Stick

All too often the idea of responsibility accounting is put forth in such a way that dollars are supposed to be the only usable language in responsibility reporting which, of course, is false. Thus we should consider some of the nondollar measures of performance. It might be quite useful to add data on units produced, pounds of materials used, direct labor hours and even machine hours to the performance reports in a manufacturing operation. To a certain extent this information is covered by the dollar data, but dollar data often tend to summarize out of existence certain facts which are better expressed in physical terms. Therefore, it is recommended that consideration be given these additional data in the performance reports of responsibility accounting in the manufacturing area. In the distribution area, the following type of data might be useful in performance reports: working days, days on road, calls, orders, and car mileage.

Still further possibilities for useful measures of performance in the manufacturing area as well as in the distribution area are listed below. No reasonable person can deny that there is at least some utility in these measures of performance. In many instances these additional measures of performance could actually be considered more significant than the basic dollar data presented in responsibility reports.

Additional measures of performance in manufacturing:
Hours available for production.
Hours regularly used for production.
Overtime hours.
Number of employees.
Average hours worked per week.
Units produced per hour.
Units produced per pound or yard of material.
Units rejected or classified as seconds.
Percent of units rejected or classified as seconds to good units.
Cost per unit for significant elements of material, labor and/or factory overhead, classified by area of responsibility.

Additional measures of performance in distribution:

Sales, gross profit and/or profit contribution per order received.
Sales, gross profit and/or profit contribution per day on the road.
Percent of orders to calls.
Percent of orders to customers.
Percent of calls to customers.
Percent of days on road to working days.
District expenses per order, per call and/or per day on the road.
Miles traveled per call.
Miles traveled per day on the road.
Number of new customers.

SOME CONCLUSIONS

Perhaps the most important idea contained in the preceding comments is that responsibility accounting is in essence a communication system which is designed to aid an enterprise in achieving its cost and profit goals. Within this communication system, extreme care must be taken to make sure that the planning and the measurement of performance revolve around the areas of responsibility.

Further, those who construct the communication system must be mindful of the many useful ways in which performance can be measured. Certainly not all of them should be used in every case, but those who construct the system must be aware of the variety of measurements available in order that the most suitable combination of dollar and nondollar measures is selected for each area of responsibility. Suitability in these cases will ultimately depend on the costs vs. the benefits of each measure as well as the personal idiosyncracies of report preparers and report users.

Finally, any company using responsibility reporting must inculcate in its organization a positive control attitude. Errors and mistakes are the stuff of which progress is made, but this will never be accomplished unless responsibility reports are used to pinpoint the people or groups who need help in order that adequate assistance may be rendered.

12. MANAGEMENT ACCOUNTING
IN THE AGE OF SYSTEMS *
John A. Beckett †

Today, books on managerial accounting line the shelves of libraries. Articles on how to use accounting to help run businesses fill periodicals. Speakers cry from many lecterns the theme that accounting, focusing on probability of operations and using direct costing, can improve management decisions.

Despite this, some sophisticated and discriminating business managers, skilled and knowledgeable specialists, and other perceptive observers of the business scene believe, more than ever before, that accountants are living in the past. It may serve some purpose to consider this view and to see not only what is in the minds of those who hold it but also whether there is, in fact, any merit in the charge.

It is ironic that accounting should be newly chastened with an accusation which was often made in the era before managerial accounting came alive. Those who have watched, and to some extent participated in, a major change in the emphasis of accounting in the last 20 years, are acutely aware of the way in which its practice has been elevated and strengthened in the hope of making it a more effective instrument of business management. Why, then, the charge that accounting is out of date? Can there be any truth in the claim?

OBJECTIVES OF MANAGERIAL ACCOUNTING

The principal objective of managerial accounting has often been said to be "to serve the needs of management" or "to enable managers to manage better." Responsibility accounting, direct costing, and other approaches to the use of data through accounting procedures have been developed with an eye to bringing before the manager the kinds of information that will enable him to know the things that are important to know, in order that he may make more intelligent deci-

---

* From the *N.A.A. Bulletin* (April, 1964). Reprinted by permission of the National Association of Accountants.

† John A. Beckett, Forbes Professor of Management, Whittemore School of Business and Economics, University of New Hampshire, Durham, New Hampshire.

sions. In short, management accounting has been striving to provide a means for bringing meaningful knowledge promptly to those persons who presumably are vested with the authority and the capacity to do something about it. Management accounting has also been trying to assist in the establishment of ways of controlling operations, i.e., to provide a means for conveying knowledge promptly from persons who are vested with the authority to those whose duty it is to react to those messages.

Today there are new terms for these two kinds of activities. Using the terms in the context of the objectives of modern accounting, it may be said that accounting has been striving to develop itself into an information retrieval system, on one hand, and an information (or command) disseminating system on the other. Notice that both of these systems deal with the getting and the giving of information. This is the essence of information systems as well as of managerial accounting.

Of course, applying new names to recognized processes does not change anything. Yet, in this case the new terms characterize management accounting as essentially an information system and stimulate full consideration of the implications of the activities involved, the more so because so much has been learned in recent years (and is still being learned) about systems, their meaning, and their implications.

THE PRESYSTEM ERA

To set the stage for appraising managerial accounting as an information system, it is helpful to review the evolution of business systems and, in that way, to get a deeper insight into their meaning and implications for the present and near future.

The first thing to notice is the growth which has taken place in business operations; the magnitude and nature of that growth has such importance that it has required the development of business information systems.

In the past 20 years both the national income and the gross national product of the United States have increased over 500 percent. In the same period, the number of business firms in operation has increased less than 50 percent. It is apparent that the average firm is carrying on much more business than ever before.

As business grew in size in the early decades of this century, so did the number of people who, in effect, comprised the business transacting machinery. Volume increases meant increases in people employed. As manufacturing economies were achieved through improved production techniques and equipment, these advantages were often dissipated by the need to add to payrolls. In the case of service industries, such as railroads and life insurance companies, gains in business meant almost proportionate increases in the number of people needed. It was a great era for the manufacturers of desks and chairs!

Early improvements in companies' abilities to handle increased volume of business came with the introduction of business equipment. These were individual units, such as the register, the counter, and the sorter. They brought the first real improvements in the productivity of individuals whose efforts were devoted to keeping in motion the machinery of operations. With further growth, however, better tools for the human being who comprised a cog in the business transacting machinery proved inadequate.

The growing complexity of business was creating more difficult problems. Increased need for coordinating the work of people became apparent. The need for coordinating materials inventories with production, production with finished product, and finished product with sales, presented greater difficulties than ever before. Opportunities for achieving major improvements in operations through specialization, integration, standardization, and other efficiency producing techniques and equipments, all coordinated, were beginning to be apparent to a few people. New tools were developed—tools which promoted as well as met the needs of specialization in the business transacting functions. But the really important evolutionary development that was beginning to take place in this era was the development of the elements of business systems. The tide of business systems began to flow.

FUNCTIONAL SYSTEMS—AND CONFORMITY

At first, crude systems were developed for those activities which involved the greatest volume of repetitive activity—payroll, accounts receivable, accounts payable, etc. These partial and rudimentary subsystems employed equipment in many cases. What was more important, they required integration of activities and recognition of a cycle, from beginning to end, which used common forms, procedures, methods, equipment, and appropriately trained people. A whole new field of research in business was opening up, but few companies got very far with it at the start.

One impediment was that, at the very beginning, improvement efforts generally encountered a wide and well-entrenched diversity of existing activities, forms, records, procedures, methods, and reports, all attesting to the deep-felt need for systems and all representing partial solutions worked out by any number of people for any number of reasons. They had one thing in common: they were not coordinated. Dealing with them so that they would yield to an integrated approach to systems work required a lot of time if only because of the size of the problem presented. This was the finding in companies of all sizes. Still, existing partial routines were not the principal cause of slow progress in system building. The main reason was the fact that improved operating systems inevitably cut across established organizational lines.

Payroll is a good example. To get a good payroll system in operation, it is necessary to integrate and standardize the activities of all people who have anything to do with it. The worker must perform his part by handling his clock card in a prescribed manner at a prescribed time if just the first step of the system is to be made operative. The time clerk must perform his standardized operation at the appropriate time. The same is true for the foreman, the payroll clerk, and the treasurer. In order for the system to work, each participant must perform his standard task at the proper time and in the proper sequence according to instructions established in advance in a detailed procedures manual. The activities of the several participants are prescribed by this system; as individuals, they have no alternative but to perform those activities.

The essential point here is that the system establishes rules governing the work of people in different functional jurisdictions of the organization. The system is the set of operating rules that binds all activities together. A functional organization chart may show that the foreman exercises jurisdiction over the worker but, as regards timekeeping and piece-count, he does not. The payroll system controls that. The chart may show that the production superintendent is responsible for the work of the foreman but, as regards payroll practices, he is not. Again the payroll system controls that. The chart may show that the controller is responsible for the work of the payroll clerk but, as regards payroll practices, he is not. Once more, the payroll system controls. The controller may have been instrumental in establishing the system, in concert with others, but his main function as regards payroll is simply to see that an appropriate, essentially self-operating system is designed and installed.

Three functional jurisdictions are involved in this simple example. The treasurer, the controller, and the production manager are all integral to the operation of the system. All of them and their subordinates are bound together by the system. They are wholly the servants of the operating plan which is expressed in the system. They have only one function with respect to it. That is to make it work by playing their respective roles routinely and promptly, in harmony with all others. Most payroll systems involve more than three functional jurisdictions. The greater the number of organizational jurisdictions, the greater the number of managers who must play their unvarying and disciplined roles precisely according to instructions.

Payroll systems are simple to install. Almost everybody understands that the functions of payroll require integration. Few managers are disturbed by the realization that the system runs the timekeeping and payroll activities. They do not think of this as an unfair encroachment on their prerogatives nor as an inappropriate reduction of their managerial responsibilities. Therefore, although the installation and the constant improvement of integrated payroll systems have, in many cases, taken years to accomplish because of the need to coordinate them throughout a large organization, they have not, in most companies, been delayed by obstructive attitudes. The same cannot be said about other systems installations.

A system for sales order and billing, simple as it may seem, has been at once the battlefield and the burial ground for many systems people. In the past, it has not been uncommon for sales managers to resist having their assistants placed in what they describe as the straitjacket of systems. Some of them have actively and effectively opposed efforts to require their subordinates to supply the system with standard input. Many well-conceived, integrated systems of order entry and billing have stood idle, waiting for the day when the sales force could be reconciled with them.

Production control is another area of difficulty. It supervises, among other things, the levels of materials inventory and the timing of replenishing orders. Some corporate purchasing officers have perceived in this a challenge to their traditionally secure position in functional organizations. As they see it, if a system determines precisely what should be ordered—and in what quantity and at what time—their jobs are reduced in importance. Many of them resisted the establishment of any such system.

It is inevitable that systems will take some of the traditional prerogatives of decision making away from individuals. Top management personnel have been reluctant to recognize this, because it puts them "on the spot." It asks them to decide whether to preserve a traditional functional organization or to attempt substantially to change people's responsibilities and activities.

Toward Total Systems

Many managers hedged on the decision for a long time. Others are still hedging. However, time and necessity have changed a lot of minds. There are evidences that the systems point of view has been widely accepted and utilized with breathtaking results. Stock and order controls have been so developed that, on a nationwide basis, all features of checking stock, activating manufacturing, and filling orders are programmed into the procedure so that virtually no "human" managing is done once the system is in motion. This is a mere aspect of thousands of business systems that are already installed. Thousands more are in the development stage and will be in effect in the next few years. Individual business systems are growing into total systems for business. The tide of systems is in flood.

A most significant discovery from all this effort has been that systems really have no start and no end; they are circles, and they are interrelated within a business. They are wheels within wheels within wheels.

For instance, a check pays for a product which was ordered in response to a requirement for materials which are converted into products, or for labor which is used in making new products which are advertised, stored, shipped, and sold to get more bank deposits on which other checks can be written to start the cycle again.

In earlier years, systems for each aspect of a function were designed and developed, but it soon became apparent that the objective of systems work is a total system, an all-embracing formalized system for the operation of business as a whole. Probably no American business has reached this formalized total system yet, though many are working on it.

Military Systems

It is worth noting, however, that total systems actually do exist outside the business world. One example is an antisubmarine warfare system. In it, a warhead by itself is of no significance at all; its effectiveness depends entirely on programs for its employment—programs that make use of both equipment and people. Some operating decisions are routinely made by automatic equipment; some are routinely made by men. Servomechanisms aid the actions and reactions of both. The system is the interaction of machines and men, all operating in accordance with plans that are put into effect by choice of the man at the top.

Another example is the Strategic Air Command. As a whole, it has the characteristics of a total system. Every aspect of its operation is preplanned. Every action has a right way to be done. There is continuous feedback and measurement of every action, and there is a plan for almost instantaneous correction of nonstandard performance. All subsystems are keyed to the operation of the overall system. The actions of machines and men are wed in perfect harmony in a total system designed for total destruction.

Note that in both of these examples there is an underlying plan that takes effect at the will of the commanding officer. His is either a "go" or "no go" decision. When he decides to "go" in a certain way, the machinery of the system is routinely put into effect. The system is conditioned to respond and interact according to a multitude of possibilities that have been predetermined and programmed for action in the long months and years that have preceded the event of its becoming operational.

The commander's decision, to "go"—whether it is on a training mission or on a real aggressive or defensive mission—in a very real sense means that the operational plan is in control. He is completely unable to make, with the split-second timing that is needed, all the decisions that are necessary to accomplish the mission. The system makes those decisions. The decisions that have been programmed for machine making are made by machines; the decisions that have been delegated to human beings are made by human beings who are part of the operational system. If the mission is going according to plan, the commander can keep his hands off, knowing that the system is in control.

This does not mean that the commander has abdicated his responsibility to the system. He must watch it in operation, perfect it in practice, and stand prepared to shift momentarily from plan to plan within the system, as circumstances dictate. But it seems clear that the commander can never again in modern warfare abrogate the existing plans and take over as an individual, making the decisions as he goes along. That day is past. The amount and the speed of information involved in the operation of the system simply exceeds the capacity of the human nervous system to accept, digest, or act upon. The commander is a manager only insofar as he is capable of seeing that adequate alternative plans are designed and made operative, and that he can make the choice of the plans within the system to put into effect at any one time. But when he has made his choice, the system takes over.

In military operations, total system is the inevitable and imperative objective. It is also a reality.

Is it possible that, for business, the objective is the same?

THE IMPACT OF SYSTEMS

Two of the most striking of the implications of systems are their impact upon the nature of business organization and upon the activities of management.

Systems breed coordination and, with it, a de-emphasis of the planning function and of the decision making power and personal responsibilities of all but the top planners and decision makers. As a result, whatever use traditional organization charts may have had as means of describing human interrelationships and individual responsibilities in business organization, they are fast losing their value as visual expressions of those interrelationships and responsibilities. Jobs down the line are no longer becoming centers of significant cost or profit responsibility as they may once have been or, at least, have been supposed to be. They are not centers at all but more like functions of subsystems, no one of which is either more or less important than all the others.

Business organization, under advanced systems, is due to become more centralized, the statements of public relations-minded presidents to the contrary notwithstanding. This means that responsibility, and any other than merely servomechanistic decision making, is also becoming more concentrated at and near the top. Business organization is changing fast under the irresistible pressure of systems development. With it are coming changes in management too, both in concept and in practice.

Some managers are now redefining their jobs in the light of these new developments. New emphasis is being given to the manager's responsibility for studying systems opportunities, standardizing and routinizing more and more functions, tightening the coordination of subsystems and building in self-checking procedures for human and mechanical servomechanisms.

It may come as a surprise to many people—and certainly to treasurers, controllers, and accountants—to learn that the board of directors of one of this country's largest and most progressive companies recently took its most promising young man (at the age of 34) out of the managership of a principal subsidiary, and assigned him the job of manager of its corporate systems department! They reasoned, in a manner consistent with the times, that, to be a president of the corporation in the years ahead, he must have the training of a systems man!

Potentially even more startling is the new talk of a "lost generation" in the management of one of the largest companies in the United States. In that company, the decision has just been made that, in view of the fact that the type of training needed for top management tomorrow was, figuratively, not available until just yesterday, there will be no promotions to significant management positions in the next decade for any men over the age of 40! The members of one whole generation of men in this mammoth company are being lost as candidates for important managerial positions at the top!

Another sobering implication of modern systems development is the speed with which information is now being retrieved and disseminated for systems operation and managerial guidance. We need only reflect momentarily to see how compressed is the action-reaction cycle in modern systems operation. And the implications are obvious; this speed is an indispensable ingredient of systems management.

MANAGERIAL ACCOUNTING IN THE REAL WORLD

Now, with some understanding of the history of systems development, its present and prospective impact, and some insight into its implications for organization and management, we may appraise managerial accounting in terms of its potential for being of effective service to the management of American business in the near future.

That managerial accounting is an information system goes without saying. However, is it a good information system in concept and design—as good an information system as others that are available today or will become economically available for most businesses in the near future? Is it, in fact, keyed to the kind of intercoordinated operating and centralized systems management structure that is fast becoming a reality in business organization today? And finally, is managerial accounting attuned to the new management, the kind of management that will be commonplace tomorrow?

That depends on whether books of account, periodical financial statements, and variance reporting are useful information for operations management and strategic planning. It depends on whether managerial accounting is relating itself to the new structure of organization and the new functions of managers that are fast taking shape under the pressures of systems development.

It depends on other considerations, also.

Consider first the issue of speed of information flow. Its critics believe that managerial accounting is essentially an off-line information system whose reaction time is painfully slow. They consider monthly reports to be preposterous, weekly reports to be absurd, and even daily reports of operations to be virtually useless—at least for the needs of tomorrow. The process of passing information from the bottom up to tell the president what is going on and from the top down to get subordinates to understand what the president wants them to do has been aptly described as "a modern bucket brigade, with about 50 percent slop." [1]

The unswerving purpose of information systems development is to achieve instant information. The step beyond that is the achievement of on-line automatic reaction, a step that has already been taken for many business operations and will be more and more commonly taken in the future.

In the matter of speed, many activities of managerial accounting are being weighed (as information systems) and are being found wanting.

Consider next the type of information gathered and disseminated by a managerial accounting information system. Here it must be acknowledged that managerial accounting, with its traditional emphasis on cost behavior, cost and performance standards, and economic analysis has actually provided much of the foundation on which the structures of modern information systems are being built. Managerial accounting gets a generally good mark on this score.

But now consider organization and managerial responsibility within systems managed companies. The idea of individual operating managers throughout an organization having identifiable packages of responsibility for cost experience and even for general performance is, to the average systems analyst, ridiculous. He is convinced that the planners of whatever system has been implemented in a given instance are the ones who exert the greatest influence on its cost and

---

[1] Bernard J. Muller-Thym, "The Real Meaning of Automation," *Management Review* (June, 1963).

performance, and he looks upon the organizational premises of responsibility accounting as something akin to modern fairy tales.

This criticism strikes a nerve end for managerial accountants, because they have been increasingly uncomfortable, of late, trying to prove to themselves and others that there really are a good many factors of operation over which the middle or lower managers exercise true cost or managerial control.

Can it rightly be said, in an integrated and coordinated system, that the responsibility of any person in the system is clear? Is it not more clear that the true responsibility—even for the operation of the system—rests on the shoulders of those who planned and built it? If its implementation in operations is faulty, may that be caused more often than not by the failure of the architect of the system to build it in such a way that it will operate effectively under the conditions in which it is intended that it shall operate? Or else, may it not be caused by the assignment of inadequately prepared men or inadequately engineered tools to assure effective operation of the system?

As systems are perfected, responsibility for standard performance in operation is more and more being shifted from the manager to the planner. Trying to pin this responsibility back on the operating manager is an exercise in futility. Yet it seems that this is what managerial accounting is still striving to do in an era in which reality is becoming quite different from what the advocates of responsibility accounting have traditionally assumed that it is. As regards its relationship with present and future organization patterns in business and as regards its concepts of the responsibilities of managers in the unfolding age of systems, managerial accounting cannot be said to be in tune with the times.

A CRITICAL JUNCTURE

Managerial accounting stands challenged and accused just at a time when its practitioners had begun to feel that they had raised their profession to its highest stature in value and service to American business. The accusation is in three parts. It alleges that accounting does not:

1. Serve as an information system with nearly the precision, speed, and effectiveness of other modern means.
2. Mesh with the new realities of business organization.
3. Relate to the new realities of business management.

Managerial accounting will have to prove these accusations untrue. In doing so, it may have to change its focus, its methods, and perhaps even its philosophy in some respects. It may even have to embrace new developments of the information revolution—and make them its own.

It has faced challenges before and has not only survived but flourished in the face of advertisity. Now is the time for it to be shown that it can do so again.

13. ACCOUNTING FOR
DECISION MAKING *
H. Justin Davidson and Robert M. Trueblood †

For many years, the management community has regarded the accounting discipline as one of its principal tools in the decision making process. The accounting systems of business have traditionally provided much of the financial data and much of the analysis of that data applicable to decision making purposes. Today, however, there are symptoms of management dissatisfaction with current accounting systems. Many managers believe the accounting function has failed to adjust its objectives and activities to the decision making requirements of a changing business world.[1]

This charge—that the accounting profession has not kept itself up to date—could be the subject of an acrimonious debate. The purpose of this article is not, however, to debate the merits of what accountants have done in the past. We assume neither that accountants are so out of touch with the management process as to be obsolete, nor that accountants are so far in the vanguard of newer management movements as to be complacent. Instead of finding fault with the past, we propose to discuss some of the challenges that accounting faces today and in the future. We believe that one of these challenges may be characterized as "accounting for decision making."

WHAT IS ACCOUNTING FOR DECISION MAKING?

Accounting for decision making involves a particular way of viewing the decision making, or managing, process in business. As

* From *The Accounting Review* (October, 1961). Reprinted by permission of the American Accounting Association.

† H. Justin Davidson, Touche, Ross, Bailey and Smart; Robert M. Trueblood, Partner, Touche, Ross, Bailey and Smart.

The authors gratefully acknowledge the assistance of Richard M. Cyert, Graduate School of Industrial Administration, Carnegie Institute of Technology. Dr. Cyert's counsel and criticism have been particularly helpful in structuring the ideas involved. The subject matter of the article was first presented in an address by Mr. Trueblood to the Federal Government Accountants Association, Detroit, Michigan, May 23, 1959.

[1] For a statement of this position, see C. West Churchman and Russell L. Ackoff, "Operational Accounting and Operations Research," *The Journal of Accountancy* (February, 1955), pp. 33-39.

characterized in a recent monograph by Herbert A. Simon, the decision making process does not consist solely of the choice involved between two or more alternatives. The decision maker is not "the alert gray-haired businessman, sitting at the board of directors' table with his associates, caught at the moment of saying 'aye' or 'nay.' " [2] Decision making involves something more than the final choice which is the culmination of the decision process.

As first described by John Dewey,[3] decision making, problem solving, or managing may be viewed as involving a three-stage process aimed at answering the following questions:

1. What is the problem?
2. What are the alternatives?
3. Which alternative is best?

What relevance does this decision making process have to accounting?

The tie between the accounting process and the decision making process described above is basically one of information. In its broadest and most fruitful sense, accounting is an information or data providing function—and information of one kind or another is required at each stage of the problem solving process.

Consider, for example, the first stage of the problem solving process: What is the problem? A standard cost system is an information system designed to answer this kind of question in a specific, although limited, area. One of the uses of a favorable or unfavorable variance generated by a standard cost system is simply to tell management that it has a problem, a decision to make. A standard cost system doesn't define the alternatives—that requires investigation of the reasons for variance—nor does it tell which alternative is best. The standard cost system is an information device to indicate when there is a problem.

As a further example of the information link between accounting and decision making, consider the third stage of the decision making process. Choice of a best alternative requires criteria against which to judge various possibilities. Choice requires information concerning the various alternatives—information cast in a form consistent with the criteria. For example, the choice of investment alternatives may be judged against a rate-of-return criterion, and information about the alternatives must be provided in rate-of-return form. Here we

[2] Herbert A. Simon, *The New Science of Management Decision* (New York: Harper & Brothers, 1960), p. 1.

[3] John Dewey, *How We Think* (2d ed.; Boston: D. C. Heath & Co., 1933), p. 120.

have another case where accounting in the information providing sense is clearly linked to the decision making process.

In talking about accounting for decision making, we are considering perhaps two fundamental characteristics of the information system of a business. These characteristics can be summarized by the following questions:

1. *Which alternative is best?* For any given decision, which is, in fact, necessary, what information is required to make the decision?

2. *What is the problem?* For any given organization and its objectives, what information is necessary to determine what decisions are, in fact, required?

In general, these two questions are related to two management decision areas where much current attention is being concentrated.

The first question is related to "routine" decision problems— regularly recurring problems which are programmed or structured. In controlling inventory, for example, a routine decision is how much to buy. Considerable progress has been made in determining good criteria for such routine decisions and in determining the information necessary to make such decisions.

The second question is largely related to "special" decision problems—irregularly occurring problems which are unprogrammed and unstructured. How and when, for example, should a business undertake a thorough review of its plant location policy or its organizational structure? When should a firm consider switching from a policy of price following to a policy of price leadership? How does a business recognize that its routine decisions are uncoordinated?

These two questions, their related problem areas, and current research pose many challenges for the accounting profession. We will first discuss challenges in the routine decision area.

ROUTINE DECISIONS

In assessing the challenges that accounting information systems present in the routine decision area, it is profitable to review some of the common deficiencies of information systems today.

Overinformation

This is the situation where too much information is made available to the decision maker. Detailed or refined data are supplied when summary or gross data would suffice. This situation frequently exists where detailed information is required at one decision point, but summary information would be adequate for a decision at another point. As a result, complete detail is given to all users of the data. An example of overinformation in military accounting is the detailed costing of nuts and bolts for the indirect reason that detailed unit information is required for inventory control.

On the matter of overinformation, a note of alarm should be sounded. Massive quantities of detailed information are available with current electronic data processing systems. Unless these data are properly screened and summarized, the individual manager can easily become flooded with unnecessary information. The manager can spend the bulk of his day ferreting out or summarizing those facts which are required in order to make a decision.

In many installations of data processing systems made to date, there is the serious question whether the needs for information have been adequately considered in the systems design. It is often easier to generate an abundance of data than to go through the difficult process of deciding which data are necessary.

Underinformation

Another characteristic of some present-day information systems is the lack of adequate information to make an appropriate decision. This condition we can refer to as *underinformation*. Traditionally, accounting systems have recorded only data stated in terms of dollars. For many situations, however, such data are not particularly useful, and other data are required. In item inventory control, for example, unit information is perhaps most important and helpful; dollar data are larger irrelevant. Another example of underinformation relates to unfilled orders or lost sales. Information regarding lost sales is apt to be more significant for many decisions than are carefully quantified data on completed sales transactions.

In order to correct problems of underinformation, there are two approaches. First, the new methods of processing data are making it relatively easier to supply information which might not normally be accumulated in a typical accounting system. Second, accountants can broaden their interest and responsibility for information stated in nondollar units of measurement—information typically needed and required to make adequate decisions in many operating areas.

Untimely Information

There are two kinds of untimely information. There is that information which comes too late, or is supplied less frequently than necessary. There is information which is supplied too often simply because it is prepared routinely. In the first case, accountants have considerable responsibility for getting data to management in a prompt and useful fashion. Monthly financial statements or monthly budget status reports which come out too late to be useful as a basis for corrective action might as well not be generated. In the second situation, there is no need to supply, routinely or regularly, data which are needed only at irregular or sporadic intervals.

There are generally two corrective approaches to the problem of untimely information. There is the concept of exception reporting, which has gained much acceptance today. There is also the proper use of analytical studies. Information systems should be capable of developing an analytical report which is useful in making a particular decision—if and when it is necessary to make that decision. Detailed analytical reports should not be supplied routinely, however, with the idea that they *may be* required for a decision which *may have* to be made.

The Decision Making View

At the present time, many applications of the accounting for decision making point of view to routine decision problems are being made in business. These applications are often made in the name of operations research, management sciences, management services, or some other title. Whatever the title, the accountant applying this viewpoint must consider the following series of questions:

1. What is the decision that needs to be made?
2. What is the best rule for making the decision?
3. What information is required in making the decision?
4. How accurate must that information be?
5. How frequently should the information be supplied?
6. What is the most logical source for generating the information?
7. How can the information best be obtained and transmitted to the user?

An information system which is developed after consideration of these questions will not, of course, guarantee that the answers to each problem will be the best possible answers. Rather, this approach to system design guarantees only that the right questions are being asked.

Assume, for example, a particular area of control which has always been a problem—inventory—and consider the relationship of the stated questions to an analysis of a typical inventory control problem.

Decisions which must be made in the routine management of each item of inventory may be stated as follows: How much to buy? When to buy?

Much progress has been made in the spreading use today of the standard lot size formula and reorder point formulas—improved decision rules for determining how much of an item to buy and when to buy it. These improved decision rules create, however, a host of new information problems. It is important to know that these rules require the explicit consideration of certain information which heretofore has often been considered intuitively:

1. The cost, in the opportunity sense, of running out of an item.
2. The cost, in the opportunity sense, of holding an item in inventory.
3. The cost, in the money sense, of procuring an item.
4. The expected future demand for the item.

The accounting function is presented with a need for new kinds of information not generated in conventional accounting systems. In addition, the task of evaluating accuracy, timeliness, source, and transmission requirements for these new kinds of data must be performed.

The fact that routine decision rules can be improved by scientific analysis has already been demonstrated in the inventory control, production control, and investment fields. Improved decision procedures, based on such logical analysis as we have described, are being increasingly accepted by business. Current research can be expected to produce further improvements in methods of making routine business decisions.

The implications of these developments for the accounting information function seem fairly clear. Accounting within the firm must concern itself more with integrating information flows with decision requirements. Information flows must be tied directly into decisions which are to be made. Information flows to decision points must be accurate and timely, whether the decision point be a machine, a man, a department, or a board of directors.

In the future, we can expect to learn more about the effects of information frequency (and accuracy) on routine decisions. Tremendous technical strides in methods of information transmission and information reduction can be expected. In particular, electronic data processing and statistical sampling promise revolutionary changes in information processing methods.

SPECIAL DECISIONS

In our discussion of accounting for decision making as applied to routine decisions, we have assumed the decisions to be made by an organization must first be specified before an intelligent design of the information flow is possible. Determination of the decisions to be made comes properly before specification of the data which should be supplied. Since the decisions which must be made are not always obvious, this brings us back to the first question posed: What is the problem?

To determine what decisions should be made—What is the problem?—is perhaps the essence of the present art of management. It may be considered the highest management art for, in most instances, it carries with it the highest penalty for failure. An organization which does not recognize that it has a poor system for routine inventory decisions will suffer reduced profits. An organization which fails to recognize in time the necessity for a major investment decision may go bankrupt. An organization which fails to integrate routine decisions with each other and with the objectives of the organization may suffer the same fate, even though the routine decisions are independently well made. But how can management recognize such special problems? At the present time, there are no satisfying answers to these questions.

Although our present fund of knowledge about how problems are recognized is exceedingly meager, we do know a few things, and current research is promising some breakthroughs in this decision area. We know, as we have previously pointed out in connection with a standard cost system, that information of one kind or another is required to recognize problems—to signal that the determination of a lower level decision is required. At the present time, managers acquire the information which spurs problem recognition in many haphazard and random ways. Often the manager must hunt for and search out the information leading to problem recognition.

Nonetheless, it is not too optimistic to hope that, in the future, information systems can be devised which will aid the manager in the problem recognition stage of decision making. Information systems of the future may be commonly applied to the problem recognition phase as well as to the alternative choice phase of the decision making process. Under the title of *heuristics* or *heuristic programming*, a considerable amount of management service research directed toward such a goal is being conducted today.[4]

Again, we believe the implications of these developments for accounting for decision making are clear. As business organizations structure their decision activities, it will be with the help of more complex and sophisticated information systems. The responsibility of the accounting information function must, of necessity, increase.

Perhaps the primary implication of the notion of accounting for decision making is that accounting practice of today must move ahead, with new thinking and new methods. In the past, the accounting function has been a principal source of information flows within a business. The accounting function in the future will assume an expanded responsibility for information flows. Accounting has an obligation to take a significant part in the development of new quantitative information systems.

As a part of this development, accounting must divert itself from its preoccupation of the past with fiduciary and stewardship responsibilities. Responsibility for fiduciary decisions is a proper and major concern of the accountant. However, if the accountant is to comprehend and contribute to the decision making, information flow process within tomorrow's business organizations, he must integrate his stewardship responsibility with a responsibility for broader management decisions.

---

[4] A. Newell and H. A. Simon, "Heuristic Problem Solving," *Operations Research*, Vol. 6 (January-February, 1958), pp. 1-10.

PART II

THEORY OF COST ACCOUNTING
FOR INCOME DETERMINATION

In recent years, the bulk of the literature in the accounting field seems to be concerned with the problems of information for planning and control, but through history there has been a major and continuing concern with the problem of accounting for costs in the income determination problem. The basic issue is the identification of costs which have expired and should be matched against revenue, recognized as losses, or which should be carried forward for future matching.

A classic in this area is the monograph by Paton and Littleton in which they describe the concept that costs attach or cohere and that they should be matched with the effects attributable to such costs. More recently a committee of the American Accounting Association reexamined the matching concept and concluded that it should be emphasized in financial reporting. They then proceeded to establish criteria for the matching process considering direct costs, indirect costs and losses, their measurement, and certain specific problems. There are two sides to the matching process. Costs are either matched against revenue in the current period or they are carried forward as assets to be matched in future periods. The relevant costing approach places the emphasis upon the future aspects of matching, carrying forward only those costs which have "a favorable economic effect on expected future costs or future revenues." [1]

Granted the validity of some theory of matching, there remain the need for consistent supporting theories of fixed cost allocation to products, loss concepts in cost accounting, and the matching of marketing costs. These are explored in the last article.

---

[1] Article 17, page 212.

14. AN INTRODUCTION TO CORPORATE ACCOUNTING STANDARDS *   W. A. Paton and A. C. Littleton †

Costs Attach [1]

The economic activity of a business enterprise consists in uniting materials, labor, and various services to form new combinations having new utilities. This it does without regard to accounts. Accounts, however, are useful adjuncts to the economic process, since they trace the shifting movements and conversions that are constantly occurring within the enterprise, as well as record the changing relations of the enterprise with the outside world.

Whereas production activity uses material things and varied services, accounting employs the price aggregates of exchange transactions to represent objects and services. When production activity effects a change in the form of raw materials by the consumption of human labor and machine power, accounting keeps step by classifying and summarizing appropriate portions of materials cost, labor cost, and machine cost so that together they become product costs. In other words, it is a basic concept of accounting that costs can be marshaled into new groups that possess real significance. It is as if costs had a power of cohesion when properly brought into contact.

It is not necessary to assume a cost theory of value in order to explain the concept that costs cohere. Costs are not marshaled to show value or worth. In their new position they are still costs, that is, price aggregates of exchange transactions; they have merely been regrouped. The purpose of reassembling is to trace the efforts made to give materials and other components additional utility.

If cost of production were to represent "value," it should include an amount for the added utility given to the product by the process of business operation itself. But this is not attempted. The producer may think that utility has been added and that the product is worth

---

* Excerpts are from *An Introduction to Corporate Accounting Standards*, a monograph published by the American Accounting Association. Copyright 1940 by the American Accounting Association. Reprinted by permission of the American Accounting Association.

† W. A. Paton, Professor of Accounting, *Emeritus*, University of Michigan; A. C. Littleton, Professor of Accountancy, *Emeritus*, University of Illinois.

[1] This reading is excerpted from Chapter II, "Concepts."

more than the sum of the several costs; but he does not know. One's own judgment of added utility is not conclusive; the test comes when a sale is made. If the price accepted by the buyer is greater than related costs, it can be said that the presence of added utility in the product has been independently confirmed and that its measurement has become possible. Therefore, costs are assembled by products or time intervals as if they had a power of cohesion, not because, as regrouped, they express values, but because they express parts of the total effort made to bring about a subsequent advantageous sale.

The realization of revenue from sales, therefore, marks the time and measures the amount of (1) recapture of costs previously advanced in productive efforts, and (2) capture of additional assets (income) representing amount of compensation for capital service rendered, responsibility taken, and risk assumed in the process of production. Inventories and plant are not "values," but cost accumulations in suspense, as it were, awaiting their destiny. In order to learn what costs have already met the test (recapture) and what costs still await the test, accounting assumes that acquisition costs are mobile and may be apportioned or regrouped, and that costs reassembled have a natural affinity for each other which identifies them with the group. Some costs, like manuufacturing overhead, in which an affinity with a product can be detected, are allocated directly to a product; but other costs, like administrative overhead, in which it is difficult to detect an affinity with a product, are commonly allocated only to time periods, that is to say, against total revenue for the period.

Effort and Accomplishment

The flow of business activity has a long continuity; the ultimate outcome of the activities lies in the future. But decisions cannot await the ultimate outcome; management, investors, government, all of the interested parties, need "test readings" from time to time in order to gauge the progress made. By means of accounting we seek to provide these test readings by a periodic matching of the costs and revenues that have flowed past "the meter" in an interval of time. For this purpose cost and revenue data are selected because of the belief that the study of the acquisition price aggregates and disposition price aggregates of transactions will be useful in comparing the efforts to produce results with the results produced.

Costs are considered as measuring effort, revenues as measuring accomplishment. Costs are traced carefully from the first acquisition of goods or services through various regroupings for the specific object of having available, at the time of sale of the product, information regarding relevant costs—that is, those costs related to a specific segment of revenue because they are technically or economically associated with a corresponding segment of product, or unit of time in which such product appears.

Ideally, all costs incurred should be viewed as ultimately clinging to definite items of goods sold or service rendered. If this conception could be effectively realized in practice, the net accomplishment of the enterprise could be measured in terms of units of output rather than of intervals of time. This ideal condition, indeed, can be approached in some types of construction projects and other single, terminable undertakings. But in the more typical situation the degree of continuity of activity obtaining tends to prevent the finding of a basis of affinity which will permit convincing assignments, of all classes of cost incurred, to particular operations, departments, and—finally—items of product. Not all costs attach in a discernible manner, and this fact forces the accountant to fall back upon a time period as the unit for associating certain expenses with certain revenues. Time periods are a convenience, a substitute, but the fundamental concept is unchanged. The ideal is to match costs incurred with the effects attributable to or significantly related to such costs.

Matching Cost and Revenue [2]

It was pointed out earlier that accounting for costs involves three stages: (1) ascertaining and recording costs as incurred, appropriately classified; (2) tracing and reclassifying costs in terms of operating activity; (3) assigning costs to revenues. The third stage is crucial from the standpoint of periodic income measurement; it likewise comprehends most of the difficult problems of accounting analysis. Matching costs and revenues requires more than careful procedure and accurate compilation. Recording the inflow of cost is in large measure a matter of close observation and efficient clerical process; recording the outflow of costs as embodied in revenue is essentially a matter of judgment and interpretation.

The revenues of a particular period should be charged with the costs which are reasonably associated with the product represented

---

[2] This reading is excerpted from Chapter V, "Income."

by such revenues. In this connection it should be emphasized that physical use or consumption is not a satisfactory test of assignability to revenue, notwithstanding the usual assumption to the contrary. The fuel cost to be associated with revenue for the period need not be the cost of the coal burned during the period. The cost of fuel consumed becomes a charge to benefited operations, and the amount to be attached to the revenues of the period depends upon the amount of cost (partly fuel) of such operations which is associated with unfinished product and hence with future resources. In other words, the cost of any factor utilized in operating activity is chargeable to revenue only as the resulting product is recognized as having produced revenue.

The general point of view expressed here is widely accepted by accountants and business managements with respect to the original costs of primary materials or merchandise and—in manufacturing —the direct labor charges incurred. Under many cost systems the flow of materials and labor is scrupulously and effectively traced in terms of particular departments, activities, and units or classes of output. Considerable progress has also been made in the development of theories and methods of associating the so-called indirect or overhead production charges with operations and—by this route— with revenues. It remains true, however, that in many enterprises the handling of manufacturing overhead costs in relation to revenue is still on a rough percentage basis, and for most enterprises in all fields it is also true that the costs of general administration and the costs associated with marketing the product are deemed to be chargeable to revenues as incurred, with no attempt at periodic apportionment.

The point is that the costs of direct materials and labor as a rule can be followed in relation to activity and output in a fairly satisfactory manner by careful observation of objective physical relationships; whereas such tracing is impracticable or impossible for many elements of manufacturing overhead, general administration, and distribution charges. Particular difficulty is presented by long-range advertising and other indirect selling charges which are now so important in many lines. Costs of general administration and of selling represent efforts to produce revenue just as truly as do costs of direct labor and materials, and one class of charges is just as legitimate and significant as the other, but the accounting treatments accorded cannot be expected to be strictly comparable unless and until the means of effecting association with particular quantities of revenue are equally well developed.

In view of the work being done in certain quarters some improvement in the assignment of general and selling charges may be anticipated. Growing recognition of the fact that costs may well be classed in two main pools, production and distribution, into which the costs of general administration can be absorbed upon proper analysis, has been helpful. Another important development is the trend toward the application of the tools of functional analysis (budgeting and standard costs) to administrative and selling charges as well as to so-called production costs. There is also an occasional indication in accounting and business practice of a realization of the inherent propriety of accumulating distribution costs as a form of cost "inventory" to the extent that the charges involved are incurred on account of future sales rather than on account of current business.

The problem of properly matching revenues and costs is primarily one of finding satisfactory bases of association—clues to relationships which unite revenue deductions and revenue. As suggested above, observable physical connections often afford a means of tracing and assigning. It should be emphasized, however, that the essential test is reasonableness, in the light of all the pertinent conditions, rather than physical measurement. Even in the handling of direct material charges, for example, it is often necessary to recognize that the problem of assignment is a matter of economic rather than of physical flow. Thus the entire cost of a sheet of leather consumed in making shoes is charged to the product notwithstanding the fact that a considerable portion of the sheet becomes waste material.

Matching does not imply cancellation. Occasionally commissions, shipping costs, or other charges incurred at the point of sale are subtracted from the total of revenue and only the balance is recognized in the accounts. This practice is objectionable. All costs actually incurred by the enterprise, whatever the point at which incurred and whatever the method of effecting payment, should be recorded as costs; similarly the full price of the product should be reported as revenue. To ignore this rule results in a definite obscuring of the essential factors in income measurement, even if there is no modification of the net amount.

In general, only costs which have been definitely incurred are assignable to revenue. It was pointed out in the preceding chapter, however, that in cases in which revenue is measured in terms of sales and in which charges clearly applicable to current revenue can be anticipated, a precise accounting requires the adjustment of gross revenue as otherwise determined, by the amount of reasonable estimates of the costs of billing, collecting, etc. Likewise, if the sales agreement provides for the rendering of service by the vendor without additional compensation it is necessary to modify recognized revenue by means of an estimated liability to effect a sound periodic apportionment. Another case requiring similar treatment is that of land sold with the understanding that the vendor is to take care of contemplated improvements such as installing water mains, building roads, and the like.

Under some circumstances an anticipated expenditure must be accrued over a period of years. Ideally, the estimated cost of removing plant assets at the end of service life, if in excess of anticipated salvage, should be accrued through appropriate charges to revenue. In practice this special cost is often assumed to be cared for in the regular depreciation accrual—not a seriously questionable assumption if the amount of the net removal cost will presumably be small. Again, the contract under which property is leased may provide for the removal of improvements made by the tenant when the use of property is restored to the owner. For such situations accountants can see nothing unreasonable in a periodic accruing of the anticipated special expenditure, reliably determined, with corresponding credits to a liability reserve, for the purpose of a proper matching of revenue and cost incurred. Indeed, in such a situation it is perhaps permissible to say that the cost is incurred, on an accrual basis, as the date of actual expenditure and satisfaction of the obligation to the owner approaches.

Deferred Charges

The process of applying costs incurred to revenues, as explained, consists essentially of the division of charges into those to be reported in the current income sheet and those assignable to future periods. The general problem, therefore, can be stated in either of two ways. Under what circumstances are costs chargeable to immediate revenues? Under what circumstances should costs be accumulated for application to future revenues? At this point some attention will be given to the second approach.

According to the position taken here all costs incurred prudently and in good faith are reflected at least momentarily in the total of assets, broadly conceived, and through this avenue attach to business activity, the effort to produce revenue. The acceptance of this point of view means that any type or kind of cost may contribute, under appropriate conditions, to the total of charges deferred at the end of the particular period. Costs to be deferred, in other words, are not confined to the charges specifically represented by land, materials, merchandise, buildings, equipment, and other tangible properties; they may properly include charges for necessary services of every nature and description, assuming that reasonable means of determining the amounts to be deferred are available.

It follows that the tendency of some people to view with suspicion deferred charges representing service costs not readily assignable to physical property is not altogether justified. If determined on a sound basis such charges are just as legitimate a member of the family of asset balances as the unamortized costs of plant. A business enterprise is a complex economic institution, and its status cannot properly be reckoned purely in terms of brick and mortar or other physical characteristics, or only on the basis of its apparent ability to pay its debts. It may well be agreed that assets should be reported conservatively, but the adoption of this attitude does not preclude careful consideration of each class of charge incurred on its merits, in the light of the conditions prevailing in the particular situation. Thus organization costs need not be viewed as a questionable element, to be written off as incurred or as soon as they can be absorbed without reducing the reported net income to a level which is objectionable to the management. Similarly, technical development costs in mining operations (for example, exploratory drilling, stripping, etc.) and such general charges as costs of training personnel, developing records, and the like are subject to treatment as deferred charges, with subsequent assignment to revenues in accordance with a reasonable policy of amortization. In connection with such suggestions it must of course be borne in mind that apportionment of many classes of cost is easier said than done, and that if convincing means of periodic spreading are lacking the practice of "charging off" as incurred may be expected to persist.

The general test or tests to be applied to the various costs incurred in the particular period to determine their disposition as deductions from current revenue on the one hand and deferred charges on the other may be readily indicated. First, does the charge in question represent a bona fide cost, an expenditure reasonably justified under all the circumstances? If the answer is in the affirmative the charge cannot well be treated as a loss, although it may still be a current deduction. Second, does the charge represent a factor from which a future benefit or contribution can reasonably be anticipated; that is, is the charge intrinsically associated with future revenues? If the answer is again in the affirmative the cost under consideration may properly be deferred. A minor test of some value is suggested by the question: Is the charge of the regularly and frequently recurring type? For costs of this nature there is a presumption in favor of absorption in current operations, due allowance being made for ordinary inventories and prepaid balances.

It is sometimes assumed that no expenditure may be capitalized (that is, deferred) unless an increase in the volume of revenue or decrease in cost per revenue unit may be expected to appear as a result. This position is untenable. Not infrequently additional investment in plant facilities is required when there is no prospect of either an expansion of revenue or a reduction of operating costs. In working the lower levels of a mine, for example, it may be necessary in order to continue operations to install equipment not needed at earlier stages of the process of extraction. To refer again to the general test: all costs prudently incurred which can reasonably be associated with future production are subject to deferment. Needless to say, no additional investment should be made unless the available data indicate that the enterprise will be advantaged thereby—will be in a more favorable condition than would be the case if the proposed charges were not incurred.

In corporate reporting the term "deferred charge" is often used in the balance sheet to designate such dissimilar things as short-term prepayments for service, organization costs, costs of experiment and development, security discounts, balances in suspense, and actual losses. This is bad practice. Prepaid insurance, rent, etc., should be labeled as such and listed either as current or semicurrent resources; organization costs should be separately and distinctly reported after the tangible fixed assets; security discounts should be shown as contras on the equity side of the statement; so-called suspense balances should be analyzed and defined in terms of their principal characteristics; actual losses should be charged off. This leaves general development costs, not readily assignable to tangible factors, as the principal candidate for reporting under the special caption "deferred charges."

15. CONCEPTS OF INCOME
UNDERLYING ACCOUNTING *   A. C. Littleton †

A survey of accounting literature would lead most observers to the conclusion that, on the whole, capital has received more attention in accounting than income. Yet fundamentally income produced, not capital in use, is the central theme of account keeping as it is the focal center of the business enterprise. Capital is only a means to an end; income is that end. . . .

One of the keenest critics of accounting theory has said with much justification that "accountants have no complete philosophical system of thought about income." [1] That statement is all too true. Accountants, like businessmen, are too deep in practical affairs to be philosophers. But that does not prevent accounting records from giving expression, piecemeal as it were, to definite concepts of profit and income.

Bookkeeping has given quantitative expression to various aspects of profit ever since income and expense accounts have been used, and that has been at least for five hundred years. Few indeed are the companion disciplines which have served more effectively for as long with so little change in their fundamental doctrines or methods. Businessmen, and accountants as well, have indeed been rather inarticulate in expressing a theory of profit. They have left it to economists to explain why there was such a thing as a profit margin, and to jurists to deliberate upon restricting dividends in a way to protect the creditors of limited-liability corporations. But businessmen and their bookkeepers, working within the limits of their tradition, have for a very long time been *living* a theory of profit even if they wrote little about it. They, not economists or jurists, undertake day by day to quantify profits; they have to do so for they are

* From *The Accounting Review* (March, 1937). Reprinted by permission of the American Accounting Association.
† A. C. Littleton, Professor of Accountancy, *Emeritus*, University of Illinois.
[1] J. B. Canning, *The Economics of Accountancy*, p. 160.

unable to await the outcome of ultimate liquidation before making decisions. Businessmen cannot escape acting with regard to profit one way or another without much time to rationalize their acts in advance.

Accounting, which we may call the art of keeping accounts, is the means of giving definite quantitative expression to many accepted customs of business.[2] And public accountants are constantly scrutinizing the details of these "profit customs" and criticizing their reasonableness in the light of sound principle. Accounting and accountants, therefore, are supplementary to business activities. Even if their service proves useful to investors, creditors, or tax collectors, such service is secondary to a dependable record; a correct record comes first if only as a point of departure for subsequent interpretations.

Bookkeeping is first of all a record methodology for an economic enterprise as a producing unit. And since accounting is but expanded and refined account keeping, we must conclude that the true base of the most useful ideas of accounting is economic rather than legal, even though accountants, as well as businessmen, are under the necessity of conforming to the law of the land so long as it is law.

The concept of income, then, which underlies accounting may be expected to be closer to that of economics than to that expressed in statutory law or court decisions.

There is, I believe, a concept of profit, or as I prefer to say, a concept of net income, inherent in double-entry bookkeeping as it has been refined by the accrual system of accounting. What follows is an attempt to describe that concept. It is an effort to interpret out of business customs and accounting practices the concept of net income which is lived day by day in business and which necessarily constitutes the most basic concept in accountancy.

This purpose leads first to a brief consideration of what may be termed the economic condition of an enterprise in contrast to its financial condition, and then to the larger question of whether the cost outlays (including expenses) made in business and recorded in

---

[2] The English courts, in decisions under the income tax law, have repeatedly taken the view that what is profit is to be determined by the practices of businessmen. . . . The development of accounting, like the development of business law, should be determined by the best practices of businessmen. George O. May, *The Influence of Accounting on the Development of an Economy* (New York: American Institute of Accountants, 1936), pp. 4, 41.

General accounting practice (is) based largely on the customs of prudent businessmen . . . . M. E. Peloubet, *Journal of Accounting* (March, 1936), p. 190.

the accounts may reasonably be thought of as causally related to the revenue incomes secured.

Whenever debtors and creditors enter into contractual relationships, financial condition becomes an important consideration. This is very largely a legal matter. But a business enterprise is more basically an economic unit than it is a legal institution; finance and debt are secondary to the primary economic activity of producing an output which will be acceptable to customers. Therefore, it is possible to say that economic condition, not financial condition, is of first importance in a business enterprise.

The appearance of output in a business is not the result of the simple speculative adventuring of an investment—the providential casting of bread upon the waters. And income is more than the chance realization of a gain arising out of an ownership now transferred to another.

The assembly and union of selected elements of input form the units of final output of a business enterprise. Presumably the manipulative processes add new utilities beyond the mere sum of the utilities of the previously separate elements. How much is thus added will be tested by the market's acceptance or rejection of the product at the price asked. Insofar as money costs can measure the sacrifices made in producing the output, it may be said that the calculated cost of production expresses the sum of the utilities of the separate elements of input. The sum (cost), compared with the market's expression of opinion regarding output utility (revenue), will presumably measure the utility added by the productive processes.

It is necessary to qualify the statement by the word "presumably" because monopoly, if present, could hold selling prices artificially high, thus adding a sum to the profit margin which could not properly be described as a producer added utility. But in the absence of outright monopoly control of price, the effect of "natural" scarcity factors would be transmitted to high-cost and low-cost producers alike or they would both receive the same price for their product. Consequently, in the absence of monopoly, the profit of those producers who are above the margin must be due to their lower costs. And lower costs, for the most part, are expressive of the producer's skill and efficiency.

We may say, therefore, that the point of view of the businessman is that *output* is the result of definitely planned work—the consequence of a prior *service input* made with intent to create output;

money income is the earning flowing from the planned work—the consequence of a prior *money outlay* made with intent to generate income.[3]

From the businessman's point of view, and hence the point of view also of accounting theory, the key to this doctrine is the word "intent." Service input and its money counterpart, outlay, are entered upon with the clear intention of establishing a relationship with subsequent service output and its money counterpart, income; that is to say, input has the objective of producing an effect on the economic condition of the enterprise. Hence cost outlays are more than mere cash disbursements or liabilities incurred; outlays for cost express in homogeneous money price the heterogeneous service input made in the effort to produce an acceptable service output. And in a similar way revenue and earnings (incomes) are more than mere cash collections or accrued assets receivable. Incomes express in money price the fruition of the enterpriser's efforts—the ripening harvest as it were from a prior planting carefully cultivated. Quite a different condition this from a mere speculative venturing, even though the outcome of the husbandry may be subject to unpredictable and uncontrollable risks.

Economic condition, then, is a relationship, as financial condition is a relationship. Whereas the latter is a relationship of debt to debt-paying capacity, the former is a relationship of income produced to the cost of producing it. For many purposes a knowledge of financial condition is important, but economic condition is a foundation to financial condition and to many other matters besides. Wherever business management or investors attempt to think of results in terms of causes, it is details of economic condition which should receive major attention.

The clue to the concept "economic condition" is found in the term "net income"; and the explanation of net income is found in the conjunction of two elements: one is the acceptance of the service output by customers *at a price,* and the other is the preparation of the service output for customers *at a cost.*

---

[3] John R. Commons (*Institutional Economics,* pp. 253, 257, and elsewhere) stresses the economic distinction between output, an engineering concept of quantity devoid of price, and income, an economic concept of the aggregate from multiplying quantity and price; and the distinction between input, related to services acquired and used, and outgo, the aggregate costs incurred to acquire the input. Also see John D. Black, *Introduction to Production Economics* (1926), especially Chapters XI, XII.

Imagine a pair of shears in the hands of a tailor; the lower blade moves only forward on the tabletop but the upper blade also moves up and down in the cutting stroke. Net income, like the cloth under the tailor's hand, is shaped as by the interaction of the blades of a pair of shears—revenue as one, cost as the other. It is obvious that both blades are necessary to produce the result. But their action is not necessarily equal. One blade may rest passively on the table while the other blade moves actively up and down under pressure from the operator's fingers. The passive blade represents revenue—the element under little direct managerial control; the active blade represents costs—the element under considerable managerial control in the activity of producing net income.

Cost outlays are much more subject to the enterpriser's decisions and choices than is revenue; he controls the timing of his cost outlays and their apportioning among types; he selects the quantity and agrees to the buying price; by following his selections with expenditures or contracts, he induces a flow of service input. We may say then that the costs thus incurred express quantitatively the *causes* which actuate the inflow of services, or that the chosen input of services *causes* the outflow of cost expenditures. But whichever way the proposition is stated, the result is that costs represent "solidified" managerial choices made with specific intent.

The shears illustration clearly expresses the thought that net income is the result of a favorable or unfavorable *relation* between revenue and cost. But the relation changes more readily under the influence of costs than revenues; profit is likely to accompany low costs, and loss to be associated with high costs. If "A" is a marginal producer, he is so because his costs are high in relation to the price the market is willing to pay; if "B" makes a good profit with a similar product in the same market, he does so because he has been able to get his costs low in relation to market price.

One should no doubt refer to "cause and effect" circumspectly in these scientific days, for effects are usually considered to emerge out of a complex of antecedent conditions rather than from specific causes. Yet it is difficult to contemplate the complex conditions antecedent to the appearance of earned net income and not try to see at least some distance into the tangle.

What lies back of the revenue which flows from the customer's acceptance of a product? As "causes" of demand, consumers' wants will probably stand first. But the wants behind demand are not wholly beyond the influence of an enterpriser's expenditures. Many managerial decisions are made with the definite intention of influencing demand. Improvements in old products, devising new products, forceful and truthful advertising, skillful styling and designing, attractive price-quality ratio—the enterpriser's cost expenditures for such as these cannot change human nature perhaps, but they can uncover latent wants and make effective many wants formerly unsatisfied. In this sense even an individual seller's costs can lead to the ultimate acceptance of that seller's output and to a consequent inflow of revenue. If outlays can "cause" a demand for specific services, they can be considered causally related to the revenues which flow from the services rendered.

Besides wants as primary causes of demand there is also the matter of consumer purchasing power. Wants are fulfilled only at a price. The price which will convert wants into purchases depends upon the intensity of the want and the ability to pay. Can the seller's expenditures influence these? Intensity of want can be influenced probably very little, but ability to pay can be influenced a great deal. For example, wherever ingenious policies and wise expenditures result in low costs and consequent low prices, the effect upon the customer's purchasing power is direct and beneficial. In that sense also, business expenditures can "cause" demand and lead to acceptance of the product.

But demand and even sale do not of themselves yield a profit; they can only offer a chance to profit. The opportunity to earn a profit appears with the customer's acceptance of the product, but profit realization to an important extent depends upon how successfully the costs have been kept below the revenues. This accomplishment is seldom accidental. To be sure, cost is partly the result of the state of the supply-market at the time, but to a large extent, as suggested above, costs are subject to the choices and the resourcefulness of the producer. Good buying, high worker efficiency, inventiveness—expenditures for these elements and many others, if made with clear foresight and wise intent, do have the planned result, namely, costs which are lower than the corresponding revenues.

Managerial policies are made effective through costs. Costs, therefore, are quantitative measures of policies translated into action. Management, having recognized wants to be satisfied and being desirous of contriving a supply to fill the need, can effectively express itself only in expenditures made or expenditures avoided. By that means management succeeds or fails in its objective of providing a desired economic service at a cost which is less than the price set by marginal producers in a competitive market.

How can management know when and what to cease producing except by learning to distinguish the successful from the unsuccessful attempts at supplying a service? It has been said, "It is only when past plans for production and past costs have been accurately adjusted to the demand that exists when the goods finished arrive at the consumer's market, that goods sell for prices that agree with past costs of production." [4] Since the manager cannot foretell the future, and therefore cannot at the moment judge the wisdom of his present costs, he can become "accurately adjusted to the demand . . ." only upon the basis of a comparison of his past plans, partially expressed in his costs, and present market demand, partially expressed in his revenue.

The enterpriser's problem then is twofold: first, to discover economic wants which he believes he can be the means of satisfying; second, to choose the necessary elements of service input and to direct the production and distribution of the service output accordingly. Market analysis, it is true, may be able to express some elements of economic wants in quantitative terms for the enterpriser's guidance; but the most important quantitative data of business are the cost of input and the revenue from output. Of these two, cost is the more useful to the enterpriser because it is more directly under managerial control and more expressive of causal factors. Because costs are thus closely identified with the vital aspect of business operations they take on great importance in accounting.

Cost in business is the special province of cost accounting, and it is in cost accounting that we find the clearest conception of cost as representing causal factors. Cost accountants are unwilling to add overhead costs related to idle equipment to the products from busy equipment. They are opposed to spreading total factory overhead over whatever production exists. The reasoning is that idle equipment has made no physical contribution to the appearance of the new products and that consequently none of the costs congealed in the idle equipment can properly be attached to the product of other equipment.

This example indicates that a theory of causation lies at the basis of cost accounting calculations. This theory is also discernible in the

---

[4] Garner and Hansen, *Principles of Economics*, p. 167.

opposition in accounting to deferring the unabsorbed overhead costs from idle equipment into the future where the deferred costs could be attached to the product then produced by the formerly idle equipment. It is reasoned that equipment idleness now can no more contribute to the appearance of later production than could idle labor today create product tomorrow.

By way of partial summary we may say that the chief points of contact between enterprise economics and accounting come at three places: (1) wherever accounting theory seeks to establish suitable bases for uniting cost and revenue as representing input and output respectively, (2) wherever accounting practice performs the operations necessary to disclose the causal relationships, and (3) wherever auditing makes a critical examination of individual applications of accounting theory and practice.

The chief problems of accounting can be stated with equal conciseness. They are (1) to record details of revenue income in such analytical form that they will be useful in distinguishing the results of differing causes, (2) to record details of expenditure outlay in such analytical form that they will be of service in distinguishing the causes of differing results, and (3) to marshal analytical details with such skill as to reflect with high fidelity the association of known results with their causal factors.

If, as I believe, substantial progress has been made in establishing correct calculation of profit produced as the central theme of accounting as it has always been the theme of bookeeping, then perhaps the time has come to consider the possibilities of refining the profit concept in order to make it still more serviceable. Therefore, I should like to indicate briefly how a more distinct recognition may be given in accounting theory to refinements already begun.

Accrual accounting is not properly considered to mean profit accounting, if profit is thought of merely as the difference between two specific prices. Accrual accounting is better described as income accounting for the reason that accounting is a method of computing the net result produced by two price streams rather than a way of comparing pairs of individual prices. One stream is the outflow of services given, the other is the inflow of services received.

It is only as a practical expedient for securing a common denominator that these service streams are expressed in money prices and called "revenue" and "expense" respectively. The essential thought is the comparison, as it were, of two physical streams one tending to raise the level of a lake and the other to lower the level. Insofar as accounting operates from the capital or balance sheet point of view it looks at the lake levels at different dates. But business is much more concerned with the income point of view which looks at the waxing and waning influences themselves. It is a case of the dynamic versus the static; accounting must be primarily dynamic because business is dynamic.

Accrual accounting has two important parts. One of them directs us in distinguishing expense from disbursement, and income from receipt, the other directs us in the careful separation of assets and expenses. Both of these elements of accrual accounting are parts of the process of allocating cost outlays to time periods where they will meet income revenues similarly allocated to time periods.

But accruals according to the periods wherein benefit is conferred and realization takes place may not be enough to show the full facts. The emergence of revenue and the incidence of expense are stressed in accounting in order to bring together the elements which belong together. But what is the clue to "belonging"?[5] Is periodic revenue linked to periodic cost in an association of cause and effect that is as close as would be desirable?

The intent of accrual accounting is to associate *related* costs and revenues; allocation to equal fiscal periods is the present, accepted method. But occasionally the impression arises that we use time periods for this association merely because more positive means are lacking for linking cost more directly with the revenue it helped to produce.

It, therefore, seems probable that the principle of distinguishing income from receipts could be further refined by rules for better classifying income by sources, for sources provide a clue to causes. One of the principles of accrual theory is that income is considered valid only after it has been tested as to its reality—the rule of realization. But it would be a most acceptable refinement to distinguish earned income produced and derived profit received.

In order to distinguish these two we may say that a concern earns income to the extent that it produces revenue which may reasonably be considered to have arisen because of the costs currently

---

[5] Alfred Marshall mentions a report on the income tax by a committee of the British Association as early as 1878 wherein deductions from gross income were referred to as "the outgoings that belong to its production." *Principles of Economics*, 8th ed., p. 72. John B. Canning gives point to the problem in this question, "How much of any given dollar of outlay is spent to obtain any particular dollar of receipt?" *Econometrica* (January, 1933), p. 57.

incurred in the performance of the enterprise's particular economic function; and we may say it receives derived profit merely by alienation of property, adjustment of debts or capital structure, or other activities unrelated to the direct performance of the enterprise's particular economic function.[6]

Because of the obviously different indications that these two kinds of realized gains give of managerial skill and activity, they should be separately reported in the first instance. Probably only one of them should be lodged in earned surplus so that the balance of that account will reflect only undistributed earned income which was produced as the result of outlays made with the intent of generating earned income. Earned surplus thus treated will not be strictly analogous to the older concept of undivided, realized profits; rather in the interest of distinguishing earned income and realized profits it will be a new extension of the normal accounting impulse to break down every complex into its constituent elements.

It is also probable that the principles which distinguish asset and expense can be further refined by suitable rules for drawing a more careful distinction between expense and loss, and between different kinds of losses.

It is no doubt an acceptable generalization to say that cost allocation is the fundamental process of accounting. And it is clearly recognized that original outlay costs may be deferred (as assets), amortized (as expenses), or abandoned (as losses). It is the duty of accounting theory in this connection to lay down the rules and reasons for making these distinctions. In the present treatment of original costs the clue to the status of a given item is its relation to a time period. It would be better if the clue were the relation of a particular cost cause to its corresponding revenue source. Thus original outlay costs should become deferred costs only when they may be reasonably considered as causally related to future revenue

---

[6] This theory of the distinction between income and profit is close to that found in the legal and accounting views of estate accounting, wherein the life tenant is entitled to the net income earned by the trust assets, that is, gross income less "all expenses properly incurred in earning or collecting the income or preserving the trust fund in order that it may earn income" (Langer and Greeley, "Estate Accounting," *Accounting Principles and Procedure*) and the remainderman is entitled to capital gains, these being increments to corpus rather than income. In contrast to this theory, which carries over the essential distinction between corpus and income into a similar and wholly consistent distinction between earned income and increment to corpus, it is to be noted that general accounting, income tax practice, and dividend law are only partially consistent, for therein a parallel distinction between capital and income is not accompanied by a clear distinction between income produced (earnings) and realized increments (capital gains).

sources; they should become amortized costs only when they may be reasonably considered as causally related to current revenue sources; and they should become abandoned costs only when they may be reasonably considered as unlikely ever to be causally related to the production of any revenue. If reasonable causal connections are established between revenue sources and cost causes, the allocation of costs and revenues to equal time periods becomes incidental rather than the controlling feature of the calculation of net income.

But it is an open question whether even this basis for associating revenue and its cost would alone serve to carry the refinement of accrual theory far enough to distinguish also between different kinds of losses. Therefore, certain other sharp distinctions must be added.

An abandoned item of equipment represents one type of loss; another and quite distinct type of loss is a deficiency of current revenue to cover the cost which must be currently amortized against that revenue. The latter loss is definitely related to the performance of the enterprise's particular economic function and is significant of the unacceptability in the market of the economic service offered or of a failure to keep the supply cost below the demand price which the market affords. On the other hand, costs abandoned or disposed of, other than in a way to affect the appearance of earned income currently or later, are significant of a managerial change of capital policy—a decision not to try to enter the market with an output derived from that particular outlay.[7]

If these distinctions are made, we would then have something that could be called "earned net loss" (to parallel "earned net income"), and something that could be called "derived loss" (to parallel "derived profit"). A deficiency of revenue, or an earned loss, should logically be entered in earned surplus; an abandoned cost, or derived loss, could probably be best recorded in an account reflecting reserved surplus.

In this paper I have tried to make two main points: first, that businessmen and accountants should not be charged with having a vague concept of profit, or net income, either because various details of the calculations are still debated or because some of their theory

---

[7] Physical depreciation, the consumption of equipment used to facilitate production, creates an expense expressive of an active cause; completed obsolescence, the retirement of useful but unused service capacity, creates a loss expressive of factors not causally related to actual production. See also the clear distinction between "expense" and "loss" very forcefully made by Donald Horne in "The Annual Allowance for Depreciation," *Management Review* (May, 1936), p. 139.

must be inferred out of business methods and accounting practice; second, that the businessman's concept of net income grows out of his productive activity and his inability to defer decisions until ultimate liquidation or final consumption place their seal of reality on the values concerned.

I hope that economists will see that, through a long evolution in the field, a thoroughly dependable accounting technique of calculating interim income has been developed upon the foundation of a real concept of net income. And I hope that accountants will see that their acceptance of interim income as a primary consideration in their work also involves their acceptance of economic ideas as being more basic to accounting concepts than are legal ideas.

16. THE MATCHING CONCEPT *

1964 Concepts and Standards Research Study
Committee—The Matching Concept †

A primary function of accounting is to accumulate and communicate information essential to our understanding of the activities of an enterprise.[1] The information so communicated is used by management, by owners, and by other interested parties in making judgments relating to the operation of the entity. Any judgment regarding performance is facilitated by information disclosing the extent of progress toward an objective. Furthermore, historical financial data are recognized as being of limited value except as they may be used to help predict the results which can be expected from a duplication of or planned deviations from the operating plan followed in achieving the historical results.

Working from these premises, the committee has sought to define some of the pertinent questions relating to the matching concept and to suggest theoretically logical answers for them. The conclusions reached are in the nature of practices judged to be preferable by the committee rather than a dogmatic statement of practices required for the presentation of useful financial reports.

MATCHING AND THE PROFIT OBJECTIVE

The committee first considered whether the matching convention is still a useful concept to guide financial reporting practices. Since the fundamental long-term objective of a business entity is to earn a profit, this financial data, to be most meaningful, should include information about profit determinants, including costs and revenues. Only by including these data can the reasons for and the extent of progress of the entity toward its primary objective be disclosed.

* From *The Accounting Review* (April, 1965). Reprinted by permission of the American Accounting Association.

† Members of the committee were W. G. Berg, Luther College; C. H. Griffin, University of Texas; Emerson Henke, Baylor University; Paul Kircher, University of California, Los Angeles; W. S. Mitchell, University of Kansas; and W. J. Schrader, Pennsylvania State University.

[1] *Accounting and Reporting Standards for Corporate Financial Statements* (1957 Rev.; Madison, Wis.: American Accounting Association), p. 1.

Following this thought a bit further, one's judgment regarding the effectiveness of a specific effort is improved if it can be related to its contribution toward the recognized objective of the entity. In business operations, costs, defined as resources given up or economic sacrifices made, are incurred with the anticipation that they will produce revenue in excess of the outlay. Within this frame of reference, one can then say that costs constitute one measure of business effort, and revenues represent accomplishments coming from those efforts. Appropriate reporting of costs and revenues should, therefore, relate costs with revenues in such a way as to disclose most vividly the relationships between efforts and accomplishments.

All activities are inexorably tied to the passage of time. The use of roughly equivalent time intervals can constitute a common basis for the measurement of business activity. Since comparison is one of the most effective analytical devices known to accountants today, it is desirable to use similar time intervals for measuring the efforts and accomplishments of a business entity. Thus, specific time periods, preferably of equal length, do represent a useful and an appropriate framework within which to relate achievements with efforts.

For the reasons cited in the preceding paragraphs, the committee concludes that it is desirable to emphasize the matching concept in financial reporting. The extent of progress of a business enterprise toward the profit goal within a specified period of time should be disclosed. Accomplishments and their related efforts should be matched quantitatively on a periodic basis.

The committee further concludes that an appropriate application of the matching concept requires recognition of the fact that the product and service factors to be matched against revenue can be considered separately from the technique of measuring them. This represents a significant departure from conventional thought and practice. Such an approach to the problem led the committee to give special consideration to the following questions:

1. What criteria shall be used as a basis for associating costs (product and service factors given up) with present and future periods?

2. How shall the expirations of product and service factors be measured?

After having considered these two areas, the committee gave some attention to the actual application of the proposed practices to the solution of matching problems relating to some specific outlays.

CRITERIA FOR MATCHING

The allocation of accomplishments, reflected in the form of revenues, to specific periods requires an appropriate interpretation of the point of realization. (This problem is being examined by another research committee and, therefore, was not studied by this committee.) Efforts, in the form of related costs, should be matched with these accomplishments. Ideally, then, a cause and effect relationship should be discernible as the basis for matching costs with realized revenues. The time of revenue recognition is, therefore, a primary determinant in distinguishing between expired and deferred costs. From a practical point of view, however, it may be virtually impossible and perhaps unnecessary to identify some specific costs with related revenues in a cause and effect sense. Therefore, the committee advocates that costs (defined as product and service factors given up) should be related to revenues realized within a specific period on the basis of some discernible positive correlation of such costs with the recognized revenues.

Positive Correlation

Costs related to period revenue are judged to fall into three categories. The first group includes product and service factors that may be characterized as direct costs in that they can be associated directly with specific results. Direct materials and direct labor are examples of such costs. These items are relatively easy to correlate with their accomplishments because of the observable cause and effect relationship. Insofar as these costs are concerned, the flow of goods or services from the entity to customers is an appropriate justification for allocating them against the realized revenue when the point of sale is judged to be the instant at which income is recognized. Various devices (lifo, fifo, etc.) have been used to identify the acquisition costs of these items with the goods or services given up. From the point of view of associating specific resources given up with revenues realized from them, it seems that first-in, first-out would most nearly reflect the planned buying and selling relationship. Undistributed product and service factors of this type should be deferred as part of inventory to be matched against the revenue realized at the time the inventory is given up. Another group of outlays may be labeled indirect costs. They are associated with a group of results rather than with a specific revenue recognition. These are in effect joint costs having little in the way of an identifiable causal relationship with any specific segments of revenue.

Certain overhead items and many of the general operating costs of business fall into this category. In allocating service factors of this type, the committee feels that positive correlation with current period revenue can be presumed to exist when, on the basis of past experience and reasonable expectations for the future, no objectively discernible ability to produce future revenue is associated with them. When, on the basis of the above-mentioned test, there is an apparent ability to produce future revenue, the costs would be deferred and matched with the revenue of subsequent periods.

A third group of costs may be characterized as losses. They are product and service factors which lose their ability to produce future revenue within a period, without being either directly or indirectly associated with the production of revenue during that period. The same test for positive correlation as that suggested for indirect costs should be applied to these items Thus, the point where a product or service factor loses its discernible ability to produce future revenue would be the point where it should be charged against period revenue. Losses within this framework of thought may also be recognized as product or service factors given up in return for a zero quantity of revenue, a result of the risks associated with business ventures.

Measurement of Expired Product and Service Factors

The committee also considered the problem of measuring the expired portions of product and service factors to be matched with revenues. Traditionally, the original outlay (or a conservative interpretation of it, in the case where inventories were valued at the lower of cost or market) has been used to measure efforts in the form of costs, to be matched against accomplishments in the form of revenue. Accountants have defended the use of original outlay as a measurement of cost by maintaining that it is an objectively determined amount. It appears, however, that original outlay is an objectively determined basis for measuring the value of product and service factors only at the time of the outlay. Market value, determined as a result of current bargaining between suppliers and buyers, is probably a more objective measurement at the point where the product or service factor is given up than is the amount of the original outlay.

Another factor which suggests that original outlay is not the most desirable measuring device is the fact that businesses operate in an environment where the dollar is not a stable measuring unit. Much has been written and said in support of the contention that inflationary tendencies and their effect on the dollar as a unit of measure have been such as to make the original dollars of outlay a poor measure of product and service factors other than at the time of their acquisition. The committee has recognized this problem as a factor supporting the use of market value as the basis for evaluating product and service factors given up.

Another consideration at this point centers around the ways in which financial reports are used. One of the most important uses of these data is to evaluate the effectiveness of management actions by relating achievements to efforts. Typically, revenue may be related to at least two efforts of management. One of these is the effort to operate effectively in carrying out the production and/or service functions of the business. The other is the effort to occupy an advantageous position in the market. Present methods of financial reporting tend to mingle the results of management's efforts in such a way that neither effort may be evaluated separately. As a result, judgments and decisions made from such reported results are likely to be similarly less precise and less effective in evaluating efforts against achievements.

In the light of these observations the committee proposes that, within the limits of practicality, the *directly related product and service factors* given up be measured in terms of their replacement value at the time they are positively correlated with period revenue. The residual amount resulting from matching these items may be labeled "net margin realized from operations" or designated by some similarly descriptive term. The matching of this amount with the revenues yielded by the sacrifice provides a more meaningful basis for evaluating the effort to operate effectively in carrying out the production and/or service functions of the business.

The committee further proposes that the difference between the replacement value allocated against revenue and the original carrying value of product and service factors given up should be designated within the income statement as "realized gains or losses from market fluctuations and price level changes." This would help interested parties to evaluate the effectiveness of management insofar as its buying efforts were concerned; but more importantly, it would remove from the data pertaining directly to operations those amounts realized simply as a result of market fluctuations.

The committee felt that the report of the 1963 American Accounting Association committee on inventory measurement could be reconciled with the proposed application of the matching concept if original carrying values were retained in the records. This would require the use of valuation accounts to reflect that committee's proposed adjustments to replacement values. Our committee suggests that "holding gains" arising from the revaluation of inventory be treated as unrealized revenue. When realized, revenues could then be divided into "net income from operations" and "gains or losses arising from market fluctuations and price level changes" as discussed in the preceding paragraphs.

APPLICATION TO SPECIFIC PROBLEM AREAS

Certain problem areas were explored in the light of the proposals cited above. The implications of the concept suggesting that costs be measured by the use of replacement values is reasonably obvious. For that reason particular attention was given to changes in present practices suggested by the positive correlation concept.

After Costs

The matching of *"after costs"* (defined as costs expected to be incurred in periods subsequent to the one in which the benefits or accomplishments from them were received) with revenue was the first to be considered. The anticipated costs of providing such previously sold services can be estimated by the use of sound statistical and quantitative procedures based on past experience. In this situation, the positive correlation concept requires that such anticipated costs either be recognized as an addition to the cost of sales at the time of sale or that a portion of the sales price be deferred until the future services are performed. The point of revenue recognition should, therefore, determine which of the two possibilities would be followed. A majority of the committee felt that more realistic periodic net income figures would be reflected if revenues were deferred in amounts which would allow the firm to realize a normal margin over "after costs" in the periods in which the product or service factors are given up.

General and Administrative Expense

General and administrative expenses were examined in the light of the positive correlation concept proposed by the committee. It was generally agreed that some of these items, presently matched with revenue of the period in which they are incurred, may have objectively discernible future benefits associated with them. The committee, therefore, suggests that more attention be given to determining the periods during which the accomplishments of these outlays are expected to be realized. There may be justification for deferral of more than the customary amounts of these items within the positive correlation concept.

Pension Costs

Pension costs were recognized as additional employment costs. Once a contractual obligation has been created, actuarial calculation is recognized as a sound statistical basis for establishing positive correlation with the revenues of present and future periods.

Income Taxes

Application of the positive correlation concept to income taxes requires that they be matched with the revenue responsible for them. Such taxes represent a cost of being allowed to operate within the environment created by the governmental services. Since the amount of taxes is usually determined by the amount of taxable income earned, a direct relationship can be established between such taxes and the revenues reported in the income statement. This seems to require that the appropriate amount of income taxes be matched with the reported revenue. The amount to be recorded in anticipation of taxable income deferred would then be based upon the application of statistical procedures considered appropriate in the light of past experience, supplemented by reasonable judgment as a basis for determining future expectations. Such a line of reasoning would generally call for reflecting a provision for anticipated taxes as an offset against unrealized holding gains. It would also seem to call for the creation of a deferred tax obligation in cases where depreciation for tax purposes is in excess of that allocated against reported income on the basis of the positive correlation concept.

Statements of the Concepts and Standards Research Study Committee—The Matching Concept represent the reasoned judgment of at least two thirds of the committee members and are approved for publication by the director of Research. They are not official pronouncements of the American Accounting Association nor of its Executive Committee.

1964 Concepts and Standards Research Study Committee—The Matching Concept:

W. G. BERG	W. S. MITCHELL
C. H. GRIFFIN	W. J. SCHRADER
PAUL KIRCHER	EMERSON HENKE, *Chairman*

17. ASSET RECOGNITION AND ECONOMIC ATTRIBUTES—THE RELEVANT COSTING APPROACH *

George H. Sorter and Charles T. Horngren †

INTRODUCTION

Some of the most controversial areas in accounting—direct costing, selection of inventory valuation methods, lower of cost or market, capitalization of research, and other nonmanufacturing costs—revolve around a central problem that permeates theory and practice. It is the asset versus expense problem that must be resolved on a most fundamental level before hoping to find answers to specific accounting controversies. In this paper we will (1) define the problem, (2) examine the assumptions that have been made by accountants in dealing with this problem, (3) compare and evaluate the assumptions in detail, and (4) illustrate how our suggested approach —the relevant costing approach—is distinct from other commonly used approaches.

THE PROBLEM

The Central Issue of Expiration

The central problem we must examine is found within the asset-expense dichotomy. If we accept the notion that original acquisitions always represent assets (why acquire expenses?), the central problem narrows to the expiration problem. Should the original asset be carried forward as an asset in some form, or should it be recorded as an expiration (an expense or loss)?

Basic Definitions and Concepts

Before analyzing the expiration problem, we should define a basic term—asset. Although many definitions of assets have been advanced, there seems to be wide acceptance of the concept of assets as service potential:

* From *The Accounting Review* (July, 1962). Reprinted by permission of the American Accounting Association.
† George H. Sorter, Associate Professor of Accounting, Graduate School of Business, University of Chicago; Charles T. Horngren, Professor of Accounting, Graduate School of Business, University of Chicago.

Assets are economic resources devoted to business purposes within a specific accounting entity; they are aggregates of service potential available for or beneficial to expected operations. The significance of some assets may be uniquely related to the objectives of the business entity and will depend upon enterprise continuity.[1]

When assets have "no discernible benefit to future operations" they are expired and "may be classified as 'expense' or 'loss.' "[2]

Working with these basic definitions and with the widely accepted concept of enterprise continuity, accountants have adopted two concepts to deal with the expiration decisions: (1) costs attach and (2) match costs and revenue. Certain qualifying assumptions are needed to make these concepts operational. These qualifying assumptions are basic sources of disagreement among accountants.

Costs Attach. Paton and Littleton have stated:

> . . . It is a basic concept of accounting that costs can be marshaled into new groups that possess real *significance*. It is as if costs had a power of cohesion when *properly* brought into contact.
> . . . Accounting assumes that acquisition costs are mobile and may be reapportioned or regrouped, and that costs reassembled have a natural affinity for each other which identifies them with the group. . . . Some costs, like manufacturing overhead, in which an affinity with a product can be detected, are allocated directly to a product. . . .
> . . . The purpose of reassembling is to trace the *efforts* made to give materials and other components additional utility.[3]

The "costs attach to product" proposition has been widely misinterpreted. For example, accounting literature is peppered with the notion that manufacturing costs somehow cling, adhere, stick, or fuse to the physical product to be sold. Although such picturesque thinking may be helpful for certain purposes, this is a good example of how Paton and Littleton's fundamental ideas can be misinterpreted. As they point out:

> In a broad sense, all costs of factors which contribute to the grand total of objects and conditions making up the economic structure of the enterprise are represented in the physical structure of the enterprise, even though it may not be expedient to assign all of them to specific sections or elements of such physical structure. Accountants have undoubtedly been unduly preoccupied with the view that assets are properly recognizable only in terms of definite units. Accounting is concerned

---

[1] Committee on Concepts and Standards Underlying Corporate Financial Statements, "Accounting and Reporting Standards for Corporate Financial Statements," Rev. 1957, *The Accounting Review* (October, 1957), p. 538.

[2] *Ibid.*, p. 541.

[3] W. A. Paton and A. C. Littleton, *An Introduction to Corporate Accounting Standards* (Madison, Wis.: American Accounting Association, 1940), pp. 13-14. (Emphasis supplied.)

with economic attributes and measurements, not with the physical layout as such.[4]

Matching Costs and Revenue. Paton and Littleton describe the
matching concept as follows:

> Costs are traced carefully from the first acquisition of goods and
> services through various regroupings for the specific object of having
> available at the time of sale of the product information regarding
> *relevant* costs—that is, those costs related to a specific segment of
> revenue because they are *technically* or *economically* associated with the
> corresponding segment of product. . . .
>
> The ideal is to match costs incurred with the effects *attributable* to
> or *significantly related* to such costs.[5]

THE ASSUMPTIONS

Clearly, to make these concepts operational, accountants need
workable assumptions about the italicized portions of the above quotations. When do new groups of cost possess *real significance?* When
are costs *relevant?* What is *proper* contact? How are costs *technically* or *economically* associated with product? How are costs
significantly related? To us, the formulation of convincing answers
to these questions is not at all as clear-cut as many accountants
maintain.

As a point of departure, let us examine and evaluate the assumptions or rules that are usually followed by three groups labeled as
follows: conventional costers, variable costers, and relevant costers.
We have included variable costers because the "direct" costing controversy highlights the fundamental issues. These three groups agree
on the basic concepts just discussed. The question in dispute is which
working assumptions or rules are most likely to result in a *valid*
application of the basic accounting concepts to the realities of our
economic world.

A. Conventional Costing

Conventional accounting has followed a physical interpretation
of attach and match. Two general implicit rules have been adopted,
one negative and one positive:

*Rule (1). If a cost cannot be associated with a physical object
or a contractual right, it cannot be considered as an asset.*[6] This rule

---

[4] *Ibid.,* p. 32. (Emphasis supplied.)
[5] *Ibid.,* p. 15. (Emphasis supplied.)
[6] Accounting for goodwill is an exception to this rule.

leads to current write-off of such costs as research, employee training programs, advertising, sales promotion, and so forth. In general, all selling and administrative expenses are accorded such treatment. Manufacturing costs receive elaborate treatment for asset-expense determination purposes, while the other costs continue to be expensed with little ado.

Rule (2). A cost that is necessary for a class of physical product must be allocated to each member of that class. For example, the cost of a machine is obviously a part of the cost of the *total output* of that machine. It seems obvious that the cost of the machine is "relevant" and "technically or economically associated with" its total output. What is not so obvious, and where the differences arise, is whether this cost must also be relevant for each specific unit of output. By adopting Rule (2), conventional costers have decided that generally what is relevant to the whole must also be relevant to each part.[7]

B. Variable Costing

Proponents of variable costing seem to have either accepted Rule (1) or else remained silent on that point. However, they have adopted a totally different and conflicting Rule (2):

Rule (2). A cost is relevant to (and allocable to) a unit of product if, and only if, the cost varies with the number of units produced.

This rule has been challenged and discussed repeatedly in the profuse antidirect costing literature. It also is too narrow and too shallow to meet head-on the broad issue of asset recognition which must be confronted.

C. Relevant Costing

Under relevant costing, only one basic assumption is needed: *Any cost is carried forward as an asset if, and only if, it has a favorable economic effect on expected future costs or future revenues.*[8] Under relevant costing this rule is completely general; no distinction is made between physical product and economic attributes because *only* the economic attributes are important and governing.

---

[7] Practically, in some instances underutilization of a machine or plant will be recognized as a loss and will not be allocated to inventory.

[8] In a previous article (Horngren and Sorter, " 'Direct' Costing for External Reporting," *The Accounting Review* [January, 1961], pp. 84-93) we advocated this same assumption (pp. 86, 88-89) as a proper criterion for asset valuation. However, our preoccupation with direct costing per se evidently obscured our

A prime task of the accountant is to report financial results in the historical sense. But the asset-expense measurement problem is inextricably linked to future expectations as well as to past performance. Here is where the concept of relevancy appears. To have a bearing on the future, to represent service potential, a given cost must be an index of future economic benefit in the form of a reduction of *total* expected future costs or an addition to *total* expected future revenue in the ordinary course of business.[9] Expressed another way, if the total expected future costs or revenue of an enterprise will be changed favorably because of the presence of a given cost, that cost is relevant to the future and is an asset; if not, that cost is irrelevant and is expired.

In contrast, the conventional view is that future cost recoupment is the general criterion for asset measurement. But our goal, within the limits of historical cost, is to reflect economic realities. Then no cost can represent a future benefit if its absence will not influence the obtaining of future revenues or the incurrence of future costs. For example, if an item can be replaced and used in normal operations at zero incremental explicit or opportunity cost, its presence or its physical amount does not represent service potential; in other words, its absence would have no impact on total future costs or revenues.

---

arguments for relevant costing as a principle distinct from both conventional and direct costing. For example, two recent articles critical of our earlier paper are heavily aimed against variable costing rather than against relevant costing as a concept. Furthermore, we considered future revenue as an important aspect of our relevant costing approach. Yet we apparently failed to make the breadth of our cost concept (it included opportunity cost!) clear because James F. Fremgen ("Variable Costing for External Reporting—A Reconsideration," *The Accounting Review* [January, 1962], pp. 76-77) and Philip E. Fess and William L. Ferrara ("The Period Cost Concept for Income Measurement—Can It Be Defended?" *The Accounting Review* [October, 1961], p. 601) mistakenly asserted that our position confined itself to future outlays and ignored future revenues.

Our colleague, David Green, Jr., uses the coinage "cost obviation" in his discussion of these issues. See his "A Moral to the Direct Costing Controversy?" *Journal of Business* (July, 1960), pp. 218-26.

[9] An expenditure for a machine is an asset because it has impact on future revenue and/or costs. This impact could be quantified in two ways: (a) by the earnings lost if the machine were absent or (b) by the alternative costs that would have to be incurred to produce these earnings if the machine were absent. Thus, the cost of the machine can be viewed as the present value of the revenue attributable to the machine, or, as Canning stated (*Economics of Accountancy* [New York: The Ronald Press Co., 1929], pp. 187-88) as "the present worth of future outlays necessary to obtain like services in like amounts by the best available alternative means." These two concepts would give identical results in a world of perfect knowledge. Ideally, assets should represent present values of future streams of income (future rents, cost savings, net earnings). However, translating this economic notion into meaningful, objective measurements is too difficult, so accountants have used historical costs as a maximum limit of these present values. Working within this historical cost framework, the question becomes one of deciding when costs represent future economic benefit and when they do not.

In sum, the test for asset recognition under relevant costing is quite simple. If a given cost will not influence either *total* future revenue or *total* future costs, it is not an asset. We maintain that this is completely consistent with the attach-match concepts. We cannot see how a "significant relationship," how "relevance" or "economic association," can be said to exist between two attributes (historical cost and future results) if the absence of one will not affect the other.

COMPARISONS OF ASSUMPTIONS

Relevant Costing and Conventional Costing

Emphasis on Economic Benefit Rather than Physical Form. A major weakness in the conventional costing approach to asset recognition is its emphasis on physical form rather than economic substance. The working rules used in applying the concepts described so lucidly by Paton and Littleton have been too concerned for too long with appearances—with physical objects or contractual rights— instead of the underlying fundamental reality of economic benefits.

This preoccupation with physical evidence often results in expensing expenditures that should be capitalized. Thus, expenditures for research, advertising, employee training, and the like are usually expensed, although it seems clear that in an economic sense these expenditures represent future benefit.[10] The difficulty of measuring future benefits is the argument usually advanced for expensing these items. Although the measurement problems are admittedly imposing, predictions as to future benefits are explicitly or implicitly made to warrant these spending decisions. There is some justification for using these predictions as a basis for measuring unexpired costs.

Of course, one ostensible reason for immediate expensing is that any capitalization of these expenditures is arbitrary. But is it not more arbitrary and more erroneous to favor immediate write-offs? By doing so these assets are shown, implicitly if not explicitly, as assets with zero valuation. Is a classification of an expenditure as asset 0 percent and expense 100 percent any less arbitrary than, say, as asset 20 percent and expense 80 percent, or as asset 60 percent and expense 40 percent? Immediate write-off is in fact more arbi-

---

[10] This seems especially obvious in the case of employee training programs. The expensing of these costs implies that they represent no future benefit. This means that training costs benefit the training period, i.e., make the employee a better trainee rather than a more effective employee in the future.

trary and in many cases much further from economic reality than some positive asset figure obtained through the principle of relevant costing.

Another practical reason for immediate expensing is that the resulting effects on net income are undistorted because most non-manufacturing costs are recurring in nature. Besides having no conceptual merit, this argument frequently fails on practical grounds. For example, immediate expensing can seriously distort the reported incomes of growing companies.

The conventional emphasis on physical form also often results in capitalizing costs that should be expensed. For example, consider a paper manufacturing company, a going concern. Assume that Batch A-1 of inventory is carried on the balance sheet at $100,000, consisting of $40,000 of variable production costs and $60,000 of fixed factory overhead. Also assume the following:

1. If Batch A-1 were not on hand, a similar batch, Batch A-2, could be produced next period by utilizing otherwise idle capacity. Therefore, no additional fixed costs would have to be incurred and the total expected incremental cost of Batch A-2 would be the $40,000 of variable production costs.

2. Batches A-1 and A-2 cannot both be sold. The outlook is such that only one batch can be sold.

The conventional approach maintains that the production of physical Batch A-1 results in a valuable asset. The full cost of A-1 is an asset as long as it can be recaptured in the form of future revenue. This asset-expense technique is dependent on a physical rather than an economic identification of Batch A-1 and the forthcoming revenue.

The relevant costing approach would recognize only $40,000 as representing economic benefit. Under the circumstances described, the $60,000 fixed cost is a cost incurrence that cannot qualify as an economic good. If Batch A-1 can be replaced in normal operations at variable cost, its presence or its physical amount represents economic benefit only in the amount of the variable costs that will *not* have to be incurred in the future. In other words, if Batch A-1 were not on hand, $40,000 would be the only future outlay necessary to restore the enterprise to an equivalent *economic* position.

Indeed, we need only ask ourselves, "What is the maximum price that a purchaser of this business would be willing to pay for the inventory?" It seems obvious that he would be willing to pay a maximum equal to the present value of the inventory's expected impact on future cash flows—no more than $40,000 in this instance.

Conventional costers may severely doubt the proposition that Batches A-1 and A-2 cannot both be sold. Then no quarrel exists. If there is a strong probability that the presence of A-1 will really have a favorable impact on *total* future revenue, then the fixed cost relating to A-1 should also be carried forward as an asset measure.

Emphasis on Future. The relevant costers take the position that future sales outlooks, future availability of capacity, and future expected costs have a bearing on asset valuation. Conventional costers, however, maintain that it is irrelevant whether Batch A-2 can be produced next period, whether Batch A-2 can be produced at certain specified costs, whether both A-1 and A-2 can be sold. Assertions such as the following are made frequently:

> Future benefits have nothing to do with the valuation of inventories. Inventories are simply an expression of all costs used up in the process of acquiring revenue which has not yet been recognized.[11]

In other words, even if the suppositions made above concerning A-1 and A-2 were accepted by conventional costers as valid and accurate, the conventional approach would nevertheless treat the full cost of object A-1 as an asset.

Fess and Ferrara also state, "If the service potential has been used in the production of income the recognition of which is delayed, the cost must be delayed. . . . If the service potential has been wasted . . . the cost must be treated as a loss. . . ."[12] The relevant coster agrees with every word in the last quotation. But the relevant coster and the conventional coster do not agree on the meaning of "production of income (revenue)." Fess and Ferrara maintain that production of income is delayed if a physical object is produced now and sold later. The corollary to this position is their assumption that waste of fixed facilities can be avoided by producing objects that can later be sold. To the relevant coster, "production of income" is delayed if, and only if, income is different in the future because of the decision today. He would maintain that "waste of fixed facilities" cannot be avoided merely by physical production. The waste can be avoided only if production today means more revenue or less costs tomorrow. If production today fails to change revenue or costs

---

[11] Fess and Ferrara, *op. cit.*, p. 601.
[12] *Ibid.*, p. 602.

tomorrow, then economically the production is meaningless—regardless of how many units are produced.

Effort and Accomplishment. The attempt to match costs and revenue is said to be an attempt to match "effort" and "accomplishment." The relevant coster maintains that no rational relationship exists between effort and accomplishment if the amount of accomplishment (revenue) is independent of and unaffected by the amount of effort (cost). Proper matching prohibits the linking of costs that have no *economic* effect on future revenues with such revenues. Proper matching calls for the deferral of all costs that have an economic impact on future events. Conceptually, such deferrals should be measured by the present value of the necessary alternative expenditures that would be needed to maintain the projected level of income.

Furthermore, it seems to us that the relevant costing approach makes "value added" operational. Only costs representing scarce resources add value to the product. Utilization of fixed facilities in one period to accumulate inventories does not represent the utilization of "scarce resources" if the fixed facilities will stand idle during the subsequent period.

Comparisons of Asset Measurements. How does the application of relevant costing affect asset measurement for the "average" company? Asset measures will not necessarily be different. Let us make a tabular comparison as illustrated at the top of page 221.

Relevant Costing and Variable Costing

As our analysis in the previous section indicated, the relevant costing approach often will lead to asset and income measurements that coincide with results under the controversial direct costing approach. However, the relevant costing approach to fixed factory overhead is distinct from both the conventional and the direct costing approaches. While conventional costers will say that fixed factory overhead is an asset, and direct costers will say that it is a period cost, the relevant coster will say, "It depends."

For example, let us examine the relevant coster's approach to depreciation on machinery.

If depreciation is most closely related to time expiration (due to obsolescence, supersession, technological change, etc.), it is not an asset unless the utilization of the machine in a particular period will make possible future sales that would otherwise be lost forever.

	Approach to Measuring Unexpired Cost	
	Recoverability	*Relevancy*
Merchandise inventory	√	√ (1)
Prepaid rent, taxes, etc.	√	√ (1)
Patents	√	√ (1)
Fixed assets	√	√ (1)
Inventories carried at market when lower than cost	√	√ (2)
Manufactured goods:		
Direct material (variable)	√	√
Direct labor (variable)	√	√
Variable indirect manufacturing costs	√	√
Fixed indirect manufacturing costs	(3)	(3)
Selling costs	(4)	(4)
Research costs	(4)	(4)

Note: Where check marks are shown, the results of both approaches should generally coincide; but the logic applied in measurement is different.

(1) Merchandise inventory, prepaid rent, patents, and fixed assets all represent valuable rights to future services. These rights are assets because their absence would require new acquisitions of the same kinds of rights in order to sustain operations as a going concern.

(2) In the case of the lower of cost or market inventory method, our maximum cost will be historical dollar outlay. Write-downs are justified where events subsequent to acquisition show an opportunity cost to be lower than historical cost. Unless written down, the historical cost overstates the expected economic benefit. If the cost were reincurred at the balance sheet date, it would be less than the historical cost. Current market quotations on inventory provide an objective means of measurement.

(3) Relevant costing would often lead to expensing more quickly.

(4) Relevant costing would often lead to expensing less quickly.

If depreciation is most closely related to production rather than time, it is properly treated as an asset because the decision to produce a unit in Period 1 rather than in Period 2 affects the service potential of the fixed asset. Each decision of this kind affects the asset's useful life, while in the former case such a decision has no effect on useful life.

In summary, if production today will in no way affect either the number of units to be sold in the future or the cost (including opportunity cost) of those units, the relevant coster would maintain that the depreciation conventionally allocated to such units is not an asset.[13] Of course, in many practical situations, it is nearly impos-

---

[13] This is similar to the Keynesian concept of user cost, which is the expected change in the value of an asset due to use from the beginning to the end of some time span. Myron H. Ross, "Depreciation and User Cost," *The Accounting Review* (July, 1960), pp. 422-28, and J. M. Keynes, *The General Theory of Employment, Interest and Money* (New York: Harcourt, Brace & Company, Inc., 1936), p. 53.

sible to measure with assurance what portion of depreciation is related to time expiration and what portion is related to physical use. The point is that, depending on the circumstances, the evidence of economic realities should dictate the accounting treatment of depreciation.

ILLUSTRATION OF THE RELEVANT COSTING APPROACH

The B. E. Company

The following is the B. E. Company income statement for the year 1961:

Sales (17,000,000 units @ $2.00)		$34,000,000
Cost of goods sold (no opening or closing inventories):		
Variable (17,000,000 units @ $1.00) ..	$17,000,000	
Fixed	8,400,000	25,400,000
Gross margin		$ 8,600,000
Selling and administrative expenses:		
Variable (17,000,000 units @ $.50)	$ 8,500,000	
Fixed	600,000	9,100,000
Net operating loss		$ —500,000

The "normal capacity" per year (based on three- to five-year demand) is 30,000,000 units. Maximum production capacity is 40,000,000 units per year.

The board of directors has approached a competent outside executive to take over the company. He is an optimistic soul, and so he agrees to become president at a token salary; but his contract provides for a year-end bonus amounting to 10 percent of net operating profit (before considering the bonus or income taxes). The annual profit was to be verified by a huge public accounting firm.

The new president, filled with rosy expectations, promptly raised the advertising budget by $3,500,000 and stepped up production to an annual rate of 30,000,000 units. As soon as all outlets had sufficient stock, the advertising campaign was launched, and sales for 1962 increased—but only to a level of 25,000,000 units.

The verified income statement for 1962 contained the data shown at the top of page 223.

The day after the statement was verified, the president resigned to take a job with another corporation having difficulties similar to those that B. E. Company had a year ago. The president remarked, "I enjoy challenges. Now that B. E. Company is in the black, I'd

```
Sales, 25,000,000 × $2.00 ..............                      $50,000,000
Production costs:
  Variable, 30,000,000 × $1.00 ........  $30,000,000
  Fixed ...........................       8,400,000
    Total .......................       $38,400,000
  Inventory, 5,000,000 units, (⅙ of
    $38,400,000) ....................       6,400,000
  Cost of goods sold .................                        32,000,000
Gross margin .......................                         $18,000,000
Selling and administrative expenses:
  Variable ..........................   $12,500,000
  Fixed .............................     4,100,000   16,600,000
Net operating profit ..................                     $ 1,400,000
```

prefer tackling another knotty difficulty." His contract with his new employer is similar to the one he had with B. E. Company.

Let us consider the following questions:

1. As a member of the board, what comments would you make at the next meeting regarding the most recent income statement?

2. Would you change your remarks in (1) if (consider each part independently):

   a) Sales outlook for the coming three years is 20,000,000 units per year?

   b) Sales outlook for the coming three years is 30,000,000 units per year?

   c) Sales outlook for the coming three years is 40,000,000 units per year?

   d) The company is to be liquidated immediately, so that the only sales in 1963 will be the 5,000,000 units still in inventory?

   e) Maximum production capacity is 40,000,000 units per year, and the sales outlook for 1963 is 45,000,000 units?

Analysis of the Illustration

Our analysis should help show how the relevant costing approach differs from both conventional costing and direct costing.

Answer 1. Depending on the business outlook, we would object strenuously to the most recent income statement because the $1,400,000 profit is represented by $1,400,000 share of fixed production costs (5/30 × $8,400,000). The $1,400,000 which was plowed into inventory is an asset only if it represents a future economic benefit in the form of added sales that would otherwise be lost or decreases in future production costs.

Under relevant costing, the $1,400,000 profit could easily be zero because $1,400,000 of fixed production costs might be written off immediately instead of being held back as an asset.

On the other hand, the profit may be some other figure because some of the selling and administrative expenses might properly be capitalized.

Fixed indirect manufacturing costs are unexpired only when the utilization of these costs in production this period will reduce total future costs or enhance total future revenue. When will the latter situation occur? Only if failure to produce now would lead to additional costs (or lost sales) in the future in order to conduct contemplated operations.

What assumptions are necessary to justify treating fixed indirect manufacturing costs as unexpired? (a) Future production must be at maximum capacity with future sales in excess of capacity by the amount of increase in ending inventory; or (b) variable production costs are expected to increase; or (c) future sales will be lost forever because of lack of inventory; [14] that is, the absence of inventory at a certain place at a certain time will result in a permanent loss of certain sales.

Note that this approach to whether fixed indirect manufacturing costs are expired or unexpired may yield answers in favor of treatment as assets in some cases (for example, seasonal businesses, building base stocks of new products) or as expenses in other cases (for example, operations of a seasoned company at less than maximum capacity, increases in inventory stocks because of a slowdown in sales).

Answer 2. (a) (b) (c) No. As long as the sales outlook is 40,000,000 units per year or less, the company can meet its sales needs out of current production. The fixed costs do not represent assets because no future economic benefits are forthcoming unless either Condition (b) or (c) specified in our Answer 1 above is met.

(d) If the fixed costs must continue to be incurred during liquidation, and selling prices remain the same, the answer would be no. If the fixed costs do not continue and the regular selling price can be attained, the answer would be yes.

(e) Yes. If the 5,000,000 units were not held in stock, the future sales would be only 40,000,000 units. Therefore, the case for recognizing $1,400,000 of fixed production costs as an asset is strong because Condition (a) in our Answer (1) is fulfilled.

Further, the case may also be strong for recognizing some advertising and other selling costs as an asset.

---

[14] For an expanded discussion, see Horngren and Sorter, *op. cit.*, pp. 88-90.

Conclusion

The controversial issues in accounting have led us to quest for a workable assumption about asset valuation that will bring convincing and universally applicable answers to the problem of asset expiration. We believe that the relevant costing approach is more likely to result in a *valid* application to accounting practice of the basic accounting concept (enterprise continuity, attach, match). Conventional accounting rules are too often preoccupied with physical form instead of economic substance. In contrast, the relevant costing rule emphasizes the "economic attributes and measurements" with which, according to Paton and Littleton, accounting is primarily concerned. The implementation of relevant costing will often result in expensing certain costs that are conventionally capitalized and capitalizing certain costs that are conventionally expensed.

18. ACCOUNTING THEORY AND
COST ACCOUNTING *

L. J. Benninger †

At the beginning of this century there was no consensus concerning the inclusion of the cost accounts within the framework of the general ledger. There were many who argued that two complete and independent sets of books be kept, one to obtain product and process costs and the other to keep the financial or commercial records of the firm. On the other hand, there were the exponents of integrated cost and financial accounts. Although, as pointed out by Garner, arguments were posed in favor of separate books as late as 1921, the inclusion of the factory accounts with the financial accounts had become generally accepted by 1910.[1] Consequently, as we begin any appraisal of accounting theory relative to cost accounting, we must keep in mind the background of the partnership between the two areas.

Although cost accounting became fully absorbed into the formal accounts, it has, nevertheless, retained over the years something of its original and esoteric nature. Data incorporated in the cost accounts receive a transforming action sometimes not clearly encompassed in guidelines set forth for the practice of financial accounting. Thus, there arises a dilemma of both description and theory formulation. Cost accounting, when well developed, represents a highly specialized segment of the accounts. At the same time, however, its data become an important aspect of many problems facing the general accountant. The cost accounts as an integral portion of the general ledger affect the general purpose statements, and at the same time they are in turn affected by the point of view and interest of the prevailing attitude of the accountant towards accounts in general.

The word "theory" as employed in this paper offers both a stumbling block and an avenue enabling a broad exploration. Kohler

* From *The Accounting Review* (July, 1965). Reprinted by permission of the American Accounting Association.
† L. J. Benninger, Professor of Accounting, University of Florida, Gainesville, Florida.

[1] S. Paul Garner, *Evolution of Cost Accounting to 1925* (University, Ala.: University of Alabama Press, 1954), pp. 255-75.

defines theory as a "set of propositions, including axioms and theorems, which, together with definitions and formal or informal rules of inference, is oriented towards the explanation of a body of *facts* or treatment of a class of concrete or abstract operations." [2] Definitions of the word "theory" in *Webster's New International Dictionary* range from those which state simply two words—"contemplation" and "speculation"—to the use of phrases such as "a general principle, formula, or ideal construction, offered to explain phenomena. . . ." *The Oxford English Dictionary* attempts to explain the word theory by use of phrases such as "a conception or mental scheme," "a systematic statement of rules or principles to be followed," "a scheme or system of ideas or statements held as an explanation or account of a group of facts or phenomena," and "a hypothesis that has been confirmed or established by observation or experiment and is propounded or accepted as accounting for the known facts."

Devine states, "Some writers feel that the term 'theory' is so poorly defined that it must be reconstructed or abandoned." [3] I like the statement that he cites from *Theory and Methods of Scaling* by Torgerson:

> A fact is regarded as an *empirically verifiable observation . . . theory refers to the relationship between facts* or to the ordering of them in some meaningful way. . . . Theory is a tool of science in these ways: (1) it defines the major orientation of a science by defining the kinds of data which are to be abstracted; (2) it offers a conceptual scheme by which the relevant data are systematized, classified, and interrelated; (3) it summarizes facts into (a) empirical generalizations and (b) systems of generalizations; (4) it predicts facts; and (5) it points to gaps in our knowledge. [4]

I like particularly the statement that theory refers to the relationship between facts or to the ordering of them in some meaningful way.

Consequently, I take the point of view that when I use the term "accounting theory formulation" I am referring to the ordering of economic facts or representations of them in some meaningful way. I would argue that this ordering process calls for a range of definitions, classifications, and guiding instructions. Further, since we are

---

[2] Eric Kohler, *A Dictionary for Accountants* (Englewood Cliffs, N.J.: Prentice-Hall, Inc., 1963), p. 493.

[3] Carl Thomas Devine, "Accounting Semantic Difficulties," *Essays in Accounting Theory*, Vol. I (Published in mimeograph form, 1962), p. 122, Footnote 15.

[4] Warren S. Torgerson, *Theory and Methods of Scaling* (New York: John Wiley & Sons, Inc., 1958), p. 4.

dealing with the product of the effort of human beings, economic and other activities undertaken must need be pointed towards some rational end. Accounting and accounting theory formulation are concerned with this problem of recording and portraying human activities seeking a definable goal or goals.

With respect to cost accounting, a paper tiger of some age is that cost accounting deals with accounting data on the level of procedure and, therefore, has little or no theoretical significance. This is in part an inheritance from a period when cost accounting was considered as simply a procedural affair of the lowest level. On the other hand, it also stems from those who would construe theory only in the broadest terms as something far above the level of procedure and rules. It is my contention that whenever there are alternatively acceptable rules or procedures which make for significantly divergent reporting results, this is a matter for which theory formulation should afford a guide. This has been done in various instances in connection with general accounting theory formulation. For example, the accounting literature is replete with discussions relating to revenue recognition and inventory pricing rules. By the same token, it seems proper therefore to question the use of alternative concepts, rules, and procedures specifically identifiable with cost accountancy, particularly those which are intimately tied in with financial reporting.

RECENT THEORY FORMULATIONS

Little of the voluminous writings on accounting theory in recent decades has had specific applicability to the transforming action of cost accounting and its impact upon financial reports. Discussions which might have had relevance to cost accounting often have either been made in such general terms or have been presented along with concepts of such a conflicting nature that their impact upon the solution of cost accounting problems of methodology has been negligible. Statements presented by the major accounting associations as well as those written by individuals on their own are altogether indicative of both the gaps in theory and the gulf which remains between accounting theory in general and the solution of specific cost accounting problems. The 1957 Revision of the American Accounting Association's statement on standards, for example, did give a directive to the effect that manufacturing cost "is the sum of the acquisition costs reasonably traceable to that product . . ." and that "no element of manufacturing costs should be omitted from product." [5] On the other hand, it also posed the loss concept as "expired cost not beneficial to the revenue producing activities of the enterprise." [6] Costs placed in the latter category are not to be capitalized but expensed.

Other statements concerning cost accounting made by persons representing the major accounting associations run along the following lines. Typically, lip service is given to the service potential or benefits basis of asset valuation; however, when writers are faced squarely with the problem, for example, of manufacturing inventory dollar measurement, they hastily take refuge in an "acquisition cost basis or some derivative thereof." [7] Committee statements generally approve of the transforming action of cost accounting, however, that transforming action takes place as well as the subsequent recognition of cost in changed form. Committees typically have argued that an unfruitful transforming action may take place, i.e., that no benefits are apparent from the transforming process, and hence the expired cost is a "loss." Major committees have indicated that cost of product purchased may include invoice and related costs and that cost of goods manufactured must include all elements of manufacturing expense. Accounting associations generally cast a benign eye on standard costs. In fact, it seems that the 1957 Revision of the American Accounting Association's statement on standards inadvertently went to an extreme concerning the use of standard costs, for after posing the following objectives in connection with the measurement of expense:

1. Report in current terms the cost of products and services, transferred to customers during the period;
2. Report in current terms the cost present in inventories at the end of the period;
3. Identify the gains or losses resulting from price change;

it states, "Standard cost methods can accomplish the objectives set forth above, but the results of these procedures typically are adjusted to historical outlay cost in published financial reports." [8]

The American Institute demonstrates its interest regarding standard costs in the following quotation:

---

[5] *Accounting and Reporting Standards for Corporate Financial Statements* (1957 Rev.; Madison, Wis.: American Accounting Association), p. 4.
[6] *Ibid.*, p. 8.
[7] *Ibid.*, p. 4.
[8] *Ibid.*, p. 6.

. . . When standard cost methods of inventory valuation are used, the balances in variance accounts may be used to adjust cost of goods sold if the amounts are immaterial; otherwise they may be allocated between inventories and cost of goods sold.[9]

The Institute committee gives us the dicta, "Selling expenses constitute no part of inventory costs" and "It should also be recognized that the exclusion of all overheads from inventory costs does not constitute an accepted accounting procedure." [10]

Accounting Research Study No. 3, *A Tentative Set of Broad Accounting Principles for Business Enterprise,* represents a refreshing change in approach, though perhaps giving little guidance to the cost accountant. The authors view "the revenue of an enterprise during a period of time" as "a measurement of the exchange value of the products (goods or services) of that enterprise during that period." [11] Were objective means of measurement available, they would like to identify revenue "with the period during which the major economic activities necessary to the creation and disposition of goods and services have been accomplished. . . ." [12] Thus Sprouse and Moonitz seem to indicate that if major marketing activities precede production or delivery, these activities should be recognized as revenue creating in the period of activity. Similarly, production efforts represent a major activity and should likewise give rise to revenue recognition. Finally, the writers of *Accounting Research Study No. 3* state that wealth producing activities may take place following the process of production. With respect to an inventory of metal having a ready market at a known price:

> Accordingly, any inventory of that metal should be measured by its net realizable value (i.e., estimated selling price, less costs to complete and sell) and the revenue from the mining and smelting activity of the current period measured by the net realizable value of the metal produced during the current period.[13]

Where there are no objective means for measuring the contribution of productive efforts to net realizable value, Sprouse and Moonitz would retain the cost basis of inventory valuation. In such instances,

---

[9] Paul Grady, *Inventory of Generally Accepted Accounting Principles,* Accounting Research Study No. 7 (New York: American Institute of Certified Public Accountants, Inc., 1965), p. 102.

[10] *Accounting Research and Terminology Bulletins,* Bulletin No. 43, (Final ed.; New York: American Institute of Certified Public Accountants, 1961), p. 29.

[11] Robert T. Sprouse and Maurice Moonitz, *A Tentative Set of Broad Accounting Principles for Business Enterprise* (New York: The American Institute of Certified Public Accountants, 1962), p. 46.

[12] *Ibid.,* p. 48.

[13] *Loc. cit.*

however, they urge an accounting for inventory in terms of current (replacement) cost with a consequent reporting of gains or losses prior to validation by sale. Their approach to the term "loss" is apparently similar to that presented by the AICPA Committee on Accounting Procedure, for they end their discussion on losses with the statement that their conclusions "seem to be consonant with those of the committee on accounting procedure, at least in broad outline." [14]

Sprouse and Moonitz enumerate types of losses more comprehensively than is usually the case:

> Losses may result from (1) the sale of assets, other than inventory for less than book value; (2) the decline in the current value of inventories; (3) the diminution or elimination of assets other than as the result of use or sale (e.g., as the result of flood, fire, or abandonment); (4) the settlement of liabilities for a consideration in excess of book value (e.g., bonds issued at par, reacquired at a premium); or (5) the involutary incurrence of liabilities (e.g., as the result of a lawsuit).[15]

In one sense, they diminish the cost accounting task; for if it should become possible to recognize revenue on a production basis, then *ipso facto* as costs appear, revenues are recognized. If an objective basis is found for measurement of revenue, then periodic costs need only be dumped into the annual revenue-expense hopper and income will be ascertained. Insofar as financial statements are concerned, the need for a precise tracing of costs to inventories becomes less evident. Arguments concerning absorption costing, direct costing, and normal overhead accounting will, therefore, become inconsequential or less significant. On the other hand, were their recommendations capable of general application, they might on occasion complicate the costing problem. In qualifying the words "realizable values," the authors use such terms as "with known or readily predictable costs of disposal," or "less costs of completion and disposal," and "less costs to complete and sell." [16] Presumably, these costs refer to specific products rather than products in general, and, consequently, it seems an association of these costs must be made with products. What statistical assuredness is required to come within the confines of the word "predictable?" Do the authors envisage an expanded cost accounting for marketing costs by products to enable a forecast of marketing costs yet to be undergone?

---

[14] *Ibid.*, p. 52.
[15] *Ibid.*, p. 51.
[16] *Ibid.*, p. 27.

THREE CURRENT PROBLEM AREAS

The writer is of the opinion that the accountant needs further guidance particularly along the lines of the following three problem areas. Each represents a basic methodology situation in cost accounting which significantly affects the makeup of general financial statements. Alternative procedures used in connection with the first two of these epitomize one of the principal barriers to interperiod and intercompany comparisons cited by the 1957 Revision published by the American Accounting Association. The third problem area, marketing costs, represents an area of neglect.

The problem areas to be discussed are the following:

1. The utility of expressing fixed costs in terms of a particular concept of normal overhead.
2. The utility of the loss concept as applied to cost accumulation and allocation procedures.
3. Whether or not theory formulations concerning product costs should be extended to some of the marketing costs.

In connection with the first two points, some reference will by necessity be made to direct costing.

Normal Overhead Rates

As you know, two major ideas concerning normal overhead accounting have come down to us through the years. One is that we select a numerical measurement of output, which is representative of maximum or practical capacity, and that we divide the annual fixed manufacturing costs by this quantity to obtain a fixed manufacturing cost per unit of output. The reasoning here is clear. Fixed costs over a series of years will provide potential benefits in terms of potential maximum capacity over those years. By means of what is often called a practical capacity rate, a representative cost per unit of activity is constructed. Failure to utilize capacity in any period means that the applicable fixed costs have been wasted, and that a loss due to idleness has occurred. This loss is in the nature of an expired cost and is consequently deducted from periodic revenues. Except for its possible separate identification as a loss, it appears in the income statement like any other expense (and thus is broadly construed by most writers). Practical capacity ordinarily gives a unit fixed overhead cost smaller than that emanating from use of average capacity.

The average capacity method of computing normal overhead rates divides annual fixed costs by a quantity which is thought to be representative of average use of capacity over a period of years or sometimes by a quantity indicative of something called representative activity which will probably be lower than the maximum. The general reasoning is that management obligated itself to incur certain annual fixed costs of manufacturing and did so in the light of its production-sale estimates and that these estimates would for a variety of reasons be less over a period of years than the maximum production obtainable from these facilities. Despite the fact that capacity is not expected to be utilized in full continuously, the reasoning is that cost is at least equal to the discounted value of such usage.

The practical capacity method bolsters, either by intent or by accident, the doctrine of conservatism. An NAA research study reports that the great majority of the companies studied treated year-end overhead variances of any kind as period charges.[17] Shillinglaw, Neuner, and other textbook authors commonly mention as favored practice the closing of overhead variances at the end of the year to cost of goods sold.[18] Such variance disposition is contrary to the AICPA recommendation previously referred to.

It is interesting at this point to note that the practical capacity approach (under a sales basis of revenue recognition), except in years when there is a radical buildup or diminishment of inventory, gives results quite similar to that afforded by direct costing. If the bulk of a particular year's production is sold, whether that output be large or small, under both the theory and the practice of the practical capacity rate, the fixed costs become a period charge. If the proposal suggested by *Accounting Research Study No. 3* concerning a production basis of revenue recognition were commonly adopted in practice, then employment of a practical capacity rate would produce results identical to those achieved by an accounting for fixed costs under direct costing.

The average capacity proponent, on the other hand, follows a management expectations doctrine of value, and argues for an allocation of fixed costs over anticipated production. Because under the theory of average capacity costing the year-end capacity variance is deferred, in theory the use of the average capacity approach should, under conditions of fluctuating annual output, give results quite different from those obtained under practical capacity account-

---

[17] *N.A.A. Research Report Series, No. 13,* "Standard Costs for Inventories," as cited by Robert I. Dickey, *Accountants Cost Handbook* (2d ed.; New York: The Ronald Press Co., 1960), pp. 10-27.

[18] Gordon Shillinglaw, *Cost Accounting* (Homewood, Ill.: Richard D. Irwin, Inc., 1961), p. 71.

ing and direct costing. However, perhaps also as a matter of conservatism, the user of average capacity rates has been reluctant at year-end to defer capacity variances. Consequently, where the bulk of a year's production is sold, the dollar effects of the use of average as contrasted to practical capacity overhead accounting, or even to direct costing, relative to income reporting under any of the suggested bases of revenue recognition, are apt to be negligible. It is only where there are distinct lags between production and sale that the dollar effects upon income from use of one normal overhead method or another or direct costing become significant.

A curious side issue in connection with the use of average capacity (not ordinarily raised) is what should be done under the theory of the method if managerial expectations change with respect to capacity utilization of a given plant over a number of years. Staubus who is a proponent of the practical capacity concept comes into this problem obliquely in discussing the relationship between idle capacity cost and inventories:

> . . . It is the fixed facilities . . . that should be written down below full cost. The plant embodies a bundle of potential services which, based on the forecast of idleness, will expire without having a favorable economic effect on expected future costs or future revenues.[19]

He suggests, therefore, that if the plant is in excess supply, it should be written down.

Returning to the problem of the use of an average capacity rate, if the average use of facilities over time is expected to be 60 percent rather than 70 percent, should this in terms of benefit theory or service expectations affect the carrying cost of plant and facilities or alter the overhead rate? Or, if it becomes evident that benefit expectations are changing from original anticipations of 70 percent to an average of 80 percent, should this information lead to a change in the carrying cost of the plant and/or a change in the overhead rate? My own view on this point with regard to average capacity is similar to that held by Staubus on practical capacity. If the value of a firm is related to expected net receipts and the stream of expected benefits declines from original expectations, management has erred. If the average capacity rate is utilized, and expectations decline, from the point of view of management a loss in value has occurred. If, therefore, our judgments of value are management oriented, then it would seem that a loss should be recognized to the

---

[19] George J. Staubus, "Direct, Relevant or Absorption Costing?" *The Accounting Review* (January, 1963), p. 73.

extent possible. Depending upon the relationship of fixed charges to plant, a writedown is in order; or the fixed cost rate should be increased, or both. If expectations improve materially, it would seem that some type of gain should be recognized.

Let us give the direct coster a moment or two. There has been so much duplication of writing effort on this topic that it has become quite allergenic to me. By 1950, the developing school of direct costers had evolved from a wisp of a breeze into a full-fledged and enervating gust of wind. I do not feel that this is the place to continue the long harrangue over the relative merits of direct and absorption costing. This is the place, however, to point to a basic dichotomy in belief, if not in practice, that direct costing may give drastically different reporting results from average capacity costing, and, under conditions of extensive inventory change, different reporting results from what would be obtained by using practical capacity costing.

Devine has commented sagely that the direct coster operates under the premise either that maximum benefits are rendered by facilities periodically irrespective of periodic use of capacity or that fixed costs represent, as a matter of ascertained truth, costs which are period rather than product related.[20] As he points out, use of direct or full costing ought not to be premised upon vague feelings or doctrinaire assertions, but upon the utility of the resulting presentations. Staubus follows a short discussion concerning practical capacity accounting and closes with the observation: "The direct costing system makes no distinction between productive use of the services embodied in fixed assets and their waste."[21]

The Loss Concept

This last comment by Staubus leads us appropriately into a topic which is not only related to practical capacity overhead accounting and direct costing but has further implications to other cost accounting problems. The loss concept has been adopted within the body of generally accepted accounting principles with little or no study concerning its basic implications to cost accounting. The Paton-Littleton monograph defines loss "as an expiration of cost incurred without compensation or return, in contrast to charges which are absorbed as costs of revenue."[22] The two writers caution discretion in the use of the concept:

---

[20] Carl Thomas Devine, "The Direct Costing Controversy II," *Essays in Accounting Theory* (Mimeograph, 1962), p. 343.

[21] Staubus, *op. cit.*, p. 69.

[22] W. A. Paton and A. C. Littleton, *An Introduction to Corporate Accounting Standards* (Madison, Wis.: American Accounting Association, 1940), p. 93.

It should be recognized that business is not carried on under ideal conditions; the actual circumstances of operations must be faced. Many units of labor services, considered critically, may not be productive. Are the corresponding items of wages to be segregated as losses? Maintenance charges are heavy because "green" men are handling the machines. Is the excess over normal a revenue charge or a loss? [23]

Despite the limitations of the concept, association committees have continued to bring it into their presentations. The Committee on Terminology of the AICPA, in Bulletin No. 4, discussing "Cost, Expense, and Loss," allowed the word "loss" to represent the result of deducting expenses from revenues as well as the excess of the cost of assets over proceeds. The committee stated that when such losses of the latter type "are deducted from revenues, they are expenses in the broad sense of that term." [24]

Accounting and Reporting Standards for Corporate Financial Statements (1957 Revision) defines the term losses within the context of expired costs: "Loss is expired cost not beneficial to the revenue producing activities of the enterprise." Sprouse and Moonitz define losses as "decreases in net assets, other than (a) those resulting from distributions to owners or (b) those resulting from expenses." [25] Their itemization of various types of losses was given earlier in this paper.

If we now add together statements made by persons representing or sponsored by the AAA and the AICPA, we have a comprehension of the word "loss" which indeed covers the waterfront. In connection with his own discussion of varied definitions of loss, Devine recalls Gilman's famous statement: "Accounting does not require an apologist even though it often requires an interpreter." [26]

A Study Group at the University of Illinois examined the loss concept and came to this conclusion concerning its utility:

> It is common in accounting to make a distinction between those revenue charges which actually make a constructive contribution to the appearance of revenues and those which fail to contribute. Thus the cost of material sold is considered to be an expense whereas the cost of assets destroyed by fire is considered a loss. At first such a distinction appears to be a useful one, but its application in accounting has been so inconsistent as to raise serious doubts concerning its validity.[27]

---

[23] *Ibid.*, p. 94.
[24] "Cost, Expense, and Loss," *Accounting Terminology Bulletins*, Bulletin No. 4 (July, 1959), p. 42.
[25] *Op. cit.*, p. 50.
[26] "Loss Recognition," *Accounting Research*, Vol. 6 (October, 1955), p. 312.
[27] A Statement of Basic Accounting Postulates and Principles," Study Group, University of Illinois, R. K. Mautz, Chairman (University of Illinois, 1964).

Despite these perambulations, this paper is less interested in the problem of manifold definitions; it is instead concerned with the fact that, conceptually, accountants utilize some variation of the loss concept in connection with cost accounting problems. Most accountants are familiar with the application of the loss concept to inventories and have carefully considered its effect upon a presentation of assets and a showing of revenue deductions. This is the Paton and Littleton emphasis, and correspondingly this is the stress given by Devine which would permit write-downs, i.e., based on standards of loss recognition.[28] Few accountants have considered the extent and implication of a philosophy of this concept applied to problems beyond the sale, disposal, or evaluation of certain asset categories. The concept, however, extends beyond the asset write-down realm into a variety of cost accounting processes. Its application here has significant effects upon income determination. Let me undertake a few examples.

We have already discussed the case of idle capacity loss. A second instance in cost accounting where we meet the unfruitful expenditure idea is in connection with the interpretation of overhead budget variances in the operation of an actual or a standard cost accounting system. Depending upon the tightness of the budget and the efficiency of management, variances will or will not arise. If the budget is tight, less overhead expense will be capitalized. The overwhelming tendency is to treat debit overhead variances of any kind as revenue reductions. If the budget allows for considerable inefficiency and as a consequence the budget variance is negligible or even favorable, more expense is capitalized.

Both of these instances of the application of the loss concept are expanded in a thoroughgoing system of standard cost accounting. In standard costing, an extremely broad conceptual range exists for the establishment of standards in general, and in the construction of specific standards for materials, types of labor, service department costs, and general overhead. These extend from idealistic standards, stating costs in minimum terms, to lesser standards that anticipate and allow for a variety of inefficiencies. One research study reports a tendency toward "tight" labor cost standards.[29] But even without such a study, the prevalent view that standard costs should be utilized as performance controls, that they should serve as incentives, indi-

---

[28] Devine, "Loss Recognition."
[29] "Standard Costs for Costing Inventories," *N.A.A. Research Report Series*, *No. 13, N.A.A. Bulletin*, Section 2 (June 1, 1948).

cates the nature of standards in use and their proneness to give rise to unfavorable variances.

It has been noted that were a production basis adopted for revenue recognition, productive effort as expressed in dollars would be expensed in the period of revenue recognition. Consequently, the undercapitalization and expense matching problems occasioned by employment of the loss concept in cost accounting processes would largely disappear.

It is my view that if an objective of cost accounting is to improve the process of matching expense against revenue, there is little justification for the exclusion of most costs commonly defined as losses from product costs. The doctrine of managerial *intent* as applied to income determination and asset valuation is not one of wishful thinking nor of motivational incentive. Under the present sales basis of revenue recognition, accountants capitalize cost. In the cost capitalization process there is a presumption of value recognition. Successful organizations over the long run cover their costs. Over the long run, therefore, costs in these firms represent minimum inventory values. To set up unrealistic goals stated in dollars of expense incurrence and then delete from the costing process costs representing a failure to meet these goals is a negation of the idea of the cost principle and its relationship to value accounting.

Although the loss concept has never been clearly posed with reference to financial accounting problems, it has been applied to cost accounting problems interpreted in the sense of cost incurred because of inefficient conditions of production. This application generally has been in the direction of assuming that management will be motivated by stating target costs at a lower level than is currently achieved. Although such an interpretation may be useful as a type of performance control, it is inimical to both the doctrine of management intent and the cost principle and should not be generally employed in connection with revenue-expense matching problems. Where costs are truly high from the point of view of managerial intent, there is a presumption that, for want of ameliorating factors, inclusion of such costs in product costs would distort product cost, i.e., a showing of product value. Such costs could therefore, if desired, be expressed as "losses." Prior to loss recognition in cost accounting, however, there must be a realistic understanding of cost construed in the light of managerial intentions.

Marketing Cost Accounting for Products

Concerning the question of capitalizing marketing costs on a cost accounting basis, *Accounting Research Bulletin No. 43* gives the following guidance:

> As applied to inventories, cost means in principle the sum of the applicable expenditures and charges directly or indirectly incurred in bringing an article to its existing condition and location.[30]

The foregoing is qualified as follows:

> The definition of cost as applied to inventories is understood to mean acquisition and production cost. . . . Selling expenses constitute no part of inventory costs.[31]

Grady, in commenting on *Accounting Research Bulletin No. 43*, presents a more satisfactory statement concerning expenses and costs than is given in the above:

> Expenses are costs which have expired in the process of producing revenue or with the passage of time. The term "cost" here means the sum of the applicable expenditures and charges, directly or indirectly incurred in acquiring a good or service in the condition and location in which it is used or sold. Initially, cost incurrence produces an asset or provides a service, the benefits of which are expected to produce present or future revenue. As the benefits are used up or expire, the portion of the cost applicable to the revenue realized is charged against revenue. The identification and measurement of costs which have expired and matching them against applicable periodic revenue is a primary consideration in accounting.[32]

Two other sentences should be cited from the *Inventory of Generally Accepted Accounting Principles for Business Enterprises*:

> . . . When a cost is incurred the benefits of which may reasonably be expected to be realized over a period in the future, it should be charged against income over such period.[33]
> Substantial uncertainty as to whether benefits may reasonably be expected to be realized in the future are resolved by charging the costs against current revenue. . . .[34]

There are some exceedingly good expressions here, e.g., espousal of a benefit basis of cost allocation and the caution regarding substantial uncertainty. However, with respect to marketing cost accounting,

---

[30] Page 28.
[31] *Ibid.*, pp. 28-29.
[32] Paul Grady, *op. cit.*, pp. 99-100.
[33] *Ibid.*, p. 100 (citing *ARB No. 43*).
[34] *Ibid.*, p. 101 (citing *ARB No. 43*).

the value of these expressions is partly negated by the statement, "Selling expenses constitute no part of inventory costs." [35]

What is meant by "selling expenses"? I cannot find a definition either in the original *Accounting Research Bulletin No. 43* or in *Accounting Research Study No. 7*. Does *selling* mean the same as *marketing* as employed by the National Association of Accountants?

> Broadly defined, marketing includes all activities involved in the flow of goods from production to consumption. "Distribution" is also widely used with the same meaning although some companies limit it to the physical handling of finished goods in storage and transportation. In general, marketing activities consist of finding potential customers, persuading them to buy, and delivering the goods at the place and at the time wanted by the customer.[36]

Marketing costs broadly defined include, therefore, such items of cost as warehousing, packing, shipping, outgoing transportation, advertising, personal promotion, order processing, billing, and accounts receivable credit and collection operations. Are all of the items to be construed as "selling expenses" and, thus, at all times and in all places not a part of inventory costs?

Are storage costs at the manufacturing location, shipping costs to a regional warehouse, receiving and handling costs properly inventoriable? Would the dictum on selling expenses forbid the capitalization of the foregoing costs? Would it prohibit the capitalization of specific promotional expenses undertaken to secure a particular customer's order which is now in process of production? Accounting theory formulation as codified by the *Inventory of Generally Accepted Accounting Principles for Business Enterprises* has given positive theoretical constructs and a negative assertive guide to the cost accounting for marketing costs.

The 1957 AAA statement is even less enlightening on the subject. It ignores marketing costs completely. In its discussion of the cost of a manufactured product, by omission it defines product costs as excluding marketing costs. The Sprouse-Moonitz report with its flexible approach to revenue recognition expressed the value implications of any cost effort and, therefore, allowed for the recognition of value increases due to marketing efforts. In effect it sanctioned the capitalization of marketing costs in those instances where its standards of objectivity were met.

---

[35] *Ibid.*, p. 245 (citing *ARB No. 43*).
[36] "Cost Control for Marketing Operations," *N.A.A. Research Report Series, No. 25, N.A.A. Bulletin* (April, 1954), p. 1255.

The Sprouse-Moonitz report, however, stands out as an exception to statements made by authoritative persons and groups. Presumably, too, its expressions concerning accounting theory were largely countermanded by the publication of the *Inventory of Generally Accepted Accounting Principles for Business Enterprises.* It is the writer's opinion that clarification of the term *selling expense* is in order and that the profession needs to make more explicit its recommendations for an accounting for marketing costs.

Broadly speaking, what apparently is needed in accounting theory formulation is a study leading to a comprehensive and unified statement concerning accounting theory as a whole. Such a statement should integrate a presentation of purposes, a coherent general theory rationale, and guiding standards which would apply to the broad outlines of the accounts. Theory expressions made in this statement must be capable of extension to all accounting processes. Finally, as regards the subject of this paper, steps need to be taken to extend accounting theory formulation to specific problems encountered in the area of cost accounting.

PART III

PROBLEM AREAS OF ACCOUNTING FOR PRODUCT AND PERIOD COSTS

There are many problems which may be encountered in the application of the theory or theories of income determination which were discussed in Part II.

One consideration is the view taken by the public accounting profession as formulated by the American Institute of Certified Public Accountants. The public accountant's concept of costs which are inventoriable not only influences the client's public reporting but may, indirectly, have a strong bearing upon statements for internal purposes.

Many writers stress a dichotomy of costs as product costs and period costs. Product costs may be defined as those which vary with production volume and these may be matched with revenue in the year in which the goods are sold. All others are period costs and lodged against revenue in the current period. This is essentially the direct costing theory, discussion of which has been so extended in the past 15 years. However, the direct costing controversy involves not only issues of income determination but also the development of information for planning and control.

When absorption costing is used, there is a multitude of theoretical and practical problems involved in overhead allocation. All these must be considered in trying to establish a figure for net income.

When the accounting period is the month, instead of the year, the income determination problem is further complicated by monthly variations, for example, vacation pay. In this case, one solution is to use an annualized rate with a base point labor distribution system.

19. INVENTORY PRICING *

Committee on Accounting Procedures, AIA

1. Whenever the operation of a business includes the ownership of a stock of goods, it is necessary for adequate financial accounting purposes that inventories be properly compiled periodically and recorded in the accounts.[1] Such inventories are required both for the statement of financial position and for the periodic measurement of income.

2. This chapter sets forth the general principles applicable to the pricing of inventories of mercantile and manufacturing enterprises. Its conclusions are not directed to or necessarily applicable to non-commercial businesses or to regulated utilities.

STATEMENT 1

The term *inventory* is used herein to designate the aggregate of those items of tangible personal property which (1) are held for sale in the ordinary course of business, (2) are in process of production for such sale, or (3) are to be currently consumed in the production of goods or services to be available for sale.

Discussion

3. The term *inventory* embraces goods awaiting sale (the merchandise of a trading concern and the finished goods of a manufacturer), goods in the course of production (work in process), and goods to be consumed directly or indirectly in production (raw materials and supplies). This definition of inventories excludes long-term assets subject to depreciation accounting, or goods which, when put into use, will be so classified. The fact that a depreciable asset is retired from regular use and held for sale does not indicate that the

---

* Committee on Accounting Procedure of the American Institute of Accountants, *Accounting Research Bulletin No. 43, Restatement and Revision of Accounting Research Bulletins* (New York: American Institute of Accountants, 1953), Chapter 4. Reprinted by permission of the American Institute of Accountants.

[1] Prudent reliance upon perpetual inventory records is not precluded.

item should be classified as part of the inventory. Raw materials and supplies purchased for production may be used or consumed for the construction of long-term assets or other purposes not related to production, but the fact that inventory items representing a small portion of the total may not be absorbed ultimately in the production process does not require separate classification. By trade practice, operating materials and supplies of certain types of companies such as oil producers are usually treated as inventory.

STATEMENT 2

A major objective of accounting for inventories is the proper determination of income through the process of matching appropriate costs against revenues.

Discussion

4. An inventory has financial significance because revenues may be obtained from its sale, or from the sale of the goods or services in whose production it is used. Normally such revenues arise in a continuous repetitive process or cycle of operations by which goods are acquired and sold, and further goods are acquired for additional sales. In accounting for the goods in the inventory at any point of time, the major objective is the matching of appropriate costs against revenues in order that there may be a proper determination of the realized income. Thus, the inventory at any given date is the balance of costs applicable to goods on hand remaining after the matching of absorbed costs with concurrent revenues. This balance is appropriately carried to future periods provided it does not exceed an amount properly chargeable against the revenues expected to be obtained from ultimate disposition of the goods carried forward. In practice, this balance is determined by the process of pricing the articles comprised in the inventory.

STATEMENT 3

The primary basis of accounting for inventories is cost, which has been defined generally as the price paid or consideration given to acquire an asset. As applied to inventories, cost means in principle the sum of the applicable expenditures and charges directly incurred in bringing an article to its existing condition and location.

Discussion

5. In keeping with the principle that accounting is primarily based on cost, there is a presumption that inventories should be stated at cost. The definition of cost as applied to inventories is understood to mean acquisition and production cost,[2] and its determination involves many problems. Although principles for the determination of inventory costs may be easily stated, their application, particularly to such inventory items as work in process and finished goods, is difficult because of the variety of problems encountered in the allocation of costs and charges. For example, under some circumstances, items such as idle facility expense, excessive spoilage, double freight, and rehandling costs may be so abnormal as to require treatment as current period charges rather than as a portion of the inventory cost. Also, general and administrative expenses should be included as period charges, except for the portion of such expenses that may be clearly related to production and thus constitute a part of inventory costs (product charges). Selling expenses constitute no part of inventory costs. It should also be recognized that the exclusion of all overheads from inventory costs does not constitute an accepted accounting procedure. The exercise of judgment in an individual situation involves a consideration of the adequacy of the procedures of the cost accounting system in use, the soundness of the principles thereof, and their consistent application.

STATEMENT 4

Cost for inventory purposes may be determined under any one of several assumptions as to the flow of cost factors (such as first-in first-out, average, and last-in first-out); the major objective in selecting a method should be to choose the one which, under the circumstances, most clearly reflects periodic income.

Discussion

6. The cost to be matched against revenue from a sale may not be the identified cost of the specific item which is sold, especially in cases in which similar goods are purchased at different times and at different prices. While in some lines of business specific lots are clearly identified from the time of purchase through the time of sale

---

[2] In the case of goods which have been written down below cost at the close of a fiscal period, such reduced amount is to be considered the cost for subsequent accounting purposes.

and are costed on this basis, ordinarily the identity of goods is lost between the time of acquisition and the time of sale. In any event, if the materials purchased in various lots are identical and interchangeable, the use of identified cost of the various lots may not produce the most useful financial statements. This fact has resulted in the development of general acceptance of several assumptions with respect to the flow of cost factors (such as *first-in first-out, average,* and *last-in first-out*) to provide practical bases for the measurement of periodic income.[3] In some situations a reversed markup procedure of inventory pricing, such as the retail inventory method, may be both practical and appropriate. The business operations in some cases may be such as to make it desirable to apply one of the acceptable methods of determining cost to one portion of the inventory or components thereof and another of the acceptable methods to other portions of the inventory.

7. Although selection of the method should be made on the basis of the individual circumstances, it is obvious that financial statements will be more useful if uniform methods of inventory pricing are adopted by all companies within a given industry.

STATEMENT 5

A departure from the cost basis of pricing the inventory is required when the utility of the goods is no longer as great as its cost. Where there is evidence that the utility of goods, in their disposal in the ordinary course of business, will be less than cost, whether due to physical deterioration, obsolescence, changes in price levels, or other causes, the difference should be recognized as a loss of the current period. This is generally accomplished by stating such goods at a lower level commonly designated as *market.*

Discussion

8. Although the cost basis ordinarily achieves the objective of a proper matching of costs and revenues, under certain circumstances cost may not be the amount properly chargeable against the revenues of future periods. A departure from cost is required in these circum-

---

[3] Standard costs are acceptable if adjusted at reasonable intervals to reflect current conditions so that at the balance sheet date standard costs reasonably approximate costs computed under one of the recognized bases. In such cases descriptive language should be used which will express this relationship, as, for instance, "approximate costs determined on the first-in first-out basis," or, if it is desired to mention standard costs, "at standard costs, approximating average costs."

stances because cost is satisfactory only if the utility of the goods has not diminished since their acquisition; a loss of utility is to be reflected as a charge against the revenues of the period in which it occurs. Thus, in accounting for inventories, a loss should be recognized whenever the utility of goods is impaired by damage, deterioration, obsolescence, changes in price levels, or other causes. The measurement of such losses is accomplished by applying the rule of pricing inventories at *cost or market, whichever is lower*. This provides a practical means of measuring utility and thereby determining the amount of the loss to be recognized and accounted for in the current period.

STATEMENT 6

As used in the phrase *lower of cost or market* [4] the term *market* means current replacement cost (by purchase or by reproduction, as the case may be) except that:

(1) Market should not exceed the net realizable value (i.e., estimated selling price in the ordinary course of business less reasonably predictable costs of completion and disposal); and

(2) Market should not be less than net realizable value reduced by an allowance for an approximately normal profit margin.

Discussion

9. The rule of *cost or market, whichever is lower* is intended to provide a means of measuring the residual usefulness of an inventory expenditure. The term *market* is, therefore, to be interpreted as indicating utility on the inventory date and may be thought of in terms of the equivalent expenditure which would have to be made in the ordinary course at that date to procure corresponding utility. As a general guide, utility is indicated primarily by the current cost of replacement of the goods as they would be obtained by purchase or reproduction. In applying the rule, however, judgment must always be exercised and no loss should be recognized unless the evidence indicates clearly that a loss has been sustained. There are, therefore, exceptions to such a standard. Replacement or reproduction prices would not be appropriate as a measure of utility when the estimated sales value, reduced by the costs of completion and disposal, is lower,

---

[4] The terms *cost or market, whichever is lower* and *lower of cost or market* are used synonymously in general practice and in this chapter. The committee does not express any preference for either of the two alternatives.

in which case the realizable value so determined more appropriately measures utility. Furthermore, where the evidence indicates that cost will be recovered with an approximately normal profit upon sale in the ordinary course of business, no loss should be recognized even though replacement or reproduction costs are lower. This might be true, for example, in the case of production under firm sales contracts at fixed prices, or when a reasonable volume of future orders is assured at stable selling prices.

10. Because of the many variations of circumstances encountered in inventory pricing, Statement 6 is intended as a guide rather than a literal rule. It should be applied realistically in the light of the objectives expressed in this chapter and with due regard to the form, content, and composition of the inventory. The committee considers, for example, that the retail inventory method, if adequate mark-downs are currently taken, accomplishes the objectives described herein. It also recognizes that, if a business is expected to lose money for a sustained period, the inventory should not be written down to offset a loss inherent in the subsequent operations.

STATEMENT 7

Depending on the character and composition of the inventory, the rule of *cost or market, whichever is lower* may properly be applied either directly to each item or to the total of the inventory (or, in some cases, to the total of the components of each major category). The method should be that which most clearly reflects periodic income.

Discussion

11. The purpose of reducing inventory to *market* is to reflect fairly the income of the period. The most common practice is to apply the *lower of cost or market* rule separately to each item of the inventory. However, if there is only one end product category the cost utility of the total stock—the inventory in its entirety—may have the greatest significance for accounting purposes. Accordingly, the reduction of individual items to *market* may not always lead to the most useful result if the utility of the total inventory to the business is not below its cost. This might be the case if selling prices are not affected by temporary or small fluctuations in current costs of purchase or manufacture. Similarly, where more than one major product or operational category exists, the application of the *cost or market, whichever is lower* rule to the total of the items included in

such major categories may result in the most useful determination of income.

12. When no loss of income is expected to take place as a result of a reduction of cost prices of certain goods because others forming components of the same general categories of finished products have a market equally in excess of cost, such components need not be adjusted to market to the extent that they are in balanced quantities. Thus, in such cases, the rule of *cost or market, whichever is lower* may be applied directly to the totals of the entire inventory, rather than to the individual inventory items, if they enter into the same category of finished product and if they are in balanced quantities, provided the procedure is applied consistently from year to year.

13. To the extent, however, that the stocks of particular materials or components are excessive in relation to others, the more widely recognized procedure of applying the *lower of cost or market* to the individual items constituting the excess should be followed. This would also apply in cases in which the items enter into the production of unrelated products or products having a material variation in the rate of turnover. Unless an effective method of classifying categories is practicable, the rule should be applied to each item in the inventory.

14. When substantial and unusual losses result from the application of this rule it will frequently be desirable to disclose the amount of the loss in the income statement as a charge separately identified from the consumed inventory costs described as *cost of goods sold.*

Statement 8

The basis of stating inventories must be consistently applied and should be disclosed in the financial statements; whenever a significant change is made therein, there should be disclosure of the nature of the change and, if material, the effect on income.

Discussion

15. While the basis of stating inventories does not affect the over-all gain or loss on the ultimate disposition of inventory items, any inconsistency in the selection or employment of a basis may improperly affect the periodic amounts of income or loss. Because of the common use and importance of periodic statements, a procedure adopted for the treatment of inventory items should be consistently applied in order that the results reported may be fairly allocated as between years. A change of such basis may have an important effect

upon the interpretation of the financial statements both before and after that change, and hence, in the event of a change, a full disclosure of its nature and of its effect, if material, upon income should be made.

STATEMENT 9

Only in exceptional cases may inventories properly be stated above cost. For example, precious metals having a fixed monetary value with no substantial cost of marketing may be stated at such monetary value; any other exceptions must be justifiable by inability to determine appropriate approximate costs, immediate marketability at quoted market price, and the characteristic of unit interchangeability. Where goods are stated above cost this fact should be fully disclosed.

Discussion

16. It is generally recognized that income accrues only at the time of sale, and that gains may not be anticipated by reflecting assets at their current sales prices. For certain articles, however, exceptions are permissible. Inventories of gold and silver, when there is an effective government controlled market at a fixed monetary value, are ordinarily reflected at selling prices. A similar treatment is not uncommon for inventories representing agricultural, mineral, and other products, units of which are interchangeable and have an immediate marketability at quoted prices and for which appropriate costs may be difficult to obtain. Where such inventories are stated at sales prices, they should, of course, be reduced by expenditures to be incurred in disposal, and the use of such basis should be fully disclosed in the financial statements.

STATEMENT 10

Accrued net losses on firm purchase commitments for goods for inventory, measured in the same way as are inventory losses, should, if material, be recognized in the accounts and the amounts thereof separately disclosed in the income statement.

Discussion

17. The recognition in a current period of losses arising from the decline in the utility of cost expenditures is equally applicable to similar losses which are expected to arise from firm, uncancelable,

and unhedged commitments for the future purchase of inventory items. The net loss on such commitments should be measured in the same way as are inventory losses and, if material, should be recognized in the accounts and separately disclosed in the income statement. The utility of such commitments is not impaired, and hence there is no loss, when the amounts to be realized from the disposition of the future inventory items are adequately protected by firm sales contracts or when there are other circumstances which reasonably assure continuing sales without price decline.

> *One member of the committee, Mr. Wellington, assented with qualification, and two members, Messrs. Mason and Peloubet, dissented to adoption of Chapter 4.*

Mr. Wellington objects to Footnote 2 to Statement 3. He believes that an exception should be made for goods costed on the *last-in first-out* (LIFO) basis. In the case of goods costed on all bases other than LIFO the reduced amount (market below cost) is cleared from the accounts through the regular accounting entries of the subsequent period, and if the market price rises to or above the original cost there will be an increased profit in the subsequent period. Accounts kept under the LIFO method should also show a similar increased profit in the subsequent period, which will be shown if the LIFO inventory is restored to its original cost. To do otherwise, as required by Footnote 2, is to carry the LIFO inventory, not at the lower of cost or current market, but at the lowest market ever known since the LIFO method was adopted by the company.

Mr. Mason dissents from this chapter because of its acceptance of the inconsistencies inherent in *cost or market, whichever is lower*. In his opinion a drop in selling price below cost is no more of a realized loss than a rise above cost is a realized gain under a consistent criterion of realization.

Mr. Peloubet believes it is ordinarily preferable to carry inventory at not less than recoverable cost, and particularly in the case of manufactured or partially manufactured goods which can be sold only in finished form. He recognizes that application of the *cost or market* valuation basis necessitates the shifting of income from one period to another, but objects to unnecessarily accentuating this shift by the use, even limited as it is in this chapter, of reproduction or replacement cost as *market* when such cost is less than net selling price.

20. DIRECT COSTING AND
PUBLIC REPORTING *

Maurice Moonitz †

On pages 87-88 of *N.A.A. Research Report No. 37,* "Current Application of Direct Costing," a statement is made with reference to the American Institute of Certified Public Accountants' Committee on Accounting Procedure which, we believe, should have some comment and clarification. The statement reads as follows:

> A statement issued in 1947 by the American Institute of Certified Public Accountants' Committee on Accounting Procedure is often cited as an opinion to the effect that direct costing is not an acceptable practice in external income reporting. However, careful reading of the statement does not seem to bear out this impression. Beyond stating that the exclusion of all overheads from inventory costs does not constitute an accepted accounting procedure, the opinion gives no specific indication with respect to what expenditures and charges are considered applicable to inventories. That direct costing was not considered in the statement is not surprising because very few accountants were then acquainted with the technique.
> A substantial proportion of the accountants with whom the question was discussed in the course of this study expressed the opinion that the statement can reasonably be interpreted to include direct costing as an accepted procedure. Moreover, while 17 of the 50 companies participating in the study report to stockholders on a direct costing basis, in none of these cases had auditors given a qualified opinion or taken exception to the practice.

The report refers to and quotes from the statement issued by the American Accounting Association in 1957 and then says:

> Neither of the foregoing committee statements disclose any evidence which was examined or any reasoning which led to the conclusions stated. Consequently, the statements remain as unsupported opinions which offer little guidance to the accountant who seeks to arrive at a judgment of his own as to acceptability of direct costing in reporting to stockholders.

Accounting Research Bulletin No. 29, from which the quotation was obtained, was reconsidered by the committee, and the same

---

* From the *N.A.A. Bulletin* (October, 1961). Reprinted by permission of the National Association of Accountants.

† Maurice Moonitz, when he was Director, Accounting Research, American Institute of Certified Public Accountants, New York City.

language now appears in Paragraph 5 of Chapter 4 of *Accounting Research Bulletin No. 43*, published in 1953. It is also pertinent to note that this paragraph is preceded by "Statement 3" which reads as follows (emphasis supplied) :

> The primary basis of accounting for inventories is cost, which has been defined generally as the price paid or consideration given to acquire an asset. As applied to inventories, cost means in principle the sum of the applicable expenditures and charges *directly or indirectly* incurred in bringing an article to its existing condition and location.

Although the committee did not express its opposition to the use of direct costing in the external financial reports in so many words, there is no doubt but that it did react unfavorably to such a procedure. The minutes of the committee and the clear recollection of staff members who were present at the meetings through the years indicate that the question of direct costing was raised from time to time. That the committee did not express itself at length on the subject is not surprising in view of the small number of instances in which attempts have been made to use this method of inventory costing in the balance sheet, and in the light of the committee's negative attitude toward it.

Mr. Carman G. Blough, writing in the April, 1955, issue of *The Journal of Accountancy,* page 64, said that "by implication" the committee opposed direct costing insofar as it affected the financial statements. This statement of the committee's position was discussed at a meeting of the committee shortly before the publication of the article, and the decision was made to pursue the matter no further.

In my opinion, nothing in the accounting research bulletins issued by the Committee on Accounting Procedure can or should be used to support the use of direct costing in published financial statements.

21. WHAT CAN WE EXPECT OF DIRECT COSTING AS A BASIS FOR INTERNAL AND EXTERNAL REPORTING? *

Herman C. Heiser †

In the spring of 1952 the N.A.C.A. National Committee on Research approved a study to explore the subject of direct costing. While the idea of direct costing is not new and while it has not been generally accepted by management in the past, there appears to be a growing interest in the subject, as evidenced by an increasing number of companies which have or are planning to adopt it as a basis for internal reporting.

With costs rising and, as a result, unit profit margins shrinking, attention is being directed by management toward a better and fuller understanding of cost-volume-profit relationship. The realization of adequate profit return on capital employed will depend to a very large extent on the ability of management to procure greater sales volume and to capably perform its profit planning function. Direct costing, as a method of reporting upon the results of operations, is designed to satisfy the need for a simple presentation of operating results, clearly indicating the cost-volume-profit relationship. This, in all probability, is the underlying reason for the growing interest in direct costing.

The purpose of *Research Series No. 23* on direct costing, issued in April, was largely to summarize articles dealing with the subject, which have been published since 1936, and to relate the experiences and plans of the companies now employing or contemplating the use of direct costing. Since this research study is based upon field interviews with companies which are "sold" on direct costing, it must be expected that emphasis will be found to have been placed upon its advantages. However, the number of companies using direct costing at this time is very small and it must be remembered that, until a large number of companies adopt the principle, it cannot be con-

* From *N.A.C.A. Bulletin*, 1953 Conference Proceedings. Reprinted by permission of the National Association of Cost Accountants.
† Herman C. Heiser, Specialist in Industrial Accounting with the public accounting firm of Lybrand, Ross Bros. & Montgomery.

sidered as being generally accepted. Further research and development is necessary in this field and I should like to discuss some matters pertaining to the evaluation of the prospects for the general acceptance of direct costing. This will have to develop in two fields, the field of internal reporting and the field of external reporting. In the field of internal reporting, which deals primarily with the reports and data prepared and presented for management's use, it will be necessary for management to decide that the use of direct costing produces more useful statements and reports upon operations. The major portion of this paper will bear on this phase. A final section will be directed to the applicability of direct costing to the field of external reporting, which deals primarily with reports designed for use outside the management circle.

EVALUATION OF ACCEPTABILITY OF DIRECT COSTING
FOR INTERNAL REPORTING

The industrial accountant has the responsibility of investigating the advantages and disadvantages of direct costing as applied to his company, to determine whether or not the use of direct costing will furnish management with more useful accounting reports. It should be recognized, of course, that direct costing is not a "cure-all" and that its universal application can no more be expected than the universal application of "lifo," or any other specific costing method.

Absorption Costing Compared with Direct Costing

In connection with our evaluation of direct costing as a basis for internal reporting, let us review for a moment what direct costing is. As pointed out in the *Research Series No. 23,* direct costing is an alternate method to absorption costing. I have prepared a series of three cost flow charts comparing absorption costing with direct costing. These charts make up Exhibit 1 to this paper. They illustrate a simplified income statement under three sets of conditions:

1. Both sales and production at normal volume.
2. Sales at normal volume, production at one-half normal.
3. Sales at one-half normal, production at normal.

These charts show how variable and fixed manufacturing costs flow into inventories and into costs of goods sold. Cost of goods sold is plotted on a bar representing total sales income. In each of the sections of the flow chart, comparison is made of results under absorp-

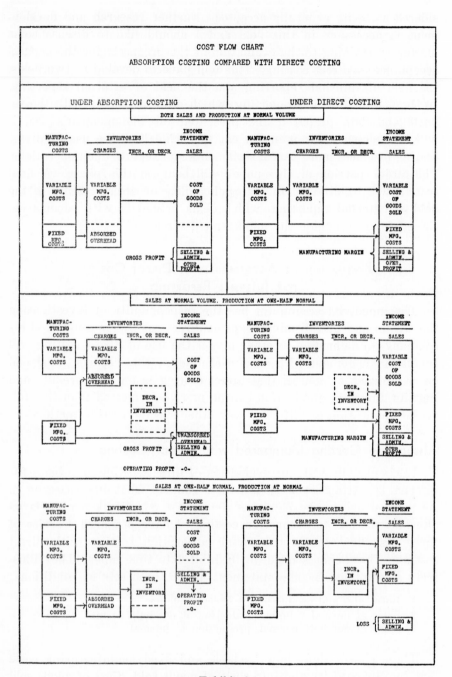

Exhibit 1

tion costing and under direct costing. Under the first set of conditions, operating profits are the same under both methods. **Under the second set of conditions, operating profit is zero under absorption costing and 10 percent of sales under direct costing.** Under the third set of conditions, operating profit is zero under absorption costing and an operating loss of 10 percent of sales results under direct costing.

These charts emphasize the one essential difference between the two costing methods. Absorption costing measures higher profits than direct costing when production is the dominant factor, whereas direct costing measures higher profits than absorption costing when sales are the dominant factor.

Direct Costing and the Break-Even Chart

It is a truism that reports to management should be simple and should conform to management's concept of the operations with which the reports deal. Today, managements generally are fairly well informed concerning the relationship of sales, variable costs, fixed costs, and profits and many managers are quite familiar with the break-even chart, a sample of which is included as Exhibit 2 to this paper. This chart has a vertical scale in thousands of dollars and a horizontal scale showing percent of capacity. Plotted on the chart are three lines:

Line A—Total Sales, Line B—Total Cost, and Line C—Variable Costs.

Consequently, the area from the horizontal axis to Line C represents the variable costs at indicated percentage of capacity. The area between Lines B and C, which are parallel, represents fixed costs which are the same in amount at all levels of capacity. The areas between converging Lines A and B represent losses before the break-even point and profits after the break-even point.

Direct costing adheres to the concept illustrated in the break-even chart, in that it provides the needed marginal income figures to measure the profit value of changes in sales volume in accounting statements received regularly by management. Absorption costing, on the other hand, recognizes the effect of not only sales volume but also of production volume.

Direct Costing in Multiple Department and Product Situations

It is true, of course, that the cost-volume-profit relationships are more complex than illustrated by the simple break-even chart, since

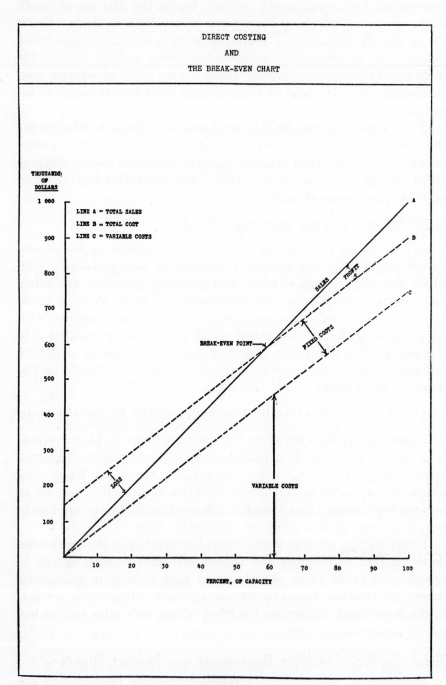

DIRECT COSTING

AND

THE BREAK-EVEN CHART

THOUSANDS
OF
DOLLARS

LINE A = TOTAL SALES
LINE B = TOTAL COST
LINE C = VARIABLE COSTS

SALES FRONT

BREAK-EVEN POINT

FIXED COSTS

LOSS

VARIABLE COSTS

PERCENT. OF CAPACITY

Exhibit 2

almost every company manufactures more than one product in more than one department, shop or plant. Therefore, let us consider the effect of using direct costing in preparing operating statements for a company with several products and departments. Exhibit 3 shows a profit flow chart, under direct costing, for a company with multiple department and product operations. This hypothetical company has two departments, or plants, and manufactures three products (A, B, and C) in Department 1 and two products (D and E) in Department 2.

Illustrated on the chart in the upper section are bars representing the total sales volume of each of the products, on which has been plotted the variable manufacturing costs for each product as a percentage of total sales and the resulting manufacturing margin over variable costs. In the second section of the chart, departmental manufacturing margins have been accumulated, showing the contribution by each product. Each department's manufacturing margin is then charged with departmental fixed costs and the chart shows the remaining plant manufacturing margin. Each department's contribution to the plant manufacturing margin is shown in the lower section of the chart. Against this margin have been charged plant fixed costs, selling and administrative expenses, and the resulting operating profit.

You will note the distinction between departmental fixed costs and plant fixed costs. This illustrates the need of allocation of fixed costs to operating cost centers. Departmental fixed costs are joint costs to all products made in each department. It is perfectly possible, and perhaps likely, that some of the fixed costs are not joint costs and should properly be allocated to products. Consequently, such costs should be shown as a direct charge to products in order to determine the product contribution to departmental manufacturing margin.

Comparative Statements under Direct Costing

The value of the marginal income approach in the preparation of statements for management use can be demonstrated by the use of comparative statements of operations, whether they be comparisons of historical data or comparisons with budgets. Reference to Exhibit 4 discloses comparative income statements under direct costing for two periods. Let us assume that Period A represents the six months ended June 30, 1952, and that Period B represents the six months ended June 30, 1953. It will be noted that the profit has increased

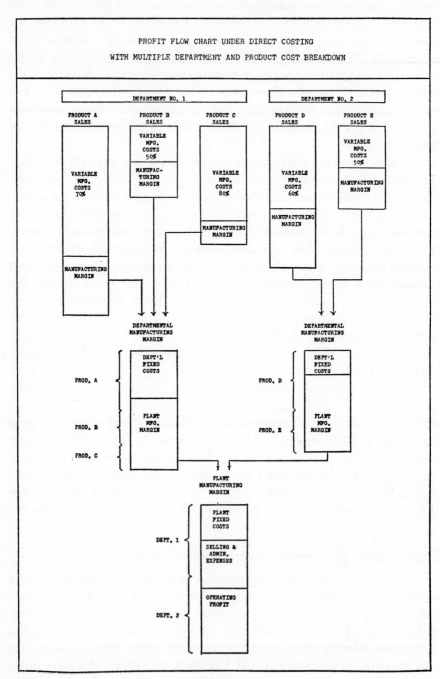

Exhibit 3

COMPARATIVE STATEMENTS OF INCOME

BY DEPARTMENTS AND BY PRODUCTS

UNDER DIRECT COSTING

PERIOD B
IN THOUSANDS OF DOLLARS

	PLANT TOTAL	DEPARTMENT NO. 1				DEPARTMENT NO. 2		
		TOTAL	PRODUCT A	PRODUCT B	PRODUCT C	TOTAL	PRODUCT D	PRODUCT E
Sales	$5 100	$3 200	$1 600	$600	$1 000	$1 900	$1 200	$700
Variable cost of goods sold	3 250	2 200	1 100	300	800	1 050	700	350
Pct. to sales	64%	69%	70%	50%	80%	55%	60%	50%
Departmental mfg. margin	1 850	1 000	$500	$300	$200	850	$500	$350
Departmental fixed costs	600	400				200		
Plant manufacturing margin	1 250	$600				$650		
Plant fixed costs: Manufacturing	300							
Selling & admin.	400							
Operating profit	$550							

PERIOD A
IN THOUSANDS OF DOLLARS

	PLANT TOTAL	DEPARTMENT NO. 1				DEPARTMENT NO. 2		
		TOTAL	PRODUCT A	PRODUCT B	PRODUCT C	TOTAL	PRODUCT D	PRODUCT E
Sales	$3 340	$915	$375	$290	$250	$2 425	$1 625	$800
Variable cost of goods sold	1 895	520	225	145	150	1 375	975	400
Pct. to sales	57%	57%	60%	50%	60%	56%	60%	50%
Departmental mfg. margin	1 445	395	$150	$145	$100	1 050	$650	$400
Departmental fixed costs	600	400				200		
Plant manufacturing margin	845	($5) LOSS				$850		
Plant fixed costs: Manufacturing	300							
Selling & admin.	400							
Operating profit	$145							

Exhibit 4

from $145,000 to $550,000, as a result of an increase in sales volume from $3,340,000 to $5,100,000 and in spite of an increase in variable cost of goods sold from 57 percent to 64 percent.

The comparative statements show quite clearly that the increase in profit is due to a profit contribution of $600,000 by Department No. 1 as compared to a $5,000 loss for the previous period, while Department No. 2 contributed $650,000 as compared to $850,000 for the corresponding period a year ago. Reference to the comparison by products indicates that Products A, B and C have substantially increased their profit contribution, while the contribution by Products D and E has decreased. Further reference to the comparative statements indicates the effect of increased sales of Products A, B and C, which has more than offset the increased percentage of variable costs to sales, and also shows the effect of decreased sales of Products D and E. Time will not permit a complete review of these statements as compared with similar statements prepared under absorption costing, but such a review can be made from the statements and should prove interesting.

Monthly Profits under Direct and under Absorption Costing

As discussed in connection with Exhibit 1, the basic difference between absorption costing and direct costing with regard to reported profits is that absorption costing gives effect to both sales volume and production volume, while direct costing gives effect primarily only to sales volume. Therefore, the selection of one of the two methods will depend on whether management prefers that operating profits follow variations in sales volume or whether they prefer to weight operating results by both sales and production volume. The effect of direct cost on reported operating profits might be considered undesirable by some companies, particularly those which have high peaks of sales volume within the annual cycle.

An illustration of this point appears in Exhibit 5. In the preparation of this graph, we have assumed that the company has highly seasonal sales during midsummer, as indicated by the plotted sales curve. Since it is management's objective to level the activity curve as much as possible for production purposes, we have plotted the production ideally as a straight line. Now let us see how operating profits show under direct costing and under absorption costing. Since direct costing recognizes primarily the effect of sales volume, it will be noticed that the operating profits vary in proportion to sales from

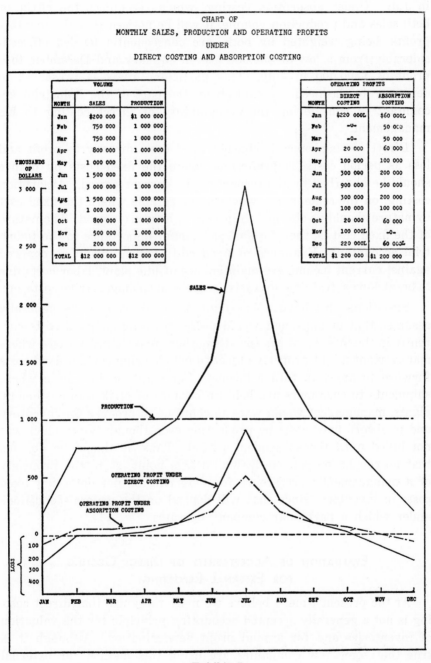

Exhibit 5

a low of $220,000 loss in January and December to a $900,000 profit in July. Under absorption costing, which recognizes the effect of both sales and production volume, it will be noticed that the monthly profits, being weighted by both, are consequently leveled off considerably from a low of $60,000 loss in January and December to a profit of $500,000 in July. This particular study is presented to demonstrate the need for caution on the part of the industrial accountant in considering the acceptability of direct costing to his management.

Direct costing, since it charges fixed costs directly to profit and loss as period costs, is preferable where the fixed costs by nature should be absorbed by the income of the current period. Absorption costing, on the other hand, would be preferable where the fixed cost by nature should be charged to income of a future period. The nature of the fixed cost is, therefore, of paramount importance to the industrial accountant. Examples of fixed costs which should be charged against current income are maintenance of idle plant, labor costs due to breakdowns, training, excessive waste and spoilage, strike costs, etc.

Situations also have a bearing. Although it may be generally assumed that management would prefer to write off fixed costs currently in the interest of conservatism, there may be many cases where management might properly object to not carrying certain fixed costs forward to apply to future income. For example, in a case where shipments to customers are held up because of strikes in customers' plants, management would want to continue to produce for inventory and to absorb fixed costs by production even though the product was not billed until the subsequent period. Thus, it should be obvious that no conclusion can be drawn, at this point, as to the propriety of a management's preference for deferring or not deferring fixed costs in inventory, since that will depend on the general conditions under which a particular company operates.

EVALUATION OF ACCEPTABILITY OF DIRECT COSTING FOR EXTERNAL REPORTING

At the present time, I believe we must recognize that direct costing is not a generally accepted accounting principle for the valuation of inventories and for annual profit determination. Although it is true that some few companies are using this method for external reporting, direct costing will not become an accepted accounting principle until a larger number of companies have adopted it. Acceptance of the method is necessary in four general areas. These, not necessarily in order of importance, are acceptance by:

1. Management.
2. The certifying public accountants.
3. The investing public and the Securities and Exchange Commission.
4. The Treasury Department.

In practically all cases, acceptance in any of these areas is dependent upon acceptance in the others. Management will be reluctant to adopt direct costing if the independent public accountants, the SEC, and the Treasury Department will not accept it. On the other hand, neither the independent public accountants nor the Treasury Department will accept direct costing if only a handful of companies have adopted it. How, then, will the question of acceptability of direct costing for external reporting be resolved? It must not be supposed to be an insoluble problem. It would appear that, if a large number of companies have thoroughly evaluated the usefulness of direct costing and demonstrated its acceptability by its adoption for internal reporting purposes, general acceptance by the public accounting profession, the investing public, and the Treasury Department is quite possible.

What Fixed Costs to Exclude from Inventories?

In connection with the evaluation of the prospects for general acceptance, it must be recognized that there are some all too real practical problems involved, with respect to clearly defining the fixed costs which are to be excluded from inventories. The principal basis for excluding these costs is that they are costs of providing the capacity to produce and that they expire with the passage of time, regardless of the extent to which the facilities are actually utilized. Hence these fixed costs are treated in their entirety as period costs. In view of this interpretation, the industrial accountant must review each item of fixed costs to determine whether, in fact, it does expire with the passage of time.

For example, depreciation includes an allowance for wear and tear and an allowance for normal obsolescence. Although it is true that the allowance for obsolescence may expire with the passage of time, the allowance for wear and tear actually is based on facility use. In other words, the decision to charge off depreciation on a straight line basis for accounting purposes does not automatically classify depreciation as a fixed cost to be excluded from inventory under direct costing.

Another example of the necessity to clearly define fixed costs to be excluded from inventories might involve productive labor. Analysis of direct labor in some companies indicates that there is a goodly sum of direct labor cost which is, in fact, fixed and will not vary with production volume. This is usually true of the highly skilled groups of workers. As a matter of fact, I know of one company employing highly skilled workers, in which the size of the labor force governs production rather than production governing the labor force. Of course, direct costing could not contemplate the exclusion of such labor cost from inventories, even though such cost did not vary with volume. In addition, as is well known, there is increasing agitation on the part of organized labor for a guaranteed annual wage, which would certainly have an influence on the fixed or variable cost characteristics of direct labor.

Squaring Direct Costing with Accepted Valuation Basis

Up to this point, we have been thinking of reported results of operations, when we have mentioned inventories. The effect of direct costing on inventory valuation is likewise important from the balance sheet point of view. The Committee on Accounting Procedure of the American Institute of Accountants, in formulating general principles applicable to the pricing of inventories, stated in its Bulletin No. 29 issued in July, 1947, "As applied to inventories, cost means in principle the sum of the applicable expenditures and charges directly or indirectly incurred in bringing an article to its existing condition and location." Whether or not the principle of direct costing is ultimately accepted will depend to a very large extent on whether the fixed costs to be excluded from inventories can be clearly defined and whether such fixed costs can be considered not to have been incurred in bringing an article to its existing condition and location.

In connection with any discussion of this kind, the question is soon raised, "Well, how much money are we talking about?" The answer to this question depends, of course, on many variable factors. Exhibit 6 accompanying this paper shows a chart of relationship of fixed cost included in inventories to various bases. This chart contains purely hypothetical figures but I believe them to be in reasonable proportion. It may prove quite interesting. It will be noted that the chart assumes a net worth of $20,000,000 and sales of $50,000,000.

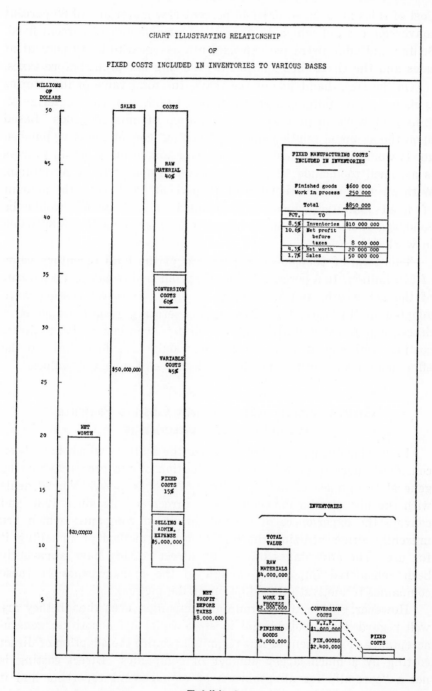

Exhibit 6

Cost of sales is assumed to be 40 percent raw material and 60 percent conversion cost, of which 45 percent is variable and 15 percent fixed. Selling and administrative expenses are assumed to be 10 percent of sales and the chart then shows the resulting net profit before taxes.

On the right-hand side of the chart, the total value of inventories is shown as $10 million, assumed to be $4 million of raw material, $2 million of work in process, and $4 million of finished goods. Based upon the assumed relationship of 60 percent conversion cost, finished goods would include $2,400,000 of conversion costs. Work in process is assumed to include 50 percent of conversion costs or $1 million. With an assumed relationship of 15 percent fixed costs, the amount of fixed manufacturing costs included in inventories would be $850,000, of which $600,000 is included in finished goods and $250,000 in work in process.

This total of $850,000 is 8.5 percent of the total inventory value of $10 million, 10.6 percent of the net profit before taxes, 4.3 percent of the net worth, and 1.7 percent of sales. If direct costing were adopted in this case, the effect upon operating results would be a decrease of $850,000 during only the first year of conversion to direct costing. Subsequent years, of course, would be subject only to the effect upon profits of the increase or decrease of inventory values.

GENERAL ACCEPTANCE OF DIRECT COSTING PRINCIPLE CONTINGENT ON DEVELOPMENTS

In conclusion, we might summarize the matters which have been considered here to pertain to an evaluation of the prospects for the general acceptance of direct costing. *Research Series No. 23* deals with the history and development of direct costing since 1936 and conveys the experiences of a small group of companies which are presently either utilizing the direct costing method or installing it for use. The advantages offered by direct costing have apparently been considered important enough to the managements of these companies to motivate the adoption of the method.

However, such a small group of companies, even though they are well regarded and substantial in size, would not constitute general acceptance. Fulfillment of this term will require the adoption of direct costing by a much larger number of companies. Direct costing is not a "cure-all" for all problems of management reporting and it cannot be expected to replace the absorption costing method satisfactorily serving the needs of most managements at the present time.

However, there is considerable merit to some of the advantages of direct costing, particularly for internal reporting purposes, and it would be desirable if more companies devoted further study as to its application to their reporting problems.

Whether or not direct costing becomes a generally accepted accounting principle will depend not only on its merits but also on the ability of industrial accountants to develop sound accounting practices and procedures for its practical application to the reporting of business results. There are some highly regarded accountants who believe that the principle of direct costing is fundamentally unsound and if that viewpoint is shared by a large segment of industrial management, then the prospects for general acceptance are poor.

On the other hand, in view of the enthusiasm of the companies now using direct costing it would seem likely that a greater number of companies might find it equally desirable. If a large number of companies adopt direct costing for internal reporting purposes, it may be assumed that such wide-scale use would influence the Treasury Department, the certified public accountants, and the investing public to recognize direct costing as one of the acceptable bases of cost accounting and inventory valuation.

I believe that the present is too soon to evaluate the chances that direct costing will, or will not, become an accepted accounting principle.

22. ALTERNATIVES TO
DIRECT COSTING *   Howard Clark Greer †

The vigor and enthusiasm of the current debate on direct costing is unmitigated by the fact that it is not at all clear just what is being debated. The proponents of direct costing describe it in such diverse terms that it is difficult to determine exactly what one is accepting or rejecting in lining up for or against the proposition. Of the contentions advanced by direct cost advocates, some are plainly true and some are extremely doubtful. It is going too far to demand their acceptance on an "all or none" basis.

This paper presents the results of an effort to separate the several elements of the direct cost philosophy and examine them individually for merits and defects, and also to relate them to other cost procedures of longer standing. After such a study of this new philosophy, there is a temptation to suggest that what is good about it is not new and what is new about it is not good. That, however, would be unfair. Several valid and important conclusions have received needed emphasis from the direct costing approach. It has thus served a very useful purpose, whether or not it deserves an all-inclusive acceptance.

DIRECT COSTING—WHAT IS IT?

There seems to be no simple straightforward definition of direct costing. The available descriptions of the procedure are vague and rambling, with the authors by no means precise as to the essentials or the boundaries of the suggested method. The more dubious aspects of the theory are introduced as optional and secondary, but so emphasized as to make them appear fundamental. This is confusing.

However, there appear to be two principal elements in the philoso-

---

* From *N.A.C.A. Bulletin* (March, 1954). Reprinted by permission of the National Association of Cost Accountants.

† Howard Clark Greer, Treasurer of The Chemstrand Corporation, Decatur, Alabama, and Director and Vice President of the Chicago, Indianapolis and Louisville Railway (Monon Route).

phy, one having to do with cost analysis for management control and price comparison purposes, and the other with cost assignment for inventory valuation and profit determination purposes. Some of the recent pronouncements on the subject, though not following any such clear-cut lines, can be separated into these two primary idea groups. For example, the statement of "essential characteristics" quoted with approval in the Association's excellent research study on this sub- ject [1] can be rearranged to emphasize the basic association of ideas, as follows:

COST ANALYSIS

Direct costing should be defined as segregation of manufacturing costs between those which are fixed and those which vary directly with volume. . . . The point to be empha- sized is that direct costing is pri- marily a segregation of expenses and only secondarily a method of inven- tory valuation.

COST ASSIGNMENT

Only the prime costs plus vari- able costs are used to value inventory and cost of sales. The remaining factory expenses are charged off currently to profit and loss. . . . By this approach, full attention can be devoted to the effect which direct costing has on the profit-and-loss statement and supplementary opera- tion reports.

In case you do not understand that, you can proceed through the following paragraph, in which the researchers explain what they think is meant:

. . . The prime objective of the plan is provision of information about cost-volume-profit relationships . . . not a reversion to earlier cost- ing practices which omitted some or all indirect costs from product costs because accountants did not then know how to allocate them or failed to see their importance as product costs.

Direct costing has sometimes been described as a plan for elimi- nating fixed costs from inventories. This description stresses an inci- dental feature. . . . Under direct costing, variability with volume de- termines whether a manufacturing cost should be classified as a product cost or as a period cost.

If this leaves the definition still somewhat obscure, one may turn to the papers on this subject presented at the most recent National Cost Conference [2] which again offer contrasting concepts of the essentials of direct costing in such comments as the following (lan- guage altered slightly for sake of brevity):

---

[1] *N.A.C.A. Research Series No. 23, N.A.C.A. Bulletin* (April, 1953), pp. 1079-80.
[2] *N.A.C.A. Bulletin,* 1953 Conference Proceedings, Section 3 (July, 1953), pp. 1534-35, 1946-47.

Direct costing . . . is designed to satisfy the need for a simple presentation of operating results, clearly indicating the cost-volume-profit relationships . . . adheres to concept of the break-even chart in providing marginal income figures to measure profit value of changes in sales volume.

Basic concept is . . . to make a careful classification or division of expenses between fixed and variable, and then pull all fixed expenses out of product costs and treat them as costs of the period . . . only variable costs will be included in cost of sales . . . difference between cost of sales and sales is marginal contribution to period costs.

Basic Propositions

Mind reading is a hazardous occupation, but it appears that these authors, and others, are advancing two basic propositions which may be stated briefly in the following language:

In the presentation of cost comparisons, the essential distinction, for all purposes, is between expenses considered as variable and expenses considered as fixed.

In the determination of profits and inventory values, only variable expenses may be included in product costs, and all fixed expenses must be treated as period costs.

The validity of these propositions can be better assessed if they are reframed in the form of questions, as follows:

1. Is a simple distinction between apparently variable and supposedly fixed expenses all that is necessary for managerial cost control, pricing policy, operations planning, etc.?
2. Is periodic profit measurement improved by charging all fixed expenses against current sales revenues, regardless of production volume, inventory accumulation, etc.?

The answer to both these questions is obviously no. Cost problems are far from being that simple, as even the most ardent advocate of direct costing would doubtless agree. To clarify the problem, two additional questions may be posed:

3. In pricing, is it essential to distinguish between (a) marginal income contribution (excess of sales revenue over direct out-of-pocket costs) and (b) net income contribution (excess of sales revenue over fully apportioned costs)?
4. In operation, is it essential to distinguish between (a) controllable expenses (those related to the degree of departmental activity and efficiency) and (b) fixed expenses (those resulting from factors and decisions beyond the influence of the departmental supervisor)?

The answer to both of these questions is clearly yes. If that is what the proponents of direct costing are trying to prove, there should be no one to dispute their contention, even if there is nothing strikingly novel about it.

Since the issue has been joined on both grounds, it may be worthwhile to explore the entire field somewhat further, to determine what elaboration of conventional procedures is desirable and how management decisions can be improved through consideration of facts developed by direct cost presentations.

Variable Costs—Variable with What?

Management difficulties in adjusting selling practices to direct cost facts are complicated by accounting difficulties in developing the facts. These arise from the impossibility of making a clear distinction between variable and fixed costs.

Proponents of marginal income calculations, break-even charts, and similar devices, usually start with the convenient assumption that every expenditure, in relation to the volume of output, either varies directly with that volume or is completely independent of it. Grant the assumption and numerous conclusions become easy. Unfortunately for theory, the assumption is manifestly false in most cases.

While certain costs obviously are influenced by volume to a greater extent than others, it is broadly correct to say that over the entire potential volume range (from maximum to zero) almost no costs are precisely uniform per unit of output or per unit of time. At the one extreme, even such supposedly fixed costs as insurance, taxes, and depreciation can be reduced when there are radical reductions in output. At the other extreme, even such direct costs as materials and labor may be larger per unit when volume is down.

This well-understood fact is not itself a bar to the establishment of "variable" and "fixed" as broad classifications of costs, however rough and arbitrary they may be. Within rather narrow ranges of overall volume (e.g., 60-80 percent of capacity) assumptions as to relative variability and fixity can be made without risk of serious error, but, in a large manufacturing operation, there are further complications.

Production on a broad scale entails not merely the conduct of the direct operations of processing the materials into finished products, or parts, but also the performance of numerous auxiliary functions of independent character. For example, there may be power plants, pumping stations, waste disposal units, analytical laboratories, mechanic shops, medical facilities, cafeterias, plant guard forces, firefighting units, etc. There also may be supervisors, personnel men, time study engineers, inspectors, paymasters, and others.

Each of these activities may comprise variable and fixed expenses —variable with the service performed by that unit or fixed in relation to it, but not necessarily bearing a similar relationship to the output of any product item or production center. Informative classification of such costs can become a very intricate and puzzling affair.

Even within a production center, variations in volume have often unpredictable effects on cost incurrence. Discontinue the output of one machine from a battery of ten and supervision cost may be unaffected, but discontinue one whole battery from a group of three and supervision may be cut one third. Volume increase up to the point of maximum single shift output may leave overheads fixed, but the addition of a second shift may suddenly magnify such overheads in a startling manner. Maintenance costs often are higher when volume is down and machinery available for repair.

Thus, even the direct cost of a given activity often cannot be determined unless it is known what other activities are going to be conducted at the same time. Numerous classes of expenses are sometimes fixed and sometimes variable, depending on conditions. When major decisions are to be made, it becomes necessary to make a forecast of results through the entire manufacturing operation, with integrated assumptions as to both the amount and the character of the anticipated output, before a safe conclusion can be reached.

This does not weaken the direct cost argument. It merely broadens its scope and exposes the dangers of oversimplification of either the analyses or the conclusions they suggest. The problem is still one of combining in one enterprise a group of productive activities which in the aggregate will produce the largest possible return on investment. This end is not to be achieved by seeking uniform profit margins over fully apportioned costs, but neither is it to be attained by treating certain cost components as unalterably fixed or undeviatingly variable under all possible manufacturing conditions.

ADEQUATE COST AND EXPENSE CLASSIFICATION

The most important contribution of the direct cost philosophy is its emphasis on more intensive analysis and more effective presentation of product costs and operating expenses. It has been apparent that many cost accountants, in their preoccupation with the assignment of all classes of costs to individual units of output, have failed to give adequate emphasis to the nature of the cost components themselves.

The first step in classification is the selection of suitable primary expense categories. This is sometimes assumed to consist solely of establishing a single "code of accounts," in which analysis is extended merely by establishing further subdivisions of the categories initially selected.

In a large operation, the inadequacies of such procedure are soon apparent. Intelligent managerial study of expense data requires that they be classified not merely according to one characteristic (e.g., expense type), but also according to possibly two or three others (e.g., function, controllability, basis of assignment). There must be, not just a one-way expense analysis, but a two-way or three-way summary, analyzing the various aspects of the outlays made, for the various interpretations requisite to effective management.

A two-way classification, so universally needed that it is fast becoming standard practice, identifies expenses first by type and second by function. Through this device, a distinction can be made between such expense-type groups as materials, labor, security, supplies, outside services, insurance, taxes, and depreciation, and such functional activity subdivisions as production, utilities, maintenance, supervision, etc. Separate recognition of both characteristics prevents either from obscuring the other.

This, however, is only the beginning of an adequate analysis of costs and expenses. As to each activity (cost center), a distinction must be made between direct and apportioned charges, between standard and allowable expense, between fixed current and fixed sunk costs, and between those outlays which are presently controllable at the local level and those which reflect management decisions made at some earlier time or in some higher echelon.

Such analyses give rise to a series of internal cost reports which are vital to intelligent control of activities and evaluation of results, while, at the same time, contributing the elements necessary to a calculation of product costs, stated in whatever terms may be most useful for the management's immediate purposes. A glance at the report for any individual cost center will show the probable cost influence of any additions to (or reductions in) the volume of any product utilizing the facilities of that center and will suggest the advantage or disadvantage of any price decision of either short-range or long-range import.

This supports, but again modifies, the direct costing contention that cost elements must be known when price and profit calculations are made. The important point is that margin contributions must be measured, not simply in their relation to some simple composite cost figure (supposedly comprising only the two elements of direct-variable and overhead fixed expense), but rather in their relationship to an overall production and sales program, and to other similar income contributions obtainable at the same time. It would be convenient if the simpler concept would suffice, but unhappily it often does not, and its indiscriminate acceptance may be more dangerous than constructive.

DIRECT COSTING IN PRICING AND SELECTIVE SELLING

What cost information is needed for pricing purposes? Is a single fully apportioned cost figure sufficient as a guide to sound pricing policy? If not, what additional facts will be most useful to the pricemaker?

It is plain to every manager that any sale which covers the out-of-pocket cost of the goods sold and contributes something toward the general overhead of the business will add to the total profit of the enterprise. It usually is also plain that all products cannot be expected to provide income contributions of exactly equal amounts. Thus the extent of the contribution of each becomes a management fact of major significance.

It follows that the management should be informed of the out-of-pocket cost of each product as distinguished from its fully apportioned cost. This out-of-pocket cost presumably will consist of the expenditures for material and direct labor, which will occur only if this product is made, plus such additional expenditures for manufacturing and selling activities as tend to vary directly with the volume of production and sales.

The importance of isolating and reporting these facts is now well recognized. It has been emphasized in another fine association research study,[3] in one of the author's own previous literary efforts,[4] and in numerous other recent contributions to cost literature.

---

[3] *N.A.C.A. Research Series No. 24, N.A.C.A. Bulletin* (August, 1953), pp. 1671-1729.
[4] *Harvard Business Review* (July, 1952), pp. 33-45.

Does the direct costing technique add substantially to our effectiveness in dealing with this problem? If it brings essential facts to management attention more effectively, yes. If it merely gives bookkeeping expression to a set of already familiar calculations, probably not.

A point which seems to be overlooked by direct costing advocates is that cost-price decisions are made not on the basis of periodic cost summaries, but from individual unit cost data, developed from moment to moment as circumstances require. The desired price is one insuring a full overhead contribution and a liberal profit. If this is not obtainable, what lesser price can be considered? The question must be answered for each item separately, according to its own cost-price-volume characteristics.

It can be taken for granted that any concern which approaches the pricing problem scientifically will have developed a "standard" cost for each product. If the establishment of the standards has been through careful and thorough cost analysis, each unit cost should disclose its components—prime cost, variable expense, fixed overhead, etc. If this has been done, the facts necessary for intelligent pricing are already at hand.

Recasting the general income statement in the same form adds little to management comprehension of price relationships. It is a common error to suppose that analytical data used in making decisions are comparable with post facto summaries of the results of those decisions. The purpose of periodic recapitulations is not to aid in current decisions but rather to "prove out" the validity of the standard cost data used in the day-to-day conduct of the business and thus lay a groundwork for accuracy in such future cost calculations as become necessary.

Selective selling, concentrated on profitable items, can be an important aid to expanded profit. Most product lines contain a variety of items with differing profit potentialities. Identification and promotion of high-margin items is often a vital management function. It is a little naive, however, to suppose that managements deprived of direct cost data have remained in ignorance on this subject.

Most companies, in most industries, are vigorously attempting to develop more business in their more profitable lines, through their more profitable channels, in their more profitable trade areas, etc. They are striving, in other words, to improve the sales pattern, or "mix," to obtain the maximum total profit contribution. They have been long aware, from the conventional cost data furnished to them, or by other means, what pays best. A precise measure of the differences in marginal income contribution is less important than some ingenuity in applying the information already available.

What are the management actions to be taken when analysis discloses that a given item stands high (or low) in profit contribution? If it is a high-margin item, how do you sell more of it? The very availability of a high margin may indicate the difficulty of selling it, the small quantities in which it normally moves, the large expenditure it entails in costs of stocking, solicitation, order filling, delivery, etc. Margins often reflect hidden cost components and, if any such costs are mistakenly treated as "fixed" or "general" overhead, the analysis may lead to the wrong conclusion.

When it comes to dropping or subordinating low-margin items, an even more difficult task presents itself. These unsatisfactory articles may be by-products, companion items, "fill-ins," high-turnover staples, etc. The same is true of customers. Small volume buyers may be adjacent to large ones and thus servable at low incremental cost. Any revenue is welcome from a freight car that would otherwise move empty.

All this is not to decry the value of full exposition of the margin contribution from each item of product and each class of trade, but merely to point out that the whole problem of selective selling is immensely complicated, and not to be quickly solved, even with the best of cost-price analyses.

Writing off Fixed Costs—A Forward or Backward Step?

This brings the inquiry down to the final question of whether profit measurement is improved and management facilitated by treating all fixed expenses as period costs rather than product costs (i.e. charging them in total against revenues from current sales, rather than against revenues from sales of the product manufactured during the period to which the costs relate).

The principal arguments for this procedure seem to be that the benefits of fixed costs expire with the passage of the period to which they relate, and they must therefore be absorbed by the revenues of that period, and that it is simpler and more understandable to treat all fixed expenses as profit reduction items rather than as value creating items.

These contentions again greatly oversimplify the problem. Do all fixed costs in fact relate to periods of time rather than units of output? This is not demonstrable. Charges for insurance, taxes, maintenance, and depreciation are commonly treated as relating to such short-term periods as individual months, but this is largely a matter of convention and convenience. The costs of facilities usage may be as logically apportioned to units of output as to periods of time. Either basis is arbitrary and largely theoretical. Are vacation costs related to the period when the vacation is taken, or to some other period, or to the output of some other period? Answers reflect preference rather than fact.

It seems clear, however, that even if the "period" argument is accepted, it is the *production* of the period rather than the *revenue* of the period that supplies the test of the benefits obtained. Machine rental may relate to a specific time period, but it is hardly arguable that the company has sustained a loss of the amount of the rental because the product made in that period was not sold in that period. Facilities are utilized to create values, not to reduce profits. The values stored up in manufactured goods are sacrificed when the goods are sold, not lost when the goods are produced.

Concededly, it might be simpler merely to write off all fixed charges as incurred and management might readily understand what had been done. Simplicity, however, is not the exclusive or even the major goal of cost analysis. If it were, it would be very simple to write off all costs as incurred, carrying inventories at zero value. Simpler, still, all cash disbursements might be treated as expenses, and all cash receipts as revenues. These seem like logical extensions of a philosophy that charges should be treated as losses whenever it is easier to do it that way.

Would management be helped or strengthened by adoption of the "immediate write-off" theory? It is hard to see why or how. The profit and loss variations which normally accompany the rise and fall of sales volume would be exaggerated by the deduction from revenue of a heavy burden of fixed manufacturing expense, in addition to the normal burden of fixed selling expense. Months of low sales volume would bring criticism from owners, even though a busy factory might presage expanding profits in the near future. There could be pressure for greater sales during unfavorable market conditions, unreasonable optimism during seasonal sales peaks, etc.

Illustrations of supposed improvement in interpretation of results, under direct costing, are unimpressive. Under certain conditions, the emphasis on deficient sales revenue might be constructive, but often it could be merely confusing. A factory which produces in the spring and summer for sale in the fall and winter would show startling losses for six months and illusory profits for the next six, contrary to logic and reason. Facilities usage does not involve a loss if the goods manufactured are worth what they cost, including the fixed charge component. Why tell people it does?

More than Two Alternatives

In the argument for direct costing, that method is often contrasted with what is termed "absorption" costing, with an accompanying inference that the only alternative to charging off the total of period fixed charges is the inclusion of the total of such charges in the cost of the goods produced, with a pro rata share finding its way into inventory valuations.

This, of course, is not the common practice in the handling of fixed charges, under conventional cost procedure. Most manufacturers employ something in the nature of standard or other predetermined unit costs for inventory valuation purposes, and such unit costs include not more than a "normal" fixed charge component, based on production at some selected level (maximum, average, expectable, budgeted, or what have you). Costs are "absorbed" in inventory values only to that extent.

When production is less than the amount on which the standard cost is based, some portion of fixed overhead expense remains "unabsorbed," and thus is charged off to profit and loss as a production variance. To this extent, conventional procedure parallels the direct costing approach, the difference being that conventionally the profit and loss charge represents only the amount of fixed cost not assignable to production, while, under direct costing, the profit and loss charge would include all fixed charges, whether production was at maximum or at zero.

The choice then lies among three alternatives rather than two, as follows:

1. Write off all fixed charges (direct costing).
2. Include all fixed charges in product cost (absorption costing).
3. Include normal fixed charges in product cost and write off any excess due to subnormal production (standard costing).

It is difficult to discover either theoretical or practical considerations which make the first of these procedures preferable to the third.

Apologists for the direct costing approach concede that the exclusion of fixed overhead from inventory costs is not yet an "accepted method of accounting," and with good reason. They have injected an occasional suggestion that such exclusion was unwarranted when it occurred because the accountant once did not know any better but that it may be appropriate now that he has thought up a more elaborate defense of his action in valuing inventories at prime cost plus "variable" expense.

Perhaps this is intended to be humorous. It is doubtful that a method esteemed wrong when adopted for one purpose can become right when adopted for another. Auditors have trouble enough with objective measurements. They can hardly be expected to certify to the mental state or intellectual attainments of the fellow who did the figuring. The question is whether the procedure contributes to a better understanding of results and more constructive management decisions. Direct cost inventory valuation seems unlikely to do so.

ALTERNATIVES TO DIRECT COSTING

Alternatives to direct costing as commonly defined may be stated as follows:

1. Emphasize the marginal income contribution of any present or prospective piece of business, at any proposed selling price, by calculating the excess of the additional costs it will entail.
2. Maintain the data required for such calculations in the form of detailed reports, by cost centers, designed to facilitate the quick computation of changes in total costs which will result from any major change in the production and sales pattern.
3. Classify expenses as to type and function, for all activities, so that the relative fixity or variability of each can be determined for any prospective operating condition or volume level, for each cost center affected.
4. Retain the orthodox practice of absorbing in product costs and inventory values only such fixed charge component as is reasonably related to the facility utilization reflected in actual manufacturing operations for the period in question.

With these modifications, the direct costing philosophy can make an important contribution to better management, while retaining the advantages of presently accepted methods of inventory valuation and profit determination.

23. DIRECT COSTING
AND THE LAW *   R. W. Hirschman †

The fact that direct costing is an interesting and controversial topic is apparent. Numerous articles on the subject [1] have appeared in print since the term *direct costing* was first used in 1936.[2] And the debates continue to go on!

Advocates of direct costing maintain that it simplifies the interpretation of financial results and that it is particularly useful for profit planning, pricing decisions, and cost control. Opponents do not generally deny that the system has advantages; they are more concerned with its application to external reporting.[3]

The purpose of this article is not to discuss the arguments for or against the use of direct costing. It is instead to focus attention on some of the legal implications a company should keep in mind with respect to taxation, securities regulation, and antitrust and other legislation if it is considering the use of direct costing as an all-purpose accounting technique.

DEFINITIONS

A *direct cost,* as defined in *A Dictionary for Accountants,* is "the cost of any good or service that contributes to and is readily ascribable to the product or service output of the organization by which it is incurred, any other cost incurred by the organization being regarded as a fixed or period cost." [4] *Direct costing,* as defined, is "the doc-

---

* From *The Accounting Review* (January, 1965). Reprinted by permission of the American Accounting Association.
† R. W. Hirschman, Controller-Europe for IMS, Inc., New York City.

[1] See bibliography of more than 50 articles contained in Cecil Gillespie's *Standard and Direct Costing* (Englewood Cliffs, N.J.: Prentice-Hall, Inc., 1962), pp. 141-43.
[2] In Jonathan N. Harris's "What Did We Earn Last Month?" *N.A.C.A. Bulletin* (January, 1936), pp. 501-57.
[3] James M. Fremgren, "The Direct Costing Controversy—An Identification of Issues," *The Accounting Review* (January, 1964), p. 43.
[4] Eric L. Kohler, *A Dictionary for Accountants,* (2d ed.; Englewood Cliffs, N.J.: Prentice-Hall, Inc., 1961), p. 178.

trine that *direct cost* is the basis of valuing output." [5] Its counterpart is *absorption costing,* an accounting plan that requires each product unit to bear its proportionate share of the fixed manufacturing costs [6] calculated on either a full or modified basis.

As pointed out in the most recent NAA Research Report on direct costing, "Costs are not inherently direct or period in nature, but acquire these characteristics as the result of managerial decisions with respect to organization and control of cost factors." [7] Wages, for example, are usually considered to be product costs, but in several companies they are classified as period costs because it is company policy to maintain a steady labor force.[8]

Many recent articles suggest that a more appropriate term than direct costing would be *variable costing.*[9] In this paper the term *direct costing* will be used throughout to mean the inventory costing method which relates only variable production costs to a product.

Taxation and Accounting Practice

Federal income tax reporting is by far the most important in the area of taxation. It establishes the landmarks for tax acceptability since many other taxing bodies tailor practices to fit the federal pattern.[10] Let us look, therefore, at the Internal Revenue Code of 1954. In the Code it is stated that the inventory shall be taken on a basis "conforming as nearly as may be to the best accounting practice in the trade or business and as most clearly reflecting the income." [11]

Reference should also be made to a definition which has been included in tax regulations in almost identical form since those issued under the Revenue Act of 1918: [12]

> In the case of merchandise produced by the taxpayer since the beginning of the taxable year, cost means (1) the cost of raw materials and supplies entering into or consumed in connection with the product, (2) expenditures for direct labor, and (3) *indirect expenses incident to and*

[5] *Ibid.*
[6] *Ibid.,* p. 179.
[7] "Current Application of Direct Costing," *N.A.A. Research Report Series No. 37* (New York: National Association of Accountants, 1961), p. 11.
[8] *Ibid.*
[9] See, for example, Charles T. Horngren and George H. Sorter's " 'Direct' Costing for External Reporting," *The Accounting Review* (January, 1961), p. 84.
[10] Frank L. Traver, "Direct Costing Has Been Allowed for Tax Purposes but Caution in Making Shift Is Urged," *The Journal of Taxation* (November, 1961), p. 200.
[11] IRC Sec. 471.
[12] T. M. Kupfer, "The Tax Status of the Direct Costing Method," *N.A.C.A. Bulletin* (April, 1955), p. 1042.

necessary for the production of the particular article, including in such indirect expenses a reasonable proportion of management expenses, but not including any cost of selling or return on capital, whether by way of interest or profit.[13]

Accounting Practice

In considering the first requirement of the Code mentioned above, the question arises as to what constitutes the best accounting practice, and one can look to the expressed opinions of professional accounting groups such as the American Institute of Certified Public Accountants and the American Accounting Association.[14]

The Committee on Accounting Procedure of the AICPA has stated that "the exclusion of all overheads from inventory costs does not constitute an accepted accounting procedure." [15] The Committee also specifies that a portion of general and administrative expenses clearly related to production should constitute a part of inventory costs.[16]

The AICPA statement was originally issued in 1947 and does not use the term *direct costing*; however, this is not surprising in view of the fact that probably few accountants were acquainted with this method at that time.[17] Although there is much disagreement on this point, the writer does not believe one can interpret the Committee's pronouncement in such a way that direct costing can be considered an accepted and approved procedure.

The AAA maintains that "the cost of a manufactured product is the sum of the acquisition costs reasonably traceable to that product and should include both direct and indirect factors. *The omission of any one element of manufacturing cost is not acceptable.*" [18] There is no question about the Association's stand on direct costing.

James M. Fremgen, in an interesting examination of the issues surrounding the present controversy over direct costing, discusses the possibility that direct costing might become accepted as a technique of inventory measurement in external reporting. He believes that there would be nothing unique about there being two acceptable,

---

[13] Regulations Section 1.471-3. Emphasis supplied.
[14] Reference is not made to the National Association of Accountants because this organization does not issue judgments on accounting practices.
[15] *Accounting Research and Terminology Bulletins* (Final ed.; New York: American Institute of Certified Public Accountants, 1961), p. 29.
[16] *Ibid.*
[17] National Association of Accountants, *op. cit.*, p. 88.
[18] Executive Committee of the American Accounting Association, *Accounting and Reporting Standards for Corporate Financial Statements and Preceding Statements and Supplements* (Madison, Wis.: American Accounting Association, 1957), p. 4. Emphasis supplied.

but different, methods of measurement—particularly where inventories are concerned.[19] He refers to another proposal being given much attention in current accounting literature, that is the one suggested by Sprouse and Moonitz for valuating inventories at net realizable value.[20]

Although the AICPA and the AAA may disapprove—tacitly or otherwise—of direct costing, there are companies which use this method of valuation for both internal and external reporting. The National Association of Accountants reported that 17 of the 50 companies participating in a research study report used direct costing in preparing financial statements for stockholders. In none of these cases had auditors given a qualified opinion or taken exception to the practice.[21] Apparently the CPA's performing the examination believe that the use of direct costing results in financial statements which present fairly both the financial positions of their clients as well as the results of operations for the periods under review.

Tax Rulings

One example where direct costing has been used both internally and externally is The Kaar Engineering Company of Palo Alto, California, which has always valued its inventory at direct cost on a first-in, first-out basis.[22] In this case, the Internal Revenue authorities accepted the company's calculations, their decision being based not on the valuation method used but, instead, on the doctrine of consistency.[23]

The applicable tax regulations state that:

> . . . In order clearly to reflect income, the inventory practice of a taxpayer should be consistent from year to year, and greater weight is to be given to consistency than to any particular method of inventorying or basis of valuation so long as the method used is substantially in accord with Regulations 1.471-1 to 1.471-9. An inventory that can be used under the best accounting practice in a balance sheet showing the financial position of the taxpayer can, as a general rule, be regarded as clearly reflecting his income.[24]

[19] James M. Fremgen, *op. cit.*, p. 51.
[20] Robert T. Sprouse and Maurice Moonitz, *A Tentative Set of Broad Accounting Principles for Business Enterprises* (New York: American Institute of Certified Public Accountants, 1962), p. 20.
[21] National Association of Accountants, *op. cit.*, p. 88.
[22] Oswald Nielsen, "How Direct Costing Works Internally and Externally for a Small Manufacturer," *The Journal of Accountancy* (August, 1953), pp. 197-205.
[23] Oswald Nielsen, "Tax Court May Not Reflect Best Accounting Practice," *The Journal of Accountancy* (December, 1953), p. 672.
[24] Regulation Section 1.471-2.

In the writer's opinion it does not automatically follow that the "best" inventory valuation results in a "clear" reflection of income. The Court has stressed, incidentally, that the Kaar case should *not* serve as a precedent.

A second example of a company using direct costing for all external reporting is the Geometric Stamping Co.,[25] a clear-cut case of a company which changed to direct costing without requesting permission in advance.[26] The favorable decision in this case was also reached primarily on the basis of the consistency doctrine. There was no contest as to the propriety of the direct costing method as such.

A clear reflection of income, as mentioned earlier, is the second of the two requirements prescribed by the Internal Revenue Code. It is true that direct costing methods have been successfully used by some companies for tax purposes on the grounds that in such situations they have reflected income *better* than conventional costing systems that add all overhead costs to inventory. *Better* has been described as being "more understandable and meaningful." [27]   In assessing the validity of this interpretation, however, and in defining *clear reflection of income,* one must revert to the pros and cons of the main argument.

Not all companies have been as successful as **Kaar** and **Geometric** in their reporting, for example the Wikstrom Company [28] which had valued part of its inventory under the direct cost principle used by The Kaar Company.[29] As described in the Court's statement of facts, inventories included "only direct labor and material charges attributable to specific contracts as costs of production. All other expenses were treated as general expenses in the year incurred, deductible as operating expenses of that year." The company's overhead expenses consisted of officers' salaries, rent, taxes, depreciation, repairs, light, heat and power, insurance, employees' welfare, factory stores, indirect factory labor, vacation, holiday and bonus pay, freight inward, and "miscellaneous." In this case the Commissioner refused to allow this method of inventory valuation even though the method had been consistently used by the taxpayer since incorporation.

---

[25] *Geometric Stamping Co.,* 26 TC 301, 1958.
[26] Frank L. Traver, *op. cit.,* p. 263
[27] *Ibid.,* p. 260.
[28] *Frank G. Wikstrom & Sons, Inc.,* 20 TC 45, 1953.
[29] Sidney J. Fenton, "Tax Court Decision Seems to Disallow Direct Cost Valuation of Inventories," *The Journal of Accountancy* (December, 1953), pp. 670-72.

One might argue that the Wikstrom case is an example of a company using *prime costing* rather than *direct costing* inasmuch as *all* overheads were excluded; nevertheless, one must conclude that the acceptability of using direct costing for tax reporting has not been decided by the courts. As one observer has pointed out, "The odds are against the company changing from absorption to direct costing."[30]

SECURITIES REGULATIONS

Let us now discuss securities regulations as they might relate to direct costing. Although the Securities and Exchange Commission has the authority to prescribe its own accounting principles, it has not done so except in a few selected instances. For the most part the SEC has been content to rely on generally accepted accounting principles.[31]

As indicated earlier, the consistent use of direct costing may have the approval of the tax authorities. But tax accounting, as is often pointed out, is not necessarily good accounting!

A company filing statements with the SEC must correct its statements if a particular item is "material." It does not suffice merely to disclose in the prospectus that overhead, for example, has been omitted, if the omission is wrong in principle. It is a fundamental rule in SEC work that disclosure of an improper accounting practice will not obviate the need for correcting the statement.[32]

The Chief Accountant of the SEC, Andrew Barr, in discussing the fact that financial statements prepared on a tax basis are often included in registration statements, stated that one of the recurring subjects for debate is that all overhead, and sometimes even direct labor, may be omitted from inventory.[33]

Louis H. Rappaport, in his book *SEC Accounting Practices and Procedure*, states that:

> Sometimes the omission of overhead from inventory does not have a material effect either on the financial position or on the results of operations during the period under report. In that case the SEC has accepted registration statements containing financial statements which disclosed the facts and stated that the statements had not been adjusted.[34]

---

[30] Frank L. Traver, *op. cit.*, p. 264.
[31] Louis H. Rappaport, *SEC Accounting Practice and Procedure* (2d ed.; New York: The Ronald Press Company, 1963), pp. 3.1-3.2.
[32] *Ibid.*, p. 9.3. Also see *SEC Accounting Series Release No. 4* (1938).
[33] Andrew Barr, "Current Practice with the SEC; Duties and Responsibilities of the CPA," address before California Society of CPA's, June 26, 1961.
[34] Louis H. Rappaport, *op. cit.*, p. 21.20.

In an article cited in the preceding section of this paper, reference was made to a company which had applied for and received permission to use direct costing for tax reports.[35] This company, whose name was not given, subsequently adopted direct costing for all external reporting, including SEC filings.

The writer has been unable to determine if there are many similar filings but believes they would be few in number. Reports of companies which have been prepared with an omission of manufacturing costs from inventory calculations would be subject to close scrutiny by the SEC in its determination of material effect.[36]

Rappaport also refers to Rule 2-02(c)(iii) of Regulation S-X which requires the accountant to state in his certificate the nature of any material differences between the accounting principles and practices reflected in the financial statements and those reflected in the accounts and his opinion as to such differences. He writes that:

> One of the most frequent causes of adjustment is the omission of overhead from inventories. Although they are willing to prepare their financial statements to meet the requirements of their CPA's and the SEC, these companies are often not willing to enter the adjusted inventories in the records for fear that this would subject them to tax on the increased value of the inventories.[37]

In a typical case, a company disclosed in its prospectus the adjustment of its inventories as follows:

> For many years, in computing cost of goods sold, the company has consistently stated inventories at the lower of (1) cost (first-in, first-out) of raw materials plus direct labor without addition of any manufacturing overhead cost, or (2) market. Total inventories on this basis as recorded in the accounts have been retroactively adjusted to reflect the addition of manufacturing overhead cost, less related tax effect, which adjustment has not been reflected in the books and records of the company.[38]

SEC regulations, like tax regulations, fail to state whether or not direct costing is acceptable. It would appear, however, that a company using direct costing might be able to omit fixed cost allocations from its inventory only if such omission did not materially affect the financial position or the results of operations and provided that

---

[35] Frank L. Traver, *op. cit.*, p. 261.
[36] In a letter dated June 15, 1964, Andrew Barr, SEC Chief Accountant, stated, "We have not accepted financial statements from which all overhead is omitted in the valuation of inventories if we are aware of such practice and its effect on net income is material.
[37] Louis H. Rappaport, *op. cit.*, p. 21.20.
[38] *Ibid.*

proper disclosure was made. It seems doubtful, however, that many companies could meet such provisions.

ANTITRUST LEGISLATION

Many companies may not be concerned with antitrust legislation, particularly if they are not engaged in interstate commerce, but it might be well to review antitrust laws to see how they relate to costs.

Antitrust laws have been enacted to protect and encourage competition. The first of these, the Sherman Antitrust Act, 1890, declared contracts, combinations and conspiracies in restraint of trade to be illegal, and an attempt to monopolize to be a misdemeanor. The Federal Trade Commission Act, 1914, provided for the creation of the Commission as an administrative and quasi-judicial agency and declared illegal unfair methods of competition and unfair or deceptive acts or practices in commerce. The Clayton Act, 1914, contained provisions dealing with a wide variety of trade matters, including price discrimination, tying arrangements, exclusive dealing, and acquisitions and mergers.[39]

The Robinson-Patman Act was passed in 1936 in order to strengthen the provision of the Clayton Act pertaining to price discrimination. Its purpose, as stated in the preamble to the Bill when it was introduced in Congress, was:

> To make it unlawful for any person engaged in commerce to discriminate in price or terms of sale between purchasers of commodities of like grade and quality; to prohibit the payment of brokerage or commission under certain conditions, to suppress pseudoadvertising allowances; to provide a presumptive measure of damages in certain cases; and to protect the independent merchant, the public whom he serves, and the manufacturer from whom he buys, from exploitation by unfair competitors.[40]

Jerrold Van Cise, a member of the New York Bar, has concluded from a review of the Act that three negative and three affirmative issues must be resolved before one can determine whether an alleged discrimination is in violation of the Act.[41] First, it must be determined if any one of the three facts essential to establish an unlawful discrimination is *not* present. These are:

---

[39] Otto F. Taylor, "Cost Accounting under the Robinson-Patman Act," *The New York Certified Public Accountant* (June, 1957), pp. 386-94.
[40] Wright Patman, *The Robinson-Patman Act* (New York: The Ronald Press Company, 1938), p. 3.
[41] Jerrold J. Van Cise, "The Robinson-Patman Act and the Accountant," *The New York Certified Public Accountant* (May, 1958), p. 352.

1. A discrimination in price,
2. Between purchasers of commodities of like grade and quality,
3. Where the effect may be substantially to lessen competition, tend to create a monopoly, or injure competition with any person.

Secondly, it must be determined if any one of the three affirmative justifications for such a discrimination *is* present. If so, the otherwise unlawful discrimination becomes lawful. These justifications are:

1. The discriminatory lower price is in response to changing conditions affecting the market for or marketability of the commodities involved,
2. The discriminatory lower price is made in good faith to meet an equally low price of a competitor, or
3. The discriminatory lower price makes only due allowance for specified cost differences.

Cost Justification

The third affirmative justification is of particular importance to accountants. The so-called cost proviso states:

> That nothing herein contained shall prevent differentials which make only due allowance for differences in the cost of manufacture, sale, or delivery resulting from the differing methods or quantities in which such commodities are to such purchasers sold or delivered.

The problem is to identify those costs which differ when the methods or quantities of sale differ. Costs which do not differ with such differing methods and quantities may be disregarded. Cost accounting, for Robinson-Patman purposes, is, indeed, a selective matter!

The Honorable Wright Patman, coauthor of the Act, wrote a book hoping to clarify the intent and scope of the Act. In a section devoted to situations when price discriminations are lawful, Patman discusses *costs*:

> Costs enjoy the paradoxical position of being definite and at the same time variable. Every article in commerce has accumulated certain definite elements of cost in the process of its production and distribution. At the same time the elements of pricing with which we are concerned must include also a forecast of what costs will accumulate in an article by the time it passes out of our hands into the hands of a purchaser. Thereupon we encounter the *variable* factor arising out of future processes.
> . . . It is not sound to argue that, because present overhead is absorbed by present production, a producer could make 10,000 extra units at no cost for overhead and hence could sell them to a favored buyer at a less cost than other units sold. The increased production merely reduces the overhead cost *on all* units equally. The same applies to the cost of handling or warehousing.

As the volume of business increases, the cost per unit recedes all along the line. Every unit handled must bear its share. As the units increase in number, the individual share becomes less and the selling price may be lowered in direct proportion to the decrease in cost of each unit.[42]

Although Patman advocates a predetermination of overhead costs,[43] he also states that "costs will not be theoretical or estimated. They will have been incurred or recorded." [44]

It appears that Patman did not anticipate any major problems in overhead allocation because he states that:

> ... There is little danger that a seller will invite prosecution because of price discriminations that may arise out of minor errors in the allocation of overhead in the determination of standard costs. Discriminations due to such minor errors will hardly result in injury among competing purchasers, nor would the charge of intent or negligence be tenable.[45]

The words *cost of manufacture, sale or delivery* in the cost proviso seem to include *every sort* of cost actually incurred except one which represents a fair return. *Costs,* per Robinson-Patman interpretation, do not mean *direct* or *variable* costs, because the savings which result from additional volume of production should be shared pro rata among all those who contribute to that volume.[46]

To illustrate, let us suppose a company makes 50 units of a product, each of which requires $5 of variable costs. If fixed costs of $50 are allocated to each unit produced, the total unit cost will be $6. If the company then sells at a 50 percent markup, its selling price will be set at $9 per unit.

Let us now suppose that the company receives an additional order to make 50 items of identical grade and quality. Because the additional direct costs will be only $5 per unit, the company might want to set its selling price at $7.50. Pricing on this basis, however, could lead to a charge of unlawful discrimination.

In quite a different situation, a company might be able to rely on a direct costing approach. Let us assume that all orders are shipped in carload quantities. If an order is received for less than a carload quantity, the shipping charges will be higher. In this case the company, with good justification, might vary its price upward because of the fact that additional direct costs are involved.

---

[42] Wright Patman, *op. cit.*, pp. 13-14.
[43] *Ibid.*, p. 18.
[44] *Ibid.*, p. 19.
[45] *Ibid.*
[46] Jerrold C. Van Cise, *op. cit.*, p. 356.

As indicated earlier, the real accounting problems arise in separating and allocating the costs, and the burden of cost justification is on the seller.[47] Rarely do Commission accountants develop cost studies from field investigations of their own; they ordinarily confine themselves to checking the respondent's figures, securing mere data, and refiguring costs in their own way.[48]

Cost justification studies should always be prepared prior to granting a price differential. As one authority has pointed out, "No charge can reasonably be made that advance cost planning, as contrasted with a study made during litigation, is more a lawyer's afterthought hastily improvised by facile accountants to give a color of legality to an arbitrary discrimination." [49]

Herbert F. Taggart, who was Chairman of the Advisory Committee on Cost Justification set up in 1953, has stated that, "The cost defenses which have been presented are as varied as the companies which have presented them. They agree in only one thing: cost justification is a complex procedure." He adds: "Part of the difficulty with cost justification is the lack of definition of terms and the complete absence of rules of the game. The Act itself defines neither the word *cost* nor any of its modifiers." [50]

OTHER LEGISLATION

Companies using direct costing as a basis for pricing should be familiar with various state unfair practices acts which in many states prohibit sales at less than cost. In California, for example, *cost* for manufactured items is defined to include "the cost of raw materials, labor, and all overhead expenses of the producer."

Companies which have foreign subsidiaries should also be familiar with foreign customs and tariff laws.

For additional information in this area, the reader is encouraged to read Williard E. Stone's "Legal Implications of Intracompany Pricing," which appeared in the January, 1964, issue of *The Accounting Review*.

---

[47] See discussion by William J. Warmack, "Cost Accounting Problems under the Robinson-Patman Act," *Robinson-Patman Act Symposium, 1947* (New York: Commerce Clearing House, Inc., 1947), p. 107.

[48] Otto F. Taylor, *op. cit.*, 389.

[49] Jerrod J. Van Cise, *op. cit.*, p. 359.

[50] Herbert F. Taggart, "Cost Justification under the Robinson-Patman Act," *The Journal of Accountancy* (June, 1956), p. 53.

CONCLUSION

A company considering the use of direct costing as an all-purpose accounting technique cannot afford to overlook the threat of all possible legal entanglements. Although the use of direct costing might be condoned for tax reporting purposes, there have been few successful rulings to date. There is even less likelihood that the SEC will accept financial statements prepared from direct costing records. And the relationship of direct costing to Robinson-Patman accounting is still another area characterized by uncertainty.

The use of direct costing at this time cannot be considered a generally acceptable accounting practice. Until such time as the issue is clarified and legislative rulings definitively stated, a company would be well advised to proceed with extreme caution if it plans to adopt solely direct costing methods for inventory valuations used in both internal and external reporting.

24. LIMITATIONS OF
OVERHEAD ALLOCATION *   William J. Vatter †

> In the case of an industry producing, from the same plant and equipment, a variety of kinds and grades of products, the exact determination of costs of production is impossible. All that is possible under such circumstances is . . . the reaching of an estimate resting on theoretical assumptions of necessarily disputable validity. . . .[1]

> Cost allocation at best is loaded with assumption and in many cases, highly arbitrary methods of apportionment are employed in practice. Certainly it is wise not to take the results of the usual process of internal cost computation too seriously.[2]

These statements certainly indicate that cost accounting methods fall far short of perfection as a means of establishing unit costs of product. Yet, the dependence placed upon cost accounting methods for determining inventory balances in financial reporting and income tax calculations, the use of costing techniques for establishing fair compensation on wartime procurement contracts, and the applications of cost criteria to problems of price and production control in the individual firm, as well as in social control legislation, combine to present conclusive evidence of the necessity for and the usefulness of cost accounting.

Necessity and usefulness, however, are not sufficient criteria for judging the acceptability of results; nor do these concepts determine in more than a vague and uncertain way the directions in which cost analysis should be developed. The techniques of costing overhead, especially, have real limitations that cannot be waved aside on grounds of necessity and usefulness. A recognition of these limitations may serve to reduce misunderstandings as to the content of costing techniques; but such a recognition may also be an important step toward improvement and refinement of methods. This paper is an attempt to point out those limitations by considering in turn

---

* From *The Accounting Review* (April, 1945). Reprinted by permission of the American Accounting Association.

† W. J. Vatter, Professor of Accounting at the University of Chicago.

[1] Jacob Viner, *Dumping, a Problem in International Trade* (Chicago: University of Chicago Press, 1923), p. 243.

[2] W. A. Paton and A. C. Littleton, *An Introduction to Corporate Accounting Standards* (Madison, Wis.: American Accounting Association, 1940), p. 121.

the problem of joint cost, the procedures commonly employed to assign joint costs to costing units, and the conflicts that arise from varying objectives of cost calculation.

THE PROBLEM OF JOINT COST

When the financial effects of individual external transactions are recorded for historical purposes, the meaning of cost as the "release" side of an exchange is generally clear, even though there may be disagreements as to the basis of measurement. But when transactions are viewed from within the matrix of operations, entwined in a maze of interrelated and interdependent activities, the meaning of cost becomes so indefinite that the term must be qualified if it is to convey much sense. The need for abstracting data from such a matrix is the basis for adding to the cost concept those modifying phrases that make costs the cost of *something*. Some of the major factors that contribute to that "large grist of unsettled problems on the cost side of accounting" [3] are to be found in those prepositional phrases.

Ordinary conversation exhibits an almost spontaneous appearance of such phrases; this suggests that, somehow, "cost" is incomplete, and requires elaboration and association with other ideas to complete the conveying of thought. The notion that "costs attach" [4] is basic to extant concepts of relationship between assets and expenses. The assignment of cost to discrete bundles of economic service (assets) and the subsequent tracing of cost expirations to specific time periods (correlative with the production and recognition of revenue) constitute a large part of the entire process of accounting. For some students of business behavior [5] the association of cost with aim, accomplishment, or alternative is an inevitable and fundamental principle. William Morse Cole [6] suggested that the basis of double-entry bookkeeping demands such associations on grounds of principle; he wrote:

> A basic principle, one that is too often neglected [is] that there is no such thing as an abstract cost—a *mere* cost. A cost is always the cost *of* something.

---

[3] Paton, "Recent and Prospective Developments in Accounting Theory," *Bureau of Business Research Studies, No. 25*, XXVII, No. 2 (Boston: Harvard University, March, 1940), p. 7.

[4] Paton and Littleton, *op. cit.*, pp. 13 ff.
Research Bulletin No. 9 (New York: American Institute of Accountants), pp. 70 ff.
Research Bulletin No. 22 (New York: American Institute of Accountants), pp. 179-80.

[5] John Maurice Clark, *Economics of Overhead Cost* (Chicago: University of Chicago Press, 1923), pp. 36-37.

[6] "Theories of Cost," *Accounting Review*, XI (March, 1936), p. 4.

State the basis for it in whatever terms you will—conversational habit, convention, or principle—the association of costs with related aims, ends, or accomplishments is a feature of business and accounting thought. The acceptance of this fact establishes the concept of a "costing unit"—some activity, thing, event, or other phenomenon, to which cost bears the positive relation of correspondence or association. In the recognition of the "costing unit" concept lies the origin of cost accounting, and the root of the problems of cost assignment.

Although it may be convenient (perhaps even necessary) to assume a direct correspondence between certain releases of measured consideration and the designated costing unit, it is not always true that in fact such a relation exists. On the contrary, those phenomena that are paired as cause and effect, effort and accomplishment, or cost and the costing unit, are but seldom so simply and directly connected. Every cause has a number of effects, every event arises from many causes; all incidents and observations are bound together by many ties.[7] All costs are more or less interwoven in a complex fabric; in large measure costs are joint as to their incurrence, as well as to their associations with various costing units.

The joint nature of costs is apparent at the point of their incurrence. The process of production is an assimilation of various kinds of economic service into a new combination; the operations of trading as well as manufacturing businesses are but conversions of those services acquired from one set of exchanges into new forms represented by tangible or intangible products that are exchanged in turn. The service product is often very different from any of the component items; the services measured by input costs are not contributory to the product, but complementary to each other. Appropriations of services, whether measured by asset expirations, accruals, or disbursements, do not stand individually and alone in the process of assimilation, for the way in which the service factors are combined is at least as important as the nature of the specific items themselves. Changes in the service potentialities of any factor may

---

[7] The validity commonly ascribed to simple and direct association arises from the overwhelming human desire for simplicity, and consequent analogies (usually but loosely drawn) between our direct experience and the "causal systems" of science. Scientific laws, however, derive their validity from repeated and controlled experiments, the statistical validity of which is never based upon individual observations as such. Even then, scientific data are never so positively and finally associated as to preclude alternative interpretations, for such new interpretations are frequently the source of progress. See E. W. Hobson, *The Domain of Natural Science* (London: Cambridge University Press, 1926), pp. 740-98.

entail alteration in the product; it is frequently true that the absence or the alteration of a single factor may make the continuance of operations difficult if not impossible. In this situation, costs are often incurred because other costs have been incurred; one item of outlay trails others along with it, either concomitantly or in sequence. There is no point in hiring workers unless tools and materials are available, unless sheltered working space (heated, lighted, and ventilated), power supply, storerooms, inspection and maintenance crews and facilities, supervisory and administrative staff are also provided. The combination of resources inherent to the processes of business has the effect of making costs joint at the very point of incurrence.

But costs are incurred jointly in still another and more important sense. The cost of one factor of production may be affected by alterations in the other factors, stemming from quality, efficiency, or other variables in the composite picture. For instance, the labor cost of a particular operation may be increased or decreased by changes in the quality of materials; differences in machine setups, layouts, or speed; shifts in maintenance policy or procedure; more or less intensive inspection; differences in the alertness and intelligence of supervisors. Even a change in the personal associations of worker groups may have considerable effect on labor cost. The addition of extra items of cost may actually reduce the net unit outlay for labor; incentive wages, quality bonuses, and overtime premiums—certainly additional costs from the isolated item point of view—may actually be the means of reducing aggregate unit costs.

The failure to recognize jointness of cost at the point of incurrence, and the treatment of joint outlays as direct costs, may result in unit costs that are difficult to interpret. If overtime premiums are treated as direct costs, the activities of normal working hours are charged with none of the overtime; the work done in overtime periods bears the full brunt of the premiums. The prime reason for overtime is the presence of work to fill the normal schedule, yet a direct tracing of the overtime item gives just the opposite effect in the final cost calculations.[8]

Viewing the joint cost problem from the point of view of the costing unit, there are several aspects of cost interrelation that should be observed. The commonly recognized coproduct situation illustrates some of this. A given set of costs may be associated with

---

[8] Cf. J. J. W. Neuner, *Cost Accounting* (Rev. ed.; Homewood, Ill.: Richard W. Irwin, Inc., 1942), pp. 194-95.

a conglomeration of costing units in the form of service products that cannot be produced independently. Chemical and extractive industries offer numerous instances of the eventual appearance of several products from a single set of operations. These coproducts often appear in fixed proportions, quite irrespective of man's interest in them. Sometimes, the insignificant items are considered "by-products" and are treated either as having no assignable cost or as having costs equal to their net sales value. Either procedure is difficult to justify except on grounds of expediency. But, no matter how the costs may be allocated, the fact remains that all costs of producing the entire conglomeration of output are joint with respect to the costing units represented by the individual products.

To be sure, coproducts are not always produced in fixed and unalterable proportions; something can be done to increase the yield of wool, gasoline, or high-grade lumber by improvements of method or by technological research. Then too, means have been found for increasing the usefulness of products of lesser importance, so that by-products otherwise disposed of at nominal prices are specially processed to meet demands previously unrecognized. Nevertheless, the problem of joint cost remains, so long as more than one product results from given productive operations.

The coproduct situation, however, is not confined to processes of physical production. It also exists in the form of those intangible products referred to as "services." In the sense of being end results of business activity, services are often joint products. The product of a railroad company is "transportation"; this, however, can be broken down into smaller groupings with respect to commodities, passengers, divisions, classes of accommodation, specific trains, or particular runs. If such breakdowns are attempted, the problem of joint cost is immediately apparent. This is parallel to the breakdown of physical product into components with respect to classes of products, or to jobs identified with production order numbers.

An even more difficult problem is posed by the fact that the concept of service embodied in the end product of the railroad is itself a conglomeration of things. Passenger travel by railroad involves a great many things besides physical transportation; the end product of the railroad is a peculiar combination of convenience, timesaving, comfort, entertainment, and perhaps other things. In this sense, even the direct costs of departments of manufacturing enterprises are joint. The "products" of service departments are intermediate products, required for the furtherance of activity in the "producing" centers. But the nature of those intermediate products is often fully as complex as the concept of transportation applied to the railroad company. Personnel departments, research and production planning units, and other service centers turn out a variety of individual products that are seldom recognized and separated so as to facilitate accounting for them in concrete terms. Certainly, hiring a new employee is different from adjusting a grievance of one already on the payroll; establishing reasons for not carrying out a plan of product design is different from working out the standard procedures and specifications for new products; each service department may turn out products of several kinds, and the costs are joint costs when this is the case.

Perhaps it is also worth noting that joint cost is not merely a peculiar problem of overhead cost allocation. The assignment of costs to time periods—the fundamental operation of calculating expense— is not free from joint implications. Even in those trading enterprises in which the internal tracing of cost has not been considered essential to the measurement of expense, there are instances of joint cost. Depreciation, with the attendant items of repairs, maintenance, replacements, additions, and betterments, is but one phase of joint cost allocation with regard to time periods. Bond discounts or premiums, and financing costs related thereto, are joint factors in the calculation of income charges. Selling expenses, because of the difficulty of establishing proper costing units, are seldom traced through internal organization for allocation to time periods. But, because of the lag between cost incurrence and the production of revenue, there are questions as to how some of these costs should be divided. The problem of assigning inventory charges to expense, brought to view in the discussions of alternative merits of first-in first-out, last-in first-out, and other methods of cost assignment, is from one point of view but another problem in the allocation of joint cost.

Granting the ubiquity of joint cost, the reader may ask: What is the difficulty involved in joint costs, and why do joint costs create a problem? The answer to this question is that costs are not assigned for the mere sake of dividing them; the results of cost allocation must be logically defensible if they are to be accepted as objective and acceptable data. This raises the question as to the bases or criteria upon which are established the allocations of overhead that appear in expense and inventory balances.

The fundamental criterion for cost assignment is the identification of cost with costing units in terms of physical accompaniments. An examination of definitions of direct cost shows this quite clearly. For example, Reitell [9] defines direct costs as "those which are known to have been incurred because of a particular unit of product or group of units." Blocker [10] states that "direct materials are those materials and supplies that can be identified with the manufacture of a product or a group of products," and uses similar phraseology in defining direct labor cost. In the *Cost Accountants' Handbook* [11] we find the following:

> Generally speaking, materials present in the finished product are classed as direct materials. However, there are exceptions in the form of materials not physically present in the finished article . . . finishing or polishing material consumed in the operation . . . can be logically treated as direct material cost, and this . . .
>
> If a labor cost cannot be identified with some particular production cost order number, or if it cannot be identified with some productive operation, then it cannot be classified as direct labor.

Dohr, Inghram and Love [12] define direct costs as "those elements of cost which can easily, obviously, and conveniently be identified with specific units of product, processes, jobs, departments, etc."

Underlying the idea of physical identification is the fact that in an isolated transaction cost and the costing unit are paired in an obvious way. The thing parted with (cost) and the thing acquired (costing unit) are so obviously connected that little question arises as to the allocation of the cost within the framework of that transaction. Even when transactions are considered in aggregates, identification in most cases is still supported by those statistical patterns that can be observed readily between the physical and the financial aspects of these transactions. For instance, the physical unit of material can be seen and examined; if a high positive correlation between the total cost of materials and the physical quantities can be established, there is some justification for the allocation of the cost to the physical units on a direct basis. If, in addition, a similar correlation exists between units of materials and units of product (or service) direct allocation is logical and feasible.

Whether direct allocation by physical identification is actually carried out is, however, a matter of expediency. Sometimes it is not

---

[9] *Cost Accounting* (Scranton: International Textbook Press, 1937), p. 22.
[10] *Cost Accounting* (New York: McGraw-Hill Book Co., Inc., 1940), p. 16.
[11] (New York: The Ronald Press, Co., 1944), pp. 629, 839.
[12] *Cost Accounting* (New York: The Ronald Press Co., 1935), p. 603.

worthwhile to strive for objective procedures in allocating costs of small amount, and many items that could be allocated directly (on the ground of correlations such as have been suggested) are treated as indirect costs for economy of effort. The costs of electric power purchased from a utility company, social security taxes, and minor supplies such as tacks and glue are illustrations.

But when costs are joint—when the cost is associated with more than one costing unit—the simple correlations described above do not exist. Instead, the services or products that are employed as costing units are so closely interrelated that precise relationships cannot be established among cost, physical units of time or space, and the end products. Then the criterion of physical identification fails; other criteria must be sought for, in terms of actual or assumed correlations that can be substituted. At the present time, it is not possible to establish by any simple means those relationships that must be available for an objective allocation of cost among co-products, because there are no known variables that are correlated with cost on the one hand and the individual coproducts on the other. The search for such criteria is the only means of improving and objectifying indirect costing procedures.

If there can be established and verified by statistical means those relationships that tie together the incurrence of cost and the physical measures of product attributes, the measurements based on these criteria will be objective and acceptable, however indirect may be the means of measurement employed. The problem of joint cost allocation does not arise from indirect methods of measurement; [13] rather, the problem originates in the fact that the relations implied in making allocations have not been, or are not, capable of independent verification. Some of the criteria now employed in the form of "bases" for allocation have been developed on purely utilitarian lines, without support other than appeal to judgment. So long as no better approach is made, so long as the basic relationships are but a matter of conjecture or assumption, joint cost allocation will remain unobjective, unsatisfactory and inconclusive.

---

[13] The lack of confidence that many writers express in indirect measurements is an error; especially is it incorrect to say that the problem of joint cost arises from the methods of measurement employed. Most of the extremely precise measurements that exist are the results of indirect methods. Astronomical measurements are all indirect, yet the forecasting they make possible is certainly precise. All really sensitive instruments for measurement of very small variations operate on principles of indirect measurement. The difficulty is not one of method, but of the errors that may occur from unwarranted or unverifiable assumptions.

Methods and Procedures

Before attention is turned to those criteria that are currently employed to allocate joint cost, a few general points should be stressed to make more clear the situation in which overhead costing methods are used.

In the first place, the costs of modern business activity cannot be classified sharply as between direct costs assignable by physical identification and those costs that must be traced by other means. The *Accountants' Handbook* states on this point:

> The two divisions are not mutually exclusive. Thus a particular cost may be direct as related to the overall operations of a department, yet be indirect with respect to any particular product unit or activity within the department. As implied in the definition of direct costs, certain costs which can be identified with specific end results may nevertheless be treated as indirect because of the inconvenience involved in measurement.

There are many patterns into which directness or indirectness may fall; the following are typical illustrations:

1. An electrotype plate purchased by a job printing firm for use on one specific job for a one-time customer. This is a direct cost of that job.
2. Wages earned by a worker who tends several semiautomatic machines working on similar, but not identical, lots of goods. This cost is direct as to the operating center, but indirect as to the product lots.
3. Salary of an operating department foreman. This is direct as to the department, but indirect as to the operating centers within that department, and also indirect with respect to product units.
4. Fuel consumed in the production of electric power by a company-owned plant. This cost is direct as to the power plant (save for the inventory charge problem referred to previously) but it is an indirect cost so far as the producing departments, operating centers, and product lots are concerned.
5. Factory building operating costs, such as elevator service, are direct manufacturing charges, but are joint costs of the various service and production departments, operating centers, and product.
6. Service of watchmen and guards patrolling a plant site within which are housed the general administrative and sales offices as well as the factory buildings. This is a direct charge only for the enterprise as a whole; it is joint with respect to manufacturing, sales and general administration, and that part which is traceable to manufacturing is still joint with regard to departments, operating centers, and product lots.
7. Research activities having to do with product design, manufacturing methods, sales appeal, etc., are joint costs that are indirect even with respect to time periods. In addition, such a cost must be allocated to the major functions, service and production departments, operating centers, and product lots.

The patterns mentioned are not exhaustive, for there may be a number of combinations of these situations. For instance, the cost of power produced in the company's plant, though it originates as a manufacturing charge, may be assigned in part to general administrative and selling functions, as well as to manufacturing activities. A firm that produces some of its own tools or supplies will experience a similar combination of cost allocations. Then, too, there are circular or reabsorbed cost situations, in which joint cost allocation must be made by extended computations or by algebraic methods.[14]

In all these cases, joint costs cannot be assigned by physical identification; instead, costs are divided by reference to "bases" that reflect in some form one or more of the criteria now to be examined in detail.

The Criterion of Origin

One method of dealing with joint costs is to assign costs to the units or centers in which they originate. In the case of social security taxes, for example, those taxes that represent cost to the employer are calculated on an aggregate payroll, and consequently are joint with regard to the various activities of the firm. To divide cost of taxes among operating and service departments on the basis of direct and indirect payroll costs is to apply to criterion of origin. If the payroll figures employed for this allocation are adjusted to exclude amounts paid to employees in excess of $3,000 during the year, the correlation between the base and the tax cost is complete and verifiable; the assignment of cost is thus correct. But if, as is likely to be the case, the payroll figures are not so adjusted, the assignment of the tax cost is biased toward charging more tax than should be charged to those departments in which higher salaried employees happen to be employed.

In some cases, an item of joint cost may be assigned as a whole to one department on the ground of origin, and reliance placed upon subsequent apportionment of that department's total cost to effect the division of this item. Maintenance and janitor supplies, payroll and the miscellaneous costs of production control departments are illustrations. This may or may not be a correct treatment of such cost items, depending upon how the ultimate division of the total department cost is worked out. But it is conceivable that very different results would be had by this means than would ensue from specific

---

[14] Cf. Stephen Gilman, *Accounting Concepts of Profit* (New York: The Ronald Press Co., 1939), pp. 325-28; and Dohr, Inghram, & Love, *op. cit.*, pp. 150-51.

assignment of individual items. The criterion of origin is often employed to assign costs purely as a matter of expediency.

The Criterion of Use

Particularly helpful with problems of apportioning "service department" charges, the use made of a given service or facility is the basis for assigning the cost of providing it. An example of this is the apportionment of internal transportation costs to operating departments on the bases of pieces hauled, ton miles, or truck hours. Such a division is equivalent to making a unit charge for specific services used. The difficulty with this criterion is that the costs of providing service are not always correlated with the use made of that service. One of the important elements in this situation is the fact that standby facilities are often maintained in anticipation of use that does not materialize.[15] Fixed costs can hardly be said to be divided objectively on the basis of use of service if some of the facilities provided are idle, however necessary such excess capacity may be for the overall smooth operation of the plant.

The Criterion of Facilities Provided

Some overhead costs are divided on bases that reflect the provision of facilities rather than the use made of them. Apportionment of personnel department costs on the basis of number of employees or man-hours of operation and distribution of building maintenance costs (depreciation, property taxes, heating, lighting, ventilating, repairs, and janitor service) on the basis of floor area or cubic volume are cases in point.

The distinction between the criterion of facilities provided and that of use is that the use made of a service may or may not correspond with the availability of that service. Costs of maintaining capacity to serve, in terms of fixed or standby costs, would seem to be more equitably distributed by the criterion of provision than by that of use of the service. One of the difficulties here is, however, that costs of service departments are seldom segregated into fixed and variable categories for each department, at least partly because the meaning of "fixed" or "variable" costs for the department is not always clear. Even if this were done, there would still remain the problem of separating the costs of providing facilities from those costs representing excess capacity for the service department over and above normal requirements.[16]

---

[15] Fred V. Gardner, *Variable Budget Control* (New York: McGraw-Hill Book Co., Inc., 1940), especially pp. 171-89.
[16] *Ibid.,* pp. 203-05.

It is interesting to observe that one common approach to the selection of bases for cost assignment is stated to be that of "benefits received." This, at least in terms of the bases selected by this means, is really a combination of the criterion of use with that of facilities provided. "Benefits," unless measured in terms of the use or provision of facilities, is too vague a term to result in objective division of joint cost among departments or other costing units.

The Criterion of Ability

Some cost assignments are established upon bases that reflect an ability to withstand or to absorb charges. The validity of such cost assignments rests on grounds that are highly colored with ethical considerations. Illustrations are to be found outside accounting: e.g., the theory of taxation based on the principle of "ability to pay" as exemplified in progressive tax rates, and the setting of prices in terms of "what the traffic will bear." From the point of view of accounting method, there is some question as to the acceptability of this criterion for assigning joint costs, even as a last resort. The distribution of department store costs on the basis of net sales or of aggregate gross margins seldom adds anything to the information already at hand before the distribution is made. The allocation of joint cost to coproducts on the basis of net sales value is another application of the capacity criterion. Although this allocation is made only to establish inventory valuations, the inventory figures could be better and more logically justified in terms of a valuation at net sales value less the average normal margin, this margin, of course, serving to exclude selling expenses as well as the income to be realized upon final sale. The latter calculation will give results almost identical with cost allocations based upon net sales value, but it is to be preferred on logical grounds.

According to Blocker, there are other criteria that may be applied to the problem of assigning overhead. He mentions two in particular: efficiency (or incentives) and the survey of conditions. The first of these, he says, "is the newest approach to the scientific distribution of overhead costs." [17] Although it must be admitted that such bases are employed in the newest designs of costing systems (in terms of standards, budgets, and quotas) the efficiency criterion is not related to cost assignment in terms of expense measurement; rather, the use of incentive or efficiency bases is related to managerial aims. Such an approach to cost analysis illustrates the "conflict of objectives" to

---

[17] *Op. cit.*, p. 153.

be discussed in the third section of this paper. The survey basis suggested by Blocker is a combination of the criteria suggested above, plus some unspecified application of judgment on the part of the cost accountant or the management. The fact that most cost accountants think that surveys need to be made only at irregular intervals to obtain a sample or cross section of the prevailing conditions [18] is itself an indication that the procedure is heavily weighted with factors of judgment and expediency. Blocker's illustration of this approach is that of delivery service in a department store. It is justifiable to give consideration to the number of packages delivered, the size and weight of items transported, the number of deliveries and pickups made, and the mileage traveled. This should be on the ground that these factors reflect the use made of the service. However, the real problem lies in the complexity of the departmental product; the case is similar to that of defining the transportation product of a railroad.

A list of criteria for cost assignment would not be complete without some reference to arbitrary divisions of cost. One of the simplest of these is to spread cost equally, on the ground that, in the absence of other considerations, "equality is equity." This principle may be a means of solving otherwise hopeless situations, but it cannot be defended as having logical relation to the problem of cost assignment. Sometimes, arbitrary bases of allocation are established after due consideration of a number of factors that have some bearing on the problem of cost allocation; and, since judgments based upon adequate study of the problem are presumed to be sound, these bases may be acceptable. However, judgment, even sound judgment, is not objective!

A consideration of the bases that are employed to allocate overhead cost brings us to three rather important conclusions. The first is that criteria for overhead cost allocation have not yet been developed which are capable of statistical verification. Extant criteria of origin, use, facilities provided, or ability have not been subjected to the kinds of tests that they must satisfy if they are to be considered objective. Among these extant criteria, the choice is usually one of individual preference or judgment; this means that uniformity of principle does not obtain in the assignment of overhead costs.

A second generalization is that the bases chosen for cost assignment are frequently but imperfect expressions of the criteria them-

---

[18] *Ibid.*

selves. The choice of bases such as floor space, ton miles, or number of employees is often a matter of accepting or adapting available statistics to the problem, so long as the choice looks reasonable. The use of percentages of direct labor cost as bases for allocating overhead to product units is admittedly imperfect; such procedure is justified in practice because of the availability of the direct labor cost figures as against the extra work of calculating man-hours, or setting up procedures to tabulate machine hours or other bases more closely related to the problem of cost assignment. The major influence that determines the choice of bases for cost assignment is expediency.

The third generalization has to do with the notion of averaging. Overhead costs must be averaged to be assigned at all. For, when we assign a cost on some basis, we are in effect calculating a cost per unit of the basis that is adopted; this unit cost calculation is implicit in every distribution, apportionment, or allocation. Since averaging is based upon certain assumptions, and has certain limitations, those limitations are inherent in overhead cost assignment, even though no explicit unit costs are recognized. Averaging always assumes a degree of homogeneity in the data that are brought into an average. The wide range of activities engaged in by some service departments and some operating centers raises a real question of whether such activities are sufficiently homogeneous to be averaged with logical consistency. Certainly the failure to separate fixed and variable elements when overhead is apportioned and allocated produces error and bias if the proportions of fixed and variable cost vary as among different departments or over different periods of time.

Furthermore, if the cost of 100 units of service product is $1,000, it is not correct to infer that the cost of each and every unit is $10. If the true costs of individual units were known, they would be seen to form a statistical frequency distribution of considerable range. When this distribution is symmetrical and leptokurtic (i.e., when there are few deviations from the average, and those deviations are equally distributed above and below that average) the arithmetic mean is a useful indication of probable unit cost. The usefulness of the average, however, depends upon these features of the distribution. Even then, the average unit cost is only a probable cost, not the specific cost of each unit. A recognition of these points does not imply that averages are to be avoided, nor that they are necessarily untrustworthy. In the absence of contrary evidence, no harm results from assuming those conditions which validate the averaging process. But unless this assumption can be verified, the accountant should be careful to specify his unit cost as an average, not an "actual" unit cost. This is particularly true with respect to overhead costs that are averaged over months of varying production rates, and when seasonal or erratic fluctuations exist in the pattern of overhead costs incurred. To specify the unit cost as a "normal average" cost is merely to recognize the quoted figure as an approximation, rather than a verifiable and actual cost of the item in question.

CONFLICTING OBJECTIVES

Accounting data are used for many purposes, only one of which is the "measurement of income" in the sense that that phrase is employed by accountants. The position taken by J. M. Clark (that "there are different kinds of problems for which we need information about costs, and that the particular information we need differs from one problem to another" [19]) is entirely sound. However, one of the very practical difficulties in the way of allocation of overhead is the fact that the content of an accounting system tends to be affected by the aims of at least two important groups: accountants, who are interested in income determination; and managers, whose primary interests lie in directions other than an income figure. Of course this difference is partly one of emphasis, for managers are indirectly interested in the reported income; management is to some extent judged as to its effectiveness by the operating statement and the balance sheet. But the primary emphasis of management is upon control—that complex of planning and administrative activities aimed at the individual steps to be taken to produce income and to attain whatever other objectives may be important to the progress of the enterprise.

The usefulness of accounting systems as means of establishing and maintaining control of operations requires no demonstration in this paper. The thing that does need to be emphasized is that the interests of management are not always the same as those of the accountant engaged to record and present the financial results of operations. Quite apart from the fact that management may have a more personal interest in the presentation of financial summaries than does

[19] *Op. cit.*, p. 35.

the accountant, there are certain differences in the kinds of classifications that would be desirable, and the kinds of treatment that would be accorded to operating data, from these two points of view. And, since management determines to some extent what kind of accounting activities shall be carried on, it is but logical that there would be at least some expression of the managerial viewpoint in the cost accounting system. One example of this is the use of "incentives" in the departmental distributions and apportionments of overhead costs, referred to previously in the discussion of criteria for cost allocation. There are numerous instances of the fact that managerial requirements affect the methods of accounting that are employed. What are the significant elements in this problem of objectives?

Prospective versus Historical View

The traditional viewpoint of the accountant (interested in measuring income) is that he records, interprets, and presents the financial aspects of business events. From this position, the task of the accountant is primarily historical; and the data that he is willing to accept and incorporate into his summaries are historical data. The interest of management is not, and cannot be, purely historical. Management is concerned with present and prospective information upon which to base today's decisions; whether the past record is good or bad cannot be allowed to influence the present analysis and the action to be taken, for management must solve problems in terms of making the most of available resources, present opportunities, and expected events. Although it is true that the historical record serves to indicate and (within limits) to measure the effects of past actions, historical records do not serve managerial ends beyond this. The narrative aim of financial reporting is inconsistent and incompatible with the prospective viewpoint of managerial policy.

Short-Run versus Long-Run Interpretations

Managerial policy and accounting are both spoken of as being concerned with long-run points of view, but the content of the long-run notion is different in the two cases. Accounting is concerned with long-run implications in the sense that any error in accounting is bound to show up, ultimately; and, since the problem of accounting is fundamentally one of breaking up the continuity of the enterprise into short periods for financial reporting purposes, it is but logical that the accountant should bear in mind the fact that there is an eventual day of reckoning for all costs, whatever their nature.

The accountant, when he strives to measure income, must keep in mind the long-run implications of the figures he places upon reports.

Managerial policy, if it is "long run" at all, embraces a different kind of long-run view. Past decisions do not determine future managerial actions in the mathematical fashion that applies to accounts. Poor policies are constantly being replaced by better ones, and although the policies of management may be shifted only slightly by a given action, *policies evolve through time*. The two long-run notions are not the same; it is possible that occasionally they may conflict. To illustrate: the management may decide as a matter of policy that replacements of equipment must be justified in terms of demonstrated ability to "pay for themselves" over a period of three or four years; such items are, however, depreciated at usual rates once they have been acquired. There is a difference between the managerial and the accounting views of replacement policy, however much emphasis on long-run notions may be made on either side.

Alternative versus Absolute Costs

Perhaps the most striking instance of the difference in point of view between management and narrative accounting is the fact that managerial discussions are replete with references to "savings" and "wastes"—words that have but small place in the terminology of financial accounting. Savings and wastes are alternative concepts; they have to do with a comparison of observation with what should have happened or what might have happened. To management, savings are the stuff of which profits are made; to the financial accountant, they have no existence except as they may offset cost or expense.[20] To management, wastes are losses that might have been avoided; these, too, are "elements in the profit pattern." The notion that conventionally recorded expenses include dissipations as well as applications of resources—that there are loss elements in operating charges that should be separated from expense—is almost entirely a managerial idea. Discussion of such "interim" losses has appeared in accounting literature almost solely within works on cost accounting,[21] sometimes being confined to analysis of standard cost variations. Financial accounting views an operating loss merely as the excess of total operating expense over total operating revenue.[22]

---

[20] Cf. H. A. Finney, *Principles of Accounting* (New York: Prentice-Hall, Inc., 1936), p. 115; also, see the discussion of purchase discounts in Paton, *Essentials of Accounting* (New York: The Macmillan Co., 1938), pp. 267-68.

[21] Dohr, Inghram and Love, *op. cit.*, pp. 410-37.

[22] Paton, *Accounting Theory* (New York: The Ronald Press Co., 1922), pp. 176-77.

The practice of "converting" standard cost variations to "actual" costs by prorating variations when statements are prepared illustrates the conflict between the absolute and the alternative view of cost. Standard cost accounting emphasizes alternatives in terms of efficiency; financial statements, on the other hand, require absolute measurements of cost, which necessitate adjustment or conversion of the figures produced by the accounting system so as to meet the norms and standards for income determination.

The extreme case of conflict between alternative and absolute viewpoints is the overtime premium case cited by J. M. Clark.[23] He states that the overtime bonus should be counted not once, but as many times as there are opportunities for saving this outlay. This, from the absolute standpoint of income determination, seems absurd; yet it is perfectly sound from the alternative point of view.

Control of Cost versus Expense Measurement

One of the important tasks of management is to fix responsibility. A practical means of furthering this end is to associate costs with the operations of specific administrative units. However, the association of cost must fall within the limits of organization principles, one of the most fundamental of which is that the responsibility exacted from an executive must be commensurate with the authority granted him. The application of this principle to cost assignments for managerial purposes establishes the concept of "controllable" costs. If the administrator is to be held accountable for the costs of his department, those costs must consist only of the items over which he has control— i.e., costs that he can alter by his own decisions. The costs of manufacturing vary to a considerable degree as to their controllability; many of the allocations that would be made in one way for financial reporting would have to be made differently for control purposes. Further, it must be recognized that many costs are controllable only at the higher levels of organization; some are almost completely beyond control even by top executives. Changes in prices for materials and supplies are not controllable except as adjustments may be made with respect to purchasing policy, manufacturing methods, or the quality and quantity of product. Even then, there are limits to the degree of control that may be exercised. Indirectness of relations between cost and cost control creates a special class of problems, beyond the scope of this discussion.

---

[23] *Op. cit.*, p. 247.

However, the difficulty that arises from the use of control criteria is that control classifications are simply not relevant to the problem of costing product for financial reporting. If costs are assigned for management purposes on the basis of their controllability, there will be some costs that will remain unallocated, and those that are divided will be divided with reference to criteria that may have little reference to the problem of measuring income.

Enough has been said to indicate that the problems of management are different from the problem of income measurement, and that allocations that may serve one purpose cannot and will not serve the others. Yet it is fairly obvious that management may be expected to favor those methods of cost allocation that answer its questions rather than procedures that are aimed strictly at the expense measurement objective. The amount of outlay required to operate an accounting system is itself a reason for requiring managerial information from it.

Simple, one-dimensional, and standardized procedures can meet the problem of conflicting objectives only by compromise. To mix management control data with expense measurement procedures is to confuse one or both of these viewpoints, perhaps to present a cost figure that is unsatisfactory for any purpose. The compromises that exist in current cost systems limit the value of the resulting unit costs both for management purposes and for the calculation of expense.

Conclusions

The writer has no quarrel with cost accountants and their methods, nor is it implied that cost figures, because of their imperfections, are hopelessly useless. By and large, the cost accountant performs well a function that is essential to carrying on accounting in general and basic to the furtherance of intelligent management. There are, however, three general conclusions that may be drawn from the exposition presented in these pages; these should be emphasized.

First, there is a real need for research directed toward the establishment of principles for cost allocation, especially with regard to the allocation of overhead costs. The search for more objective and defensible bases of allocation, and the development of methods of handling masses of data to meet special purposes, are promising fields for improvement in extant costing methods.

Second, there is good reason for broadening the concepts that have been applied to the field of cost accounting, to embrace techniques of statistical and mathematical analysis. Cost accounting is more than expense measurement, and the problems of cost analysis are too complex, and of too many dimensions, to be confined wholly within the limits of double-entry bookkeeping. A wider familiarity with ancillary techniques would be a happy addition to the accountant's tool kit.

Third, and most important: the limitations of available methods, the compromises of expediency, and the conflicting objectives that enter into cost calculations should make the accountant more careful as to his terminology with respect to unit costs. Readers of financial operating and cost reports, unless they are technically trained, are prone to accept terms used in accounting reports at their face value. The distinctly observable tendency toward emphasis of actuality [24] in terminology is unfortunate. In view of what has been said above, it is questionable whether there can be much hope of calculating an "actual" unit cost. Hence, terms that are used to describe costs should be chosen carefully to avoid an unnecessary implication of precision or objectivity that may be grasped and misused by the uninitiated. Pending those developments of costing technique that will solve some of the present problems of cost allocation, the accountant should be careful to avoid misunderstanding and misinterpretation of his work. He should avoid as a plague any reference to actuality in his presentations of unit cost. Cautious applications of terminology to figures that are subject to so many weaknesses, yet which can be taken to mean so much, are demanded by that prudence and judgment upon which the accountant's reputation depends.

---

[24] If the reader has any doubt as to the existence of this tendency, let him examine the available text materials on cost accounting, to observe the frequency with which the words "actual" and "cost" appear in context; further, the absence of definitions of "normal" cost in cost accounting texts is notable, despite the fact that the unit costs produced by the methods outlined are always normal, not actual, costs.

25. MISMATCHING OF COSTS AND REVENUES *

John G. Blocker †

The accounting practices and the periodic financial statements of many business concerns are confusing, and in some cases grossly misleading to management, investors, creditors, students, and the general public. In fact, it seems on occasions that only the accountants who originated the techniques or inherited the procedures from those who preceded them can explain the logic behind the accounting methods in use.

When confronted with the blunt question of why a particular accounting practice continues to be followed, in spite of the confusion and misrepresentation of accounting data which it creates, the frank executive confesses that his accounting techniques are governed by one or more of the following: (1) tradition or established custom, which discourages change in accounting methods or financial statements in order to avoid confusion to employees or recipients of the company's statements; (2) conservatism; (3) cost involved in a change in methods; (4) tax savings; (5) lack of understanding of accounting principles; and (6) desire of management to present a particular financial picture.

In order to correct one or more of the many confusing, misleading, or unacceptable accounting practices which are to be found in daily use, a periodic reexamination of the accounting policies and procedures of every business concern should be undertaken at least once a year and each should be tested for compliance with accepted accounting standards and principles. Such remedial action has been encouraged by the recent Report of the Committee of the American Accounting Association on Revision of the Statement of Principles which was presented at the annual meeting of the American Accounting Association in September, 1947, and printed in the January, 1948, issue of *The Accounting Review*.

* From *The Accounting Review* (January, 1949). Reprinted by permission of the American Accounting Association.

† John G. Blocker, Professor of Accounting at the School of Business, University of Kansas.

While each of the fundamental concepts or principles which are contained in the Committee's report is worthy of careful consideration and elaboration, one in particular, viz., the matching of costs with revenues, is selected because of its importance in the preparation of the profit-and-loss or income statement which, during the past ten years, has been given priority over the balance sheet when conflicting policies and concepts require that a choice be made as to the more important of the two statements. If management, investors, creditors, and the general public base their decisions and actions upon the profit-and-loss statements which are submitted to them monthly, quarterly, or annually, it is imperative that the data presented in these statements be accurately prepared with as careful a matching of costs with revenues as is possible.

It seemed to be an interesting project to contact executives of industrial enterprises and public accountants in the midwest for the purpose of ascertaining their opinions as to what extent profit-and-loss statements do not reflect an accurate matching of costs with revenues and are therefore misleading in their presentation of profit or loss figures. No formal questionnaire was circulated, but 25 interviews were conducted. The interviews suggested the following presentation in this paper: (1) consideration of the importance of the problem of matching costs and revenues in the operation of business enterprises; (2) presentation of concepts of revenue and cost expirations; (3) examination of established accounting policies and practices which result in improper "matching" and the presentation of inaccurate profit-and-loss data; and finally, (4) suggestions as to remedies that will result in more reliable and valuable profit-and-loss statements.

IMPORTANCE OF MATCHING COSTS WITH REVENUES

The accounting period concept is relatively a recent development in business. In antiquity the accounting period was the life of the business venture. The round trip of the sailing vessel or caravan required many months, and the accounting period represented the span of life of the trading venture. As business became more complex and competitive, regular reports covering shorter periods of operation were demanded by the entrepreneur so that the financial progress of the concern could be presented in an orderly manner, and comparative studies of costs and income could be made.

It became the custom to present financial data for periods not to exceed 12 months with preference for an accounting period which would coincide with the natural business year. Gradually the demand for more frequent accounting reports has resulted in the trend toward the preparation of quarterly or monthly profit-and-loss statements. This demand has been of much concern to those who desire to prepare accurate financial statements, because it is generally accepted as a fact that the shorter the accounting period the more difficult is the task of preparing profit-and-loss statements. The procedure is complicated because of the many problems encountered in matching cost expirations against revenues identified with the period. It is only by proper matching that the profit or loss for any given period can be accurately stated.

REVENUE

A wealth of material has been written on the subject of revenue, but the recommendations of the Committee on Revision of the Statement of Principles can be adopted:

> The present committee would make the basic principle provide for recognition of revenue at the time of legal transfer of assets whether by delivery or otherwise, the performance of services, or the use of resources of one enterprise by another, provided there is concurrent acquisition of assets or a reduction of a liability.[1]

The accrual basis of allocating revenue to the proper accounting period is generally identified with the sales basis of measuring revenue. Receipts are taken up in the accounting period in which the goods are sold or services furnished. The Committee recognizes that there must be certain modifications of the basic rule. These modifications are founded in the belief that in certain lines some activity may be more important than the delivery of goods or performance of services. These modifications are exemplified by enterprises producing for special order, construction, production of staples, and the accretion of natural resources. There is a further modification of the basic rule founded in the hazard of installment collections.

Regardless of which method is adopted for allocating revenue to the accounting period, the costs necessary to create such revenue must be allocated to the identical period if the income is to be accurately measured. Income, as the term is generally used, is computed by matching revenues realized with costs consumed or expired, in accordance with the cost principle.

---

[1] Thomas W. Leland, "Revenue, Expense and Income," *The Accounting Review* (January, 1948), p. 18.

Cost Expirations

The Committee gives accounting recognition to expenses in the particular period in which there is (1) a direct identification or association of the asset expiration with the revenue of the period, as in the case of merchandise delivered to customers; (2) an indirect association with or applicability to the period's revenue of the deduction or charge, as in the case of office salaries and rent; or (3) a measurable expiration of resources even though not necessarily associated with the production of revenue, past, present, or future, as in the case of losses from flood or fire. The Committee believes that the expense of a particular period should include all accounting costs not previously deducted from revenue and not reasonably applicable to future periods.[2]

Accounting Practices Which Result in Improper Matching of Costs with Revenues

The following examples of improper matching of costs with revenues are not isolated instances, but were found to be common procedures in many business enterprises. The list could be extended, but the executives and public accountants who were contacted agreed that the most common infractions are included. In general, they also agreed to the corrective measures that are suggested in each instance.

Inventory Valuation

Inventory valuation methods have been a common topic of discussion in textbooks and periodicals for many years so it is only necessary to review the two generally accepted methods, i.e., (a) cost, and (b) cost or market whichever is lower, in connection with the proper matching of costs with revenues.

Cost or market whichever is lower has received wide acceptance because it is a conservative inventory method. Its use results in the recording of losses but not profits prior to the sale of merchandise. The interviews indicated that it is still widely used in retail establishments, but that it is being supplanted by cost methods in industrial enterprises. The method results in the reduction of profits of one period but the inflation of the profits of the next period in a corresponding amount. Mismatching of cost and revenues cannot be avoided and the profit or loss of each accounting period is incorrectly stated.

---

[2] *Ibid.*, p. 18.

Receiving and Handling Costs

It is generally agreed that inventory costs should include all costs up to the point where goods are placed in the storeroom or are in a salable state. The invoice price at the vendor's shipping point, less all trade and cash discounts offered, plus transportation costs, cartage costs, insurance, receiving, testing, temporary storage, and purchasing costs, represents a correct cost of inventories which should remain in asset status until matched against the revenues identified with their sale. The survey indicated wide variations in the policies adopted in the treatment of purchasing, receiving, and handling costs with freight-in being the only commonly included item. Generally the other items are treated as expenses or cost expirations in the periods in which they are vouchered.

Few concerns purchase materials or supplies in the same quantities during each month of the year. Likewise, production and sales are seasonal. If purchasing, receiving, and various forms of handling costs are treated as current expenses, the charges to profit and loss are overstated, the value of inventories in stockrooms is understated, and there is a resulting understatement of profit during periods when heavy purchases are being made. The situation is reversed when there are few purchases, but production and sales are large. Thus failure to use an accounting technique which will provide for the inclusion of purchasing, receiving, and handling costs in inventories, or which will defer such costs, results in the mismatching of revenues and cost expirations.

A practical accounting device to remedy this situation is the use of a normal, predetermined purchasing and handling rate. In the majority of concerns it is possible to prepare a yearly budget of freight-in, cartage, receiving, testing, storage, insurance, and purchasing costs and to divide the total by the estimated net cost of purchases (or number of units such as tons) for the year to obtain a percentage to be applied to the net cost of each purchase as it is received and vouchered each day. As a result, purchasing and handling costs are attached to goods received so that the total costs can be treated as inventories until they are properly matched with revenues when sold.

Purchase Discounts

A common recommendation of accountants is the adoption of an accounting technique which will treat purchase discounts as a reduction in the vendor's invoice price. However, the survey indicated that in the majority of enterprises purchase discounts are treated as "other income." Income is not realized upon the initiation and receipt of a purchase, nor through payment of an invoice. Furthermore, inventories are not carried at a proper cost valuation if purchases are booked at the invoice price and a cash discount is subsequently taken. There is no justification for recording inventories at an amount greater than their cash outlay. Clearly then, if cash discounts are not treated as a reduction in cost there will be a misstatement of inventory cost, inventory cost expirations in future accounting periods will be overstated, a mismatching of revenues and costs will result for both the present period and the succeeding periods and the profit-and-loss statement will reflect inaccuracies.

If purchases are recorded at net cost, there remains the problem of treating cash discounts lost. Should the discount lost be considered a period charge, or should it be added to the cost of materials purchased? The period charge may be considered proper if the discounts are lost because of inefficiency. Future accounting periods should not be burdened with cost expirations resulting from the deferment of all or a .portion of the purchase discount lost due to a weak financial position of a prior period which is considered to be the fault of management. Likewise, if discounts are lost because of mismanagement, such as an oversight or inadequate internal control, the amount lost should be a period charge. Future periods should not be charged with a cost expiration greater than the actual cost of materials merely because of the mistakes in an earlier period.

However, it might be argued that if the discounts are lost due to reasons beyond the control of management, the amount lost should be associated with and be made a part of the cost of any material remaining in ending inventories. Inadequate working capital is an example.

Inventory and Sale of By-Products

Current practice is to treat income from the sale of by-products as "other income" and to ignore the inventory values of quantities on hand at the end of the accounting period. Records only of quantities of scrap and other residues are generally maintained for purposes of internal control. Since the accumulation of by-products is subject to seasonal conditions of production, and in many concerns represents a substantial revenue factor, the "other income" method results in revenue being identified with a different accounting period than that of the major commodity with which the by-product was created. Other important infractions of good accounting principles which result from the "other income" method are the overstatement of the inventory value of the major product and the failure to recognize the inventory value of by-products at the close of each accounting period.

Any plan of accounting for by-products which does not attempt to inventory by-products and which does not relieve the major commodity of this value at the point of separation results in mismatching of revenues and cost expirations. A satisfactory plan, which is a distinct improvement over the "other income" method, is found in the treatment of income realized from the sale of by-products as a reduction in the cost of production of the major commodities. In job order plants, if the work in process involves large jobs from which are obtained by-products of considerable value, the best method is to credit the job with the estimated market quotations of by-products which are recognized as inventory valuations on the balance sheet until sold. If the by-products cannot be identified with a particular job, their inventory value can be treated as a reduction of manufacturing overhead. If a process cost system is used in an industry, the value of by-products may be credited to the process or operation responsible for the creation of such residues.

Selling Costs

It continues to be the practice to consider selling costs as charges to operations in the period in which the expenditure is made. Only under unusual circumstances, such as an advance payment to an advertising agency or the purchase of sales pamphlets to be distributed to customers in the future, are selling costs generally treated as deferred charges or prepaid items. It is readily admitted that selling activities such as radio advertising, magazine and newspaper copy, schools for salesmen, promotional travel, extra clerical help, and printing of circulars require large expenditures during the launching of a sales campaign and that the impact of the sales effort may result in a large sales volume in succeeding accounting periods after the completion of the promotional efforts, but accountants seem reluctant to defer any of these selling costs or to treat any portion of them as finished goods inventory values. As a result the monthly or quarterly profit-and-loss statements frequently show high selling costs and low profits in one period followed by correspondingly low costs and large profits in the succeeding periods.

One remedy for such bad matching of revenues and cost expirations is the careful analysis of each selling cost and the recognition of the prepaid and deferrable elements as balance sheet items. The analysis will generally result in exceptionally large and unusual items being segregated, but the method does not result in the systematic and accurate identification of selling costs with units or dollars of sales and ignores the irregularity and seasonal character of sales.

A second plan that requires the use of a normal, predetermined selling cost distribution rate (or a separate rate for each sales territory) is being used by a few concerns as a more effective means of matching selling costs and sales. A system of budgetary control permits the preparation of estimates of selling costs for each of the 12 months of the budget period. Likewise sales estimates, in terms of dollars or units, can be prepared for each month. A normal, predetermined selling cost distribution rate for the year is obtained by adding together the 12 monthly selling cost estimates and dividing the total by the 12 monthly sales estimates as shown by the following formula:

$$\frac{\text{Total estimated selling costs for budget period}}{\text{Total estimated sales for budget period}} = \text{Normal selling cost distribution rate.}$$

A separate rate can be computed for each sales territory if selling costs and sales are classified by territories. The percentage rate is used each accounting period to apply a normal amount of selling cost to the sales for the period. Thus, the same amount of selling cost is matched against a dollar of sales in each month of the year thereby leveling the seasonal factors of selling costs and sales. The amount of selling costs transferred to profit and loss in any one period may be more or less than the actual selling expenditures for the period since the emphasis has been placed upon cost expirations in terms of sales rather than upon expenditures made. Variances are treated each month as deferred items and should be eliminated automatically by the end of the budget period due to counteracting conditions of selling costs and sales in other months of the year.

Research and Development Costs

Research costs are normally thought of as the costs of discovering a new idea, while development costs are those necessary to place the research findings on a commercial basis. Included in research and development costs are engineers' and technicians' salaries, new tools and dies, blue prints, laboratory supplies, and associated costs. Occasionally the costs of securing patents are included, although this practice is not common.

The question was asked as to whether these research and development costs are considered to be a period cost, or whether they are charged to a research and development account and amortized over the life of the product discovered and developed.

It is apparent from the answers obtained that in the majority of companies no attempt is made to match research and development costs against the revenues realized and recognized from these cost expirations. The effect of treating such costs as charges to current operations is to relieve future accounting periods of their proportional share of the cost expirations and to misstate the profit or loss in all periods concerned.

If the research and development costs are deferred so as to be amortized over the life of the developed product, then an approach is made to a true matching of cost expirations and revenues. The question of how to estimate the life of the developed product may be difficult to answer, but should the development result in a patent, then the patent's life of 17 years may be used; or if it is a "fad" item the estimated life may be shortened. In any event the estimate can be based upon experience and judgment and the amortization of the costs over this estimated life will result in a more accurate profit or loss figure than is obtained by arbitrarily charging research and development amounts as period costs.

The costs for research and development, which have been deferred for products that are subsequently abandoned, should be treated as a loss in the period of abandonment. Care should be exercised so as not to include such losses in factory overhead which subsequently becomes a cost expiration through inclusion in inventories, because if such a procedure is followed, future periods will be burdened by cost expirations properly chargeable to a prior period. The losses should be treated as charges to surplus as a correction of a prior period's error in judgment.

Strikes, Lockouts, Material Shortages, and Other Abnormal Losses

A sharp line should be drawn between normal and abnormal losses. Normal losses are those that naturally result from business operations and tend to be a recurring charge exemplified by loss due to idle labor time resulting from the uneven flow of the product through the production processes, or the loss due to material waste resulting from pattern cuts. Such losses are normal and are anticipated by management. Their disposition is either through the absorption of increased labor or material cost, or if recorded separately, as an increase in the factory overhead or burden. In either instance they become a product cost and are subsequently properly matched against recognized revenues.

Abnormal losses include not only losses resulting from strikes, lockouts, material shortages, fires, and floods, but all other losses which are beyond the control of and not anticipated by management. The survey indicated that such losses are generally treated as nonoperating items and therefore are not included in the cost of the product or as current operating costs. However, noncatastrophe losses such as strikes, lockouts, and material shortages have tended to be included in operating figures. Such a procedure inflates the cost expirations for the current period as well as for future periods if part of the loss is deferred through inventories. The profit or loss for all periods concerned is misstated.

The "clean surplus" theory is not at issue here. Whether or not such losses should be charged directly to surplus or cleared through the profit-and-loss statement in a separate section to be shown after operating results is not important. Such abnormal losses should not be included in the cost of the product or be allowed to influence the operating results. The inclusion of abnormal losses as operating cost expirations may be damaging to the enterprise. It is conceivable that when the product unit cost is overstated because of the inclusion of abnormal loss, management may erroneously abandon production or change its policies, investors may lose interest in the company's stock, or management may be replaced because of its failure to meet the competitive market.

Vacation Time, Bonuses, and Gifts to Employees

There is a wide variation in the treatment of vacation pay, bonuses, and gifts to employees. Weekly or monthly bonuses for above-standard production or for overtime are properly included as a direct labor cost or as overhead costs and are matched through inventories against recognized revenues. Some variations are found, however, in methods of handling vacation pay, irregular bonuses, and gifts to employees. Some companies consider such costs as direct labor charges, with the result that the cost of production during periods in which bonuses are paid or vacations are given will be higher than production costs in other accounting periods. Thus, production costs for December may be higher and profits lower than in other months because of the end-of-the-year bonuses paid to employees.

A few companies treat these costs as nonoperating items. There is little merit in this position. Vacation pay and bonuses are recurring costs and are considered necessary to maintain satisfactory personnel relations. They are an important factor of production and unit costs should properly reflect such expenditures.

It is more logical to charge these seasonal and irregular costs to factory overhead or burden. Since such payments can be estimated with reasonable accuracy for the year in advance of the budget period, they can be included in the budget of factory overhead costs and can be spread equitably over production for the year by means of normal, predetermined overhead distribution rates which spread overhead costs over all plant operations, thereby equalizing seasonal conditions of costs and production. Such a procedure properly matches cost expirations against recognized revenues.

Seasonal Plant Operations

Many concerns are confronted with seasonal operations consisting of some months of peak activity and other months of idle plant or low production. Some accountants continue to treat the maintenance costs of idle plant as regular operating costs, and, consequently, profit-and-loss statements prepared for periods of idle plant reflect a loss or low profits. In a similar manner, all plant costs are charged to the small quantity of production that flows through the plant during slack periods of operation. The result is the presentation of extremely high unit costs of production during some months and low unit costs during other periods. The resultant matching of costs and revenues is improper and the profit or loss figures are misleading because, during the slack periods, the few units produced are charged with costs that should be shared by the entire production of the natural business year.

The solution to the problem is not a difficult one. Expenditures made during seasonal shutdowns and planned stoppages are a necessary part of production costs and should be included in inventory values. However, these costs should be spread equitably over all production for the year by means of normal, predetermined overhead distribution rates. In this manner, cost expirations will be matched through inventories with recognized revenues in the proper accounting period and more accurate and dependable profit-and-loss figures will be available.

Factory Overhead Variances

There is agreement among accountants that the proper way to allocate factory overhead or burden to production is to use normal, overhead distribution rates. However, there seems to be no unanimity concerning the disposition of the variances which may result when applied and actual overhead costs are compared at the end of a monthly or quarterly accounting period. A majority of accountants consider such variances as general profit-and-loss items to be charged off as a period cost regardless of the causes of their existence. Such an unscientific approach is an acknowledgment of a lack of understanding of the objectives of using normal distribution rates and the importance of matching revenues and cost expirations.

The proper disposition of overhead variances requires a careful analysis as to the underlying conditions which created them. When the budgets of factory overhead and production are compared in detail with actual overhead costs and production at the end of each accounting period, it is generally found that the variances are due to one or more of the following causes:

1. The normal overhead distribution rate may be incorrectly computed; the estimated overhead may be too high or too low, or the estimated direct labor hours, direct labor cost, or machine hours (depending upon the distribution base used) may be too large or too small.
2. The overhead distribution rate, which is a normal rate, may be correctly computed, but there may be seasonal conditions of overhead costs and production.
3. Abnormal circumstances may have resulted in unusually high overhead costs or unexpectedly low production; the former may be caused by an uninsured fire loss, flood damage, or sabotage while the latter may be attributed to a labor strike, a lockout, or a boiler explosion.

If all or a portion of the variances are due to the use of incorrect overhead rates, goods produced during the period have been costed at an erroneous figure and an adjustment should be made to work-in-process inventories, finished goods inventories, and cost of goods sold. If revenues and cost expirations are to be properly matched, the goods produced during the period must be recosted to correct for the errors in the overhead rates.

If the variances are due to seasonal factors, they should be treated as deferred items to be shown on the balance sheet. They are absorbed in future periods through the use of the normal overhead rates.

If the variances are the result of unusual and abnormal circumstances which are beyond the control of management they should not be included in inventory costs but should be charged directly to surplus, or if charged to profit and loss, shown as "nonoperating" items.

Variances from Standard Costs

There is no uniformity of opinion among accountants as to the proper disposition of variances between actual and standard costs. One group believes that all variances, regardless of cause, should be transferred directly to profit and loss at the end of each accounting period. They reason that all forms of variances represent conditions of waste, inefficiency, idle time, and changes of business fortune, none of which is correctly included in production costs.

A second group believes that all variances except the material price variance should be charged directly to profit and loss. An exception is made of the material price variance because it is generally due to market and business conditions which are beyond the control of management. It is the policy of this group of accountants to prorate the material price variance over work in process inventory, finished goods inventory, and cost of goods sold.

The first group ignores entirely the fact that some of the variances due to off-standard operations may be applicable to future accounting periods and that there is a mismatching of revenues and cost expirations unless each variance is analyzed carefully and disposed of in accordance with sound accounting principles. The second group is correct in recognizing that the material price variance may be applicable to inventories and cost of goods sold, but these accountants fail to recognize that other variances may also be applicable to future periods and legitimately included in inventory values.

A third group of accountants believes that each variance should be carefully analyzed, the causes for its incurrence determined, and disposition methods, which recognize asset elements and expired elements, should be adopted. In accordance with this policy, each variance requires individual treatment.

The material price variance may be due to inefficient purchasing, improper shipping, failure to take discounts, or to changes in market conditions. If it is due to various types of inefficiency, it should be taken to profit and loss. If it is due to changes in market prices, beyond the control of management, it should be prorated over inventories and cost of goods sold, so that inventories will be revalued at an adjusted standard cost.

The material quantity variance (usage variance) indicates that there has been an excess or saving in quantities of materials used compared to standard. It is usually accounted for by the inefficiency or efficiency of handling and processing materials. This variance should be transferred directly to profit and loss, since one objective of the use of standard costs is to remove such losses or gains from the cost of production and inventories. Future periods should not be burdened with losses due to inefficiency which arose in the current period.

The labor wage variance is analogous to the material price variance. If due to changes in labor rates, it should be prorated over inventories and cost of goods sold. If the variance is due to inefficient employment procedures or refusal to recognize accepted wage rate standards, it should be charged directly to profit and loss.

The disposition of the labor time variance (labor usage or efficiency variance) follows the general plan outlined for the treatment of the material quantity variance. Either a debit or credit balance, which may be the result of substandard performance or gain in efficiency, should be transferred to profit and loss. Such losses or gains are properly recognized in the current accounting period.

The overhead budget variance may be due to a seasonal condition of overhead costs, to the incurrence of costs in excess of, or lower than, standard requirements, to improperly prepared standards, or to all three. If due to seasonal conditions, the variance should be treated as a deferred item, since it will be automatically adjusted by offsetting conditions in future periods. If the variance is attributed to an excess or savings over standard costs, it should be charged directly to profit and loss. Variances due to improperly prepared standards should be adjusted to inventories and cost of goods sold.

Idle or overcapacity variance (utilization variance) may result from seasonal conditions of production, from off-standard conditions of production, or from improperly prepared standards. As in the case of the overhead budget variance, this variance should be deferred if due to seasonal conditions, transferred directly to profit and loss if resulting from inefficiency or efficiency, and adjusted to inventories and cost of goods sold if the cause is improperly prepared standards.

The production efficiency variance is an indicator of the efficiency with which the plant has been operated and should be charged directly to profit and loss.

It is evident from the preceding discussion that if an illogical disposition is made of the variances from standard costs, a mismatching of revenues and cost expiration results. Under such circumstances the accuracy of the profit-and-loss statement should not go unchallenged.

Other Examples of Improper "Matching"

The previous discussion has introduced some of the problems of the accounting analysis traditionally referred to as "capital vs. revenue" or "asset vs. expense." There are other problems which are not presented in detail in this article because their importance in the matching of revenues and cost expirations has been discussed for many years and their proper treatment is generally recognized by accountants.

One group of costs includes depreciation of tangible fixed assets, depletion of natural resources, and amortization of intangible fixed assets. If an improper method is used to determine depreciation, depletion or amortization, or ultraconservatism or the lack of conservatism results in the expired elements being too large or too small, there will be a mismatching of cost expirations and revenues and the reporting of inaccurate profit or loss figures.

Other estimated items which result in mismatching when improperly computed are bad debts, sales discounts, sales returns and allowances, insurance, and various types of taxes.

CONCLUSIONS

Management, investors, creditors, and the general public are interested in obtaining the most accurate profit-and-loss statements each month or quarter that it is possible for accountants to prepare, because important operating plans, investor and creditor decisions, and public policies are dependent upon the data presented. An investigation of the accounting practices of any group of business enterprises in any section of the country would supply examples of the use of illogical and unscientific accounting procedures which are contrary to generally accepted accounting principles and which produce profit-

and-loss figures that are unreliable and misleading. It is in the mis-matching of costs and revenues that most of the errors and confusion are to be found.

Each accountant should conduct a periodic reexamination of the accounting practices of the business concerns in which he is interested for the purpose of assuring the management and himself that every accounting procedure has been reviewed and corrected for the pur-pose of obtaining the most accurate matching of cost expirations and revenues that it is possible to obtain. Then and only then can the accountant, with a clear conscience, present a profit-and-loss state-ment that is worthy of his profession.

26. BASE POINT LABOR
DISTRIBUTION *

C. W. Bastable †

Unless an accounting system is designed so as to allocate costs accurately, its products cannot be used with confidence. Inasmuch as labor costs are generally significant percentages of total costs, they must be handled with particular care. Frequently, there are major deficiencies in the methods used to allocate labor costs in the accounts. Most of these deficiencies can be eliminated through the use of a base point labor distribution system that is explained hereinafter.

DEFINITION OF LABOR COSTS

Labor costs should be defined carefully before any consideration is given to the mechanics of processing them in the accounts. There once was a time when the cost of engaging a worker's services consisted entirely of his gross earnings. Sociological developments have changed this. Gross earnings are now but a part of the cost of engaging personal services. The other parts are social security taxes paid by employers, voluntary contributions to pension plans, workmen's compensation insurance, etc., and they are becoming increasingly larger percentages of total labor costs. They are no longer immaterial in amount, and they should not be excluded from any meaningful computation of true labor costs.

In the base point labor distribution system, as should be the case in all systems, labor costs are defined as all the costs mentioned above that an organization assumes when it hires employes.

HOURLY DISTRIBUTION RATE BASED ON ANNUALIZED COMPENSATION

Complete and accurate labor cost allocation, on an individual employe basis, requires the computation of individual hourly distribution rates based on annualized compensation. The first step in

---

* From *The Controller* (March, 1959). Reprinted by permission of the Controllers Institute of America, Inc.

† C. W. Bastable, Professor of Accounting at Columbia University.

determining these rates is to compute the normal number of expected working hours in the year for each employe, as follows:

Number of days in year		365
Less:		
Saturdays and Sundays	104	
Holidays observed	9	
Vacation days granted	10	
Average number of days lost through illness (based		
upon average experience)	6	129
Normal workdays in year		236
Hours worked per day		x7
Normal work hours per year		1652

The next step is to compute the total annual cost for each employe on the basis of current conditions rather than future payroll changes. Assuming that the sum of gross compensation and other costs amounts to $5,400 for a given employe, his expected hourly employment cost would be $3.269 on the basis of 1,652 anticipated hours of actual work per year. This is his hourly distribution rate. One such rate is computed for each employe.

When multiplied by hours worked, the hourly distribution rate provides the labor cost to be allocated to work in process or to departments other than the one in which an employe is based. It should be noted that the product of hours worked and the distribution rate can be expected to exceed the total outlay for an employe's services in an average week or month. The excess, as is later explained, absorbs leave costs when they occur.

THE BASE POINT CONCEPT

In order to understand the base point concept, it will be helpful to review the practice of accruing vacation leave. This practice serves two purposes. First, it discloses the liability for accrued vacation time in the balance sheet. Second, it allocates the full annual salary of an employe over those days during the year when he is actually on the job. These points are readily illustrated by a simplified case. Assume that an employe earns $100 per week, that he works 50 weeks, and that he takes an authorized two-weeks vacation at the end of the year. If he is paid weekly, the following entry would be made each week for the first 50 weeks:

Dr. Work in Process	104.00*	
Cr. Cash		100.00
Cr. Accrued Wages Payable		4.00

    Annual salary of $5200 ÷ 50 work weeks

At the end of 50 weeks, accrued wages payable (measuring liability for vacation leave) would amount to $200. Thus, when the employe is in a vacation status for the next two weeks, the following entry would be made each of those weeks:

```
Dr. Accrued Wages Payable .....................  100.00
     Cr. Cash ......................................            100.00
```

The mechanics of the above, however, tend to obscure an important concept.

In the process of accruing vacation time, the accrued wages payable account is a focal point, or base point as it will be called later, in the allocation of wage costs to proper accounts. It may help to visualize the accrued wages payable account as a sort of clearing account. Revision of the first of the preceding entries may facilitate understanding. Instead of one entry each of the first 50 weeks, two entries might be made. One entry would record the effective cost of employment and the related liability:

```
Dr. Work in Process .........................  104.00
     Cr. Accrued Wages Payable ..................            104.00
```

The other entry would record how much of the liability is discharged by a current payment to the employe:

```
Dr. Accrued Wages Payable .....................  100.00
     Cr. Cash ......................................            100.00
```

These revised entries indicate how the accrued wages payable account is in effect a base point through which labor costs are cleared. Once this base point concept is recognized, it can be extended to achieve better labor distribution *in cases where vacation leave is not accrued as a liability.*

EXTENSION OF THE BASE POINT CONCEPT

The accrued wages payable account does not have to be the base point. Any other logical account may be so designated. The most logical one is, of course, the one through which salary costs are normally cleared. It is hard to name this account unmistakably because of the lack of standardization in accounting terminology and because of variations in different kinds of businesses. It might be the labor account, the salaries expense account, the payroll account, or any other similarly named account.

Regardless of the name of the account that is designated as the base point, the account is handled in only one way. All labor costs (gross salaries and related labor costs) are charged to it when periodic payrolls are prepared. Then the real labor costs are determined by multiplying hours worked by hourly distribution rates. The resulting costs are allocated to appropriate accounts, and their total is credited to the base point account. (In practice, all this may be accomplished by means of one combined entry.) As has previously been noted, costs allocated will exceed outlays for labor in some periods. This creates credits in the base point account. These credits absorb the costs of authorized leave, which is always charged to the base point account.

Theoretically, there should be no balance in the base point account at the end of a year because of the way in which the hourly distribution rate is computed. As a practical matter, however, there will be balances. Some employes will get raises. Thus, they will take vacations at rates of pay higher than those that created credits in the base point account for the purpose of absorbing vacation costs. Also, actual experience with sick leave cannot be expected to agree precisely with the sick leave allowance used in computing the hourly distribution rate. Notwithstanding, any debit or credit balances in the base point account at the end of the year are likely to be small. As such, they can be disposed of as manufacturing cost adjustments.

Although the preceding paragraph suggests that the base point concept is limited in its application to manufacturing personnel, such a limitation is by no means intended. If a business keeps records of departmental costs, it will have to keep its salary costs by departments. Problems arise when employes are transferred either temporarily or permanently from one department to another.

In the case of a temporary transfer, the department to which an employe is temporarily assigned should bear its pro rata share of the real cost of the employe's time. This is accomplished by charging that department for the employe's time on the basis of the hourly distribution rate. Since this charge will always exceed the straight time, plus related employment costs, for the same number of hours, the difference is automatically credited to the employe's permanent department. It is the contribution of the temporary department to the cost of annual and sick leave taken by the employe.

When an employe is transferred permanently to a new department, he may have a significant leave accumulation. The current value of this accumulation (hours of leave accumulation multiplied by the employe's straight hourly rate, plus proportionate related employment costs) is a cost for which the old department is responsible. Adjustment can be made for this under the base point concept by charging the amount to the old department and crediting it to the new department.

Should there be any overtime costs, it is intended that they be distributed at their actual amounts to the jobs or departments for which overtime was necessary. If overtime is regularly scheduled, then no one job or department is necessarily responsible for it. Neither a job nor a department should, through chance, be charged for overtime premiums under such circumstances. Instead, the cost of regularly scheduled overtime should be included when hourly distribution rates are computed. This will insure equitable distribution of overtime costs.

Rather than risk misunderstanding on another point, mention should be made of the method of dealing with holidays. No time is reported for holidays on time cards. If, for example, there is a holiday in a given week, individual time cards should account for only 28 hours (4 days of 7 hours). The employes are paid for the holiday, and the hourly distribution rate allocates the cost of holidays over all the normal work hours during a year.

This extension of the base point concept may be understood more readily by means of an actual case. The corporation in point, though small, had a variety of diverse activities. It engaged in some manufacturing, accumulating costs on a job order basis. It also maintained other departments that conducted business unrelated to the manufacturing activities. Employes were paid monthly. Some employes were frequently transferred from job to job, from job to department, and from department to department. Employes permanently assigned to one department were sometimes temporarily reassigned to other departments. Although each employe kept a time report, accurate labor cost distribution posed a number of problems.

One problem was created by the practice of paying employes monthly. The number of work hours, exclusive of any overtime, varied from 140 in some months to 154 in others. Past practice had been to distribute labor costs by dividing each employe's monthly compensation by the actual number of work hours in each month. This meant that the compensation of any given employe was distributed on the basis of varying hourly rates from one month to the next. Thus, a given amount of time for one employe might be charged to a job at one amount in January and a different amount in February.

Another problem existed with respect to vacation time. *To what account should vacation costs be charged for those employes who worked on various jobs and/or in various departments?* The difficulty was aggravated by the need to be consistent. Vacation costs of permanent departmental employes were charged to salaries expense and identified as to department. Vacation costs of persons employed to work on long-term jobs were charged as direct labor costs to the jobs. *How could the vacation time of the "transients" be handled so that the cost would be allocated to jobs and departments in a comparable manner and with reasonable precision?*

The corporation did not care to accrue vacation time, but it did wish to allocate labor costs on a sound basis. The objective was for each job or department to bear its fair share of all costs related to the employment of personnel, including the cost of annual and sick leave.

The objective was achieved by means of the base point concept and the hourly distribution rate based on annualized compensation. Because department cost statements were to be prepared, the salaries account was subdivided, in a subsidiary record, into 13 categories: e.g., general administration, accounting, shipping and receiving, periodicals, research staff, etc. These categories conformed precisely with the plan of organization. Each employe was based for accounting purposes in his appropriate category. Monthly, each category of the salaries account was charged for the full costs of employes based in it and credited for the proper cost of the time that any of these employes worked elsewhere.

An example may help to convey what the foregoing accomplished. Assume that employment of a hypothetical individual entails a total monthly outlay of $345.75 in the month of March, which has 147 working hours. The employe is based in the research staff, but he worked 120 hours on Job No. 409 and 27 hours in the periodicals department. His hourly distribution rate is $2.501. Theoretically, two entries would be made. One entry would record cost allocation:

Dr. Work in Process (Job No. 409) 300.12
Dr. Salaries (Periodicals) 67.53
    Cr. Salaries (Research Staff) 367.65

The other entry would record payment:

Dr. Salaries (Research Staff) 345.75
    Cr. Cash 345.75

It should be noted that these entries create a credit balance of $21.90 in the research staff subdivision of the salaries account. This credit, along with credits from other months, will absorb leave costs subsequently charged to the salaries account (research staff). In actual practice, shortcuts in processing labor costs merge the two entries into one, as follows:

Dr. Work in Process (Job No. 409)	300.12	
Dr. Salaries (Periodicals)	67.53	
Cr. Salaries (Research Staff)		21.90
Cr. Cash		345.75

It should be noted that base point labor distribution, as applied to the salaries account, creates credit balances within the salaries account, against which there are charges when employes take their vacations. Needless to say, it would be better to accrue the liability rather than to hide it in the salaries account. However, in business firms where employes are regularly required to take their vacations during the year, the taking of vacations generally results in cancellation of any credits that are built up during a year.

ADVANTAGES OF BASE POINT LABOR DISTRIBUTION

Base point labor distribution insures that every department will bear its fair share of the complete costs of any employes temporarily assigned to it from other departments. Conversely, base point departments are relieved of bearing such portion of leave costs as related to the time any of its employes are temporarily assigned to other departments. With respect to employes assigned to manufacturing activities, base point labor distribution also guarantees that each job will bear the full costs of direct labor despite the length of time that workers are assigned to it.

Regardless of when employes may be transferred permanently to new departments, every department can be charged for the correct amount of annual leave costs. The manner in which this is done has been explained.

Annual and sick leaves are charged to overhead accounts in some accounting systems. This may result in distortion of overhead and overhead rates—especially if employes are permitted to favor certain months. Base point labor distribution eliminates this distortion.

The hourly distribution rate based on annualized compensation, which is used in connection with base point labor distribution, results in four important advantages. First, it establishes a true hourly labor cost for each employe that is very useful when budgets and cost estimates have to be made. Second, it enables labor costs to be posted, subject to availability of time reports, as currently as desired without the need for making any other payroll computations. Third, it enables labor costs to be applied at consistent rates from month to month regardless of distorting factors such as varying work hours in pay periods and the payment of social security taxes in some months and not in others. Fourth, costs are allocated in terms of the actual costs of the individuals involved, rather than on the basis of an average rate for a group of employes:

LIMITATIONS OF BASE POINT LABOR DISTRIBUTION

Base point labor distribution has some limitations of a minor nature. They are

1. The hourly distribution rate is based upon the annualized cost of employment, which includes social security taxes levied upon the employer. Because these taxes are not paid on an annualized basis, the amount of tax paid in a year can exceed the amount allocated as cost if an employe is severed during a year.

2. If the base point is not accrued wages payable, credits may build up *during* the year in departmental divisions of the salaries account. Such balances have a nuisance value when interim departmental statements are prepared. (This limitation is of little or no significance in companies where vacations are spread evenly over the year.)

3. A definite company policy with respect to vacations is needed. Best results are obtained in cases where a fixed amount of vacation time is earned for each month (or other period) of employment.

4. Whenever an employe's rate of compensation changes, accumulated credits do not measure the value of accumulated vacation leave.

SUMMARY

Base point labor distribution is simply a method by which the full costs of employes' services are allocated equitably in the accounts. The practice of accruing vacation leave as a liability is but one way in which such allocation may be accomplished. When leave is so accrued, the liability account is in effect the base point. However, it is not necessary to recognize accrued vacation leave in order to achieve the same kind of labor cost allocation. Such can be done by the simple expedient of shifting the base point to another account.

Under the method of base point labor distribution, individual labor costs are identified. The cost of any employe's time is allocated on the basis of costs relating to him alone. The method, as presented, does not imply the application of an average rate for a group to the time of one individual. However, such a modification is feasible.

The current trend is toward more leisure and increased benefits for employes. The more liberal that time-off policies become and the more that supplementary employment costs rise, the more important it becomes to recognize the value of base point labor distribution.

PART IV

PROBLEM AREAS OF PLANNING AND CONTROL

In Part I were readings selected to provide a groundwork in the function of management and to relate accounting and budgeting to that groundwork in a very basic way. The process of decision making was explored and related to cost concepts in developing a conceptual framework for planning. In a like manner, a framework for thinking about control was established by the series of readings which reviewed the control process, and considered its elements of goal establishment, performance measurement, and feedback.

In this Part are readings dealing with particular problems in the area of planning and control. One group deals with the problems of organizing the planning and control functions, and includes the definition of functions, the role of systems, long-range planning, and the relationship to the disciplines of mathematics and behavioral science. A second group deals with the common planning problems of pricing, inventory management, cost-volume-profit analysis, and capital budgeting. A third group deals with control problems in many areas including the control of costs of manufacturing, marketing, research, administration, the control of cash flow, and the monitoring of capital investments.

In many instances, the placement of the reading in one group rather than another is arbitrary because planning and control are both discussed. Though it presents difficulties in organizing the readings, the fact underscores the close relationship between planning and control.

SECTION A

ORGANIZING THE PLANNING AND CONTROL FUNCTIONS

With the groundwork of management planning and control established and some theories of accounting and budgeting laid upon that groundwork, it is time to turn to some of the problems involved in organizing the planning and control function.

The practitioners' concepts of their function are found in the statements issued by the Budget Executives and by the Financial Executives. In the latter case a distinction is made between the Controller and the Treasurer.

The Controller has the responsibility for establishing certain subsystems (see Article 28) for planning and control. The article on "Characteristics of Management Control Systems" discusses, relates, and contrasts the several subsystems.

Long-range planning is not new but there is a quickening of interest in it. The Controller may be responsible for this function or, if not, must coordinate with it.

Several relatively recent developments are of concern to the Controller in organizing the operations of his department. These include studies in employee behavior as it relates to budget development, mathematical modeling of the budget, and network techniques applied to the budgeting and accounting processes. Operations research has had a healthy growth in recent years, yet the relationship of operations research to accounting is the subject of much disagreement. It is the subject of the final article.

27. STATEMENT OF DUTIES AND RESPONSIBILITIES OF THE BUDGET DIRECTOR *

Budget Executives Institute

A. The function of the budget director is to facilitate the direction and control of the enterprise by:

1. Insuring the generation and dissemination of information needed for decision making and planning to each person in the organization having such responsibilities. The information may include, but is not limited to, forecasts of economic and social conditions, government influences, organization goals and standards for decision making, economic and financial guidelines, performance data, performance standards, and the prerequisite plans of others in the enterprise.

2. Establishing and maintaining a planning system which:
   a. Channels information (1 above) to each person responsible for planning.
   b. Schedules the formulation of plans.
   c. Structures the plans of subsections of the enterprise into composites at which points tests are made for significant deviations from economic and financial guidelines and from goal achievement, and repeats the process for larger segments to and including the enterprise as a whole.
   d. Disseminates advice of approval, disapproval, or revision of plans to affected individuals in accordance with established lines of authority and organizational responsibilities.

3. Constructing and using models of the enterprise, both in total and by subsections, to test the effect of internal and external variables upon the achievement of organizational goals.

4. Insuring that performance data be accumulated, related to responsibility centers within the organization, measured against the plans (whether period or project) for each center, transmitted to each center, and the analysis of deviations of actual from planned performance.

B. The budget director may utilize the services of others in the organization (including but not limited to accountants, data proces-

---

* Statement prepared by committee consisting of D. R. Borst, Joseph T. Ryerson and Son; W. R. Bunge, Jos. Schlitz Brewing Co.; R. Guthrie, I-T-E Circuit Breaker Co.; H. Mason, S. C. Johnson and Son; A. Moor, United Airlines; and W. E. Thomas, University of Illinois, Chairman. Approved by the National Board as a statement of the Budget Executives Institute, September, 1966. Reprinted by permission of the Budget Executives Institute.

sors, economists, market analysts, financial analysts, and engineers) and/or may perform them himself, but he has the overriding responsibility for insuring that the functions described above are integrated into a consistent and comprehensive system which facilitates the planning and control of the enterprise by those members of the organization bearing such responsibilities.

28. CONTROLLERSHIP AND TREASURERSHIP FUNCTIONS DEFINED BY FEI *

The first formal official statement of the responsibilities of the corporate treasurership function was approved by the Board of Directors of Financial Executives Institute (established in 1931 as Controllers Institute of America) at its meeting in French Lick Springs, Indiana, on May 17.

For many years the Institute and its predecessor body had published an established list of functions of controllership. The newly approved list of treasurership functions was developed coincident with the change of scope and name of the Institute from Controllers Institute to Financial Executives Institute. (See The Controller for May, 1962: "CIA Becomes FEI," page 228.)

FINANCIAL MANAGEMENT

CONTROLLERSHIP

PLANNING FOR CONTROL

To establish, coordinate, and administer, as an integral part of management, an adequate plan for the control of operations. Such a plan would provide, to the extent required in the business, profit planning, programs for capital investing and for financing, sales forecasts, expense budgets and cost standards, together with the necessary procedures to effectuate the plan.

REPORTING AND INTERPRETING

To compare performance with operating plans and standards, and to report and interpret the results of operations to all levels of management and to the owners of the business. This function includes the formulation of accounting policy, the coordination of systems and procedures, the preparation of operating data and of special reports as required.

EVALUATING AND CONSULTING

To consult with all segments of management responsible for policy or action concerning any phase of the operation of the business as it relates to the attainment of objectives and the effectiveness of policies, organization structure, and procedures.

TAX ADMINISTRATION

To establish and administer tax policies and procedures.

GOVERNMENT REPORTING

To supervise or coordinate the preparation of reports to government agencies.

PROTECTION OF ASSETS

To assure protection for the assets of the business through internal control, internal auditing, and assuring proper insurance coverage.

ECONOMIC APPRAISAL

To continuously appraise economic and social forces and government influences, and to interpret their effect upon the business.

TREASURERSHIP

PROVISION OF CAPITAL

To establish and execute programs for the provision of the capital required by the business, including negotiating the procurement of capital and maintaining the required financial arrangements.

INVESTOR RELATIONS

To establish and maintain an adequate market for the company's securities and, in connection therewith, to maintain adequate liaison with investment bankers, financial analysts, and shareholders.

SHORT-TERM FINANCING

To maintain adequate sources for the company's current borrowings from commercial banks and other lending institutions.

BANKING AND CUSTODY

To maintain banking arrangements; to receive, have custody of, and disburse the company's monies and securities; and to be responsible for the financial aspects of real estate transactions.

CREDITS AND COLLECTIONS

To direct the granting of credit and the collection of accounts due the company, including the supervision of required special arrangements for financing sales, such as time payment and leasing plans.

INVESTMENTS

To invest the company's funds as required, and to establish and coordinate policies for investment in pension and other similar trusts.

INSURANCE

To provide insurance coverage as required.

* Reprinted by permission of the Financial Executives Institute.

29. CHARACTERISTICS OF MANAGEMENT
CONTROL SYSTEMS *   Robert N. Anthony †

Since dogs and humans are both mammals, some generalizations that apply to one species also apply to the other. It is for this reason that some new surgical techniques can be tested on dogs before being risked on humans. But dogs and humans differ, and unless these differences are recognized, generalizations that are valid for one species may be erroneously applied to the other. For example, canine behavior can be largely explained in terms of reflexes, but human behavior is much more complicated. Similarly, some generalizations can be made about the whole planning and control process in a business; however, there actually are several quite different types of planning and control processes, and mistakes may be made if a generalization (principle, rule, technique) valid for one type is applied to the other.

This note suggests a classification of the main topics or "species" that come within the broad term Planning and Control Systems as well as the distinguishing characteristics of each topic. It is hoped that such a classification will lead to a sorting out and sharpening of principles and techniques applicable to each species. The particular classification chosen has been arrived at after careful analysis of how well various alternatives match statements made in the literature and, more important, what is found in practice. It is, however, tentative. Better schemes may well be developed, and we expose this one primarily in the hope that discussion of it will lead to agreement on *some* scheme, not necessarily this one. The classification is discussed in more detail in my book, *Planning and Control Systems: A Framework for Analysis.*

* From *Management Control Systems* (Homewood, Ill.: Richard D. Irwin, Inc., 1965). Reprinted by permission of Richard D. Irwin, Inc., and Robert N. Anthony.

† Robert N. Anthony, while serving as Ross Graham Walker Professor of Management Controls, Harvard Graduate School of Business Administration, Boston, Mass. (since appointed Assistant Secretary of Defense, Comptroller), compiled the data in this material based on research sponsored by the Division of Research at Harvard Business School. See R. N. Anthony, *Planning and Control Systems: A Framework for Analysis* (Boston: Division of Research, Harvard Business School, 1965).

In this note, we shall focus on a process labeled management control. We shall describe its main characteristics, and distinguish it from other processes labeled strategic planning, operational control, financial accounting, and information handling. Obviously, we do not assert that these processes can be separated by sharply defined boundaries; one shades into another. Strategic planning sets the guidelines for management control, and management control sets the guidelines for operational control. The complete management function involves an integration of all these processes, and the processes are complementary. We do assert that the processes are sufficiently distinct so that those who design and use planning and control systems will make expensive errors if they fail to take into account both the common characteristics of a process and the differences between processes. This note describes these similarities and differences and points out some of the errors made when they are not recognized.

MANAGEMENT CONTROL

Management control is the process by which managers assure that resources are obtained and used effectively and efficiently in the accomplishment of the organization's objectives.

Management control is a process carried on within the framework established by strategic planning. Objectives, facilities, organization, and financial factors are more or less accepted as givens. Decisions about next year's budget, for example, are constrained within policies and guidelines prescribed by top management. The management control process is intended to make possible the achievement of planned objectives as effectively and efficiently as possible within these givens.

The purpose of a management control system is to encourage managers to take actions that are in the best interests of the company. Technically, this purpose can be described as *goal congruence*. For many reasons, perfect goal congruence is not achievable; the most we can realistically aim for is a minimum amount of conflict between individual goals and corporate goals. Clearly, if the system increases this conflict—as happens when a certain course of action makes the reported performance of an individual appear better, even though it is detrimental to the best interests of the company—something is wrong with the system. For example, if the system is structured so that a certain course of action increases the reported profits of a division and at the same time lessens the profits of the company as a whole, there is something wrong. Psychological considerations are dominant in management control. Activities such as communicating, persuading, exhorting, inspiring, and criticizing are an important part of the process.

Ordinarily, a management control system is a *total* system in the sense that it embraces all aspects of the company's operation. It needs to be a total system because an important management function is to assure that all parts of the operation are in balance with one another; and in order to examine balance, management needs information about each of the parts.

With rare exceptions, the management control system is built around a financial structure; that is, resources and outputs are expressed in monetary units. Money is the only common denominator by means of which the heterogeneous elements of output and resources (e.g., hours of labor, type of labor, quantity and quality of material, amount and kind of products produced) can be combined and compared. Although the financial structure is usually the central focus, nonmonetary measures such as time, number of persons, and reject and spoilage rates are also important parts of the system.

The management control process tends to be rhythmic; it follows a definite pattern and timetable, month after month and year after year. In budgetary control, which is an important part of the management control process, certain steps are taken in a prescribed sequence and at certain dates each year: dissemination of guidelines, preparation of original estimates, transmission of these estimates up through the several echelons in the organization, review of these estimates, final approval by top management, dissemination back through the organization, operation, reporting, and the appraisal of performance. The procedure to be followed at each step in this process, the dates when the steps are to be completed, and even the forms to be used can be, and often are, set forth in a manual.

A management control system is, or should be, a coordinated, integrated system; that is, although data collected for one purpose may differ from those collected for another purpose, these data should be reconcilable with one another. In a sense, the management control system is a *single* system, but it is perhaps more accurate to think of it as a set of interlocking subsystems. In many organizations, for example, three types of cost information are needed for management control: (1) costs by responsibility centers, used for planning and controlling the activities of responsible supervisors; (2) full program costs, used for pricing and other operating decisions in normal circumstances; (3) direct program costs, used for pricing and other operating decisions in special circumstances, such as when management wishes to utilize idle capacity. ("Program" here is used for any activity in which the organization engages. In industrial companies, programs consist of products or product lines, and "product costs" can be substituted in the above statements.)

Line managers are the focal points in management control. They are the persons whose judgments are incorporated in the approval plans, and they are the persons who must influence others and whose performance is measured. Staff people collect, summarize, and present information that is useful in the process, and they make calculations that translate management judgments into the format of the system. Such a staff may be large in numbers; indeed, the control department is often the largest staff department in a company. However, the significant decisions are made by the line managers, not by the staff.

STRATEGIC PLANNING

Stategic planning is the process of deciding on the objectives of the organization, on changes in these objectives, on the resources used to attain these objectives, and on the policies that are to govern the acquisition, use, and disposition of these resources.

The word strategy is used here in its usual sense of deciding on how to combine and employ resources. Thus, strategic planning is a process having to do with the formulation of long-range, strategic, policy-type plans that change the character or direction of the organization. In an industrial company, this includes planning that affects the objectives of the company; policies of all types (including policies as to management control and other processes) ; the acquisition and disposition of major facilities, divisions, or subsidiaries; the markets to be served and distribution channels for serving them; the organization structure (as distinguished from individual personnel actions) ; research and development of new product lines (as distinguished from modifications in existing products and product changes within existing lines) ; sources of new permanent capital, dividend policy, and so on. Strategic planning decisions affect the physical, financial, and organizational framework within which operations are carried on. Briefly, here are some ways in which the stategic planning process differs from the management control process.

A strategic plan usually relates to some part of the organization, rather than to the totality; the concept of a master planner who constantly keeps all parts of the organization at some coordinated optimum is a nice concept, but an unrealistic one. Life is too complicated for any human, or computer, to do this.

Strategic planning is essentially *irregular*. Problems, opportunities, and bright ideas do not arise according to some set timetable, and they have to be dealt with whenever they happen to be perceived. The appropriate analytical techniques depend on the nature of the problem being analyzed, and no overall approach (such as a mathematical model) has been developed that is of much help in analyzing all types of strategic problems. Indeed, an overemphasis on a systematic approach is quite likely to stifle the essential element of creativity. In strategic planning, management works now on one problem, now on another, according to the needs and opportunities of the moment.

The estimates used in strategic planning are intended to show the *expected* results of the plan. They are neutral and impersonal. By contrast, the management control process and the data used in it are intended to influence managers to take actions that will lead to *desired* results. Thus, in connection with management control it is appropriate to discuss how tight an operating budget should be. Should the goals be set so high that only an outstanding manager can achieve them, or should they be set so that they are attainable by the average manager? At what level does frustration inhibit a manager's best efforts? Does an attainable budget lead to complacency? And so on. In strategic planning, the question to be asked about the figures is simply: Is this the most reasonable estimate that can be made?

Strategic planning relies heavily on external information—that is, on data collected from outside the company, such as market analyses, estimates of costs and other factors involved in building a plant in a new locality, technological developments, and so on. When data from the normal information system are used, they usually must be recast to fit the needs of the problem being analyzed. For example, current operating costs that are collected for measuring performance and for making pricing and other operating decisions usually must be restructured before they are useful in deciding whether to close down the plant. Another characteristic of the relevant information is that much of it is imprecise. The strategic planner estimates what will probably happen, often over a rather long time period. These estimates are likely to have a high degree of uncertainty, and they must be treated accordingly.

In the management control process, the communication of objectives, policies, guidelines, decisions, and results throughout the organization is extremely important. In the strategic planning process, communication is much simpler and involves relatively few persons; indeed, the need for secrecy often requires that steps be taken to inhibit communication. (Wide communication of the decisions that result from strategic planning is obviously important; this is part of the management control process.) Strategic planning is essentially applied economics, whereas management control is essentially applied social psychology.

Both management control and strategic planning involve top management, but middle managers (i.e., operating management) typically have a much more important role in management control than in strategic planning. Middle managers usually are not major participants in the strategic planning process and sometimes are not even aware that a plan is being considered. Many operating executives are by temperament not very good at strategic planning. Also, the pressures of current activities usually do not allow them to devote the necessary time to such work. Currently, there is a tendency in companies to set up separate staffs to gather the facts and make the analyses that provide the background material for strategic decisions. These and other differences between management control and strategic planning are summarized in Exhibit 1 on page 351.

Strategic planning and management control activities tend to conflict with one another in some respects. The time that management spends in thinking about the future is taken from time that it could otherwise use in controlling current operations, so in this indirect way strategic planning can hurt current performance. And, of course, the reverse also is true. More directly, many actions that are taken for long-run, strategic reasons make current profits smaller than they otherwise would be. Research and some types of advertising expenditures are obvious examples. The problem of striking the right balance between strategic and operating considerations is one of the central problems in the whole management process.

Consequences of Confusion

Following are statements illustrating some of the consequences of failing to make a distinction between strategic planning and management control.

"We should set up a long-range planning procedure and work out a systematized way of considering *all* our plans, similar to the way we construct next year's budget." A long-range plan shows the estimated consequences over the next several years of strategic decisions already taken. It is part of the management control process. Although it provides a useful background for considering strategic proposals, it is not strategic planning. Strategic proposals should be made whenever the opportunity or the need is perceived in a form that best presents the arguments.

"The only relevant costs are incremental costs; pay no attention to fixed or sunk costs." This is so in strategic planning, but operating managers are often motivated in the wrong direction if their decisions are based on incremental costs—for example, in intracompany transactions.

"We may be selling Plant X someday. We should, therefore, set up the operating reports so that management will have at its fingertips the information it will need when it is deciding this question.

SOME DISTINCTIONS BETWEEN STRATEGIC PLANNING
AND MANAGEMENT CONTROL

Characteristic	Strategic Planning	Management Control
Focus of plans	On one aspect at a time	On whole organization
Complexities	Many variables	Less complex
Degree of structure	Unstructured and irregular; each problem different	Rhythmic; prescribed procedures
Nature of information	Tailor-made for the problem; more external and predictive; less accurate	Integrated; more internal and historical; more accurate
Communication of information	Relatively simple	Relatively difficult
Purpose of estimates	Show expected results	Lead to desired results
Persons primarily involved	Staff and top management	Line and top management
Number of persons involved	Small	Large
Mental activity	Creative; analytical	Administrative; persuasive
Source discipline	Economics	Social psychology
Planning and control	Planning dominant, but some control	Emphasis on both planning and control
Time horizon	Tends to be long	Tends to be short
End result	Policies and precedents	Action within policies and precedents
Appraisal of the job done	Extremely difficult	Much less difficult

Exhibit 1

For example, we should show inventory and fixed assets at their current market value." Operating reports should be designed to assist in the management of current operations. Special compilations of data are needed for such major, nonroutine actions as the sale of a plant. Collection of such data routinely is both too expensive and likely to impede sound operating decisions.

"Our ultimate goal is an all-purpose control system—integrated data processing—so that management will have all the data it needs for whatever problem it decides to tackle. We should collect data in elemental building blocks that can be combined in various ways to answer all conceivable questions." This is an impossible goal. Each strategic proposal requires that the data be assembled in the way that best fits the requirements of that proposal. No one can foresee all the possibilities. The building block idea is sound within limits, but the limits are not so broad that all problems are encompassed.

"All levels of management should participate in planning." All levels of management should participate in the planning part of the management control process, but operating managers typically do not have the time, the inclination, or the analytical bent that is required for formulating strategic plans. Furthermore, such plans often must be kept highly secret.

OPERATIONAL CONTROL

Operational control is the process of assuring that specific tasks are carried out effectively and efficiently.

As the definition suggests, the focus of operational control is on individual tasks or transactions: scheduling and controlling individual jobs through a shop, as contrasted with measuring the performance of the shop as a whole; procuring specific items for inventory, as contrasted with the management of inventory as a whole; specific personnel actions, as contrasted with personnel management; and so on.

The definition does not suggest another characteristic that applies to most activities that are subject to operational control; namely, that these activities are capable of being programmed. In order to explain what these activities are, we need first to develop the concept of outputs and inputs.

Outputs are the product, services, or other effects created by an organization. *Inputs* are the resources the organization consumes. Every organization has, or at least is intended to have, outputs, even though they may not be readily measurable or even clearly definable; that is, every organization does something, and that something is its output. In a business, outputs are goods, services, and other intangibles. In a school, the output is education; in a hospital, patient care; in a law office, advice and counsel; in a government, public service or defense posture. Similarly, the inputs may range from easily valued items, such as purchased parts, to such intangible items as executive thought.

Moreover, every unit within an organization has outputs. In the case of factories, the output is a product. In all other units—personnel, transportation, sales, engineering, administration, and so on—it is a service. Since these services are often not priced, the amounts are difficult to measure. Nevertheless, the outputs exist.

One of the important management tasks in an organization is to seek the *optimum* relationship between outputs and inputs. In many situations, it is rarely if ever possible to determine the optimum relationship between outputs and inputs objectively; instead, the choice of a relationship is a matter of subjective judgment. This is true because there is no scientific or objective way of determining how output will be affected by changes in inputs. How much should a company spend for advertising? Are additional fire trucks, or schoolteachers, or policemen worth their cost? Informed people will disagree on the answers to questions of this type.

The term *managed costs* is descriptive of the type of inputs for which an objective decision cannot be made as to the optimum quantity to be employed. An important management control function is to make judgments as to the "right" amount of managed costs in a given set of circumstances. These are, by definition, subjective judgments, and such judgments fall within the management control process.

In other situations, there is at least the possibility that an optimum relationship between outputs and inputs can be found. It is unrealistic to imply that this relationship ever can be determined in an absolute sense, inasmuch as new and better ways of doing things are constantly being developed; therefore, a more realistic meaning of optimum is this: The optimum is that combination of resources, out of all *known* combinations, that will produce the desired output at the lowest cost. If the optimum input-output relationship for a given activity can be predetermined, then the inputs that should be employed in a given set of circumstances can be described and reduced to rules; that is, they can be programmed.

As an example of an activity to which operational control is applicable, consider the inventory area. If the demand for an item, the cost of storing it, its production cost and production time, and the loss involved in not filling an order are known, then the optimum inventory level and the optimum production or procurement schedule can be calculated. Even if these factors cannot be known with certainty (as, of course, is the case with all future events), sound estimates nevertheless can be made, inventory levels and production or procurement schedules based on these estimates can be calculated, and reasonable men will agree with the results of these calculations. An inventory control system using rules derived from such calculations is an example of operational control.

By contrast, consider the legal department of a company. No device can measure the quality, or even the quantity, of the legal service that constitutes the output of this department. No formula can show the amount of service the department should render or the optimum amount of costs that should be incurred. Impressions as to the "right" amount of service, the "right" amount of cost, and the "right" relationship between the service actually rendered and the cost actually incurred are strictly subjective. They are judgments made by management. If persons disagree on these judgments, there is no objective way of resolving the disagreement. Yet the legal department, as a part of the whole organization, must be controlled; the chief counsel must operate within the framework of policies prescribed by top management. The type of control necessary in this situation is management control.

Examples of activities that are susceptible to operational control are automated plants, such as cement plants, oil refineries, and power generating stations; the directly productive operations of most manufacturing plants, but often not the indirect, overhead items; production scheduling; inventory control; the order taking type of selling activity; and order processing, premium billing, payroll accounting, check handling, and similar paperwork activities.

Examples of activities for which management control is necessary are the total operation of most manufacturing plants, which includes such judgment inputs as indirect labor, employees' benefit and welfare programs, safety activities, training, and supervision; most advertising, sales promotion, pricing, selling (as distinguished from order taking), and similar marketing activities; most aspects of finance; most aspects of research, development, and design; the work of staff units of all types; and the activities of top management.

The control appropriate for the whole of any unit that carries on both programmed and nonprogrammed types of activities is management control. Thus, the control of one division of a company is management control. The control of the whole accounting department is management control, even though operational control is appropriate for certain aspects of the work, such as posting and check writing.

Some people believe that the distinction between the two classes of activities described above is merely one of degree rather than of kind; they say that all we are doing is distinguishing between situations in which control is easy and those in which control is difficult. We think the distinction is more fundamental, and hope this will be apparent from the following brief list of characteristics that distinguish management control from operational control.

Management control covers the whole of an organization. Each operational control procedure is restricted to a subunit, often a narrowly circumscribed activity. Just as management control occurs within a set of policies derived from strategic planning, so operational control occurs within a set of well-defined procedures and rules derived from management control.

Control is more difficult in management control than in operational control because of the absence of a scientific standard with which actual performance can be compared. A good operational control system can provide a much higher degree of assurance that actions are proceeding as desired than can a management control system.

An operational control system is a *rational* system; that is, the action to be taken is decided by a set of logical rules. These rules may or may not cover all aspects of a given problem. Situations not covered by the rules are designated as exceptions and are resolved by human judgment. Other than these exceptions, application of the rules is automatic. The rules in principle can be programmed into a computer, and the choice between using a computer and using a human being depends primarily on the relative cost of each method.

In management control, psychological considerations are dominant. The management control system at most assists those who take action; it does not directly or by itself result in action without human intervention. By contrast, the end product of an inventory control system can be an order, such as a decision to replenish a certain inventory item, and this order may be based entirely on calculations from formulas incorporated in the system. (The formulas were devised by human beings, but this is a management control process, not an operational control process.)

In a consideration of operational control, analogies with mechanical, electrical, and hydraulic systems are reasonable and useful, and such terms as feedback, network balancing, optimization, and so on are relevant. It is perfectly appropriate, for example, to view an operational control system as analogous to a thermostat which turns the furnace on and off according to its perception of changes in temperature. These analogies do not work well as models for management control systems, however, because the success of these systems is highly dependent on their impact on people, and people are not like theromostats or furnaces; one can't light a fire under a human being simply by turning up a thermostat.

The management control system is ordinarily built around a financial structure, whereas operational control data are often non-monetary. They may be expressed in terms of man-hours, number of items, pounds of waste, and so on. Since each operational control procedure is designed for a limited area of application, it is feasible to use the basis of measurement that is most appropriate for that area.

Data in an operational control system are often in real time (i.e., they are reported as the event is occurring) and relate to individual events, whereas data in a management control system are often retrospective and summarize many separate events. Computer specialists who do not make such a distinction dream about a system that will display to the management the current status of every individual activity in the organization. Although this *could* be done, it *should not* be done; management does not want such detail. Management does not need to know the time at which Lot 1007 was transferred from Station 27 to Station 28; rather, it needs to know only that the process is, or is not, proceeding as planned, and if not, where the trouble lies.

Similarly, operational control uses exact data, whereas management control needs only approximations. Material is ordered and scheduled in specific quantities, employers are paid the exact amount due them, but data on management control reports need contain only two or three significant digits and are, therefore, rounded to thousands of dollars, to millions of dollars, or even (in the United States government) to billions of dollars.

An operational control system requires a mathematical model of the operation. Although it may not always be expressed explicitly in mathematical notation, a decision rule states that given certain values for parameters $a, b, \ldots n$, Action X is to be taken. Models are not so important in management control. In a sense, a budget and a PERT network are models associated with the management control process, but they are not the essence of the process.

The formal management control *system* is only a part of the management control *process,* actually a relatively unimportant part. The system can help motivate the manager to make decisions that are in the best interests of the organization, and the system can provide information that aids the manager in making these decisions; but many other stimuli are involved in motivating the manager, and good information does not automatically produce good decisions. The success or failure of the management control process depends on the personal characteristics of the manager—his judgment, his knowledge, his ability to influence others.

In operational control, the system itself is relatively more important. Except in fully automated operations, it is an exaggeration to say that the system *is* the process, but it is not much of an exaggeration. An operational control system ordinarily states what action should be taken; it makes the decisions. As with any operation, management vigilance is required to detect an unforeseen foul-up in the operation or a change in the conditions on which the technique is predicated, and to initiate the necessary corrective action. And management will be seeking ways to improve the technique. In general, however, the degree of management involvement in operational control is small, whereas in management control it is large.

As new techniques are developed, there is a tendency for more and more activities to become susceptible to operational control. In the factory, the production schedule that was formerly set according to the foreman's intuition is now derived by linear programming. And although not very long ago it was believed that operational control was appropriate only for factory operations, we now see models and formulas being used for certain marketing decisions, such as planning salesmen's calls and planning direct-mail advertising. This shift probably will continue; it is a large part of what people have in mind when they say, "Management is becoming increasingly scientific."

Consequences of Confusion

Following are statements illustrating the consequences of failing to distinguish between management control and operational control.

"Computers will make middle management obsolete." Although computers can replace human beings in operational control, they are not a substitute for the human judgment that is an essential part of the management control process.

"Business should develop a management control system like the SAGE and SAC control systems that work so well for the military." The military systems mentioned are operational control systems. They are not related to the management control problem in the military, let alone that in business.

"The way to improve the management control process is to develop better management decision rules." This implies that mathematics, rather than human beings, is the essence of management control.

"Transfer prices should be calculated centrally." This gives no recognition to the importance of negotiation and the exercise of judgment by divisional managers in many situations.

"If you follow the planning and control techniques described in this book, your profits are a near predictable certainty." This, from an advertisement for a well-known book, implies that the technique, rather than the quality of management, is the principal determinant of success.

FINANCIAL ACCOUNTING

Financial accounting is the process of reporting financial information about the organization to the outside world.

The purpose of financial accounting is to provide financial information about a business or other organization to outside parties—investors, lending agencies, regulatory bodies, and the public. The reader should be entitled to assume that the information is presented "in accordance with generally accepted accounting principles." An important criterion in devising these principles is that of objectivity; that is, it is considered essential that financial statement data be predominantly derived from objective evidence, rather than the subjective, and hence unverifiable, judgments of management.

Management accounting is the term used for the type of accounting done in connection with the processes already described—strategic planning, management control, and operational control. Management accounting differs from financial accounting in that it is not bound by the generally accepted principles of financial accounting. In devising its management accounting structure, management may prescribe whatever rules it finds useful, without regard to whether these are consistent with generally accepted principles.

Even so, the management accounting structure will resemble the financial accounting structure in most respects, both because the prin-

ciples useful in reporting to outside parties are often equally useful
in reporting to management and because the internally generated
data are the raw material for the published financial statements,
which makes it desirable to have the differences kept to a minimum.

Consequences of Confusion

Following are statements illustrating the consequences of confusing management accounting and financial accounting.

"Management makes judgments regarding fixed assets on the basis
of estimates of the present value of their future earnings; therefore,
fixed assets should be valued in this way on published balance sheets."
Regardless of how useful such estimates may be to management, this
principle is inappropriate for financial accounting because of the impossibility of obtaining objective estimates of present values.

"In measuring divisional return on investment, fixed assets should
be shown at their balance sheet amounts." This is the opposite of the
above error. The criterion for management accounting is this: What
method will encourage division managers to make the best decisions
regarding the acquisition, utilization, and disposition of fixed assets?
The way in which assets are shown on the published balance sheet
is not governing.

"Direct costing is not permitted under generally accepted accounting principles; therefore, we shouldn't use direct costing in our management system." Again, financial accounting principles are not
governing in management accounting.

"Information that is useful to management is also useful to investors; therefore, there should be no difference between management
accounting and financial accounting." This statement implies incorrectly that the objectivity criterion is of no consequence.

INFORMATION HANDLING

Information handling is the process of collecting, manipulating,
and transmitting information, whatever its use is to be.

Space permits only a brief mention of this process here. Clearly,
there is much that can be said about the most efficient ways of collecting and transmitting information without reference to the use
that is to be made of it. Such generalizations range all the way from
the statement, "manual copying should be avoided," up through
matters relating to the design and programming of computer systems.
In recent years, systems specialists, computer specialists, forms
designers, and others have developed an expertise that they can apply

to a wide variety of problems in any of the areas already discussed. It is this expertise that constitutes the subject matter which is here labeled information handling.

Summary

We have described several subsystems that come under the general heading, "Planning and Control Systems." Although related to one another, they have different purposes and different characteristics; different ways of thinking about each of them are therefore required. Generalizations about the whole area are, if valid, so vague as not to be useful. By contrast, useful generalizations, principles, and techniques can be developed for each of the subsystems. Mistakes are made when those valid for one subsystem are applied to another.

30. MAKING LONG-RANGE COMPANY PLANNING PAY OFF *

George A. Steiner †

This article is devoted to a thumbnail sketch of two major aspects of long-range planning. First is the methodology or procedure for long-range planning. The second concerns the payoff to a company that does long-range planning.

I have chosen to dwell on these two points for several reasons. First, while long-range planning has grown rapidly in recent years and has paid off handsomely for many companies, there still are questions raised about its value. Second, while important progress has been made in the techniques of long-range planning, there are comparatively few detailed case studies and principles which are available for those who wish to initiate the process or improve their planning.

These two factors are related, I suspect, although solid proof is not available that the major reason for the fact that more companies do not engage in long-range planning is that they do not know precisely how to go about it. Not wishing to admit this even to themselves, other reasons are given for the lack of long-range planning.[1]

WHAT IS LONG-RANGE PLANNING?

Planning, in general, is the conscious determination of courses of action to achieve preconceived objectives. It is deciding in advance what is to be done, when it is to be done, by whom it is to be done,

---

* Reprinted from the *California Management Review* (Winter, 1962). Reprinted by permission of the Regents of the University of California. (This article, translated into Italian, appeared abroad under the title "Il rendimento della Programmazione d'impresa a lungo termine" in a recent issue of the *Rivista Internazionale di Scienze Economiche e Commerciali*, a periodical published by the Università Bocconi in Milan.)

† Professor George A. Steiner, Director of Division of Research, Graduate School of Business, University of California, Los Angeles, California.

[1] For example, other reasons given are: Our business is too cyclical. Our customers do not know their plans, so how can we know ours? Long-range planning is too vague. Not enough time exists for short-range planning, let alone long-range planning. We cannot afford specialists needed to do the job. It costs more than it is worth.

and how it is to be done. It can range from the detailed, specific, and rigid to the broad, general, and flexible design.

Long-range planning does this for extended periods of time. Long-range planning is a process for establishing long-range goals; working out strategies, programs, and policies to achieve these goals; and setting up the necessary machinery to insure that the company gets where it wants to go.

It is a process of choosing from among alternative courses of action and charting the use of time, resources, and effort to achieve the objective sought. The further into the future the plan stretches the less detailed are its specific parts. The subject matter of long-range plans should cover products, services, facilities, manpower, research and development, organization, marketing, financial matters, and various aspects of management itself.[2]

How Long Is Long Range?

How long a time should a long-range plan cover? The answer to this question is much like the response of Abraham Lincoln when asked how long a man's legs ought to be. "Long enough to reach the ground," said the President.

Similarly, the length of a planning period will vary considerably from company to company and subject to subject. It is not fixed or rigid. The time span of a plan should cover the period encompassing important financial commitments and their payoff.

For example, depending upon subject matter, coverage should embrace product development time and period of major financial impact following development; resource development time (e.g., sources of supply, management talent, or labor skills) ; and time required to develop physical facilities plus payoff period for major capital investments. For most businesses such factors will establish a minimum long-range planning period of from five to ten years.

Formal Long-Range Planning in Industry

All managers engage in long-range planning—if only to increase their own salaries. If they do not plan they are not doing their jobs.

---

[2] For other definitions see George A. Steiner, "What Do We Know about Using Long-Range Plans?," *California Management Review* (Fall, 1959); Peter F. Drucker, "Long-Range Planning, Challenge to Management Science," *Management Science* (April, 1959) ; Bruce Payne and James H. Kennedy, "Making Long-Range Planning Work," *The Management Review* (February, 1959); and William H. Newman and Charles E. Summer, Jr., *The Process of Management* (Englewood Cliffs, N. J.: Prentice-Hall, Inc., 1961), pp. 430-36.

In the past, when top managers needed help in planning they often hired an assistant or created a vice-president for administration.

Large and complex organizations centuries ago had staff positions for planning. Long-range planning, therefore, is not new. What is new is charging someone with full-time responsibility for planning and giving him a staff to do the job. It is the growth of planning departments and staff specialists at the top levels of corporations and major divisions that is new.

Pressures on American companies to establish such formal organizations have been most strong during the past ten years. Among the major pressures are the following:

1. Business has become increasingly complex because of expanding enterprise size, decentralization of authority, diversification of product lines, mergers, and the growing sensitivity of internal operations to uncontrollable environmental forces.

2. Technological rates of change are increasing and placing a premium on those organizations which can foresee and adapt to them.

3. A variety of forces is squeezing profit margins.

4. End use markets (domestic) are altering significantly and rapidly with geographic population shifts, changes in population composition, new social trends influencing market behavior of consumers, and growing competition for consumer savings.

5. End use markets (abroad) are changing rapidly with new commercial alignments, and efforts to industrialize the underdeveloped countries of the world.

6. There has been a rapid development of tools for planning and a growing recognition of the need for skilled technical competence to apply them to long-range planning. This trend promises to accelerate. In mind are not alone the new powerful mathematical tools which have been adapted to business decision making (e.g., linear programming, game theory, probability theory, etc.), but the application of computers, simulation and systems concepts, and new developments in economics, psychology, and other social sciences.

7. Competitors are devoting more attention to long-range planning.[3]

Under such pressures more and more companies in the past ten years have been developing long-range planning programs and extending the field of inquiry further into the future. I believe, however, that effective long-range planning in industry is not as widespread as it ought to be.

---

[3] Charles E. Summer, Jr., "The Future Role of the Corporate Planner," *California Management Review* (Winter, 1961).

Facts about the growth of formalized long-range planning are not plentiful nor reliable. *Nation's Business* concluded that about 20 percent of businesses had long-range planning in 1953 compared to about 50 percent in 1958.[4] The National Industrial Conference Board concluded in 1956 that of 189 manufacturing companies participating in its survey only one out of four had no formalized forward planning or failed to plan ahead beyond one year. About half of those having long-range plans said they included all the major elements of the enterprise in their planning. Only half said they placed much reliance on the plans.[5]

A survey made by *Management Methods* in 1958 revealed that among its respondents, only 18 percent had formal advanced plans while another 52 percent had informal advanced plans. No advanced plans were made in 30 percent of the companies covered. When asked whether respondents felt they were doing as much advanced planning as they should, 72 percent replied in the negative. Practically all planning in companies in this survey was for five years or less.

Professors Sord and Welsch found in a study published in the same year that two thirds of the number surveyed had long-range plans, but the subject matter varied greatly. Two thirds had long-range sales plans, but only about one third had long-range research or expense plans. Only about half had long-range profit or cash plans. Practically all plans were for five years or less.[6]

These data, while not conclusive, are helpful. My own empirical observations, together with the data cited, lead me to conclude that, while formal long-range corporate planning has grown by leaps and bounds in the past ten years, the practice is heavily concentrated in larger enterprises, and it is centered there on a few major problem areas (capital expenditures, product development, and sales) for periods less than five years. The coverage, time span, and usage are not great enough in light of potential value.

HOW TO MAKE A LONG-RANGE PLAN

In developing long-range plans it is helpful to think in terms of a series of steps. But, since the planner must always think in terms of retracing his thinking, allowance must also be made for some overlapping of these steps.

---

[4] "Planning Tomorrow's Profits," *Nation's Business* (August, 1958).
[5] "Long-Range Planning Pays off," *Business Record* (October, 1956).
[6] Burnard H. Sord and Glenn A. Welsch, *Business Budgeting* (New York: Controllership Foundation, 1958).

The sequence of steps presented in the next few paragraphs illustrates one concrete framework upon which a company may plan. It is flexible and has been used successfully. This particular sequence has the virtue of focusing attention on product which is usually, although not always, the principal theme of a business long-range plan.

The specific methodology of planning may vary much from one company to another whether or not the steps presented here are followed. This arises because the process must be flexible to accommodate an unusually complex intermeshing of variables which are subject to constant change. In mind are such factors as the technical knowledge and wisdom of the planners, the particular needs of the enterprise, the organization for planning, availability of strategic facts, subject matter of the plans, and uses to be made of the results.[7]

First: Plan to Plan

First is *planning to plan*. As the Cleveland Electric Illuminating Co. has so well documented, company planning must be planned.[8] This may seem as redundant as Cole Porter's "Begin the Beguine." But planning does not just happen. It must be planned!

A suitable planning climate must be established, and the organization made planning conscious. Policy decisions must be made about who will do what in planning. And, step-by-step procedures must be worked out. In one major planning program of a large corporation in which I participated the first thing we did was to prepare a detailed letter covering the entire planning procedure for signature by the president. The letter was addressed to all parties involved. In this way everyone knew what was the plan to plan. The newer the plan the more important the thoroughness with which this step should be taken. But even where planning is well established the procedures

[7] For other operational planning sequences see David W. Ewing, *Long-Range Planning for Management* (New York: Harper & Brothers, 1958); William E. Hill, "Planning for Profits: A Four-Stage Method," *California Management Review* (Spring, 1959), which is a method much like that presented here; Bruce Payne and James H. Kennedy, "Making Long-Range Planning Work," *The Management Review* (February, 1959); *Westinghouse Planning Guide* (Westinghouse Electric Corporation, 1959); *Guide to Profit Improvement Program* (American Brake Shoe Company, 1959); and Arthur W. Lucas and William G. Livingston, "Long-Range Planning and the Capital Appropriations Program," *Financial Planning for Greater Profits* (New York: American Management Association, 1960), Report No. 44. For a detailed analytical planning sequence see Preston P. Le Breton and Dale A. Henning, *Planning Theory* (Englewood Cliffs: N. J.: Prentice-Hall, Inc., 1961).

[8] Ralph M. Besse, "Company Planning Must Be Planned!" *Dun's Review* (April, 1957).

should be carefully spelled out, as in, for example, the *Westinghouse Planning Guide.*[9]

On the other hand, care should be taken to avoid overdoing this step. It is easily possible to preplan too long, in too much detail, and to spend too much time on clarification of procedures. There is too much feedback in going through the sequences of planning to warrant more than just enough detail in this step to get the process moving.

Basic assumptions must be made at various stages in the planning process. At the outset, however, some of the overall assumptions upon which planning rests should be set forth. In mind, for example, are premises which provide a framework for planning, such as the course of the cold war, population movements, or competitors' activities.

Purely methodological premises may also be established, such as —plans will be based upon constant rather than actual anticipated prices. But, whatever the premises determined, the point is that standards must be developed to guide the planning program. Otherwise, lack of coordination, unnecessary emphasis and study on less important subjects, excessive planning costs, and confusion in drawing conclusions are predictive consequences of poorly devised or neglected premises.

Second: Define Objectives

Second, *objectives of planning must be clearly specified.* The purpose of the plan, the objectives to be sought in the planning process, and the relation of planning goals to other goals and objectives in the enterprise must be clarified. Setting objectives provides the key to how planning will be done, the strategic factors to be emphasized in plan development, and methods by which planning will become the basis for action.

The objective of every business, of course, is to make a profit. Otherwise the business will not survive. But saying this is far from developing a set of goals which will best serve a company and its long-range planning program.

Be Specific. Goals should be established as concretely as possible. What does this mean? Is the goal to be an aggregate absolute volume of profits? Is the goal to be expressed in terms of a percentage of sales? Is it to be in terms of percentage of investment? If it is return on investment, how is this to be calculated? Is it the E. I. du Pont de

---

[9] See Footnote 7.

Nemours and Company or the Monsanto Chemical Company formula? Will a rising rate of return on investment be accepted even if sales do not increase?

Is sales growth in itself a goal? Is sales stability a goal? How are conflicts among goals to be resolved? Are there other objectives which need be expressed as a guide to the planning program?

Defining Corporate Goals. There has recently been a growing interest in defining corporate goals, probably in part as an outgrowth of long-range planning needs. Often stated economic type objectives, besides those mentioned in preceding paragraphs, are growth, expressed in terms of sales, assets, employees, profits, or product line; stability, usually expressed in terms of sales, manpower, and profits; flexibility, expressed in numerous ways, such as ability to innovate, speed of response to new environment, especially competition; diversity in preparedness to compete; sensitivity to technological and market changes; and acquisition of a given status of technical skill.

Very frequently goals express ethical or moral considerations. These are generally described in terms such as leadership of the firm in the industry, integrity and honesty in dealing with others, maintenance of amicable community relations, and assumption of social responsibilities with respect to community problems.[10]

Must Be Realistic. Long-range company goals should be given the greatest thought and formulated as realistically as possible. The validity of goals for planning should be tested upon the basis of past experience of the company and its industry, and future prospects for both. Unrealistic goals are not very helpful.

Sometimes an immediate problem will serve as the focal point for planning. If, for example, rate of return on stockholders' investment for a company has been well below the industry average for the past five years the prime goal for the company planning may be to achieve the industry average or better.

Similarly, actual or anticipated trouble with a product may provide the basis for a concrete goal; e.g., "eliminate the product and substitute others," "undertake new research on the product to improve its salability," or "cut costs of the product by X percent of sales so that it will attract a new level of demand."

---

[10] See Stewart Thompson, *Management Creeds and Philosophies* (New York: American Management Association, 1958), Research Study No. 32; Richard Eells, "Corporate Goals," *The Meaning of Modern Business* (New York: Columbia University Press, 1960), Chapter 6; Peter Drucker, "The Objectives of a Business," *The Practice of Management* (New York: Harper & Brothers, 1954), Chapter 7; and George R. Terry, "Management Objectives and Ethics," *Principles of Management* (Homewood, Ill.: Richard D. Irwin, Inc., 1956), Chapter 9.

Realistic projections of company operations must be placed against any goals established for the future. The difference between the two sets of numbers will reveal the magnitude of the tasks that lie ahead for the corporation. If, for example, a sales objective of 1,000,000 units is established for five years in the future [from 1962], and 1,500,000 for ten years ahead, and a realistic forecast shows 750,000 units in 1967 and 1,150,000 in 1972, the magnitude of the problem for the company is revealed.

Through this process long-range company goals should be established for sales, profits, capital requirements, new and old product requirements. Then, for each of these, the gap between aspirations and projections on present plans and trends must be measured or defined.

Third: Explore Possible Strategies

The third step is to *develop strategies to fill the major gaps.* The problem here is to bring to the foreground and examine the principal alternatives open to the company in filling the gaps and then to choose from among them those most acceptable. There obviously are many ways to do this.

In this step companies must come face to face with major questions of policy. If there is a sales gap, for example, to what extent will it be filled with old products, by further penetration of old markets, or entrance into new markets? If this is not enough to what extent should the old product be importantly modified by research? Where can and should costs be reduced or increased? Should new products be introduced? If so, should they be developed by the present company or acquired through merger? Should all new acquisitions have an affinity with present product lines, or is this not necessary?

While the central focus of planning is naturally on products, the question of strategies is not exclusively concerned with products. Strategies may be developed, for example, for management training, management succession, organization, investments of surplus cash, dividend policy, or public relations.

The precise steps to be followed in developing strategies to answer the kinds of questions given above obviously vary from case to case. One illustrative approach is as follows.

To begin with, tentative alternative courses of action may be set forth for testing in the planning process. These may be suggested by managers at different levels. A planning group itself may, and probably will, think up alternative strategies. The planning process will apply several screenings to the suggestions, the sifting measures which will become more rigorous in successive planning stages.

It is also healthy and often indispensable to undertake an objective and honest appraisal of company strengths and weaknesses in relevant areas. For example, if a company is planning a diversification program, analysis is important in the following areas: management competence to digest proposed mergers; financial capability; marketing abilities for the new product; and, if stock is used to acquire a new company, the ability of the present management to continue control of the enterprise. Other areas of review might include basic research and engineering competence, advertising and promotion skills, labor relations, quality of mangement, capacity to control costs and production, and product and service acceptability.

Elemental, of course, is the buildup of information important in choosing between alternative courses of action. This is a critical stage in planning because it is frequently difficult to acquire reliable information about the most crucial strategic factors in decision making. It is most important at this stage to concentrate on the strategic data, or those which will have the most significance in choice conclusions.

The range of phenomena about which data should be collected is very wide. For a new product possibility, for example, the analysis may cover technological matters, ranging from projection of prospective scientific advances affecting the product to costs and timing of research, development, tests, and engineering for the product. There are many economic matters of interest, including market changes, possible demand at different pricing levels, estimated fixed and variable costs, break-even volume, prospective return on investment, and probabilities of profit amounts at different price-volume-cost ranges. Where applicable, there are also, of course, social, political, military, and internal administrative matters demanding attention.

The next step is to *select strategies from among alternative possibilities*. More or less simultaneously four analytical processes merge at this point. The first is the application, where appropriate, of new mathematical techniques to get a quantitative optimization of objectives.

The second is a modification of quantitative conclusions by a broad range of qualitative factors which will have a determining impact on final choices. Included in the latter, for example, would be estimates of what competitors are likely to do under given circumstances.

Break-Even Calculations. Third, to the extent practicable, the financial impact of decisions should be measured individually and in their entirety. This should be done by the preparation of break-even calculations, cash flow analyses, and balance sheet and profit-and-loss statements. The detail of analysis should naturally be tailored to fit the need and importance of the data to the reliability of conclusions. Computer simulation, while not now used very extensively in this step, is a fourth process which promises to grow in importance.

The net results of this stage should be the development of strategies to fill the gaps apparent in Step 2. These broad plans of action should be either the best possible solutions to the problems or, at the very least, suitable ones. They should be tested for feasibility in terms of management, manpower, finances, competitor actions, technical expectations, and market acceptability. Broad magnitudes and timing should be established.

Resulting strategies can be broad or relatively narrow. One important aerospace company in the United States recently matched a frank appraisal of its strengths and weaknesses in various disciplines of knowledge used in the industry against prospective new product developments. It reasoned that it could not maintain strength in all the areas of knowledge which it now covered. The result was an increase in strength in some areas and an elimination of many other areas.

Some companies have decided to expand through merger even though the resulting product line is heterogeneous. Other companies feel it a better strategy to acquire new products through merger only when there is a close relationship with present product line. Some companies mix these two strategies. Certain companies have decided to lead their industry in research and development. Others are content to follow.

A manufacturer of ceramicsware recently decided to concentrate only on products requiring advanced scientific and engineering skills and to abandon mass production of dinnerware. One electronics producer recently decided, following an agonizing appraisal, to abandon his computer line.

A medium-sized California food processor worked out a completely new detailed strategy for timing of annual sales promotion and new product development. A large oil company recently completed a detailed strategy covering its foreign investment program. These are illustrations of results from this step.

Fourth: Subplan to Fit Strategy

The fourth step in long-range planning is to *develop derivative operational plans*. A planning process is not complete until subsidiary plans are made to put into effect the strategies developed in Step 3. This seems elementary but is not always followed in practice. Decisions made without methods to carry them out are ineffective. The following cover the most important functional areas where derivative plans must be made.

Research and development programs should be supported, timed, and controlled to achieve the new product or other requirements needed to reach goals. These other requirements may, for example, include improving old products, reducing production costs, hiring new scientific skills, or increasing basic research.

Production programs should reflect digestion of new equipment, scheduling, new quality controls and inspection methods, and associated activities.

Marketing and promotion plans would, of course, include new selling efforts, advertising programs, reorganization of sales territories, pricing, and perhaps packaging.

Organizational changes may be required as a result of the new program which in turn, of course, needs detailed planning before implementation. Included here might be new management training programs.

Financial plans would include preparations for new equity financing or borrowing, budgeting of capital, and detailed financial forecasts to support the feasibility of the operational plans.

Parallel Planning. An important feature of long-range planning is parallel planning. It would be a waste of time and resources to insist that production await engineering before beginning its derivative plans, or that marketing await production, or that organization await all of them. It is true that what is decided in one functional area will have a determining impact on other areas. But planning in all areas must proceed in parallel to the fullest extent practicable to save time. This can be accomplished by good communications in planning and sharpening of abilities to guess correctly what is going on in other functional areas that will affect planning in another area.

Naturally, the nearer-term plans should be sufficiently detailed to permit operations and control. For this purpose detailed budgets or other planning and control techniques should be prepared. The further away in time the less detail should be needed or justified in terms of cost.

Fifth: Integrate Plan

The fifth and final step is to *assure the integration of long-range and short-range plans and to introduce the necessary controls to be sure operations take place in conformance with plans.*

Sequential Stages. Short-range plans must, of course, be prepared in light of longer-range goals. Meshing the two can be accomplished by developing sequential stages to meet long-range goals, as for example, promotion plans, the near-term aspects of which would be included in specific budgetary items. Where long-range plans are not specified in concrete terms, as for example, outlines to improve the quality of management, the connection is looser.

In such instances, short-range plans should reflect the longer-range goals and policies set to achieve them. In some companies the problem of meshing short-range and long-range plans is accomplished by developing five-year plans in which the first year is the current operating budget.

The control process designed to insure that operations take place in conformance with plans extends too far beyond the planning function discussed in this paper and will not be treated here. It is perhaps unnecessary to say that plans which are not executed are only exercises. They may be important as exercises but they are not plans in the sense the term is used here. Reciprocally, efficient control of operations is rather difficult without the goals and standards of performance which plans establish.

ORGANIZATION FOR PLANNING

Too large a field of inquiry for extended treatment here is the subject of business practices and principles in organizing for long-range planning. But, since it has a direct bearing upon the way planning steps such as the above are performed, a few observations are in order.

First of all, organization for planning is not a simple matter of working out procedural or data flows. It must face the fundamental question of who is going to do what about basic decision making in an organization.

Boards of directors have superior authority but there is great variation in the extent to which they choose to use this power. At E. I. du Pont de Nemours and Company, for example, the board has delegated great power to subcommittees of the board, principally the executive committee. Long-range planning at Du Pont centers in this group. In other companies the board has delegated its planning powers to the president. In some, the president in turn has delegated his powers in varying degrees to committees, departments, or individuals.

Top Management Support

Second, and closely associated with the above issue, long-range planning will be most useful and effective if the top executives of the company have confidence and faith in it. A long-range planning program is not likely to be of much value if the chief executives do not support it actively.

Third, rather widespread participation in the process should be encouraged, but not to the extent that timetables cannot be met, objectivity in analyzing facts is lost, or strategic decisions become known to too many people. Long-range plans are usually rather important to a great many people in an enterprise. Their participation in and execution of the plan will be enhanced if they can point to some contribution of theirs in it, or if they can find in it a goal worth striving for.

Effective planning requires decentralization. It is true that top management itself may define basic long-range planning strategies. But the execution of these programs requires effective coordination of many people. As Peter Drucker has pointed out, planning and doing are separate parts of the same job. They are not separate jobs. Planning proceeds best when both top management and operating people participate fully in it.

Does Planning Pay Off?

Determining payoff is a matter of relating the value of planning results to the costs of planning. Every planning program should be examined to determine the margin between value and cost. On the whole, payoff calculations are probably more easily determined for short-range than for long-range plans.

Long-range planning may not pay off for five, ten or more years. It is because of the difficulties in making cost-value calculations, together with the length of time needed to draw conclusions, that questions often arise about payoff for long-range planning.

"Extinct by Instinct." Two extreme approaches seem to be taken by companies that either ignore or improperly face the question of payoff. One approach is to minimize costs by ignoring basic steps in planning. This method depends upon conclusions derived without encumbrances of carefully developed facts or lines of reasoning. For this approach the practitioner feels little need for a conscious and deliberate assessment of relevant considerations upon which judgments can be developed. In common parlance this is called "flying by the seat of your pants." I prefer to call it the road to becoming extinct by instinct.

"Paralysis by Analysis." At the other extreme is overemphasis of value in relation to cost. With this approach there is recognition of the need for planning. An assignment is made to a dedicated hardworking soul with a reputation for thoroughness. Work is begun without much reference to the complexities of the task and before long a large number of people are involved at substantial cost.

Somewhere along the line, usually later than sooner, a voluminous report is prepared and promptly filed away "for future reference." Either the need for decision has long since passed or the report is too complex and bulky for busy people to read and digest. This I call the road to "paralysis by analysis." [11]

Cost-Value Equation. For planning to pay off, a happy balance between the two extremes must be struck. The precise payoff for any particular planning operation is difficult to determine. No one can do this without examining the cost-value equation for that program. But planning has paid off for companies that have considered this equation and achieved the balance required.

The Stanford Research Institute studied the question, "Why Companies Grow." One major conclusion of the study was that: "In the cases of both high-growth and low-growth companies, those that now support planning programs have shown a superior growth rate in recent years." [12]

---

[11] Charles R. Schwartz, "The Return-on-Investment Concept as a Tool for Decision Making," *Improving the Caliber of Company Management* (New York: American Management Association, 1956), General Management Series, No. 183, p. 46.

[12] N. R. Maines, *Why Companies Grow* (Palo Alto, Calif.: Stanford Research Institute, 1957), p. 4.

The Stanford study observed that most companies with formalized planning programs were enthusiastic about their value. Well might they be if, partly as a result of planning, their growth rates have been exceptional. For these companies planning has clearly paid off.

Ford's Experience

Ernest Breech, former chairman of the board of the Ford Motor Company, has observed: "We believe it is our business, and that of other large companies, to make trends, not to follow them. A confident aggressive spirit, backed up by intelligent planning and hard-hitting management, can be contagious." [13] For Ford, planning has paid off handsomely as the last ten years of that company's history will testify.

On the other hand, the path to bankruptcy is strewn with corpses who failed to plan or planned poorly. A study by the Bureau of Business Research at the University of Pittsburgh concluded that among the ten companies chosen for intensive study every one was guilty of poor planning, and this shortcoming was the major cause of failure in the majority of cases.[14]

It is probably true that the only certainty about long-range planning is that the conclusions will prove to be in error. There is no such thing as 20/20 foresight. But one great advantage of forward planning is that coming to grips with uncertainty by analysis and study should result in a reduction of the margin of doubt about the future. Despite the fog enshrouding the future many companies have planned ahead and hit goals surprisingly accurately.

Forward Planning

Ralph Cordiner, commenting on this point in his book *New Frontiers for Professional Managers,* has observed that one of the three principal new horizons ahead for managers lies in the area of long-range planning. As he put it, "In a time of radical worldwide change, when every day introduces new elements of uncertainty, forward planning may seem to be nearly impossible—an exercise in futility. Yet there never was a more urgent need for long-range planning on the part of every business, and indeed every other important element of our national life." [15]

---

[13] Ernest R. Breech, "Planning the Basic Strategy of a Large Business," *Planning the Future Strategy of Your Business,* ed. Edward C. Bursk and Dan H. Fenn (New York: McGraw-Hill Book Co., 1956), p. 17.
[14] A. M. Woodruff and T. G. Alexander, *Success and Failure in Small Manufacturing* (Pittsburgh: University of Pittsburgh Press, 1958), pp. 48 and 100.
[15] (New York: McGraw-Hill Book Co., 1956), p. 82.

The argument is often presented that for large companies the choices for investing funds are many and necessitate advance planning. But, since a range of choice in investment of funds in a small single product company does not exist, for it, advance planning is a waste of time.

This idea is most erroneous. Small companies have just as great a need for long-range planning as large ones. They may not have the cash to support technical specialists, but there are other means to acquire the needed expertise. Many small companies, through long-range planning, have opened the door to successful expansion, new products, and new markets by multiplying ranges of desirable choices.

In considering payoff for long-range planning, value is generally considered to lie in the areas of improved profit stability, growth, more efficient sales, capital expenditure, inventory, research and development, or cost reduction programs. Or long-range planning may prove its worth in better management replacement and improvement programs, or some other tangible and concrete activities of the enterprise.

Ancillary Benefits

It should also be pointed out that a number of important ancillary and intangible benefits have accrued to companies having formal long-range planning programs. A brief list of them would include the following points. The planning process constitutes an excellent channel of communication throughout the organization. It identifies problems ahead for a firm long before they become acute. It focuses attention on the principal determinants of the business. It provides an organized mechanism for testing value judgments.

It opens new horizons for profitable study. It prevents piecemeal solutions to problems. It is a good training ground for future managers, and it brings to those responsible for running the business a comprehensive, coordinated, and uniform picture of present and future business.

CONCLUSIONS

Despite the phenomenal growth of formal long-range planning, and its important payoff to many companies, there are still too many companies that do not employ the process effectively. The reasons are often anchored in their lack of knowledge about how to do it, misunderstanding of its cost-value calculation, or both.

Five operational steps for long-range planning have been set forth and examined. They are recapitulated below in graphic form.

For long-range planning to pay off a balance must be struck between minimizing cost by ignoring basic steps and principles of effective planning and incurring overly heavy cost by excessive analysis. While full benefits may not be derived for many years, efforts should be made to measure them and offset them against costs. This article has been devoted to the proposition that available knowledge about how to undertake long-range planning is quite sufficient, and full understanding of the cost-value equation is so pervasive, that all businesses, large and small, should have a more or less formal long-range planning program and reap rich rewards from it.

FIVE STEPS FOR LONG-RANGE PLANNING

—1—

Planning to Plan

—2—

Specifying objectives of enterprise

- *forecasting future prospects*
- *measuring the gaps between aspirations and projections*

—3—

Developing strategies

- *to fill in the major gaps*

—4—

Developing derivative or detailed plans in major functional areas to fit the strategies

- *research and development*
- *production*
- *marketing and promotion*

—5—

Integration of long-range and short-range plans

- *introducing necessary controls*

31. BUDGETING AND EMPLOYEE
BEHAVIOR * Selwyn Becker and David Green, Jr.†

Writing in *Number, the Language of Science,* Tobias Dantzig observed: "The concrete has ever preceded the abstract. . . . And the concrete has ever been the greatest stumbling block to the development of a science. The peculiar fascination which *numbers as individuals* have exerted on the mind of man from time immemorial was the main obstacle in the way of developing a *collective* theory of numbers, i.e., an arithmetic, just as the concrete interest in individual stars long delayed the creating of a scientific astronomy." [1]

And so it has been with budgeting, where for some there is still question on whether or not a theory has developed. Business budgeting is a twentieth century innovation; its development has been characterized by a fragmentary literature and an emphasis on technique. A review of its history indicates that progress has largely been through learning from mistakes—a "cut-and-try" aproach. In this paper we will review this history as a background toward an understanding of the relation of the budget to the motivations of those who effect and are affected by it. In a sense this will be an excursion—an attempt to determine "what the behavioral scientists can tell us or find out for us about . . . the impact [of budgets] on people and on their aspirations." [2] In the process, we will point out that the attempt to make use of motivational factors in the budgeting construct raises many difficult and imperfectly understood problems. Further, we will attempt to explain why the style of managerial

* From the *Journal of Business* (October, 1962). Reprinted by permission of the University of Chicago.
† Selwyn Becker, Assistant Professor of Psychology, Graduate School of Business, University of Chicago; David Green, Jr., Professor of Accounting, Graduate School of Business, University of Chicago.
The authors are indebted to the members of the Workshop in Accounting Research, Institute of Professional Accounting, Graduate School of Business, University of Chicago, for helpful comments—especially Charles T. Horngren and George H. Sorter.

[1] (4th ed.; New York: The Macmillan Co., 1956).
[2] David Solomons, "Standard Costing Needs Better Variances," *N.A.A. Bulletin,* XLIII, No. 4 (December, 1961), p. 30.

leadership is of critical importance in the choice of budget procedures —an issue largely overlooked. Also, we will consider the role played by the communication of performance results and the timing of budget revisions.

In the United States, budgeting by state and local government started with the municipal reform movements around the turn of the century. At the outset, the budget was viewed as an instrument of control—"control over the officers . . . of administration by placing limitations on their authority to spend." [3] These early budgets were, and for the most part still are, authorizations to spend—appropriations—for particular "objects of expenditure" such as personal services, commodities, travel, and the like. The appropriation was the "upper limit" much like a thermal control on a furnace—when the limit is reached the fuel, or, in the fiscal sense, the money is stopped. The upper limit was imposed through the approving of the budget by the governing body—the board, the council, the legislature, etc.

These governmental budgeting procedures provided for a second type of control—a restraint control. Each claim presented had to be approved for payment by the chief financial officer. The question of "what is a legal or bona fide obligation?" was resolved by considering (1) whether the budget document provided for such an expenditure, (2) whether sufficient funds were left in the appropriation to pay the claim, and (3) whether the necessary documents were on hand. To know if the remaining appropriation was sufficient, fairly elaborate records were maintained. To these were posted the dollar amounts of issued purchase orders as well as the specific expenditures. Both types of transactions reduced the "available" balance. This was a practice of *clerical* control—a technique employed to insure the completeness of record and one that is still unique to governmental accounting (with the possible exception of retail "open-to-buy" records). To the extent that interim reports were prepared and distributed to department heads, rudimentary *communicative* control was practiced.

Governmental purposes were served well enough by these budget procedures. Revenue and expense forecasts were relatively simple. Because changes were not contemplated, the budgets were for fixed amounts for the designated time period. Where actual revenues fell

---

[3] Frederick A. Cleveland, *Chapters on Municipal Administration and Accounting* (New York: Longmans, Green & Co., 1909), p. 72.

short of the estimates, unilateral demands to cut expenditures by a designated percentage were issued—sometimes by resort to payless paydays.

Early business budgeting largely imitated governmental practice and technique. It began with "imposed" budgets [4] and the obvious controls—limit, restraint, clerical, and communicative. During the early and middle 1930's, it became fashionable to speak of "budgetary control" and to view the budget as both (1) a financial plan and (2) "a control over future operations." [5] Also in the thirties, the inadequacies of the static budget became obvious when business activity took a sharp downturn and profits disappeared.[6]

A budget form that provided for intraperiod changes in the level of sales or manufacturing was introduced and was called a flexible or variable budget. It attempted to provide "bench mark" numbers for a range of contemplated activity.

Primarily, budgetary control has been the attempt to keep performance at or within the acceptable limits of the predetermined flexible plan. In a sense the plan controls—but for how long? And how is the plan to be modified?

Budget Periodicity

The recurring cycle of early governmental and business budgets was simple. The budgets were imposed, there was performance, and the comparison of the performance against the budget influenced the next budget. The cycle could be depicted as follows:

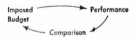

Ordinarily, the budget period was one year or two. The comparison of performance and budget often had curious results on the subsequent budget. Where expenditure was less than budget, there was a tendency to revise the subsequent budget downward. As a result,

----

[4] Imposed budgets have been characterized as ones "dictated by top management without the full participation of the operating personnel" (R. N. Anthony, "Distinguishing Good from Not-So-Good Accounting Research," *Proceedings of the 22nd Annual Institute on Accounting* [Columbus: Ohio State University, 1960], p. 68).

[5] Eric Kohler, *A Dictionary for Accountants* (Englewood Cliffs, N. J.: Prentice-Hall, Inc., 1957), p. 75.

[6] F. V. Gardner, "How About That 1935 Operating Budget?" *Factory Management and Maintenance* (November, 1934); C. E. Knoeppel and E. G. Seybold, *Managing for Profit* (New York: McGraw-Hill Book Co., Inc., 1937), p. 206.

managers would engage in a spending spree the last few weeks of an appropriation year to avoid being cut down next year.

The budget period in business has also been calendar oriented— the quarter or 12-week period extended 12 or 15 months. Ordinarily, budget revisions are restricted to future periods. Later in the paper we will discuss reasons for cycling budget revisions on a basis other than the calendar.

BUDGET MODIFICATION

By 1930 it was recognized in business circles that imposed budgets "resulted in some dissatisfaction and advice was given to prepare them in the departments and have them revised or edited in the central offices." [7] Thus *participation* was introduced into the budgeting construct. It has been said that the "real values of participation at all management levels . . . , aside from better planning, are the psychological values that accrue as the result of participation. A high degree of participation is conducive to better morale and greater initiative." [8]

There is some evidence of the extent (and degree) to which participation is currently employed in business. Sord and Welsch interrogated managements of 35 companies to determine the level at which principal budget objectives were developed. No companies said they used totally imposed budgets. Six firms (17 percent) prepared objectives at higher levels and allowed subordinate managers to consider and comment on them before final adoption. Twenty-nine firms (83 percent) said they requested subordinate managers to prepare their own goals and objectives for review and approval at higher levels. [9]

Theirs obviously was a very small sample. Furthermore, it is questionable that the interrogatories used did, in fact, investigate participation. As Chris Argyris discovered, there is such a thing as "psuedoparticipation" "that is, participation which looks like, but is not, real participation." [10]

Participation may have great value in improving budgets by drawing together the knowledge diffused among the participants, although we do not treat this objective here. Our interest is in participation

[7] *Budgetary Control in Manufacturing Industries* (New York: National Industrial Conference Board, 1931), p. 52.
[8] B. H. Sord and G. A. Welsch, *Business Budgeting* (New York: Controllership Foundation, Inc., 1958), p. 97.
[9] *Ibid.*, p. 95.
[10] *The Impact of Budgets on People* (New York: Controllership Foundation, Inc., 1952), p. 28.

as a useful technique for dealing with the psychological problems of employee satisfaction, morale, and motivation to produce, that is, the belief that increased participation can lead to better morale and increased initiative. The evidence supporting this belief will be evaluated, as well as other psychological effects associated with participation that may be of even greater importance. But first the question: What is participation? We will use the following definition: Participation is "defined as a process of joint decision making by two or more parties in which the decisions have future effects on those making them." [11]

A collateral question: How does the introduction of participation affect the budget cycle? At first glance, it seems that the chart would appear as follows:

However, we believe this is too simple. Participation adds a separate "psychological path." Participation is *not* a single value variable but rather is a concept encompassing several explicit variables. Instead of a simple cycle we have a sequence that might be depicted as follows:

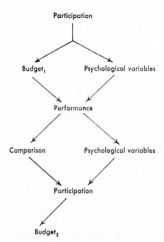

---

[11] J. R. P. French, Jr., J. Israel, and D. As, "An Experiment on Participation in a Norwegian Factory," *Human Relations*, XIII (1960), p. 3.

In paragraphs that follow we will attempt to identify these unspecified psychological variables by examining what we consider to be the relevant available research results. Before proceeding it is imperative to make one fundamental point: *Participation is not a panacea.*[12] Indeed, there is evidence to suggest that it is inappropriate in certain "environments." When participation is employed, the concept of control, as outlined above, requires modification. Instead of the budget being the plan to which performance is conformed, compared, and evaluated irrespective of changes in environment (other than those provided for in the flexible budget), the plan is influenced, at least in part, by the environment; that is, control limits and informs those operating under the budget; in turn, they determine and limit the succeeding budget.

PARTICIPATION, MORALE, AND PRODUCTIVITY

In an industrial setting Coch and French investigated the effects of prior participation on production after work changes were introduced.[13] Difficulty of work and percentage of work changes were equated for a no participation group (NP); for participation by representation (PR); and for a total participation (TP) group. With a prechange standard of 60 units per hour, after relearning, the NP group reached a level of 50 units per hour; the PR group 60 units per hour; and the TP group 68 units per hour, or an improvement of about 14 percent over the standard rate. Another important finding was that 17 percent of the NP group quit their jobs in the first 40 days after the change, and the remaining members of the group filed grievances about the piece rate, which "subsequently was found to be a little 'loose.' " There was one act of aggression against the supervisor from the PR group, none from the TP group, and no quits in either the PR or TP groups

If employee turnover and stated grievances can be taken as a measure of morale, then it seems clear that the two groups that participated in the initiation of change were better disposed toward their job situations than was the no participation group.

Based only on this study one cannot decide if participation directly increased incentive to produce, as measured by subsequent productivity, or only improved morale, which in turn led to increased

[12] A useful discussion—"Participation in Perspective"—appears as Chapter IX in *The Human Side of Enterprise* by Douglass McGregor (New York: McGraw-Hill Book Co., Inc., 1960).

[13] L. Coch and J. R. P. French, Jr., "Overcoming Resistance to Change," *Human Relations,* I (1948), pp. 512-32.

motivation. This is a point worth considering since morale is not perfectly correlated with productivity.

An inference about this relationship can be drawn after examination of a study by Schachter *et al.* on group cohesiveness and productivity.[14] (Group cohesiveness is usually defined as attraction to the group—desire to become or remain a member—and reluctance to leave the group. Another way of looking at cohesiveness might be the amount of "we" feeling generated in an individual as a result of his association with others.) Schachter and his associates experimentally created high and low cohesiveness in two groups. A task was chosen in which output could be easily measured. In half of each group subjects were individually given instructions designed to induce production at a high rate; the other half instructions designed to induce production at a low rate. It was found that group cohesion and acceptance of induction were significantly related. The high cohesive groups more frequently accepted induction than did the low cohesive groups. This was especially true of the negative induction, or "slow-down" situation.

The Coch and French study suggests that morale and/or productivity are enhanced as a result of employee participation in the initiation of change. The Schachter *et al.* study suggests that with participation held constant (all groups worked under constant conditions) change in productivity is related to group cohesiveness. Cohesiveness, it can be seen from the definition, is related to morale. Morale is most frequently defined as satisfaction with one's job, supervisors, and working associates. It has also been defined as the *degree* to which an employee identified himself as part of the organization. In either case morale and cohesiveness with a group imply some similar reactions and attitudes toward an organization or group.

Since participation affects morale (cohesiveness) and productivity, but cohesiveness without participation affects production, the most likely conclusion is that cohesiveness is dependent on participation but that changes in productivity are more directly related to cohesiveness.

ELEMENTS OF PARTICIPATION: PROCESS AND CONTENT

Let us consider participation as conceptually divisible into process and content. Process means the *act* of participating with the possible

---

[14] S. Schachter, N. Ellertson, D. McBride, and D. Gregory, "An Experimental Study of Cohesiveness and Productivity," *Human Relations*, IV (1951), pp. 229-38.

consequences stemming from the act; content is the *discussion topic* toward which are generated the positive or negative attitudes. The *act* of participating enables the participants to know one another, communicate and interact with one another—conditions that easily can lead to increased cohesiveness. As we have seen, however, increased cohesiveness also can result in lower production if that is the sentiment of the cohesive group. Thus it becomes clear that the content of participation is an important determinant of final production levels. What should the content consist of and what should it accomplish? These questions can be answered on the basis of some data on group decision making collected by Kurt Lewin and his students.[15] One experiment was designed to induce housewives to use previously unused foods (sweetbreads, etc.). Positive communications describing the foods were presented to two groups: one by the lecture method, the other by a group discussion method. A subsequent check revealed that 3 percent of the women who heard the lectures served one of the meats never served before, whereas after group discussion, 32 percent served one of the meats. This experiment was repeated with a different leader, different groups, and a different food—milk —and yielded essentially similar results.

As compared to individual instruction and the lecture method, group discussion was superior in inducing change—a result attributed to the hesitancy of individuals to accept goals that depart from the group standard. (Psychological nonacceptance of a goal by an individual virtually precludes its attainment by him.) The group discussion method allows the group member to assess the standards of all other members so that, if the group apparently accepts a change, he, too, can accept it and retain his group membership.

It is clear that the content of participation should be directed toward setting a new goal with discussion of a sort sufficient to enable each participant to realize that the goal is accepted by the others in the group. The fulfillment of these conditions could serve as a definition of successful participation by (1) providing the opportunity for enough interaction so that a cohesive group can emerge and (2) directing the interaction so that each participant's analysis of the content will enable him to accept as his own those goals adopted by the group. Thus, we can see that the process and content of a participation program interact, and that such interaction can lead to one of several outcomes:

---

[15] D. Cartwright and E. Zauder (ed.), "Studies in Group Decision," *Group Dynamics* (Evanston, Ill.: Row, Peterson & Co., 1956), pp. 287-88.

1. High cohesiveness with positive attitudes (goal acceptance), a condition of maximally efficient motivation;

2. Low cohesiveness with positive attitudes, an unlikely but possible condition that probably would result in efficient performance;

3. Low cohesiveness and negative attitudes, a condition resulting from unsuccessful participation that would tend to depress production within the limits of the integrity or conscience of each individual; and

4. High cohesiveness and negative attitudes, the occurrence most conducive to a production slowdown.

Level of Aspiration and Performance

Ideally, in the budgeting process, participation results in a plan of action including a proposed amount of accomplishment and an estimate of the costs to achieve it. If participation has been successful, then these proposed levels of cost and accomplishment are accepted as goals by the participants. In effect, these projected levels of achievement become the levels of aspiration of the managers of the organization. (In a smoothly running organization the managers induce acceptance of the same levels of aspiration in the members of their departments.)

Level of aspiration has been defined in the psychological literature as a goal that, when just barely achieved, has associated with it subjective feelings of success; when not achieved, subjective feelings of failure.[16] From an extensive review of the literature Child and Whiting summarize many findings into five conclusions:

1. Success generally leads to a raising of the level of aspiration, failure to a lowering.

2. The stronger the success the greater is the probability of a rise in level of aspiration; the stronger the failure the greater is the probability of a lowering.

3. Shifts in level of aspiration are in part a function of changes in the subject's confidence in his ability to attain goals.

4. Failure is more likely than success to lead to withdrawal in the form of avoiding setting a level of aspiration.

5. Effects of failure on level of aspiration are more varied than those of success.[17]

---

[16] K. Levin, T. Dembo, L. Festinger, and Pauline Sears, "Level of Aspiration," *Personality and the Behavior Disorders*, I, ed. J. McV. Hunt (New York: The Ronald Press Co., 1944), pp. 333-78.
[17] J. L. Child and J. W. M. Whiting, "Determinants of Level of Aspiration: Evidence from Everyday Life," *The Study of Personality*, ed. H. Brand (New York: John Wiley & Sons, Inc., 1954), pp. 145-58.

Recently Stedry has utilized this psychological variable in an attempt to establish some relations between level of aspiration, imposed budgets, and subsequent performance.[18] Stedry, not a psychologist, may have overlooked some of the revelant psychological literature. Seemingly, he selected an inaccurate method of measuring aspiration level which weakens his several conclusions and recommendations. For his measure of level of aspiration, Stedry asked his subjects to express what they "hoped to achieve" on the next set of problems. Festinger found that the D score (the difference between performance and aspiration) was greater between performance and expressions of "like to get" than between performance and expressions of "expect to get." [19] Diggory found the correlation between "hope" statements before and after failure significantly higher than statements of expectations before and after failure.[20] In other words, "hope" and "expect" represent different attitudes. Since level of aspiration is defined as the goal one explicitly undertakes to reach rather than the goal one hopes to achieve, it seems clear that Stedry's conclusions are based on an inaccurate measure of his major variable. Subsequently, Stedry has indicated his belief, based on questionnaire information, that his "subjects appeared . . . to have given the right answer to the wrong question." [21] In any event, his attempt is valuable heuristically because it highlights a possible relation between budgets, budgeting, and human motivational performance.

We have already hypothesized a relationship between participation and the formation of levels of aspiration. There remains a specification of the effects of level of aspiration on the remaining segments of the budget cycle.

After the budget has been adopted, the attempt to translate it into behavior constitutes the performance part of the cycle. The degree of effort expended by members of the firm as they attempt to achieve budgeted goals is partially dependent upon their levels of aspiration. Maximum effort will be exerted to just reach an aspired-to goal. In fact, according to level of aspiration theory if, for example, five units of effort are required to reach goal $x - 3$, ten units to reach goal $x - 2$, 15 units to reach goal $x - 1$, and 25 units to reach goal x, the

---

[18] Andrew C. Stedry, *Budget Control and Cost Behavior* (Englewood Cliffs, N. J.: Prentice-Hall, Inc., 1960).

[19] L. Festinger, "A Theoretical Interpretation of Shifts in Level of Aspiration," *Psychological Review*, XLIX (1942), pp. 235-50.

[20] J. C. Diggory, "Responses to Experimentally Induced Failure," *American Journal of Psychology*, LXII (1949), pp. 48-61.

[21] Stedry, "Aspiration Levels, Attitudes, and Performance in a Goal-Oriented Situation," *Industrial Management Review*, III, No. 2 (Spring, 1962), p. 62.

level of aspiration goal, an individual will expend the disproportionate amount of energy to achieve at level x to derive that subjective feeling of success. Thus, we can see how a budget that is partially derived through a successful program of participation can result in greater expenditure of effort on the part of employees to reach goals specified in the budget.

Such expectations are not without foundation, of course. Bayton measured the levels of aspiration of 300 subjects of roughly equivalent ability prior to their performance on seven arithmetic problems. He found that subjects with higher levels of aspiration followed with higher performance.[22] From a finding of this sort one cannot conclude that greater motivation to achieve is associated with the level of aspiration goal, but it is well known that increased motivation leads to increased effort, a condition usually followed by an increase in performance. We can thus find indirect support for our contention. Another bit of evidence may illustrate the point further. Siegel and Fouraker set subjects to bargaining under bilateral monopoly conditions.[23] With no control of levels of aspirations, the subjects maximized the joint profits and split the profits nearly equally. However, when high and low levels of aspiration were induced into the bargaining pairs (despite the fact that a better bargain meant more money for the subject), those with a low level of aspiration gained only about one third of the joint profits. Thus, it seems clear that level of aspiration not only describes a goal for future attainment, but also it partially insures that an individual will expend a more than minimum amount of energy, if necessary, to perform at or above that level.

Depending, then, on the conditions under which a budget is drawn the budget can act as a motivating force and can induce better performance from the members of the organization. On the other hand, the budget can specify aims and goals so easy of attainment that the organization's members will be induced to produce at less than their usual capacity.

After the performance phase of the cycle a comparison is made between the costs and income previously predicted in the budget and the actually attained income and costs. We are not here concerned

---

[22] J. A. Bayton, "Interrelations between Levels of Aspiration, Performance and Estimates of Past Performance," *Journal of Experimental Psychology*, XXXIII (1943), pp. 1-21.

[23] S. Siegel and L. Fouraker, *Bargaining and Group Decision Making* (New York: McGraw-Hill Book Co., Inc., 1960).

with how the comparison is made but rather with its utilization, since that may have considerable effect on employee behavior and morale.

Much has been written on the effect of communication within an organization. With reference to the comparison, or control, function of the budget, the use or misuse of communication can be critical especially when viewed in the context of participation and level of aspiration.

First and foremost, it is imperative for each participant to know whether he should feel subjective success or failure. If he is not informed of the results of the comparison he cannot know whether his striving for a particular level was worthwhile or not. Nor can he, in turn, pass on the word to his subordinates in whom he induced specific levels of aspiration. They, too, will not know whether to feel success or failure. We can see that communicating knowledge of results acts, in this case, as reward or punishment. It can serve either to reinforce or extinguish previous employee behaviors. Where subjects were given a learning task and provided knowledge of results, learning increased; but when knowledge of results was withheld performance fell; that is, learning not only stopped but performance was decreased.[24] In discussing these results, Munn argued that "the rapid drop in performance which followed this point may be attributed to the loss of motivation which came with withdrawal of knowledge of results, not from forgetting what had been learned up to this point." [25]

Failure to communicate knowledge of results adversely affects not only performance but also morale. Leavitt and Mueller, in an investigation of effects of varying amounts of feedback, found that task accuracy increased as feedback increased. They also found that zero feedback is accompanied by low confidence and hostility while free feedback is accompanied by high confidence and amity.[26]

The question may now be asked: "So what if the employees don't know how they did? They already performed and the profit is recorded." The answer obviously concerns the effects this lack will produce on subsequent behavior and, more specifically, on the goals to be set in the succeeding budget.

The next budget will be affected because omitting feedback not only precludes certainty regarding a previous level of aspiration but

---

[24] J. L. Elwell and G. C. Grindley, "The Effect of Knowledge of Results on Learning and Performance," *British Journal of Psychology*, Vol. XXIX (1938).
[25] N. L. Munn, *Psychology* (Boston: Houghton Mifflin Co., 1946).
[26] H. J. Leavitt and R. A. H. Mueller, "Some Effects of Feedback on Communication," *Human Relations*, IV (1951), pp. 401-10.

also affects the subsequent level of aspiration. Most generally an individual will raise his level of aspiration after success and lower it after failure.

In the budgeting cycle, after the comparison phase, the new budget is started. The participating supervisors bring to the new participation situation all their new aspirations resulting from past feelings of success or failure. If they have been deprived of a rightfully achieved feeling of success, their subsequent aspirations are likely to be lowered. This could result either in a less efficient budget, that is, lower goals than could easily be achieved or, after disagreeable argument, an imposed budget from an adamant management. In the first case succeeding performance will be unnecessarily low; in the second, participation will be ineffectual with the possible result of poor performance and, almost certainly, lower morale. The *proper* budget cycle then is really a dual, interacting sequence of budgeting and psychological events. It can be depicted as follows:

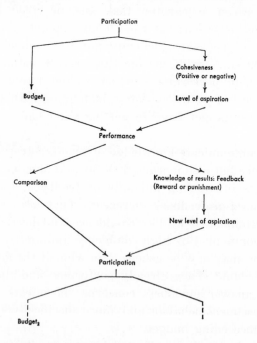

A successful participation budget does two things: (1) it induces proper motivation and acceptance of specific goals, and (2) it provides information to associate reward or punishment with performance. These lead to new aspirations and motivations that set the stage for the next participation budget.

Conclusions

An understanding of the psychological variables stemming from participation is valuable, perhaps, for its own sake, but it is hardly likely to provide concrete assistance in a decision to institute such a program. We have seen that participation can lead to either increased or decreased output. It is not unlikely that the setting in which participation occurs is one determinant of the production outcome. Some organizations can be characterized as operating under relatively authoritarian leadership. By definition, participation is essential to democratic process and very probably is antithetical to an authoritarian organization. To illustrate the latter, assume that the various department heads participate in the decision making process, prepare a budget, only to have it rejected by upper management without explanation other than that a more satisfactory budget is necessary. The best prediction here is that the participating group will be highly cohesive and hold negative attitudes toward management, a precondition to lowered output.

It is also likely that under authoritarian management status differences will be rigidly adhered to. If the participants in the budgeting process occupy different status levels, influence on decisions will be directly related to status—the more status the more influence. Status differences would probably mitigate against high cohesiveness. Presumably, status differences that did not affect the decision making process would not preclude either a cohesive group or positive goal acceptance, especially if the occupants were secure in their positions or perceived the possibility of upward mobility.[27]

We do not wish to enter the controversy over the relative merits of various styles of leadership but merely wish to point to some possible limitations on the use of participation. In order to be successful, the participants must participate, that is, must have influence on the adopted decisions. If participation can be achieved under more or less authoritarian conditions, it is likely to be effective, just as it can be undermined (by disregard) with democratic leadership. Only management itself can determine whether it is worthwhile to initiate or continue the participation segment of the budgeted cycle.

At any rate, presuming an organization has determined that it can benefit from participation, are the psychological effects such that participation simply can be "grafted" onto existing procedures or are

---

[27] Harold H. Kelley, "Communication in Experimentally Created Hierarchies," *Human Relations*, IV (1951), pp. 39-56.

other changes necessary? Or indeed, if no changes are necessary, are there any that can be made so that efficiency, motivation, and productivity will be enhanced?

Suggested changes in budgeting are not difficult to find. Stedry, recognizing the possible motivating forces produced by budgets, seems to suggest that "phony" budgets be prepared while the real budget is kept secret.[28] The "phony" ones would be designed to induce maximum motivation through a manipulation of level of aspiration. This plan would require different phony budgets for each department and, indeed, for each individual. If different budgets are viewed as discriminatory and unfair devices, company morale might suffer. Further, if already disgruntled employees learn that they were striving to attain phony goals the effectiveness of future budgets, real or phony, might be seriously impaired.

A knowledge of the effects of level of aspiration may lead to changes designed to increase employee motivation and output. The budget cycle characteristically is tied to an arbitrary time schedule. Even with no other information, this is defensible logically and perhaps economically as well. If, however, the budget is to be used as a control device (in the sense of prohibiting excessive expenditures) as well as a motivating device, then it clearly should be tied to the level of aspiration cycle rather than to a time schedule. We know that success leads to a rising level of aspiration and, generally, failure to a lowering. Failure can also result in "leaving the field," that is, psychological or physical withdrawal from the goal oriented environment.

It is suggested here that much more frequent comparison of performance and budget be made, including feedback to the employees of the results of the comparison. This recommendation is made for the following reasons: (1) If the performances meet or slightly exceed expectation, then level of aspirations will rise and budgets can and should be revised; otherwise employees will perform at the budget level when they could be performing at a higher budget level. Maximum efficiency can be achieved only by revising the budget upward. (2) If performances are just slightly below the budget expectations, budget changes are not necessary, but feedback is so that employees will continue to strive for the budget goals. (3) If performances are well below the budget, it may be well to revise the budget downward. If such revision is not made, employees' level of aspiration will fall,

---

[28] *Budget Control and Cost Behavior*, pp. 5, 17, 41-42, and 71. Stedry does not use the term "phony."

the budget wil be viewed as unattainable, and output will fall. The danger here is that levels of aspiration and output may fall much more than are necessary. If the budget is revised downward just enough so that it is perceived as being attainable, then maximum output will be achieved again.

32. A MATHEMATICAL MODEL
FOR BUDGET AND OTHER
COMPUTATIONS *

Edward E. Hoffman †

This paper describes the application of a mathematical model and of computer techniques to a budgeting system at Esso Research and Engineering Company. The basic problem was making the many interrelated calculations required to develop, and revise, detailed divisional operating expense budgets for Esso Research and Engineering Company. The calculation problem existed primarily because accurate, equitable cost accounting and, therefore, budgeting required a considerable amount of "cross-charging." This occurs when company divisions or divisional sections first charge each other for goods or services rendered, with subsequent charges against the product(s).

The approach was to express the entire divisional budgeting system in some equation form which would reflect all pertinent accounting rules for allocation of actual expenses. The basic form chosen was a system of simultaneous linear equations. This matrix consists of about 130 equations in 130 unknowns. There is one equation for each division, or where appropriate, divisional section. The sum of the terms in a given equation is the total operating budget for a given division or section.

SETTING UP THE COMPUTER PROGRAM

The budgeting model is solved on an IBM 7094 computer in about 20 minutes. The computer program used consists of three major parts:

1. Preparation of the basic input data for insertion into the matrix model.

2. Solution of the matrix.

3. Preparation of a number of summaries of the detailed matrix solutions.

---

* From *Budgeting* (March, 1965). Reprinted by permission of the Budget Executives Institute.

† Edward E. Hoffman, Budget Analyst, Esso Research and Engineering Company, Linden, New Jersey.

The approach and techniques used are general enough to apply to other computational situations involving charges or allocations among and between cost centers and products or customers. Other computer systems could be used as well.

The project reflects the joint efforts of Esso Research and Engineering Company's Budget and Finance and the Applied Mathematics Divisions. Specific mention is due Mr. Del Heuser of Applied Mathematics Division. His computer programming efforts not only made the project possible but resulted in an unusually flexible system.

Using the Mathematical Model

Initial experience with the use of a mathematical model for budget calculations has been gratifying. Something less than six man months of effort was required from conception to actual use. Using Esso Research and Engineering Company's experience, others might develop a similar model tailored to their special needs, using other computers, with even less effort. Initial use of the ERE model was for 1964 budget revisions. To date, the model has been used five times for this purpose. In addition, the 1964 input deck was simply machine reproduced and revised, based on decisions by management, to produce an initial set of 1965 budget figures. The model and the computer program which permits its use have offered:

1. *Speed* of operation. Since the model is solved on a computer, massive recalculations are made and printed out in a matter of minutes.

2. *Flexibility* to meet changing needs, because the model itself is easily modified. Cost centers may be added, deleted, split, combined, or distributed in new ways simply by changing a few cards in the basic input and/or program decks.

3. *Economy*. Recurring costs are essentially made up of computer time. While this may run $5-$10 per minute, the total cost for a budget revision has compared favorably with manual alternatives, where they existed.

4. *Accuracy*. Manual approximations can be made of the correct budgets to reflect subsequent cross-charging of actual expenses between divisions. However, even the magnitude of the error of approximation cannot be known without having the computer-produced, exact answers. The model and the computer eliminate the computational error question altogether.

Others have made use of mathematical models and computer techniques for such purposes as allocating charges among and between the various overhead and process units of a petroleum refinery. However, there is some reason to believe that the subject model may be the first to encompass an entire divisional budgeting system. Further, it is speculated that the programming techniques employed yield a more flexible system than others that may be in use.

COMPUTERIZING THE BUDGET SYSTEM

Recent refinements in the cost accounting system at Esso Research and Engineering Company and the need to reflect these in budgets, while reducing the initial and recurring clerical effort required, led to efforts to computerize the budgeting system. The first step was to express the entire system in terms a computer could deal with. In doing this, there was one aspect of the budgeting and accounting systems which required particularly careful attention. This was the need to provide for "cross-charging" or "recycling" of costs between certain cost centers, e.g., company divisions and sections within a division.

Except when done on a very limited basis, cross-charging presents a particularly difficult computational problem when attempted manually. The following example is typical of the general problem in this area. Assume the situation where company Cost Centers A and B each charge the other for goods or services rendered. Assume further that the output of both A and B can be measured in some kind (or combination) of units so each can determine the proportion of its total output going to the other. Suppose the portion of A's output going to B is 10 percent; B's to A, 20 percent. The next step normally would be to apply these percentages to the totals (budgeted or actual expenses) for A and B to determine the appropriate charge from each to the other. But the total for either A or B depends, to the extent of the cross-range, on the total of the other. The charge *to* each from the other depends, in part, on the charge *from* each to the other.

EQUATIONS FOR "CROSS-CHARGING"

Accurate answers can be produced only by calculating the totals for both cost centers simultaneously. This is done easily enough by setting up two simple equations.

1. A Total $= 10\%$ (B Total) $+$ Other A Expenses

2. B Total $= 20\%$ (A Total) $+$ Other B Expenses

Equation 1 says that A's total is made up of its charge from B plus the rest of its expenses. Equation 2 is interpreted in a similar manner. The algebraic solution to those two equations in this simple example is very easy. The solution would remain simple even if A and B made both fixed (e.g., materials) *and* prorata (e.g., percent of total labor provided) charges to each other.

However, the situation becomes vastly more involved when charges between a larger number of cost centers, even, say, ten, must be considered. Of course, one approach with a larger number of cost centers is to approximate the real situation by freezing charges into one cost center and then distributing its costs to the others, and/or product lines, projects, etc. This step would then be repeated with a second cost center, then a third, and so on. The problem here is that this approach introduces some error in each computation. If the net result of all of these errors could be known, it might be quite acceptable in many situations. However, the size of the error of approximation cannot be known without having the exact answers for each situation. To do this, when more than just a few cost centers are involved, i.e., make charges to each other, requires a computer.

The need to deal with the cross-charge situation on a relatively large basis, and the fact that it can be defined by "simultaneous" equations, led to consideration of a large group of such equations as the model to express the budgeting system. Most of the larger computers can readily deal with this type of mathematical model. In many cases, the basic programming work has already been done and is available.

The Budget Model

It turned out to be quite simple to build such a model for budgeting purposes. This is because budgeting (and accounting on a more complex scale) is essentially the description and assignment of resources, in dollar terms, to cost centers, be they company divisions, their sections, products, or projects.

The Esso Research and Engineering Company model currently considers about 130 separate cost centers each of which falls into one of three categories:

1. Company divisions or, in some cases, sections within a division.

2. Expense classifications which collect costs associated with the various areas of Company effort. In a manufacturing company these would be product lines or projects.

3. "Dummy" cost centers which are used to:
   a. Collect totals for certain cost center groupings.
   b. First collect and then distribute certain expenses of an overhead nature which must be known both in detail and in total and which are distributed in numerous ways.

To provide an all encompassing, and therefore extremely flexible form which a computer can readily deal with, the budgeted cost for *each* cost center is expressed in terms of a single equation having 130 elements, i.e., type of expense. Each element would represent a part of a cost center's total budgeted expense. These elements fall into two categories:

1. Elements whose budgeted dollar values are fixed and, therefore, known prior to the computer solution. The computer merely reads these into the matrix, keeps track of them by type of expense *and* cost center, and distributes them according to the desired cost accounting concepts. Examples might include salaries, materials, equipment rental, and *fixed* charges from one cost center to another.

2. Elements whose budgeted dollar values are initially unknown and must be determined by the computer. These consist of charges or allocations from other cost centers which are of a variable nature, viz., they are initially stated as a percentage (of total chargeable effort) of an unknown total (cost to be recovered). Charges made via direct labor rates would be a good example; i.e., Cost Center A charges Project Z for 20 percent of its costs recoverable through its labor rate.

The current program at Esso Research requires the computer to solve for about 1,700 unknown elements. The total number of elements in this model is $(130)^2$ or 16,900. However, about 90 percent of them are known to be zero from the start because nearly all cost centers only charge to a selected and small group of others. While this may appear to be an unnecessarily cumbersome model, it is convenient for the computer and very easily modified, generally with no additional programming, to meet changing cost accounting requirements.

The Use of "Schemes"

There is one special technique built into the program which is of particular timesaving value and, therefore, worthy of special note. It permits the computer to develop a large part of the information it must have to solve the equations in the matrix model. The technique involves the use of "schemes" to distribute costs collected by various cost centers, both to other cost centers and to expense classifications (types of work or products). For example, one scheme distributes all costs associated with occupied space. This scheme simply lists the space units, i.e., square feet, associated with each cost center. The computer collects budgeted space costs against the appropriate center designated to hold all such expenses and then spreads them to the centers listed in the scheme in direct proportion to each center's part of the scheme's total. This setup is much easier to revise than if the whole distribution (percentages of total occupied space) had to be manually recalculated for the computer.

The entire program requires about 1,800 pieces of basic input data, and something less than 20 minutes on an IBM 7094 computer. An expansion of this program is foreseen which may ultimately lead to the use of about 350 cost centers (equations). In addition to divisional budgets, this would also provide expense classification (product or project) budgets, which are currently built up, or calculated, on a manual basis.

Conclusions

Initial experience with the subject model and related computer techniques has more than rewarded their relatively modest development efforts. The use of simultaneous equations appears to be well suited to a whole class of computational needs which are, in the broadest sense, of an accounting or cost nature. Any resource distribution or allocation concept, which can be objectively and sharply defined, can be incorporated into a model built from such equations.

The most obvious application is in accounting systems. However, it is clear that accounting needs require a considerably more elaborate model than the corresponding budgeting needs. This is because accounting is done in much more detail than budgeting. For example, a divisional budget for materials might consist of only one annual figure. However, the accounting system must be capable of recording, storing, and reproducing possibly hundreds of transactions chargeable against that one budget figure. Further, each of these transactions must be described as to exact cost, item(s) purchased, vendor, date paid, authorizing individual, etc.

Still, most of the differences between accounting and budgeting systems appear to fall into one of two classes:

1. Number of cost centers and categories of expense which must be dealt with. The subject model for budgeting could possibly be expanded to meet this need. Additional detail could be accommodated by increasing the model matrix size.

2. Data storage and retrieval requirements for such things as paid invoices and receipts from customers. The subject model for budgeting was not designed to meet this accounting need. However, existing accounting input storage systems might be modified to feed summary information to such a model, while preserving all of the required basic detail.

Given the basic simplicity and flexibility of the budgeting model, there is some reason to foresee its use by others.

33. NETWORK TECHNIQUES AND ACCOUNTING—WITH AN ILLUSTRATION *

Gordon B. Davis †

Judging by such criteria of the interest of businessmen as numbers of articles, seminars, etc., one of the most interest provoking developments in recent years is the network technique for planning and scheduling. The systems which use network analysis and critical path methods for planning and scheduling the completion of a given task are variously referred to as PERT (Program Evaluation and Review Technique), CPM (Critical Path Method) or PERT/CPM. Many companies are now using these methods in planning and scheduling such diverse projects as construction of buildings, installation of equipment, and research and development assignments. All major computer manufacturers have computer programs to do network analysis. Although the origin of CPM is industrial and PERT is military, the basic concepts are similar. There has tended to be a merging of the two systems although a distinction which remains is the use of probabilities by PERT and not by CPM.

PERT and CPM both make use of two basic tools—the network description and the critical path. Together, these tools constitute a single management control tool for defining and integrating events and activities necessary for the timely completion of program objectives. This formidable task requires that activities and events be arranged in a proper sequence, that time and resource requirements be estimated for each element in the sequence, and that available resources be assigned.

Network Description: Critical Path

A program or project can be thought of as consisting of a number of specific results to be accomplished in a certain sequence so that

---

* From the *N.A.A. Bulletin* (May, 1963). Reprinted by permission of the National Association of Accountants.
† Gordon B. Davis, Associate Professor of Accounting and Data Processing, University of Minnesota.

an objective may be attained. These results are defined as the specific fulfillment of some part of the plan and are referred to as events. An event is always a distinguishable point in time. It may be a decision, availability of a part, ending point of an activity, etc. Since each event is associated with a definite point in time and is identified by a specific accomplishment, the events provide a basis for measuring the progress of a program.

Events are typically shown as nodes in a network. The activity culminating in an event is described by an arrow. Since the events are interdependent, the arrows also show the sequence in which events must be accomplished. Except for the last, each event has one or more succeeding events whose occurrence depends upon the prior completion of the given event. The events themselves occur at a point in time; they do not require time. Time is occupied by the activity necessary to proceed from one event to the succeeding one. The network description consists, then, of arrows which represent activities and nodes which represent events (or completion of an activity).

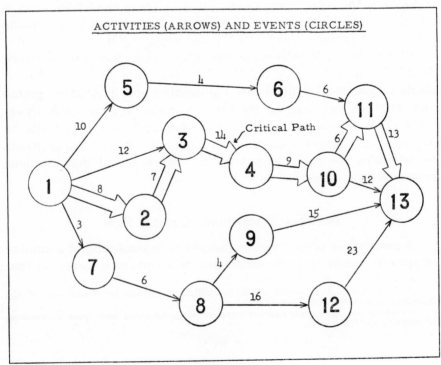

Exhibit 1

Exhibit 1 illustrates this method for describing a program. The activity which ends with Event 4, for example, cannot be begun until Event 3 has occurred, and Event 3 is dependent on activities between Events 1 and 3 and 2 and 3. Note that the network adds the interrelationship dimension to the sequencing relationship presented by bar-graph methods. In fact, the exercise of preparing a network describing the events in a program is itself often a valuable step in clarifying planning and scheduling problems.

The next step is to find the critical path through the network. An event is on the critical path if, when it is not completed on time, the entire project is delayed by the amount of time that the event is delayed. In other words, the sequence of events which cannot be delayed without delaying the entire project constitutes the critical path. For example, if the activities between Events 1 and 2 and 2 and 3 of Exhibit 1 are extended, the entire project will be delayed, whereas the activity between Events 1 and 3 can be delayed somewhat without affecting the overall schedule. The amount of time which an event can be delayed without affecting the project completion is known as "slack" or "float."

The advantages to be gained from this analysis are significant. It means that extra resources, overtime, etc., can be deployed on the critical path. Proposals that will shorten the time for certain events may be evaluated in terms of the effect on the network. Resources may be shifted and specifications altered in order to improve the capacity of the system to meet the deadlines set for it. When events on the critical path are delayed, the project is delayed by a like amount.

This does not, however, necessarily work in reverse. A reduction in the time of completion of an event on the critical path, instead of causing a like reduction in the project time, may alter the critical path. Another activity sequence may now be the one requiring the most time. The critical path is not, therefore, to be considered as fixed. It may shift if resources are shifted and time estimates are changed, and it may change as the project progresses and the actual times deviate from the estimated times.

On small networks, the critical path and amount of slack can be calculated manually. For a large network, say more than 50 events, it is unwieldy to make the calculations manually. An electronic computer is then employed. In practice, the computer analysis is a major factor in the success of network techniques.

PERT Probabilities; Extensions of PERT/CPM

The analysis presented thus far has depended on having suitable time estimates. Network analysis does not eliminate the problem of making time estimates. However, the PERT approach to time estimates provides a means for including within the analysis the uncertainty which is part of most time estimates. This is done by obtaining three separate time estimates for each activity—the optimistic, pessimistic, and most likely. These time estimates are then used to construct a probability distribution for the occurrence of the event or completion of the activity. In other words, it is more to be expected that the actual time will be close to the most likely time than it will to one of the extreme estimates. However, there is a possibility that the actual time will occur at or near the extreme, and these, therefore, may be important in assessing the probabilities of meeting a given schedule. The importance of recognizing the distribution of possible outcomes is greatest where the range and uncertainty of the estimates are greatest.

Where the estimates have a fairly high degree of precision, the use of probabilities does not seem to be warranted. For those cases in which PERT probabilities are used, the probability analysis allows for the computation of the probability of achieving an objective by a given completion date. The PERT probability approach was developed for a weapons development program in which an assumption of a precise completion time would have been unrealistic. It appears that the probabilities are most valuable in similar cases of highly uncertain time estimates. The CPM approach, using a single time estimate, is a satisfactory and simpler approach when time estimates are reasonably precise.

Time is the key element in network methods. It is used as the basis for describing progress and evaluating performance. Cost is not considered in the basic structure. A logical extension of the technique is to include the cost element, so as to be able to keep costs low and, at the same time, meet the completion date. Since there is usually a cost associated with any shortening of the schedule, there is an advantage in being able to determine the costs associated with various alternative means for reducing the completion time. Given this data, one can select the least cost alternative. Most of the more recent computer programs for critical path analysis offer this cost extension. The additional cost resulting from reducing the time required for an activity and the cost savings from allowing greater time are specified. The computer analysis determines the least cost schedule and the cost associated with a schedule that is not least cost.

Another feature found in many of the PERT/CPM computer programs is a compilation of manpower requirements by skill for each time period. For example, the schedule as originally formulated may call for more asbestos workers is a given time period that can be made available. Either rescheduling to spread out the time for the work of this skill or some other alternative action would be necessary.

These extensions of PERT/CPM illustrate what can be done to make the basic system more valuable. The electronic computer is a key element in such variations, for without the computer, the techniques would be too cumbersome for anything but very small problems. The real payoff from the technique has tended to be in application to large problems which cannot be solved satisfactorily by traditional methods.

CRITICAL PATH NETWORKS IN ACCOUNTING SYSTEMS

The successful application of network analysis to compel scheduling tasks in research and development and in construction leads one to believe that this tool may have further applications. The problem to be considered here is its applicability to accounting systems problems. Criteria for a PERT/CPM-type network may be summarized in the following points:

1. There is a definite *objective* that can be achieved at a given point in time (objective event).
2. There is a *completion date* requirement for the objective event.
3. There are many *identifiable and interdependent* activities and events that must be completed in proper sequence before the objective event can be achieved.
4. *Time estimates* can be made for the events and activities in the network.
5. *Resources* can be *shifted* from one activity to another in order to affect the completion date of activities in the network.

As indicated by the following discussion, certain segments of the accounting system qualify as critical path networks under these criteria. We will consider each of the above five points in as many paragraphs below.

The accounting system, as a whole, has an *objective* of providing information, either routinely or on request. This is essentially a statement of purpose and it does not tell us how to recognize when the objective has been reached. If one inquires as to what information, for whom, and when, several objective events emerge, such as the issuance of a set of periodic reports to management, a custodial financial statement for stockholders, or a profit plan. In addition to these objective events, there are also activities such as file maintenance and file inquiry services which have objectives, but lack a single objective event. This excludes them from application of the technique. Examples of these are providing customer billing and answering customer inquiries as to account status.

The events in a network are sequenced toward a *completion date* for the objective. Progress through time toward the completion date is basic to the network methods. This criterion also eliminates certain recurrent activities, such as file maintenance, from the PERT /CPM analysis. On the other hand, objective events which are periodic may be considered as having completion dates. Examples of this type would be the preparation of managerial reports by a certain day following the close of the accounting period and the preparation of custodial statements by a scheduled date after the end of the year.

One must be able to *identify* the existence of an event. Since an event may be the completion of an activity, the requirement is essentially that one must be able to know when a task has been completed. For instance, whereas accounts receivable file maintenance is never really completed, the taking of an accounts receivable balance ends in an identifiable event which is necessary for the issuance of a periodic report. *Interdependence* is also a requirement. If the events necessary to the completion of the objective event are not interdependent and in a certain sequence, they can still be drawn as nodes and arrows, but no network will result and there will be no critical path. The sequencing of interdependent events adds complexity to the problem and justifies the network analysis in arriving at a solution. Therefore, simple problems having few interrelationships between events and having little or no sequencing are eliminated from consideration.

Each event or activity in the network must have a time assigned to it. The time estimates are necessary in order to calculate the critical path and amount of slack. If PERT probability analysis is to be performed, there must be three time estimates: likely, optimistic, and pessimistic. The requirement of time estimates is satisfied by those accounting system problems which appear to be amenable to network analysis.

One of the ideas behind the network approach is to identify critical events and then to deploy resources to ensure the timely achieving of these events. The ability to do this is based on an ability to *shift resources* from one activity to another. Most accounting activities are of the type which can be accelerated by the addition of more manpower. This is especially true if advance planning and training have taken place.

What conclusion shall we draw from the foregoing association with accounting of the five criteria for a PERT/CPM network? An accounting system as a whole does not comprise a PERT/CPM-type network. It has features in which necessary characteristics are lacking. However, there are such networks in the accounting system. Examples would be a program culminating in the issuance of a managerial or custodial financial report and a program which produces a profit plan. This second example will be dealt with later.

The design and installation of a new or improved accounting system may also be considered to be a PERT/CPM network. The problem of system design and installation is analogous to many successful PERT/CPM applications. For the most part, these successful applications have been engineering, research and development, and construction projects. The design and installation of an accounting information system fits the criteria for a PERT/CPM network. The system must be properly sequenced. There is a time schedule to be met. There are interdependent events. There is the possibility of reallocating resources or altering specifications in order to meet the schedule date. There is also usually a reasonable measure of uncertainty in most system programs. A highly integrated data processing system is quite interdependent, more so than a system which retains traditional processing compartments. If the design and installation of a given system is sufficiently complex, it may make good use of PERT/CPM. For a simpler system, the network approach may be more trouble than it is worth.

Installation of a computer is a PERT/CPM application that has been tried with some success, although there may be some propensity to use the technique because it makes use of a computer. This application is similar to a construction or systems problem. It is also appealing in that a computer is used in installing another computer.

A Profit Plan Described by Network Methods

Those activities and events which result in a budget or profit plan may be described by a network. The objective event is the issuance

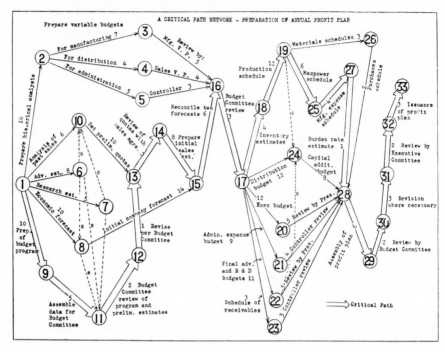

Exhibit 2

of the completed, approved document. There is usually a required completion date and there are apt to be serious consequences if it is not completed as scheduled. The events are, to a certain extent, interrelated and there are sequencing considerations. The sales forecast needs the results of the advertising decision which, in turn, needs a preliminary sales forecast. Each major step in preparing the profit plan is an activity in the network.

A hypothetical and somewhat simplified profit plan is used for this illustration. The completed network is shown in Exhibit 2. In addition to drawing the network, the problem was run on a UNIVAC 80 computer. The program uses the CPM concept of a single time estimate. Time is shown in hours on the activity lines. No probabilities were calculated. This network is activity oriented rather than event oriented, but either approach would have been satisfactory. The critical path as analyzed by the computer is marked on the exhibit by use of double-line arrows. The computer analysis on the profit plan network provides not only the critical path but also the earliest possible start and completion time for each activity, the latest possible time the activity can start and be finished in order to avoid slippage in the schedule, and the amount of float each activity has associated with it.

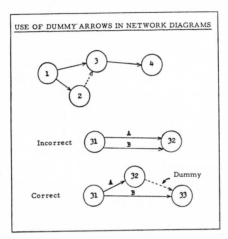

Exhibit 3

The network can be used both in planning and in controlling a program. It can, for example, be reviewed for activities which might be changed in order to reduce the total time required. If desired, the computer can be used to compute the effect on the completion date of various changes in the network. Having decided upon a particular network, it is then possible to use the network to review the progress of the program. Critical activities which begin to slip may be speeded up by the addition of resources. Other activities which are delayed can be reviewed in the light of slack available for the activity.

An Aside on Technique

It will be noted there are arrows drawn as broken lines in Exhibit 2, rather than solid lines. These are called "dummy" arrows. They are used for clarity and precision in the network diagram. They may be used to show interrelationships where no activity link exists, to clarify ambiguous networks, and to avoid having two parallel arrows. The use of dummy arrows to show interrelationships is illustrated by the diagram in the upper portion of Exhibit 3.

The activity between Nodes 1 and 3 must be completed before the activity between Nodes 3 and 4 can begin. Although there is no activity link between Nodes 2 and 3, it is necessary that the activity link between 1 and 2 be completed before the activity between 3 and 4 can begin. The dummy arrow between 2 and 3 indicates this relationship. In the above example, each activity can be described by the nodes between which it lies. The activity between Nodes 3 and 4 can be described as Activity 3, 4.

The computer analysis depends on such unambiguous designation for each activity. Therefore, it would be incorrect to have two activities with a designation, starting and ending at the same nodes, like Activities A and B in the first of the two lower illustrations in Exhibit 3. To show the proper relationship and yet have unique numbers assigned to each activity, a dummy arrow is used, as shown, in the second illustration. A is 31, 32 and B is 31, 33. The dummy arrows can be used wherever there is ambiguity in the network. They are always assigned a zero time.

Use PERT/CPM or Something Simpler?

It is likely, in most cases, that the drawing of the network will be valuable in planning and scheduling a profit planning program. However, a technique should not only be useful, but also more useful than alternative methods, and useful enough to justify the time and effort required to use it. Because the network approach is most useful when the program is complex and the analysis is done by computers, a program has to be reasonably complex to justify PERT or CPM. Networks with few interrelationships can be handled just as easily by bar-chart scheduling methods. In development type defense contracts, PERT is required if the contract is expected to exceed $1 million.

A profit plan network that is as simple or simpler than the illustration in Exhibit 2 should probably not consider PERT/CPM. As a network of events required to prepare the profit plan becomes more complex, the possibility of benefit from the network technique increases.

K. L. Dean makes the following statement in regard to the use of network techniques:

> The key as to whether or not to use the technique lies in the *uncertainty* involved. New proposals, one-shot jobs, projects of long duration—all well qualify. Short jobs, 30, 60 or even 90 days, if the *uncertainty* is relatively small, *may* not qualify. (The technique *has* been used with resounding success on two- and three-day jobs of massive proportions). Also, jobs of a repetitive nature, such as follow-on or mass production, might not find the technique as useful as many of the existing techniques such as bar charts or line of balance.[1]

[1] K. L. Dean, *Fundamentals of Network Planning & Analysis* (Remington Rand Univac Military Dept., July, 1961), pp. 7-8.

The uncertainty connected with a program to produce a profit plan is usually moderate, but this varies considerably from firm to firm. It is possible that a complex profit planning procedure might justify the network approach for structuring the program, but the uncertainty might be so low as to rule out anything but the simplest procedures for controlling the progress of the program.

In short, the network techniques have proved very successful in planning, scheduling, and controlling various types of programs, especially development and construction programs. As such, they are of interest to accountants. With respect to whether or not the approach would be useful in accounting problems, the final answer will come when there has been a number of attempts, either successful or unsuccessful. The analysis in this article suggests that there are several likely candidates for PERT/CPM. These are the preparation of the profit plan, the design and installation of a new accounting system, and the installation of a computer system. Other possible applications, such as the preparation of a set of managerial or custodial reports, would seem to justify PERT/CPM only if the particular application were fairly complex. At this juncture, the proper course of action would be for accountants to try the network technique if they have a problem which appears to justify its use.

34. OPERATIONS RESEARCH AND ACCOUNTING:
COMPETITORS OR PARTNERS? *   Richard V. Mattessich †

For centuries accounting has dominated the area of practical quantitative problems in business administration. In actual practice the accounting department was the major source for quantitative financial information until the emergence of the operations research team challenged this monopoly position. Such a challenge is a serious one. For not only do operations analysts pretend to have solutions for problems which accountants refuse to attack, the OR men even claim the ability to solve less forbidding tasks *better* and *more accurately* than accountants do. In consequence, some of the radical members of this new discipline suggest that in time they will replace accountants altogether—a threat that comes close to a declaration of war. This controversy is by no means purely academic; it intimately concerns the welfare of American industry, and an objective look at this problem may be of benefit to practice as well as to theory. But first, it seems opportune to outline the genealogy of the two disciplines.

THE CASE OF ACCOUNTING

Trade, manufacturing, and governmental activities require internal and external control systems that traditionally have been provided by accounting. There have been two decisive criteria: (1) *custodianship*, control primarily directed toward checking the honest stewardship of the person subject to it, and (2) *objective evidence*, control based on documentation of a highly "objective" nature.

Control with regard to the efficiency or ability of an enterprise or person was long restricted to crude and global evaluative criteria such as sales or profit figures. Even then the accounting system could not and did not need to indicate what better sales volume or

* From *The Quarterly Review of Economics and Business* (August, 1962). Reprinted by permission of the Bureau of Economics and Business Research, College of Commerce and Business Administration, University of Illinois.
† Richard V. Mattessich, Associate Professor, University of California, Berkeley, California.

amount of profit could have been attained under a more efficient operation. In many cases the manager was the entrepreneur and, above all, the industrial structure was simple enough to let experience and intuition control the aspect of efficiency. With the increasing complexity of industry, the problem of efficiency control became more urgently felt. Obviously it was the accountant's task to remedy the situation by extending and articulating the bookkeeping system. Thus control and cost figures for individual departments, products, and so on were generated on a large scale and have proved useful— even if not always "correct." Because of the lack of precision, allocation assumptions have had to be made more on grounds of thrift than of accuracy, a fact that limits the usefulness and validity of cost accounting data. Thus, accounting has been confronted with a problem (which it shares with OR and any other "practical" quantitative discipline) that has not yet found a systematic solution: the question of the optimal relationship between the amount to be spent on measurement and the degree of accuracy to be desired. The difficulty in determining this point of equilibrium between these two "conflicting" variables lies not so much in the lack of analytical thought as in finding a measure for the degree of accuracy of an accounting system, and above all in relating various accuracies to the benefits attained from them by the enterprise. In other words, the setting up of a reliable function between "degree of accuracy" and "yield" is the major hurdle.

As a result of this difficulty and the traditional methodology, accountants (even cost accountants) have restricted themselves to tasks of a quantitative descriptive nature. Thus, the activities of classification and allocation, as well as the definitional and evaluative problems connected with them, have constituted the main concern of the accountant. This is comprehensible in the face of the bearing which accounting has upon many legal aspects, the taxation system, and the credit rating, as well as the security trading procedures. Even cost accounting occasionally affects these areas more than the realm of managerial decision making. The choice between the fifo and lifo inventory evaluation methods and the controversies connected with it amply illustrate this assertion. Traditional cost accounting, however, does perform functions of direct use to the various echelons of management, and the emergence of "managerial accounting" (about ten years ago) was no surprise. This term is still not clearly defined—some identify it with cost accounting, some with accounting in general, and others with something in between these two concepts.[1] It has, however, succeeded in deceiving many laymen and even some accountants about the capability and range of this discipline.

Thus, accounting grew out of the immediate need of actual practice and was chiefly developed by practitioners who adjusted the accounting model (1) to the availability of documentary and documentable material, (2) to their relatively unsophisticated mathematical abilities, and occasionally (3) to the need of a particular purpose or department without regard to general or overall managerial considerations. Therefore, accounting and its effectiveness can be understood much better from a psychological than from a logical point of view. It may be farfetched to compare its main function to that which Tolstoy assigned to General Kutuzov in his *War and Peace,* but a certain analogy undoubtedly exists. There, an institution (the commanding general of the Russian Army) was painted as one whose importance lay in the representation of a stable (but perhaps purely fictitious) authority in the midst of chaos. It would be too dangerous to carry this analogy further but it is notable that this commander, whose actions were not backed by any systematic strategy and whose actions usually defied logical analysis, ultimately carried the victory over the precisely logical and highly strategical war machinery of Napoleon. Certainly, it was not Kutuzov but the Russian winter that won the war. The lesson of Tolstoy, however, consists in the implication that in spite of the winter Napoleon might have won had it not been for the *belief* of the Russian people in an undefeated—though constantly retreating—army. Likewise, the effectiveness of traditional accounting lies not in the preciseness of information to management for maximizing profit or any other entrepreneurial goal, but in its authoritative character. The institution of control checks upon people and enables the depiction of the firm's financial structure in a simple and crude but overall model which constitutes a mighty bulwark against chaos. This comparison is by no means intended as a defense of irrationalism or unscientific methods; it has been presented merely in the hope of facilitating the understanding of accounting by OR men and other people in whose logical system accounting seems to constitute a stumbling block. There can be no doubt that more scientific methods are better, absolutely speaking. There is merely the question about the threshold where they become more profitable for a certain firm.

---

[1] Cf. the definition of management accounting in R. I. Dickey (ed.), *Accountants' Cost Handbook* (2d ed.; New York: The Ronald Press Co., 1960), pp. 1-5.

The Case of Operations Research

Operations research emerged from the wartime need for solving decision making problems of a military nature by way of mathematical-scientific methods. In many complex situations the intuition of the strategist was inferior to the solution which the mathematicians provided by means of their models. Thus, it is understandable that OR methods came into vogue, not only with regard to military problems, but especially within the realm of business where the problem structure is similar or at least amenable to the same methodology. The main feature of this approach is the construction of analytical models that permit the determination of maximum or minimum solutions.[2] Some of these methods are nowadays well known under the names of linear, nonlinear, integer, and dynamic programming; solutions are occasionally attained in an iterative way only (e.g., the simplex method). This trend to substitute, in highly complex situations, purely analytical devices by iterative, heuristic, or even simulation approaches (which usually are restricted to "satisfactory" instead of optimal solutions) is another characteristic of modern OR and was strongly furthered by the advent of electronic data processing.

Out of all this grows an additional idiosyncrasy which OR shares with activity analysis[3] and which may be covered by the term "systems approach." This is the conceptualization of the problem under a viewpoint that considers the interdependence of all variables incorporated in the model. Charnes and Cooper call such models *mutatis mutandis*, in contrast to the *ceteris paribus* models.[4] The latter assume all but one variable constant whereas the former take all possible feedback reactions to other variables into consideration. This contrast in methodology is familiar to us from traditional economics where we encounter it in a less general version through the juxtaposition of Walras' general equilibrium to Marshall's partial equilibrium analysis.

---

[2] There exist various approaches to this problem and it may be worth adding that in OR these maxima or minima do not always rely on a straightforward differentiation method, but on a method that utilizes a peculiar form of the Lagrangian multiplier under the consideration of a series of constraints. Thus, the result is the maximization of a function (frequently a linear function) over a convex set (often a convex polygon), a method which at first glance bears little resemblance to the calculus maximization approach encountered in high school, yet one that is ultimately based on it.

[3] In the case of applying this new approach to macroeconomics one usually speaks of activity analysis.

[4] A. Charnes and W. W. Cooper, "Management Models and Industrial Applications of Linear Programming," *Management Science*, Vol. 4, No. 1 (October, 1957), pp. 40-41.

With respect to these mathematical tools Herbert Simon offers a "general recipe for using it in management decision making." [5]

1. Construct a *mathematical model* that satisfies the conditions of the tool to be used and which, at the same time, mirrors the important factors in the management situation to be analyzed.
2. Define the *criterion function*, the measure that is to be used for comparing the relative merits of various possible courses of action.
3. Obtain *empirical estimates* of the numerical parameters in the model that specify the particular, concrete situation to which it is to be applied.
4. Carry through the mathematical process of finding the course of action which, for the specific parameter values, maximizes the criterion function.[6]

Operations research may, then, be regarded as a field of applied mathematics and statistics whose concern is the developing of sets of standard models, as well as their modification for practical application, in the microeconomy (e.g., inventory, queuing, replacement, game, transportation, learning and search theory, and so forth) which control the efficiency of particular, limited areas within an organization. The last part of this description will be stressed because it hints at one of the major shortcomings of OR: the inability (at least so far) to provide models for overall optimization. This is partly conditioned by the technical limitations that a huge number of variables imposes even on a computer and partly by the unfortunate fact that the sum total of a series of suboptima does not necessarily yield the overall optimum. A thorough analysis even reveals something more embarrassing; namely, that in order to optimize a part correctly, the whole ought to be optimized first. The ambition toward a global model of the firm is thus restricted to the area of simulation and to "satisficing" instead of optimizing. Attempts are under way to construct comprehensive control models of the firm,[7] and all persons interested in this area expect great theoretical insight from the final results. With regard to the practical application of such complex models, however, skepticism is justified, for the huge number of unwieldy variables and the exceedingly high costs of such a project exclude any hope for establishing in the near future a control model of this sort for most of the industry. It seems instead that a combination of OR models with the accountant's budgeting model as an

---

[5] Herbert A. Simon, *The New Science of Management Decision* (New York: Harper & Brothers, 1960), p. 16.

[6] *Ibid.*, pp. 16-17.

[7] E.g., the construction of Mark I, a management control model of the System Development Corporation, Santa Monica, California.

overall frame [8] is, from the point of view of practicality of realization, a more promising solution.[9]

THE SOURCE OF CONFLICT

From the preceding description of the two subjects it would not appear that their interests clash to an extent that makes conflict unavoidable.[10] Therefore, the existing tensions and differences of opinion have to be demonstrated separately. The literature dealing with this borderline problem of accounting and OR is relatively scarce, and a listing of the arguments will have to rely primarily on Churchman's *Prediction and Optimal Decision* [11] and my own personal experience in conversation with operations analysts and accountants.

The main objections made against accounting may be summed up in four items: first, the cost accounting models (in spite of standard cost systems) are still too closely tied to the approach of historical costing, while considerations of alternatives in the form of a variety of opportunity costs are not sufficiently taken care of. Above all, accounting does not reveal the profit which would have occurred had alternative decisions been made.

Second, the accounting models are chiefly of a quantitative descriptive nature instead of a quantitative analytical nature and are not designed to search systematically for optimal solutions.

Third, on one side the accounting models apply concepts and collect many data which are irrelevant to decisions of the higher

---

[8] R. V. Mattessich, "Budgeting Models and System Simulation," *The Accounting Review*, Vol. 36, No. 3 (July, 1961), pp. 384-97. Excerpts reprinted in *The Executive*, Vol. 5, No. 7 (December, 1961), pp. 27-29.

[9] This is confirmed by a management scientist in the following sentences: "But primarily management science has failed to assist top management because the philosophy and objectives of management science have often been irrelevant to the manager. Mathematical economics and management science have often been more closely allied to formal mathematics than to economics and management. . . . In many professional journal articles the attitude is that of an exercise in formal logic rather than that of a search for useful solutions to real problems." J. W. Forrester, *Industrial Dynamics* (New York: John Wiley & Sons Inc.; and Cambridge: Massachusetts Institute of Technology, 1961), p. 3.

[10] The existence of common ground between the two disciplines, however, is sufficiently evidenced in practice as well as in the literature. For example, see D. W. Miller and M. K. Starr's discussion on the difficulty of defining OR, where, with regard to Morse and Kimbal's definition, the following assertion is made: "Replace operations research in the definition by cost accounting and it holds equally well." *Executive Decisions and Operations Research* (New York: Prentice-Hall, Inc., 1960), p. 104.

[11] (New York: Prentice-Hall, Inc., 1961) primarily Chapters 3 and 13; see also C. W. Churchman and R. L. Ackoff, "Operational Accounting and Operations Research," *Journal of Accountancy*, Vol. 99, No. 2 (February, 1955), pp. 33-39.

echelons of management, but on the other side they do not generate many data urgently needed for decision processes. In this way, accounting ignores goals other than profit and related aims and identifies the profit goal with the goal of the organization.

Fourth, accounting uses allocation procedures that are not based on a knowledge of the optimal organization structure; this distorts the measures that serve managerial decision making.

Thus, accounting does not supply an objective scale of values that can be used for selecting optimal decisions or for evaluating managerial performance. Further arguments and subarguments are that the time over which profits are being calculated is not sufficiently defined; that psychological factors which would seem significant because of the stimulus that costs exercise upon human actions are rarely considered; that the balance sheet is not comprehensive enough and its inclusive criterion of "measurable" is too superficial; that the goodwill of the enterprise, if taken into consideration at all, is incorrectly measured; that the additivity assumption with regard to many assets is unrealistic; that accounting measures are not accompanied by error estimates; and so on.

After a penetrating analysis of many of these points Churchman concludes:

> It isn't that accounting systems are "slightly" defective here and there, and that the wise manager will ignore some figures and add or subtract from others. In view of the fact that asset utilization and nonutilization, and organizational policy, are both highly critical in managerial decisions, and because the values of these policies are not measured by accounting information, it is safe to say that cost and profit information is seriously defective relative to a scientific understanding of policy information.[12]

To parry some of these attacks, accountants have asserted that their major concern is not prediction but measurement of past performance. This rejoinder, however, will hardly do, for even the correct measurement of past performance needs asset valuation through opportunity costs, value allocations based on an optimal organization structure, and so forth.

Another argument, that the center of the universe is not necessarily management but, alternatively, the consumer, the investor, or the government, seems somewhat stronger but abandons cost accounting and provokes the answer that even the investor wants to get reports of past performances which are based on opportunity

---

[12] *Prediction and Optimal Decision*, p. 66.

rather than on historical costs; only then can he continue to make the "correct" investment decisions. The argument, however, points in the right direction by indicating the existence of diverse and occasionally conflicting goals which accountants have tried to satisfy by a compromise that in future might not do.

But the strongest counterargument to the criticisms listed lies, to my mind, in the fact that, surprisingly enough, such criticism ignores the previously mentioned relationship between the costs of operating an accounting system and the yield from it. All these arguments seem to assume that the way of creating more accurate information by operations analysts costs no more, in relation to its marginal yield, than the way of creating less accurate information by accountants. I imply, of course, that both accounting and OR can attain only approximations to reality, approximations of lesser or greater accuracy, under lesser or greater costs, of a relative benefit that is not necessarily in proportion to these costs. It can well be argued that accounting is what it is, not because accountants reject analytical thinking but because under past circumstances every more sophisticated approach would have been financially unbearable to the enterprise.[13]

In close connection with this problem is a dilemma of OR which cannot remain unmentioned: the difficulty of creating the raw material of OR analysis in the form of input data. Many of these data are not regularly supplied by the accounting department. A fairly accurate measurement of most of these data is still, and will be in the future, forbiddingly expensive. Some cannot be measured at all, and accountants mock the OR men with the question of whether the crystal ball that might supply them with the required information has already been found. The only way out of this dilemma is obviously to make a crude, and often very arbitrary, estimate of the magnitude

---

[13] This does not contradict my previous statement that the search for an optimal proportion between costs for accounting and yield has not yet found a systematic solution. In the past the discrepancy between cost and yield of sophisticated methods was so large as to be obvious even without "systematic" investigation. In support of this, the example of separating fixed and variable costs may be mentioned. There exist many refined studies that employ the econometrical estimation of empirical cost curves. But these "theoretical" studies were financed for the sake of research, and though they may have been with us for a quarter of a century, and though they have greatly enhanced our theoretical understanding, they have not influenced actual practice. Accountants still estimate cost curves by the very crude method of determining two arbitrary extreme points and connecting them. Everyone is aware of the weak degree of approximation such an approach secures, yet it does supply some notion of the magnitude of fixed costs; owing to its ease of determination it seems to have a higher marginal yield than more sophisticated methods.

of these variables; this, however, defeats the operations analyst's claim to supply more accurate information than the accountant does. Therefore, even if cost accounting and OR were direct competitors, the problem would be more complex than it appears to the operations analyst who sees only the mathematical superiority of his own approach. The question must be posed in a different fashion: We have to ask, instead, where in a particular enterprise does the golden middle lie between "the pitfalls of oversimplification and the morass of overcomplication." [14] Since this middle road is differently situated in every firm, no pat answer is available. It will take considerable time to find the critical size of enterprise for which the mathematical overcomplication and "technical" oversimplification of OR models are less disadvantageous than the mathematical oversimplification and "technical" overcomplication of the accounting model. This in itself is an optimization problem and one we hope will be solved some day by OR's own methods, such as learning theory and so on. Until then the superiority of OR methods will have to find its proof by trial and error, which means through the evidence of practical results on a large scale. Thus, the hope for abandoning accounting or an immediate general acceptance of a "universal" information system of the firm, in accord with the suggestion of some operations analysts, is not great.

POSSIBILITIES OF RECONCILIATION

However, once accountants and OR men learn to recognize their own deficiencies and discover that their strong points are not of a competitive but of a complementary nature, the "optimal solution" might be found in a cooperative effort of both groups. The advent of management science may be interpreted as a start in this direction, since the founders of this interdisciplinary field have recognized that a close collaboration between scholars from many disciplines is required to develop tools which master the everincreasing complexity of our economic environment. Above all, a coordination between applied mathematics, behavioral economics, and accounting seems to provide the ingredients required to make the envisaged vehicle run properly. Hereby mathematics may be compared to the chassis and body, behavioral economics to the motor, and accounting to the

---

[14] Richard Bellman, *Dynamic Programming* (Princeton: Princeton University Press, 1957), p. x.

brakes. This very limp analogy may convey the important function of an element that can prevent a fatal crash in actual practice.

Thus, the more moderate advocates of management science recognize that cost accounting provides an effective control mechanism and supplies important raw material to the operations researcher; they are well aware that implements as well entrenched as those of cost accounting cannot be displaced overnight without serious damage to the whole economy. Another category of operations researches seems to share this attitude toward accounting but propagate a very radical opinion against business administration in general, inasmuch as they proclaim operations research as the exclusive realm of industrial engineering.

If we now examine the camp of the accountants we observe here, too, various reactions to the new movement of management science. One group, and it appears to me that it still is the dominating one, wants to disregard or deny the impact which this new development makes upon accounting; they refuse to acquire even the basic mathematical knowledge necessary to understand operations research methods and behave in a manner which is erroneously attributed to the African ostrich. The second group, which seems to grow slowly but steadily in number, recognizes the importance of the achievements of operations research for the field of accounting, is willing to sacrifice enough time and energy to learn and understand the working methods of management's new science, and admits that major revisions are due in managerial accounting, but firmly believes that the main structure of accounting will survive in this process of reformation. Most of the members of this group do not favor sudden and radical adjustments, and some believe that a first step toward cooperation with operations research is the translation of accounting models and submodels into mathematical terms. On one hand they are aware that the future accounting system of the firm cannot do without many technical and often trivial appearing details, but on the other hand they are skeptical of the idea that a central information system of the firm—in which are also stored and elaborated the innumerable, purely technological personnel, psychological, and market data—can fulfill all the functions of traditional accounting. In my opinion such an information system may perform useful services to many departments, but can neither be identified with what is commonly understood as accounting nor replace it overnight. Finally, those few accountants must be mentioned who have lost all hope for the future of their discipline and hasten to abandon what they believe to be a sinking ship.

The call for a novel approach to accounting comes from several directions and the need for a broadening of this discipline has many facets. Thus accountants are confronted with choosing one of the following alternatives:

1. To acquire a profound knowledge of many aspects of jurisprudence (civil law, commercial law, corporation and partnership law, and tax law) and develop their discipline into a *purely* legalistic-dogmatic field of knowledge; or
2. To acquire proficiency in modern quantitative analytical methods and try to maintain the old status of their discipline; namely, that of the most important quantitative tool of economic practice.

I do not believe that these will become alternatives for the profession as such rather than for the individual accountant. The past has revealed clearly the importance of accounting as an instrument for the fulfillment of legalistic requirements. Our present system of financial accounting, however, constitutes a compromise that neglects some legal aspects almost as much as some managerial aspects. This anticipated diversification of accounting need not create a chasm within accounting, but may well lead to a close cooperation between specialists.

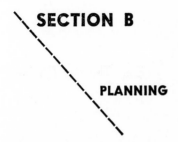

SECTION B

PLANNING

In Part I, Section A, the basic nature of decision making and planning was examined, and cost concepts for management use were delineated and related to the management planning function. Because of the nature of these readings there was little use of business problems as illustrative material.

Therefore, this section has been included to illustrate some of the complexities of applying the theories of planning to actual business situations. Any of a wide range of problems could have been chosen for this purpose. The three selected involve the important problems of capital budgeting, inventory planning, and pricing, with an examination of pricing in some depth.

The accountant is a major source of information for the management planning process. A careful reading of the articles in this section should provide valuable insight as to information requirements.

Problems of structuring of the information for planning purposes is discussed in the readings on cost-volume-profit and the assignment of nonmanufacturing costs.

35. COST ACCOUNTING
AND PRICING POLICIES *   Carl Thomas Devine †

There is abundant evidence that the cost accountant's traditional approach has been strongly influenced by classical and neoclassical economic theory. With the possible exception of specific order industries the general prescription that management should concentrate on those items which yield the largest markup is based squarely on the assumption of pure competition. Clearly in pure or near pure competition with unlimited demand for the firm's products at going prices management is well advised to push—in a production sense—those items which yield the largest markup. The extension of this prescription to products to be sold in areas of imperfect competition seems to be just as clearly unwarranted. Businessmen, and accountants particularly, have often argued that production and distribution cost accounting gives the key to decisions as to which lines, products, territories, etc. should be pushed through increased advertising expenditures and other sales pressure. The fact that sales effort is necessary is an indication that the products are differentiated and that the demand for each product is not completely elastic. Intelligent pricing and sales pressure decisions must give full consideration to estimates of demand elasticities and to the probable reaction of demand schedules to changes in (and different types of) advertising and other selling methods.[1]

Cost accountants seem also to follow orthodox economics with regard to the necessity for long-run recovery of costs by firms that

* From *The Accounting Review* (October, 1950). Reprinted by permission of the American Accounting Association. This paper was presented at the 1949 meeting of the Pacific Coast Economic Association.

† Carl Thomas Devine, Professor of Accounting at the University of Southern California.

[1] There is some evidence that accountants, with their cost approach and going concern value, tend to follow a modification of classical economic theory that was in vogue prior to 1870, but in the above connection it is probably more reasonable to assume that originally they based their arguments on the doctrine of pure or perfect competition. Yet it is difficult to understand how the profession could follow the assumptions of pure competition when its members were so well aware of specific order costing.

remain in business. It is easy to misapply the rules for long-run behavior to short-run problems, and it is perhaps to be expected that businessmen and accountants would assume that prices in the short run should be high enough to cover total unit costs. Such an expectation seems justified because orthodox economists of the day tended to disregard the short run and to assume that depressions were temporary and unimportant for overall policy decisions.

To be sure, during depressions distressed firms in their frantic search for solvency often found it necessary to use drastic pricing measures. If the more stable concerns followed with similar price reductions, the result was cutthroat competition, and businessmen rightly or wrongly wished to avoid such competitive measures. The fear of cutthroat competition and the knowledge that successful businessmen covered their costs in the long run no doubt worked together to support the pricing position taken by most cost accountants. The advent of the new economics of approximately 1930 left the philosophical supports for this pricing policy somewhat weakened.

For approximately two decades economists, a few accountants, and businessmen have been sure that the cost accountant's intricate compilations are worse than useless if not downright nonsense. Robinson, Chamberlain,[2] and their fellow economists had with devastating logic pointed out the limitations of perfect competition and along with other observations had offered a set of rules for pricing to attain maximum profit. An oversimplified statement of the fundamental rule follows: Each producer should produce and sell until marginal costs are equal to marginal revenues, and for differentiated products marginal selling costs must be given consideration.

The marginal cost, marginal revenue formula is, of course, short run in nature and reflects the general viewpoint taken by the economic theorists of the time. Thinking economists were not without doubts regarding the generality of the rule, and certainly Robinson and Chamberlain were properly cautious. Even the most inflexible were willing to admit the difficulty of estimating entire demand schedules, marginal cost structures, and the softness or hardness of demand schedules in response to various amounts and types of selling effort.

More serious assaults on the foundations of the simple rule were not long in coming. At the very beginning of the trend (1930)

---

[2] Joan Robinson, *The Economics of Imperfect Competition* (London: Macmillan and Co., Ltd., 1933). Edward Chamberlain, *The Theory of Monopolistic Competition* (Cambridge: Harvard University Press, 1933).

Evans pointed out the possible influences of current prices on demand and costs of the future.[3] It is clear that a businessman who maximizes profit for each short period, for example a season, may not maximize his profit over the life of the enterprise. To the extent that customers speculate wisely when prices are low the demand for the product in the immediate future may shrink, and it is highly probable that a price that leads to large profits today will lead to increased wages and other costs in the future. Costs and demand should be represented by surfaces extending along an axis representing time. The businessman's problem is then to maximize the volume representing profits through time. Most economists have been guilty of gross oversimplification.

Sweezy introduced the kinked demand curve that is common to oligopoly.[4] If one producer raises his price and competitors fail to follow, his demand is certain to be highly elastic for prices higher than the going level. If a large producer lowers his price, others are likely to follow, and Sweezy concludes that the schedule is more inelastic for prices lower than the existing level. The marginal revenue curve is, of course, discontinuous, and the intersection of marginal cost with marginal revenue is indeterminate.

Colberg and others have pointed out the complications resulting from joint costs and multiprocess production.[5] A coherent generalization of the economics applicable to specific order production has apparently not been written. Many economists seem to have lost faith in the assumption that businessmen invariably try to maximize profits. Gordon calls attention to the tremendous motivating influence—at least on the downswing of the cycle—arising from fear of insolvency.[6] On the practical level Dean and Eiteman have ques-

---

[3] G. C. Evans, *Mathematical Introduction to Economics*, pp. 143 ff. Evans was not interested in determining the degree of the temporal relationships. See also, R. G. D. Allen, *Mathematical Analysis for Economists* (New York: The Macmillan Company, 1938), pp. 533-36. It is, of course, possible to use the short-run marginal rule with estimates of future repercussions included in the current representations of marginal costs and revenues. Apparently Fritz Machlup favors this approach. "Marginal Analysis and Empirical Research," *The American Economic Review* (September, 1946), p. 521 ff.

[4] Paul Sweezy, "Demand under Conditions of Oligopoly," *Journal of Political Economy* (1939), pp. 568-75.

[5] M. R. Colberg, "Monopoly Prices under Joint Costs: Fixed Proportions," *Journal of Political Economy* (February, 1941), pp. 103-10. See also, R. H. Coase, "Monopoly Pricing with Interrelated Costs and Demands," *Economica* (November, 1946), pp. 278-94.

[6] R. A. Gordon, "Short-Period Price Determination," *The American Economic Review* (June, 1948), pp. 265-89. This article is an excellent critical summary of the limitations of present thinking in the pricing field. See also, Moses Abramovitz, "Monopolistic Selling in a Changing Economy," *Quarterly Journal of Economics* (February, 1938), p. 201.

tioned the assumption that marginal costs per unit vary perceptibly with changes in output.[7]

Economists are examining critically the assumptions underlying the marginal approach, but the remaining body of marginal theory is worthy of the closest study by businessmen and cost accountants. In many cases the approach may be rejected. Ignorance, however, is not a proper cause for rejection.

COSTS AS PARTIAL DETERMINANTS OF PRICE

It should be emphasized that costs are often only one of many determinants of price. Clearly in pure competition the costs of an individual firm are not a factor to be considered in setting prices.[8] If a stock of goods is already in existence and is not to be replaced for the current market, past costs are certainly not price determining. In other instances expected future costs of replacement are given more weight than the actual cost of existing stocks.

It is sometimes assumed that short-run prices will not fall below variable costs, but there are so many exceptions that this generalization is practically worthless. If the costs of shutdown and resumption are important, it is obviously more profitable to price below variable costs for a short period than to stop production. If the products are differentiated and identified by brand names, businessmen may sell far below variable costs in order to keep the brand names before the public. Contract suppliers, even when business is good, will sometimes bid a job at less than marginal cost with the hope of getting more profitable business from the customer at a later date. Finally in spite of the fact that altruism is not expected in a self-interest economy, some managers feel a responsibility for worker welfare and will continue to operate at prices far below variable cost. It seems clear that there is no discernible lower limit (except perhaps zero) to short-period prices.

Some economists have assumed that the upper limit for short-run prices is determined by the demand schedules, and that in many

---

[7] Joel Dean (especially) *Statistical Cost Functions of a Hosiery Mill* (Chicago: University of Chicago, 1941). W. J. Eiteman, "Factors Determining the Location of the Least Cost Point," *The American Economic Review* (December, 1947), pp. 910-18.

[8] Good cost accounting for all or a large number of firms does influence prices in an indirect manner. If accountants fail to record all pertinent costs, the reported profits for the industry will be too high and new firms will be encouraged to enter the field and existing firms will be expanded. The supply therefore increases, and the price tends to fall. An overstatement of costs throughout an industry in the same manner leads to increased prices. In either event there is an improper allocation of economic resources.

cases businessmen will charge what the traffic will bear. In most cases this too turns out to be an oversimplification. High reported profits even in the short run sometimes lead to the entry of new firms into the industry and thus decrease each concern's share of the long-run demand. Labor organizations are becoming more aware of reported income and are encouraged to press their demands for wage rate increases by large operating profits.

Reynolds has suggested that a firm's own variable costs are not as important as competitors' costs in bringing about price increases. "If the costs of only one firm had increased it is unlikely that a price increase would follow. The firm raises prices when it is able to, and it is able to when the costs of other producers have risen sufficiently that they will concur in a price increase." [9] If prices are increased by all members of an industry without an increase in cost, there is danger that the larger profits will encourage new firms or the enlargement of existing plants.

There is little doubt that businessmen have tended to disregard the short-period pricing pronouncements of the economists.[10] One explanation for their failure to follow these suggestions is that managers have been ignorant and have not understood the terms and logic of the marginal doctrine. In some cases ignorance is probably a factor, but, inasmuch as cost accountants have been preparing differential cost studies and firms on occasion have been quoting prices on variable costs for many decades, ignorance is probably not an important factor.[11]

Businessmen have been impressed with the difficulty of making accurate estimates of marginal revenues. The knowledge of some

---

[9] Lloyd G. Reynolds, "Relations between Wage Rates, Costs, and Prices," *The American Economic Review Supplement* (March, 1942), p. 280. It should be observed that this argument is useful in justifying the inclusion of the cost of normal lost units with the cost of good units. If lost units are to be expected throughout the industry, the cost of these units is likely to be price determining and the sales possibilities of the unsold units should, therefore, be higher and support the increased cost of such units as a proper inventory value.

[10] The committee, appointed by the American Accounting Association to prepare a statement of cost accounting concepts (principles), holds—tentatively at least—that the cost accountant's function in pricing is to prepare special differential cost studies for particular occasions. There is little doubt that the Committee has been influenced by the marginal approach to pricing and has not been impressed by such legislation as the Robinson-Patman Act. "Cost Accounting Concepts," *The Accounting Review* (January, 1948), p. 41.

[11] For practical purposes variable costs may be considered equivalent to marginal costs. The accountant's differential cost is also essentially equivalent except the unit used for differential cost studies traditionally has been large— usually an entire prospective order. In utility accounting incremental cost is sometimes used.

is no doubt limited to the fact that a firm can price itself out of the market and that a price decrease not matched by competitors will result in increased volume to the firm making the cut. On the other hand it is reasonable to assume that most managers do experiment with demand elasticities in the neighborhood of their current prices. Some chains have attempted to find comparable markets and have compared the results of particular price experiments in each. It is the policy of many firms to ask their salesmen to estimate the increase in sales that might reasonably be expected if a price allowance of say 10 percent is made. Such estimates must, of course, take into consideration the probable reactions of competitors and are subject to serious error. The point to be emphasized here is that many organizations are fully aware of the importance of demand and are making attempts to measure its price elasticity and its response to advertising and sales pressure.

In the distributive trades it is common to base prices on the largest of their variable costs—merchandise cost. Tarshis has made use of Robinson's relationship between optimum price, marginal cost, and the elasticity of demand and has concluded that successful firms no doubt approach the results of marginal cost, marginal revenue pricing through trial and error in setting markups. These relationships should simplify considerably the application of marginal techniques to pricing by permitting occasional comparisons of markup policies with estimated elasticities as determined by sales estimates for a few alternative prices[12]

PRICING ON THE BASIS OF TOTAL UNIT COST

The cost accountant has developed a costing policy which no doubt has been influenced by the pricing problems of management. The assumptions underlying cost distributions are comparatively simple and may be quickly reviewed. Specific jobs are charged with the costs for which they are directly responsible. For practical pur-

---

[12] Lorie Tarshis, *The Elements of Economics* (Boston: Houghton Mifflin Company, 1947), pp. 198-99. Joan Robinson (*Op. cit.*, p. 36), has pointed out the following relationship: $A = Me/(e - 1)$, which may be stated: $e = A/(A - M)$, where A equals average revenue or price, M equals marginal revenue, and e equals the elasticity of demand. Tarshis notes that if the marginal cost curve is horizontal and if the elasticity of demand is constant, it follows that marginal cost plus a fixed percentage is a reasonable approach to pricing. If the elasticity is three, the appropriate markup is 50 percent; for an elasticity of two, the most profitable short-run markup is 100 percent on cost, etc. In a similar way a markup of 40 percent on sales may be reduced to 66⅔ percent on cost and is proper only if the elasticity is 2½. Observe that Tarshis assumes that short-run marginal pricing is a, if not the, proper pricing policy.

poses variable costs may be assumed to be equivalent to responsibility costs.[13] Unless the job or order is extremely large and requires additional facilities, it is clear that the concept of responsibility cost is a short-run concept, and it is clear also that it is related to the notions of marginal and differential cost.

Any first-rate cost accounting system is able to divulge reasonably accurate responsibility (marginal) costs. As a matter of fact, the accountant is considerably in advance of the economist in this regard. Marginal costs for diverse products and even for specific orders may be approximated through the use of bills of materials, standard labor estimates, and through the use of cost centers and common denominators of labor hours, etc., for units of factory output.

The merits of assigning fixed charges to products, territories, types of customers, etc., are not so clear-cut. The cost accountant's defense is often based on the ethical judgment that equity should be preserved among customers—that each should bear his pro rata share of fixed overhead. It is usually assumed that if Job A receives twice the amount of benefit from the facilities whose costs are fixed, then Job A ought to bear twice as much of the fixed costs of these facilities.[14] Certainly the need for preserving equity among customers has been emphasized by various federal and state laws— notably the Robinson-Patman Act. The implied relationship between costs and prices remained in the background until the comparatively recent definition of discrimination in terms of prices not justified by differences in cost.

The desirability of assigning fixed costs to products, size of order, territories, methods of sale, etc., has been questioned many times.[15] Do such distributions aid in the control of fixed costs? Do they determine whether to continue or to abandon a product or territory? Negative answers seem justified in both instances. Do these assignments aid in pricing for profit and financial security? Economists in general have returned an unfavorable verdict, but businessmen have long felt that such procedures have proved useful.

---

[13] That they may not be equivalent is clear. Depreciation for buildings on an activity basis makes the charge a variable cost, but only in rare cases can a particular job be said to be responsible for building depreciation. Observe that responsibility costs are not equivalent to direct costs. In general the distinction between direct and indirect is unimportant except in a recording sense.

[14] The ethical assumption—the so-called benefit doctrine—should not be confused with the practical problem of measuring relative benefits received. The measurement is usually based on a further assumption: that relative necessary factory time is a measure of relative benefit.

[15] Jonathan N. Harris, to my knowledge, was one of the earliest critics. "What Did We Earn Last Month?" *N.A.C.A. Bulletin* (January 15, 1936).

The assignment of fixed factory costs to products and the quotation of prices related to these costs tend to stabilize prices throughout the industry at any given time. If businessmen are "educated" to set prices with reference to total unit costs, the cutthroat tendencies that are present in an economy in which there are numerous producers and numerous by-products are less likely to develop. Moreover, the assignment of fixed costs to lines and products tends to stabilize unit costs over the business cycle. Businessmen, in their search for simple rules to guide them through the bewildering complexity of relevant pricing factors, have—except in the field of distribution—favored the cost accountant's total unit cost with semi-flexible markups. The marginal approach may or may not lead to greater long-run profits.[16]

Although the orthodox arguments (including those given above) for fixed cost assignments are usually applied to firms and industries operating at low levels of activity, it is possible to build a defense for such distributions during periods of high production.

Suppose as a basis for illustration that a firm is operating at full capacity. A file of unfilled orders is on hand and salesmen are able to write more orders than the plant can fill. Management wishes some relatively simple rule that would permit its salesmen consistently to quote prices that will yield close to a maximum return. The usual approach that utilizes the contribution of the selling price over variable costs must be modified drastically before it can be applied with benefit. To illustrate, Job A may be quoted at a price that will yield $300 above the costs for which it is responsible and Job B may cover its variable costs and contribute $200 toward the recovery of fixed charges and the formation of profit. It does not follow of course that A should be accepted for production and that B should be rejected. If Job A requires twice as many hours of scarce factory facilities, it is clear that two B jobs contribute $100 more than one A and may be produced with no more utilization of

---

16 It is not safe to generalize with regard to relative stability when marginal pricing is compared with the total unit cost approach. Marginal costs, as a rule, decrease per unit in depression periods, and it is usually assumed that demand curves shift downward and to the left. Professor Leonard A. Doyle, in an unpublished discussion, has suggested that if demand curves during depression years become more inelastic in the relevant areas of output, pricing on total unit cost may approximate the results yielded by application of the marginal doctrine.

It is also not safe to assume that inflexible prices tend to accentuate the business cycle. Due to differences in the propensity to consume it is probable that flexible prices—except for wage rates—might limit the severity of the depression. For a highly technical discussion of the necessary conditions see Oscar Lange, *Price Flexibility and Employment* (Bloomington, Ind.: Principia Press, 1944).

limited factory time. This direct approach to the problem of accepting or rejecting orders may usually be applied to the problem of setting relative prices. For each item usually produced time estimates may be prepared and prices may be scheduled to yield identical contributions per unit of scarce factory time.

The businessman's traditional tendency to quote prices on the basis of total unit costs as compiled by cost accountants is in fact an imperfect approximation of the method outlined immediately above. The distribution of fixed overhead to jobs or products is normally on a time basis, and the relative total fixed overhead charges to jobs do therefore measure more or less imperfectly the relative usage of the firm's scarce factor of production. The obvious shortcoming of this procedure is that the fixed overhead rate is not an accurate measure of the contribution to profit made by an hour's use of the factory. Unfortunately, markup is usually based on total unit cost so that the fixed burden rate plus the markup that is applied to the fixed burden is not large enough to accomplish the desired selection of products. That part of the markup which is applied to direct labor and materials confuses the issue and tends to favor those jobs that use less direct costs. To the extent that facilities for handling materials and accommodating labor are limited the usual markup procedure based on total unit cost may provide a simple rule for pricing for high profits at full capacity.

36. COST FACTORS IN PRICE MAKING *

Howard Clark Greer †

Price making is one of management's most important tasks. The success or failure of an enterprise may depend on the ability of its management to select the right prices for its goods.

This is a difficult and delicate operation. The successful price maker needs a knowledge of economics, an understanding of markets, a familiarity with distribution techniques, and a grasp of the relevant cost facts. This last aspect of the problem is the particular subject of this discussion.

The attempt here is to describe the price making function as the writer has come to know it, through a quarter century of close association with such activities, as an accountant, analyst, adviser, executive, and director, serving numerous business enterprises in a variety of industries. The discussion is based on observation and interpretation of what actually takes place in the price making process. Accordingly the conclusions are derived from practical experience rather than abstract reasoning.

How does a manager go about the job of establishing a price? What conditions confront him? What considerations influence him? What facts does he require? In particular, what cost information is significant, and what bearing will it have on his decisions?

PART I: IN A FREE ECONOMY

These questions may be answered first in terms of what happens under a free price system. The problems of establishing prices in a controlled economy require separate consideration and will be treated in Part II of this discussion, in the next issue of the REVIEW.

* From *The Harvard Business Review* (July-August, 1952). Reprinted by permission of the President and Fellows of Harvard College. EDITOR'S NOTE: This article is based on the first of the author's Dickinson Lectures (1952) before the Harvard Graduate School of Business Administration. An article in the September-October *Harvard Business Review* completed the publication of Mr. Greer's discussion of "Cost Factors in Price Making."

† Howard Clark Greer, Treasurer of The Chemstrand Corporation, Decatur, Alabama, and Director and Vice President of the Chicago, Indianapolis and Louisville Railway (Monon Route).

The Price-Cost-Volume Equation

An understanding of prices requires some understanding of costs. Prices and costs are indissolubly connected. Each affects the other. Both prices and costs, in turn, affect volume. Accordingly, the three factors of price, cost, and volume are fundamental to virtually every business activity, every business decision.

The interrelation of these factors is a subject of great confusion and misunderstanding, in business as well as out of it. Because certain influences are commonly significant, it is often assumed that they are universally controlling. Because simple conclusions are craved, interpretations are oversimplified and become misleading. Thus laymen come to believe that they can comprehend price-cost problems which actually baffle the experts.

For example, it is commonly asserted that costs control prices—that the businessman computes his costs, adds a profit, and establishes a price. Acceptance of this postulate leads to assumptions that prices are controlled by producers, that every cost change will be reflected in a price adjustment, that profit margins are optional with sellers, that inflation stems from cost increases, and so on.

Conversely, it is sometimes contended that costs must be governed by prices—that the producer can pay out for materials, wages, taxes, rents, and other costs only what he can collect from his customers, less a reasonable return on the capital employed. This leads to beliefs that consumers may be exploiting producers, forcing down wages and commodity prices, destroying investments, and so on.

It is not that simple. Costs do influence prices, but seldom control them (in the sense of exercising the final, exclusive dominance over their precise level and variation). Prices do influence costs, but cannot regulate them (in the sense of forcing adjustments of specific amount in any particular component). Both costs and prices influence the volume of goods that will be produced and distributed, and it may be volume that is affected when the cost-price relationship changes.

The fact is that prices and costs are in a continuous process of becoming adjusted to each other, with neither in absolute control. When costs rise, there is a tendency for prices to be raised, provided the conditions which produced the cost increase will also warrant a price increase. In many cases, however, a higher cost (e.g., one due to shrinking volume and higher overhead) cannot be "passed on" to the buyer. Likewise, product price reductions put pressure on cost elements like raw material values, wage rates, and taxes, but some of these are rigid and inflexible charges which yield to pressure very little and very slowly, if at all.

The third factor in the equation, and the one most likely to fluctuate, is the volume of business done. For most products there is no single, uniform, invariable price. Rather there is a range of prices within which some sales can be effected. A limited amount of business can be done at the top of the range, a larger amount at the bottom. The question is how much sales volume can be generated, and how much production stimulated, at any particular price level.

Price Maker's Choice. What the price maker must do, when considering the proper adjustment to a change in either the strength of demand or the level of costs, is to decide how much of the gain or loss should be reflected in margins and how much in volume. The combined reaction of all the individual price makers in an industry determines the change for the industry as a whole.

For example, if demand is strong, sellers may elect to raise prices (widening unit margins) or to seek increased volume (possibly lowering costs and raising total margins). If demand weakens, sellers may choose to cut prices (in an effort to maintain volume, even at lower unit margins) or to "hold the line" and let sales decline (in the hope that maintained unit margins may offset shrinking volume).

Similarly, if costs rise, sellers may attempt to raise prices proportionately (at the risk of curtailing volume if demand is not likewise rising), or may "absorb" the increases (on the theory that lower volume might raise costs even more than higher wage or material costs). If costs decline, sellers may reduce prices to get more business (figuring they can afford it), or may try to reflect the savings in wider margins (accepting current volume as adequate).

Thus the price effect of a cost change on prices cannot be predicted with assurance. The reaction of sellers will vary with the circumstances. If the cost increase occurs during a generally rising level of wages and consumer incomes, prices are quite likely to be advanced, because a strong level of demand is indicated. If the cost increase occurs in a period of shrinking volume and heavier unit fixed charges, prices are unlikely to be adjusted upward—in fact they are more likely to be reduced.

It is most certainly *not* true, as so often contended, that all cost increases bring about commensurate price increases, or even that costs are the chief element in market level advances. Growing demand does more to raise prices than do advancing costs. The inflationary effect of wage advances is to give people more money to spend rather than to make products cost more. Prices do not go up and down, and cannot be put up and down, simply because costs have risen or fallen. Many other factors influence the result.

Ceilings and Floors. One reason why prices are not immediately, or necessarily, responsive to cost changes is that for most products there is a fairly wide range within which prices may be established with moderately satisfactory results. There usually is no single, inevitable "right" price, which cannot be either higher or lower. There is likely to be a top and a bottom for permissible quotations, but often these limits are quite far apart.

This being the case, a cost increase or decrease may not necessitate an immediate price adjustment. An increase can perhaps be absorbed, a decrease retained as profit. Costs change constantly, and prices may have to be quoted for a whole season at a time. When an adjustment is postponed, it may ultimately prove unnecessary.

It is noteworthy that price ceilings are established by consumer demand and the absence of competitive pressure, while only price floors are created by production and distribution costs. If the product is scarce and in strong demand, the price may be pushed up far above the highest conceivable cost. If the product is plentiful and has acceptable substitutes, the price may be driven down close to the out-of-pocket cost of the most efficient producer.

Obviously a cost change is not necessarily a price influence unless prices are already so close to costs that there is no room for absorption. In all other cases the result is speculative, depending on numerous factors, a few of which are mentioned later.

Product Type Influences

Some of the confusion about price-cost relationships arises from lack of understanding of the price characteristics of products of different types. The controlling factors in the establishment of a price vary according to the nature of the article priced. Attempts at generalization breed confusion, since the principles applicable to one group of products are not necessarily significant in other groups.

A few illustrations may help to clarify this point.

Basic Commodities. This group consists of the primary raw materials obtained from field, forest, mine, and ocean (such as grains, livestock, timber, and petroleum), and the products resulting from their initial processing (like flour, meat, lumber, and oil). While the volume of such products is immense, the number of enterprises in these industries is relatively small, and the nature of their pricing problems is unfamiliar to the average citizen, and even to most businessmen.

For all such products the controlling factor in price determination is the size of the supply and the state of the demand. Except as it influences supply (often remotely and indirectly), cost is not a factor in the short-run price movements affecting such products. They sell for what buyers will pay, irrespective of what they may have cost.

Meat furnishes a good example. The supply is regulated by the amount of livestock produced for market, often determined by producer decisions made a year in advance. The demand is a function of consumer incomes. The product is perishable and therefore must be moved promptly. The composite meat price is the total of the family meat budgets of all households in the country divided by the total quantity of meat available for sale.

The cost to any producer, processor, or dealer has no bearing whatever on the price he will be able to obtain. He is completely at the mercy of his customers. They pay what they wish, and he must accept it. What he offers for his raw materials may be based on what he thinks he can resell them for in processed form; but once he has made his purchase, he is helpless against the decisions of his clientele.

This compulsion of demand fixed selling prices in controlling costs is more widespread than is generally recognized, though in many lines of activity the effects are obscure, complex, and delayed. With basic commodities the effects are prompt and unmistakable. When flour sales are poor, the price of wheat goes down. When textiles are dull, cotton declines. When gasoline moves slowly, petroleum slumps.

In such industries cost calculations work backward. The seller subtracts his expenses from his obtainable selling prices to determine what he can afford to pay for his raw materials. The collective ability of raw material processors in any such industry to guess right and figure accurately determines the amount of profit they can obtain. The important factor is the margin which the markets afford. All other influences are secondary.

By-Products and Joint Products. Many basic commodities, when processed, yield one major product and several by-products, or a number of joint products. Livestock, for example, produces meat, skins, fibers, greases, and pharmaceuticals. Petroleum is converted into gasoline, fuel oil, and a myriad of basic chemicals. Cotton supplies fiber, oil, meal, and livestock feed.

The ineffectiveness of costs in influencing prices is even more clearly evident where by-products or joint products are concerned. Cattle costs have no bearing on hide prices, and what is paid for cotton has no influence on what can be charged for cottonseed oil. For the individual items in a group of joint products (like ham, bacon, chops, and lard), no true cost can be determined. The price of lard, for example, has varied over the years from double to half the cost of the live hogs from which it was produced.

What *is* true is that the combined price of all the products has a strong and direct effect on the price which will be paid for the raw material. Processors of agricultural commodities make frequent calculations of total prospective realizations, minus probable processing and marketing expenses, to determine what material cost can be incurred with some promise of a profit. The collective result of such calculations is a market influence of no mean proportions. It is not solely controlling, but highly important.

It is noteworthy that in such industries the burden of processing expense increases tends to fall first on the raw material producer, not on the product purchaser. Higher milling costs are more likely to depress the price of wheat than to raise the price of flour. High transportation costs may hold down raw material values rather than put up product prices. The cost of the box is more important to strawberry growers than to shortcake eaters.

Processed Commodities. When secondary processing occurs, costs (in the form of conversion expenses) begin to be a greater factor in price determination. Here the processor normally has some choice about doing the conversion job. When there is a market for the commodity he owns, he is unlikely to incur the expense of converting it into something different unless the finished product can be sold at a price which will cover the basic commodity value plus at least the out-of-pocket expenses involved.

Thus, in setting the price on a processed commodity, the manufacturer begins to work forward as well as backward in his cost-price calculations. He reflects the *raw material market plus processing expense* in his asking price for the finished product, while at the same time he considers the *product price less processing expense* in appraising the raw material market.

When the two markets get out of relationship, as they often do, it suggests that a corrective change may be in prospect, or that an abnormal competitive condition exists, or that the public demand for the article has become exceptionally strong (or weak), or that some other unusual element is present in his situation. Deciding which of these conditions prevails is the essence of successful management in enterprises of this type.

Since most commodity processing industries are highly competitive, with margins narrow and market fluctuations severe, knowledge of processing cost data is an indispensable element in the development of sound price making policies. Often a sequence of processing operations is involved, with the product salable at various stages of completion. Allocation of joint costs among the processes becomes an important factor. The influence of volume is a vital one.

Under normal conditions each stage in the processing will produce an increase in value equal to the conversion cost plus some margin of profit. Manufacturers thus naturally seek to extend their processing as far as possible. Flour millers go into the breakfast food and bake mix business; meat packers make sausage and canned meats; cotton oil processors become producers of packaged shortenings; steelmakers turn out rails, pipe, and wire—even fences, bridges, and houses. The price influence of these "integrated operations" is important and particularly difficult for an outsider to comprehend.

Alternative Uses and Sources. Many raw materials have several alternative uses. Animal and vegetable oils, for example, may be processed into edible products (lard, shortening, margarine, salad dressing) or into inedible products (soap, paint, lubricants, cosmetics). Conversely, many needs can be met from alternative sources. Meat, for example, may be replaced on the menu by fish, poultry, eggs, or cheese; for many purposes, metal and wood are interchangeable with glass or plastic.

The availability of substitute outlets and sources is an important influence on prices. Nothing can be purchased for less than it will bring if diverted to its next most valuable use. Nothing can be sold for more than the price of its most acceptable alternate. Gasoline will bring not less than fuel oil, not more than benzene. Rough lumber must command more than firewood, less than finished flooring.

A whole series of prices may be influenced in this way. In the packing business, for example, it is said that the price of grease may affect the price of pork chops, since lard is a substitute for grease, salt pork for lard, bacon for salt pork, ham for bacon, and pork chops for ham. All meats affect each other; cheap beefsteak may mean lower ham prices, high veal chops strengthen lamb chops, and so on.

In transportation the effects of such competition are striking. Barges compete with pipelines, railroads with barges, trucks with railroads, airplanes with trucks. The cost of the service is less significant in its price than the availability of an alternative facility. High cost of an unsatisfactory service will not necessarily raise its price, though it may ultimately eliminate it from competition. The bus and the private automobile put the electric interurban out of business. Labor and materials flow into trucks and planes if freight cars cost too much to be a profitable investment.

For the past generation most agricultural by-products have been under pressure from synthetic substitutes of chemical origin. Petroleum products crowd the inedible oils of animal and vegetable derivation; rubber and plastics push leather aside; man-made fibers elbow cotton and wool in the textile field; oil and gas have ousted coal from its monopoly of the fuel business; and asphalt roofing has made the wood shingle obsolete.

Fabricated Articles. Somewhat different conditions prevail in the broad field of fabricated articles, such as automobiles, appliances, furniture, clothing, personal goods, and industrial equipment. Because of the huge number and wide variety of such items, they tend to be regarded as typifying price formation in all lines of business, which is an unfortunate misapprehension. These products do, however, furnish the most numerous (and therefore the most impressive) examples of price making activity, and call for extremely careful attention.

With all such products, cost becomes an important factor in price determination. These goods do not exist in nature, merely awaiting cultivation or extraction; they come into being only as created by man to satisfy an apparent need. Since man expects a compensation proportionate to his efforts and risks, he normally will undertake production only if reasonably assured of an adequate return. He must know his costs and their probable relation to his potential selling prices before he devotes his capital and his energies to the undertaking.

This condition exists, however, only at the initiation of the venture. Once facilities are provided, an organization created, and a trade established, the venture becomes subject to all the hazards of competitors' activities, public preference, and cost fluctuations that beset commodity processing or any other form of commercial endeavor. The first price may recover the first cost, but it does not follow that subsequent prices will reflect subsequent costs. Cheaper, more attractive merchandise may appear. Advances in material costs, or wage levels, or tax rates, or promotional services may raise costs faster than values rise. Continuing profit is far from assured.

On the other hand, the value created may be far in excess of the *cost plus normal return on investment.* New discoveries in fields such as chemicals and drugs may provide goods which sell (initially at least) for double or treble their cost. A brand name may create more profit than a brand-new factory. A trademark may sell for more than a transit system.

Again it becomes apparent that costs affect prices but seldom control them. For fabricated articles, cost may establish a floor, never a ceiling. Wide profit margins stimulate increased production and attract competitors. More goods and more sellers tend to lower prices until margins shrink to normal or less. Demand, however, is still the most significant factor in determining the price.

Individual Projects. At the far extreme from the basic commodity stands the individual project—the once-and-for-all, not-to-be-repeated job of constructing an object or performing a service on a special contract, unique in its characteristics, beginning and ending with itself.

Here, and here alone, cost normally becomes the solely controlling factor in the establishment of the price. Since no labor, materials, or facilities are committed to the job in advance, it is evident that no one is likely to acquire and supply them unless he feels sure of getting his money back. Since other contractors are normally awaiting the same opportunity, it is unlikely that anyone can include an abnormal profit in his bid without losing the business to some competitor who is willing to work for less.

Unusual conditions (such as labor and material shortages), peculiar circumstances, or extraordinary demand may stretch or shrink the normal margins, and exceptional efficiency or good fortune may lower costs; but on the whole the selling price of construction, investigation, development, and promotion tends to be related very closely to the costs incurred. It is unfortunate that this well-known fact should lead to the conclusion that the same principle applies to the sale of goods and services of other kinds.

Cost Influences

For those industries in which cost calculations form at least the primary basis for determining what prices should be charged (i.e., will be profitable), what cost data are useful and how are they employed?

Here again the answer is far from simple. The "cost" of a product is not some single precisely calculable figure. Cost is a composite of numerous elements—some direct and some imputed, some fixed and some variable, some provable and some theoretical. No two cost finding procedures are identical, and no one procedure will produce continuously identical results.

Thus cost finding for pricing purposes is necessarily the assemblage of a variety of cost facts, which can be combined in a variety of ways to produce a variety of answers. The price maker can use them only as a guide and a point of reference. In constructing his price list, he will apply cost facts more or less conscientiously according to his philosophy and his circumstances.

Every seller would prefer a price list in which the price of each item fully covers the total computed cost of that item. Such a list would consist of "safe" prices, involving no risks of loss if adequate volume is obtained.

In practice, however, it is often found that not all items will carry full overhead. Competition may limit the obtainable price for certain products. Staple items, turning over rapidly, may justify narrow margins. Overhead analysis may indicate that apportionments have been faulty, with some products bearing more than a fair share. It may be even argued that available prices should dictate the overhead distribution. Should by-products carry full costs? The variations are endless.

Price lists ultimately may be forced into patterns established by competition. The question then becomes one of how much cost is recovered by any given price. The slim margin items are tolerated; the wide profit numbers are actively pushed. Price-cost relationships must be constantly checked, as a basis of production and sales policy, even when prices themselves seem immune to the influences of cost computations.

Cost Components. Price making, of course, is not wholly (or even mainly) the job of establishing general price levels or constructing price lists. Almost every seller is constantly confronted with individual selling opportunities requiring him to arrive at a quotation for a particular piece of business involving some one item, or order, or quantity, or customer. Here the knottiest cost-price problems occur.

The normal condition is one in which the seller is anxious to make the sale. In ordinary times, thanks to this country's enormous natural resources and productive capacity, business is conducted in a so-called "buyers' market." The seller must be the aggressor; he must go after the business. To get it he must match, or better, competitors' prices. How low can he afford to go?

This raises the broad and important question of what elements of cost are significant in establishing prices for individual transactions where more volume is needed, competition is severe, and close figuring is essential. The right answer depends on a full knowledge of the components of costs, a shrewd appraisal of the probable effect of the decision, and a generous portion of ordinary good luck.

In the typical enterprise the total of the costs assignable to an individual product or sale comprises cost elements of several types, usually including the following:

1. Costs which are directly connected with that one product or sale and which occur if that product is made or that sale consummated and not otherwise—so-called *direct* costs.
2. Costs which are related to the total volume of business done, but not specifically to any individual fraction of that total—sometimes referred to as *variable overhead* costs.
3. Costs which are predetermined and constant, irrespective of individual transactions and even of all transactions combined—commonly known as *fixed overhead* costs.

The first group is made up of such elements as materials and direct labor; the second, of costs of such services as maintenance, power, communications, travel, and operating supplies; the third, of such facility and organization costs as insurance, taxes, depreciation, advertising, and executive salaries. How much of each of these costs must be reflected in an acceptable selling price?

The orthodox answer is that every price should cover the full cost of the article, including not only direct out-of-pocket costs but a full apportionment of fairly allocated variable and fixed overhead. It is argued that unless each sale returns its share of such costs, all sales combined are unlikely to prove profitable. The dangers of below cost selling are widely advertised.

The trouble with the advocated principle is the impossibility of applying it. Overhead costs relate to individual items only in theory, and the amount properly assignable to some one unit of goods or services is never precisely measurable. Even when the philosophy of cost apportionment can go unchallenged, the size of the overhead burden per unit cannot be determined unless the number of units is known. Getting or losing a particular order may in itself affect the cost of filling it. The manager is almost bound to assume the acceptance of his bid in figuring his overhead, even though his past experience suggests that higher average costs are probable.

Taken by itself any order is desirable if the price will cover its direct costs and contribute something to the overhead. In few cases, however, can an order be taken entirely by itself. A low price on one sale may involve low prices on others. The order which our low price takes away from a competitor may be canceled out by some other order which his low price takes away from us. Too much cheap business may crowd out more profitable orders obtainable elsewhere. The business might ultimately consist of orders which were individually desirable but collectively unremunerative.

It spite of all this, the fact remains that not all business can be obtained at exactly the same price and that some concessions from top prices are commonly necessary to meet many situations. How far such concessions can extend is an ever present problem of price making.

Apportionment of Joint Costs. An invaluable aid in the solution of such problems is a clear understanding of the principles underlying the apportionment among products and activities of those costs which apply jointly to many products and transactions. Which will be greater or less if a certain pricing policy is adopted, and by how much? From which classes of business can fixed overhead costs be recovered, and at what rate?

The first task of the cost accountant confronting a pricing problem is to study all the indirect costs connected with production, distribution, and administration in an effort to determine which ones are positively affected by the amount and kind of business taken. These may then be grouped according to the *factor of variability* influencing each, and a cost *per unit of activity* may be developed.

In a factory, for example, certain costs may vary with the man-hours operated, others with machine hours operated, others with quantities processed, and others with values invested. In a transportation system costs may vary with miles of track maintained, with locomotive hours operated, with car miles run, with tons hauled, or with passengers carried. In a store or warehouse costs relate to sales volume, inventory volume, space occupancy, personnel employment, promotion, supervision, and so on.

The cost data so developed are not necessarily those incorporated in product or departmental costs, assembled for bookkeeping purposes. They must consist of basic cost elements—"building blocks" from which any specific cost computation can be made to meet whatever need may arise. Even the contents of a block may have to be varied according to the circumstances. The job must be done over and over, with costs assembled in a variety of combinations, to meet the requirements of each particular situation.

Normally the calculation of total cost is a two-stage operation. The first step is to add to the known direct out-of-pocket costs an appropriate allowance for variable overhead costs of all types—the amounts by which the aggregate expense of conducting the business will be increased if this particular order, or class of orders, is obtained and filled. The second step is to add a reasonable (or perhaps the maximum obtainable) share of fixed overhead costs—those charges which will continue in substantially unchanged amount whether or not this particular business is handled. The resulting figure is the basic "sold" cost which a price must attempt to recover.

Unfortunately the distinction between variable and fixed overhead costs is often difficult to maintain. Few overhead costs are uniformly variable or wholly fixed. The principle is easy to state, often difficult to apply. While the mechanics of applying it cannot be fully described here, at least some further attention to the influence of fixed costs on prices may be in order.

Sunk Costs. Businessmen, apprehensive of price-cutting by competitors, commonly argue that every price quoted should reflect a "fair" share of all costs, including those fixed charges which result from the maintenance of an investment and an organization and which are not directly related to any individual activities in which the business may subsequently engage. Economists, however, recognize that many of these outlays create what are sometimes termed "sunk" costs, irrevocably committed to the enterprise and therefore not necessarily an element in the future price decisions of its managers.

While every manager strives mightily to price his goods so that these costs, with all others incurred, will be fully recovered, he usually recognizes that there is no fixed or determinable fraction of the total which is necessarily assignable to, or recoverable from, any individual transaction or group of transactions. While he will use as a guide some possibly arbitrary apportionment of such costs to particular units or classes of products or orders, he must remain conscious that the profitableness of a price, or a price schedule, is not adequately measured by its relationship to costs thus determined.

The reasons are obvious, though they seem often to escape both managers and cost accountants. First, the basis of apportionment is necessarily theoretical and subject to wide variations according to the theory adopted. Secondly, the unit amount of such overhead costs is more closely related to total volume than to the size of the costs themselves. Thus the determination of the fixed cost component in a total cost involves both a theory as to apportionment and an assumption as to volume. Such a cost factor has no intrinsic veracity, stability, or dependability. It constitutes merely a guide, a measuring stick, or an objective—not a controlling element in price calculations.

The manager's task, broadly considered, is to establish a pricing program which will insure the recovery *in the aggregate* of all costs incurred, plus a maximum of return for the use of the capital employed. Sound pricing usually involves quoting for each item an amount high enough to cover its direct cost, plus its proper share of variable costs, plus its maximum contribution toward fixed overhead and profit. To determine the latter amount it is necessary to estimate the size of the volume obtainable at any level of prices, the probable influence of competition, and many other factors.

Distribution Costs. With attention long concentrated on manufacturing costs, inadequate consideration is frequently given to the expense of marketing the product after its manufacture is completed. Yet distribution accounts for a large percentage of all costs incurred and commonly has more influence on pricing policy than the bare cost of production.

Distribution may include any or all of the following activities: publicity, contact, solicitation, warehousing, display, order filling, delivery, service, credit extension, market research, and the related supervisory and administrative functions. Costs of such activities differ according to products, quantities, channels, locations, customers, and methods of sale. The cost differences vitally affect the price which will be remunerative under varying conditions.

The skillful price maker must know accurately what cost variations are involved in the offering of goods under the widely differing conditions which may be met in a typical marketing program. One product may differ from another in frequency of sale, rate of turnover, breadth of customer demand, and so on. Unit selling cost for quantity orders is normally far less than for small transactions. Selling to wholesalers is usually much cheaper than direct-to-retailer merchandising. Distance and congestion increase delivery costs. Some customers require more service than others.

Most enterprises develop a pattern of price differentials designed to reflect these cost differences. Quantity discounts are common, and functional (i.e., customer-class) discounts apply in many fields. Delivered prices may include transportation charges. Extra service may rate a special charge.

In no field, however, are there greater temptations toward abuse of the differential cost principle or toward price-cutting of an indiscriminate character. Knowledge of the differences in distribution costs is frequently inadequate; many of the costs are "joint," or seemingly in the category of fixed overhead; the lure of the big order is ever present. The sales temperament plays a part. "If our competitor can do it, so can we" becomes a comfortable excuse for any kind of careless or damaging price making.

This subject has had intensive study in recent years, but most businesses still have a lot to learn about it. Sound cost calculation is an invaluable aid to sound organization of the selling program. The right selection of customers and channels and the right differentials between classes of service may mean the difference between success and failure for the entire enterprise.

Prior and Current Acquisitions. A particularly perplexing price-cost problem arises from the ownership of materials or facilities acquired at prices substantially above or below those currently prevailing. Should cost calculations (and the related price quotations) be based on actual original costs or on current replacement costs?

Should the advantage of the fortunate acquisition be retained by the owner or passed on to the buyer? Should resale prices originally established be maintained even though the goods can now be bought for less?

This is a highly controversial issue, fraught with supposed moral implications as well as real, practical complexities. Is a dealer a "profiteer" if he raises his prices to correspond with changes in replacement costs and sells his low price inventory for more than he expected to get? Is he a "chiseler" if he marks down his high cost goods when he learns that lower markets are on the way?

The moralist's response is likely to depend on which theory of price making appeals to him. If he is a cost recovery advocate, he may contend that higher replacement costs should not be reflected in higher selling prices till the old low cost inventory has been sold. This theory comfortably ignores the fact that public demand is expressed in rising prices, and that there is no more justification for denying a seller the advantages of a higher level of purchasing power than there is possibility of protecting him from the penalty of shrinking incomes among his prospective customers. People have to be charged more when they can pay more, and less when they have less to spend.

Oddly enough, sellers often refuse to take advantage of the opportunities for abnormal margins resulting from fortunate acquisitions, using their favorable position instead to "undersell the market" and thus grab some business away from not-so-fortunate competitors. This causes great indignation throughout the trade. The merits and dangers of such a course must be carefully weighed by each seller in the light of his own particular circumstances.

One aspect of this problem is the competitive influence of low cost and high cost productive facilities, existing side by side and turning out goods for the same market. Should the owner who acquired his plant at a bargain price—either from a distressed seller or during a period of deflation—use correspondingly reduced depreciation allowances in computing his costs (and setting his prices)? Or should he incorporate in his charges a provision for replacement at current price levels?

The answer again is not properly one of morality or philosophy, but one of judgment, depending on manufacturing conditions, market demand, available trade, volume and profit objectives, and other factors. The utilization of low cost facilities often involves high operating and maintenance costs, and an inflated depreciation provision may raise the hypothetical product cost to an irrecoverable level. On the other hand, the refusal to recognize a higher level of plant replacement costs may result in "giving away" the economic values inherent in the facilities, when higher prices and wider profit margins are essential to provide the funds needed for replacements.

"Follow the market" is normally the soundest pricing policy. Here again, as in so many other cases, the seller's own actual cost will not constitute the sole (or even an important) determinant of what should be charged. Cost is simply one factor to be considered, receiving greater or lesser weight according to the circumstances.

Incidence of Costs. Despite all the uncertainties as to how much cost can be recovered in any given price, one important fact can never be disregarded, namely, that all costs ultimately burden someone. When the buyer does not pay them, someone else must. Who that someone is depends on circumstances.

It is plainly *not* true that all costs are eventually passed on to the consumers of the products in question. Excessive costs, abnormal losses, and higher income taxes are *not* merely added to selling prices. More than one fourth of the country's business enterprises normally lose money and thus are obviously not recovering all their costs. Even whole industries may sell their output below the cost of production.

Who takes those losses, carries those burdens?

Most of them, of course, fall on the owners of the enterprises through reduction in, or elimination of, the hoped for profit—perhaps eventually through dissipation of their capital investment. Others, however, may also be involved.

Unprofitable sales (i.e., those not recovering the costs incurred) in due course put pressure on both volume and costs. The least remunerative business is dropped; special services are discontinued; quality may be lowered. Suppliers are pressed to reduce their quotations for materials and parts. Workers may be forced to accept lower wages, fewer "fringe" benefits. Rents are cut, by using less space or taking cheaper quarters. Tax payments are pushed down, income taxes disappear, and authorities are petitioned for lower property tax assessments.

Thus prices may put pressure on costs as often as costs exert influence on prices. In the long run, for broad segments of the economy, there must be some relationship between the two, but in individual cases it is often difficult to determine which is cause and which effect.

Trade-Position Influences

Costs, then, influence prices, but seldom control them. Costs, moreover, show wide variations according to the basis of computation, which may be altered according to the objectives of the costing process. The conclusion will differ depending on whether the perspective adopted is short range or long range, particular or general, aggressive or defensive, complacent or concerned. A price-cost relationship which is acceptable under one set of conditions may be wholly unattractive under another.

It is obvious, moreover, that many considerations other than current and immediate costs have a profound influence on price making. The trade position of the enterprise is a vital factor. Some of the elements in this position deserve attention.

Competitors' Prices. Run-of-the-mill price making probably is more strongly influenced by the known (or supposed) prices being quoted by competitors than by any other one factor. Sensitiveness to other people's prices is one of the most marked characteristics of the typical sales representatives. "We can't ask more than they do," the argument runs; "and if they can make money at such prices, so should we."

Pursuaded by such flimsy arguments, many enterprises do little more than imitate or adapt their competitors' price lists or individual quotations. Many managers have a blind faith in the soundness and profitableness of a price offered by anyone whom they consider a leader in the field. Others, convinced that competitors are ignorantly or maliciously selling below cost, still feel constrained to meet the price regardless of consequences.

The interpretations of competitors' pricing policies are often unjustified. We cannot assume that any given price is adding to (or subtracting from) a competitor's profits, or that, if adopted, it will add to (or subtract from) our own. There are too many uncertainties, too many differing interpretations, to permit a clear-cut conclusion about the probable effects of a policy on either party concerned.

Competitors' prices may frequently be found unprofitable, in the sense of making less contribution to margins than we consider necessary for the success of our own enterprise. Some concerns consistently underprice their goods, and eventually go broke. On the other hand, the fact that a competitor's price is below *our* cost is far from proving that it is below *his* cost. Some people can and do produce more cheaply than others, and use their cost advantages to establish lower prices, thus either broadening the market or obtaining a larger share of it. Either condition must be presumed possible.

The price maker's difficulty is in appraising the profitableness of any given quotation he is called on to match. Is it an unwarranted, "flash-in-the-pan," loss-leader type of price, which cannot be consistently maintained, or is it symptomatic of someone's ability to make money on a lower price level than our own cost position appears to justify? Should the lead be followed or disregarded?

While few concerns are in a position to know the details of a competitor's costs, it may be possible, from a study of one's own cost experience, to form useful hypotheses as to the facts which may underlie the other fellow's decisions. For example, it is possible to set down all the numerous components of our own calculated cost for the item in question, and then to guess at the probable elements in the competitor's figuring by seeking answers to such questions as the following:

Has he an advantage in raw material cost; and, if so, how much? Are his labor and facilities more efficient; and, if so, what is his maximum saving? What volume may he be enjoying (or seeking), and what fixed overhead cost per unit would our factory have if operated at the same percentage of capacity? What distribution methods does he employ, and how costly are they? Is this item one of his major products, or a by-product, or a sideline? How large a contribution to overhead and profit might he normally be expected to seek from such an item? What is his stock position, and what is that of the trade generally?

The answers may be conjectural, but often even a conjecture is illuminating. Furthermore, our own costs take on additional meaning when viewed in the light of what we believe other people's may be. Much as we may desire to realize a price which will compensate us for all our costs, justified or unjustified, we cannot expect our customers to pay us a premium to cover inefficiency, wastefulness, or disadvantageous position.

If we have bought our materials too high, or employ our labor carelessly, or use obsolete equipment, or fail to attain adequate volume, or spend too much on maintenance or supervision or advertising, we create no values through those expenditures—none, certainly, that a customer will recompense us for if similar goods are being produced for less by aggressive competitors who are willing to work on narrow margins to improve their volume and increase their turnover. Under such conditions an excess cost becomes a loss, not something that can be recovered in a price. When it is one thing and when the other is one of management's perennial $64 questions.

Continuity of Operations. It is significant that just as cost factors influence prices, so also do price decisions influence costs. This is so because the production volume generated by a given price is itself one of the important factors in determining what the product will cost.

This is not merely a matter of the size of the unit overhead cost, which is strongly influenced by the overall volume level, but it is also a question of continuity and orderliness in the scheduling of production and distribution. In most lines it is not possible to stay in business by accepting prices (making sales) only when margins look favorable. Continuous, uninterrupted activity is one of the most important elements in effective cost control.

For this reason many concerns plod patiently along through what are sometimes long extended periods of unremunerative prices, taking business at whatever price level they may obtain, because the penalties of price reductions on business done are less than the penalties of cost increases resulting from business refused. Conversely, the enterprise which tries to protect its margins by refusing orders at substandard prices may find those margins impaired and its maintained prices no longer profitable if its production schedule is too often disturbed by interruptions.

As production has become more highly mechanized, and as labor costs have become more and more inflexible, the effect of this factor has become more pronounced. Set-up and start-up expenses for short runs become prohibitive. Guaranteed minimum weekly pay rates prevent savings from the layoff procedure once widely employed. Labor shortages and high training costs make it essential to preserve a skilled labor force, even when profitable employment for all of it cannot currently be found.

The exact cost significance of these factors can be measured only with great difficulty and considerable uncertainty. Their importance is, however, rather generally recognized, and they become a compelling influence on pricing policy.

Maintenance of Trade Position. Even more important than continuity of operations is maintenance of trade position—that is, holding one's normal share of whatever business is available. For every regular article of commerce there is an established pattern of distribution, and neither sellers nor buyers want it disturbed to their own disadvantage. Normally they will make substantial sacrifices to maintain it.

For a seller, building up trade is a costly and difficult job. He must make his goods known to potential customers through advertising, publicity, promotion, and display. He must form acquaintances, create confidence, solicit orders, and establish a method of transportation and delivery. He must pave the way for repeat orders, provide customer service, and aid in secondary distribution. Eventually he has a heavy investment in his trade position, perhaps comparable in size with his investment in plant facilities.

The position thus established is one not lightly to be abandoned, and an agressive seller will defend it stubbornly. He is too conscious of the cost of "getting in" to let himself be easily pushed out again. To maintain his position he may have to make price concessions which appear unwarranted from a cost and profit standpoint, but this step may be cheaper in the long run than to let someone else take his place in the market and then try to win it back at some future date.

The hard choice between selling at a loss and not selling at all may be forced by several different conditions. A competitor's advantage in cost, in location, in service, or in some other factor may make his offerings more attractive and compel us to make a price concession to retain the business. Again, a competitor's willingness to sell at a loss to obtain a "first order" may make our prices look high. The customer may find his own resale margin squeezed by similar competitive factors in his own field, and may demand reductions in the prices he is paying. Substitute goods of a new type may threaten the whole fabric of our trade.

Whatever the cause may be, the effect is often to push prices disturbingly far away from the level which would prevail if current costs and desired profit margins were the only considerations in price making.

Market Level Equilibrium. Much of the foregoing has emphasized the pressures toward lower prices which are exerted on the seller by his desire to expand volume, broaden markets, maintain production, and protect trade. These "trade considerations," however, are by no means all on the side of price reductions. Several powerful influences work in the opposite direction.

One of these is the inherent tendency of management to lean to the "high side" in computing costs. Businessmen instinctively fear "close prices." They prefer guides which allow for possible unanticipated cost increases or other contingencies. Accountants are typically conservative. They abhor costs which may turn out to be understated. They like to "forget" possible cost savings in the hope that they will form a welcome, if unexpected, addition to profits.

More important, however, is the disinclination of the average seller to upset an established market equilibrium. Often there is a strong prevailing demand for all the goods currently being produced at prices which are reasonably remunerative to everyone concerned. Why disturb a favorable situation?

True, a lower level of prices might broaden the market, stimulate greater sales, lower costs, and widen the opportunity for profitable employment of capital in expanded plant facilities. When margins are wide and demand apparently insatiable, the pressure for increased competition becomes irresistible. But the typical situation is the one on the border line, where today's prices are barely satisfactory and any reduction seems likely to damage the profit position of the enterprise, perhaps of the entire industry.

Sellers in such cases are characteristically wary. They know that price reductions on their own part may lead to retaliatory price-cutting by others. Often they see little possibility of substantial expansion in the overall volume of the industry and fear that lower prices will mean simply lower margins and no improvement in trade position. A sort of trade stigma may attach to a seller who "breaks the line."

The fear of the consequences of price-cutting sometimes has become so great as to encourage collaboration among sellers to maintain existing price levels through formal or informal agreements not to lower them. The foolishness, the ineffectiveness of such joint undertakings has been amply demonstrated, and for half a century they have been legally outlawed, but a wistful desire for "protection" of this sort still lingers in the minds of many businessmen.

Lacking the opportunity for outright price-fixing schemes within the law, apprehensive sellers resort to moral preachments on the evils and dangers of price reductions; and the atmosphere thus created does definitely discourage individual adjustments, thus sometimes offsetting the pressures toward lower prices which come from cost and other considerations previously mentioned.

To cut or not to cut, that is the question. There is no formula which will provide an answer. Each seller must assemble, analyze, and evaluate the available trade information, reaching a solution which seems calculated to give him the best profit possibilities for both the immediate and the long-term future. The decision is likely to be a sound one only if it is based on comprehensive factual data, among which the particulars of costs, both actual and potential, are of prime importance.

Conclusions

Costs influence prices but do not control them, except in a limited and special sense. Goods sell for what buyers think they are worth, whether this price is more or less than cost. Business must recover from its total revenues its total costs, but not every sale will show an adequate individual profit. A contribution to overhead is all that can be expected from some classes of business.

Most enterprises will go to great lengths to maintain volume, continue operations, protect trade position. Sales will be made close to cost (or even below cost) before the operation is abandoned. On the other hand, wide profit margins are eagerly accepted, actively exploited.

In a free economy no seller is "entitled" to a price which will cover his costs. He is entitled only to the price the market affords. He must learn to live on that price, or quit. He cannot burden the buyer with excess costs; he must absorb them himself.

In a free economy the buyer is king. He buys what he wants, pays what he chooses. He must offer enough to bring out the production he desires, but no more. He takes nothing not wanted, and supports no one not needed. He makes his own price controls, and it is surprising only that he should imagine anyone else could do it better.

This, it should be emphasized, is his experience in a free economy. His experience under the "protection" of government regulations is the subject of Part II of this discussion, published in the following issue.

37. COST FORECASTING
AND PRICE POLICY *

Joel Dean †

The central question of this paper is: "How should cost estimates be used to do a better job of setting prices?" In dealing with this question, our concern will be with the way to get answers to pricing problems, rather than with the answers themselves; and our focus will be on principles rather than techniques. This analysis will be confined to costs of production (i.e., *handling* the business); it will exclude selling costs (i.e., costs of *getting* business).

COST CONCEPTS AND COST FUNCTIONS

There is a variety of cost concepts, each useful under some circumstances and misleading or worse under others. Effective use of costs for setting prices requires a clear understanding of the principle of different costs for different purposes.

Future costs, not current or past costs, are relevant for most price policy decisions. A strategy of using price as an instrument of market development requires bold action in anticipation of higher sales and consequent economies of volume. There are, normally, practical impediments to frequent changes in price. Moreover, it takes time for its full volume effects to be felt. A basic price, decided on today, is likely to far outlast the conditions that determine today's costs. Therefore it is forecasts of tomorrow's costs that are needed.

Cost behavior is the result of many forces. Determination of the functional relationships of costs to each major force provides the informational foundation for the various cost forecasts that are useful for pricing decisions.

* From *The Journal of Marketing* (January, 1949). Reprinted by permission of the American Marketing Association. Presented before the New York meetings of the American Marketing Association, June, 1947.

† Joel Dean, of Joel Dean Associates, Yonkers, N. Y., in addition to his work as an economic and management consultant, is Professor of Business Economics in the Graduate School of Business, Columbia University.

Knowledge of cost functions provides a foundation which has the necessary flexibility to develop the multiple condition conjectures that are needed. Practical demand estimates usually cover a range of sales volume, because of estimating error and uncertainty about fluctuations in national income and other influences; hence it is necessary to be equipped to conjecture costs for various volumes and for different combinations of cost conditions; e.g., 15 percent higher wages, 20 percent less output, 10 percent greater efficiency.

Clearly, forecasts, based upon these cost functions, are subject to estimating error. But this does not destroy their usefulness. It is impossible for management to escape guessing about future costs when it makes a pricing decision. The choice lies between forecasting explicitly and adopting the viewpoint of the ostrich. No careful forecast could be as inaccurate as the tacit assumption that current costs will continue indefinitely. Yet that is exactly the assumption that is made when price decisions are reached on the basis of "actual costs."

Now let us briefly examine some of the most important kinds of cost functions and see how each can be used for more scientific

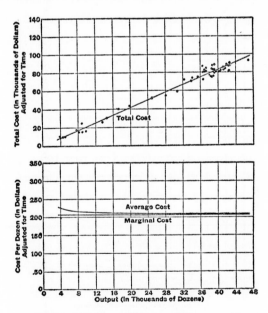

FIG. 1. Hosiery mill—monthly costs. Total average and marginal combined cost derived from partial regression on output.[1]

[1] Reproduced from Joel Dean, *Statistical Cost Functions of a Hosiery Mill*, (Chicago: University of Chicago Press, 1941), p. 34.

pricing. We shall confine our attention to the relation of costs to
(1) rate of output, (2) size of lot, (3) size of plant, (4) wage rates
and material prices, and (5) technology.

Rate of Output Curve

The cost curve for output rate is illustrated by three charts.
Figure 1 shows results of a statistical determination of costs for a
hosiery mill. Total cost rose at a constant rate over the prewar range
of output. This resulted in an average cost which declined over the
whole range and a marginal production cost which was constant.
There is some reason to expect that this kind of cost behavior is
quite general in manufacturing industries in normal times. Figure 2
shows how various components of cost behave when output is varied.
You will note wide differences in sensitivity to output. Findings for
the coat department of a large New York store are shown in Figure 3.

This sort of short-run cost curve has several valid uses for
pricing: (1) It provides the groundwork for short-run comparative
income statements to test the profit effects of alternative basic prices.
(2) It is the basis for estimates of short-run incremental costs

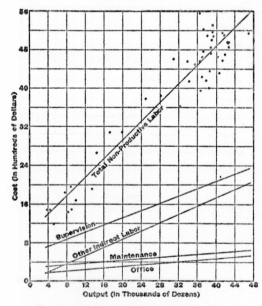

FIG. 2. Hosiery mill—monthly costs. Simple regressions of nonproductive labor cost
and its elements on output.[2]

---

[2] Reproduced from Joel Dean, *Statistical Cost Functions of a Hosiery Mill*,
(Chicago: University of Chicago Press, 1941), p. 23.

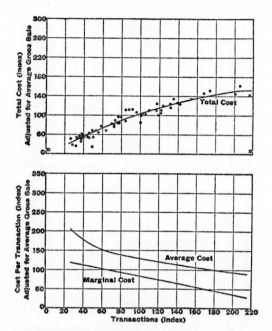

FIG. 3. Coat department. Total average
and marginal combined cost derived from partial regression on transactions.[3]

which are useful for setting various kinds of price differentials and
for market segmentation. (3) It is also useful in estimating how
much volume increase would have to result from price concessions in
order to obtain specified levels of profitability. A high proportion of
companies can develop, quite cheaply, a short-run production cost
curve of this type, which is accurate enough for pricing purposes.

Lot Size Curve

The relationship between cost and the number of units in a production (or distribution) lot is easy to understand and to estimate.
If the set-up costs (or other constant costs) are large and the economies of lot size are therefore marked, then projections of cost
curves for lot size have wide usefulness for price policies. It may be
a factor in determining the basic price level. Pricing to develop
volume markets frequently contemplates economies of lot size as
well as of scale, output rate, and technology. Forecasts of lot size
economies also underlie quantity discount structures and package

---

[3] Reproduced from Joel Dean "Department Store Cost Functions," published
in Lange, *et al. Studies in Mathematics, Economics and Econometrics* (Chicago:
University of Chicago Press, 1941), p. 242.

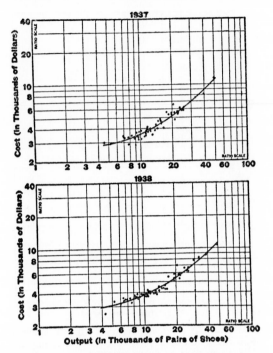

FIG. 4. Shoe store chains. Simple regressions of selling expense on output measured by shoe sales in pairs.[4]

size differentials. Also such economies are responsible for some of the differences in costs among models and hence affect price differentials for quality, size, use, etc.

Size of Plant Curve

The way unit costs will behave as plant size is expanded is illustrated by the empirical cost curve for size of store shown in Figure 4, in a shoe chain. Another method that is more appropriate for many situations is engineering estimates of a plant's expansion path.

Long-term cost estimates play an important role in decisions on the basic price because plant expansion is often entailed. When price is used as a major instrument of long-range market development, estimates of the economies of scale play a major role in testing the probable profitability of reductions. For example, when a major insurance company was deciding whether to reduce the price of policy loans, it projected costs at various volumes far beyond the

    [4] Reproduced from Joel Dean and R. W. James, *The Long-Run Behavior of Costs in a Chain of Shoe Stores* (Chicago: The University of Chicago Press, 1942), p. 27.

range of past experience. These were paired with revenue estimates to test the earnings consequences.

Wage Rates and the Price Level

Should your price move up and down with the general price level? The general price level is a statistical fiction. A glance at the individual price relatives that are summarized in the various indexes of the price level shows the bewildering disparity among the individual price movements. They move not only at different rates but also in different directions.

The impact of the price level upon your price works through various kinds of goods: (1) products that are substitutes (direct or indirect) for your product, (2) goods that siphon off purchasing power otherwise available for your product, and (3) goods and services that are components entering into the cost of making your product. Instead of keeping your price in some arbitrary relationship to the general price level, it is far more useful to recognize and study each of these types of impact separately and arrive at a pricing decision. They differ in degree and even in direction. Moreover, the first two affect demand estimates and the third affects your costs.

Projections of future costs on the basis of changed wage rates and material prices are needed for many pricing problems. For most decisions, replacement costs, rather than costs historically incurred, are needed. This principle applies with equal force to equipment and plant (where they are relevant) as to finished inventory and goods in process.

In applying this principle, the first step is to make some estimates. What will happen to your material prices and wage rates in the near and distant future? The next step is to determine the impact of these estimated changes upon your costs. In the near term, when substitutes and improved methods and technology can be virtually ignored, this is largely a matter of arithmetic. Even here these factors price changes do not affect all costs proportionately. Hence their consequences should be estimated separately for various concepts of cost and for various products. For the most distant future, the estimates should take account of the possibility that cheaper materials will be found, methods will be improved, and technical advances will displace man-hours.

Technological Cost Curve

Since pricing decisions of today stretch into the distant future they must be made in contemplation of continued technological advance. Guessing technical improvements is bound to be inaccurate, yet it is likely to be far less wrong than operating on the tacit assumption that technology will stand still. But this is exactly the assumption that is made when no effort is made to project innovations. Methods for estimating technical advance include (1) surveying the specific technical advances that are now upon the horizon and tracing their cost reducing consequences for your company and (2) projecting the past trend of technical advance in your industry.

This brief survey of cost curves shows that different problems call for different kinds of cost conjectures. Projection on a scientific basis involves knowledge of the relationship of cost to each of these factors. This framework of knowledge of cost curves makes it possible to combine factors flexibly and thus produce without special research a variety of cost estimates suitable for various purposes.

How to Use Costs for Setting the Basic Price

A useful distinction can be made between the problem of setting the *basic price* and of setting the structure of *price differentials*. The basic price, for a single product firm, is a price bench mark for stating price differentials for differing quantities, locations, distribution channels, etc. For a multiple product company the basic price is less definite. But frequently the price of the prototype product of the high volume product serves as a bench mark for model differentials among a group of closely related products as well as for quantity and channel discounts.

Let us first look at determination of the basic price for a firm making several products.

Cost Plus Is Wrong

Only in the last decade have economists had sense enough to sit at the feet of businessmen and try to find out systematically how executives really go about setting prices. Two studies of this type have been made in England, and two comprehensive ones have been under way for several years in this country. The most striking finding is that an overwhelming majority of businessmen say they set prices on the basis of cost plus a fair profit. By "cost" they usually mean full cost at current levels. By a "fair profit" it is hard to know what they mean. No one ever seems to want more than a fair profit.

The respondents probably tend to overstate the rigidity of this pricing rule, for many of them introduce the afterthought of "adjustment to take account of competitive conditions." Hence the cost formula may be a pricing ideal which is actually attained less frequently than these surveys indicate.

The popularity of the cost plus method does not necessarily mean it is the best available method. In most situations it is the wrong attack on the pricing problem, for several reasons: (1) It ignores demand. What people will pay for a product bears no necessary relationship to the costs incurred by the manufacturer. (2) It involves circular reasoning: unit cost depends on volume but sales volume depends on the price charged. (3) It fails to adequately reflect competition. Buyers' alternatives in the form of substitute products are all omitted from this simple formula and the effect of a price upon rivals' reactions and upon the birth of potential competition is also neglected. (4) It concentrates on the wrong cost. Not current cost and certainly not past cost but forecasts of future costs are needed for the limited role of costs in setting prices.

Types of Valid Uses

The dominant factor in pricing should be the estimated effect of price on sales volume; the effect on buyers' actions and attitudes, rivals' reactions, potential competition, etc. Cost estimates play a secondary, facilitating role. What are the valid uses for pricing? They may be roughly classified into three groups:

1. To measure the effects of the alternative prices upon profits.
2. To guess what people will do in response to a proposed price.
3. To justify a course of price action already decided upon.

1. *Effects on Profits.* Measurement of the effects of proposed prices on profits presupposes estimates of expected volume at different prices. But cost estimates are an essential element in choosing between proposed prices, since they make it possible to project and compare the probable profits from alternative price-volume combinations.

This can be done by drawing up comparative operating budgets that show the probable earnings that will result from each potential price under consideration. To get these comparative budgets, cost projections based upon the relationships of cost to output rate, plant size, technology, price levels and to other conditions are needed.

2. *Effect on Actions of Buyers and Competitors.* There are several kinds of practical uses of cost estimates to aid in guessing what people will do in response to proposed price: (a) estimating the

demand for some types of producers' goods by making an analysis of users' probable cost savings; (b) guessing rivals' reactions; (c) predicting impacts on potential competition.

(a) *Buyers' Alternative Costs.* The demand for capital goods is largely governed by the way the product affects the buyers' costs. Hence prices should be geared to buyers' alternative costs by estimating the amount of cost savings of various types of customers. Price thinking should be focused upon the customer's payout period, and upon user costs as compared with his existing and alternative equipment. An example of the approach is a producer of a petroleum additive who bases his price, not on his costs, but on what it will cost his customers to obtain the same product properties by alternative means.

(b) *Guessing Rivals' Reactions.* More direct methods of predicting competitors' concurrence in price action are probably widely used. But when they are not used, or when they still leave uncertainty, cost estimates can be of some help.

For this purpose it is the competitor's probable costs of the supplies rather than your own costs that are relevant. Your costs serve merely as a point of departure in estimating theirs. Knowledge of the cost hierarchy of your industry and the technology and size of rivals' plants is important for translating your cost figures into estimates of competitors' costs. A major oil company in setting prices in its leadership area estimates the costs of its best situated competitor to indicate the likelihood that its price lead will be followed. Recently one of the large magazines contemplated an increase in advertising rates. To guess whether this lead would be followed by competitors, it developed cost estimates and conjectural income statements at present prices and at proposed prices for its major rivals. This analysis indicated that a cost squeeze would force rivals to follow the increase.

(c) *Potential Competition.* The effects that your price will have upon entry into your industry and upon expansion is a long-term factor of importance in pricing. You can price competitors *into* your market as well as yourself *out* of it. Here again cost estimates are useful in guessing the effect of your price upon unborn competitors.

Stay-out pricing is the cornerstone of the pricing philosophy of many leading producers of automotive parts and accessories. Their big customers stand at the threshold of producing the product themselves. Some already have one foot in the door. Projections of the costs of these potential invaders should be a major pricing factor.

Only if your own current costs are really the best estimate you can make of potential competitors' cost, should this consideration lead to prices based solely on your own average costs. Costs of existing plants are sometimes significantly higher than those of new entrants with up-to-date technology.

3. *Justification of Price Action.* Cost is frequently used to justify a course of price action already decided upon. Examples include satisfying the government that the provisions of the Robinson-Patman Act have been met, justifying prices before a regulatory commission, and convincing customers that the price rise was "necessary."

Costs have become a sort of social conscience in pricing. This notion springs from the precept of the classical economists that price tends to equal cost of production under conditions of perfect competition. Because this dream of atomistic competition has been used by economists as a norm of desirable price behavior, costs have grown to perform a normative function. In public utility regulation, for example, full cost plus a fair return on capital is a regulatory standard. This public utility thinking has been carried over into business in a distorted form in the practice of full cost plus a fair profit. Yet an aggregate earnings standard and a unit margin standard are not the same thing at all. This guide at most stills complaint and yields peace of mind. But it is a hazardous standard of practical price making. It yields a price which you perhaps "ought to get," but not one that you necessarily can get. As a social conscience it ought to be *expected* replacement cost by the most technically advanced plant—not "actual costs."

Inverted Relation of Cost to Price

Frequently the relation of cost to price is, in practice, inverted. The practical problem is to tailor costs to fit a predetermined selling price. A manufacturer of model airplane building sets, for example, starts with a target retail price and works backward by first deducting estimated retail and wholesale margins, then deducting desired manufacturers' profit, and finally selecting the components whose costs will not exceed what money is left over. Similarly, the economic strategy of product development for many firms, notably chemical companies, is similarly inverted. The problem is to develop a substitute which will capture the market presently held by a specified chemical in a specific industrial use. This means that the unborn chemical must sell at a predetermined displacement price, and that the guide for the entire process of product search, development, production, and costing is a predetermined price.

This approach, though fully usable only in special situations, has important pricing lessons for most manufacturers. First, it starts with market price realities and looks at the problem from the viewpoint of what the buyers want and will pay for. Second, it views the seller's costs as susceptible of reduction—not as immutable facts. Third, it views the product, not as sacred but as modifiable vehicle for satisfying specified consumer wants.

SETTING THE STRUCTURE OF PRICE DIFFERENTIALS

What is the role of cost in reaching decisions about the structure of price differentials and what concepts and projections of cost are useful and valid? Most practical problems involve a *change* in the existing differentials, rather than the creation of a new pattern from whole cloth. Incremental costs, accordingly, play a strategic role. They make it possible to compare the additional revenue with the resulting additional cost in order to maximize the incremental contribution to profits and overhead.

The kinds of price differentials that present practical pricing problems may be classified as follows: Quality differentials (e.g., standard vs. deluxe models; regular vs. "fighting" brands); Size spreads (e.g., three-ton vs. five-ton trucks); Use differentials (e.g., royalty leasing of patents and machinery; fluid milk vs. cheese milk); Load factor differentials (e.g., morning movie prices and off-peak electric rates); Style cycle progressions (e.g., merchandise markdowns and edition differentials); Trial discounts (e.g., introductory subscriptions to magazines and to services); Quantity discounts (e.g., order size discounts and package size differentials); Distribution channel differentials (e.g., wholesale vs. retail prices; private brand vs. house brand); and Geographical differentials (e.g., zone pricing, basing point pricing, etc.).

Product Line Pricing

The problem is to fix the relationships of prices among your products. What kinds of products need to be priced in relationship? What kinds independently? In principle, only products whose demands are importantly interrelated must be considered together in pricing. Relationship on the cost side, through common production of distribution processes, has no bearing here. Common costs reduce the accuracy of estimates of the costs of individual products, but should not affect the relation of product prices. Joint products should be priced independently unless they are related in demand. Demand interdependence includes products that are similar in use and hence are potential fringe substitutes, or products that complement one another in use or in the sellers' market strategy.

A common way of setting the price of such kindred products is to estimate the full costs, including overheads, of each and apply a uniform percentage markup. This is easy and definite, but it is usually not the best way to go about it. The various qualities, sizes, editions, etc., of the product are likely to tap market sectors differing in demand elasticity and in competitive intensity. These demand differences should be the controlling determination of price differences.

A constructive approach to problems of this type is to view the product variants as opportunities for market segmentation in order to tap added markets and to separate sectors of the market which differ in demand elasticity. For example, multiple editions of books are a means of successively exploiting more and more elastic sectors of the market. Viewed thus the technical problem of product line pricing is to obtain the most profitable degree and kind of price discrimination.

Relevant consideration for setting product differentials includes (1) Relative buyer benefits obtained from the product variants (i.e., the use value in different applications and sections of the market). (2) Degree of competitive superiority of your product. (3) Intensity of competition. (4) Comparative elasticity of demand of the market segments tapped by each product. (5) Cross-elasticity of demand among your products. (6) Future revenue consequences upon customer goodwill. (Prices that are proportional to sellers' allocated costs are sometimes thought to have magical effects upon buyers' goodwill.) (7) Promotional effects of introductory model pricing (e.g., loss leaders, introductory subscriptions, equipment subsidies to stimulate sales of parts). (8) Effects upon profits of alternative schedules of differentials best studied by effects on total contribution to overhead and profits.

From this list it is apparent that the role of cost estimates in product line pricing should be a secondary one. Their most important job is to help project the earnings consequences of contemplated product differentials. Estimates of total cost before and **after**, paired with comparable estimates of total receipts, **are** needed for this job. The impacts upon total costs of more sales or of less sales of the various products can often be most practically projected by using the incremental cost of the various products.

Incremental cost has other important uses here. It can be used as a bench mark for finding the best pattern of market segmentation and price discrimination. The spread between incremental cost and price represents the product's contribution to overhead and profits. This spread should be studied in measuring the profit effects of alternative prices and in deciding upon product additions and product deletions. Hence incremental costs play a strategic role in maximizing this marginal contribution by price structure decisions.

Where common overhead costs are important, increment costs can often be approximated by using traceable costs. The allocation of overhead costs to individual products is quite arbitrary and is subject to wide errors; moreover many of the overhead items may not vary with output and hence have no short-run marginal cost. Orthodox allocations are often more misleading than useful in estimating incremental costs. This approach does not imply that prices should be *equal* to incremental costs—far from it. Nor does it mean that prices of related products should be *proportionate* to their marginal costs. The margin between price and incremental cost should normally differ among related products. And these differences should not be determined by the theology of cost accounting. Instead they should be governed by the demand and competitive considerations cited above. Thus, estimated incremental cost is a practical economic sill—it sets the minimum of bedrock pricings; it serves as a valid point of departure for demand pricing, and provides an efficient vehicle for tracing effects on total costs and profits.

Cost estimates sometimes have still another function in product price differentials. A study of the comparative costs of various kinds of users gives a clue to the use value and buyers' benefits of producers' goods.

Royalty licensing represents in some respects a sort of ideal of market segmentation pricing that is keyed to user costs and user benefits and is admirably divorced from irrelevant sellers' costs.

Quantity Discounts

A sound quantity discount policy requires estimates of the relationship of your cost to the relevant dimensions of quantity. The Robinson-Patman Act is construed as limiting quantity discounts to the savings of the seller (although it makes an exception "to meet competition"). Key questions in studying this relationship include: Does cost vary more closely with account size (i.e., the volume of annual purchases), or with the size of the individual order? How big are the savings of case lots?

Many prewar cost analyses now badly distort the present and future cost relationships. The universality of the unprofitable small customer problem (e.g., 80 percent of the customers accounting for 20 percent of the volume and 10 percent of the profits) may indicate that many quantity discount structures need a checkup. Possibly price has not been adequately used as an instrument of selective selling.

Cost estimates should not *determine* the quantity discount structure; instead they should be used (1) to help select the *basis* of discounts that is appropriate for your business (e.g., annual sales or order size); (2) to mark out legal limits for the amount of discounts; (3) to estimate the impact on your profits of adopting alternative schedules of quantity discounts.

As stated at the outset, cost estimates should play second fiddle to demand in pricing decisions. But even though demand estimates are rudimentary and have wide error ranges, it is usually helpful to have the relevant cost estimate for each type of price decision, provided they are not too expensive. For most established enterprises with normally adequate records, cost functions may be developed quite economically that will give adequately accurate cost forecasts— by almost anyone who takes the trouble to find out what is known about cost curves and who employs some ingenuity and insight in developing simplified short cuts. The expense of cost estimates is further reduced because the basic cost relationships have clear usefulness for other kinds of business policy.

38. WHY SCIENTIFIC INVENTORY MANAGEMENT
HAS PROVED USEFUL *   Joseph F. Buchan †

In such diverse businesses as department stores, supermarkets, wholesalers, electroplaters, aircraft manufacturing, and paper manufacturing, the systematic application of explicit, scientifically based ordering rules has significantly improved inventory management decisions. The development of various inventory management systems using such rules in these industries has been documented.[1] The typical result of installing such a system in a company which did not already have one has been one or both of the following:

1. A reduction in inventory of from 10 percent to 30 percent.
2. A decrease in stockouts of from 25 percent to 70 percent.

Frequently these changes have been accompanied by increased sales, and often they have required no increase in the continuing amount of effort devoted to inventory management once the system has been installed. Although the most sophisticated systems make use of a computer, some quite successful systems have been manual, while others have used tabulating equipment.

The reason for the results obtained from the installation of scientifically based inventory systems lies partially in the large number of reordering decisions which have to be made when managing inventories ranging from several hundreds to many thousands of items, with differing and changing demands. It is unrealistic to expect that all of these decisions will be made in a consistent manner without

* From *The Quarterly* (Touche, Ross, Bailey & Smart, March, 1964). Reprinted by permission of Touche, Ross, Bailey & Smart.
† Joseph F. Buchan, Management Services Division, Touche, Ross, Bailey & Smart.
[1] Joseph Buchan and Ernest Koenigsberg, *Scientific Inventory Management* (Englewood Cliffs, N.J.: Prentice-Hall, Inc., 1963).

explicit rules for "when" and "how much" to reorder and a formal system to ensure that the rules are followed. And the rules are not likely to be set properly without an understanding of the relationships between order quantities and inventory costs on the one hand and between inventory levels and stockouts (or customer service levels) on the other. It is in the setting of the rules that an element of the "scientific method" is brought to bear on the inventory management problem.

The concept of "making a model of a system (or operation)" is a fundamental technique in science which turns out to be quite useful in inventory management. A model is a simplified reproduction of the important relationships in an operation or a system. It may be a set of equations, a simple flow chart, or an elaborate computer program. If the model adequately represents the operation, we can often learn how to improve the operation by experimenting with the model.

The basic inventory model illustrated in Exhibits 1 and 2 is somewhat of a classic, having first appeared in the literature more than 30 years ago.[2] It illustrates the typical assumptions and simplifications of a model, but one which has proved widely useful despite its simplicity. The model shown, which is variously referred to as an Economic Order Quantity system, a reorder point system, or a trigger system, is made up of two parts . . . a model of cost behavior for determining how much to reorder and a model of inventory behavior for determining when to reorder.

THE ECONOMIC ORDER QUANTITY (HOW MUCH)

Exhibit 1 illustrates the cost model which is used to determine the most economic, or minimum cost, order quantity. The model assumes that the total cost of managing inventory consists of two kinds of costs:

1. Ordering cost (Co) is the additional cost of placing an order—a cost which is considered to be independent of the size of the order. This might include set-up costs in manufacturing, but only purchase order processing costs in retailing. As shown in Exhibit 1, the *annual* cost of ordering decreases at a decreasing rate as the order quantity increases. In other words, a specific cost per order is spread over more units per order.
2. Carrying cost ($Cu \; x \; i$) is the cost of storing inventory plus the opportunity cost of the money tied up in inventory. This is usually

    [2] R. H. Wilson and W. A. Mueller, "A New Method of Stock Control," *The Harvard Business Review*, Vol. 5 (1926-27).

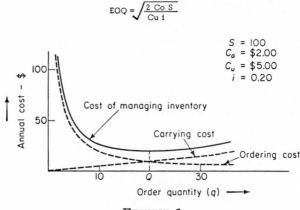

$$EOQ = \sqrt{\frac{2\ Co\ S}{Cu\ i}}$$

$S = 100$
$C_o = \$2.00$
$C_u = \$5.00$
$i = 0.20$

EXHIBIT 1

expressed as the unit cost of an item multiplied by an annual per-centage, such as 20 percent per year. The *annual* cost of carrying inventory increases in direct proportion to one half of the quantity ordered ($q/2$), because the average level of the inventory will be about halfway between the level just before a reorder is received and the level just after a reorder is received.

As is shown in Exhibit 1, the total annual cost of managing inventory first decreases as the order quantity increases because of the rapid reduction in the unit ordering cost. At some point, this total annual cost begins to increase again as the reduction in ordering cost gets progressively smaller and is eventually outweighed by the increase in carrying cost. The mathematics of this particular model are such that the minimum total annual cost occurs where annual carrying cost equals annual ordering cost, and the order quantity which results in minimum cost can be determined from the formula in Exhibit 1, where S is the annual unit sales.

Based on this cost model, the formula shown will permit determination of the most economic order quantity. Note that the total annual cost curve is rather flat near the minimum point. Thus, the reorder quantity can be varied over some range near the minimum without significantly changing total costs. And because of the square root relationship, a 21 percent error in determining the carrying cost or the ordering cost will introduce only a 10 percent error in the determination of the economic order quantity.

THE REORDER POINT (WHEN TO REORDER)

Having determined "how much" to reorder, it is also necessary to determine "when" to reorder. The model on which this is based is shown in Exhibit 2. With ideal behavior, a new order quantity would be received just as inventory reached zero. This quantity would be used up at a constant sales rate until another order was received just as the inventory reached zero again.

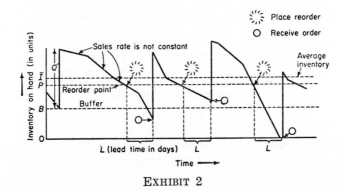

EXHIBIT 2

INVENTORY BEHAVIOR UNDER A REORDER POINT SYSTEM

Since this kind of idealized behavior does not happen in the business world, the model of inventory behavior is made a bit more sophisticated. First, the time lag between placing a reorder and receiving it is recognized. To compensate for this, the average expected sales during this lead time are calculated and that amount is added to zero in computing the reorder point—the level of inventory at which a reorder should be placed.

This is still inadequate because actual sales would exceed average sales in about half of the time periods. Every time this happened there would be a temporary out-of-stock condition (or back order) and probably lost sales. Therefore, a buffer (B) or safety stock is added to expected sales during lead time. The result is the reorder point (P) which is used in this model.

A basic understanding of how buffer stock is determined can be acquired by referring to Exhibit 3, which shows one distribution of individual weekly sales about average weekly sales for 100 weeks. This happens to be a retail item with fairly small weekly sales which fit a particular statistical distribution known as the "Poisson." The pattern of demand on manufacturing or wholesale inventories is likely to fit other distributions such as the "normal" or the "exponential," but the way in which the distribution is used is much the same. It is used to determine the buffer stock required to meet a specific, desired level of protection against stockouts.

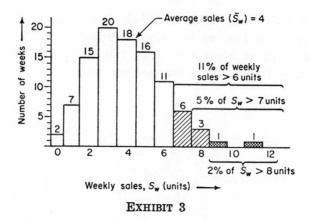

EXHIBIT 3

A DISTRIBUTION OF INDIVIDUAL WEEKLY SALES
ABOUT THE AVERAGE

When lead times are fairly constant the distribution of sales about the average sales can be used directly to determine a buffer level with an associated probability of stockout or back orders. If, for example, the lead time in Exhibit 3 were a constant one week with the average weekly sales of four units, and actual weekly sales only exceed eight units in two weeks out of 100, setting the buffer stock at four (reorder point of eight minus average weekly sales of four) should insure that stockouts would not occur more than 2 percent of the time. If lead times also have a significant variation about the average, the determination of buffer levels and stockout probabilities can be made by a Monte Carlo simulation. In this, tables are set up for the relative occurrence of various lead times and various sales rates. By randomly and repeatedly selecting a combination of a lead time and a sales value from these tables, and plotting the effect on inventory level if the reorder point and quantity rules are followed, the frequency with which inventory would drop to any given level below the reorder point can be approximated. Consequently, the percentage of stockouts which would occur for any given level of buffer stock can be approximated.

BALANCING INVENTORY AND STOCKOUTS

Regardless of the method used to determine buffer stocks, the significant fact is that the relationship between inventory levels and stockouts is not linear. As can be seen from Exhibit 3, the proportionate reduction in stockouts gets smaller as we increase inventory from six units to seven and then to eight. A kind of "law of diminishing returns" sets in.

This is shown more clearly in Exhibit 4 for one pattern of sales distribution. Reducing stockouts from 2 percent to 1 percent required only a $200 increase in average inventory, while reducing stockouts from 1 percent to ½ percent requires an additional $500 increase in inventory.

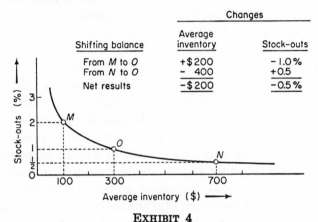

Shifting balance	Changes	
	Average inventory	Stock-outs
From M to O	+$200	−1.0%
From N to O	− 400	+0.5
Net results	−$200	−0.5%

EXHIBIT 4

BALANCING INVENTORY AND STOCKOUTS

In any large inventory, several items may have similar sales—both as to average and as to distribution. The Points M and N in Exhibit 4 show the existing stockout and average inventory levels for two such similar items at one company. Obviously these two items were not being controlled to the same extent. Yet there was no good reason for the difference except the large number of items which had to be controlled and the lack of a formal system for controlling them.

By letting management select 1 percent stockouts as a satisfactory level and by applying the reorder point and reorder quantity rules, the balance of inventory to service levels was shifted to Point O for both items. As is shown in the exhibit, the overall stockouts for M plus N and the overall average inventories for M plus N were both reduced.

Undesirable disparities in treatment of different inventory items, similar to that shown in Exhibit 4, are quite common in businesses which process a large volume of inventory transactions, but lack a formal inventory management system. That is why the installation of such a system is often accompanied by simultaneous reductions in stockouts and inventories, however paradoxical this may seem at first glance.

THE PROPER INVENTORY TO SALES BALANCE

Lack of understanding of the relations among the inventory variables is also the reason for many companies following an inventory policy which is not the best one; namely, that a fixed time supply of each item will be kept on hand. For example, all inventory items may be maintained at a level equal to two months' sales.

The reasons why this is a poor policy can be grasped by a look at the two components of inventory, buffer stock and reorder quantity. Consider the buffer stock. A fixed time supply of items with widely differing sales will not give equal protection against stockouts. For items with a Poisson sales distribution, for example, the buffer stock required to give a particular protection against stockouts varies with the square root of sales. Hence, use of a constant proportion of sales overprotects the high volume items and underprotects the low volume ones. The previous discussion of reorder quantities in connection with Exhibit 1 indicated that the most Economic Order Quantities varies, not in direct proportion to sales, but in proportion to the square root of sales.

Exhibit 5 shows how the time supply of inventory should vary with sales. Note that the scales are logarithmic so that the straight,

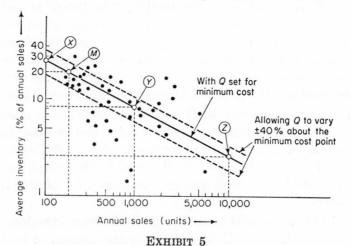

EXHIBIT 5

THE PROPER BALANCE OF INVENTORY TIME
SUPPLY TO SALES

slanted line relating the proper inventory level to the sales volume actually represents a nonlinear relationship. But it is definitely a relationship in which the time supply decreases as sales increase. For Item M with $200 annual sales, inventory should be at 20 percent of annual sales, while inventory of Item Z should be at 2.5 percent of annual sales of $10,000.

The scattered dots on the exhibit represent the actual relation between sales and inventory time supply for a number of different items under existing inventory procedures at a company which did not attempt to maintain a constant time supply. After the application of Scientific Inventory Management rules, all of these relationships were shifted to fall within the slanted dotted lines, which represent the EOQ plus and minus 40 percent. (As mentioned in connection with Exhibit 1, the total inventory cost changes relatively little for a range of values about the EOQ, and carrying and ordering costs are seldom known precisely enough to warrant insistence on the exact EOQ.) The net result was a reduction in both inventory and stockouts.

SELECTIVITY

Almost every inventory, regardless of type, displays one characteristic which should be mentioned because it often enables inventory management to be significantly improved without increasing the total amount of effort spent, by selective reallocation of effort. This characteristic is illustrated in Exhibit 6, which shows the results of classifying all items in an inventory into three groups based on their relative activity. Group A, which includes only 7 percent of the items, accounts for 51 percent of the sales and 49 percent of the inventory dollars.

Class	No. of Items	% of All Items	% of Sales	% of Average Inventory
A	156	7%	51%	49%
B	835	35	38	37
C	1409	58	11	14
	2400	100%	100%	100%

EXHIBIT 6

A TYPICAL CLASSIFICATION OF INVENTORY ITEMS

Reallocating a limited amount of inventory management effort so that more of it is concentrated on the Class A items will often improve the overall inventory picture. In a system relying on periodic inventory counts, for example, the A items might be counted every two weeks while the C items are counted only every six weeks. In addition, the customer service (or instock) levels might be set at 98 percent on the A items and 85 percent on Class C items. The existence of a pattern much like that shown in Exhibit 6 is so common that an opportunity for selective allocation of effort nearly always exists.

Variations from the Basic Model

There are many useful variations on the basic inventory model which was just discussed. The foregoing model assumes that perpetual inventory records are continually reviewed so that knowledge of reaching the reorder point is instantaneous. Where inventories are periodically reviewed, a provision can be made for sales during the review period (time between physical counts).

In another situation, where periodic inventory reviews are made and ordering costs are unimportant, a replenishment level system may be appropriate. Such a system might be used, for example, where reorders merely transfer company owned inventory from a central warehouse to decentralized selling locations. In the replenishment system, the order quantity is not constant, but is equal to the difference between a fixed replenishment level and the actual inventory level at the time of the review.

Conclusion

These variations need not concern us. The main purpose of this discussion is to indicate, by specific reference to one simple but useful inventory model, how the application of Scientific Inventory Management has been of use in improving inventory management. Its utility stems from the fact that it provides specific inventory reorder rules, based on an explicit analysis of their effect on inventory costs and customer service levels, which can ensure consistent inventory management practices in conformance with inventory management policies.

39. COST STRUCTURES OF ENTERPRISES AND BREAK-EVEN CHARTS *

Joel Dean †

I. INTRODUCTION

One of the important practical uses of empirically determined cost functions is to project the impact of output rate upon profits by means of a break-even chart. In recent years break-even charts have come into wide use by company executives, investment analysts, labor unions, and government agencies. The purpose of this paper is to appraise the reliability and usefulness of this alarmingly popular gadget. Primary attention is given to the validity of its profit projections, but its usefulness for price determination and expense control is examined briefly as well.

We shall consider, first, the nature of break-even analysis; second, its limitations; third, its principal contributions; and, fourth, ways to make this kind of analysis more useful.

II. NATURE OF BREAK-EVEN ANALYSIS

A break-even chart is a diagram of the short-run relationship of total cost and of total revenue to rate of output. These relationships should be conceived of as static. The total cost function, like its parallel in theory, is drawn on the assumption of constant factor prices, plant scale and depth, technology, and efficiency. The total revenue function assumes selling prices and product mix unchanged.

The spread between these two lines defines the profit function, which is the empirical counterpart of the short-run relationship between profits and output rate, with traditional constancies. This family of conjectural income statements is more important than is indicated by the name "break-even chart," which places unfortunate emphasis on the zero profit member of the family.

* From the *American Economic Review, Papers and Proceedings* (May, 1948). Reprinted by permission of the American Economic Association.

† Joel Dean, of Joel Dean Associates, Yonkers, N. Y., in addition to his work as an economic and management consultant, is professor of Business Economics in the Graduate School of Business, Columbia University.

Break-even analysis (which will refer not only to the presentation device, but also to the basic relationships themselves and the methods generally used to determine them) produces flexible projections of the impact of output rate upon expenses, receipts, and profits, assuming other things equal. It thus provides an important bridge between business behavior and the theory of the firm. If determination of this profit-output relationship will produce reasonably accurate predictions, then break-even analysis has considerable significance for economic research and public policy, as well as for investment analysis and company management.

Most break-even analyses are based on the concept of static cost and revenue functions, but they differ in attainment of this ideal. At one extreme are charts which involve an all-out attempt to remove dynamic influences. In statistical studies this is done by rigorous sampling, deflation, lag corrections, multiple correlation, and other statistical refinements.

At the other extreme stands the "migration path" break-even chart which is developed from annual data that cover a long period of years, with no correction for the substantial changes that have occurred in dynamic factors such as prices, efficiency, technology, and plant. Output is measured by sales volume in current dollars rather than by an index of physical production. A sort of dynamic total cost function, which appears to be linear and which often shows only moderate scatter, has been obtained for many enterprises. Sometimes subgroups of consecutive years show different lines of fit. The result is not a static total cost function but a movement path on a series of shifted static functions.[1] A possible explanation for the linearity of this path is cost plus formula pricing by the enterprises studied. A sort of dynamic profit function can also be determined directly by correlation of historical profits and output, with constancies abandoned. Scatter diagrams of this sort are used in investment analysis.

Break-even analysis should be distinguished from two other managerial tools: flexible budgets and standard costs. The variable expense budget is built on the same basic cost-output relationships, but it is confined to costs and is primarily concerned with the components of combined cost, since the purpose is to control cost by

---

[1] The pioneering work of Walter Rautenstrauck is an example of this sort of analysis. See his *Economics of Enterprise* (John Wiley & Sons, Inc., 1939), Chapters VI and VII.

developing expense standards that are flexibly adjusted to activity rate. This purpose often leads to measures of activity that differ among costs and operations, so that they cannot be readily added or translated into an index of output for the enterprise as a whole. Standard costs, on the other hand, are quite foreign to break-even analysis. Typically, they are unchanging unit costs, which are used as expense goals or as a substitute for current unit costs. The analysis of departures of current costs from standard cost usually attempts to segregate the variance attributed to rate of activity (as well as that due to other causes). This analysis of variances involves some knowledge or assumptions concerning the basic relationship of expenses to rate of utilization.

III. Limitations of Profit Projections

For profit forecasting the static break-even chart has serious limitations which its users have frequently ignored. These limitations arise from four general sources: errors of estimating the true static cost function, oversimplification of the static revenue function, dynamic forces that shift and modify these static functions, and managerial adaptations to the altered environment. Awareness of these sources of error can improve the analysis and sharpen interpretation and application of the resulting projections.

A. Determination of Cost Functions

The principal problem area of break-even analysis is empirical determination of the enterprise's cost curve. Typically the static cost function has not been established with much sophistication or precision. Since profits are residuals, the profit function gets the full impact of these inaccuracies. To understand the nature and importance of this source of forecasting error let us see how successfully break-even analysis has solved the chief problems of empirical cost determination; namely, measuring cost, measuring output, matching cost with output, holding other things constant, and finding functional relationships.

Measuring Cost. Enterprise cost data are largely the by-product of the requirements of financial accounting. They are, therefore, collected, classified, and apportioned under fairly rigid conventions which impose serious qualifications on the meaning of the resulting

cost and profit functions. Errors from this source are of three types:
exclusion of imputed cost, wide discretion in the timing of semi-
investment expenditures, and valuations and allocations that are
necessarily arbitrary.[2] Thus, the profit function is a mixture of
interest, rent, and economic profits; it usually includes inventory
value gains, which are nonrecurrent; and it is probably today inflated
by a serious understatement of capital wastage arising from prospective replacement values that are now far above original cost.

The inclusion of selling costs also impairs the accuracy of the
estimate of total cost, and this makes profit prediction more unreliable. There is no necessary functional relation between output
and costs incurred to modify the firm's demand curve. Selling
activity may remain substantially constant yet the demand curve
may shift with fluctuations in national income and tastes. Moreover,
there is much latitude for manipulating the amount and timing of
many kinds of selling expenditures.

A high correlation between output and selling outlays does not
necessarily mean a stable or meaningful relationship. To be sure,
some selling costs, such as salesmen's commissions, may be a function
of sales. But sales may depart from current production for short
periods, so that even these expenses may not be related to output.
When the advertising appropriation is determined by mechanistic
standards (e.g., x percent of expected or past sales) this expense
is often projected as proportionate to output. This is not, however,
evidence of a true functional relationship. Output may depart from
history and from forecasts without causing changes in the advertising plan or commitments. Moreover, the effect of advertising will
be spread indeterminately over future output as well as present.[3]

---

[2] Valuation errors can be serious in a period of rapid rise in the price level.
Valuations based on cost depart seriously from replacement value. This gives
rise to inventory gains which, unless removed, magnify and distort the cost and
profit functions. Rising prices also cause understatement of depreciation, assuming that prices will be higher than the purchase level at the end of economic
life of the equipment.
  Allocation errors arise from the necessarily arbitrary proration of common
costs among operating units, and the allocation of capital wastage over time
periods. Depreciation is a good example of the problems of time allocation.
When, as is common, depreciation is recorded as a straight line function of time,
it is treated as a constant cost and is thereby excluded from the estimate of
marginal cost. The amount of error from this omission depends on the extent
to which obsolescence exceeded the loss of value due to use deterioration that
was not made up by properly recorded maintenance.
  [3] Even when budgeted as a fixed percentage of expected sales, much advertising should be treated as a fixed cost, since once the advertising plan is
established its total is unaffected by the actual output rate of the period. Better
still might be to view some advertising as a capital investment, since benefits
stretch into the future, and there is wide discretionary latitude in its timing.

Even the empirical production cost function is likely to be somewhat nebulous in a large enterprise because of disparity among constituent plants. Typically, plants differ considerably in size, technology, factor prices (due to geographical variation), and other locational advantages. For example, a large gypsum company has geographically scattered board mills which embody the history of various stages of technical advances and which also differ in scale, in depth, and in wage rates, and material prices. These plants form a hierarchy in respect to marginal cost and average unit cost. The costs associated with a specified company-wide output rate are thus a composite of the costs of those mills which are operated at that time. Since it is not possible to move up the cost hierarchy as output rate expands, because of the uncontrollable geographical distribution of demand, cost will not be the same for any given composite output rate.

Measuring Output. Perhaps the most difficult problem of empirical cost research is to get a good index of output for a multiple product plant with variable product mix. A specially constructed index of physical output with weights based on inputs at constant prices is usually the best solution.

Output indexes used in most break-even analyses are not very satisfactory. Sales volume in current dollars is generally used. This kind of index, which weights diverse products in ratio to selling price rather than to inputs, is unreliable if articles differ in contribution margin [4] and if the product mix varies. It is also erroneous if selling prices change during the analysis period.

The use of sales (in properly weighted physical units) rather than production to measure output is satisfactory only if selling is the dominant activity of the firm, or if the production and sales rate are closely synchronized. Otherwise serious error is introduced, particularly if the analysis period is short. Normally it is better to measure activity by production, and to reconstruct any expenses that are a function of sales or orders, on the assumption the output is sold in the period produced.

Activity is sometimes measured by input, such as direct labor hours. Through-put of crude oil in a refinery is another example. This is a good solution when, as in a refinery, the output is diffused over a host of products whose proportions can be varied over broad

---

[4] Contribution margin is the difference between price and marginal cost. It can be approximated often by price minus traceable (direct) cost.

ranges. Direct labor is the most common input index. If deflated or measured in hours, this index is satisfactory when the input of other factors, notably material and equalized equipment hours, has about the same ratio to labor hours for various products. Under these circumstances, it amounts to an output index with constant input weights.

Expressing the activity index in terms of a percentage of capacity is common practice. This conversion camouflages but does not solve the problems we have just discussed. Capacity is generally conceived in physical rather than in economic terms. And physical capacity cannot normally be determined accurately.[5]

Theory has viewed economic capacity (defined as the low point of the unit combined cost curve) as considerably less than physical capacity. I doubt that the disparity is great for production costs under modern technology. If total production cost remains linear up to the point of extreme crowding of plant, the two kinds of capacity are not far apart, and are probably well within the error range of estimating either.[6]

What benefits come from expressing output as a percentage of "capacity"? This ratio is an easily understood common denominator for a variegated output; it shows an upper limit and it may be compared over periods when plant size has changed. But these benefits can be obtained by other means. Capacity percentages imply a more rigid and determinable upper limit of output than usually exists. The notion that there is some standard of a safe break-even percentage makes little sense. The peril of a particular break-even point is a function of the probability that output rates will go below it and the probability function for shifts in the firm's demand curve has no logical relationship to its capacity. Thus, little is added and much may be lost by expressing the output index as a percentage of physical capacity.

---

[5] Presumably it is based on three-shift operation, even though labor or material shortages limit potential output more narrowly. Moreover the time distribution of demand frequently keeps output far below equipment capacity at stable rates (e.g., electric power). Physical capacity is also affected by operating conditions such as product mix and how long one is able and willing to defer maintenance. Relatively minor capital outlays on bottleneck operations can, furthermore, expand capacity considerably, so that it may change frequently.

[6] A more meaningful economic concept of capacity in imperfect markets might be the businessman's notion of "all I can sell." This would be the point set by rising marginal selling cost or the limit of the firm's resources for market aggrandizement. This concept has the limitation of being unstable, since it shifts with income and taste and market imperfections. But the orthodox concept of economic capacity is also somewhat variable, with changes in relative prices.

Matching Cost with Output. To find the relation between cost and output the costs must be synchronized with the output to which they contributed. This problem has not been recognized or solved in most break-even analyses. The importance of the resulting error differs among establishments and depends on the length of the record period in relation to the production cycle. A production gestation period of any length results in a recording of costs to some degree in a period earlier than the recording of the output for which they were incurred. Removal of this error is tedious and never entirely satisfactory for short analysis periods. The use of annual data largely obviates the problem but hides important variations of cost and output within the year.

The wide latitude in timing many expenditures also causes errors of matching. Outlays for maintenance and for many administrative and selling activities are properly attributable to past and future outputs as well as that of the current period. Hence true costs associated with any output have a penumbra of indeterminacy. Outlays, however, may be made to have a fairly definite relationship to output by company policy that controls the timing of expenditure. Thus railroad management has often "controlled" maintenance outlays to conform much more closely to fluctuations in traffic than the timing of their true incurrence would justify.[7]

Holding Other Things Constant. The problem of actually obtaining the assumed constancy of plant, technology, methods, product, and prices cannot be satisfactorily solved in workaday break-even chart analysis. Analysis of past cost behavior underlies, in some degree, all empirical cost functions (unless the whole projection is based on engineering conjecture). Yet no past period can be found with the assumed constancy of dynamic factors.

In the empirical work of the economists, chief reliance has been placed on careful selection of the enterprise and the sample period. In normal break-even chart analysis, this kind of sample selection is out of the question. Much use must be made of conjectures that imagine away these difficulties. Multiple correlation analysis has

---

[7] The cost function derived from such expenditures may do a good job of forecasting future expenditures and short-term recorded profits. But even so, profits will differ materially from a concept of "real" profits over the long term. Hence it may be argued that the source of distortion should not be removed since it is the timing of expenditures, not of cost incurrence, that is relevant for expense control and possibly for profit forecasting. But this assumes that the change in output (and other sources of distortion) will always follow the same pattern in arriving at a specified output rate.

been used with some success in removing the influence of "other factors." But its widespread use in break-even analysis is limited by its expense and unfamiliarity.

In most break-even analyses adjustments for changes in factor prices have not been made carefully or at all. The use of current dollar sales as an output index does not solve the problem. The direct impact of changes in factor prices can be easily removed by tailored index numbers; but indirect influences through substitution among input factors cannot. Rigid limits upon such price motivated substitutions are, however, imposed by modern technology.

Determining Relation of Cost to Output. Three general types of methods have been used to get the relation of cost to output: classification of accounts; engineering projections; statistical analysis of past behavior.

Classification according to volume variability is the most common method. Expenses are classed as constant, proportionately variable, or semivariable. Semivariable expenses are then broken into a constant component and a variable component. Variability is determined largely by inspection and experience.

Engineering projections are the only feasible method for enterprises without usable operating experience or records. Such estimates are usually based on rated characteristics of equipment and on parallelism with other operations.

Statistical analyses cover a wide range of refinement. Rough scatter diagrams of a few uncorrected observations at the extremes of the output ranges are used by some practitioners. Simple correlation analysis of annual cost data, uncorrected for dynamic changes, and of output measured in current dollar sales has also been widely employed. Farther up the ladder of refinement are academic studies which employ all the available techniques of data adjustment and multiple correlation analysis. Although refined methods of this type cannot be widely used in break-even analysis, visually fitted lines to carefully selected samples of roughly adjusted cost observations should be more widely used to get and to verify relationships of cost components to output.

Linearity of Total Cost. The linearity of the total cost function in break-even charts disturbs many economists because it conflicts with the generalized curves of theory. But rising marginal production cost is not needed to determine the output which would theoretically maximize profits under imperfect competition. Moreover, many meticulous statistical investigations have found the total production cost function to be linear for several enterprises. To be sure, the extremes of the potential output range were not explored, since the samples largely covered operations in the thirties.[8] Had wartime outputs that pressed hard on physical capacity been included, it is possible that the curve would have turned up. Doubtless operations that would crowd capacity to the point of rising marginal production costs are conceivable. The real question, however, is whether they are likely. The cost penalties of superfull production may be so great and so apparent that output in this area is unlikely.

There are severe limitations on the research refinements that are practical for break-even analysis. It is costly to get precise estimates of cost functions by careful research. The error range from cheaper methods is often tolerable practically, particularly when shifts of the cost functions cause estimating errors that are much wider. These shifts often have more practical interest than the function's precise shape, at least over the range of normal operations, for changes in factor prices are dramatic in their impact today and changes in technology and product design often take place continuously.

B. Validity of Revenue Functions

The revenue function of break-even analysis holds selling price constant over the range of output, an assumption that is practical for many enterprises because of the inflexibility of selling prices and the existence of an area of price discretion. This departure from the assumptions of economic theory is made because break-even analysis is not concerned with the effect of price or quantity sold, but is confined to projections of the effects on costs and profits of various outputs that result from shifts in the firm's demand function. Analysis of demand is viewed as a separate problem.

The accuracy of a profit projection based on this constant price revenue line will be impaired by changes in list price, concessions, product mix, and distribution channel ratio. Changes in list price call for a new sales line which alters the profit function and the

---

[8] The range of output sampled looked wide in terms of the ratios of its high to its low and in terms of the experience of the preceding decade. Moreover, at least under "normal" conditions, imperfections of the market and rising marginal selling costs usually set limits on output considerably short of physical capacity. Differential and overtime pay, which might cause marginal cost to rise if not removed as factor price changes, were not significant in my published studies.

break-even point. Changes in price concessions, which in some industries are great and are likely to be correlated with output, will also vitiate the profit forecast, and are harder to allow for.

Changes in the composition of demand impair the accuracy of the static sales line and may vitiate the profit projection. Whenever products differ in contribution margin and there is variation in product mix from period to period, profits will vary at a given output rate, if output is measured by an index that is appropriate for getting a production cost function. Under these circumstances, the constant price sales line is inaccurate, even as a static function. Two different combinations of products that are equal in amount as measured by the output index will not yield equal revenue. Only by measuring output in current sales dollars can total revenue be a single valued function of output. But if this is done, cost will not be the same for output of different product composition.

Changes in the proportion of output that goes through the various distribution channels have serious effects in some firms, where the contribution margin differs greatly among channels (for example between original equipment and retail dealer sales of automobile accessories). The channel proportion is often neither stable nor precisely correlated with output.

One way out of these difficulties that I have found helpful is to set up a family of revenue lines, each one applicable to a specified product mix and distribution channel ratio.

C. Dynamic Forces

Dynamic forces impose added limitations on profit projections from static and partial cost and revenue functions, however accurately determined. Concentration on short-run cost functions has led to neglect of other elements of the cost structure of the enterprise. Changes in factor prices, technology, and scale and depth of plant, shift and modify the static cost function. These changes take place continuously and their impact is intertwined so that it is normally not possible to separate them empirically from short-run adjustments.

The distinction between short-run and long-run cost, for example, is continuously blurred. Conceptually, the basis of the distinction is the degree of adaptation of cost to output rate. This conventional dichotomy of long run versus short run should be expanded in theory to envision a whole family of cost curves that differ in the degree of adaptation, with the conventional long-run cost curve as the limit of perfect adaptation. Adjustments to higher output take a variety of forms short of adding an entire balance plant unit. They represent jumps from one short-run curve to another, not just movement along one curve.

The relation of technology to cost behavior is also more subtle than implied in theory. Changes in scale, in flexibility, and in management methods are often all represented in a single technical improvement.

These dynamic changes in costs and selling prices are likely to be highly correlated with the firm's output. This will reduce the reliability of forecasts of profits that are based upon assumed independence. A single company's volume decline is not likely to be independent of a downturn of a general business activity. And it is improbable that management's adaptation to this changed situation would produce an output expenditure pattern just like that produced by the operating plans of today's volume expectations.

Break-even analysis is virtually useless for some firms. This is particularly likely when materials that fluctuate widely in price are a predominant cost, when the product mix varies greatly and profit margins differ among products, when advertising or sales promotion are important and highly shiftable, or when the product design or technology changes continuously over short periods.

D. Profits Controllable

Profits in modern enterprise are not as purely passive as economic doctrine implies. Profits are controllable by management to an important degree. Costs are more reducible and manipulable than economists have recognized. Profit maximization in the short-run sense is seldom the dominant objective and the pressure for efficiency is not, as assumed in theory, constant and always sufficient. It varies dramatically over the cycle and with the fortunes of the firm. There are, therefore, significant fluctuations in the intensity of the compulsion to attain the least cost combination. Top management of a major railroad estimates that two years of systematic indoctrination at all management levels will be required to get the efficiency drive back to the prewar level.

This can affect costs because there is much room for improving efficiency in even the best managed concerns, and because a wide area of uncertainty exists as to the least cost combination for specified conditions of output, factor prices, and technology. For example, the methods for determining economic lot size differ greatly and cannot all be best.

Another condition that makes reported profits significantly controllable has been mentioned; namely, the wide time latitude that exists in the incidence of real cost upon expenditures. Important parts of production, selling, and administrative expense relate to past or future output and can be postponed over long periods.

Price jurisdiction provides another means of controlling profits. Big business under monopolistic competition does not continuously set prices to maximize profits in the short run. There are many indications that prices in many industries are lower than would be most profitable today. In many companies prices that were high enough to retain the prewar break-even point would put profits so high at current output rates that they would have serious consequences for public and labor relations. The postwar shift in the profit function is probably due in large part to the changed relation of cost prices and selling prices. A rise in break-even point frequently indicates that price advances have not kept pace with shifts in cost.

This controllability of short-term profits means that the empirical profit function is less reliably determined and forecasted and has less economic meaning than has been supposed. It also suggests that a doctrine of respectable profits should replace our notions of a continuous and uniform drive to profit maximization.

E. Summary of Limitations

The projection of the short-run, static profit output function of break-even charts is not a reliable forecast of future profits. The break-even point indicated by charts presupposes continuation of today's relative prices and expenditures patterns. Hence, it does not accurately forecast the probable future break-even point in the event of a business decline. A break-even chart is an oversimplified analysis of expected profits at various levels of output. The basic premise that profit is a single valued function of output is wrong. Profit will, of course, vary with changes in output; but it also will vary with changes in production plans and in the intensity and kinds of selling efforts. The profit function will also be buffeted about by the vast impersonal forces of the market. Hence, at best, any single break-even chart can only show profit expectations under a single set of assumptions regarding external market conditions and internal management strategy.

In typical break-even analysis, the static cost function has not been determined with much precision. Concentration on short-run cost functions has led, moreover, to neglect of other elements of the enterprise cost structure, which impairs the accuracy of projections of the short-run cost function. Changes in the composition of demand and in costs and in prices are, moreover, likely to be highly correlated with the firm's output. Despite rigidities of prices and of wage rates, a decline in general business activity will shift the functional relationships that were presumed to be independent.

IV. Usefulness of Break-Even Analysis

The empirical short-run profit function has more stability than the foregoing discussion of its limitations might imply. One reason is that shifts in the cost function tend to be accompanied (with some lag) by similar changes in selling prices in many imperfectly competitive enterprises. This is partly the result of the use of cost plus formulas to set and adjust prices. Another reason is that the pressure for efficiency is intensified in periods of adversity. The controllability and postponability of expenditures can in some degree compensate for uncontrollable shifts in selling prices and stickiness in factor prices.

Under modern competitive conditions, selling price and the intensity of selling efforts are not normally adjusted frequently to short-term shifts of the firm's demand. Hence the assumptions of constant selling price and essentially passive selling cost adjustments are more realistic and useful for short-run adjustments under normal conditions than economic logicians might think.

Contributions to Economic Analysis. Break-even analysis can make solid contributions to the development of enterprise economics. The importance of fixed costs makes total cost and profits vary significantly as a function of output rate. Projections of this short-run relationship can be useful. Break-even charts and flexible budgets have been responsible for a vast amount of inductive investigation of the short-run cost and profit functions which dwarfs the pitifully few empirical studies made by economists.

This kind of analysis can also provide insight into the bases of business decisions which should lead to reexamination of some tenets of received doctrine. For example, it provides added evidence that cost behavior patterns in a modern enterprise differ in important respects from the theoretical model, that knowledge of these behavior patterns by management is far less precise than assumed, and that the things maximized by business executives may differ greatly from theoretical assumptions.

Managerial Usefulness. Ambitious claims have been made concerning the managerial usefulness of break-even charts. They include not only profit projections but also expense control and price determination. For these added purposes, as for profit projection, the limitations discussed above impair but do not destroy their usefulness.

Empirical cost functions can be highly useful for expense control. But for this purpose they must deal with components of cost, and should be confined to those costs that are controllable at each area of responsibility. Although this kind of flexible budget may be built up to a break-even chart, it is not a by-product.

Thus conceived, the break-even analysis no longer concentrates on the break-even point or on a single static profit function. Instead, it provides a flexible set of projections of costs and revenue under expected future conditions and under alternative management programs. Profit prediction under these multiple conditions becomes then a tool for profit making.

40. COST-VOLUME-PROFIT ANALYSIS UNDER CONDITIONS OF UNCERTAINTY *

Robert K. Jaedicke and Alexander A. Robichek †

Cost-volume-profit analysis is frequently used by management as a basis for choosing among alternatives such decisions as (1) the sales volume required to attain a given level of profits, and (2) the most profitable combination of products to produce and sell. However, the fact that traditional C-V-P analysis does not include adjustments for risk and uncertainty may, in any given instance, severely limit its usefulness. Some of the limitations can be seen from the following example.

Assume that the firm is considering the introduction of two new products, either of which can be produced by using present facilities. Both products require an increase in annual fixed cost of the same amount, say $400,000. Each product has the same selling price and variable cost per unit, say $10 and $8 respectively, and each requires the same amount of capacity. Using these data, the break-even point of either product is 200,000 units. C-V-P analysis helps to establish the break-even volume of each product, but this analysis does not distinguish the relative desirability of the two products for at least two reasons.

The first piece of missing information is the *expected* sales volume of each product. Obviously, if the annual sales of A are expected to be 300,000 units and of B are expected to be 350,000 units, then B is clearly preferred to A as far as the sales expectation is concerned.

However, assume that the expected annual sales of each product are the same—say 300,000 units. Is it right to conclude that management should be indifferent as far as a choice between A and B is concerned? The answer is *no, unless* each sales expectation is certain. If both sales estimates are subject to uncertainty, the decision process will be improved if the relative risk associated with each product can

---

* From *The Accounting Review* (October, 1964). Reprinted by permission of the American Accounting Association.

† Robert K. Jaedicke, Associate Professor of Accounting, Graduate School of Business Administration, Stanford University, Stanford, California; Alexander A. Robichek, Professor of Accounting, Graduate School of Business Administration, Stanford University, Stanford, California.

somehow be brought into the analysis. The discussion which follows suggests some changes which might be made in traditional C-V-P analysis so as to make it a more useful tool in analyzing decision problems under uncertainty.

Some Probability Concepts Related to C-V-P Analysis

In the previous section, it was pointed out that the *expected* volume of the annual sales is an important decision variable. Some concepts of probability will be discussed using the example posed earlier.

The four fundamental relationships used in the example were (1) the selling price per unit, (2) the variable cost per unit, (3) the total fixed cost, and (4) the expected sales volume of each product. In any given decision problem, all four of these factors can be uncertain. However, it may be that, *relative to* the expected sales quantity, the costs and selling prices are quite certain; that is, for analytical purposes, the decision maker may be justified in treating several factors as certainty equivalents. Such a procedure simplifies the analysis and will be followed here as a first approximation. In this section of the paper, sales volume will be treated as the only uncertain quantity. Later, all decision factors in the above example will be treated under conditions of uncertainty.

In the example, sales volume is treated as a *random variable*. A random variable can be thought of as an *unknown quantity*. In this case, the best decision hinges on the value of the random variable, sales volume of each product. One decision approach which allows for uncertainty is to estimate, for each random variable, the likelihood that the random variable will take on various possible values. Such

TABLE I

PROBABILITY DISTRIBUTION FOR PRODUCTS A AND B

Events (Units Demanded)	Probability Distribution— (Product A)	Probability Distribution— (Product B)
50,000	—	.1
100,000	.1	.1
200,000	.2	.1
300,000	.4	.2
400,000	.2	.4
500,000	.1	.1
	1.00	1.00

an estimate is called a subjective probability distribution. The decision would then be made by choosing that course of action which has the highest *expected monetary value*. This approach is illustrated in Table I.

The expected value of the random variables, sales demand for each product, is calculated by weighting the possible conditional values by their respective probabilities. In other words, the expected value is a weighted average. The calculation is given in Table II.

Based on an expected value approach, the firm should select Product B rather than A. The expected profits of each possible action are as follows:

> Product A:
> $2(300,000 units) — $400,000 = $200,000
> Product B:
> $2(305,000 units) — $400,000 = $210,000

Several observations are appropriate at this point. First, the respective probabilities for each product, used in Table I, add to 1.00. Furthermore, the possible demand levels (events) are assumed to be mutually exclusive and also exhaustive; that is, the listing is done in such a way that no two events can happen simultaneously and any events *not* listed are assumed to have a zero probability of occurring. Herein are three important (basic) concepts of probability analyses.

TABLE II

EXPECTED VALUE OF SALES DEMAND FOR PRODUCTS A AND B

(1) Event	*(2)* P(A)	*(1 × 2)*	*(3)* P(B)	*(1 × 3)*
50,000	—	—	.1	5,000
100,000	.1	10,000	.1	10,000
200,000	.2	40,000	.1	20,000
300,000	.4	120,000	.2	60,000
400,000	.2	80,000	.4	160,000
500,000	.1	50,000	.1	50,000
	1.00		1.00	
Expected Value		300,000 units		305,000 units

Secondly, the probability distributions may have been assigned by using historical demand data on similar products, or the weights may be purely subjective in the sense that there is no historical data available. Even if the probability distributions are entirely subjective, this approach still has merit. It allows the estimator to express his uncertainty about the sales estimate. An estimate of sales is necessary to make a decision. Hence, the question is *not* whether an estimate must be made, but simply a question of the best way to make and express the estimate.

Now, suppose that the expected value of sales for each product is 300,000, as shown in Table III. In this example, it is easy to see that the firm would *not* be indifferent between Products A and B, even though the expected value of sales is 300,000 units in both cases. In the case of Product A, for example, there is a .1 chance that sales will be only 100,000 units, and in that case, a loss of $200,000 would be incurred (i.e., $2 × 100,000 units − $400,000). On the other hand, there is a .3 chance that sales will be above 300,000 units and if this is the case, higher profits are possible with Product A than with Product B. Hence, the firm's attitude toward risk becomes important. The expected value (or the mean of the distribution) is important, but so is the "spread" in the distribution. Typically, the greater the "spead," the greater the risk involved. A quantitative measure of the spread is available in the form of the standard deviation of the distribution, and this concept and its application will be refined later in the paper.

TABLE III

Demand	P(A)	E.V.(A)	P(B)	E.V.(B)
100,000 units	.1	10,000	—	—
200,000 units	.2	40,000	—	—
300,000 units	.4	120,000	1.00	300,000
400,000 units	.2	80,000	—	—
500,000 units	.1	50,000	—	—
	1.00		1.00	
Expected Sales Demand	300,000			300,000

THE NORMAL PROBABILITY DISTRIBUTION

The preceding examples were highly simplified and yet the calculations are relatively long and cumbersome. The possible sales volumes were few in number and the probability distribution was discrete; that is, a sales volume of 205,762 units was considered an impossible event. The use of a continuous probability distribution is desirable not only because the calculation will usually be simplified but because the distribution may also be a more realistic description of the uncertainty aspects of the situation. The normal probability distribution will be introduced and used in the following analysis which illustrates the methodology involved. This distribution, although widely used, is not appropriate in all situations. The appropriate distribution depends on the decision problem and should, of course, be selected accordingly.

The normal probability distribution is a smooth, symmetric, continuous, bell-shaped curve as shown in Figure 1. The area under the curve sums to 1. The curve reaches a maximum at the mean of the distribution and one half the area lies on either side of the mean.

On the horizontal axis are plotted the values of the appropriate unknown quantity or random variable; in the examples used here, the unknown quantity is the sales for the coming periods.

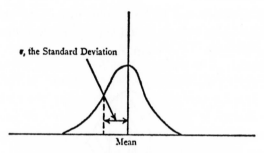

The Normal Probability Distribution

FIGURE 1

A particular normal probability distribution can be completely determined if its mean and its standard deviation, σ, are known. The standard deviation is a measure of the dispersion of the distribution about its mean. The area under any normal distribution is 1, but one distribution may be "spread out" more than another distribution. For example, in Figure 2, both normal distributions have the same area and the same mean. However, in one case the σ is 1 and in the other case the σ is greater than 1. The larger the σ, the more spread out is the distribution. It should be noted that the standard deviation is not an area but is a measure of the dispersion of the individual observations about the mean of all the observations—it is a distance.

Since the normal probability distribution is continuous rather than discrete, the probability of an event cannot be read directly from the graph. The unknown quantity must be thought of as being in an interval. Assume, for example, that the mean sales for the

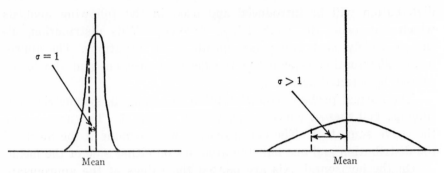

Normal Probability Distributions with Different Standard Deviations

FIGURE 2

coming period is estimated to be 10,000 units and the normal distribution appears as in Figure 3. Given Figure 3, certain probability statements can be made. For example:

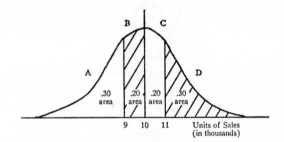

FIGURE 3

1. The probability of the actual sales being between 10,000 and 11,000 units is .20. This is shown by Area C. Because of the symmetry of the curve, the probability of the sales being between 9,000 and 10,000 is also .20. This is shown by shaded Area B. These probabilities can be given a frequency interpretation; that is, Area C indicates that the actual sales will be between 10,000 and 11,000 units in about 20 percent of the cases.

2. The probability of the actual sales being greater than 11,000 units is .30 as shown by Area D.

3. The probability of the sales being greater than 9,000 units is .70, the sum of Areas B, C, and D.

Given a specific normal distribution, it is possible to read probabilities of the type described above directly from a normal probability table.

Another important characteristic of any normal distribution is that approximately .50 of the area lies within ± .67 standard deviations of the mean; about .68 of the area lies within ± 1.0 standard deviations of the mean; .95 of the area lies within ± 1.96 standard deviations of the mean.

As was mentioned above, normal probabilities can be read from a normal probability table. A partial table of normal probabilities is given in Table IV. This table is the "right tail" of the distribution; that is, probabilities of the unknown quantity being greater than X standard deviations from the mean are given in the table. For example, the probability of the unknown quantity being greater than the mean plus $.35\sigma$ is .3632. The distribution tabulated is a normal distribution with mean zero and standard deviation of 1. Such a distribution is known as a standard normal distribution. However, any normal distribution can be standardized and hence, with proper adjustment, Table IV will serve for any normal distribution.

For example, consider the earlier case where the mean of the distribution is 10,000 units. The distribution was constructed so that the standard deviation is about 2,000 units.[1] To standardize the

TABLE IV

AREA UNDER THE NORMAL PROBABILITY FUNCTION

X	0.00	0.05
.1	.4602	.4404
.3	.3821	.3632
.5	.3085	.2912
.6	.2743	.2578
.7	.2420	.2266
.8	.2119	.1977
.9	.1841	.1711
1.0	.1587	.1469
1.1	.1357	.1251
1.5	.0668	.0606
2.0	.0228	.0202

distribution, use the following formula, where X is the number of standard deviations from the mean:

$$X = \frac{\text{Actual Sales} - \text{Mean Sales}}{\text{Standard deviation of the distribution}}$$

---

[1] To see why this normal distribution has a standard deviation of 2,000 units, remember that the probability of sales being greater than 11,000 units is .30. Now examine Table IV, and it can be seen that the probability of a random variable being greater than .5 standard deviations from the mean is .3085. Hence, 1,000 units are about the same as ½ standard deviations. So, 2,000 units are about 1 standard deviation.

To calculate the probability of the sales being greater than 11,000 units, first standardize the distribution and then use the table.

$$X = \frac{11,000 - 10,000}{2,000}$$
$$= .50 \text{ standard deviations}$$

The probability of being greater than .50 standard deviations from the mean, according to Table IV, is .3085. This same approximate result is shown by Figure 3, that is, Area D is .30.

The Normal Distribution Used in C-V-P Analysis

The normal distribution will now be used in a C-V-P analysis problem, assuming that sales quantity is a random variable. Assume that the per unit selling price is $3,000, the fixed cost is $5,800,000, and the variable cost per unit is $1,750. Break-even sales (in units) are calculated as follows:

$$S_B = \frac{\$5,800,000}{\$3,000 - \$1,750} = 4,640 \text{ units}$$

Furthermore, suppose that the sales manager estimates that the mean expected sales volume is 5,000 units and that it is equally likely that actual sales will be greater or less than the mean of 5,000 units. Furthermore, assume that the sales manager feels that there is roughly a ⅔ (i.e., .667) chance that the actual sales will be within 400 units of the mean. These subjective estimates can be expressed by using a normal distribution with mean $E(Q) = 5,000$ units and standard deviation $\sigma_q = 400$ units. The reason that σ_q is about 400 units is that, as mentioned earlier, about ⅔ of the area under the normal curve (actually .68) lies within 1 standard deviation of the mean. The probability distribution is shown in Figure 4.

The horizontal axis of Figure 4 denotes sales quantity. The probability of an actual sales event taking place is given by the area under the probability distribution. For example, the probability that the sales quantity will exceed 4,640 units (the break-even point) is the shaded area under the probability distribution (the probability of actual sales exceeding 4,640 units).

The probability distribution of Figure 4 can be superimposed on the profit portion of the traditional C-V-P; this is done in Figure 5.

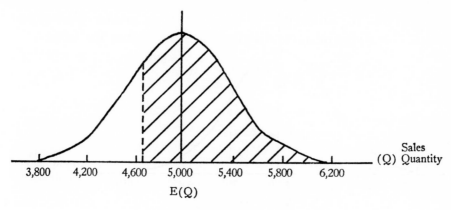

FIGURE 4

The values for price, fixed costs, and variable costs are presumed to be known with certainty. Expected profit is given by:

$$E(Z) = E(Q)(P\text{-}V) - F = \$450,000$$

where

$$\begin{aligned}
E(Z) &= \text{Expected Profit} \\
E(Q) &= \text{Expected Sales} \\
P &= \text{Price} \\
V &= \text{Variable Cost} \\
F &= \text{Fixed Cost}
\end{aligned}$$

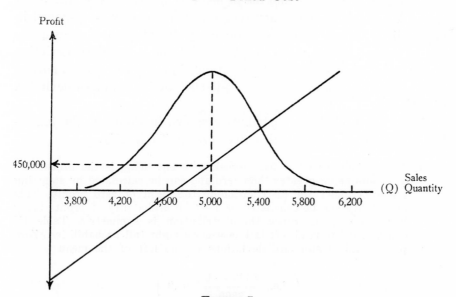

FIGURE 5

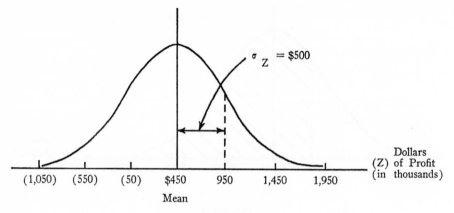

FIGURE 6

The standard deviation of the profit (σ_Z) is:

$$\sigma_Z = \sigma_Q \times \$1,250 \text{ contribution per unit}$$
$$= 400 \text{ units} \times \$1,250 = \$500,000$$

Since profits are directly related to the volume of sales, and since it is the level of profits which is often the concern of management, it may be desirable to separate the information in Figure 5 which relates to profit. Figure 6 is a graphical illustration of the relationship between profit level and the probability distribution of the profit level. A number of important relationships can now be obtained in probabilistic terms. Since the probability distribution of sales quantity is normal with a mean of 5,000 units and a standard deviation of 400 units, the probability distribution of profits will also be normal with a mean, as shown earlier, of $450,000 and a standard deviation of $500,000.

Using the probability distribution shown in Figure 6, the following probabilities can be calculated (using Table IV).

1. The probability of at least breaking even: This is the probability of profits being greater than zero and can be calculated by summing the area under the distribution to the right of zero profits. This probability can be calculated as 1—(the probability of profits being less than zero). Since the distribution is symmetric, Table IV can be used to read left tail as well as right tail probabilities. Zero profits fall .9 standard deviations to the left of the mean

$$\left(\text{i.e., } \frac{\$450 - 0}{\$500} = .9 \right)$$

Hence, the probability of profits being less than zero is:

$$P \text{ (Profits} < .9\sigma \text{ from the mean)} = .184$$

Therefore

$$P \text{ (Profits} > 0) = 1 - .184 = .816$$

2. The probability of profits being greater than \$200,000.

P (Profits > \$200,000)

$$= 1 - P \left(\text{Profits} < \frac{450 - 200}{500} \sigma \text{ from the mean} \right)$$

$$= 1 - P \text{ (Profits} < .5\sigma \text{ from the mean)}$$
$$= 1 - .3085 = .692$$

3. The probability of the loss being greater than \$300,000.

P (Loss > \$300,000)

$$= P \left(\text{Loss} > \frac{450 - (-300)}{500}, \text{ or } 1.5\sigma \text{ from the mean} \right)$$

$P = .067.$

The question of how the above information can be used now arises. The manager, in choosing between this product and other products or other lines of activity, can probably improve his decision by considering the risk involved. He knows that the break-even sales are at a level of 4,640 units. He knows that the expected sales are 5,000 units which would yield a profit of \$450,000. Surely, he would benefit from knowing that:

1. The probability of at least reaching break-even sales is .816.
2. The probability of making at least \$200,000 profit is .692.
3. The probability of making at least \$450,000 profit is .50.
4. The probability of incurring losses, i.e., not achieving the break-even sales volume, is (1.816, or .184).
5. The probability of incurring a \$300,000 or greater loss is .067, etc.

If the manager is comparing this product with other products, probability analysis combined with C-V-P allows a comparison of the risk involved in each product, as well as a comparison of relative break-even points and expected profits. Given the firm's attitude toward and willingness to assume risk (of losses as well as high profits), the decision of choosing among alternatives should be facilitated by the above analysis.

SEVERAL RELEVANT FACTORS PROBABILISTIC

It is evident from the above discussion that profit, Z, is a function of the quantity of sales in units (Q); the unit selling price (P); the fixed cost (F); and the variable cost (V). Up to this point P, F, and V were considered only as given constants, so that profit was variable only as a function of changes in sales quantity. In the following discussion, P, F, and V will be treated in a manner similar to Q, i.e., as random variables whose probability distribution is known. Continuing the example from the preceding section, let

Variable	Expectation (Mean)	Standard Deviation
Sales Quantity (Q)	$E(Q') = 5,000$ units	$\sigma_Q' = 400$ units
Selling Price (P)	$E(P') = \$3,000^2$	$\sigma_P' = \$50^2$
Fixed Costs (F)	$E(F') = \$5,800,000^2$	$\sigma_F' = \$100,000^2$
Variable Costs (V)	$E(V') = \$1,750^2$	$\sigma_V' = \$75^2$

For purposes of illustration, the random variables will be assumed to be independent, so that no correlation exists between events of the different random variables.[3] In this case, the expected profit $E(Z')$ and the related standard deviation $\sigma_{Z'}$ can be calculated as follows:

$$E(Z') = E(Q')[E(P') - E(V')] - E(F')$$
$$= \$450,000$$
$$\sigma_{Z'}{}^{[4]} = \$681,500$$

Note that when factors other than sales are treated as random variables, the expected profit is still $450,000 as in the previous cases. However, the profit's risk as measured by the standard deviation is

---

[2] The mean and standard deviation for P, F, and V can be established by using the same method described earlier; that is, the sales manager may estimate a mean selling price of $3,000 per unit and, given the above information, he should feel that there is roughly a ⅔ probability that the actual sales price per unit will be within $50 of this mean estimate.

[3] This assumption is made to facilitate computation in the example. Where correlation among variables is present the computational procedure must take into account the values of the respective covariances.

[4] For the case of independent variables given here, $\sigma_{Z'}$ is the solution value in the equation:

$$\sigma_Z = \sqrt{[\sigma_Q{}^2(\sigma_P{}^2 + \sigma_V{}^2) + E(Q')^2(\sigma_V{}^2 + \sigma_V{}^2) + [E(P') - E(V')]^2\sigma_Q{}^2 + \sigma_F{}^2]}$$

TABLE V

COMPARISON OF EXPECTED PROFITS, STANDARD DEVIATIONS OF PROFITS,
AND SELECT PROBABILISTIC MEASURES *

| | *Products* | | |
	(1)	*(2)*	*(3)*
Expected profit	$450,000	$450,000	$ 450,000
Standard deviation of profit	$500,000	$681,500	$1,253,000
The probability of:			
(a) at least breaking even	.816	.745	.641
(b) profit at least +$250,000	.655	.615	.564
(c) profit at least +$600,000	.382	.413	.456
(d) loss greater than $300,000	.067	.136	.274

* Note: The above probabilities, in some cases, cannot be read from Table IV. However, all probabilities come from a more complete version of Table IV.

increased from $500,000 to $681,500. The reason for this is that the variability in all of the components (i.e., sales price, cost, etc.) will add to the variability in the profit. Is this change in the standard deviation significant? The significance of the change is a value judgment based on a comparison of various probabilistic measures and on the firm's attitude toward risk. Using a normal distribution, Table V compares expected profits, standard deviations of profits, and select probabilistic measures for three hypothetical products.

In all three situations, the proposed products have the same break-even quantity—4,640 units. The first case is the first example discussed where sales quantity is the only random variable. The second case is the one just discussed, that is, all factors are probabilistic. In the third case, the assumed product has the same expected values for selling price, variable cost, fixed cost, and sales volume, but the standard deviations on each of these random variables have been increased to $\sigma_{Q''} = 600$ (instead of 400 units); $\sigma_{P''} = \$125$ (instead of $50); $\sigma_{F''} = \$200,000$ (instead of $100,000); and $\sigma_{V''} = \$150$ (instead of $75).

Table V shows the relative "risk" involved in the three new products which have been proposed. The chances of at least breaking even are greatest with Product 1. However, even though the standard deviation of the profit on Product 3 is over twice that of Product 1, the probability of breaking even on Product 3 is only .17 lower than Product 1. Likewise, the probability of earning at least $250,000 profit is higher for Product 1 (which has the lowest σ) than for the other two products.

However, note that the probability of earning profits above the expected value of $450,000 (for each product) is *greater* for Products 2 and 3 than for 1. If the firm is willing to assume some risk, the chances of high profits are improved with Product 3, rather than with 2 and 1. To offset this, however, the chance of loss is also greatest with Product 3. This is to be expected, since Product 3 has the highest standard deviation (variability) as far as profit is concerned.

The best alternative cannot be chosen without some statement of the firm's attitude toward risk. However, given a certain attitude, the proper choice should be facilitated by using probability information of the type given in Table V. As an example, suppose that the firm's position is such that any loss at all may have an adverse effect on its ability to stay in business. Some probability criteria can, perhaps, be established in order to screen proposals for new products. If, for example, the top management feels that any project which is acceptable must have no greater than a .30 probability of incurring a loss, then Projects 1 or 2 would be acceptable but Project 3 would not.

On the other hand, the firm's attitude toward risk may be such that the possibility of high profit is attractive, provided the probability of losses can be reasonably controlled. In this case, it may be possible to set a range within which acceptable projects must fall. For example, suppose that the firm is willing to accept projects where the probability of profits being greater than $600,000 is at least .40, provided that the probability of a loss being greater than $300,000 does not exceed .15. In this case, Project 2 would be acceptable, but Project 3 would not. Given statements of attitude toward risk of this nature, it seems that a probability dimension added to C-V-P analysis would be useful.

SUMMARY AND CONCLUSION

In many cases, the choice among alternatives is facilitated greatly by C-V-P analysis. However, traditional C-V-P analysis does not take account of the relative risk of various alternatives. The interaction of costs, selling prices, and volume is important in summarizing the effect of various alternatives on the profits of the firm. The techniques discussed in this paper preserve the traditional analysis but also add another dimension—that is, risk is brought in as another important decision factor. The statement of probabilities with respect to various levels of profits and losses for each alternative should aid the decision maker once his attitude toward risk has been defined.

41. CAPITAL BUDGET FORMULAE *

William J. Vatter †

The literature of capital budgeting has presented a fair number of "different" formulae, which range from the simplest financial tabulations to fairly complicated patterns. All these formulae attempt to combine the financial factors related to an investment opportunity into a single expression; this single expression is intended to serve as the prime criterion for accepting or rejecting an investment proposal, or it may be used as a means of ranking several such proposals in some form of preference scale.[1]

To the layman, these formulae present a formidable array; there are "first year rate of return" comparisons, "rate of return on average investment," "average return on initial investment," "pay-out" (both simple and time adjusted), "investor's present worth" comparison, the "time adjusted rate of return," and the "discounted cash flow" approach—not to mention the Terborgh-MAPI formula and the sets of charts which accompany it. All these formulae and their variants lend an aura of undue complexity to investment decisions. They make an admittedly difficult problem appear even more perplexing than it is, simply because of the variety of ways in which it can be viewed.

There have been attempts to compare the results obtained from the use of various formulae.[2] Some writers give the impression that specific formulae are applicable to given circumstances; some others attribute various biases or inadequacies to the different approaches;

* Reprinted from the *California Management Review*, Vol. III, No. 1 (Fall, 1960). Reprinted by permission of the Regents of the University of California.
† Professor William J. Vatter, School of Business Administration, University of California, Berkeley, California.

[1] See, for instance, Pearson Hunt, C. M. Williams, and Gordon Donaldson, *Basic Business Finance* (Homewood, Ill.: Richard D. Irwin, Inc., 1958), pp. 477-95; Claude S. George, *Management in Industry* (New York: Prentice-Hall, Inc., 1959), pp. 255-76, Robert N. Anthony, *Management Accounting* (Homewood, Ill.: Richard D. Irwin, Inc., 1956), pp. 392-412.
[2] The most recent attempt of this kind is *Return on Capital as a Guide to Managerial Decisions, N.A.A. Research Report No. 35* (New York: National Association of Accountants, December 1, 1959), 107 pp.

still others try to relate various formulae to each other in more or less direct ways.[3]

There is no doubt that the range of problems encountered in the field of capital budgeting is wide. There are many dark and dusty corners in which confusions and frustrations may lurk. However, the situation could be made a bit more clear, to the uninitiated at least, if it were recognized that the "different" methods are not really so vastly divergent as their proponents or critics imply. There is a general approach to investment problems; this could be used to relate the various formulae to each other so as to clarify relationships and emphasis. Then one might possibly be able to see (by reference to the basic relationship) just what the various formulae have in common, to what extent and in what ways they differ, and to what degree they conflict, supplement, or substitute for each other.

This paper is an attempt to set up the basic pattern of relationships in a general formula of which the special methods are restricted cases or special applications.[4]

WHY INVEST?

Investment is the sacrifice of current financial advantage (such as purchasing power) in return for some future return; the decision to invest or not to do so involves a comparison of the current sacrifice with future expectations. The comparison may be written:

$$C = \frac{A_0}{R^0} + \frac{A_1}{R^1} + \frac{A_2}{R^2} + \frac{A_3}{R^3} + \frac{A_4}{R^4} \cdots \frac{A_k}{R^k}$$

In this expression, C is the capital commitment, the present outlay or sacrifice required to establish the investment, measured in terms of immediate dollar payment. The A's in the expression are the individual amounts expected to be received at the end of each time period in the future. These time periods are of uniform length. The subscripts thus indicate the number of periods that will pass

---

[3] The October, 1955, issue of the *Journal of Business* was a compendium of this kind of comparison. The article by M. J. Gordon, "The Payoff Period and the Rate of Return," pp. 253-61, and that by Joel Dean and Winfield Smith, "MAPI and Comprehensive Capital Control," pp. 261-74, in this issue are of especial interest.

[4] This general relationship is not a new discovery. It was clearly developed and applied to various kinds of plant investment decisions in W. N. Mitchell, *Production Management* (Chicago: University of Chicago Press, 1931). There is considerable evidence that these relationships were understood and used even earlier.

before the given A is received. Typically, the series of A's is limited, and the last one is A_k, an amount to be received k periods hence.

The economic cost of waiting is measured by R, the compound interest conversion factor; this expresses the effect of an interest rate applied to the timing of future receipts. R is $(1 + i)$; the conversion factor is applied by successive and reiterative multiplication as time proceeds into the future; *per contra*, the conversion factor is applied by reiterative division as time moves backward into the past. Thus, a future payment scheduled for one year later than the present represents an accumulated amount of XR, and the present significance of an item deferred n years (interest conversion periods) is $X \div R^n$—that is, X divided by the conversion factor n times. The exponent of the factor R indicates the number of periods of deferment, for each of which the reiterative division by R is made.[5]

The expression sketched above may be used to describe and define the financial effect of any investment proposal, by putting the relevant data into the pattern and simplifying the result. A proposition that will yield $500 at the end of one year and an additional $400 at the end of the second year, may be reduced to an equivalent "present worth" using a 5 percent annual interest rate:

$$C = \frac{\$500}{(1.05)} + \frac{\$400}{(1.05)\,(1.05)}$$

Dividing $500 by (1.05) yields $476.19; dividing $400 by 1.05 and then again dividing the result by 1.05 gives $362.81. Alternatively, we may use a table of "discounting factors" to establish that $1/1.05$ is .95238, and that $1/(1.05)^2$ is .90703; multiplying by these numbers is the same as dividing by 1.05 once and twice respectively. Either way, the computation gives a total "present worth" of $839. This means that $839 invested now at 5 percent compounded annually provides for the return of $500 one year hence, and $400 two years from now, leaving nothing to be settled thereafter.

Should the outlay required to obtain these future receipts be more than $839, the return will be less than 5 percent compounded annually. Should there be added to the proposal that an additional $200 will be forthcoming four years from now, the present worth of $200 ($200 divided by 1.05 four times, or multiplied by the appro-

---

[5] I am indebted again to Mitchell (see Footnote 4) for the symbol R^n to replace the more common but confusing $(1+i)^n$. Compound interest is always computed by the use of the conversion factor, not the rate of interest as such. For elaboration of this usage, see W. N. Mitchell, *Organization and Management of Production* (New York: McGraw-Hill Book Co., Inc., 1939), pp. 374-5.

priate discounting factor, $1/[1.05]^4 = .82270$) would be put into the calculation. This would add \$164.54 to the commuted returns; the total of \$1,003.54 is the amount which, invested at 5 percent compounded annually, would yield the indicated future receipts. At a higher price than \$1,003.54, the investment would yield less, and at a lower price it would yield more, than 5 percent compounded annually.

Thus, in general terms the investment pattern is a relationship of three sets of data: the acquisition cost, price, or capital commitment; the series of expected receipts; and the effect of the interest conversion factor which applies the "rate of return." Adjustment of any one of these sets of data entails a compensatory change in one or both of the others. Further, for any given situation, specifying two of the three sets of data permits computation of the third one. The example in the preceding paragraph established the price of an investment, using the specified future receipts and the interest conversion factor, but the rate of return may be established by using the series of future receipts and the present outlay required to obtain them. Had the data of the foregoing example been given without specifying the rate of return, we could have written the investment expression as follows:

$$\$1.003.54 = \frac{\$500}{R^1} + \frac{\$400}{R^2} + \frac{\$200}{R^4}$$

This expression could then be manipulated to "solve" for R, using interest factors from tables and trial and error computation to find that interest conversion factor which would reduce the future receipts to a present worth of \$1,003.54. This, as we already know, is (1.05) and the rate of return is thus 5 percent per annum.

VARIATIONS ON A THEME

The computations just described illustrate two of the methods of evaluating an investment. The "investor's present worth" approach assumes the rate of return as given and solves for the "price," or capital outlay. The desirability of the proposal is measured by the relation of the computed "price" to the actual one. The "discounted cash flow" method employs an identical relationship, but the solution is worked out from the given "price" to establish the rate of return. The difference in method is merely a difference in viewpoint, for the relationship is the same.

Similarly, the calculations could have been set up to leave the time factor as the one to be established. For instance, suppose that the case under discussion involved (instead of the $200 receipt four years from now) a series of $50 receipts at the end of each of the four years. The whole proposal would then involve future receipts of $550 after one year, $450 after two years, and $50 after the third and fourth years. Given a price of $1,000 for the package, how many of the $50 payments would be necessary to justify the investment? This obviously depends upon the rate of return that is required; assuming this to be zero results in the familiar "payout" calculation. By the end of two years, the receipts total $1,000, and the payout period is thus two years.

Since a zero rate of return is (or should be) an unattractive investment outlook, a more meaningful result could be had by using, say, the 5 percent annual rate to commute the prospective receipts. The first year's $550 would reduce ($550 × .95238) to $523.81, and the second year's $450 would be ($450 × .90703), or $408.16. The sum of these is $931.97, not enough to cover the capital cost. The $50 to be received after three years discounts to ($50 × .86384) $43.19, which makes the total three-year commutation only $975.16.

The last $50 receipts adds $41.13 to the previous total, making it $1,016.29. Thus, the investment will not yield 5 percent on the capital cost unless it includes this last item. This analysis, referred to as a "time adjusted payout," is based on the same general formula as was described earlier, and is in principle no different. The fact that the solution for the number of years to realize a return of 5 percent was done by approximation does not alter the validity of the general formula. Incidentally, it may be observed that we should be willing to pay exactly $12.75 more for the $50 per year arrangement than we would have paid for the $200 after four years proposal, for if the rate of return is 5 percent per year, the rearrangement of $50 per year is "worth" that much more than the $1,003.54 computed previously.

A SUMMARY FORMULA

As has been pointed out, all three of the approaches ("investor's present worth," "discounted cash flow," and "time adjusted payout") are really the same set of relationships. This may be written:

$$C = \sum_{n=0}^{n=k} \left(\frac{A_n}{R^n} \right)$$

The entire gamut of investment evaluations can be related specifically to this general formula, as will appear in subsequent paragraphs. The terms in the formula, however, require some explanation. The capital commitment (C) is a single sum, the net expenditure at "time zero," the present. This may be the cash price for the item purchased at this date, less the trade-in allowance (but increased by the cash value of what was traded in) ; but the capital commitment may also involve separate computations to bring to the present (time zero) whatever other capital contributions may be required to carry out the investment arrangement, as in an installment acquisition. The rate used to arrive at this commutation of capital outlays may be the same, or it may be a different one than that used to evaluate the investment as a whole.

The future receipts are also "net"; that is, each future receipt may be offset by such amounts as may be applicable. The returns from the use of a machine, for instance, may be reduced by the operating costs to be incurred in the respective future periods. These future net receipts are not, however, to be construed as "income" in its ordinary sense. Business income is typically calculated for a period shorter than an investment term, and it, therefore, entails accrual or deferment of certain items of receipt or expenditure to match them properly with the economic flows of revenue and expense. Future net receipts in the investment formula must be left unadjusted by such accruals or deferments.[6]

Another observation of importance is that the general investment formula does not make an explicit allowance or provision for the recovery of capital investment; this is implicit in the relationship and is automatically included in the computations. One indication of this is the fact, noted earlier, that the simple payout calculation is a zero rate of return variant of the general pattern. If the rate of return is taken as zero, every R in the general formula is reduced to unity, and the general formula reduces to:

$$C = \sum_{n=0}^{n=k} \left(\frac{A_n}{1} \right) , \text{then,} \frac{C}{\sum_{n=0}^{n=k} \left(A_n \right)} = 1$$

_____

[6] The fact that business (accounting) income is not a cash flow is not always clearly recognized. To measure income the accounting process must be such as to remove the effects of timing distortions caused by technology and by credit, so as to reflect economic events as they affect the firm from day to day.

If the annual receipts are the same in every year (A is a constant), the last mentioned relation becomes:

$$k = \frac{C}{A} \text{ or } C = kA$$

FIRST OR "NEXT YEAR" APPROACHES

Another variant of the investment analysis arises from reducing the number of future periods under consideration to one, and then, assuming that the first year receipt may be viewed as two items, (a) income for the first year and (b) full recovery of the invested capital at the end of the first year. This rearrangement makes the formula:

$$C = \frac{A}{R} + \frac{C}{R}$$

This, in turn, may be rearranged:

$$CR = A + C; R = \frac{A}{C} + \frac{C}{C} \text{ and } R - 1 = \frac{A}{C}$$

Substitution of $(1 + i)$ for R gives:

$$1 + i - 1 = \frac{A}{C} \quad i = \frac{A}{C} \text{ or } C = \frac{A}{i}$$

This last is an old friend, the "simple capitalization" formula, which makes it clear that the assumption of separate and complete capital recovery at the end of the first period is equivalent to perpetual receipt of A at the end of every period in the future. Thus the investment formula becomes identical with the present worth of a perpetuity.[7]

---

[7] Interestingly enough, the perpetuity formula is itself an open sesame to a number of other investment formulae, since the notion of an annuity is developed from it. Every terminal annuity is the difference between two perpetuities, one beginning at the inception of the annuity term, the other starting at the end of the term. The initial perpetuity, less the second one, is the annuity. Then,

$$C = \frac{A}{(R-1)} - \frac{A}{(R-1)} \left(\frac{1}{R^n}\right) \text{ which converts to } C = \frac{AR^n}{R^n(R-1)} - \frac{A}{R^n(R-1)} = \frac{A - AR^{-n}}{R-1} = A\left[\frac{1-(1+i)^{-n}}{i}\right]$$

Similarly, the "accumulation" of the terminal annuity (at the end of the term) is:

$$\frac{A - AR^n}{R-1} (R^n) = \frac{AR^n - A}{R-1} = A\left[\frac{(1+i)^n-1}{i}\right]$$

(See Mitchell, Footnote 4, for further elaboration and application of this approach to deferred, interim, and other special annuity patterns.)

Average Rate of Return

By appropriate adjustment, the general formula may be made to fit other investment notions. For example, it may be used to establish the average rate of return over more than a single period. Usually this involves the use of simple interest to express the rate of return over the multiperiod term. This is expected, if the rate of return is expected to be a simple arithmetic average rate over the term; compound interest computations do not fit simple averages of rates.

In this variant computation, R becomes $(1 + ni)$ instead of $(1 + i)^n$, and the recovery of capital is specifically provided for. The formula becomes:

$$C = \frac{\sum_{n=0}^{n=k}(A_n)}{(1 + ki) - 1} = \frac{\sum_{n=0}^{n=k}(A_n)}{ki}$$

$$C_{ki} = \sum_{n=0}^{n=k}(A_n) \quad \text{and} \quad i = \frac{\sum_{n=0}^{n=k}(A_n)}{Ck} \quad \text{or} \quad \frac{\sum_{n=0}^{n=k}(A_n)\left(\frac{1}{k}\right)}{C}$$

In ordinary language, this last expression is equivalent to stating that the average rate of return on investment is obtained by summing the receipts over the term, dividing by the number of periods (years) as well as by the capital commitment amount.

The fact that capital recovery is here specifically provided for is of some importance. In some cases, this is the actual situation; for example, a bond includes a specified maturity date when the "principal" will be returned. There are cases, however, in which the capital return is provided for in some other way.

"Depreciating Asset"

As an example of the kind of investment in which the capital recovery [8] is provided for specifically (but not at the end of the term), consider the "depreciating asset." This is also a variant of the general formula, but the definition of terms is importantly different. The capital commitment is not merely the present investment, but one that is reduced each period. If the reduction (depreciation) is assumed to occur at a constant rate, reaching zero at the end of the

---

[8] "Recovery" is the result of an assumption that "depreciation provides funds." As to this, see "Depreciation," p. 528, or "Some Misconceptions about Depreciation," *Hospital Accountant* (February, 1960), pp. 12-16.

term, the capital commitment is C_0 at the beginning, but is C_k at the end of the term, the average investment per period being $\frac{1}{2}(C_0 + C_k)$. In the case of zero terminal value, the average is simply $\frac{1}{2}C_0$.

The annual or periodic recovery is deducted from the receipts, so that the "A's" in the formula are interpreted as receipts less depreciation. Then, if the net "A's" are related by simple interest computations to the investment, the general formula reduces to:

Then,
$$\frac{1}{2}C_0 = \frac{\sum_{n=0}^{n=k} (A_n - d)}{(1 + ki)} \quad \text{and} \quad C_0 + C_0 ki = 2\left[\sum_{n=0}^{n=k} (A_n - d) \right]$$

$$C_0 ki = 2\left[\sum_{n=0}^{n=k} (A_n - d) \right] - C_0; \quad \text{and} \quad i = \frac{\sum_{n=0}^{n=k} (A_n - d) - C_0}{C_0}$$

Don't Invest by Formula Only

The foregoing paragraphs have shown that the differences in the various approaches towards dealing with the investment situation are only alternative interpretations of the same basic pattern of relationships. Whether or not any of these is "correct" is more a matter of empirical verification of the assumptions and interpretations made than it is a matter of fundamentals. Whether the force of interest is taken as an arithmetic or a geometric (exponential) pattern, whether capital recovery is specifically included or excluded, whether investment is defined in one way or another is largely a question of the situation and purposes involved.[9] The important observation is that a mere formula or its special variant does not constitute anything like a solution to the investment problem; it is only a vehicle to bring together certain data systematically.[10]

Variations in the definition and the treatment of the ingredients of the investment relationship are not, however, the only factors in the problem of investment. The measurements that are used to

---

[9] Even though it may involve assumptions that a theoretician might be unwilling to accept, the "first year" analysis might be quite satisfactory, if the decision maker is concerned only with his "showing" at the end of that year. Methods are right or wrong only in the sense that they meet, or fail to meet, the situations and objectives at which they are aimed.

[10] Although it may appear to be vastly different, the MAPI formula is another variant of the general investment formula. The chief difference is the emphasis given to the accumulative effects of operating inferiority (rising costs or declining returns as the investment progresses through time). The fact that solutions are sought which minimize the sum of operating inferiority and capital cost makes the mathematical treatment appear much more at variance with the general investment formula than it really is.

supply the data used in the variants of the formula bring their own problems. There is a number of complicating angles that ought at least to be recognized, even if they cannot be dealt with expressly. Some are worth examination.

LIMITATIONS IN FORECAST DATA

Investment analyses necessarily are forward looking, and the data used to quantify the outlook are of necessity expectations and forecasts. Perhaps this should be allowed for by recognizing that for every investment situation—for each future period, in fact—there is a range of probable net receipts. There is some chance of receiving each of a various number of amounts in any given period, at any given date. The weighting of each of these by the probability of its occurrence would give a probability array for each of the *"A's"* that we have put into the formula. If such probability distributions could be established, they would improve the validity of the entire approach.

INTRAPERIOD ITEMS

Typically, the period—the interval between receipts and the time over which a "conversion" of interest occurs—is assumed to be one year. This is in conformance with the general notion that interest is an annual affair. Rates of interests are taken to be "per year," even when there is no specification of the conversion period. If we do need to deal with periods shorter than a year, there is no great problem involved in restating interest so that the shorter period can be used. Compounding on a semiannual, quarterly, or monthly basis is an answer to this, for it makes the payment interval and interest-conversion period alike.

CONTINUOUS CONVERSION

However, an annual (nominal) rate of 6 percent is not the same thing as a rate of $\frac{1}{2}$ percent compounded monthly, for any sum invested at the monthly rate over a year will accumulate to $(1.005)^{12}$ times its initial amount; $(1.005)^{12}$ is 1.06168. Thus, $\frac{1}{2}$ percent compounded monthly is more than 6 percent per year. If we try to go around the other way to find a rate which, compounded monthly, will be 6 percent over the year as a whole, we discover that the result must be $\sqrt{1.06}$ per month, which is .004868, not $\frac{1}{2}$ percent.

The questions raised by this can be quite difficult, especially when the interim dates are irregularly spaced, or when they are unspecified. Under such circumstances it is common to simplify the problem by assumption, such as that the receipts are evenly (and thinly) spaced over the interest conversion period. If the notion of spreading is carried to the extreme of constant (instantaneous) flow, the mathematical answer is found in the "continuous" conversion concept. However, this may add more complexity than it saves.[11]

Another (and simpler) way to deal with the unspecified interim payment interval is to assume that such payments may be "averaged" to center at the middle of the year. Although this is not quite an acceptable notion from the strict mathematical viewpoint, it has the merit of easier manipulation; it pays some attention to the fact that receipts are not timed at the ends of the interest periods. The procedure would be to discount the indicated receipts as at the ends of the year in which they occur, and then to accumulate for a half year (at the effective rate) to get the "present" worth. The following diagram makes this a bit clearer.

0 = the present, "time zero."
1, 2, 3, K = ends of future years.
x = midpoints of years at which items are supposedly centered.
M = point at which centered items are commuted by discounting (one-half year before "time zero").
Accumulation of the commuted amount at M for one-half year gives "present" worth.

As an illustration, suppose our earlier example ($500, $400, and $200 at annual intervals) were due at the midpoints of Years 1, 2 and 3 respectively. Discounting at 5 percent would give the commuted value ($1,003.54) at one-half year *before* time zero. Ac-

---

[11] Continuous conversion is the limiting case of increasingly shorter interest periods. A 6 percent nominal rate of interest per year is really 6.09 percent when compounded semiannually; compounded quarterly, the 6 percent nominal rate becomes 6.136 percent. Monthly compounding makes the rate 6.168 percent; daily conversion raises the rate to 6.183 percent. But hourly conversion raises the rate to only 6.1838 percent and continuous conversion to only 6.1840 percent. For some other rates, 4 percent per year on a continuous conversion basis becomes 4.081 percent, 5 percent per year becomes 5.127 percent, 7 percent is raised to 7.251 percent, and 10 percent becomes 10.517 percent. Evidently the effect of shortening the interest conversion period is not very great, except in its initial stages. The continuous rate may be computed from log $(1 + i)$ = .434294j in which i is the continuous (effective) rate that results from compounding the nominal rate j at instantaneous intervals. See *Handbook of Financial Mathematics* (New York: Prentice-Hall, Inc. 1929), p. 1047.

cumulating at $\sqrt{1.05}$ (for the half year) would give $1,003.54 (1.0247) or $1,028.33, the corrected amount at time zero, interest at 5 percent per year.

Formula Permits Objective Comparisons

Investment proposals are seldom evaluated singly and *in vacuo*; typically, the problem is to choose between two or more alternatives, and the investment formula is a way to make comparisons in an objective fashion.

Sometimes, however, two proposals being compared do not coincide as to the investment term. One proposition may offer a series of receipts over, say, a six-year term, while the other may run for only three years. Using the rate of return evaluation provided by the "discounted cash flow" approach, it would seem that the investment offering the higher rate of return is to be preferred. But this is not without its difficulties.

For example, take a six-year proposal with annual receipts running $600, $600, $500, $500, $400, $400 in the successive years; compare it with another proposition that runs for three years and provides receipts of $600, $500, and $400 in those years. The "present worth" of these proposals on a 5 percent basis works out to $2,571 for the first, and $1,370 for the second. Although the nominal amount of future receipts is exactly half as much in the second proposition, the discounted amount of the investment is relatively greater for the shorter term; the effect of compound discount increases as the term is lengthened.

The effect noted may be expressed in another way, by noting the shift in the rate of return, if the investment commitment is made comparable. Suppose the first investment could be had for a price of $2,740—twice the price of the second (three-year) proposal—what rate of return would be indicated? The rate of return works out to a 3 percent basis:

$600 $\times$ .9709 = $582.54
 600 $\times$ .9426 = 565.56
 500 $\times$ .9151 = 457.55   Total, $2,730. This indicates a rate of
 500 $\times$ .8885 = 444.25   slightly *less* than 3 percent if the "price"
 400 $\times$ .8626 = 345.04   is $2,740.
 400 $\times$ .8374 = 335.00

Are these two investments really as different as the 5 percent and 3 percent rates suggest? Or does the length of term have some effect in the comparison? If the second investment is offered at half the price of the first ($1,286) the rate of return becomes slightly more than 8.5 percent per annum. $600 × .92166 = $553.00; $500 × .8494 = $424.73, and $400 × .78291 = $313.16. $553.00 + $424.73 + $313.16 = $1,290.89. Thus, in the first case a $159 addition to the price of $2,571 reduced the rate of return from 5 percent to less than 3 percent per annum; an $84 reduction in the $1,370 price in the second case raises the rate of return to slightly more than 8.5 percent.

If we make the investments really comparable, by comparing two successive three-year commitments with the six-year one, we get a yield of 5 percent and a price of $2,553; so it is evident the rate of return is shifted quite noticeably by variations in the term and tim-

Capital Commitment		*Commuted Returns*	
$1,370 now	$1,370.00	$600 × .95238	$ 571.43
1.370 three years		500 × .90700	453.50
hence (× .86384)	1,183.46	400 × .86384	345.53
		600 × .82270	493.62
		500 × .78353	391.77
		400 × .74622	298.49
Total	$2,553.46	Total	$2,554.34

ing of amounts. The conclusion is that comparisons of investment proposals should take into account the dissimilarity of investment term length.

It is fairly easy to handle the dissimilar term problem in a case such as has been cited. But to compare a two-year and a five-year proposal, commensurability requires a ten-year comparison. This can be quite awkward, for the comparison of a five- with a seven-year proposal requires a 35-year analysis, that of a seven- and eleven-year proposal necessitates consideration over 77 years, the least common multiple of the alternative investment terms. The difficulty becomes extreme if the question is, "Shall we buy the machine now, or wait two years and then buy it?" In this last situation, there is no hope of a comparison period commensurable with both proposals.

However, even this can be dealt with if a "terminal" value can be estimated for one of the proposals. Assuming the use life of the machine to be ten years, a net recovery or use value at the end of eight years for the deferred purchase may be treated as an investment "return" to make the comparison less inconsistent. However, there is some error in stating such a value; the *recovery* value is not really relevant even if it can be estimated, and the *use value* is not easily estimated in an objective sense.

CAPITALIZED COST COMPARISONS

Still another way to meet the dissimilar term issue is the use of "capitalized cost" comparisons. These are based on the assumption that the investment proposals may be continued indefinitely by repetition of successive identical terms and results. This is not exactly realistic, but the dissimilar terms become manageable through this procedure.

Two perpetuities are established for each proposal: (1) the capital commitment, repeated *in perpetuo*, and (2) the future receipts discounted in the same dimensions. Each of these may be viewed as an "annuity" in which the rent is the recurring capital commitment (or the commuted receipts), and the "periods" are the terms of the recurring commitments. The compound interest factor is the "rate" for the *term—$R^n - 1$*.

Adding the perpetuities to the initial capital commitment (or commuted receipts) gives the capitalized cost:

$$K = C + \frac{C}{R^n - 1}$$

Capitalized cost may be used to establish a perpetual rate of return, if desired. For the six-year investment mentioned earlier, at 2.75 percent annually, the capitalized cost computation is:

Capital Commitments	*Commuted Returns*
$2,740 due now $2,740.00	$600 ÷ 1.0275 ...... $ 583.94
	500 ÷ 1.05576 ..... 473.60
$2,740 every six years:	400 ÷ 1.08479 ..... 368.74
	600 ÷ 1.11462 ..... 538.30
$2,740 ÷ [(1.0275)^6 — 1],	500 ÷ 1.14527 ..... 436.58
$2,740 ÷ .17677 = 15,500.37	400 ÷ 1.17677 ..... 339.91
	Commuted returns
	for the first term $ 2,741.07
	For future terms,
	$2,741.07 ÷ .17677 15,506.42
Total capitalized	Total commuted
commitments .. **$18,240.37**	returns **$18,247.49**

This indicates that the rate of return *in perpetuo* is slightly too low at 2.75 percent. At 2.8 percent, however, the capitalized commitments are $17,944.48, and the commuted returns are $17,922.81. From the illustrations here presented it should be clear that investments with dissimilar terms and spacing should be evaluated with due care. Mere dependence on rates of return without considering the timing and spacing patterns may have definitely untoward effects.

COST OF CAPITAL

Another inherent difficulty with investment formulae is that they do not recognize the cost of capital as an explicit factor in the computations. This reflects the assumption that the problem to be solved is merely a relative evaluation of alternative investments, and that the differences in the gross rates of return are the important criteria. There is some reason to question this assumption.

The rate of return is inherently a kind of average; we use a single rate in any given computation, which is supposed to reflect the postponement of cash receipts and payments over various time periods. Actually, there is no such thing as a single rate for the great majority of cases; empirical rates, as they are quoted in the market, cover various kinds of arrangements over different time periods, and it is unusual to find only one way in which a venture can be financed. The problem of measuring the cost of capital as a separate variable in the investment situation is a difficult one, and we shall not be able to solve it here.[12] But capital cost is not irrelevant if it fluctuates through time or as between alternatives. Recognizing capital cost as a separate factor serves to separate the gross rate of return into

TABLE I

Amounts, Timing, and Rates of Interest Applicable to an Investment

(1) Month	(2) Day	(3) Year	(4) Amount	(5) Semiannual Interest Rate	(6) p	(7) $(1 + pi)$	(8) $\dfrac{A}{(1 + pi)}$
5	1	1	$1,950	.0250	2/3	1.01667	$1,918.03
7	15	1	1,500	.0225	1/12	1.00188	1,497.19
6	1	2	1,750	.0275	5/6	1.02292	1,710.79
11	10	2	1,800	.0300	13/18	1.02167	1,761.82
2	1	3	2,100	.0325	1/6	1.00542	2,088.68
10	1	3	2,000	.0350	1/2	1.01750	1,965.60
4	10	4	1,620	.0325	5/9	1.01806	1,591.26
9	1	4	1,200	.0300	1/3	1.01000	1,188.12
3	10	5	900	.0275	7/18	1.01069	890.48
8	15	5	500	.0250	1/4	1.00625	496.89

(1), (2), (3) Dates of future receipts.
(4) Amounts to be received.
(5) The rate which is here used to represent the cost of capital.
(6) Proportion of the semiannum by which receipts are deferred from the beginning of that semiannum.
(7) Simple interest factor for the period p and the rate in (5).
(8) Present worth, at simple interest (see Footnote 13) of the receipts as expected within that semiannum.

---

[12] See Footnote 1, *ibid*, pp. 496-523.

two parts: contractual amounts that will be based upon financing arrangements and the net return, the earnings over and above such contractual obligations.

Even if the cost of capital cannot be measured—if the investment alternatives must be appraised without an absolute and definite factor to represent financing—the approach must be to *compare* alternatives, not merely to match gross rates of return. The alternatives are different in that they involve different patterns of future receipts, over shorter or longer periods, and with respect to different capital demands. At least in theory, the cost of capital should appear within the alternatives, as explicitly as possible, not merely as reflections in the overall gross rates of return for dissimilar projects.

All of this suggests that there ought to be some way to deal with varying costs of capital over the term of a given investment, a variant of the general approach, best illustrated by a concrete example.

In the illustration to be presented, we shall assume (1) that the amounts of future receipts are of varying size and that they are expected to arise at somewhat irregular intervals, (2) that the rate of interest used to represent the cost of capital also varies from period to period. This will make it possible to see how interim receipts and varying interest rates may be handled. Table I, reproduced on page 522, gives the basic data along with figures to reduce the receipts to present worths at the beginning of respective future periods.[13]

Although it is a digression, it may be worth noting at this point that the error introduced by using simple interest instead of compound interest rates for interim calculations is not large. Table II shows the contrast between the present worth at simple interest as computed in Table I, and the result of *accumulating* the interim payment to the end of the semiannum, and then discounting by the correct compound rate.

The data in Column (1) of Table II may be discounted to compute the present worth of future receipts for comparison with capital commitment in the general formula. Because the semiannual cost of capital is different in each period, the discounting must be done one period at a time, as in Table III.

---

[13] Present worths are computed at simple interest, to avoid the complexities described earlier with interim interest rates. But this is not the same as simple discount. Present worth at simple interest is computed by dividing by $(1 + pi)$, in which p is the proportion of the interest period involved and the effective rate (in this case, per semiannum). Simple discount would require multiplication of the maturity amount by the factor $(1 - pi)$; this does not give the same result.

TABLE II

Effect of Using Simple Interest for Interim Receipts Calculations

Period	Years	(1) $\dfrac{A}{(1+pi)}$	(2) Accumulation Rate $(1+qi)$	(3) Amount, End of Period $A(1+qi)$	(4) (3) Discounted at $(1+i)$	(5) Error
1	½	$1,918.03	1.00833	$1,966.24	$1,918.28	.25
2	1	1,497.19	1.02063	1,530.95	1,497.26	.07
3	1½	1,710.79	1.00458	1,758.02	1,710.97	.18
4	2	1,761.82	1.00833	1,814.99	1,762.13	.31
5	2½	2,088.68	1.02708	2,156.87	2,088.98	.30
6	3	1,965.60	1.01750	2,035.00	1,966.18	.58
7	3½	1,591.26	1.01444	1,643.39	1,591.66	.40
8	4	1,188.12	1.02000	1,224.00	1,188.34	.22
9	4½	890.48	1.01681	915.13	890.64	.14
10	5	496.89	1.01875	509.38	496.96	.07

(1) Actual receipts expected as stated in Columns (1)-(4) of Table I, reduced to present worth at beginning of each semiannum. See Column 8 of Table I.

(2) Simple interest applicable for that part of the semiannum remaining after the date of receipt, $q = (1 - p)$.

(3) Specific receipts as given in Table I accumulated at $(1 + qi)$ to the end of each semiannum.

(4) Amounts in (3) discounted at rate i to beginning of semiannum, for comparison with (1).

(5) Differences caused by simple interest conversions, (5) less (1).

TABLE III

Discounted Future Receipts from an Investment With Varying Amounts, Timing, and Capital Costs

(1) Period	(2) To Be Received This Period	(3) Future Period Receipts = (6) Line above	(4) Total Commuted Values, All Future Receipts	(5) Capital Cost Factor for Prior Period	(6) Commuted Value Total Future Receipts Beginning Prior Period
10	$ 496.89	$ 0	$ 496.89	1.0275	$ 483.60
9	890.48	483.60	1,374.08	1.0300	1,334.06
8	1,188.12	1,334.06	2,522.18	1.0325	2,442.79
7	1,591.26	2,442.79	4,034.05	1.0350	3,897.63
6	1,965.60	3,897.62	5,863.23	1.0325	5,678.67
5	2,088.68	5,678.67	7,767.35	1.0300	7,541.12
4	1,761.82	7,541.12	9,302.94	1.0275	9,053.96
3	1,710.79	9,053.96	10,764.75	1.0225	10,527.87
2	1,497.19	10,527.87	12,025.06	1.0250	11,731.77
1	1,918.03	11,731.77	13,649.80	.....	....

(1) The periods are arranged in declining order to facilitate discounting.

(2) Figures in this column are from Column (8) of Table I.

(3) Receipts which were discounted from future periods, to present worth at beginning of this period.

(4) Sum of Columns (2) and (3).

(5) Conversion factor (cost of capital) from Column 5, Table I.

(6) Column 4 item divided by capital cost factor in Column 5.

The figures in Table III make it clear that the investment proposal we have assumed has a present worth (at the indicated capital costs) of $13,649.80. If it is acquired for that amount, the future receipts will be just sufficient to cover the costs of capital. At a higher price, it will not return its capital costs; at a lower price, it will return something more than the cost of capital.

EVALUATION OF PROFITABILITY

Suppose the investment proposal just illustrated can be purchased for $12,150. It obviously offers a profit over and above the cost of capital, indicated by the excess of "present worth" over capital commitment, $1,499.80. This can be due only to the effect of discount rates higher than those employed in the "capital cost" evaluation. But what rate or rates are involved?

We may "solve" the problem by finding a single discount rate that will equate the discounted future receipts with the capital commitment; that is, we may find (by trial and error) that discount rate which, applied to the future receipts over the entire investment term, will result in a present worth of $12,150. This is done in Table IV.

TABLE IV

Finding a Gross Rate of Return by Approximation from Adjusted Data

Discounting at Various Rates

Period	Receipts as at End of Period	3%		6%		5½%	
		Compound Discount Factor	Present Worth at Time Zero	Compound Discount Factor	Present Worth at Time Zero	Compound Discount Factor	Present Worth at Time Zero
10	$ 509.38	.7441	$ 379.03	.5584	$ 284.44	.5854	$ 298.19
9	915.13	.7664	701.36	.5919	541.07	.6176	565.18
8	1,224.00	.7894	966.23	.6274	767.94	.6516	797.56
7	1,643.39	.8131	1,366.24	.6651	1,093.02	.6874	1,129.67
6	2,035.00	.8375	1,704.31	.7050	1,434.68	.7252	1,475.78
5	2,156.87	.8626	1,860.52	.7473	1,611.83	.7651	1,650.22
4	1,814.99	.8885	1,612.62	.7921	1,437.65	.8072	1,465.06
3	1,758.02	.9151	1,608.86	.8396	1,476.12	.8516	1,497.21
2	1,530.95	.9426	1,443.07	.8900	1,362.55	.8985	1,375.56
1	1,966.24	.9708	1,908.82	.9433	1,854.75	.9479	1,863.80
Totals		....	$13,551.06	....	$11,864.05	....	$12,118.23

Receipts as at end of period are taken from Table II, Column (3), and discounted at the indicated rates. The rate of 3 percent per semiannum is found to be too low, and that of 6 percent is too high.

The rate of 5.5 percent per semiannum is nearly "correct," for the present worth comes to only $31.77 less than the capital commitment.

The calculations in Table IV result in an average gross rate of return; this rate ignores capital cost except as it is used to carry each semiannum's receipts to the end of that semiannum for discounting at the gross rate. To subtract the capital cost rates from the gross rate in an attempt to get a net rate for each semiannum is inaccurate, for the discounting has been done at a single rate over the term. Further, it should be clear that there are any number of combinations of gross and net rates that might result in a present worth equal to the capital commitment; thus, any solution is at least partially arbitrary.

As another approach to this problem, we may discount the future receipts at a variable rate, established by adding to the capital cost a constant net return factor. The gross rate will then vary, as the cost of capital changes, and the net rate will be constant. This pattern of discounting, assuming a constant net return of 3 percent per semiannum, is applied in Table V.

Table V

Present Worth Evaluation of an Investment
From Adjusted Data, to Net 3% per Semiannum over Capital Costs

				Present Worth at Beginning This Period			Present Worth at Begining Prior Period	
Period	Receipts	Gross Rate	$(1 + pi)$	This Period Receipt	Future Receipts	Total	Gross Rate	Present Worth Carried Down
(1)	(2)	(3)	(4)	(5)	(6)	(7)	(8)	(9)
10	$ 500	1.055	1.01375	$ 493.22	$........	$ 493.22	1.0575	$ 466.40
9	900	1.0575	1.02236	880.32	466.40	1,346.72	1.0600	1,270.49
8	1,200	1.0600	1.02000	1,176.47	1,270.49	2,446.96	1.0625	2,303.02
7	1,620	1.0625	1.03472	1,565.64	2,303.02	3,868.66	1.0650	3,632.54
6	2,000	1.0650	1.03250	1,937.05	3,632.54	5,569.59	1.0625	5,241.97
5	2,100	1.0625	1.01042	2,078.36	5,241.97	7,320.33	1.0600	6,905.97
4	1,800	1.0600	1.04333	1,725.24	6,905.97	8,631.21	1.0575	8,161.90
3	1,750	1.0575	1.04792	1,669.97	8,161.90	9,831.87	1.0525	9,341.44
2	1,500	1.0525	1.00438	1,493.46	9,341.44	10,834.90	1.0550	10,270.05
1	1,950	1.0550	1.03667	1,881.04	10,270.05	12,151.09	.....	12,151.09

(1) Periods shown in reverse order to facilitate discounting.

(2) Nominal receipts expected in this period, on dates earlier specified.

(3) Gross rate of return (capital cost plus net return) expressed as conversion factor, R, for this period.

(4) Interim conversion factor, applying gross rate to specified dates.

(5) Amount in Column (2) discounted at $(1 + pi)$ to beginning of this period.

(6) Receipts of all future periods discounted to beginning of this period, same as (9) in line immediately above.

(7) Sum of items in (5) and (6).

(8) Conversion factor applicable to prior period (line immediately below).

(9) Amount in Column (7) divided by conversion factor in Column (8).

In Table V, the calculations proceed as in Table III. Each period is treated separately in the discounting process, since the gross rate of return is 3 percent higher than the variable capital cost rates. The result is arithmetically comparable to that shown in Table IV, for the "present worth" as computed is close to the amount of the capital commitment. But *logically* the varying gross rate is better, for it at least recognizes the capital cost rates in determining the "average return on investment." Whether or not the average net rate of 3 percent per semiannum is realistic, in view of the fluctuations in capital cost, is another question. Perhaps it might be better to use a varying net rate that fluctuates in proportion to the capital costs. This would recognize the interdependence of related interest quotations. However, as was stated above, there is no one answer to the problem of a net return after capital cost; there are a number of combinations of gross and net rates that would yield comparable "present worths."

The calculations to establish the present worth of the investment in this situation are somewhat tedious, because of the number of variables recognized. But they recognize some of the more obvious complications in such an evaluation.

Interest factors are used to make investment evaluations in at least two senses; one of these is the recognition of capital cost, and the other is the net rate of return, or the percentage of income on the investment over the term. A gross rate which combines these elements is confusing. Each rate ought to be recognized specifically in calculations. This is apparent when it is seen that the cost of capital is not an absolute, but is likely to appear in the form of a set of alternative programs. Further, the cost of capital is likely to fluctuate through time, not only because of the force of market factors, but also because there are various shifts in the array of investment opportunities. Using a single rate of return combines the effect of two dissimilar aspects of the problem. Using a constant total rate over the entire term averages not only the cost of capital and the return rates, but also the fluctuations over time in both of them.

Depreciation, *per se,* is irrelevant for investment evaluations; the general investment formula makes no provision for spreading or amortization of capital cost. Rather, the recovery of capital commitments is built into the general formula implicitly, by matching capital commitment with discounted future receipts. Depreciation is merely the assignment of capital cost to periods shorter than the life of the commitment, to reduce what would otherwise be distortions arising from the short periods we use to establish income for most purposes.

In the attempt to measure income for a year or a quarter, there must necessarily be some adjustment of cash receipts and payments to reflect economic events. The accountant (or anyone else who attempts such a measurement) must recognize that the timing of receipts and disbursements does not coincide with economic service flows. We receive labor services now and pay for them later; we make deposits on contracts whose execution is postponed. We borrow money and repay loans in secondary financing transactions that are only indirectly related to the acquisition, usage, or delivery of economic resources.

Insurance contracts require payments for one to five years in advance, merchandise purchased in one period may be used in a second one and paid for in a third. Plant and equipment costs are long-term prepayments, the use period of which may be 20 years or more. The credit system and the technological occurrence of bundles of service used in business necessitate a number of interim adjustments and allocations, so as properly to time service flows, to match them in short reporting periods.

On the other hand, investment decisions are not concerned with annual income. The investment is evaluated as a whole over its entire term, and the timing of cash receipts and disbursements is relevant and correct data for this purpose. The borrowing and repayment transactions that are indirect and secondary for annual income determination are of the essence of investment in the broader sense. Depreciation, amortization, and other such short period corrections are of no use for evaluating a long-term investment.[14]

DEPRECIATION

No discussion of the place of depreciation in investment evaluation should fail to mention the need for clear thinking about depreciation in relation to sources of funds. Most finance textbooks, many articles in the public (and the academic) press, and a great deal of "serious" talk in business circles further this gross misconception that somehow depreciation brings money into a business. The error in this can easily be seen when it is suggested that if this were so,

---

[14] The reader may object that in an earlier connection we presented a computation which did show capital recovery explicitly, and in which depreciation was deducted in computing annual receipts. This was the one-year computation in its "first year," average year and average return on average investment variants. This is not inconsistent with what has been said about depreciation, but is actually a clear illustration of how the short period requires capital cost allocation.

we could meet any need for cash by a sufficient increase in the depreciation charge! The fact is that income (accounting income) is erroneously viewed as a source of funds. Depreciation reduces income and does not take money out of the business; since both these ideas are correct, depreciation is added back to income to get "funds provided from operations." This "internal financing" is really only a reflection that receipts from customers actually cover most operating expenses and more. The adjustments made to compute short period income (as has been explained) really make the income figure only a rough indication of cash flows, at best.

Related to this is the naive notion that, somehow, depreciation is "recovered" from the government via income taxes. It is true that income taxes are affected by depreciation allowances or deductions, but the federal government does not pay back our depreciation cost. The tax is reduced by perhaps 52 percent of the depreciation charges, but if this is "recovery," let us all campaign for larger taxes to recover more depreciation!

DEPRECIATION AND INCOME TAXES

Although depreciation is itself irrelevant for investment evaluations, it does enter into the computation of income taxation, and income taxes are an important element in any investment problem or situation. Many investments that are attractive on a before tax basis become uninviting after taxes are considered, and some that are apparently undesirable may be made interesting and remunerative after tax effects are understood.[15]

The way in which income tax considerations should enter the investment evaluation is through the annual receipts or expected savings to arise from the investment. In this, the income tax payments required in a given future year are as much a part of determining the net receipts as any other operating cost. It should also be stressed that when the use of a special provision such as accelerated depreciation defers the payment of taxes, it is possible for the income tax to turn future savings or receipts into net costs or payments, after the

---

[15] It is really surprising how many textbook and other presentations of investment analysis dismiss the tax effect as of minor and only relative importance. The argument that a proposal is not made more or less desirable by tax effects is simply wrong, when the income tax rate is as high as it is, and when it is possible to postpone, accelerate, or affect the absolute amount of taxes by considering legally available variations in the methods of reporting, or the contractual arrangements surrounding business transactions. *Management Planning for Corporate Taxes* (New York: The Controllership Foundation, 1951).

total effect of such postponements has "worked out." In other words, it is never safe to assume that income taxes are irrelevant; the tax effect is present so long as the investment situation can affect the tax liability.

Decisions to invest usually involve fairly large sums and fairly long periods of time, and they, therefore, deserve careful study and evaluation. However, it is also true that the conditions surrounding an investment at the time the decision is made may change considerably as time passes. It is, therefore, of some importance that the investment decisions as made are subjected to a certain amount of systematic review. Most companies have a regular procedure of reviewing the commitments made at intervals afterwards. This has the dual effect of unearthing errors and thus avoiding their perpetuation, and of calling attention to the changes that have occurred which may logically entail shifts in the original plan.

No investment is irrevocable in its entirety; there is always some adjustment that is possible, if only to terminate or shift the emphasis in the plan to meet changing conditions. This suggests that there ought to be some way to set up the data employed in the original decision so that they may be reviewed and that the changes that may be proposed can be related to the original pattern of evaluation.

Follow-up Is Essential

The typical present worth comparison (common to all the approaches that have been considered) proceeds from the future back to the present time, and thus permits a comparison of actual events with those anticipated in the decision only imperfectly. This suggests that there may be some merit in a forward-looking computation of investment evaluation, so that the computations may be arranged in the order in which the future events will occur.

This sort of approach is afforded by an amortization table, a not so new but overlooked device that may be of help in this connection. Its form is based upon the same evaluation as the others that have been described, but it carries through the events of the successive periods in the order in which they occur. An example is presented in Table VI, based on the illustration that was used earlier.

Value of Amortization Table

The amortization table is based on the same general formula as are all the other computations that have been presented, and

TABLE VI

AMORTIZATION OF $12,150 INVESTMENT AGAINST EXPECTED RECEIPTS TO NET
6% COMPOUNDED SEMIANNUALLY OVER VARYING CAPITAL COSTS

(1) Period	(2) Carrying Amount at Beginning of Period	(3) Gross Interest Rate, i	(4) Accumulation at End of Period	(5) Amount to Be Received in the Period	(6) Interim Period (q)	(7) A, (Column 5) Times $(1 + qi)$	(8) Forwarded at End of Period, $(4) - (7)$
1	$12,150.00	.0550	$12,818.25	$1,950	1/3	$1,985.74	$10,832.51
2	10,832.51	.0525	11,401.22	1,500	11/12	1,570.70	9,830.52
3	9,830.52	.0575	10,395.77	1,750	1/6	1,776.77	8,629.00
4	8,629.00	.0600	9,146.74	1,800	5/18	1,830.01	7,316.73
5	7,316.73	.0625	7,774.03	2,100	5/6	2,209.37	5,564.66
6	5,564.66	.0650	5,926.36	2,000	1/2	2,065.00	3,861.36
7	3,861.36	.0625	4,102.70	1,620	4/9	1,664.97	2,427.73
8	2,437.73	.0600	2,583.99	1,200	2/3	1,248.00	1,335.99
9	1,335.99	.0575	1,412.81	900	11/18	931.63	481.18
10	481.18	.0550	507.64	500	3/4	520.64	(13.00)

therefore it does not give a fundamentally different answer. However, there are some aspects of emphasis and arrangement that are worth noting. First, the amortization table is a "forward-moving" presentation. The earlier events are presented first, the later ones afterwards. This gives a pattern to the presentation that conforms to the elements in the decision. Rather than summarize the entire presentation in the form of a mere gross or net rate of return, the amortization table focuses attention on the whole set of data.

Second, the arrangement of the amortization table permits the use of specific calculations for interim receipts and for fluctuating rates of interest, both gross and net. Each line of the table may be set apart as a calculation to show the effect of interim fluctuations.

Third, the arrangement of the amortization table calls attention to the fact that the capital significance of the investment is not constant over its entire term. Not only does this indicate the amount of capital recovery as it occurs, but it serves to hint at the existence of possible disposition values. If these do in fact exist, there may be reason to restudy the available opportunities. This kind of systematic review and reevaluation is an essential part of any capital expenditure or investment program.

Fourth, the mere presence of a "carrying value" suggests the marginal nature of each successive year's participation in the total investment proposition. When future receipts or savings discount to an amount that is less than currently available recovery value, there is doubt as to the continuance of that proposition. A building or an equipment item is economically obsolete when the costs of keeping it in service are greater than the corresponding costs of providing and operating an acceptable substitute.[16]

Finally, it should be noted that the arithmetic of the amortization table is direct and uncomplicated. The interest rates are "simple" interest, for each computation concerns only one interest conversion period. It is not necessary, therefore, to have available any extended tables of compound interest factors. Neither does the use of odd or fractional rates cause undue trouble. It may be difficult to locate a compound interest table for $9\frac{1}{2}$ or $13\frac{2}{3}$ percent; these computations offer no problem in an amortization arrangement. Also the use of interest calculations made in this way removes some of the sources of mystery and confusion on the part of the uninitiated.

It has been the purpose of this paper to lay a few of the ghosts that haunt the investment analysis and capital budgeting areas. We have attempted to show that there is a basic investment formula which has been applied in various ways. The various "methods," however, are not so different that they should be regarded as possessed of exclusive virtues or faults in themselves. Quantitative data should be marshaled in whatever way serves the purpose at hand, so long as inherent biases and weaknesses are recognized. In this connection, every investment analysis necessarily lacks something in the quest for ultimate and final validity. Some of the weaknesses of investment analysis may be dealt with, but others may have to be left to intuition and judgment.

Actually, the user of any variant of the general investment formula must be his own counsel as to the use of computations versus judgment, intuition, or hunch. But a clearer understanding of what the numbers can and will do (and what they cannot do) is the best approach to useful applications of investment formulae.

---

[16] See Footnote 10. MAPI computations recognize this situation in applying that variant of the investment formula, but it is easy to lose sight of this aspect of obsolescence if rechecks are not made. And it should be stressed that the carrying value is only an indicator; the carrying value (like any other prorated figure) is irrelevant for decision making purposes if it is not supported by recoverable or disposition values. Actually, the carrying value is the capital sum on which the remaining (originally assumed) receipts will still earn the indicated gross rates of return used in the amortization.

42. ASSIGNMENT OF NON-MANUFACTURING COSTS FOR MANAGERIAL DECISIONS *

In the operation of a business it is necessary to decide what products to sell, where and to whom to sell them, how to price them, and what methods to use in selling. In making such decisions, management needs to have cost and income data for individual product lines, territories, customers, and other units which are dealt with. Since these decisions are made in the planning stage of management at which alternative courses of action are compared and choices are made, both historical and prospective future costs are needed. When reliable measures of the relative profitability of individual units in the overall picture are lacking, management may hesitate to act or it may act blindly.

Determination of costs and profit margins by products, territories, and other lines of activity requires assignment of costs to those lines of activity. Both manufacturing and nonmanufacturing costs must be assigned in order to provide complete coverage of factors which affect profitability of individual units. This report presents the results of an analytical study of the techniques available for determining the incidence of nonmanufacturing costs by products, territories, customer classes, and similar lines of marketing activity. It is based upon practices of 70 companies which were interviewed in developing the study.

INTRODUCTION

The processes of cost accounting have been developed most extensively for the purposes of producing cost figures needed in preparing periodic financial reports and for aiding management in its exercise of control over costs. Substantially less attention has been given to the determination of costs for decisions which fall in the

---

* N.A.C.A. Bulletin, Research Series No. 19, 1951. Reprinted by permission of the National Association of Cost Accountants.

realm of policy making. This study is concerned with the latter field —the development and uses of cost information as a basis for making decisions in the field of business planning and policy formulation.

Illustrative of the type of problems here under consideration are the following:

1. The products to be offered for sale, the proportions in which they are to be sold, and the prices at which to sell them.
2. Where to sell them, i.e., the geographical area in which to operate.
3. The classes of customers whose patronage is to be solicited.
4. The channels to be used in distributing the company's merchandise.
5. The services to be offered to customers.
6. The relative emphasis which is to be placed upon the various products, territories, etc.

Decisions such as those listed above fall in the planning stage of management at which alternative courses of action are compared and choices made. The resulting decisions are then expressed in the form of policies, budgets, and standards which serve as guides to subsequent actions in the day-to-day executory stage of management. The preparation of cost and income statements and analyses needed as a basis for such decisions provides a wide scope within which the accountant can be of service to management. The aim of this study is to explore the methods for getting facts on which such actions may be based.

Without minimizing the importance of manufacturing costs, this study is limited to the assignment of nonmanufacturing costs to products, sales territories, and other subdivisions of the business. Methods for ascertaining manufacturing costs have been well developed by most companies in which management is aware of the advantages of having good costs, but preliminary field interviews showed that comparatively few companies possess equally good information about nonmanufacturing costs. Since marketing costs usually constitute the major portion of nonmanufacturing costs, this study places particular emphasis upon costs of marketing. However, the broader aspects of cost assignment described here are equally applicable to other costs.

As a basis for the present report, 70 companies were visited by members of the Association's research staff to determine what methods are in use and why they are used. In addition, a survey of existing literature on the subject was made.

NATURE OF THE PROBLEM

Need for Costs by Segments of the Business

Most businessmen realize that some products, territories, customers, etc., are more profitable than others. They also know that an undue proportion of small orders, excessive product variety, and too many special services may have an adverse effect on profits. In pricing, most executives recognize both the advantages and the dangers in accepting orders which increase volume and contribute something to fixed overhead when more profitable business is not to be had. While general impressions may serve as a rough guide to decisions, measurement of the factors involved is needed before management can take effective action on specific problems. Lacking reliable measures of the relative profitability of products, territories, and customers, management may hesitate to take action or may act blindly.

Overall financial statements do not provide the data needed for decisions with respect to individual organizational or product units. Instead management needs to have costs and income by segments of the business.[1] Analysis of sales income and costs by segments of the business provides the basis for a better understanding of the elements which make up overall profit.[2] Specific products, territories, salesmen, and other units which need attention are then more readily identified and it is easier to select the areas which offer the greatest opportunity for profits. It is also possible to evaluate proposed courses of action with greater objectivity and to measure the results of action taken with more reliability. However, the difficulty encountered in finding companies which could contribute information to this study seems to indicate that comparatively few companies have the cost data needed to determine relative profitableness of products, territories, salesmen, customers, etc.

Uses for Historical Costs

Costs may represent the ways in which operations are currently being carried on, or they may be prospective costs which are expected

---

[1] The term "segment" is used in this report to designate any line of activity or subdivision of the business (e.g., a product line, sales territory, or customer class for which separate determination of costs and sales income is wanted).

[2] In this report "analysis" is used to cover the process of dividing or separating costs into the portions applicable to individual functions, products, territories, etc. The word "assign" is then used to designate the application of cost components to segments of the business. Costs of individual segments are thus obtained by analysis, followed by assignment which takes the form of accumulation of direct costs and allocation of indirect costs.

to result if a specified change is made in the future. In the first instance the breakdown of costs and sales by segments utilizes historical data. A monthly statement of profit and loss by product lines or sales territories is a typical result, although such studies are not always made at regular intervals. For example, a number of companies seen in the field study had made studies to determine the cost of handling orders of various sizes, but these studies were repeated only when some change in conditions made it advisable to bring a prior study up to date.

Determination of historical costs by segments often serves to direct managerial attention to areas where action might be taken to improve profits. For example, if a certain sales territory shows profits which are low in comparison with other territories, investigation to determine the reason would seem to be in order. This investigation may show causes beyond control of the company, as might be the case in a territory where sales potential is low and necessity for much travel between sales calls results in high selling expenses. On the other hand, it may be possible to improve profits by such means as increasing sales volume, improving the sales mix, better control of expenses, or shifting to more economical methods of delivery. Progress made in such a program can be followed from period to period by watching the territorial profit-and-loss statements and by comparing current figures with the figures from prior periods or with budgeted figures in which expected improvement has been reflected.

Opportunities for improving profits which may be disclosed by study of historical costs are not limited to finding remedies for unsatisfactory conditions. One company found that all of its sales territories were profitable, but that a few were especially outstanding. Experimentation showed that methods of promotion developed by the most profitable territories could be used to advantage in some of the less profitable territories. Other territories were found to be not responsive to heavy promotion expense, and profits in these territories were actually improved by reducing promotion expenditures.

Need for Prospective Costs

An alert management looks not only to the past, but also is constantly searching for better methods of doing things. This requires evaluation of possible alternatives to determine whether or not they promise improved profits. In the process, comparisons are made with costs expected under alternative methods rather than with previous costs or standard costs. For example, in a case where an unprofitable sales territory had been disclosed, one company had considered selling through jobbers rather than through its own salesmen. In this study it took the most recent profit-and-loss statement for this territory, eliminated those costs which could be saved, and added the jobbers' commissions which would have to be paid. An adjustment to sales income was also made to allow for an expected decline in sales volume because of less vigorous selling by jobbers. It was then possible to see what effect the change in methods of marketing could be expected to have on profit from this territory.

Illustrative material in this report is drawn largely from situations involving historical costs because methods employed in the regular processes of accounting for nonmanufacturing costs were more readily determined in the interviews. However, the same approach to analysis of costs by segments is generally applied when dealing with prospective costs, although the basic data may be drawn from sources outside the company's accounts. Moreover, while the contribution which an individual unit makes to overall profit requires that both sales income and costs be analyzed by segments of the business, determination of the costs usually presents a much more complex problem than does the parallel determination of sales income. For this reason this study is concerned largely with costs.

Selection of Segments for Analysis

There are usually numerous possible lines of analysis which may be followed in ascertaining costs by segments of a business. Among the principal ones employed in practice are:

1. Products or product lines.
2. Geographical area of distribution.
3. Administrative divisions of the sales organization.
4. Distribution channels—as wholesaler, retailer, etc.
5. Method of solicitation—i.e., by salesman's call, telephone, mail, etc.
6. Method of delivery.
7. Individual salesmen or groups of salesmen.
8. Individual customers or groups of customers.
9. Warehouses.
10. Order size.

The field study showed that analyses of nonmanufacturing costs by product lines and by sales territories are the most widely used. In practically every multiproduct company, management is interested in knowing profits by products. Territorial analyses of costs usually coincide with areas of supervisory responsibility and the same reports furnish data both for measuring operating effectiveness and for disclosing points of strength and weakness in the current pattern of operations.

Reports by products and sales territories are usually prepared regularly because management wishes to follow performance of these segments from period to period. In several instances, discussion indicated that changes occurred quite frequently in relative profitability of these segments and hence it was important to know when action should be taken to correct an unfavorable trend or to gain maximum benefit from a favorable situation. Where decisions with respect to specific segments are made infrequently, analyses of historical costs are usually made as special studies when wanted or sometimes at regular intervals of several years. Studies of prospective costs are made whenever there is occasion to consider alternatives.

Additional analyses are made where desired. For example, several companies interviewed pointed out that management needs to have current information as to profits being realized at specific points in the process of manufacturing and marketing because decisions as to alternatives are frequently made at these points. For example, one company which can convert its principal raw material into a number of different products watches the product profit-and-loss statements closely and shifts its production and sales facilities to those lines which are most profitable at a given time. Another company prepares analyses of sales income and costs by region, districts, classes of trade, and method of delivery. By comparing returns being realized through these various marketing channels and methods, it is possible to concentrate sales effort and to use those methods which yield the greatest return. While opportunity to make such decisions at certain points is present in every company's operations, it is apparent that some companies have much more flexibility than others. The need for analyses of cost and income data accordingly varies with the number of possible alternatives open to management and the frequency with which decisions can be made.

Where there is no inherent difference between units in a particular class of segments and cost variations are due to random influences which cannot be controlled, analysis serves no purpose. This condition is illustrated by a situation in which time spent by salesmen in calling on customers varies according to idiosyncrasies of the individual customer. Here a cost which averages out variations in time spent in customer calls is sufficient. On the other hand, a company has salesmen who sell a mechanical appliance to the general run of manufacturing plants, but who also sell a special item of equipment which is purchased only by smelters. The latter are usually located near mines in remote places. The distinct difference in travel expense and travel time needed for salesmen to reach the smelters makes it desirable for this company to segregate the cost applicable to this class of customers.[3]

The full range of usefulness which a particular analysis may have seldom can be foreseen in the beginning. Experience of many companies has shown that the initial study has opened up previously unrecognized possibilities for improvement. For example, a reason for cost variation by territories may be variations in product mix, resulting in higher selling costs in territories with large proportions of products with high selling costs. Here analysis of selling costs by products is needed to bring out the real reasons for differences in territorial costs. It also may be found that certain analyses which have served as the basis for changes in policy or methods are no longer needed. A company interviewed had studied the effect which the number of sales outlets in a given area had on costs and sales. As a result, granting of exclusive agencies was discontinued and the products sold to any dealer who could meet certain qualifications. In this case the analysis served as the basis for a single decision. Other analyses which seem promising when undertaken may prove to be of little value. A company seen in the field study had once made a study of differences in cost of handling orders of various sizes, but the results did not indicate need for any change in policy and the analysis was not repeated. Changing market conditions may require reconsideration of a program of analysis to keep management informed about the factors which are important under current conditions.

Some costs are direct as to the specific segments being costed while other costs are indirect. Assignment of the direct costs to segments in any designated class is accomplished by classification and accumulation of the costs in the categories desired. The indirect costs are then allocated. The remainder of this report describes methods employed in assigning nonmanufacturing costs and uses made of the resulting data by companies interviewed.

---

[3] Alden C. Brett, "The Role of the Accountant in the Control of Distribution Costs," *N.A.C.A. Bulletin* (April 1, 1940), p. 969.

CLASSIFICATION OF NONMANUFACTURING COSTS

The first step in ascertaining the incidence of costs by segments of the business is classification of the costs. Classification first separates the costs which can be treated as direct charges and reduces the problem area where costs must be allocated. Appropriate classification of the indirect costs also improves reliability of allocations which are made.

Since a clear understanding of the nature of direct and indirect costs is basic to the processes of classification and allocation employed in the analysis of costs by segments of a business, a discussion of the characteristics of these two types of costs follows.

Direct Costs

The determination of costs by segments of a business begins with those costs which can, as a practical matter, be directly identified with the unit being costed. The direct costs represent cost factors whose application to specific segments can be definitely measured and whose costs can be accumulated separately from costs of other segments. In speaking of direct costs it is, of course, essential to specify the unit being costed, for costs which are direct as to one unit are often indirect as to other units. Thus, for example, when salesmen are specialized by product lines, selling costs can be charged directly to product lines, but in costing individual items within a line the same selling costs are indirect and must be allocated.

Direct charging of costs is preferable to later allocation because the reliability of the resulting unit costs is not subject to question if the basic data have been accurately classified and summarized.

In order for costs to be handled as direct charges, individual cost items must be identified with units to be costed (i.e. with departments, products, territories, etc.) at the time the cost is incurred. Ordinarily this is accomplished by some plan for coding source records so that the cost data on them can be assembled according to desired classifications. In the factory the use of labor job tickets bearing department and order numbers is generally familiar. Invoices, expense vouchers, and other source documents can be similarly coded to permit subsequent direct accumulation of nonmanufacturing costs.

However, it is rarely if ever possible to measure directly all of the costs associated with a product, territory, or other such costing unit. Even where it is possible to employ direct methods of costing, it may be too expensive to do so. For example, the time spent in packing orders could be recorded and charged directly to products in a manner similar to that followed in accounting for direct labor in a factory, but the additional refinement in costs may not be worth the additional expense that would be incurred.

In such circumstances use of standard costs often makes it possible to obtain the benefits of direct charging without the excessive clerical expense required by routine collection of actual costs for each product or other unit for which separate costs are wanted. When this is done, the standard costs are based upon test measurements which, once made, need not be repeated until methods or other characteristics of the operation change. E. Stewart Freeman has described an application of this method as follows:

> To get the profit by merchandise lines, of course, we must have an order filling cost for each kind of product. We have worked this out in two parts (1) a cost per unit which varies according to the size of the product and (2) a cost per item of goods on an order. Our accounting gives us figures showing the total quantities invoiced each month and the number of times each kind of goods has been invoiced, that is, the number of times it has appeared as an item on the orders shipped. The total quantity shipped is multiplied by the cost per unit, and the number of items shipped is multiplied by the cost per item. By adding these together, we get the order filling cost for each kind of goods and for the shipments as a whole.[4]

By such methods the standard cost of the operation is charged directly to the segment being costed, leaving only that portion of the cost represented by variances to be allocated.

This method is applicable only to those costs which could be treated as direct charges in the first place if record keeping expense did not need to be considered. Costs of routine operations such as order writing, packing, transportation, and billing are examples of nonmanufacturing costs which can often be applied by use of standards. On the other hand, advertising, salesmen's salaries, and general administrative expenses ordinarily cannot be so treated.[5]

Indirect Costs

After charging directly those costs which can, as a practical matter, be treated as direct charges, there remain indirect costs to be

---

[4] "The Manufacturer's Marketing Costs," *N.A.C.A. Bulletin* (November 15, 1929), p. 335.
[5] For a discussion of the difficulties involved in setting standards for these costs, see Arthur H. Smith, "Distribution Analysis Points the Way to More Profitable Business," *N.A.C.A. Conference Proceedings* (1950), pp. 80-5.

allocated. These indirect costs are collected as totals and subsequently are spread over the various units to be costed. Allocation as a costing process thus proceeds by breaking down totals to arrive at separate unit costs in contrast with direct charging which classifies the costs at their source.[6]

In order to allocate indirect costs it is necessary to select a basis of allocation which serves as a common denominator for the units to be costed. The cost is then divided among the various units in proportions based upon this common denominator. For example, cubic content of goods handled is often used as the basis of allocating warehousing costs to products.

The process of allocating assumes that the cost being allocated is correlated with the basis used for allocation. Where basis and cost are unrelated and do not vary together, the resulting unit costs are determined arbitrarily. To illustrate, where warehouse space is rented and paid for according to the amount of space occupied, there is a definite relationship between the number of cubic feet in goods warehoused and cost of warehousing. On the other hand there is no such relationship between sales value of the goods and warehousing cost unless sales value is directly proportional to bulk of the goods warehoused.

The reliability of any cost figure containing an allocated portion of indirect cost depends heavily upon the character of the allocations which have been made. In many cases indirect costs can be allocated to yield unit costs which are quite as reliable as those which could be obtained by direct charging.[7] The condition under which these results can be obtained is the availability of a basis for allocating costs which is demonstrably correlated with the total amount of the cost to be allocated. Where allocations have been made on arbitrary bases, the resulting costs are also more or less arbitrary according to the relative importance of arbitrarily allocated components.

[6] A number of terms are in current use to designate the process here called allocation. For example, there are "proration," "apportionment," and "assignment." The field study failed to disclose any generally accepted distinctions in the use of these words, although a few accountants prefer to use "allocation" when a factor of variability bearing a logical relationship to the cost in question is available and to use "proration" where such a relationship is lacking. In the present report, allocation is used without such distinction because it seems to be the term most commonly employed.

[7] There are also circumstances where more significant costs are obtained by allocation than by direct charging. As an example, overtime labor is commonly classified as an overhead cost and averaged over all units produced in the period in order to avoid the distortion of individual job costs resulting from the chance incidence of overtime work.

The field study yielded numerous examples of situations in which improperly chosen bases of allocation had led to the wrong decision. As an illustration, one company stated that it sells two products, one of which is priced at $50 per ton and the other at $500 per ton, delivered to the customer's city. At one time, outbound freight charges were allocated between the products on the basis of relative sales values. A study disclosed the fact that both products were carried at the same rate per ton and that weight would be a better basis for allocating outward freight costs. When shipments were costed on this basis, it was found that sales of the lower priced product in distant territories had been unprofitable, but management had not been aware of the fact because the method of allocating costs had charged a disproportionate share of freight to the higher priced product. In addition to illustrating an error in allocation, this case raises the further question of whether it would not have been preferable in the first place to have treated the freight as a direct cost chargeable to the product, territory, or other classification involved in each shipment.

Distinction between Separable Costs and Joint Costs

While many indirect costs are separable and can be allocated with substantial reliability, other indirect costs are joint costs for which no fully satisfactory basis for allocation can be found. Circumstances under which costs are being assigned determine which costs are separable and which are joint. Many costs which are direct as to major segments such as product lines or sales divisions are joint when considering subdivisions of these segments such as individual items within a product line or individual salesman. Similarly, costs which are readily separable by product lines may be joint as to sales territories, and vice versa. Costs which are fixed with respect to volume are joint as to units making up current volume and any increment in volume which may result from a decision in question. However, this applies only within a limited range of fluctuation in volume and for the period during which commitments resulting in fixed charges remain unchanged. From the long-range point of view, the same costs can be varied with volume and hence that portion of the costs associated with an increment in volume is then separable rather than joint.

Some costs which appear to be joint when viewed superficially are separable when traced to their origin in managerial decisions. For example, an advertising appropriation may be built up by combining separate plans, each of which contemplates an expenditure to obtain a definite objective with respect to an individual product or territory. Or, an expenditure for a series of sales calls may be planned with a specific allocation of time or number of stops in view. In these instances, the costs are separable and allocation on properly chosen bases yields reliable segment costs.

In practice, the dividing line between joint costs and separable costs is often not clear, for one group shades into the other by degrees. While there may be some relationship between various bases and costs to be allocated, this relationship may be imperfect. For example, the general administrative expenses may vary to some extent with sales volume when the change in sales is substantial enough to have an impact on the complexity of the administrative function, but the variation in cost is not proportional to any measure of sales volume. With many costs, current changes in volume have no measurable effect on the total amounts spent, although some relationship may exist when individual changes are considered cumulatively and over a period of time.

Often, joint costs arise because management finds it more profitable to combine several lines of activity in order to secure fuller utilization of facilities than would be provided if operations were restricted to a single line. In the factory a special purpose machine now used for the production of a single line may be further utilized if an additional line is added. In developing costs for management's decision on whether or not to add the new line, those costs which do not vary in total amount with the decision reached (such as taxes on the equipment) can be excluded from the cost calculation.

A typical example in the nonmanufacturing field is found where a company owned truck fleet is operated to deliver finished products and also to carry raw materials on return runs which would otherwise be made without load. Similarly, salesmen sell a variety of products because the combined sales income yields a greater margin over salary and travel expenses than would be obtained from a single product. Under such circumstances the overall cost of the various activities is less when they are combined than if they were separate. Differences in this overall cost which result from expansion or contraction of any single line of activity can be determined, but the complete cost for any individual unit in the combination is determinable only on the assumption that there is some reasonable basis for assessing the segment's relative share of the composite costs and composite savings.

Difficulties which arise in allocation of some joint costs stem from the lack of relationship between any available common denominator for measuring the joint activities and the cost of these activities. A principal reason for this lack of relationship is that decisions to incur costs are often made and carried out in terms of a group of segments rather than for the separate segments. Under such circumstances the group is jointly responsible for the total amount of the cost and there may be no objective way to determine separately the responsibility which each segment has for any portion of the cost.

The prevalence of joint costs had deterred a number of the companies interviewed from attempting to determine separate costs for important segments in their marketing operations. They stated that allocations of these joint costs would necessarily be arbitrary and the results would not be useful. As an example, salesmen for one of these companies sell all of the company's products to all classes of customers. An attempt was made to find some way whereby time, effort, or other factors in the salesman's work could be separated by products and related to selling costs, but no clear and consistent pattern could be obtained. On the other hand field selling costs were readily assigned to territories as direct charges. Clear-cut lines of demarcation in an organization and specialization of selling and advertising by products, customers, or other segments make costs more readily separable. However, costing facility cannot be a dominant consideration in choosing methods of operating a business.

In the preparation of periodic profit-and-loss statements by products, territories, or other segments, there is generally a residue of costs for which no fully satisfactory basis of allocation can be found. Costs of general administration, institutional advertising, and certain types of sales promotion are likely to be among those to which this statement applies. A number of companies interviewed omit general administrative expenses and sometimes other expenses from segment statements. Other companies assign all costs but emphasize the fact that some costs have been assigned on arbitrary bases.

Where the problem confronting management calls for a choice between alternatives, it is usually sufficient to know how the costs will differ from one alternative to another. For the specific purpose of making such a decision it is not necessary to allocate those costs which will not be changed in total amount by the decision. As an example, a company which sells through its own salesmen also maintains retail outlets in the form of leased departments in large department stores. These outlets are viewed partly as a means of sales promotion but it is managerial policy to close any outlet which operates at a loss. After some discussion this company decided that an outlet was desirable if it showed a margin over the costs that could be saved by closing the outlet. Sales in such outlets are benefitted by extensive national advertising of the company's products, but they decided that there was no satisfactory basis for allocating this advertising cost to sales made through different marketing channels. Since expenditures for national advertising are not affected by the decision to close or to open an individual retail outlet, it is considered unnecessary to allocate this cost in order to arrive at a decision. However, expenditures for local advertising are allocated to retail outlets since more is spent for such advertising where retail outlets are in operation than where all sales are made through other channels.

As an illustration of the dangers inherent in the improper use of allocated joint costs, one company related that during the depression years in the early thirties, it attempted to improve an unsatisfactory profit by discontinuing production and sale of products which showed a net loss after allocating to them what was considered an appropriate share of all costs of operating the company. Despite vigorous attempts to sell more of the profitable items, overall volume and profits declined. Since the company's products were sold principally by truck delivery routes which brought a full assortment of items to the customers daily, the decision to reduce product variety had little effect on costs of operating the trucks or wages paid to driver-salesmen. Once this situation became clear it was seen that an error had been made in reasoning from cost data which included an arbitrary allocation of joint costs which were not reduced by the actions taken. Had the analysis of costs been limited to those costs which were actually affected by the decision made, or had the overall absorption of overhead and its effect on company net profit been considered, it would have been apparent that the discontinued products made a substantial contribution to the remaining joint costs and net profit. When management of this company realized that a mistake had been made, it took steps to build up sales volume again by increasing the variety of goods offered for sale even though the added items could not carry a full share of allocated distribution costs and still show a profit. Following this change the company's profits improved.

In segment profit-and-loss statements prepared by some of the companies interviewed, margins are shown before allocation of certain groups of costs which management need not consider in decisions for which the statement is used. Other companies use similar margins, but determine them by special study when the information is wanted. A fuller explanation of this technique appears in later pages of this report.

Classification for Recording and Assignment

The plan for classification employed in accounting for nonmanufacturing costs needs to be developed with consideration to the types of cost statements and analyses which will be wanted. When this has been done, the desired data can be obtained more economically and its reliability improved.

One of the companies interviewed summarized the plan it follows in classifying nonmanufacturing costs as follows:

> The accounting plan should start with the determination of responsibilities. The second step would be to set up the necessary functions within each of the major responsibilities. The third step would then be to provide the necessary natural expense accounts to correctly reflect the activities of each function.

This statement seems representative of the general approach followed by companies which have well-developed plans for using cost data in control and planning of nonmanufacturing activities. The extent to which each step has been carried out appears to depend upon the complexity of the company's organization and upon the amount of information about nonmanufacturing costs which is wanted by management in the individual company.

Each of the above bases of cost classification has its own field of usefulness; viz.:

1. Classification by responsibility provides data needed by management in current cost control.
2. Classification by function gives management the costs of performing individual functions which are the primary units in planning methods of operation. Assembly of costs by function is also an essential step in assigning nonmanufacturing costs to products, territories, customers, and any other classes of segments for which costs are wanted.
3. Classification by natural groups provides information as to items for which money is being spent, e.g., for salaries, travel, rent, etc.

Since the functional classification is most directly useful in arriving at costs for purposes of planning and policy making covered by this report, additional discussion of this basis of cost classification follows.

Classification of Nonmanufacturing Costs by Function

A function may be defined as a specific type of activity for which costs are assembled. Thus major nonmanufacturing activities are classified by one company as finished goods transportation, advertising, direct selling, warehousing, sales administration, sales accounting and credit, and general administration. While this company's classification is typical of those encountered in the field study, another company uses a distinctively different major classification in which nonmanufacturing costs are grouped into (1) costs of order filling and delivery, and (2) costs of getting orders and collecting money.[8] In a few cases certain types of costs ordinarily included in manufacturing are classified as major nonmanufacturing functions. Several companies interviewed so classify research costs. Since methods of organization and operation differ from company to company, the specific functions recognized also differ from company to company.

Subsidiary to these main functions there are usually subfunctions which serve as the basis for more detailed cost classifications by functions performed. For example, one company has the following subgroups under general and administrative expense: billing, accounts receivable, general and cost accounting, tabulating, treasury, executive.

Classification of nonmanufacturing costs by function serves two important purposes; namely:

1. It facilitates determination of costs by segments through bringing together costs which can be allocated on the same basis. When this has been done, it is also easier to find a unit with which to measure the service performed and to relate this unit of functional activity to products, territories, and other segments. For example, a company which operates a fleet of delivery trucks groups all costs of operating the trucks (drivers' wages, insurance, gasoline, etc.) and allocates them to products on a single basis.

2. When the cost of an individual function is known, management is in a position to study costs of performing the same function in alternative ways and, in some cases, to decide whether or not the function should be performed at all. As an example of the first, one company had changed from decentralized billing to centralized billing because the latter was more economical. A decision of the second type was made when a company discontinued field warehouses which had been originally established to provide quicker deliveries to customers in some areas. In this case the cost of operating the warehouses exceeded the gross profit on additional sales attributable to the warehouses.

---

[8] For a description of this plan of cost classification, see E. Stewart Freeman, "The Manufacturer's Marketing Cost," *N.A.C.A. Bulletin* (November 15, 1929).

The field study showed that the functional classification of non-manufacturing costs is often limited to a few broad categories.[9] Under these circumstances it is usual to express the amount of cost in each category as a percentage of overall sales, manufacturing cost, or some similar unit and to use there percentages in determining the amount of nonmanufacturing costs applicable to each segment. Such figures are helpful as indicators of trends insofar as management thinks in terms of relationships between sales and the purposes represented by cost categories used. However, when so broadly applied, the process of averaging obscures differences in costs of selling the various products, of covering different territories, or of serving different classes of customers. Often these differences constitute the information which management really needs in making decisions with respect to specific segments. It seems fair to say that such costs are frequently used because cost data which are more appropriate for the purpose have not been developed.

In order to throw these differences into relief so that they may be used to help explain why some segments of the business are more profitable than others, the broad functions can be broken down into subfunctions. When this has been done, it is usually possible to find units for measuring functional activity which can serve as bases for allocating costs of the function. For example, many companies include with administrative expense the costs of billing, keeping accounts receivable, and clerical operations involved in order filling. Ordinarily these costs are definitely related to and fluctuate fairly closely with sales activity factors such as number of orders, number of items billed, etc. Accordingly they are not difficult to allocate. On the other hand expenses of the president's office, the treasurer's office, and the legal department generally have no relationship to current sales activity and must be allocated on bases which are largely arbitrary.[10]

---

[9] The accumulation and application of factory costs according to a detailed plan based upon operating characteristics of equipment in cost centers in contrast to the limited attention given to classification and application of nonmanufacturing costs doubtless reflects the accountant's preoccupation with inventory costs and relative neglect of costs for other managerial purposes. A previous research study ("The Volume Factor in Budgeting Costs," *N.A.C.A. Bulletin, Research Series No. 18* [June, 1950], p. 1304) also pointed out the comparative lack of budgetary control over nonmanufacturing costs even in companies where comprehensive systems for control of factory costs are in operation.

[10] Greer and Smith (*Accounting for a Meat Packing Business*, p. 191) remark that "Most of these 'general' expenses are controllable in totals only. The amount of each outlay is determined in advance as a general policy matter; and the amounts are not greatly affected either by the volume or kind of business conducted . . . the most troublesome problem in the handling of administrative expense is its allocation to products and to sales territories. In the nature of the case any such allocation is entirely arbitrary, and in the discussions of the problem theoretical considerations and personal preferences are given full sway."

For this reason a cost system which provides for separate classification and application of these different types of administrative expenses yields more reliable costs than does one in which administrative cost is collected in a lump sum and allocated on a single basis.

In the accounts, nonmanufacturing costs are usually accumulated by nature of expenditure. These accounts, classified by nature of expenditure are, in turn, grouped by departments or other organization units corresponding to areas of individual responsibility.

Since organizational lines generally follow functions performed, functional cost classifications often tend to coincide with departments or other organizational units set up to obtain responsibility for cost control. However, a group of costs under a single responsibility may include several functions and each of the latter then should be assigned on the basis which relates it to the segments being costed. Assignment of the costs to products, territories, and other segments is sometimes made in the accounts. In other cases, assignment of historical costs to segments is made with the use of tabulations and worksheets which are apart from the accounts. Where costs are assigned to a number of segments, the multiple distributions required are more readily made by statistical processes. These are applied to the cost totals accumulated in the accounts by responsibilities. The assembly of prospective costs for a decision involving a change in methods is necessarily a special study rather than a routine accounting operation.

Usually it is considered desirable to provide for regular accumulation and reporting of costs according to those classifications which correspond to major aspects of the company's marketing program. For example, one company has a sales organization which is specialized by product lines. Salesmen ordinarily handle only one product line and the emphasis is upon developing specialists to meet intensive competition in this line. Advertising features individual product lines. As a result, the company has developed its classification of accounts to provide complete statements of profit and loss by product lines. On the other hand, salesmen for another company sell a complete line and advertising stresses the brand name. The sales organization is set up on a territorial basis and management is primarily interested in sales and profits by territories and by individual salesmen. Here the selling costs are accumulated by territories.

In decisions with respect to alternatives, management often needs to know, not how much a given product has cost, but rather how much cost will be incurred or saved if a given action is taken. This calls for determining which costs will change as a result of the decision and an estimate of how much the change will be. Change in volume is often the principal factor which causes changes in cost. Under these circumstances, separation of costs into fixed and variable components is helpful.[11] Such a classification is made in the accounts by some of the companies interviewed and a few of them carry this classification into periodic reports in order to aid management in determining what effect a given change in volume can be expected to have on costs and profits.

Analyses of costs by classifications which are not incorporated in the accounts may be wanted from time to time. In order to obtain these analyses it is desirable to organize the source records in such a way that costs can be classified in various ways with a minimum of clerical work. Coding to provide for classification according to the various bases which may be wanted greatly facilitates subsequent analysis. Most of the larger companies seen in the field study had mechanized sorting and tabulating operations required in analysis of sales and costs.

In any case, it is desirable to arrange the original data in such a way that subsequent processing operations can be economically performed.

Value of Adequate Classification

Adequate classification of costs by functions or departments serves dual purposes in that it enables management to place responsibility for control of costs and also facilitates the determination of costs by products and other segments of the business. One way in which the latter objective is accomplished is by making it possible to treat many items as direct charges when otherwise they would have to be allocated. Thus it may be possible to charge some advertising and sales promotion costs directly to specific product lines. Most of the field selling costs likewise can be charged directly to territories. In general it is advisable to design the classification of accounts in such a way that, whenever practical, costs are treated as direct charges. That accountants should devote more attention to cost classification and less attention to cost allocation was the opinion expressed by one executive who had formerly been responsible for developing accounting data for use by management in several companies.

---

[11] For a discussion of the nature of fixed and variable costs, see "The Variation of Cost with Volume," *N.A.C.A. Bulletin, Research Series No. 16* (June 15, 1949), pp. 1219-22.

ALLOCATION OF INDIRECT NONMANUFACTURING COSTS

Assignment of indirect costs to segments is accomplished by allocation. These allocations must reflect the real incidence of costs as to the segments for which costs are wanted if the resulting figures are to be reliable as a basis for managerial decisions. Allocation of indirect costs presents two problems—namely, (1) what bases should be used for allocation and (2) how far the allocation processes should be carried.

Selecting Bases for Allocating Costs

Accounting discussions concerning the choice of bases for allocating indirect costs commonly dismiss the problem with the statement that bases used should be "fair" or "equitable." [12] The idea that there should be a demonstrable relationship between basis and cost to be allocated seems to be seldom expressed, although it does underlie practices followed in many cases. Hence, further information must be sought in the examination of the practices of specific companies.

In order to serve as a satisfactory basis for cost allocation, the factor chosen must (1) fluctuate concomitantly with the activity which is the source of the cost and (2) it must itself be measurable without undue expense. Objective tests for determining how well a proposed basis for allocation meets the first of these criteria are not always available or practical, but there are methods which can be helpful. The following are representative of those employed by various companies interviewed.

1. Simple correlation analysis methods employing scatter charts are used to find which of several possible bases is most closely related to the cost. This work is commonly a part of the process of preparing flexible budgets for cost control, but a factor which serves as a good measure of activity for controlling a given cost is usually also a basis for allocating the same cost.

2. Time studies and job analyses of activities of salesmen, clerks, and deliverymen are used for those costs to which such methods are applicable. Detailed measurements are made for a test period or on

---

[12] In the field study, inquiries were directed toward ascertaining the objectives which guide accountants in selecting bases for allocating indirect costs. The following statements are typical of those received in answer to these questions:

"Bases of cost allocation must be fair and equitable."

"Equity, effort expended, and benefits conferred must all be considered."

"Resulting costs must be expressed in units which management in an industry is accustomed to use."

"The basis of allocation must be related to the sales value of the product."

"Simplicity is the essential characteristic in our cost allocations."

a sampling basis to determine what factors influence costs and what the relationships are. Such methods are more readily applicable to repetitive activities (e.g., packing, loading and shipping, billing) than they are to the more varied activities such as direct selling and administration. However, such methods must be used with discrimination. To illustrate, one of the companies interviewed found that time of sales executives was almost wholly devoted to new products, to sales territories where performance was unsatisfactory, and to similar problems which were nonroutine and highly variable in nature. Allocation of executive salary and office costs according to the distribution of the executive's time therefore produced erratic results which were considered unsatisfactory. On the other hand, another company follows the practice of having divisional executives such as the sales manager estimate the ratios in which their time is divided among product lines and in this case the ratios are found to be stable and are viewed as satisfactory bases for allocating the costs in question. Some companies also allocate salesmen's salaries and expenses on bases established by studies to ascertain how salesmen spend their time while other companies consider such studies to be of no value.

3. Where the foregoing methods cannot be applied, logical analysis based upon knowledge of operations of the company is an aid to selecting bases for allocating costs. It proceeds by searching for factors which are likely to influence the cost of the function whose cost is to be allocated. For example, in allocating the costs of a packaging operation, a company considered the use of direct labor hours, machine hours, factory cost, and sales value as possible bases for allocation. The fact that labor constituted the principal cost of the operation led to tentative selection of direct labor hours. A final decision was made to use direct labor dollars since the latter data were more readily available and correlated closely with labor hours. In another case, a company which desired to allocate expenses of a divisional administrative office defined the functions of this office as planning, developing, and operating the division to obtain the best possible return on capital invested in it. The company then reasoned that expenses of carrying out these functions were related to the capital invested in the division and that divisional administrative expenses could be properly allocated to subunits of the division on the basis of relative amount of capital invested in each. A writer on the subject has suggested that the following questions be asked in searching for a basis upon which to allocate the expenses of a function: [13]

1. What is this department set up to do?
2. What are the individual steps taken to accomplish this result?
3. Are they repetitive individually or in groups?
4. If so, can these repeated operations be segregated to products or to customers and thus constitute a proper basis for allocating expense totals?

---

[13] Alden C. Brett, "The Role of the Accountant in the Control of Distribution Costs," *N.A.C.A. Bulletin* (April 1, 1940), p. 966.

The results obtained from some expenditures cannot be controlled, but the application of effort is planned and controlled by management. Under such circumstances, accountants interviewed frequently stated that planned distribution of effort constitutes a better basis for allocation than does actual distribution of effort or actual results obtained. This point of view has been expressed as follows by a writer on the subject.[14]

> Thus, the salaries and travel expenses of salesmen, one of the major items of expense in any distribution cost budget, may be allocated on the basis of the opinion of the sales manager. He builds his sales force with certain objectives in mind and he directs their efforts in those channels. Would their own time reports show a greatly different pattern? Likewise, the second largest component of cost, advertising, is beamed at the promotion of specific products and should be so charged.

These accountants stressed the need to discover the purposes which management has in mind when authorizing expenditures. In order to accomplish this, the accountant must be familiar with marketing operations and must work closely with executives in this field of the company's work.

Several companies stated that they had found it desirable to document the selection of bases of allocation, giving all factors considered and the reasons for selection of the bases chosen. When questions arose at a later date, it was easy to determine why the decision to use a particular basis was made. The record also had served as an aid when changes in bases were proposed at a subsequent time. In some cases the reasons for choice of allocation bases were summarized in the company's accounting manual.

Provision must be made for collecting statistics needed for allocating costs on the bases chosen. These take the form of time reports, quantity movements, etc. Most of this data is recorded for other purposes as well and it is necessary only to consider economical methods for summarizing and reporting.

The basis used by other companies is not necessarily a guide to the basis that should be chosen in a specific case because conditions differ. For this reason, no attempt was made in this study to tabulate and report the frequency with which various bases are employed in allocating specific costs.

---

[14] I. Wayne Keller, "Relative Profit Margin Approach to Distribution Costing," *N.A.C.A. Bulletin* (March 1, 1949), p. 765.

Proportionality between the basis of allocation and the cost being allocated is usually assumed in making allocations. While this assumption of proportionality is sufficiently in accord with the facts to produce satisfactory costs in many circumstances, difficulties may often be traced to use of this assumption where it is not tenable. In actuality there are various degrees of relationship between costs and bases of allocation.

Bases which are likely to be influenced by changes in selling prices or volume often cause shifts in the proportions in which costs are allocated. As a result, certain segments appear to cost more or less despite the fact that no changes have occurred in the way these units are made and sold. As an example of this difficulty, one company which allocated a considerable amount of cost to products on the basis of sales dollars raised prices on certain specialty lines. At the end of the year it found that low priced products on which the prices had not been advanced showed higher profits despite the fact that unit volume and total costs for these products were very close to the same figures for the previous year. Management questioned the product profit figures because bonuses were being paid to product sales managers on the basis of net profit. Study of the situation disclosed that an increase in dollar volume of sales resulting from increased selling prices on some products had reduced the ratio between sales and costs allocated on a sales dollar basis. Since the same ratio was used in costing all products, the low priced products were not charged with as much cost as before.

When the object is to measure in terms of profits the effectiveness with which marketing effort has been apportioned, it is necessary for costs of the effort to be determined independently of the results obtained. Such commonly used bases of allocation as actual sales dollars violate this principle, for here costs of marketing are made to depend in part on sales realized. Use of such costing methods for pricing amounts to reasoning in a circle since the cost which is supposed to determine the price is also determined by the price. The real cause of a change in cost would seem to be a decision to vary the marketing effort applied to the segment and hence a good basis of allocation should reflect this decision without being affected by extraneous influences.

Such difficulties also arise from bases other than the sales dollar. For example, in costing a packaging operation a company applied indirect costs of the packaging department on the basis of direct labor hours. Hourly burden rates were high because expensive equipment was used but unit costs were low because volume was large. The sales department then designed a new display package which it wished to test for effectiveness before buying special purpose packaging machinery to handle the new design. Some of the operations were done by hand. While the unit labor cost of these operations was reasonable, addition of departmental burden to this labor made the cost of the package exceedingly high. The sales department contended that this was not a correct cost and that it would discourage improvements in packaging which might be beneficial to profits by increasing sales. This contention seems to be justified because introduction of the new package caused little, if any, increase in the total amount of indirect costs to be allocated in the packaging department. At the time of the interview the company was planning to separate the packaging department costs into fixed and variable components. This would make it possible to ascertain the additional cost attributable to a new package. It was stated that this would be a better basis for deciding whether or not a trial of the new package should be made. If the new package proved satisfactory, its production could be fully mechanized and a new overhead rate established.

Extent to Which Allocation Is Carried

The field study showed that management usually wishes to have net profit figures for products or product lines. Net profit by territories is also determined by a majority of the companies interviewed. In order to ascertain net profit by segments of any class, it is necessary to assign all operating costs.

However, there are many decisions with respect to individual segments which can be made without considering all costs. For this reason, costs assembled to serve as a basis for deciding between alternatives often are limited to the costs affected by the decision. This leads to determination of cost differentials when the change under consideration is not expected to affect sales income. Where change in both costs and income is expected to accompany the decision, costs assigned to the segments in question are deducted from corresponding sales income figures to obtain contribution margins, i.e., the contribution which each segment makes to unallocated costs and profits combined.

For purposes of exposition, the net profit approach and the contribution margin approach are discussed separately in the pages which follow. However, both approaches are commonly used together, as described in the section of this report entitled "Combining Contributed Margins with Full Allocation."

The Net Profit Approach

Some companies stress heavily the need for statements which reflect the profitability of products and product lines through the assignment of all costs. This has been expressed by W. I. McNeill as follows:

> . . . Statistical net profit obtained historically once a year and computed in advance for the year to come is an indispensable tool of management for judging the profitability of individual products, product groups, or sales branches or territories, and, if you please, it is indispensable in appraising selling prices.
>
> A discussion of the problem leads immediately to a basic concept, namely that every dollar that a company spends must find its way eventually into the cost of one of the company's products. The determination of net profit through the allocation of all dollars spent is the safest way of notifying the management of products or branches that are not producing a satisfactory return.[15]

The reasons given for carrying assignment of costs to the point of determining net profit on each segment may be summarized as follows:

1. Management is familiar with and accustomed to the use of overall net profit figures. Executives naturally follow the same mode of thought in dealing with segments of the business and apply the same profit standards (in terms of net profit after all expenses) that they have developed for the company as a whole. In a number of cases comments were made to the effect that each product line or each sales territory is viewed as a separate business that should "stand on its own feet" or "carry its share of the load."

2. Since no profit is realized until all expenses of operating the company have been recovered, many accountants reason that a cost which does not include an appropriate share of all expenses may cause management to forget the need to recover all expenses. This point of view is particularly evident in the preparation of costs as a guide for pricing policy, as can be seen in the following statement made by a member of the Committee on Research:

> . . . In the initial determination of selling price in a free market, the ideal selling price should reflect all costs allocated as equitably as possible among all products. This is the soundest position competitively both from the standpoint of competition within the product line in the same company, and from the standpoint of competitive products of other manufacturers.

---

[15] "Good Old Net Profit!" *The Controller* (July, 1950), p. 317.

Uses and Limitations of Net Profit Approach

In the field study, questions were asked to bring out both the uses which are made of segment net profit data and the limitations which such data might have. It was found that management is interested in a breakdown of historical profit by segments in order to learn how much profit (or loss) was realized on each segment. From this information it is possible to discern the relative strength or weakness of each segment. In doing this, comparisons are made with one or more of the following:

1. Other segments of the same class (i.e., one product with another).
2. Expected or budgeted profit for the same segment.
3. Desired or standard profit for the same segment.
4. Profit on the same segment in previous periods.

Such comparisons are useful because they show where managerial attention should be directed in order to improve profits.

However, it is necessary to keep in mind the fact that some of the costs which have been allocated to the various segments are essentially fixed in total amount for short periods and that these costs are not immediately reduced by the elimination, or increased by the addition, of a product or territory. Hence the fact that an individual segment shows a low net profit or even a net loss does not necessarily mean that it should be eliminated. When sales income from such a product fails to show a satisfactory margin over costs but does contribute to fixed costs, it is usually desirable to continue the product in the immediate future since to abandon it would merely leave unabsorbed that portion of the fixed costs formerly allocated to the product in question. This points out the fact that individual segment net profit figures are often not applicable as guides to managerial action in short period tactical decisions.

While certain costs are fixed for short periods, they do tend to vary with some measure of activity over a longer period. As the span of time under consideration is lengthened, management has a wider scope of action in changing methods. For this reason, segment net profit figures are used as guides in long-range policy decisions.

In contrast with manufacturing costs where commitments for buildings and machinery often extend over a period of years, the major portion of nonmanufacturing costs is usually made up of expenditures for personnel, advertising, and similar items which are planned for a period of months. This leads many companies to view practically all nonmanufacturing costs as items which can be readily adjusted to change in volume, methods of operation, or other factors. Application of this point of view can be seen in the following practices observed in the field study.

When a product, territory, or other segment does not yield a satisfactory net profit, it is not summarily eliminated, but at the same time management takes steps toward making this product yield a more satisfactory margin or toward finding something else to replace it which will both absorb its share of allocated fixed costs and show an adequate net profit. This is apt to be a gradual process in the course of which a number of proposed courses of action are evaluated by special studies to determine the effect they may be expected to have on profit from the segment. These special studies need to take account of the overall effect which a decision will have on indirect costs and profits of the company as a whole.[16]

An application of full allocation is found in the method of reporting costs to territorial sales managers followed by a company interviewed in the field study. This company operates regional warehouses which usually serve several sales territories by enabling them to make prompt deliveries and warehousing is looked upon as a service supplied to assist the territorial sales managers. Costs of warehousing are allocated to sales territories because the territorial managers' requests for such service are considered to be closely related to the warehousing facilities provided and hence to the cost of such facilities. In discussion, it was stated that a decision to use or not to use these facilities in a specific territory would not greatly affect the overall cost of operating a warehouse, but that cumulatively a number of such decisions would be responsible for changes in warehousing operations and their costs. The managers may purchase the same services from outsiders if they wish, but in this case they are charged with a share of the fixed charges on company owned facilities until some other use is found for any unused capacity created by nonuse of the company owned warehouse. The reasoning which underlies this latter practice is that unabsorbed fixed costs which result from a decision to buy elsewhere are an offset to savings from obtaining the services at a price below the company's regular charge.

---

[16] See Herman C. Heiser, "Putting Cost Accounting to Work—To Answer the $64 Questions," *N.A.C.A. Year Book* (1946), pp. 145-6.

The allocation of all costs is often employed to determine costs for individual segments which are useful in setting objectives or standards for each segment. Such a cost figure aids management in determining what combination of selling price and volume is necessary to yield a satisfactory profit. While this objective may not be realizable at the moment due to competition or need to gain buyer acceptance for a new product, the cost still serves as a basis for determining how successful the company has been in reaching its profit objective on the segment. Thus the accountant for one company interviewed stated that the practice in his company was to compare the profit on each product with a potential or standard profit for the same product rather than with profits shown by other products. In some cases, the profit objective is best attained by a policy of flexible pricing. The allocation of indirect costs here provides a long-run average cost which management often wishes to have in mind as an objective even when such a cost is not an important factor in a given price decision.

Allocation of indirect costs on reliable bases can be more complete when a long-run point of view is taken because certain costs which are largely independent of fluctuations in activity bases for short periods do tend to vary with some measure of activity over a longer period. Consequently these activity measures can be used as satisfactory bases for allocation when decisions in question relate to a period long enough for the costs to respond to changes in the activity bases employed for allocation. An illustration of this is supplied by the experience related by one person interviewed. After the beginning of World War II, sales of this company's regular products dropped rapidly due to lack of essential materials, but no immediate action was taken to reduce executive and experienced supervisory personnel in the home office because the company did not wish to lose key employees. While a substantial reduction was eventually made, expenses of sales administration declined much more slowly than sales. With the end of the war, sales recovered quickly. For a time, the expanded sales volume was handled by a sales administrative force much smaller than that considered necessary in prewar years, but gradual expansion of home office personnel took place because this action was found necessary to maintain an effective sales program on a continuing basis. The company's experience has led it to conclude that cost of sales supervision is definitely related to size of the field sales force but that this relationship is not a close one.

Hence it uses the latter as a basis for allocating home office sales supervision cost to territories, but with recognition of the fact that supervision costs do not respond immediately nor are they very sensitive to changes in number of salesmen employed.

There are, however, always some costs which must be allocated by use of arbitrarily chosen bases in order to determine net profit for individual segments. The reliability and usefulness of cost data is heavily dependent upon the proportion of such allocated joint costs. Discussion of this topic with accountants for the companies interviewed brought out the following points.

1. Determination of separate product net profit figures is limited to comparatively broad segments which are largely self-contained units of the business. For example, one company preparing net profits by product lines has a separate plant for each line and manufacturing costs are accumulated by keeping a complete set of accounts at each plant. Advertising and selling costs are also largely direct charges to product lines. Assessments to cover general company administration expenses and institutional advertising are made, but the proportion of such costs is small relative to the total of all costs. Product line income statements are prepared monthly by this company and are used by management in evaluating performance of the various lines. On the other hand, determination of costs of individual items within product lines is limited to manufacturing cost and no allocations of nonmanufacturing costs are made.

2. A number of the companies interviewed have studied their costing procedures carefully in order to reduce to a minimum the need for allocating costs and to find the most reliable bases available for those costs which must be allocated. Several companies stated that through continuing study over a period of years, very substantial improvements had been achieved in the reliability of segment costs. This was accomplished by devising methods whereby more costs could be accumulated as direct charges and by finding better methods for allocating indirect costs. With respect to the latter, emphasis is placed upon determining what objectives management has in mind when expenditures are authorized. This approach leads to the allocation of many nonmanufacturing expenses on the basis of budgeted or anticipated distribution of effort rather than upon the actual results obtained.

3. Recognition is given to the fact that some allocations are arbitrary and allowance for this is made in interpretation of costs. Accountants for several companies stated that allocations expressed the proportions in which management of their companies wished joint costs to be recovered, that selling effort was directed toward realizing this aim, and that the segment profits which resulted were viewed as measures of the success with which such a policy had been carried out. For example, one company sold an article both to other manufacturers who installed it as original equipment on their products

and to consumers who used the same article as a replacement for the original equipment. All advertising was directed toward the replacement market, but it was known that consumer acceptance developed by the advertising also aided original equipment sales. Hence management decided that 15 percent of the annual advertising appropriation would be charged to original equipment sales. While arbitrarily arrived at, this percentage expressed managerial policy as to how it desired to recover this joint cost in sales to the two classes of customers.

In the allocation of costs it seems desirable to distinguish between costs which have been allocated on bases which have a demonstrable relationship to costs and the costs which have been allocated arbitrarily. As stated by an accountant interviewed:

> A proper presentation shows the costs that are direct and those that are allocated. If there are different degrees of correlation between the allocation methods and the incidence of costs, the allocated amounts should be presented in a manner to spell out this fact. The allocation of joint costs is clearly pointed out.

When considering alternatives, management needs to know how readily costs will respond to changes in conditions under which costs are incurred. In its thinking with respect to the arbitrarily allocated costs, management should realize that the incidence of these costs on individual segments has been determined by policy rather than by objective procedures. With these facts in mind, management can act with more assurance because the effects which a decision will have on costs and profits are more readily predictable. These conclusions seem to be supported by the emphasis which accountants placed upon the need for explaining how costs have been assigned when presenting cost data for management use.

THE CONTRIBUTION MARGIN APPROACH

Where decisions of limited scope are to be made, some costs usually are unaffected in total regardless of which one of the alternatives in view is chosen. Approximately half of the companies interviewed stated that they make use of the marginal analysis in dealing with problems of this type. In some of these companies contribution margin figures appear on regular operating reports as an aid to management in making decisions with respect to individual segments. More frequently this approach is used only in special studies which involve an estimate of the effect which a proposed change will have on the company's profits.

Contribution Margins—What They Are

A contribution margin figure is computed by deducting from sales income those direct and indirect costs which are incurred in obtaining that sales income. It may relate to all sales income of a given period or to some segment of that sales income such as income from sales of a given product or income from sales in a designated territory. Moreover, the margin may be either that realized in a historical period or it may be a margin anticipated in the future under circumstances defined by a budget or special study.

The specific costs to be deducted are sometimes described as the costs which would not need to be incurred if the segment being costed were not present. Some writers also refer to them as direct costs or variable costs.[17] However, specific costs chargeable against income in computing a contribution margin often include some costs which may be treated as indirect in the ordinary processes of accounting for costs. This is perhaps best illustrated by the variable component of manufacturing overhead. Where a breakdown between fixed and variable costs has been made, the variable costs are generally used, although an exception to this arises in special studies where volume is not an important variable in the problem. These problems usually involve a proposed change in methods, of which a study to determine whether to use owned or rented warehouse space may be cited as an example. Other terms used which cover both volume and nonvolume variables are "savable costs" and "escapable costs." While often distinguished as those costs which could be saved if the product or territory were discontinued, elimination of the segment is usually not the question at issue.

Costs not deducted from income in computing contribution margins are the costs which are not changed in total amount by the decision in question. The contribution margin is, therefore, the income balance contributed by the segment toward the unallocated costs and profit combined. As defined by Atkinson, the contribution margin is the "profit contribution that each one of our 250 products contributes toward meeting company fixed expenses." [18] Similar margins may, of course, be computed for sales territories, customers, and other segments.

---

[17] W. W. Neikirk, "How Direct Costing Can Work for Management," *N.A. C.A. Bulletin* (January, 1951).

[18] "Profit Control by Territories and Products in the Food Processing Industry," *N.A.C.A. Bulletin* (March, 1950), p. 809.

The contribution margin approach views the individual segments as related units in an organization rather than as separate businesses. Some expenditures are made for the business as a whole and the individual segments share the benefits from these expenditures. Those who use the contribution margin approach reason that any separation of these common expenses is unrealistic to the extent that they cannot be allocated on a reasonable basis. Hence they prefer to have a measure of what the individual segment contributes to these joint expenses and to overall company profits rather than a somewhat arbitrary net profit figure. Proper application of the contribution margin approach does not constitute disregard of the unallocated expenses, but instead it emphasizes the contribution which each segment makes to these expenses.

Uses of Contribution Margin Data

Companies which determine contribution margins on a regular periodic basis use this information principally to aid management in determining which segments should have attention in order to improve a weak situation or to make the most of a favorable one. Evaluation of performance by operating personnel was also mentioned frequently in the field study as a use for territorial margins.

As an example, one company prepares a monthly profit contribution report by sales territories.[19] This report shows, for each salesman, figures for sales, gross profit, direct expenses (salesman's salary and commissions, traveling expenses, freight outward, etc.) of the territory, and contribution to company profit. In addition, a sales budget is prepared which provides in advance the sales and the profit contribution expected from each territory. The budgeted contribution for all territories is the amount necessary to cover the general expenses plus the budgeted profit. This total is then broken down to provide a similar budgeted contribution figure for each territory.

Monthly territorial profit contribution reports show (1) what contribution each territory has made toward general expenses and profit and (2) how this contribution compares with the contribution required by the budget. When a territory shows an unsatisfactory result, sales management can analyze the situation and plan such action as it considers desirable. Exclusion of costs not specifically incurred in the territory makes it easy to see what effect any out-of-

---

[19] This illustration is based upon Granville F. Atkinson, "Profit Control by Territories and Products in the Food Processing Industry," *N.A.C.A. Bulletin* (March, 1950).

line expenses have had on territorial operating results. When a territory fails to show a positive contribution to general selling and administrative expenses, the company often finds it desirable to determine how much fixed factory overhead has been absorbed. This information is also available and from it management can ascertain whether or not the territory is contributing anything toward any of the company's fixed expenses.

Another company prepares product margin statements which show the following items:

Net Sales (quantity and amount)
Gross Margin (after total manufacturing costs)
Direct Product Expenses:
    Transportation
    Advertising
    Sales Promotion
Margin after Product Expense

A product manager is in charge of each product line and this statement enables him to measure the effect of changes in those factors within the field of his activity—i.e., the items represented in the statement above as income and costs. In addition to comparisons with budgets to check upon current performance, the above type of analysis was stated to be useful in problems such as the following:

1. Studying the effect of proposed changes in advertising and sales promotion. The current statement is adjusted to reflect the proposed changes in expenses and then compared with subsequent statements of actual results to determine what response is obtained from the change. This response is measured by the increment in profit rather than by sales volume or gross margin alone.

2. Studying the effect of changes in transportation costs. In one example given, a new packaging method was developed for a product. This method was found to increase sales, but equipment to produce the new package was available in only one of the company's plants. Shipments from this plant to sales territories ordinarily served by local manufacturing plants increased transportation costs as well as sales in those areas. By watching the effect on product margin in each sales district, the product manager was able to determine how far this product could be shipped without sacrificing profits.

3. Demonstrating to sales personnel what the effect would be on product margins if requests for changes in promotion, advertising, and prices were made.

A somewhat different application of the contribution margin approach was made by a company which sold to two distinctly different types of customers, viz., (1) consumers who buy a nationally advertised line identified by brand name, and (2) manufacturers who buy quite different bulk goods made from the same raw material. Items in the consumer line are sold at standard prices which have been infrequently changed. However, the company makes frequent studies to determine the effect which special sales promotions have on margins returned by certain large sales outlets such as department stores. Sales to manufacturers are made primarily to absorb factory overhead and to enable the company to purchase raw materials more advantageously through quantity buying. This class of business would not be profitable by itself, but is advantageous when combined with consumer products. Each order for the manufacturer's goods is studied to determine what contribution it can be expected to make to fixed factory and general company overhead. Since manufacturing capacity is limited to that which complements the consumer product business most advantageously, the company frequently selects the most profitable industrial orders and refuses business which does not offer so large a contribution to profits.

Another company had developed a statement of policy governing classes of decisions for which contribution margin figures may be used and those decisions for which they should not be used in this company. The following decisions are listed as those in which contribution margins may be useful:

1. Pricing.
2. Determining what products to make.
3. Planning production methods.

Decisions for which they are not used cover:

1. Cost control.
2. Product selection where allocation of all costs is needed to give a comparison with what the product should absorb.
3. Overall net profit comparisons.
4. Pricing where optional business is available.

Advantages of Contribution Approach for Choosing between Alternatives

In practice, the contribution margin approach is employed primarily as a tool for use in making decisions which concern current tactics in meeting competition, pricing special orders, changing of operating methods, and other problems where alternatives are involved. Such questions generally arise under circumstances in which there are joint or fixed costs of substantial amount. The decisions are made on the assumption that these costs will not be changed in total amount by the decision and hence allocation of them is unnecessary. Accountants interviewed during the field study pointed out the following advantages possessed by the contribution margin approach.

1. It provides a direct answer to the question "What does this segment contribute to overall profit?" Where management is considering alternatives that will change relative volumes of the various segments, the net profit approach is roundabout because it is necessary to take into account the effect which a redistribution of indirect costs will have upon costs of other segments. When a product, territory, or other unit shows a net loss after being charged with a full share of all costs, dropping the unit does not increase overall profit by the amount of the loss. The reason is that fixed costs formerly allocated to the unit are not saved but instead are charged to other units or against profits as unabsorbed overhead. Similarly, the benefit from increased volume in one segment is not accurately measured by the increased net profit from that segment alone. Instead, the benefit is diffused over all segments by averaging fixed costs over a larger number of units. On the other hand the change in contribution margin measures directly the change in overall net profit which results from a change affecting one segment by itself and it is unnecessary to consider repercussions on costs allocated to other segments.

2. It avoids errors which sometimes result from failure to understand cost allocations. A member of the Committee on Research stated this idea as follows in commenting upon an early draft of this report: "In my opinion, many erroneous conclusions arise from reliance upon allocated costs. Too often management, especially an individual not trained in the accounting field, tends to regard costs so determined as actual and factual and therefore places too much reliance upon their exactness. The first proration or allocation in calculating product cost, for example, introduces an element of opinion which merely represents someone's best estimate of what the cost may be. It seems rather futile, therefore, to attempt to base far-reaching management decisions on statistical information which may not be too sound. It appears far more logical to recognize that exactness cannot be attained through allocating costs to specific items or even groups of items and consequently to present data which show the contribution of such items to the profit picture as a whole."

While some accountants emphasized that in their companies management is familiar with the bases of cost allocation used and that limitations which these bases have are carefully pointed out when costs are presented, other accountants stated that they found executives to be impatient with or confused by such procedures.[20]

---

[20] As observed by H. E. Howell (Forum letter *N.A.C.A. Bulletin*, Vol. 27, p. 1027) "Management goes ahead, using its innate business sense and ignoring the cost accountant's figures."

These executives do not understand the complex effects which changes in volume or price of one product may have upon fixed costs allocated to other products and reason that a change of a given number of dollars in the final figure on the operating statement for an individual product should bring an equal change in overall net profit. The contribution margin approach follows this same line of reasoning and hence it is readily understood by those who lack technical accounting training.

3. It avoids controversy over fairness with which allocations of indirect costs have been made. The field study provided numerous examples of situations in which disagreement over expense allocations had prevented managerial personnel from reaching satisfactory decisions or had distracted attention from the costs which were really affected by the action proposed.[21] In most cases the decisions in question could have been made with contribution margin data and questionable allocations avoided.

4. Managerial action is facilitated because the expenses which can be changed by a decision with respect to a specific segment are clearly separated from those expenses which will not be affected.[22] A company in the retail merchandising field stated that when a department in the store fails to show a satisfactory profit, management does not attack such allocated expenses as receiving, personnel, and general administration, but instead looks to the expenses incurred directly within the department such as selling and advertising, and to markdowns, shortages, and other factors affecting gross margin. Departmental contribution margin statements emphasize these items and the effect which they have on the contribution each department makes to general fixed expenses and profits.[23] Several manufacturers interviewed follow a very similar approach in statements prepared for sales territories.

5. Contribution margin figures can sometimes be obtained with less clerical work than is required to ascertain net profit figures. This is often very important when a decision must be made promptly. Several companies reported frequent use of the contribution margin approach for deciding whether or not to accept an order where delay would cause the business to be lost.

COMBINING CONTRIBUTION MARGINS WITH FULL ALLOCATION

The full allocation approach and the contribution margin approach to the assignment of nonmanufacturing costs have been discussed separately in the two preceding sections of this report. The use to

---

[21] The packaging cost problem cited on pages 555 and 556 illustrates this situation.

[22] For an illustration, see I. Wayne Keller, "Relative Margin Approach to Distribution Costing," *N.A.C.A. Bulletin* (March 1, 1949), pp. 761-62.

[23] For an explanation of the contribution margin approach applied to the retailing field see "Standard Expense Accounting Manual for Department Stores and Specialty Stores," *Controllers' Congress—National Dry Goods Association*, **p. 123.**

be made of the resulting cost data will determine which of the two approaches is most appropriate in each specific case. In budgeting and for periodic reporting of historical data management often desires a complete allocation of all costs, while problems involving alternative courses of action normally require cost data from which have been eliminated those costs which do not vary in total amount with the alternative selected.

There is no reason, however, why the two approaches cannot be combined to present in a single statement both the contributed margins and the calculated net profits for each of the segments being studied. Exhibit A illustrates how this can be done. While a statement of this sort may not be necessary or desirable where the costs are to be used for the study of a specific problem, it does have merit as a general statement for management analysis purposes. A combined statement similar to Exhibit A has the following advantages:

1. Such a statement provides information on the margins contributed by each segment. The reporting by segments of the incomes and

MARGINS AND INCOME BY PRODUCTS

	Total	Product A	Product B	Product C	Product D
Net Sales	$1,000,000	$300,000	$200,000	$100,000	$400,000
Less Variable Cost of Sales	580,000	120,000	155,000	45,000	260,000
Manufacturing Margin	420,000	180,000	45,000	55,000	140,000
Less Variable Selling and Advertising Expenses	120,000	60,000	15,000	25,000	20,000
Merchandising Margin	300,000	120,000	30,000	30,000	120,000
Less Fixed Expenses Manufacturing Direct	20,000	20,000			
Allocated per Schedule A ...	50,000	20,000	5,000	10,000	15,000
Selling and Advertising Direct	20,000				20,000
Allocated per Schedule B .	50,000	25,000	12,500	12,500	
Administrative Allocated per Schedule C ...	80,000	25,000	10,000	10,000	35,000
Total Fixed Costs	220,000	90,000	27,500	32,500	70,000
Operating Income .	$ 80,000	$ 30,000	$ 2,500	$ (2,500)	$ 50,000

(Schedules A, B, C have been omitted)

EXHIBIT A

costs which vary with volume permits ready determination of the effect on each segment's contribution and on net profits of proposed or anticipated changes in volume, prices, or costs. When a segment shows a net loss, the statement shows whether or not the segment is returning the variable and direct costs which could be saved by discontinuing it. In addition, the amount which the segment contributes to the joint fixed expenses can be determined. For example, in Exhibit A, Product C has contributed $30,000 toward expenses which would otherwise have to be charged against other products.

2. At the same time such a statement provides management with the accountant's best determination of the way in which the pool of joint cost can be assigned to the various segments, with the resulting net profit by segments after such allocation.

3. The problem of assigning those fixed costs which are not common to all segments of the business is best solved on the combined type of statement. Exhibit A illustrates the case of a company which utilizes special purpose equipment as well as common equipment in the production of one product, Product A. The fixed costs relating to such special purpose equipment have been specifically assigned to Product A, without distorting this product's marginal contribution by the inclusion of fixed costs which will not vary with the alternative selected. Exhibit A also illustrates the handling of fixed selling and advertising expenses in a situation where Products A, B, and C are consumer items to which common costs apply, while Product D is an item sold to producers by a separate sales organization with its own fixed costs.

Situations of this sort are difficult to report under the contribution approach. The accountant is faced with the alternative of either assigning such direct fixed costs to products in the calculation of product contributions, which renders the figures inaccurate for volume studies, or of including such direct fixed costs in the common pool, thus withholding information of importance to management. Fixed costs which are limited to one or more segments of the business are quite common. Failure to assign such costs to segments of the business can seriously affect the interpretation of results.

CAUTIONS TO BE OBSERVED IN USE OF SEGMENT COST DATA

Certain cautions must be observed in the use of either net profit or contribution margin figures for segments of the business. These cautions are concerned with both computation of the figures and interpretation of the results.

(1) *Use of costing tools which are not sharp enough for the purpose.* It has already been pointed out that bases of allocation should be closely correlated with costs being allocated in order to obtain reliable net profit figures by segments. Moreover, when the contribution margin approach is employed, it is important to charge

each segment with all of the costs which will be affected by the change in volume, method, or other conditions contemplated in the decision for which the costs are being ascertained. This was stated in the following words by a member of the Committee on Research:

> Just as in the allocation method the principal source of distorted information is the arbitrary allocation of joint costs on bases which have no discernible correlation with the cost being allocated, so in the contribution method the danger is in a tendency to permit too many costs to rest in the joint pool which could and should be allocated to the segments of the business which occasion them. Thus, both the amount of the joint pool is distorted as well as the contribution of the several segments of the business toward its absorption.

In some applications, segments are charged with only the costs which are treated as direct costs in the accounting records. While this yields a rough approximation there may also be a significant variable component in the indirect costs.

(2) *Need to consider all relevant costs in a decision to change present procedures.* In estimating costs of alternatives there may be important costs which do not appear in the accounts and which are sometimes overlooked in evaluating a proposal under consideration. This may be illustrated by an instance in which a company made price concessions in obtaining a large order from a chain store. While the data assembled as a basis for the decision indicated that the order would be profitable because savings in selling expenses could be made, it was subsequently found that costs of delivering small lots to widely scattered stores in the chain more than absorbed the expected savings in other costs.

Where the purpose is to compare relative costs of selling and distributing in different territories, through different channels, by different methods, etc., manufacturing costs are usually not a factor. However, many decisions respecting marketing affect the production aspects of a business. For example, a decision to promote sales to the more profitable accounts and to restrict or eliminate unprofitable customers may affect product mix and impose new problems and different cost experience in the factory. A decision to eliminate a territory may result in a reduction of production volume at the factory and hence increase unit costs or produce unabsorbed overhead. Action to get new business may require a substantial increase in fixed manufacturing costs if addition to plant must be made. On the other hand, where unused factory capacity is already available, the principal reason for seeking additional volume may be to absorb fixed overhead. Where other business is not immediately available, it may also be desirable to consider the extent to which a marginal product or territory is absorbing factory overhead before deciding to drop it. In any of these circumstances, the analysis of costs as fixed and variable must be carried back to manufacturing costs.

(3) *Assumptions underlying marginal analysis.* When interpreting contribution margin figures, it is essential to keep in mind the underlying assumption that changes, additions, or eliminations resulting from decisions made will not be important or numerous enough to cause a change in total amount of the unallocated joint costs. Fixed costs usually consist of many different items, and the facilities represented by some of them may be in use to the limit of capacity at the time. Hence what may appear at first thought to be a positive contribution may result in a profit decrease since it may necessitate adding an employee or procuring a facility to withstand even a slight additional pressure on one or more fixed facilities. This is more likely to occur if the segment in question is large relative to the rest of the business, or if a number of small changes have, when taken together, an important effect on overall operations of the company. Moreover, changes in costs sometimes lag behind the changes in volume or methods which are responsible.

(4) *Need to consider overall effects of a decision.* A change affecting one segment of the business frequently affects costs or sales income from other segments as well. Experience seems to indicate that the effect on variable costs is usually not important.[24] On the other hand, products are often related in such a way that adding, dropping, changing the sales emphasis, or changing the price of one item may affect the sales of other products. Many companies carry items which by themselves contribute little or nothing to profits because they help to sell profitable items by providing a complete line. Other products are new items which are expected to become profitable in the future. In a similar manner, certain sales outlets may have prestige or advertising value even when they do not them-

---

[24] As an example of an exception to this statement, one company found that discontinuing sales of an unprofitable bulk product increased transportation charges on other products in some cases because shipments were no longer large enough to receive carload rates.

selves contribute to profits. These possibilities must always be considered in addition to the contribution margin data.[25]

However, this is not a question which can be answered by objective accounting techniques of cost allocation. Instead the contributions which individual segments make to joint costs are determined by what can be obtained in the market and by managerial decision as to the proportions in which it wishes these costs to be recovered. In reality, allocation of joint costs on the commonly used sales dollar basis amounts to a decision to seek recovery of the costs as a uniform amount per dollar of sales. While this is not necessarily wrong, it seems that the decision should be made only after full consideration of all factors in the situation. Among these may be market conditions, competition, sales promotional values, disadvantage of taking business which cannot be discontinued later on, etc. Study of such noncost factors may lead to assessment of joint costs with results quite different from those resulting from use of the bases commonly employed by accountants.

---

[25] E. Stewart Freeman has drawn an analogy between a group of related industrial products and a human family. He states that individual products ". . . cannot be judged entirely by the contribution they make during any single year. It may be as unreasonable to expect all products to pay a like share of this year's cost as it is to expect the baby, young sister, older brother, and grandparent to contribute alike toward the household expenses. Some are relics of the past still worth preserving, some are the sustenance of the present, while others are the hope of the future." ("Pricing the Product," *N.A.C.A. Year Book* [1939], p. 31).

SECTION C

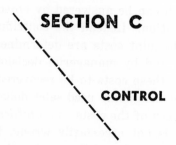

CONTROL

In Part I, Section B, the basic nature of control was examined and it was related to the accounting process. These readings were general in nature, made limited use of specific problems of control, and explored none of them in depth.

Therefore, this section has been included to illustrate and explore in depth the complexities encountered in applying the theories of control to actual business situations. The readings in this section are of three types. The first reading deals with system design considerations. The second type is primarily concerned with the analysis of variances and is represented by Articles 44 and 45 (though the learning curve is very useful in planning, also). The third type of readings is concerned with control of the various functions of the business. Included are inventory management, marketing, research, administrative, clerical, the control of cash flow, and the monitoring of investment.

43. COST ALLOCATIONS AND THE DESIGN OF ACCOUNTING SYSTEMS FOR CONTROL *

Myron J. Gordon †

I

W. L. Reed, of the American Accounting Association's Committee on Statement of Cost Accounting Principles, stated, "The purposes of cost accounting are (1) to assist in the minimization of costs of performance within the business unit, (2) to provide information basic to the determination of net income and financial position, and (3) to aid in the solution of specialized problems of business management." [1] The last two of these three purposes have been the criteria for a long and vigorous debate on the method and extent to which costs should be classified by products in the accounts. Should fixed costs, service department costs, and producing department indirect costs be carried to inventory values? If these costs are classified by product, should the allocations be at each stage in the process of production with reciprocal and multistep distributions of service department costs and with different distribution bases for each type of cost, or should less elaborate methods be used? The debate on these alternatives in the treatment of product costs has not, however, been extended to the consideration of their merits with the control of costs as the criterion.

At one time it was considered adequate for control objectives to establish and incorporate in the system standard product costs. As long as this thinking prevailed the definition of product costs [2] for

* From *The Accounting Review* (April, 1951). Reprinted by permission of the American Accounting Association.
† Myron J. Gorden, Assistant Professor of Industrial Management, Massachusetts Institute of Technology. The author is indebted to Professors W. W. Cooper and Paul Darling, of the Carnegie Institute of Technology, and to Professor Pearson Hunt, of the Harvard Graduate School of Business Administration, for their suggestions and criticisms. The article represents the personal views of the author.

[1] W. L. Reed, "Cost Accounting Concepts, Introductory Statement," *The Accounting Review* (January, 1948), p. 29.

The third purpose might be more narrowly defined as the determination of cost for price and production decisions.

[2] A unit of cost may be defined to include or exclude any element of cost depending on the purposes for which it is to be used.

control was not an issue. The standards were simply established for product costs defined for other objectives than control and placed alongside of the actual costs. This practice has not disappeared entirely. Most elementary cost accounting texts still do not go beyond this point.[3] Instances can also be found of practitioners advocating systems in which costs are summarized by product, although each product goes through a number of departments and each department works on a number of products.[4]

On the other hand, it is becoming widely recognized that the product is not the appropriate cost unit for control. A product cannot be persuaded to explain its variance, instructed to take corrective action, or fired and replaced by a product that would meet standards. For control the accounting system must provide costs classified by organization.[5] However, in developing organization costs the definition of product costs is considered given by the requirements of financial reporting and the determination of costs for pricing, or it is considered irrelevant for the development of organization costs. As a consequence, there is still no consideration of the definition of product costs which would give rise to an accounting system useful for control.

The thinking that product and organization costs are independent of each other is erroneous for three important reasons. First, the accounting system is one matrix which provides classifications of data for all purposes. Since the resources allowed the accountant are limited, using the system to develop one type of classification limits the resources available for alternatives. Also, refinements in one basis of classification frequently make it extremely difficult to develop understandable data on any other basis.

Secondly, product and organization costs are to some extent necessary for each other. To charge indirect costs to products, if it is desired, they must first be collected by departments. On the other hand, an organization produces products and their costs must be established to arrive at the organization's costs. This immediately raises the question: To what extent should costs be classified by product in order to have organizational costs useful for control objectives?

---

[3] W. B. Lawrence, *Cost Accounting* (New York: Prentice-Hall, Inc., 1946). Chapters XVII, XVIII, and XIX.

[4] Robert W. Leavitt, "Material and Labor Variances in a Sheet Metal Products Plant," *N.A.C.A. Bulletin* (May 1, 1948).

[5] An organization is one or more activities over which an individual has been assigned authority and responsibility.

Finally, the accounting system may be used as a control instrument in two fundamentally different ways. The system may be used as a source in the collection, analysis, and interpretation of data for the solution of problems, or the system may be used to provide the answers to problems directly. A different classification of costs by product is appropriate to each role. Consequently, the desirability of a definition of product costs depends upon the usefulness and the limitations of the system in the role which requires the definition.

In this paper we shall examine the use and effectiveness for control of a system in which only direct costs are carried to inventory in contrast with one in which all costs to manufacture are carried to inventory. The former system serves control objectives as a source of data. The system will be outlined and the advantages of it in this use will be analyzed. A by-product of the analysis will be the difficulties of so using a system in which indirect costs are carried to inventory.

The circulation of indirect costs between departments and to products can be explained as a control device only if the objective is to make the system provide answers. The design of a system to serve in this way will be outlined, and some limitations of such a system which the writer has observed will be presented.

The control objectives on the basis of which each of these roles will be analyzed are (1) the minimization of costs by the supervisors immediately responsible for their amount, (2) the evaluation of the performance of subordinates, and (3) the recognition and elimination of differences between actual and planned costs. The primary objective in cost control is the minimization of costs, but in a large firm where the administration of activity is carried out by a hierarchy of subordinates the system of accounts must also serve the last two objectives.

II

The major characteristics of a system in which only direct costs are carried to inventory are (1) each cost exclusive of direct labor and material is charged to only one organization account from which it is carried directly to profit and loss, and (2) a minimum of variance accounts is used. As a consequence, the system is extremely simple. Its structure may be outlined by presenting in order the treatment of direct costs, producing department indirect costs, and service department costs.

Direct Costs

Direct labor and material are charged to cost centers [6] at standard prices. The rate variances are collected in one plant account for each type of cost. Standard rates are used primarily for speed and convenience. With complicated pay plans and similar problems in the pricing of raw materials, it would be extremely difficult to charge costs currently to each cost center at actual prices. Further, actual costs need not be periodically classified by cost center, since this is rarely the level of authority immediately responsible for rate variances. A limit is placed on the overall amount of these variances as a percentage of the actual cost, and whenever this limit is exceeded or the variances run continuously in the same direction for a number of time periods a special study is initiated to determine the cause. The primary records are kept so as to allow the classification of actual costs by cost center and product, if it is desired.

Standard rates are changed periodically to reflect significant changes in wage rates or prices. This is necessary since the choice between alternative methods of production and other uses to which standard costs are put require that they be a close approximation of actual costs. These revisions are feasible due to the simplicity of the system.

The standard cost on each product of a cost center is calculated by determining the quantity of labor and material required for the operation and by valuing these quantities at standard rates. Production is credited to a cost center and charged to an inventory account or the next cost center at standard. The labor and material variances between the costs incurred by the cost center at standard rates and the standard cost of its output are charged to profit and loss. The costs are not broken down by product for the periodic reports of the cost center, and whether they are so classified perpetually in the accounts depends on the requirements of the company for an accurate measure of work in process in each cost center.[7] If the direct costs

---

[6] A cost center is the organization unit in which the individual in charge administrates his activities directly. Since the assignment of authority and responsibility is the primary objective in delineating organizations, no purpose is served by carrying organizational subdivisions below this level.

[7] If the work in process is small and stable it can be ignored and the output leaving the cost center can be taken as its entire production. If, on the other hand, the work in process is large and varies from period to period, the charges to a cost center may be classified by production order. The balances in the accounts of the cost center's unfilled orders are an accurate measure of its work in process at any moment of time. This method is generally preferable to taking a monthly or weekly physical inventory and valuing it at standard cost. However, a physical inventory is a substitute for setting up an account for each order.

are not continuously collected by product, the primary records are nonetheless organized so that this information can be determined easily by special study. It is also possible to aggregate the actual costs incurred on the different operations required for each end product.

Indirect Costs

With indirect costs, we usually run into a difficult problem of determining responsibility. The situations in which two or more people in different lines of authority affect the amount of a cost by their behavior are quite common. However, there is one individual who has the greatest influence on a cost and who is expected to inform himself of and adjust to all events, regardless of their loci, which determine cost. This individual is designated as being responsible for the cost in the organization plan, manual of accounts, etc., and in this system his account is regularly charged with the entire amount of the cost.

It thereby follows that service department costs such as maintenance, general plant administration, and power are not allocated among producing departments. Further, depreciation, rent, the supervisor's salary, and similar costs are not charged to the cost center in which they are in the customary sense of the word incurred. Some other individual than the cost center supervisor is primarily responsible for each of these costs.

The above procedure allows a great deal of flexibility and accuracy in the construction of standards. Costs are put in two categories, one for those which vary with output, and one for those which vary by management decision. For costs which vary with output it is possible to select the appropriate measure of production for each cost.[8] To illustrate, in a machine shop a good measure of output for the use of cutting tools could be machine hours. This would also be a good measure of production for set-up time only if the size of runs was fairly uniform from period to period. If the length of runs varied, the number of setups would be a superior measure of production. At less frequent intervals than the regular reporting period, setups could be compared with a standard based on machine hours to measure the cost consequences of the size of runs or poor scheduling of work.

---

[8] If indirect costs are charged to production, the same measure of output must be used for each cost. This question will be discussed further in a later section.

In the calculation of standards, statistical as well as engineering techniques may be used. By regression analysis the behavior of each cost with its measure of output may be estimated. The estimates will have a high degree of accuracy if a large number of observations on cost and output is used. The simplicity of the system is of use here also, since it allows the frequent collection of costs necessary for a large number of observations within a homogeneous period of time.

Many costs vary, but the independent variable is management policy and not output. Management will consider current or expected changes in output, but an administrative decision is necessary to secure a change in the cost.[9] It is, therefore, unrealistic to use as a standard a functional relation between the cost and output. The standard should be, and under this system is, the predetermined amount decided upon by management. In the reports these costs are segregated so as to focus attention on the source of their variability. The costs are reported at actual and standard, since it is the function of the supervisor to implement management policy.

Service Department Costs

Service departments generally have the following characteristics: (1) It is difficult to establish a meaningful measure of their production. (2) A given level of the firm's output can be realized with various levels of service department activity measured quantitatively by the cost incurred. In other words, the functional relation between a service department's costs and the firm's output is very loose, and for many services, such as research, industrial engineering, and even maintenance, there is a considerable lag in the relation. (3) Finally, service department costs cannot be made to change rapidly without serious indirect consequences. Given these characteristics no useful purpose is served by setting up a measure of output and establishing standards for various levels of output. Instead the standard is a predetermined amount set by management on the basis of expected output, financial position, and similar variables. The standard is independent of the actual level of output realized in any time period, but it may be revised by management decision as frequently as desired.

In accounting for service department costs the same procedure s followed as was given for producing department indirect costs.

---

[9] An illustration of this type of cost in a producing department would be the assistant foreman.

The periodic reports show actual and standard, but the latter is not incorporated in the accounts, and the former is charged directly to income as an expense of the period.

Some service departments do not have the characteristics outlined above. For instance, a firm's own power plant is similar in most respects to a producing department. It is quite easy to get a measure of power production, and for those costs which are a function of output the standard should be based on output. There are even some grounds for charging the cost to using departments if it is metered, if it is a substantial element of cost, and if the amount used in a producing department may vary with the efficiency of the supervisor. However, it is not certain this will contribute toward a more efficient production and use of power. The issue will be discussed further in a later section of the paper.

III

We shall now consider the use of the data provided by the system for control objectives. The use of reports by the supervisor immediately responsible for minimizing costs is fairly obvious. The standards are a means by which he can project the cost consequences of alternative courses of action. The periodic reporting of actual and standard costs provides him with a quantitative measure of the effect on costs of the events of past periods. This information increases his ability to plan activity so as to minimize costs.

An important advantage of the system outlined above is that it can be designed to provide information at the cost center level of organization without being made unmanageably cumbersome and expensive. In contrast, the circulation of indirect costs between accounts and the use of more than one or two variance accounts makes it extremely difficult to construct standards and to frequently report actual and standard costs for the large number of organizational units at the cost center level. If the system is to be of use to the individual immediately responsible for minimizing cost, this is the level at which information must be developed and frequently reported.

Another advantage of the system is the presence in the report of only those costs for which the supervisor is primarily responsible. With his attention focused on a limited number of costs, and the costs those with which he is most familiar, it is possible for him to translate between the operations he supervises and the figures contained in the report. He can be expected to determine the events which caused variances and to estimate the quantitative effect of these events on his costs without the assistance of a cost analyst to interpret the report.

The major disadvantages of the system are (1) it does not adjust cost for the effect of factors beyond the supervisor's control, and (2) it does not charge the supervisor with costs for which he is indirectly responsible. The successful use of the system, therefore, requires that the supervisor familiarize himself with all the factors which affect the costs over which he has been assigned responsibility. He is expected to recognize and influence with all the resources at his command events outside of his sphere of activity which would cause variances in his cost. This is possible only if the members of management as a whole adjust and coordinate their activities. In other words, the system is not designed so that the supervisor can consider his cost center a unit isolated from the rest of the firm and expect that variances will appear in his cost report solely as a consequence of his actions. This may be considered an advantage, because the system is not an unreal representation of the relations existing in a business enterprise.

The Evaluation of Performance

The evaluation of the performance of subordinates is a problem which vividly illustrates the contrast between the two ways an accounting system can be used. Where the evaluation is made by the collection and analysis of the relevant data, the burden of the evaluation is placed on the judgment of the person who operates on the data. The conclusion is only as good as the judgment he uses. Where the system is used to provide directly a measure of performance, the result is obtained by the application of a predetermined set of operations on the data, and the evaluation is independent of the person who carries out the prescribed operations.

A system that provides an objective measure of performance has a tremendous appeal for the harried executive. The use of judgment for evaluating performance is a difficult task. Frequently, it is distasteful and occasionally it is tainted with favoritism. In contrast, with an objective measuring device all one needs to do to set salaries and make promotions is read the report and the decisions cannot be questioned from above or below.[10]

[10] The reader may question whether anyone makes decisions in this way, but no less a person than the president of the American Management Association has complained of the bureaucratic practice. See Lawrence A. Appley, "Management Responsibility for Decision," *Management News* (February, 1950).

The proposed system does not provide an accurate measure of performance. For this a set of procedures for classifying the transactions of the firm must be specified and incorporated in the system which eliminate from the supervisor's variance account the variances due to factors beyond his control. In the system price is the only variance eliminated from the cost center variance accounts. All other variances are present in the one account for each type of cost.

The system is, however, a valuable aid in the exercise of judgment. Good judgment does not originate entirely in thin air; it follows from the collection and analysis of the relevant data. To arrive at a valid evaluation of an individual's performance the investigator must determine (1) the costs the individual actually incurred, (2) the costs he should have incurred given the conditions under which he operated, and (3) the extent to which he should have modified these conditions. The system automatically provides the investigator with the individual's actual costs and with the costs he should have incurred. The standards are for the realized level of output, for the predetermined policy of management, and for certain values of the other variables which affect his costs.

The investigator must next determine the actual values of the other variables and what costs should have been for these values. Through supplementary records the actual values of other variables such as size of orders, nonstandard specifications, and delays can be determined. The simplicity of the system facilitates establishing the required information in two ways. First, once the relevant variables are selected it is possible to proceed to the required data without delay. Secondly, the data are richly classified by types of cost and by time [11] so as to provide the large number of observations necessary for the correct use of statistical techniques in determining what costs should have been under the actual conditions of operation.

In determining what variables to look for and especially in determining the reasons why these variables took on nonstandard values there is no substitute for the exercise of judgment. To illustrate the problem, let us assume that a supervisor is provided with a new type of material and a variance occurs in the indirect labor used to prepare and deliver the material to the work place. In deciding whether the

---

[11] Costs classified by product or organization may be subclassified by type of cost, such as labor and material; by time, such as day, week, or month; and by behavior with output. The consequences of emphasizing one major basis of classification show up in the extent to which subclassifications of the data for the other unit are developed; that is, collecting product costs limits the extent to which organization costs can be subclassified.

one event caused the other and what the cost should have been, the analysis of the data by engineering and statistical techniques applied to the particular problem can be expected to yield results which would be superior to those obtained by the arbitrary application of objective procedures. In deciding who is responsible for the material—the purchasing, the engineering, or the producing department—the system breaks down completely as an instrument for providing answers.

The importance of simplicity if the data are to be used in the above way requires some elaboration. The investigation of a problem cannot begin with the original transactions as the basic data, if a solution is to be reached in a reasonable period of time. A function of the accounting system is to put the transactions in a set of general purpose classes which allow the speedy selection of the relevant data for each problem. An essential part of an accounting system, therefore, is a set of rules which allow clerical personnel to put the transactions of the firm in the general purpose classes by routine procedures. The rigid adherence to the rules in classifying the transactions makes the data objective, but it also introduces assumptions in the data which are not valid for every problem in which the data are used. The analysis of the data, therefore, requires that the effect of the assumptions in the data placed there by the system be understood. The system is simple if these assumptions are few in number and can be readily ascertained. It is then possible for the investigator to manipulate the data under assumptions he introduces because they are necessary to the solution of his problem. If, on the other hand, the data have been extensively manipulated by the system under a complicated set of rules, then the investigator becomes bogged down in the task of determining the assumptions underlying the data and their effect on the data, and he is always fearful that his conclusions are biased by assumptions which have remained hidden in the data. Only technically trained personnel could understand the findings.

Actual and Planned Activity

The recognition of and elimination of differences between actual or planned activity are cost control objectives that are not fully appreciated. The goals of an enterprise are accomplished by the formulation of plans and the administration of activity in accordance with these plans. Management can delegate to subordinates the administration of activity, but it cannot delegate the planning function without giving up control of the enterprise. It follows, of course, that control also requires that activity proceed according to plan. In a dynamic environment elements of a plan are continuously being made undesirable or untenable by the course of events. Hence, control requires that departures of activity from plan must be recognized and eliminated.

In a small firm this aspect of control can be handled informally. Management is in direct contact with activity so that information and communication are not serious problems. The data required for the formulation of plans and the recognition of events which require the revision of plans arise from management's experience.

In a large enterprise top management is divorced from activity by the very scope of the enterprise. In this situation it can formulate plans only if the great body of relevant data is organized so that a few people can analyze it in detail and as an integrated whole. A system in which costs are collected by organization and only direct costs are carried to inventory fills this need in the following way. Given a plan under consideration, it is broken down into the production or activity required of each cost center. At this level the historical data on output and costs can be analyzed to provide estimates of the costs involved in the plan. These estimates are then aggregated, finding and eliminating as they appear in the process of aggregation inconsistencies in the plan as an integrated whole for the entire firm.

This use of the system is facilitated by the absence of cost allocations between departments and to products and the variance accounts that arise therefrom. The data is not in a form that is conducive to making false assumptions about the behavior of costs with output. The same cost does not crop up in a number of accounts with the associated problems of deciding where it should be analyzed and of insuring that it is not double counted under inconsistent assumptions.

The formal and explicit statement of the plan that is adopted is a budget.[12] This budget with objectives and costs classified by organization is a set of directives to the subordinates who are responsible for the administration of activity. Each subordinate has the management function of recognizing events which jeopardize the realization of his area of the plan, and within the scope of the authority granted to him adjusting to these events. As long as the subordinates are succeeding, activity is proceeding according to plan and the enterprise is in control. However, management can be confident that activity is

---

[12] The standards that are used in the periodic cost reports to describe what *should have* happened are also used in preparing budgets to describe what *should happen.*

under control without continuously participating in its administration only if some mechanism exists which recognizes and reports when activity is departing from plan. The standard cost system in operation is this mechanism.

The variances in the periodic reports serve as warning devices by calling attention to breakdowns in the plan as they occur. The reports are frequent so that the lag between the event and its recognition is kept to a minimum. The system serves every level of management in this capacity because costs are readily aggregated and reported at every level of authority. Also the system recognizes variances in the area of activity where they have occurred—the most effective point for initiating an investigation to determine the change in methods, objectives, or in personnel necessary to restore the desired unity between actual and planned costs. Finally, the variances reported by the system are an accurate index of the relative importance of each deviation from plan. In other words, we do not have variances appearing which are false, which are removed from the activity where they occurred, or which are split up among many accounts.

The system, of course, does not tell why the variance has taken place. This can be done only by the interpretation of the data by the individual who wants to know.

IV

We now consider the design of a system for control in which all costs to manufacture are carried to inventory. It is first necessary to differentiate a system in which no control objectives are sought by carrying indirect costs to inventory. Generally, in this type of system inventory is valued at standard and not actual cost, indirect costs are inventoried by use of a simple and uniform burden rate, and the absorbed burden is not related to actual and standard costs classified by organization.[13] The use of full cost rather than of direct cost for inventory values in this situation serves no apparent purpose, since the system produces the same product cost figure that is put into it regardless of what the figure is. For the preparation of financial reports indirect costs in total can be allocated between inventory and cost of goods sold as an adjusting entry with the same accuracy that is achieved by a uniform burden rate.

---

[13] For a system which has many features in common with the one outlined in the previous section, but also values inventory at full cost in the above way, see William E. Perry, "Standard Cost System—Postwar Model," *N.A.C.A. Bulletin* (April 1, 1947).

Cost Allocation for Control

The primary control objective in carrying all manufacturing costs to inventory is the integration of organization and product costs. In preparing a budget a firm establishes prices and makes sales forecasts for its products. The difference between the sales budget and the cost budget is the planned profit for the period. It is customary to develop the cost budget by product in order to arrive at profit figures by product line. In order to insure that the realization of the planned profit is not prevented by the failure to realize the planned costs, all costs to manufacture are included in both the product and the organization costs. As a consequence, the difference between the actual and planned costs of the products will be reflected in the departmental variances.

The system which realizes this control objective is a combination of the conventional product cost accounting system and the one outlined previously. The organization units for which costs are to be collected are specified, and for each product of each organization standards are established for direct labor, direct material, and indirect costs. The direct costs are estimated as previously by time study and by review of past experience. Indirect costs, however, require a more involved procedure.

To arrive at the indirect cost per unit of product it is first necessary to make a *pro forma* allocation of the costs by type among the organizations for a normal or expected level of output. For service departments it is then necessary to establish a measure of output which will allow the allocation of their costs among producing departments. For instance, a measure of the maintenance department's output could be hours of maintenance labor. The maintenance provided to a department is measured by the hours worked for the department. A measure of the output of the plant manager's staff would be the direct labor hours incurred in other departments since it could be used to allocate the cost among the departments.

To establish a service department's costs per unit of output, the estimated total cost, including such items as salaries, depreciation, floor space, and supplies, is then divided by the estimated quantity of its output. For instance, the standard cost of the maintenance department is the average hourly rate of a maintenance worker plus the hourly amount of all other costs incurred in and the costs allocated to the maintenance department. The standard unit cost of the management's staff is the total cost of the staff divided by the estimated direct labor hours in the plant.

The output of a producing department is the products carried to inventory or to other departments, but the measure of this output is some common denominator such as the standard direct labor hours per product. To arrive at the standard indirect cost of a product the total of the indirect costs incurred in and charged to the department is divided by its normal direct labor hours and the cost per hour of direct labor is multiplied by the standard time for the product. Every element of cost is thereby converted into a cost per unit of product.

The system operates as follows. Each department is charged with (1) actual direct labor and material at standard rates, (2) actual indirect costs incurred in the department, and (3) the services of other departments. The cost of a service is the amount used, measured as indicated, multiplied by its standard unit cost. Against these charges, the producing department is credited with its production at the standard cost per unit of product. Service departments would also be charged with their actual costs and credited with the standard cost of their production both as defined above.

To review, all manufacturing costs are charged initially to organization accounts. Organizations are credited with their production at standard, but each credit is offset by an equal charge to another department or to inventory at standard. Therefore, the departments as a whole are relieved of their charges only by the amount of inventory at the standard unit cost that is delivered to the firm; and, the difference between the actual and standard cost of a period's output is exactly equal to the sum of the variances left in the department accounts.

To give this setup the flavor of reality the charges to a department are called its costs, the credits are called its earnings, and the variance is called its profit or loss. Each department is considered a separate entity which buys, produces, and sells with the object of maximizing its profit. This, of course, requires that it be charged with all of the costs to the firm required for its activity regardless of where they originate.

Limitations of System

The policy of treating each department as a separate profit maximizing entity is not carried too far. Top management does not rely on the quest for profit to insure that the supervisor will operate as efficiently as he can. Neither does it rely on sustained losses to liquidate incompetent supervisors. Instead, management uses the data provided by the system and other information to make administrative decisions which will minimize costs. However, the variances provided by the system clearly provide no explanation for their existence. In addition to all the other factors beyond the supervisor's control reflected in his variance account, the departmental variance developed in this system is affected by the level of output. In constructing standards it is assumed *all* costs including fixed and semivariable costs vary proportionately with output.

As a source of data for the analysis of costs and as a warning device the system is inferior to one free of cost allocations. The departmental accounts are burdened with a large number of costs over which the supervisor has little or no control. The data are made confusing by the assumption that all costs vary proportionately with output. The same measure of output is used for every indirect cost incurred in a department, although in many cases it is a poor measure of what the amount of the cost should be. On top of all this, the cost allocations make the system expensive to operate.

Volume Variance

A system in which all manufacturing costs are carried to inventory need not be crude as the one just outlined. Frequently, two sets of standards are constructed, one which assumes all costs vary proportionately with output and one which recognizes the behavior of fixed and semivariable expenses with output. The former standard is required if all costs are to be inventoried, and the latter standard is required to have variances that have some meaning for control. The use of both standards and the additional variance to which they give rise is sometimes justified for control as a means of providing a measure of variance due to volume. Specifically, it measures the difference in cost (the total by type or organization) between what it should have been and what it would have been if all costs varied proportionately with output.

This variance is considered useful for control for three reasons. It tells the department supervisor the amount his costs are increased by his failure to operate at normal. It tells the sales department how much costs are increased by its failure to meet the sales budget. It tells top management how much profit is being lost due to increased unit costs of production. Developing the variance for the first reason serves no control objective, because the cost center supervisor produces what he is given orders for. Failure to make deliveries may be recognized and acted upon through data less difficult to collect.

At the firm level the effect on costs of a difference between actual and planned volume can be established without allocating indirect costs between departments and to products and without developing the additional volume variance by type of cost for each department. A difference between actual and planned output requires the revision of costs and not the calculation of what costs would have been if they behaved as they could not be expected to behave. The allocations and variances only increase the difficulty of establishing the information needed to revise plans.

Variances by Cause

A more ambitious objective is to isolate the variance from standard caused by the supervisor's performance. This is accomplished by setting up standards for each nonstandard operating condition beyond his control, and by charging the difference between this and the standard product cost to the appropriate variance account. We already have the standards for nonstandard levels of production. Some of the other variances which are developed are described briefly below.

An order sometimes is produced with nonstandard material or nonstandard equipment. This will cause actual labor and material costs to be different from the standard at which the department is credited. Standards are constructed for the nonstandard practices, and the variances caused by it are charged to the appropriate variance account.

Since the measure of output for indirect costs is a simple common denominator, such as direct labor hours, costs will often vary from standard due to product mix. To cite again an instance used earlier in the paper, setting a machine for a job is classified as an indirect expense. The standard for this cost based on either machine or direct labor hours assumes a certain mix in the size of the runs and the difficulty of the settings. If the assumption is not realized, the actual cost will vary from standard for this reason. Hence, a standard time for each machine setting is established and a standard cost is established by extending the number of settings by the cost per setting. The variance between this and the standard based on a normal mix for the actual output is charged to a product mix variance.

The above are the variances most commonly developed. Space does not allow us to describe others, and, unfortunately, resources, measurement, and similar problems limit the extent to which they can be recognized in the construction of a system. Also, we have only considered the immediate effect on costs of a nonstandard value of a variable. For instance, the use of nonstandard material will cause not only a labor variance but a variance on all costs which are allowed a department on the basis of the standard direct labor hours.[14]

A system so elaborate as the one just described should itself provide control over costs. The major features in its design can be explained only by this objective. Every dollar of cost to be earned must give rise to an equivalent in good products at their standard unit cost. Thus, no element of cost escapes the watchful eye of the system. The variances between actual and standard product costs are classified by department and *by cause*. Thus, the reasons for the variances are provided by the system.

It is questionable whether this type of system realizes its objective. Management personnel with whom the writer had the opportunity to discuss the subject believed that the determination of causes for variances and the elimination of them was their responsibility. They refused to delegate the responsibility to a system. Further, management frequently found it difficult to understand the operations of so elaborate a system. This impaired their confidence in it and their ability to use the data it developed for more limited objectives than providing answers. To the extent that responsibility is delegated to the system, lower echelons of management are forced to act as if their units were independent profit maximizing entities. The devices they discover for "beating the system" are rarely of benefit to the firm as a whole.

V

To summarize the conclusions suggested by the discussion, an accounting system can serve control objectives by serving as a warning device which reports when costs are departing from plan, by directing review management to the most effective point for initiating an investigation to deal with the problem, and by providing the general purpose data that can be analyzed and interpreted by all levels of management for the solution of problems in cost control.

---

[14] For a more detailed illustration of this type of system see Joseph B. Copper, "Accounting by Causes vs. Accounting by Accounts," *N.A.C.A. Bulletin* (December 15, 1945), especially pp. 318-19 and Exhibits 1-5. The article describes the installation at the Tennessee Coal, Iron, and Railroad Company.

A system can accomplish far less than this but it cannot accomplish any more. To accomplish this the system must

1. Provide costs at actual and standard classified by organization.
2. Provide organization costs down to the cost center—the level of authority immediately responsible for incurring costs.
3. Provide in the organization report only those costs for which the supervisor is primarily responsible.
4. Provide organization costs classified by type of cost and by time in adequate detail for analysis by statistical techniques.
5. Provide data that nontechnical personnel, who must use it, can understand.

The realization of these conditions in the design of a system is made extremely difficult, if not impossible, if it is also desired to circulate costs between departments, carry all costs to inventory, and develop separate accounts for each variance.

44. THE ANALYSIS OF MANUFACTURING COST VARIANCES *

Standard costs tell what costs should be and actual costs tell what costs have been. Variances constitute a connecting link between standard costs and actual costs. Since management's goal is operation of the factory at standard cost, significant deviations from standard cost signal the need for managerial attention to conditions which are the source of variances. As a basis for deciding what action should be taken, management should know who in the organization carries responsibility for the variances, what has caused them to arise, and perhaps what effect they have had on product costs. This report presents the results of a study designed to show what the accountant can do in providing management with information which will aid in appraising the significance of manufacturing cost variances.

INTRODUCTION

The literature of standard costs has emphasized methods for establishing standards and techniques for coordinating standard costs with actual costs through variances. Methods for analyzing variances and the purposes served by such analysis have not been described with equal thoroughness. This report dealing with the analysis of manufacturing cost variances therefore supplements the Association's earlier series of research reports devoted to standard costs. Since the earlier study covered the nature of and uses for standard costs, this subject is not discussed here. The reader is referred to the reports presenting results from the prior study for a treatment of these topics.[1]

In this study, 27 companies employing standard costs were interviewed to determine how variances from standard costs are analyzed

---

* N.A.C.A. Bulletin, Research Series No. 22 (August, 1952). Reprinted by permission of the National Association of Cost Accountants.

[1] These reports were published in the N.A.C.A. Bulletin during 1948 as Research Series Nos. 11 to 15. They have since been reprinted in a separate publication entitled "How Standard Costs Are Being Used Currently." Copies of the latter are available from the National Headquarters Office.

and what benefits are realized from such analyses. In addition, records of field interviews carried out during several other N.A.C.A. research studies were drawn upon for material not previously published. The emphasis of this study has been placed upon methods employed by those companies which were judged to be making most effective use of standard costs. For this reason, the report stresses practices and viewpoints of a comparatively small group of the companies interviewed. This approach has been selected because it seems likely that members of the Association will find the most advanced practices to be more useful than those practices which are most commonly found.

THE ROLE OF VARIANCES IN COST CONTROL

Control over current costs must obviously be exercised before the fact rather than after the fact. Preventive cost control depends upon actions taken at the point where losses and waste can occur, or where savings can be made. This type of control uses basic operating standards expressed in terms of material specifications, operation methods and times, preferred equipment and facilities. Such standards need to be current at all times—i.e., they must represent the methods which should be followed when the work is done. Among the companies which were judged to be making effective application of standard costs for cost control, comments were often made to the effect that such standards "are under continuous review and are changed whenever necessary." In the words of a member of the Committee on Research:

> Standard costs serve no purpose unless the accountant is able to sell management on the merit of an installation sufficient in scope whereby manpower is provided to review and change standards whenever necessary.

Since variances are measures of performance under standards, the standards must first be good in order to yield reliable measures of performance.

While the primary aim of management should be to obtain compliance with standards, perfection cannot be obtained in either standards or practice and some variances will always arise. Past losses from failure to meet standards cannot be retrieved, but the study of variances is an important step toward improving performance in the future.

However, before management can take effective action to realize the opportunities for improving control over costs, it needs to know not only the amount of variance, but also where the variances originated, who is responsible for them, and what caused them to arise. In other words, analysis is necessary to bring out the significance of the variances in terms of sources, responsibility, and causes. When such analyses are combined with an appropriate plan of reporting, management can rely upon the principle of exceptions to disclose problems calling for attention without laborious study of many detailed facts and figures.

ANALYSIS OF VARIANCES BY RESPONSIBILITIES

Control over costs must be applied at the place and time where the cost originates. For this reason, a basic fundamental in the design of a cost system is that each cost be charged initially to the responsibility within which the decision to incur the cost is made. The same cost may subsequently be allocated to other cost centers in determining product costs, but for purposes of cost control the individual who has authority to incur a cost should be held responsible for that cost. In commenting on this, one member of the Committee on Research stated:

> To me, this is by far the most important result to be obtained from modern standard cost systems. Under responsibility accounting, the responsible operator is actually given a piece of the business to run as though it were his own. How he performs determines what results he will obtain.

Definition of a Responsibility

As defined by one company, ". . . a responsibility is an organizational unit engaged in the performance of a single function (or a group of closely related functions) having a single head accountable for activities of the unit." In this company a responsibility is established wherever the amount of cost involved or the type of operation performed makes control economically desirable and where analyses of costs as compared with standards are frequently required. A responsibility set up for cost control purposes may coincide with a cost center established to collect costs for assignment to products or it may include several such cost centers. Functional cost groups which serve solely as cost collecting centers do not constitute responsibilities.

Accounting for Costs by Responsibilities

An organization in which there is clearly defined authority and corresponding placement of responsibility is a prerequisite to effective control over costs. Delegation of authority and placement of responsibility—in other words, the development of an organization— is a management function. On the other hand, measuring the costs incurred and reporting variances from standards assigned to each responsibility is a cost accounting function.

The first step toward accounting for costs and variances by responsibilities is to prepare a cost classification in which areas of responsibility established by the company's organization plan constitute the primary basis for classifying both standard and actual costs. As described by a writer on the topic:

> Each department, as a responsibility unit, is charged with all costs over which it has control. (For the purpose of product costing, costs over which the organizational unit has no control are also allocated to it.) As represented in its controllable costs, each department thus has its own accounts. Within the department these accounts are further classified according to function. The number of such departmental accounts depends on the nature of the expense and the extent to which the expense can be classified and controlled.[2]

Inasmuch as the matching of standard and actual costs takes place as the costs are accumulated by responsibilities, the analysis of variances by responsibilities is a "built-in" feature of the cost system. Reports showing standard cost, actual costs, and variances for each responsibility are ordinarily produced as part of the clerical routine of accounting for costs.

When introducing standard costs, it is necessary to make sure that the classification of accounts permits accumulation of costs by responsibilities. Where standard costs have not been in use, it is usually found that the accounting system has been designed primarily for determining product costs and that costs controllable by two or more supervisors are merged in a single account. Under these circumstances, revisions in classification and coding must be made.

Placing Responsibility for Variances

Some factors affecting manufacturing costs can be quite readily standardized and controlled through the use of standards. Usage of direct materials, direct labor, and certain variable overhead items

---

[2] A. J. Penz, "Standard Costs in a Small Steel Company," *N.A.C.A. Bulletin* (July, 1951), pp. 1348-9.

usually fall in this category. The usage of these cost factors is generally controllable by management at the plant operations level. Responsibility for costs arising directly in productive departments is then clearly assignable to supervisors of the respective departments.

However, the field study showed that management often finds it difficult to define responsibility for costs which originate in service departments and which are subsequently allocated to productive departments. Among the companies interviewed, those which seem to be most successful in establishing responsibility for service department costs utilize plans which differ somewhat according to the nature of the service and the conditions under which it is rendered. The differences can be outlined as follows:

1. When the volume of service to be provided is fixed by decision of executive management rather than by supervisors in charge of centers in which the cost is absorbed, no responsibility for control is attached to allocated charges. For example, productive department foremen are not responsible for costs allocated to their departments for such services as cost accounting, production control, personnel, engineering, air conditioning, and other similar functional services. Here responsibility for the amount of service provided rests with executive management, for it has authority to determine how extensively such functions are to be developed. Expenditures made for such services are, on the other hand, a responsibility of the heads in charge of the respective service departments. Expenditures to be made by each of these departments are budgeted and the department head is held responsible for operating within his budget. Most costs in such budgets are considered fixed, with the amounts allowed being proposed by department heads and approved by top management as proper to provide the kind and amount of services desired. However, variable components are present in some instances—e.g., clerical costs in one company's production control department.

2. The costs of continuously available services such as power, steam, compressed air, and similar items whose consumption fluctuates with daily activity in the factory are usually charged to the consuming department at a standard unit rate when methods for measuring services consumed by individual departments are available. Responsibility for the quantity consumed, but not for the unit cost of the service, is then placed with the supervisor in charge of the consuming department. Where the consumption of such services by individual departments is not measured, supervisors of the latter departments are usually not held responsible for costs of the services used. On the other hand, the unit cost of such service is a responsibility of the service department head. Since there is usually a substantial fixed component in costs of rendering the service, a flexible budget is used and responsibility for control stresses costs variable with output of service. Measures of performance are sometimes expressed in

physical units, as for example, in a power plant where energy produced per pound of coal is employed.

3. Services rendered on demand (e.g., services of millwrights, mechanics, electricians, etc.) are charged to consuming departments at a standard hourly rate. Budgets of consuming departments ordinarily contain an allowance for such services and the department head is responsible for variances from this allowance. The costs of rendering such services are covered by departmental budgets similar to those employed for other departments. However, expenses in these budgets tend to be rough estimates because it is seldom practical to set standards for the type of operations performed. Most companies admitted that clear-cut placement of responsibility for maintenance and repair costs had not been achieved, but that methods described above had demonstrated considerable value. As an illustration, one company stated that foremen had become conscious of service costs and had tended to avoid unnecessary calls for such service since the practice of charging for such services was instituted. Other examples were also provided by companies interviewed to indicate that savings can be obtained by attempting to place responsibility for costs. In one of these examples, a general tightening of control over maintenance employees' time followed complaints by foremen even though such complaints were sometimes without foundation.

The field study seems to indicate that assignment of responsibility for control of service costs is often not distinguished from allocation of these costs for costing products. In general, accounting allocations are unsatisfactory for fixing responsibility for costs. As stated by the representative of one company in describing his company's experience, the practice "results in a chronic argument about fairness of the charges." The reason is that bases of allocation which are "equitable" for cost finding purposes are often not directly related to short period fluctuations in controllable costs.

Notwithstanding the fact that there are inherent difficulties in setting standards for some manufacturing activities and that any plan for cost control has practical limits, experience of a few companies shows that judicious attempts to place responsibility for both direct and indirect costs have yielded savings.

Separation of Operating and Nonoperating Variances

In order that variances assigned to supervisors in charge of departmental operations may be limited to variances from costs controllable by these supervisors, additional variances are needed to screen out the effect of cost changes for which management at this supervisory level is not responsible. For example, price and volume variances are needed because management responsible for the quantities of materials and services consumed in manufacturing is not also responsible for variances due to changes in market prices and for the volume of orders received by the factory. Another example is furnished by the practice of setting up special variances to segregate the effect which shortages of materials and the necessity for using substitutes have had on costs in some of the companies interviewed.

These variances usually reflect outside influences impinging on the company's operations and the company must adapt itself to existing conditions since it cannot control the causes of the variances. Authority to deal with such problems rests with top management and is exercised by initiating changes in products, methods of manufacturing, product prices, etc. In order to deal with such problems effectively, executives need information which enables them to see what effects individual conditions (such as, for example, a change in raw material prices) have had on costs.

While price and volume variances have been listed above as examples of items not controllable by operating management, there may be controllable elements in these variances. A few companies interviewed stated that price variances had a limited usefulness in evaluating purchasing activities. The following example cited by Paul C. Taylor is typical of others encountered in the field study.

> One company was purchasing a rubber grommet from an outside supplier. A standard purchase price of 32 cents per hundred had been established for it at a time when the company had just started to use a standard cost system. On the very first invoice received for the part, it was noted when the standard price was entered on the invoice and extended by the quantity for later accounting purposes, that the billing price had jumped to 49 cents per hundred.
>
> Here is where control begins. It was determined that the immediate difference was caused by the fact that purchase orders had been placed for a quarter's supply of the part at a volume large enough to obtain the best price, but faulty shipping instructions had caused deliveries in small quantities at the higher billing price. Since little was involved in storing this part and since it involved relatively little money, it was possible to discontinue the policy of numerous releases against the purchase orders.
>
> This incident led to an investigation of the ordering of other small parts such as screws, nails, taper pins, rivets, cotter keys, etc., and oddly enough, it was found that often purchase orders for these highly standardized parts were being placed as frequently as twice a week. This, of course, resulted in a backbreaking load of duplicate motions and clerical effort to follow up, inspect, receive, store, and record.[3]

---

[3] "Functioning of Standards in Cost Control," N.A.C.A. Bulletin (March, 1951), pp. 796-7.

Volume variances arise from nonstandard utilization of production factors whose costs do not vary with volume. Causes of such variances may arise outside the company (e.g., unusually good or bad business conditions, inability to obtain materials) or they may reflect internal planning and supervision in use of productive facilities (e.g., poor planning and scheduling of work or a standard which is too easily attained). To initiate action called for by volume variance usually is a responsibility of management at the executive level. However, factual information as to the sources and causes of volume variances is needed in order that those responsible may know in which direction to turn.

The field study indicates that much remains to be done in practice with the problem of determining causes of and responsibility for volume variances. However, a few companies reported methods for assembling information useful in improving utilization of facilities within the factory. Among these were the following:

1. Special studies of scheduled versus actual machine hours had been made from time to time and temporary reports rendered during the course of the study. Action based upon the most recent study had raised average machine utilization from 60 percent to 80 percent of potential capacity. This company kept a continuous record of the ratio of man to machine hours. This record was stated to be highly useful in determining how much additional output could be obtained from machines by adding more men and also in securing the optimum balance between men and machines.

2. Cooperation between accountants and engineers in establishing causes and responsibility for idle machine time was stressed by another company. Here the accounting department accumulated idle time reported in each center under a classification of causes designated by the foremen. Staff engineers were then assigned to investigate underlying conditions and to suggest methods for improvement. In such investigations it was often necessary to trace causes beyond the cost center where the delay occurred and to take actions which were beyond the authority of the individual foreman who reported the idle time. For example, excessive machine down time for setup was traced to a combination of inaccurate stores records and faulty inspection in a prior process. Changeovers made when materials ran out before an order was completed and delays for adjustment needed because materials were not uniform resulted in low production.

3. The cost accountant for this company stated that records which permitted quick accumulation of number of hours machines were operated had helped management avoid unwise decisions. Here requests for additional equipment had been denied when these records showed that machines already in the plant were being used below their capacity.

The analysis of volume variances seems to offer opportunities to the accountant, for the field study shows it has had much less attention than have direct costs of material and labor. While the latter have undoubtedly been the more important components of total cost in some companies, increasing use of expensive equipment to achieve lower production costs makes it essential to control utilization of this equipment if the expected economies are to be realized.

Administrative Decision Variances

Other variances for which responsibility rests with management at executive levels arise from administrative decisions authorizing deviations from standards. Such decisions are often reflected in costs as extra allowances or as variances caused by use of non-preferred equipment, overtime, etc. These variances may originate in actions to overcome difficulties, such as shortages of material and labor, to compensate for obsolete standards until they can be revised, or to allow for alternatives not provided for in standards. While the variances usually constitute costs in excess of standard, they are not necessarily undesirable. For example, one company stated that unfavorable material yield variances often result from use of substandard grades of material, but that yield losses can be more than offset by a favorable price on the materials. At the same time, careful analysis is needed to show management when decisions to take advantage of opportunities to buy low-priced materials will be profitable. It is also important to distinguish between yield variances due to processing efficiency (for which departmental supervisors are responsible) and yield variances ascribable to executive decisions to use different grades of material.

In summary with respect to analysis of variances by responsibility, a variance should measure success in control over cost factors assigned to a single responsibility. As expressed by Norman A. Coan:

> . . . One of the fundamental rules of utilizing the technique of variances . . . is . . . "keep them pure," i.e., unmixed with each other and a corollary to the rule is to align variance determination to the organization and to assigned responsibilities.[4]

The first step in accomplishing this objective is to separate those cost factors which are directly controllable by operating supervision from the other factors for which executive management is responsible. Among the latter, there are some which can be controlled by execu-

---

[4] "Variances Must Be Forged into Familiar Tools," *N.A.C.A. Bulletin* (June, 1950), pp. 1227-8.

tive decision and others which management cannot control. Nevertheless, top management needs to know what effect the noncontrollables have had on costs.

ANALYSIS OF VARIANCES BY CAUSES

Variances reflect the effect on costs which certain events or conditions have produced. Before management can decide whether or not action is called for and, if so, what should be done, it is necessary to know what caused the variance to arise. The analysis of variances by causes is therefore an important aspect of the use of standard costs to attain improved cost control.

However, the field studies show that in many companies using standard costs the accounting reports contain little information as to variance causes. One explanation of this fact seems to be that accountants are accustomed to the classification of costs by cost elements (i.e., material, labor, and overhead) for costing inventories and they follow the same classification in developing costs for operating cost control purposes. As a result, cost control reports display variances by items of cost rather than by cause. In commenting on this point, a writer has said:

> In most standard cost systems accounting departments have approached the subject of variance accounts almost entirely from an accounting viewpoint instead of from an operating viewpoint. The result is that variances are created to which are attached "labels" that express accounting terminology. This terminology is almost without exception foreign to the executives and operators, and it is extremely difficult for them or anyone else to understand. Furthermore, variances by accounts, such as labor, repairs and maintenance, etc., are developed which express only the fact that there is a difference between the budget and actual but give no reason therefor.[5]

While the analysis of variances according to elements and items of cost is not without service to operating management, it seems probable that more emphasis upon variance causes can add usefulness to many standard cost systems.

Who Determines Variance Causes?

Experience of the companies interviewed seems to show that the explanation and interpretation of variances is best developed through independent analysis made by the cost accountant working in close

---

[5] Joseph B. Copper, "Accounting by Causes vs. Accounting by Accounts," *N.A.C.A. Bulletin* (December 15, 1945), p. 319.

collaboration with operating supervisors. While interpretation of events in terms of variance causes is primarily a function of the operating supervisor or executive, the cost department collects and organizes statistical information relating to variance causes. By appropriate classification, the significance of the information can be brought out and through reports variance cause data are made accessible to management. In large companies, the analysis and control of variances may be assigned to one or more specialized departments. As an example, one company has a personnel efficiency department that devotes its entire time to the study of labor costs and analysis of labor variances. In other companies the work is often done by cost analysts attached to the cost accounting department but who, at the same time, are acquainted with and work as a team with production management. Where company size does not justify specialization, the function is performed by members of the regular cost accounting staff in cooperation with factory personnel.

Approaches to Analysis of Variances by Causes

Practice shows two general approaches to the analysis of variances by causes. These are:

1. To determine variance causes by special studies which are made apart from the recurrent operations of accumulating and reporting costs.

2. To incorporate the analysis by cause into the cost accounting system by providing individual variance accounts for each of the principal causes for which a variance is to be isolated. Periodic reports giving variances classified by cause are then prepared directly from the accounts.

Under the first approach variances are accumulated in the accounts by responsibility and by cost element, but not by cause. The variances developed serve to raise questions which are then answered by additional investigation to determine causes of the variances which have arisen. Under the second approach, the system is designed to provide direct answers in terms of variance causes without further analysis.

The use of variance accounts for accumulating variances by causes adds to the clerical work required in accounting for costs, although the amount of additional work depends upon the number and complexity of the variance classifications employed. However, one company stated that the desired analysis by cause could actually be made more cheaply this way than by special study because the analysis was thereby reduced to routine operations which do not require skilled cost analysts.

Repetitive analysis procedures require the use of a predetermined classification of variance causes. A system by itself does not have intelligence and hence the questions it is expected to answer and the responses it can give are limited to those provided for in designing the system. For this reason supplementary special studies are also needed from time to time to obtain information about variance causes which is not provided by the regular reports. Therefore, most companies use both approaches to some extent.

In designing a standard cost system, selection of the variances to be determined periodically is an important step. Some variances indicate opportunities for cost reduction while others measure the effect of management decisions to deviate from the established standards. Therefore each variance account provided in the chart of accounts is intended to collect information for a specific purpose. In general, the following criteria seem to be important in selecting the number and types of variances to be determined regularly.

1. The amount and relative importance of variances arising from a given cause.
2. Whether a given variance arises from recurrent or nonrecurrent causes.
3. The need to separate variances which point to opportunities for cost reduction from other variances concerning which direct action cannot be taken.

Rather obviously the periodic isolation of a variance is useful only when the amount in question is sufficiently important. Moreover, the need to avoid too much detail in reporting to management acts as a limiting factor. For these reasons, variance causes of major importance in the control of costs are singled out for attention. As an example, a company which found it especially important to control raw material costs had established a series of variances to measure usage and yields in each manufacturing process. In contrast another company uses only a single overall material cost variance account because material represents a comparatively small fraction of the total product cost and experience shows that losses of material are small.

On the other hand a variance which is too broad may fail to bring out important information about the working of individual causes in influencing costs. An illustration of this is provided by the analyses of direct labor variances shown on a single production time ticket. This ticket showed an overall variance of only 12 cents. However, when this ticket was analyzed to ascertain causes of the variance, the following results were obtained:

	Amounts	
Cause of variance	Favorable	Unfavorable
1. Rate of pay	$2.74	
2. Size of crew	....	
3. Extra setups	1.18	
4. Use of nonstandard equipment	1.24	
5. Operator efficiency	....	$5.28
	$5.16	$5.28

It was stated that management definitely should know about the efficiency variance in this case. In order to provide this information, the company makes a daily analysis of direct labor variance by causes listed above. Daily computation of the variances is feasible because they are obtained from data which the company finds essential in recording production and accounting for variances and inventory costs on a monthly basis.[6]

Examples of Variance Analysis by Cause

In practice, procedures followed in analyzing variances by cause differ widely from company to company. These differences in procedure are explained by differences in manufacturing processes employed and by differing managerial preferences as to the amount and kind of information wanted. In order to illustrate the analysis of variances by cause, the following examples have been selected from practices of companies interviewed.

Example 1: Analysis of Direct Labor Variances

This company's operations consist of machining and assembly on a job order basis. The number of employees in all operations is approximately 3,800. Labor variances, expressed in man-hours only, are analyzed according to a predetermined list of causes.

On completion of each operation, the foreman indicates the reason for labor hours over or under standard, using the code shown in Exhibit 1. Timekeepers record the information on time cards and summaries are produced by mechanical tabulation. When the variance is less than 10 percent of standard time, no explanation is required. If a

---

[6] For an illustration of the daily development of such variances as a comparatively simple and inexpensive clerical function, see Norman A. Coan, "Two Compact Forms for the Measurement of Operating Performance under Standard Costs," *N.A.C.A. Bulletin* (September, 1949), pp. 37-42.

Departmental Manufacturing Efficiency
on Completed Operations

—— Plant

Dept. No. ....

| Code | REASON FOR VARIANCE | MONTH OF | | | YEAR TO DATE | | |
		Actual Hours	Variance Hours	Cost	Actual Hours	Variance Hours	Cost
0—No reason variances less than 10 percent.		C					
1—Estimated running time too high. Reported to Stds. Dept.		N					
2—Estimated setup time too high. Reported to Stds. Dept.		N					
3—Men's effort and/or ability above average.		C					
5—New machine, standard has not been changed.		N					
6—Change in methods, standard has not been changed.		N					
7—New or improved tools, standard has not been changed.		N					
8—Used setup from previous job.		C					
9—Time set for man operating one machine. Ran two.		C					
10—Time clock registers to 0.1 hour only.		N					
11—Work done under special supervision.		C					
Total Gains							
0—No reason variances less than 10 percent.		C					
51—Standard too low. Reported to Standards Department.		N					
52—First time job was made.		C					
53—Slow or obsolete machine used.		N					
54—Planning not correct. Was changed. Stds. Dept. notified.		N					
55—Could not follow oper. as planned, delivery requirements.		N					
56—Operations in previous departments not performed as planned.		C					
57—Time set for man operating two machines. One available.		N					
58—Quantity too small.		N					
59—Extra setup result of machine break down.		N					
60—Extra work.		N					

(Continued on next page)

Exhibit 1

(Continued from preceding page)

DEPARTMENTAL MANUFACTURING EFFICIENCY
ON COMPLETED OPERATIONS

Code	REASON FOR VARIANCE	MONTH OF			YEAR TO DATE		
		Actual Hours	Variance Hours	Cost	Actual Hours	Variance Hours	Cost
61	Two men had to be assigned to job due to nature of job.	N					
62	Learner, apprentice, or student.	N					
63	Man inexperienced. Undergoing instructions.	N					
64	Different operators used due to difficulty of job.	C					
65	Assisting inexperienced operator on another machine.	N					
66	Man's effort and/or ability below average.	C					
67	Oper. not performed correctly. Add'l time required.	C					
68	Parts spoiled. Had to make additional parts.	C					
69	Tools not available at time job was started.	N					
70	Trying out new tools.	N					
71	Tools not correct when job was started. Had to be corrected.	N					
72	Broke tool. Time lost redressing and sharpening.	C					
73	Oversized material used.	N					
74	Castings warped, but are within foundry tolerances.	N					
75	Castings not to dimensions. Time lost waiting for instructions.	N					
76	Material too hard. Frequent sharpening of tools required.	N					
77	Improper supervision.	C					
79	Illegible blue prints.	N					
80	Blowholes and porous castings.	N					
81	Sheet stock—Secondary material or scrap ends used.	N					
99	Full quantity or operations not complete.	N					
	TOTAL LOSSES						
	TOTAL						
	EFFICIENCY % CONTROLLABLE BY FOREMAN	C					
	EFFICIENCY % NON-CONTROLLABLE	N					
	EFFICIENCY % OVERALL						

Exhibit 1

given variance is due to two or more causes, the foreman apportions the variance hours between the causes. Variance data recorded by the timekeepers are summarized monthly by the accounting department to produce the report shown in Exhibit 1. In the report, individual variance causes are designated as controllable or noncontrollable according to whether or not the cause is controllable by the foremen. This classification of variances was developed jointly by accounting and top factory management. While the position of some items may be questionable, the classification is sufficiently reliable to have practical usefulness. Supervision over foremen is relied upon to overcome any tendency to designate controllable causes as noncontrollable.

It was stated that supplementary explanations are seldom needed since the reports have been designed to answer most of the questions which arise in connection with labor variance causes.

Example 2: Analysis of Direct Labor Variances

This company's manufacturing operations are characterized by numerous alternative processing methods and sequences. Exacting product quality standards also make necessary a large volume of reworking operations. Managerial efforts to control costs are directed more toward attaining products of the desired quality at the desired costs than they are toward complete standardization of production processes. In order that production executives may have information needed to exercise this control, the following monthly analysis of direct labor variances is made. The company has approximately 1,600 employees in all operations and annual sales of $18 millions.

The first step in its analysis of direct labor variances is a monthly comparison between actual direct labor cost and allowed direct labor cost by product lines. Figures resulting from this comparison are reported in the initial columns of the form shown as Exhibit 2. Allowed cost includes standard operations and a normal amount of nonstandard operations. Foremen are responsible for variances from allowed cost and this comparison serves to show what effect these variances have had on costs of products manufactured. The report illustrated is prepared for executive management and reports of a different type are used in reporting variances to foremen which analyze all nonstandard costs.

The second step in this analysis is a comparison between actual direct labor cost and standard direct labor cost. Variances which result show how close actual product costs have been to standard product costs.

By a third step in the analysis, the variances from standard direct labor cost are broken down by cause, as shown in the right-hand portion of Exhibit 2. It will be noted that the variance causes are divided into two types: viz., (1) variances incurred to maintain labor standards and (2) variances incurred to maintain quality standards. Each of these types is then exemplified by such causes as operation on day work instead of piece work, authorized method changes and changes in piece rates. Variances, to maintain quality standards, arise from a variety of causes dependent upon the department in which the nonstandard operations are performed. Hence the causes reported on the form are not prelisted.

DIRECT LABOR PERFORMANCE (Left-hand side of report)

Department.................................. Month of...

PRODUCT LINE	ACTUAL	ALLOWED	VARIANCE	COST RATIO ALLOWED TO STANDARD	STANDARD	TOTAL NON-STANDARD
A	$179	$156	$23	130%	$120	$59
B	200	215	15*	110	195	5
Totals						

CAUSES OF NONSTANDARD (Right-hand side of report)

	TO MAINTAIN LABOR STANDARDS							TO MAINTAIN QUALITY STANDARDS		
	1	2	3	4	5	6A		6B		
Sub-total	Day Work	Wage Protec-tion	Std. to Piece Rate	Change in Piece Rate	Auth. Method Change	Opn. not in Std. Cost	Sub-total	Opn. not in Std. Cost		
$19	$10				$10*	$19	$40	$40		
0			7*		7		5		5	
Totals										

* Favorable.

Exhibit 2

Example 3: Analysis of Direct Material Variances

Inasmuch as direct materials constitute approximately 80 percent of manufacturing cost for this company, the company has placed major emphasis upon control and reduction of direct material cost. The stated objective was to provide a simple and flexible program for investigating causes of material losses and to stimulate action to reduce costs. In contrast with the foregoing examples, repetitive analysis following a predetermined pattern has been avoided.

Quantity variances for direct materials are available by departments with breakdowns by kind of materials used. This makes it possible for the chief cost accountant to detect and localize major variances. Analyses of these variances are made by a staff of three cost analysts permanently assigned to such studies. On assignment to a project, one of these men goes into the department concerned and studies the usage of the materials in question under actual operating conditions. An individual study may cover a period of weeks or longer and may entail a balancing of materials coming in against materials going out. Accounting for materials going out includes determining the quantities of good material in products, scrap, waste, and all other possible dispositions of material until causes of the variances are discovered.

The staff cost analyst then makes an informal report of his findings to the chief cost accountant and the latter takes the matter up with the production supervisor concerned to devise possible remedial actions. Production men have been trained to work with the cost department through company policy which emphasizes team work and oral communication. It was stated that savings directly traceable to cost analysis amply repay the costs of the analysis work.

Example 4: Analysis of Controllable Overhead

The fact that the number of actual labor hours paid for differs from the number of standard labor hours allowed for a given period tends to cause a controllable overhead variance as well as a direct labor variance. The overhead variance arises because those overhead expenses which vary with the number of hours worked are increased by excess hours. In order to emphasize the fact that efforts to control the latter portion of the overhead variance must be directed at the excess hours, this company shows among the controllable charges of each department a variance entitled "Overhead Gain or Loss Due to Direct Labor Variance." After separation of this item, the remaining controllable overhead variance is ascribable to nonstandard rates of usage in variable overhead rates.

The following hypothetical data illustrate the company's method of calculating overhead usage control figures.

BUDGET ALLOWANCE FOR MONTH

	Variable per Direct Labor Dollar	Total Variable	Fixed	Total Allowed	Actual Expense	Variance
Direct Labor				$1300	$1376	($76)
Overhead expenses	$0.60	$826	$825	$1651	$1790	($139)
Overhead loss due to excess direct labor * .				(46)		(46)
Expense controllable by departmental superintendent				$1605	$1790	($185)

* Excess direct labor times variable overhead ratio
$76 times $0.60 = $45.60 or $46.

Example 5: Analysis of All Manufacturing Cost Variances

One of the large companies interviewed prepares a monthly analysis report covering all causes of cost variances arising from manufacturing operations in the plant called upon by the interviewer. The classification of variance causes is designed to bring out information of interest to top management at the plant. A list of these causes together with an indication of the content of each class is given below. The order is that in which variance causes are listed on the company's report.

- A. Usual items (e.g., increased cost of transportation incurred to obtain raw materials needed to maintain plant output during period of unusually high production).
- B. Price and wage levels.
    (Items listed in detail with subdivisions for purchases from standard and off-standard sources.)
- C. Volume or fixed expense absorption.
    (General plant overhead shown separately from other plant fixed costs. Both are subdivided to break out significant causes contributing to volume variance—e.g., labor crew inflexibility, allowances for major repairs, vacation allowances, etc.)
- D. Noncurrent standards.
    (Variances due to changes in operation standards not yet carried through to product cost standards.)
- E. Product and facility mix.
    (Variances due to off-standard use of facilities, off-standard sources of services used.)
- F. Material substitution and mix.
    (In detail by items.)
- G. Material usage variances.
    (In detail by materials.)
- H. Direct labor performance.
    (Listed by plant divisions.)
- I. All other variances.
    (Variances of miscellaneous nature not otherwise classified above.)

Example 6: Organization for Analysis of Variances

This company provides a particularly interesting illustration because of its intensive development of variance analysis and because it utilizes a combination of periodic reports and special studies to bring out variance causes. The company had used standard costs for a number of years and had provided management with reports which classified current variances by responsibilities and by the principal causes. A review of the company's variance reports indicated that actual costs experienced were reasonably close to standard costs. However, further investigation of the existing variance reporting plan brought out the following opportunities for improvement through more intensive analysis of variances:

1. Unfavorable variances were largely offset by favorable variances within the same classification and accordingly did not appear significant in variance reports. This indicated that cost reductions could be made if these individual variances were brought to management's attention.
2. Many variances seemed insignificant when viewed in relation to total costs incurred in an individual period. Nevertheless, some

of these variances were recurrent and indicated worthwhile opportunities for cost reduction when accumulated over a longer span of time.

3. Management sometimes needed more detailed information in order to take corrective action. Since many situations were nonrecurrent, this information could not be included in routine reports, but would have to be prepared when needed.

The company then decided to establish a continuing detailed analysis of operating variances. In doing this, two important questions arose: namely, (1) how to organize the work in order to insure its being done properly and (2) how to provide for communication of the results to operating management in a manner which would enable the company to realize benefits from the analysis.

A cost analyst was already attached to the works auditor's staff at each plant, but the time of this analyst was largely taken up with routine duties in preparing monthly variance reports. It was decided that analytical study of the type desired would be most effective if unhampered by functions which had to be performed on a time schedule. Moreover, it was necessary to provide adequately for the communication of results to operating management in a manner which would insure its full participation. In order to accomplish these results the analytical accounting functions at each plant were classified into three separate groups: viz.,

1. General functions, consisting of repetitive operations such as preparation of monthly cost and variance reports.

2. Special cost variance analysis functions, consisting of intensive studies of cost variances in selected departments and collaboration with operating and industrial engineering personnel to develop methods for reducing costs and improving cost controls.

3. Special sales order analysis functions, consisting of studies of cost-sales price relationships to provide management with information useful in selling and pricing.

The resulting organization for the works accounting division is shown below.

ORGANIZATION CHART OF WORKS ACCOUNTING SECTION

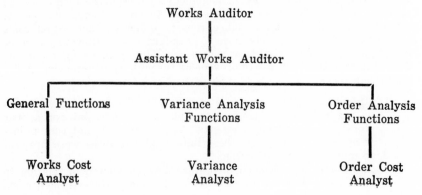

Functions of the cost analysis section are stated as follows:

1. To make intensive analysis of cost variances within selected departments and to collaborate with operating and industrial engineering personnel to develop recommendations for reductions in each element of cost.
2. To establish or revise cost controls as a result of cost variance studies.
3. To establish and maintain measurement of results for each variance analysis project presented to management.
4. To maintain close follow-up of results of corrective action on each project and to present auxiliary studies of remaining unfavorable variance causes as required.
5. To report deviations from established accounting procedures and cost principles as disclosed by intensive analysis.

Study of variances with the thoroughness contemplated made it necessary to concentrate the analysis work on selected projects. Once a specific cost has been chosen for intensive analysis, all aspects of the problem are studied to find the factors which influence the cost and to find methods for both improving control and reducing costs. After the initial investigation, the project is followed as long as seems desirable in order to gain the benefits of accumulated experience and to measure progress. Monthly operating reports to management include a section summarizing progress in the variance analysis projects under way. This information is presented under the following headings:

PROGRESS IN VARIANCE ANALYSIS PROGRAM

Project Title	Current Month's Variance	Improvement over Base Period		Number of Months Measured
		This Month	To Date	
xx	xx	xx	xx	xx
xx	xx	xx	xx	xx

In discussing the program, company representatives stressed the following points: (1) that variance analysis is a service to operating supervisors which gives them information they can use to control and reduce costs, (2) that variance analysis is an accounting function, (3) that competent personnel must be available for the analytical works, and (4) that fairly substantial expenditures must be made to carry on the program. With respect to the last point, it was stated that measured savings had justified expenditures made.

In contrast with the above examples, it seems that some companies do not fully realize the potential benefits from their standard cost systems because they have not provided the analysis needed to develop the significance of variance data and the means for effective communication of such information to operating management. These two aspects must, of course, go together, for analysis is obviously without point unless the results are put to use. While the company whose methods are described in the last example above is a large one, its manufacturing cost accounting operations are decentralized with a variance analysis section at each plant. The plant in which operation of the variance analysis program was observed by the interviewer has approximately 2,900 hourly employees. Successful operation of the same variance analysis program was reported by the company in a plant having 550 employees. At the latter location it was not found necessary to establish a new analytical section in the organization. Analyses have also been made in individual departments having as few as three employees. Hence, the same methods would appear to be as serviceable to a small company having only one plant as they are in individual plants of a large company.

REPORTING VARIANCES TO MANAGEMENT

The end product of variance analysis ordinarily appears in the form of reports which are prepared to convey to management the information developed by analysis. These reports are primarily control reports rather than financial reports, although combination of control and financial aspects is sometimes made in reporting to top management.

All of the companies interviewed which use standard costs for cost control purposes have formal reports to summarize variances by responsibilities and by cost elements. However, information as to variance causes is often communicated orally or through informal memoranda prepared in response to specific requests. On the other hand, some companies have designed their variance reports to bring out variances in terms of causes significant to management at various levels in the organization.

Summary Control Reports for Executive Management

Since top management cannot be familiar with all operating details, reports summarize variances from standards periodically. Executives characteristically rely upon checking performance at certain key control points. For this reason, the information presented in variance reports should aid the executive in appraising the effectiveness with which the organization has functioned during the period covered by the report. Moreover, the reports should, if possible, shed light upon the principal problems with which top management is concerned. All of this needs to be done in terms familiar to the executive concerned rather than in a form which implies familiarity with accounting techniques.

The field study showed that variances are usually reported to top management monthly. In addition to monthly reports, executives at middle levels (e.g., the plant manager) often receive weekly and daily summaries of variances for direct labor, direct materials, and any other costs for which frequent checks on control are desired. Case examples of the use of summary control reports by three companies are given below.

Example 1: This company, which has emphasized decentralization of manufacturing operations and diversification of products, found the classification of variances to be an important matter for top management control. A top-level monthly variance report is prepared which appears as follows:

MANUFACTURING VARIANCE FROM STANDARD COST

| | Variances— | | (Loss) | Total | | Std. Mfg. | % Variance |
	Operating	Profit or Price	Volume	Actual	Budget	Cost	ance to Std.
Division A							
Plant 1	xx	xx	xx	xx	xx	xx	xx
etc.	xx	xx	xx	xx	xx	xx	xx
Division B							
Plant 1	xx	xx	xx	xx	xx	xx	xx
etc.	xx	xx	xx	xx	xx	xx	xx

The operating classification includes direct material quantity, direct labor performance, and controllable overhead variances. Division management is held responsible for these variances. Price variance covers variances from standard direct material prices and standard direct labor rates. These are viewed as the result of outside market conditions. Volume variance, arising from under or overabsorption of fixed burden, is considered by this company to be a top management responsibility.

Example 2: A somewhat different classification of variances is employed here in a monthly report prepared primarily for the manager in charge of each plant. This report includes a comparative summary of cost variances classified under the following headings.[7]

       Variances subject to cost reduction
          By departmental supervisors
          By top management

       Variances resulting from volume of business
       Variances resulting from company policy
       Variances resulting from miscellaneous causes

In commenting on this statement, it was stated that:

       . . . The first thing the management wants to know is the *variances which are subject to cost reduction.* This should be the first

---

[7] From Joseph B. Copper, "Accounting by Causes vs. Accounting by Accounts," *N.A.C.A. Bulletin* (December 15, 1945).

item shown in an analysis of variances. This is the item which they must do something about. Therefore, this should be emphasized at all times, whether the results are being presented to a chief executive, general superintendent, or departmental superintendent.

Management is next interested in the *variances created by operating level*. This is not an item that is of interest to the departmental superintendents or to general superintendents but is of great interest to the chief executive. . . .

The next class of variances in which management is vitally interested is *variances created by company policy*. These are the variances that are created by policies laid down with respect to amortization, accelerated depreciation, obsolescence, contingencies, etc. . . .

The last section would be *miscellaneous variances*—items having to do a great deal with straight accounting, such as inventory adjustments, revision of budget standards, pension payments, etc. Generally, these variances in total should net a relatively small figure.

DEPARTMENTAL MANUFACTURING EFFICIENCY
ON OPERATIONS COMPLETED
Week Ending April 29, 1951, and Year to Date

| | | | | THIS WEEK | | | YEAR TO DATE | | |
| | | | | Efficiency % | | | | | |
DEPARTMENT	Nonstd. Hours	Actual Hours on Std.	Variance from Std. Hours	On Total	Controllable by Foreman	Variance from Std. Hours	Total	Controllable by Foreman
MACHINING								
12 Blacksmith								
21 Auto. Screw Mach.								
22 Lathe								
24 Screw Mach.								
Total Machining								
ASSEMBLY								
23 Inspection								
29 Painting								
43 Assembly								
46 "								
48 " Electrical								
Total Assembly								
Grand Total								

Exhibit 3

Example 3: A weekly summary of direct labor variances to inform top management as to performance of departments and machine centers is shown in Exhibit 3. Similar summaries by jobs and by product lines are available. Supporting these summaries is a detailed breakdown of variances by cause (illustrated in Exhibit 1). Together, these reports are intended to present the variances in sufficient detail to make them practically self-explanatory. In this company variance reports are separate from the financial statements. It was stated that this separation has been made to attract the attention of management to conditions requiring specific action.

While the terminology employed differs from company to company, it is evident that variance reports for top management commonly recognize three basic variance causes: viz.,

1. Operating causes, such as quantity of materials used, labor performance, etc.
2. Prices paid for cost factors.
3. Volume

The operating category consists largely of variances over which a substantial degree of control can be exercised and hence it measures operating effectiveness of the organization. On the other hand, the price and volume categories reflect the effect which these two external factors have had on the company's costs.

Reporting Variances to Factory Supervisors

Responsibility for directing manufacturing activities rests upon line management directly in charge of operations, although various staff specialists are provided to assist operating management in its work. The cost accounting department stands in the latter position in the organization, for one of its functions is to provide information which is useful in directing operations.

However, provision of information is not enough, for it must be actually used. This point was expressed in the following words by a speaker at an N.A.C.A. Cost Conference:

> We also recognize that we cannot achieve economical operation by sitting at a desk and devising systems, unless we secure the intelligent cooperation of the people in our organization who spend the money. These people are our foremen. Through the process of education, we have tried to develop in our foremen a cost consciousness which emphasizes the importance of getting full value for every dollar spent.[8]

Discussion with company representatives in the course of the field study indicated that strong backing from top management is the first essential in effective operation of standard costs for cost control. Given such backing, a program of education can be utilized to develop among supervisors and foremen the desired attitude of cost consciousness and skill in using standards and variances as tools with which

---

[8] Nicholas St. Peter, "How Our Profit Planning Program Works—A Case Study," *N.A.C.A. Conference Proceedings,* 1949, pp. 83-84.

to control costs. At the same time, the cost accounting department must be conducted as a service to operating men.

The information supplied to departmental supervisors usually takes the form of current cost control reports which tell the individual supervisor how his performance compares with standards. In addition to showing what variances have occurred, these reports need to point out the sources of the variances and to do this promptly in

COST CENTER ANALYSIS
FACTORY

VARIANCES			ACCOUNT	ACTUAL YEAR TO DATE	THIS PERIOD		
THIS PERIOD	YEAR TO DATE	99			EXT. BUDG. ALLOW.	CURRENT ALLOW.	ACTUAL
		01	DIRECT LABOR				
			TOTAL DIR. LABOR				
		11	SUPERVISION				
		14	OVERTIME EXCESS				
		15	INDIRECT LABOR				
			TOTAL IND. LABOR				
		22	GENERAL SUPPLIES				
		23	JIGS, TOOLS & FIX.				
		151	JIGS, T. & FIX. - LABOR				
		24	FUEL				
		30	PURCHASED POWER				
		31	WATER				
		41	REPAIRS LAND & BLDG.				
		152	REPAIRS L.& B.-LAB.				
		42	REPAIRS M. & EQUIP.				
		153	REP. M.& E. - LABOR				
		51	SOC. SECURITY TAX				
		52					
		53					
		54					
		55	VACATION ALLOWANCE				
		68	NEW METHODS EXP.				
		69	SPOILAGE				
			DEPT. TOTAL				

COMMENTS

ACTIVITY (VOLUME)	PRODUCTION	STANDARD	EFY. RATIO	T.C. RATIO
◄—— CURRENT ——►				
◄— Y. T. D. —►				

PERIOD	RECOVERY	THIS PERIOD	YEAR TO DATE
STANDARD BUDGETED RECOVERY			
RECOVERY @ INDICATED ACTIVITY			
COST CENTER		KEYMAN	

CCAF

Exhibit 4

order that action may be taken before the opportunity has passed. Exhibit 4 illustrates the form in which cost reports are prepared for foremen by one organization contributing material for this study.

In reporting variances to management at the supervisory level, emphasis is placed upon cost factors directly controllable by the individual supervisor. Many companies exclude from cost and variance reports to supervisors all items for which the supervisor receiving the report is not directly responsible. Other companies include noncontrollable items in current control reports as a matter of information or because there may be some contributory responsibility. As an example of the latter, one company which includes costs of depreciation, property taxes, and insurance in departmental cost reports stated that it does so because it wants the foreman to be aware of the importance of such costs and of the effect which requests for additional equipment have on total costs of his department.

Coordination of Reports

Discussion by the Committee on Research stressed two major points which need to be considered in developing a plan for reporting variances to management. These are:

1. Variance information must be timely.
2. Reports must provide the amount of detail needed at each level of management.

The manner in which these aims are achieved through use of carefully coordinated reports is illustrated by the following case example.

> This company has daily control reports which build up to monthly summaries. In this manner, information prepared from day-to-day operations is used to compile monthly figures for variance control. Standards in the form of allowed hours for the attained production level constitute the basis for control and variances are measured from these standards. The allowed hour standards are developed primarily from past experience modified for known correctable conditions and by elimination of ineffective operations. Stress is placed upon gaining acceptance of the standards by the factory operators.
>
> Actual production performance is reported at the end of each day on a daily production report (Exhibit 5).[9] In this report, "chargeable hours" are productive time charged directly to product cost at the standard cost per hour. "Nonchargeable hours" are nonproductive time included as burden in the standard cost per chargeable hour. Both classes are measured against an allowed hour standard for control purposes.

---

[9] Figures shown in exhibits are hypothetical.

6

DAILY PRODUCTION REPORT

FINISHING DEPARTMENT

SAN FRANCISCO DIVISION DATE 2-29-52

DESCRIPTION	MACH.	SHIFT	NO. ON	AVGE. PER HR ALL'D	AVGE. PER HR ACT	FORM NO.	PRODUCTION	CHARGEABLE HOURS MAKE READY ALL'D	ACT	L/G	RUN ALL'D	ACT	L/G	NON-CHARGEABLE HOURS SCHEDULED ALL'D	ACT	L/G	UNSCHEDULED ALL'D	ACT	L/G
MILK CTN. CARRIERS 7¼ x 25⅝		1		ACT	1775	2501	11475				6.5	6.5	-						
WEC														1.0	1.0				
Total G 1				ACT	1775		11475				6.5	6.5	-	1.0	1.0	—			
1st CRAX - 12¼ x 29¾	[illegible]	1		13000	15000	2564	60000				4.6	4.0	+.6						
2nd BUSY BAKER - 17¾ x 36¼	[illegible]	1		5750	3600	2636	1800	.7	.7		.3	.5	-.2	.3	.3				
— —	—	2		—	3400	2636	12600				2.2	3.7	-1.5	.3	.3				
WEC		2												1.5	2.0	-.5			
Total G 2				10400	9075		74400	.7	.7	—	7.1	8.2	-1.1	2.1	2.6	-.5	.1		+.1
Shift Total % all'd		1																	
" " " "		2																	
— " " " "		3													87%			41%	
Total CC-46 92 " "				6300	5825		85875	.7	.7	—	13.6	14.7	-1.1	3.1	3.6	-.5	.1		+.1
Month to Date 107 " "							5540680	63.3	63.3	—	427.1	394.2	+32.9	32.1	37.1	-5.0	3.5	8.5	-5.0

Exhibit 5

The cost department at each plant completes the daily report by entering allowed hours and variances and a copy is sent to the responsible foreman the following morning. The foreman can then spot the exceptional variances and is usually in a position to take any indicated remedial action while the order is still flowing through his department. From these departmental reports a daily summary is prepared and submitted to the plant manager and his superintendents. As these reports are reviewed each day, significant variances are checked and appropriate explanations are noted by a cost analyst working in collaboration with the responsible foreman. This routine brings exceptional items to light when they arise and therefore eliminates surprises at the end of the month. Factual information for later use in the monthly reports is also accumulated.

At the end of the month a departmental cost statement (Exhibit 6) provides a summary for the plant management. In addition, the report serves to inform the superintendent of each department as to costs and variances for which he is responsible. The subheading, "Total Controllable Costs," indicates where the superintendent's responsibility ends.

The lower sections of the report provide breakdowns of material costs by type of material and of labor costs by machine or handwork cost centers. In the latter, budget hours represent the anticipated average volume of operation upon which the standard costs per hour are predicated at the time the annual manufacturing cost budget was prepared. They are displayed on this statement to furnish a comparison

COST STATEMENT
NO. 41 Page 1
DATE February, 1952
DIV. San Francisco

Department CARTON DEPARTMENT

CURRENT MONTH		ITEMS OF COST		YEAR TO DATE		COST PER	
VARIATION FROM STANDARD	ACTUAL			ACTUAL	VARIATION FROM STANDARD	CURRENT MONTH	YEAR TO DATE
(871)	43,471	01	Direct Labor Hourly	386,305	(703)		
(2,174)	10,052	02	Indirect Labor Hourly	70,606	(2,257)		
2,489	304	04	Overtime Penalty	2,719	(5)		
(524)	6,110	69	Payroll Expense	48,563	(929)		
(2,054)			Allowed Hour Variation—Labor Cost		(36,338)		
(3,134)	59,937		Sub-Total—Labor Cost	508,193	(40,232)		
(2,897)	6,932	15	Repairs Material	38,447	(5,450)		
(688)	2,662	16	Misc. Supplies & Expense	17,576	(2,155)		
(852)	2,405	24	Major Repairs Material	15,897	(3,833)		
(1,489)	6,856	60	Maintenance Service	48,352	(4,174)		
		62	Steam Power				
(23)	188	63	Electric Power	1,473	(77)		
(58)	4,527	64	Gen. Mfg. Expense	36,892	(600)		
(711)	.		Allowed Hour Variation—Other Cost		(17,413)		
(9,852)	83,507		Total Controllable Cost	666,830	(73,934)		
(5,324)	22,498	65	Fixed Costs	151,730	(7,604)		
(15,176)	106,005		Total Conversion Cost	818,560	(81,538)		
185	161,845	95	Material Cost (See Below)	1,321,571	(1,469)		
(14,991)	267,850		TOTAL MANUFACTURING COST	2,140,131	(83,007)	x x x x	x x x x
			Units Produced				

MATERIAL COST (CURRENT MONTH)	UNITS USED ( )		ACTUAL PRICE	MATERIAL COST STANDARD	MATERIAL USAGE VARIANCE
	ACTUAL	VARIATION FROM STD.			
Chip Boards	1,049.883		41.77	43,848	
Manila Lined Boards	264.019		56.40	14,891	
Patent Coated Boards	247.757		74.48	18,453	
Other Boards	612.607		92.96	56,951	
Egg Fillers				2,583	
Misc. & Finishing Material				25,304	185
Total Material Cost	2,174.266			162,030	185

CODE NO.	COST CENTER	BUDGET HOURS	ACTUAL HOURS	ALLOWED HOURS	LABOR COST BUD. RATE		ALLOWED HOUR VARIATION LABOR	% OF ALLOWED
03	Composing	113.9	75.5	75.5	4.08			
04	Winding	503.4	330.0	334.4	1.61		7	101.3
05	Reoperation	1,992.9	1,791.5	847.5	1.52		(1,429)	(47.3)
06	Handwork	1,803.1	1,646.7	1,507.6	1.58		(219)	(91.6)
07	Die Making	877.2	672.5	680.4	2.34		18	101.2
08	Stripping	4,839.0	3,062.5	3,097.7	2.03		71	101.1
09	Finishing	2,856.2	2,636.0	2,309.7	1.86		(607)	(87.6)
49	Swift Food Pail Machine	250.2	145.1	121.9	2.13		(50)	(84.0)
50	Brightwood Gluers	1,568.7	247.2	243.5	2.19		(8)	(98.5)
51	Cu-Pak Egg Machine	643.1			2.26			
55	Cello Gluer	280.8	295.9	294.1	3.63		(6)	(99.4)
61	Quart I.C. Pail Machine	278.5	153.0	149.6	3.68		(13)	(97.8)
	TOTAL	28,816.8	20,555.4	19,126.0			(2,054)	(96.3)

( ) Denotes Red Figure

Exhibit 6

with actual volume of operation. Allowed hours represent the standard time allowance for the actual work performed during the period. The allowed hour variance represents the difference between actual and allowed hours extended by the labor portion of the standard cost per hour.

A summary of all operating variances is prepared in the form shown in Exhibit 7. This provides the plant manager with a picture of the operations of his entire plant. Furthermore, this statement serves as the medium by which the home executive office receives an analysis of each plant's operating variances with appropriate explanations.

Analysis of Operating Cost Variances
(CURRENT MONTH)

COST STATEMENT
NO. X-6 (PAGE 2)
DATE FEBRUARY, 1952
DIV. SAN FRANCISCO

NO.	OPERATING DEPARTMENTS	DIRECT LABOR BUDGET VARIANCES				ALLOWED HOUR VARIANCE	INDIRECT LABOR VARIANCE	OVERTIME PENALTY	PAYROLL EXPENSES	TOTAL LABOR VARIANCE	OTHER CONTROLLABLE		TOTAL OPERATING VARIANCES
		MISC.	NON-PRODUCTIVE	PREMIUM EXCESS	RETRO PAY						ALLOWED HOUR	OTHER	
10	Raw Mat'l. Hdlg. & Stg.	597		237			120	42	11	1,007		1,344	2,351
15	Beaters & Jordans	38					64	344	(113)	333		(975)	(642)
16	No. 1 Board Machine	46	(2)				(195)	34	(98)	(215)	3,205	(591)	2,399
17	No. 2 Board Machine	(195)	110				(209)	(98)	(83)	(475)	2,086	(980)	631
18	No. 3 Board Machine	(327)	66				(65)	68	(95)	(353)	641	1,858	2,146
20	Sheet Liner	(14)	(71)					51	(11)	(41)	39	10	8
22	Boardmill Finishing	427		(17)			81	224	56	771		371	1,142
23	Corr. Waste Baler	(45)		14				62	(4)	27		200	227
24	Carton Waste Baler	(40)		22				38	(3)	17		226	243
34	Paste Making	11						12	(2)	21		(7)	14
36	Paster	(69)	52	3				20	(11)	(5)		1,510	1,505
37	Corrugators	(2)	(191)	(688)			(226)	433	(146)	(820)	3,147	(949)	1,378
39	Corrugated Case	(179)	(197)	98	(369)		(951)	724	(364)	(1,238)		(972)	(2,210)
40	Laminator	(1)	(17)	(2)			(98)	34	(15)	(99)		(125)	(224)
41	Carton	665	(787)	(365)	(384)	(2,054)	(2,174)	2,489	(524)	(3,134)	(711)	(6,007)	(9,852)
42	Egg Filler	(171)	(11)	23			(134)	(16)	(50)	(354)	70	(143)	(427)
70	Shipping & Warehousing	(269)		220				86	(68)	(31)		1,196	1,165
		472	(1,048)	(446)	(753)	(2,054)	(3,787)	4,547	(1,520)	(4,589)	8,477	(4,034)	(146)

NOTE: BRACKETS OR RED DENOTE LOSS

EXPLANATION OF SIGNIFICANT VARIANCES:

Direct Labor — Non Productive Variance — $(1,048)

Carton Dept. — $(787)
    Training program in the die making room accounts for $(520)
    Excessive proportion on non-productive time to total time was experienced on the
    gluers due to curtailed running schedules from three shifts to two shifts
    with no change in daily and weekly cleanup time. This accounts for $(77).

Allowed Hour Variance — $(2,054)

    Too light scoring on cutting operation caused excessive reoperation costs
    of $(1,287)

Indirect Labor — $(3,787)
Carton Dept. — $(2,174)
    The addition of three inspectors to the printing centers accounts for $(1,692).

( ) Denotes red figures

Exhibit 7

The reports described above serve to inform management at three levels (viz., the plant manager, the department superintendents, and the foremen) with regard to daily and monthly performance and to provide a common ground for discussion and cooperation.

A final summary of all cost variances is prepared for each plant on the report form shown as Exhibit 8. From these statements the executive office obtains a bird's-eye view of operating effectiveness in comparison with standards. At the executive office, a cost analyst utilizes the data on these statements to prepare a statement which the president uses in his monthly report to the executive committee and board of directors.

Commenting on its plan for reporting variances, a representative of the company stated that "We feel that we have provided to successive levels of management only the details on cost variances needed for constructive action and at a time when such action can be most effective. By integrating these reports with our regular cost accounting routine, we have been able to minimize the expense of preparing special reports and analyses."

				COST STATEMENT	
				NO. X-6 (PAGE 1)	
				DATE __Feb. 1952__	
		Summary of Cost Variances		DIV __San Francisco__	

CURRENT MONTH		DESCRIPTION	YEAR TO DATE	
AMOUNT	% OF STD.		AMOUNT	% OF STD.
		681 Operating Variances		
(4,589)		1 Direct Labor—Operating (ANALYSIS ON PAGE 2)	(39,141)	
(4,034)		2 Other Controllable Costs (ANALYSIS ON PAGE 2)	(45,376)	
8,477		3 . Allowed Hour Variation (ANALYSIS ON PAGE 2)	37,393	
(146)			(47,124)	
		682 Service Department Variances		
(2,483)		1 Controllable Cost Variance (ANALYSIS ON PAGE 3)	(12,238)	
(1,976)		**683 Volume Variance**		
		1 Volume Variance (ANALYSIS ON PAGE 3)	30,935	
		684 Material Variances (ANALYSIS ON PAGE 3)		
(1,016)		1 Material Price	(12,309)	
(535)		2 Material Usage	11,795	
(1,551)			(514)	
		685 Other Manufacturing Variances		
5,893		1 Carton Department Waste (Credit)	50,579	
		2		
(2,719)		3 Loss on Defective Finished Merchandise (Per Schedule)	(16,243)	
3,174			34,336	
		687 Inventory Adjustments		
		1 Adjustment to Physical		
(242)		2 Revaluation to Market	(242)	
		3 Reclassification of Products	(1,372)	
(242)			(1,614)	
		689 Miscellaneous Cost Adjustments		
5		1 Fixed Costs (Over) or Under Budget	(8,528)	
(5,316)		2 Over or (Under) Absorbed Service Costs	(28,002)	
(399)		3 Use of Assumed Standard Product Cost	6,139	
453		4 Sale of Scrap and Junk	4,416	
(966)		5 Experimental Expense	(1,094)	
		6 Recoveries or Gains on Insurance Claims	170	
(1,096)		7 Sales and Use Taxes on Capital Additions	(13,272)	
503		9 Other Miscellaneous Cost Adjustments: (SPECIFY IN DETAIL)	3,230	
2,054		68Q) Deduct: Allowed Hour Variation Transferred to Inventory	36,338	
711		6813)	17,413	
(4,051)			16,810	
(7,275)		**TOTAL COST VARIANCES**	20,591	
		NOTE: BRACKETS OR RED DENOTE LOSS		

Exhibit 8

ANALYSIS OF VARIANCES BY PRODUCTS

Two important purposes served by product costs are (1) to cost inventories and (2) to guide management in decisions with respect to pricing, product selection, and sales emphasis. Many of the earlier writers on standard costs believed that standard product costs should be used for these purposes and that assignment of variances to products was unnecessary. In support of this point of view, they argued that where good standards and good control practices prevailed, variance balances would be unimportant. If significant variance balances did occur, it was thought that these variances would represent losses from preventable inefficiency or temporarily depressed sales volume and that they should not be reflected in product costs.

On the other hand, most of the companies interviewed assign variances to products either regularly or occasionally. This practice is, in part at least, attributable to the impact on costs of rapid changes in prices and other conditions during recent years. Under such circumstances it has been impractical to keep standard product costs current at all times.

Most of the companies review their standard costs periodically and revise them when it is found that the standard product costs in use are no longer proper ones for the purpose. The field study shows that this revision of standard product costs usually takes place just prior to the annual closing. Up-to-date standard product costs are therefore available for costing the year-end inventory and as a basis for decisions made at that time. However, when the revised standard costs reflect anticipated manufacturing costs for the coming year which are higher than current actual costs, the valuation of the inventory should not exceed actual cost of the goods on hand at the closing date. When standard costs are revised prior to the annual closing and inventories on hand are costed at the new standard costs, the effect is, of course, to charge inventories with a part of the accumulated variances. Variances which are not considered proper inventory costs are still charged in their entirety against cost of sales for the period.

However, during the interim between periodic revisions, standard product costs are not always current. It is, of course, true that standards for material usage, operation times, and other elements of cost directly controllable by operating supervisors must be current at all times if the standards are to be satisfactory tools for cost control. These operation standards are revised when necessary without changes through to the point of setting new product cost standards until the end of the year. In the meantime, differences between the operation standards and the product cost standards show as variances.

Since management usually wants current costs when decisions are to be made with respect to pricing and related questions, variances are often analyzed by products in order to arrive at current product costs. Companies producing nonstandard goods built to the customer's specifications may also analyze the variances by job orders. For such purposes the analyses are usually prepared when wanted as supplementary statistical data and are not entered in the accounts.[10]

The analysis of variances by cause is useful in deciding whether or not current variances should be allocated to products in arriving at product costs for pricing. When management knows why the variances have occurred, it usually follows the line of reasoning expressed by H. T. McAnly in the following words:

> If the variations represent losses which were avoidable and can be corrected, they represent definite charges against the profit or loss for the period, and cover cost—no part of which need be in future planned product cost for pricing and sales policies. If they represent revisions in values (material prices or wage rates) or insufficient unavoidable loss provisions in the planned burden, they represent adjustments which apply not only to the specific products in process during the period in which they occurred, but to the cost of all products affected by these necessary revisions.[11]

Among the companies interviewed in this study, there were several which use some or all standard costs solely to facilitate the process of computing actual costs of products. Some of these companies combine fixed standards for material prices and labor rates with current standards for other cost factors.[12] When cost control is not an objective in using standard costs and inventories are costed at historical actual cost, it is not necessary to revise standard costs when material prices and labor rates change. However, variances from such standard costs must be analyzed by products in determining current costs for managerial decisions and the variances need to be allocated between inventories and cost of goods sold when preparing financial statements.

Examples of Variance Analysis by Products

When analysis of variances by products is desired, suitable techniques are needed to effect the analysis without an excessive amount of clerical work. Apportionment of variances between inventories

---

[10] Another research study entitled "Product Costs for Pricing Purposes" presented a more comprehensive discussion of variances from standard costs in relation to pricing decisions. This study was conducted by the Association's Committee on Research.

[11] "The Coming Challenge to Cost Accounting," Symposium Papers (North Carolina Association of Certified Public Accountants, 1950), p. 47.

[12] For a discussion of this procedure, see John F. Mickelson, "Standard Costs Applied to the Manufacture of Silverware," *N.A.C.A. Bulletin* (December 15, 1947) and James F. Merrick, "An Application of a Basic Standard Rate to Direct Labor," *N.A.C.A. Bulletin* (August, 1950).

and cost of goods sold without allocation to individual products or product lines may be sufficient for financial reporting purposes. However, most of the companies charging a portion of the variances to inventories consider it necessary to analyze the variances by product classification because an overall variance ratio is not sufficiently accurate.

Standard product costs are converted to actual costs by applying the ratio between variance balances and standard costs to the standard costs. In this process the grouping of costs and products should not be so broad as to obscure important differences in the incidence of variances on individual product classes. Examples of the procedures followed by some of the companies interviewed are given below.

Example 1: A comparatively small number of raw materials constitutes a major portion of the total product cost. Prices of these materials fluctuate over a wide range. For these reasons, the cost of each material is individually converted from standard to actual. On the other hand, a single percentage is used for labor and overhead combined.

Example 2: This company has grouped materials, basing the groupings on similarities in materials so that actual prices of the items within a group tend to fluctuate by the same percentage. To illustrate, items made of brass are in one category and items made of steel are in another category. By using ratios to fixed standard prices, clerical work required to convert standard cost to actual cost is minimized without loss of the desired accuracy.

Example 3: In place of deriving average adjustment factors for all items in a product line, this company first selected individual items which typify the line of products to which they belong. The standard cost of each of these items is then carefully converted to actual cost by detailed computation. Ratios between standard and actual cost of these type items are applied to standard costs of all related items. This procedure has been found quicker and clerically cheaper than the more usual method of developing overall ratios for entire product lines.

Example 4: The company manufactures a wide variety of products and sales are characterized by small orders. Knowledge of product profitability was stated to be the principal key to management's success in operating the business. Moreover, operations performed in each department result in a salable commodity and inventories are carried at the various stages of manufacturing. Hence it is necessary to have a complete product cost, operation by operation. To ascertain product costs with historical job order methods would be impractical because the clerical expense would be excessive. The plan used is to issue production orders which are costed at standard cost as each operation is completed. Actual costs and standard costs are summarized monthly by operations and a single overall variance for each operation is developed. In order to determine the cost of goods sold for the monthly commodity profit-and-loss statement, shipments are first summarized by commodities and extended at standard cost. The appropriate variance ratios are then applied to the standard cost figures to obtain the actual cost of each commodity sold.

CONCLUSION

Variances serve to direct management's attention to the fact that current costs have deviated from standard costs. While cost control must be exercised before the fact and variances are ascertained after the fact, prompt review of variance history can bring to light conditions needing attention and it can also provide management with information which contributes to the making of sounder decisions with respect to the future.

Since costs are controlled by individuals, determining responsibility for variances is the first step toward making variance data useful for cost control. Accumulation of standard and actual costs controllable by each managerial responsibility in the company's organization provides a measure of managerial performance in comparison with the standards established for the purpose.

Before intelligent action based upon variance information can be taken, it is necessary to know why the variances arose. Hence analysis to determine the causes of variances makes the variance data more useful. Analyses by cause may be made regularly according to a preestablished procedure or they may be made by special studies in which the methods and objectives differ from one study to another. Examples of both of these approaches have been given in earlier pages of this report. Most companies make some use of both approaches.

While much may be learned by a well-directed analysis of variances, the ultimate value of the analysis rests upon effective communication of the results to managerial personnel. Reports which bring out the significance of variance data in terms of the problems faced by executives and supervisors are useful for the purpose. However, experience shows that reports need to be accompanied by the informal methods of communication which develop when the accountant works closely with operating management. In small companies, the latter methods largely replace formal reports.

For such purposes as pricing, management wants current product costs which include all costs which it aims to recover in selling prices. Where standard costs are current and variances are relatively small, analysis of variances by products may be unnecessary. Nevertheless, the field study shows that it is often impractical to maintain standard product costs which are continuously current or to eliminate variances from standards which are based upon preferred methods and materials, normal variety, and similar conditions. Hence most of the companies interviewed analyze variances by products before using the costs as guides to decisions with respect to pricing and product selection.

On the other hand, the common practice of revising standard costs at the end of the year provides up-to-date standard product costs for costing the year-end inventory. Consequently, assignment of variances to products for this purpose is usually not considered necessary.

45. LEARNING CURVE TECHNIQUES FOR DIRECT LABOR MANAGEMENT *

Rolfe Wyer †

For many years, the control of direct labor hours has been accomplished in most industries through the use of standard time data. The methods employed are varied but most standard labor control systems have one common feature, i.e., that the hours allowed for a given increment of labor remain constant for some period of time. Thus, when it becomes obvious that a particular unit standard is obsolete (whatever the cause), it is necessary to restudy the operation and "set a new standard."

Even a casual review of the principles underlying labor incentives and other familiar applications of standards show that there are certain underlying premises which will not always stand the test of critical evaluation. For our purpose here, the most important of these premises is that each time an operation is performed, it should require the same unit time, except as altered by operator effort. It is easy to understand that such a premise is valid in high volume, repetitive operations. Monotony alone would work against any improvement or learning in operations performed several thousand times each day. The trend of modern industry is, however, away from such routine labor functions (which are being replaced by machines) to very complex and lengthy operations, usually involving a higher degree of technical skill and performed on a limited quantity of production.

This is particularly true in the so-called defense industries, where the end product is intricate and engineered for many purposes other than low cost. In this area and in many others, it can be demonstrated by both theory and actual test that each time an operation is performed it will require less time than before, under normal circumstances. Since it would be impracticable to set a new labor standard for each unit built by customary techniques, it is clear that some type of progressive and systematic standard must be developed which will

* From *N.A.A. Bulletin* (July, 1958), Section 2. Reprinted by permission of the National Association of Accountants.
† Rolfe Wyer, Vice President and Treasurer, Airtek Dynamics, Inc., Los Angeles, California.

automatically yield a new, lower value, each time that a new unit is produced. The learning curve fits this definition and is, to my knowledge, the only example of a flexible and dynamic labor standard in use by a major segment of American industry today. Thus, the learning curve is used because it is a practical technique which is superior to constant engineered time values for control purposes. Not only is it superior because of the lower cost of developing and applying the standard values, but also because it provides a reducing daily target which is in harmony with manufacturing realities and is a continuous spur to lower cost.

Form and Construction of the Learning Curve

Having covered some of the basic premises underlying the learning curve, let us now proceed to an examination of what the curve is and how it works. Exhibit 1 is a graph which shows a plot of learning experience for an individual operator performing a simple repetitive operation for a limited time period. The number of pieces produced is plotted on the X axis and the time per unit on the Y axis. Normal graph paper has been used on which all lines are equidistant.

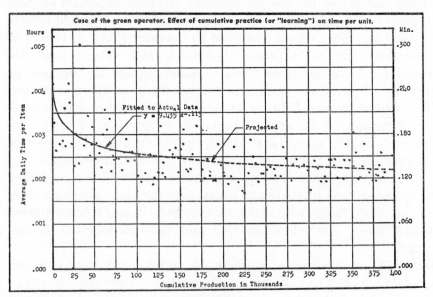

EXHIBIT 1

Next, let us look at Exhibit 2 of the same general form, which compares the learning curves found in aircraft and refrigerator manufacture. It will be noted that the curve for refrigerators is not

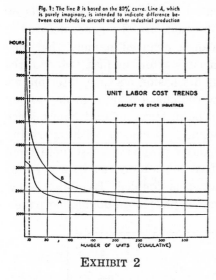

Fig. 1: The line B is based on the 80% curve. Line A, which is purely imaginary, is intended to indicate difference between cost trends in aircraft and other industrial production

UNIT LABOR COST TRENDS

AIRCRAFT VS OTHER INDUSTRIES

NUMBER OF UNITS (CUMULATIVE)

EXHIBIT 2

unlike the first one shown, since this is a mechanized and repetitive type of production. These curves are the beginning of the entire learning curve system. Fortunately, they can be reduced to straight lines on double log graph paper, since it would be very impracticable to use such curves in everyday operations if they could not be easily read and charted. Many people have criticized this use of double log paper as an unnecessary complication but, as can easily be seen from this exhibit, it is quite the opposite. From now on all of our exhibits will be on this paper, with the curves shown as straight lines.

With the form of the curve established, we can now state the proposition which is the basis of most practical applications of the curve today. The proposition reads: "Each time the quantity of production is doubled, the cumulative average unit hours will be some constant percentage of the average unit hours of the quantity that was doubled." This percentage must be more than 60 percent and is usually in the range of 80 to 85 percent. While the proposition stated may be confusing, it can be very simply presented in the following tabulation of an 80 percent curve, in which the initial quantity of production is one and the hours required for this first unit 100.

HOURS

Quantity of Production		Per Lot		Cumulative	
Per Lot	Cumulative	Total	Per Unit	Total	Per Unit
1	1	100	100	100	100
1	2	60	60	160	80
2	4	96	48	256	64
4	8	152.6	38.15	409.6	51.2
8	16	245.76	30.72	655.36	40.96

There are several important points to note about the tabulation. The cumulative hours per unit do reduce in an exact 80 percent progression. The hours per lot do not show an 80 percent progression on the first two lots (i.e., 100 to 60) but do follow the 80 percent pattern (with minor fluctuations) thereafter (i.e., 48 is 80 percent of 60). Thus, from these observations, the general form of both the cumulative and unit curve can be deduced, namely, that they are parallel lines for all practical purposes after the first two or three units. This is very important for our discussion because, later on, we will have the opportunity to see how the curve is used in day-to-day operations. Most of these charts will be in terms of unit hours, since cumulative hours cannot be intelligently discussed with operating personnel who are concerned with today's problems. Also note from the tabulation that the total cumulative hours increases by a percentage each time the quantity of production is doubled. Exhibit 3 below shows these lines as they would appear if plotted on double log paper.

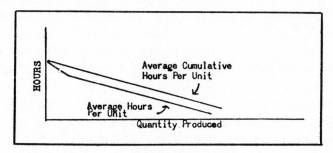

EXHIBIT 3

In presenting this basic concept, I have avoided any reference to the mathematical formulas involved because I do not believe that our discussion will be helped particularly by a lengthy explanation of equations which have already been proved. Let us, instead, list the information which we have compiled on the curve, without reference to mathematics.

1. The slope of a cumulative line for any percentage of curve can be determined by a calculation similar to the one presented earlier.
2. Conversely, a given set of data can be plotted on log-log paper and the percentage of the curve resulting calculated.
3. With a given cumulative line, a unit line can be determined without reference to any special conversion tables.
4. With a plot made, total projected hours can be calculated, either by multiplication of cumulative hours by total quantity, or by a constant percentage.
5. Job status in relation to any or all of these lines, which has been set as a budget, can be quickly determined by everyday charting techniques.

From listing these points, we can conclude that it is not necessary to understand the mathematics of the curve in order to work with it.

If you are the lazy type, I would suggest that you obtain one of the learning curve chart guides which are available. With this aid, you can determine the slope of any curve, draw a slope of your choice, or draw any cumulative line from a unit line, or vice versa.

One word of caution before leaving our discussion of the form of the curve. With a given set of data, cumulative lines can be easily calculated and drawn. However, as indicated earlier, most practical work with the curve is in terms of unit lines. Now, referring back to our original tabulation of data and bearing in mind that the unit line represents the hours per unit for each individual unit, a problem of how to plot this data arises. We can obtain hours for each individual unit or else we must plot these points for lots of more than one at the linear midpoint (since we are working on double log paper) between the cumulative quantity and the quantity doubled.

Actually the unit line is asymptotic to the cumulative line. This means it is not accurately parallel to the cumulative line but is drawing away from it at a declining rate which, after the first few units, is insignificant. However, to overcome this problem, along with getting an accurate plot on the first few units, many companies have turned the formula around so that the unit line is straight and the cumulative line is asymptotic to it, as in Exhibit 4.

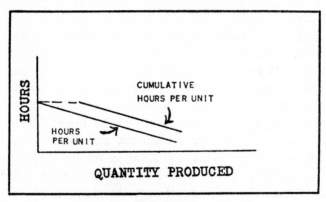

EXHIBIT 4

The principles involved are the same and you have no more difficulty working with this form of the curve than the other.

CURVES FOR ESTIMATING AND CONTROL

Our subject is the use of the curve to control direct labor. It should already be very obvious that this is not the only possible use. Even if we start our direct labor control with the job estimate, many interesting phases of curve application—such as price renegotiation and redetermination, contract termination, inventory valuation, and job costing—must necessarily go uncovered or receive too little attention. Also, space prohibits exploring the accumulation of data for learning curve plotting, which is a field in itself. Here are the main points in direct labor control in which the curve is used:

1. Original estimate.
2. Scheduling (including machine and tool loading).
3. Manpower procurement and loading.
4. Labor efficiency.
5. Methods and tool improvements.

For any or all of these phases, the curve is broken down into many segments. This means that, for a particular project, there are many curves (sometimes in the thousands) which can be combined or used separately according to the need. Starting with the original estimate will show how this works. Imagine, if you will, that you are faced with estimating a new airplane. Unfortunately, this airplane is in the preliminary design stages so that there is no bill of material, detailed drawings, or other customary comforts to the estimator. This is not an imaginary situation or one that will be rescued by cost plus. Commercial jet airlines were sold with little more, a few years ago. Now it is your job to calculate what these airplanes will cost and, most important, the break-even point for the project. With reference to past projects of this type, if any, the airplane is broken down into its various components or systems and overall curves established with reference to such factors as weight, complexity, and function according to experience. Broad as these curves may be, they are the beginning of the labor budget.

Before leaving the estimating subject, let me outline one fundamental point of controversy. Estimates, and hence curves, can be set by reference to some point well along in the production cycle (i.e., 100th airplane) or they can be set by estimating the hours for the first unit. Often it is easier to discern the shape of the "devil" you know than to picture him two or three years ahead. Hence, many estimators believe they can more accurately judge hours for Unit 1 than to predict the hours required for the airframe once in production. Hence, they will set the initial figures and extend the curve from there. This is probably more practical when a small quantity is being purchased, since a small error at Unit 100 is greatly magnified at Unit 1. Conversely, if a large quantity is being purchased, the reverse is true.

Once the initial estimate has been made and the job is in the house, then the overall curves must be broken down into great detail. These breakdowns are by both type of work (i.e., machining, welding, and assembly, etc.) and by components or subassemblies. Not all of these detail curves have the same slope. Let us look at some of the many uses to which these curves are put.

1. Total hours for the project are broken down between in-plant and subcontract. The purchasing department is given a budget for subcontract labor, which is tied to the curve. In turn, individual vendors are selected after their bids have been related to the budget.
2. Total in-plant labor requirements are scheduled by months and related to other labor needs. The personnel department is given a recruiting plan based on the curve, according to the skills needed. Incidentally, this was the very problem which first sparked the government's interest during World War II.
3. Tooling plans are coordinated with the curves so that bottlenecks will not occur. In short, elapsed time in a particular jig or fixture must be related to man-hours required.
4. Quantity schedules are tied to manpower, tools, etc., so that customer requirements will be met.
5. Budgeted hours are translated into daily or weekly targets on the floor, so that foremen or group leaders know both the unit and elapsed times which they are expected to meet and so that the manning for each work station can be set.
6. Job progress against these targets is reviewed in detail on a regular basis so trouble spots are pinpointed.
7. Overall job progress is compared to the total budget and methods effort applied to projects which are lagging.

CONCLUSION

Now this is only a thumbnail sketch of how learning curves are used to manage direct labor. Before closing, I would like to call attention to one phase of learning curves which, while not within our subject, has received far too little attention from accountants and should be discussed here. If the estimate for an airplane or any other similar complex product is really a curve, then how should this product be costed? If the so-called actual cost is applied as the product is shipped, then large losses occur early in the project. Yet these "losses" may be exactly as planned or even less than planned. Conversely, is the inventory really properly valued if these losses are written off? Conservatively, yes, but put yourself in the place of an owner selling such a business on the basis of book value, to get the proper perspective. First, look at Exhibit 5 which shows the problem graphically. The area between the cost line and the sales line is loss until about Unit 25. After this point, profits are realized.

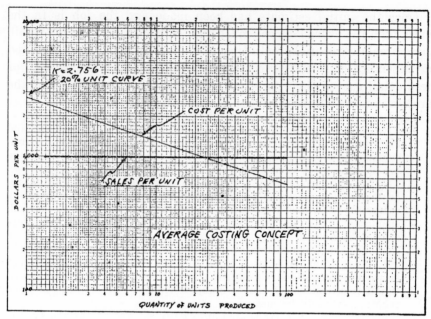

EXHIBIT 5

Next look at a tabulation (Exhibit 6) which previously appeared in the *Bulletin*, which shows how this works. Now if there were many jobs in work, it might average out but this is rarely the case with the types of products we are discussing. Something needs to be done. There are not many accountants willing to leave these losses in inventory.

MONTHLY GROSS PROFITS OVER PERIOD OF CONTRACT — LEARNING CURVE VS. ACTUAL COST METHODS

	TOTAL SALES		GROSS PROFIT LEARNING CURVE METHOD		GROSS PROFIT ACTUAL COST METHOD		CUMULA-TIVE DIF-FERENCE
Month	Monthly	To Date	Monthly	To Date	Monthly	To Date	Learning Curve over Actual
1	24,875		(2,000)		(41,374)		39,375
2	74,625	99,500	(3,375)	(5,375)	(49,125)	(90,500)	85,125
3	149,250	248,750	4,500	(875)	(29,250)	(119,750)	118,875
4	248,750	497,500	23,750	22,875	5,000	(114,750)	137,625
5	248,750	746,250	18,750	41,625	17,500	(97,250)	138,875
6	248,750	995,000	53,750	95,375	67,500	(29,750)	125,125
7	248,750	1,243,750	30,000	125,375	55,000	25,250	100,125
8	248,750	1,492,500	40,000	165,375	65,000	90,250	75,125
9	248,750	1,741,250	27,500	192,875	67,500	157,750	35,125
10	248,750	1,990,000	27,500	220,375	62,625	220,375	—

EXHIBIT 6

Briefly, we covered the fundamentals behind the curve and how it works. Then we touched on its application to the management of direct labor. I would like to leave this one thought. The learning curve is not just a poor substitute for labor standards. While in many ways less accurate, it fills a definite need and, all too rare in our accounting world, it builds improvement and progress into our figures rather than blind and rigid adherence to the past.

46. THE CRITICAL AREAS
OF MATERIAL COST
CONTROL *   I. Wayne Keller †

A survey of the published reports of a number of corporations indicates that in the average business the cost of direct materials is approximately 40 percent of the sales dollar. Certainly, in most businesses it is by far the largest component of cost. Since this is true, the control of material costs should be given relative importance by the accountant. It is the purpose of this paper to survey the many facets of material cost control and suggest policies and procedures which can be adopted in this important phase of cost accounting. While the specific treatment will be of direct material costs, referred to hereafter as material costs, indirect material costs can, for the most part, be controlled by the same or similar procedures. The "paper work" of purchase requisitions and orders, receiving reports, stores records and requisitions, etc., will be mentioned only as it is incidental to cost control policies.

The placing of responsibilities for control follows the organization structure of the Armstrong Cork Company, and much of the subject matter was suggested by material cost control problems of this company. While cork is an important raw material of the company, its value is a small percentage of the total value of raw materials. Others of the hundreds of materials used in important quantities and values are linseed oil, pigments, natural and synthetic resins, natural and synthetic rubber, plastic molding powders, metal plate, rags, sand, soda ash, pulpwood, asphalt, clay, glue, and glycerine. Most of these are bulk materials with a relatively low unit value. However, there are some others which have a high unit value and therefore require great care in storage and extremely close control in usage.

* From *N.A.C.A. Bulletin* (July 15, 1948). Reprinted by permission of the National Association of Cost Accountants.
† I. Wayne Keller, Controller of Armstrong Cork Co., Lancaster, Pa., and past president of the National Association of Cost Accountants.

ORGANIZATION FOR CONTROL

The first requisite for the control of material costs is organization, with responsibilities clearly established for all phases of the control problems. The accountant is the keystone in such an organization, for control will be no better than the accounting records and data which are established. The accountant's direct responsibility is one of recording, measuring, and reporting. His functional responsibility should have no limits and he should be alert at all times to appraise and report to management the effectiveness with which material costs are being controlled in all areas.

The size and complexity of the control organization as well as the specific assignment of responsibilities will vary with the size and character of the business. In the larger businesses, control responsibility is frequently divided among the laboratory, engineering, purchasing, receiving and stores, production planning, standards of production, and accounting departments. In the smaller businesses all of these functions may be assigned to one person or may be performed in conjunction with other functions by several persons. The specific organization structure is not important, but the clear assignment and delineation of responsibilities are.

The control of material costs will be made easier and more effective if standards are established and if the standard material costs are recorded on the books, with accounting segregation and reporting of variances from standard. However, many control devices can be operated effectively if standards are not in use.

AREAS OF CONTROL

There are eight areas of control of material costs and accounting is involved in each one of them. These areas are:

1. Specifications.
2. Purchasing.
3. Inventory.
4. Usage.
5. Scrap.
6. By-products and joint products.
7. Salvage.
8. Indirect costs.

Evaluation of Materials Specifications

The control of material costs begins with the establishment of specifications for materials. The technical experts establish the kinds of materials to be used and the yields to be expected. The laboratory is responsible for determining what kinds of raw materials shall be used and their chemical and physical characteristics. This department also establishes formulas and processing speeds which are affected by chemical reaction. Yields may be set by the laboratory if chemical characteristics are dominant or by the engineers if physical measurements are the determining factors. The engineers also establish the processing losses which may be expected because of spilling, adherence to containers, minimum possible processing damage, etc. In a larger corporation with many plants or departments, the specifications established by the laboratory and engineering departments are usually cleared through a standards of production department which is responsible for placing the specifications in the hands of those who will need them and also for inspecting the products to see that they meet the specifications.

The accounting function with respect to specifications is one of evaluation. Before a specification is finally established, the accounting department determines its effect on the profit from the product. In many instances this may extend beyond the material cost and affect such things as production speeds, capacity, processing and handling equipment, and even customer acceptance. Therefore, such evaluation cannot be limited to simple application and addition of unit costs but calls for the exercise of sound business judgment and consideration of economic factors. Specifications do not become effective until approved by the accounting department. Where there is no standards of production department, the accounting department may also be responsible for routing, filing, and revising the written production specifications.

Purchase Variances and Materials Handling Procedures

With specifications established, it is the responsibility of the purchasing department to procure materials in accordance with the specifications at the best possible price. Since purchases are made only on purchase requisitions issued by the production planning department, it is necessary for purchasing and production planning to work very closely in determining what quantities shall be purchased. A requisition for the material requirements of the next month may be for a quantity which will be more costly than standard because of less than carload transportation costs, extra packaging or necessity of placing the order with a distributor rather than the manufacturer. Purchasing brings these matters to the attention of production planning and in many instances quantities are changed in order to secure a better price. Also, purchasing keeps production planning informed of current price trends and availability of material. Quantities purchased are then governed by these factors as well as by price.

The purchasing department sets standard material prices for each year. These reflect the best possible estimate of the average price which will be paid for each material over the year. Since these standards are used for interim inventory valuation and for accounting they are approved by the accounting department. The approval procedure requires checking the price against recent purchases, analysis of the FOB and delivered price to establish the inclusion of freight and the method of transportation, determination that the price is based on delivery in the custmary form, bulk or package, and appraisal in the light of economic trends and specific industry forecasts.

Accounting control of material costs in the purchasing area is implemented through comparison of actual costs with standard as purchases are made, and through special material cost studies. Comparison with standard price is supplemented by determination that the description of the materials on the invoices is in accordance with the specifications and by a system of follow-up of the laboratory tests of inbound materials. Periodically studies are made, in conjunction with the engineering or production departments, of alternate methods of receiving and handling raw materials. Thus it may be determined that because of changes in plant layout, labor costs, or market conditions, savings can be effected by changing the purchase specifications.

Inventories: Control of Receipts and Storage

The physical receipt and storage of raw materials is the responsibility of the receiving and stores departments, and the quantities to be carried are the responsibility of the production planning department. The inventory records and values are the responsibility of the accounting department. It is in this area that the major emphasis of accounting control is frequently placed. All too often, the emphasis is placed here to the exclusion of other vital areas.

Physical loss can be detected and controlled if there are adequate records in which management has full confidence. Such physical loss is not limited to pilferage but can also result from deterioration, shrinkage, and damage. To keep each of these at an irreducible minimum requires rather detailed records but not more detailed than the records which are kept of cash. In many businesses the value of the inventories is greatly in excess of the cash of the company. Is there any reason, then, why inventories should not be controlled as carefully as is cash? Probably the only valid one is the general utility of cash as against the limited utility of inventory items. But this is offset by the fact that employees are more careless in handling inventories than they are in handling cash.

Pilferage can be eliminated through controlled receipt, storage, and issuance of the raw materials with complete transfer records through production and finished stock into shipments. The records must show quantities entering, on hand in, and leaving each storeroom or production operation. Then when shortages occur, it is possible to concentrate vigilance on a small area and thus detect the cause quickly. The very fact that a good system of control through records is in operation will provide a strong psychological deterrent to individuals who otherwise may be tempted to carry some of the products away.

The problem of shrinkage exists in many inventories and particularly with regard to raw materials. Such shrinkage may result from evaporation, seepage through the container, and adherence to the container. The accounting records should show the units received or produced in comparison with the units used or sold. By comparison of statistics of several periods, weighing "empty" containers, test gauging, etc., the amount of shrinkage to be expected can be established. An adjusting factor should be added to unit cost rates so that the units moving out of inventory will be costed at a rate higher than that at which they were charged in.

The mere passage of time causes loss in value through deterioration in most materials. If chemical and physical changes do not occur, the accumulation of dust and physical contacts through moving adjacent materials will usually cause damage. Wherever possible, all storage should be in lots or piles which are clearly identified on the inventory control records. Requisitions should be screened by the accounting department and marked to be taken from the oldest pile or lot. Then, if each is cleared completely before new material is added, there will have to be turnover. In addition to providing for good physical turnover, such records also provide automatic checks on the quantity in each location. As each pile or lot is exhausted, the records are marked accordingly and thus an automatic continuous check of physical inventories is effected.

An adequate system of securing turnover will not eliminate all obsolescence of materials. Changes in customer demand and in formulations cannot always be anticipated by the production planning department, either because the causes are outside of the enterprise or because other departments did not supply information of trends. If the accounting records indicate that a material is not moving, an investigation should be made immediately to determine whether or not the condition is likely to be permanent. If it is, possible alternate uses or sales outlets should be explored and an estimate made of the value the material would have in each of these. When the best outlet is established, the loss which will result from using or selling through the alternate outlet should be charged to an account for loss due to obsolescence. If no alternate outlet can be found, the material should be scrapped and its full value charged to the obsolescence loss account. Such charges should have the prior approval of all departments having responsibilities for materials.

Inventories: Material Movement Costs

Costs of receiving, handling, and storing material are frequently of sufficient importance to justify the expenditure of a reasonable amount of control effort on them. It is possible to set labor standards for unloading, moving, and storing materials and for establishing expense rates to be applied to such labor. The material value charged into production should include such costs to the extent of one movement into the standard storage area and from that area to point of usage. Allowance should not be made for nonstandard movement of materials.

Thus, if materials are stored in areas not normally used, the difference between the actual cost of moving them into the areas and the standard allowance for movement into the standard areas should be reflected as a variance. The aggregate of such variances at the close of a period will measure the effectiveness of scheduling purchases, the adherence to standard containers or method of transportation, and the efficiency of handling. While each of these may be computed individually through very detailed application of standards, it is usually unnecessary to do so, as reasons for variances can be established by scanning the receiving records and visiting points of storage of inventories.

When costs of storage and handling are determined, it may be found that the provision of storage space at each using operation is desirable. The possibility of more discrepancies in the inventory records because records cannot be maintained and physical movement controlled as carefully in each such operational storage area as in a central storeroom may be more than counterbalanced by tangible savings from storing materials adjacent to point of use.

Responsibility for Inventory Valuation

Inventory valuation is the responsibility of the accounting department. Since valuation directly affects the cost of goods sold, no small part of the control of material costs rests on the method used and the adequacy of the records. Valuation will be determined first by the policy established by the company and second by the operations within the policy. With the increasing election of the "last-in first-out" method of inventory valuation, the accountant has a new area in which to guide management in establishing policy. Since few companies have their entire inventories valued on this elective method, there are items in each company which should be studied constantly to determine whether or not approval of the Commissioner of Internal Revenue should be requested for adopting the method for additional items.

After the basis is established, whether it is "first-in first-out" or "last-in first-out," the timing of increases or decreases in inventory can have a substantial effect on cost of goods sold. Here the accounting and production planning departments work hand in hand in operating within the established policies. If standard costs are used, another policy decision concerns whether to value the inventory at standard or at actual. The literature of N.A.C.A. includes many detailed discussions of these matters. It should be reviewed frequently and inventory valuation policies and procedures appraised periodically so that no opportunity for control will be lost. Conditions change constantly and inventory valuation policies can become obsolete just as the inventories themselves become obsolete.

Usage: Formulation and Yield Variances

At the point of usage, material costs can best be controlled through complete and detailed physical standards. The setting of these standards is the responsibility of the laboratory, engineering, and standards of production departments. The compilation of records, measurement against standards, and reporting of performance is the responsibility of the accounting department. In many processes material usage must be controlled in accordance with a standard formula. In these, the daily reports should show the comparison of actual units used with the standard units for the actual quantity of production. If changes in formulation are authorized, the report should show the revised formula units as well as actual and standard units. In the accounts it is frequently expedient to establish a separate variance account which is charged with the actual raw material used and credited with production times the standard formula allowance. If this is done, variances due to formulation can be separated readily from variances due to yield.

If there are no problems of formulation, there will always be variances due to yield. Such variances may occur when the compounded materials are processed further, when other raw materials are put into process, or when processed materials are used in another operation. The standards should establish the amount of material to be used on standard equipment to produce a specified finished or semifinished product. If this is done, variances would occur if more or less than the standard quantity was used. The accounting records and reports should provide for the explanation of such variances as to cause and location of responsibility.

In applying standard costs to unit quantity standards, consideration should be given to unavoidable loss due to adherence to containers, spilling, and shrinkage. This can be done by adding to the inventory value of the material a percentage to cover these unavoidable losses of materials susceptible thereto. Thus, if the reported usage of plastic molding powder weighed into production is a thousand pounds and the unit raw material inventory value is 20 cents, the credit to inventory and charge to production may be a thousand pounds at 20.4 cents per pound to provide for a 2 percent loss which experience has shown will be experienced on the average against the quantities taken into raw stock.

Keeping Scrap Losses under Control

Frequently material damaged in process and nonstandard finished product is charged to plant expense and credited to inventory. While some control may be effected under this procedure, if expense budgets are used, the control will be less effective than it would be if standard scrap allowances are established. The engineers and standards of production department set the expected amounts and the standards of production department is responsible for all inspection. The accounting records show total production and the inspection reports show good production for each operation. In this way, actual scrap losses can be determined by production responsibility and dollar variances reported in the same manner. Process inventory would then be credited with actual scrap at standard value to its stage of completion which would be charged to a variance account. This account in turn would be credited with the standard allowance for scrap and process inventory charged.

Scrap or imperfect production may fall into three categories: (1) that which is of no value and is destroyed, (2) that which can be reused, and (3) that which can be sold as imperfect goods. In the first category may be mentioned material which may have no value or such a low value that it is impractical to reflect it in the unit cost of the end product. This latter is treated as salvage and is discussed later. When scrap material is destroyed, the accounting stops with the comparison of actual scrap produced and standard scrap allowed. If there is expense of disposing of the scrap, such costs are usually included in the general expense of the plant.

If the scrap can be reused in formulation or reworked, the operation creating the scrap should receive credit for the value which it will have when reused. The scrap would then be carried on inventory at this value until reworked or reused. When imperfects are produced which can be sold as such, the production of perfects should be costed at a price greater than the cost to make so as to provide for a write-down of the imperfect values. Such adjustment is usually in relation to sales prices. Thus, if imperfects are sold at 82 percent of the sales price of perfects and 10 percent of the production is imperfect, the perfects would be written up 2 percent. (Write-down of ten imperfects from cost to make of $1 to $.82 = $1.80 ÷ 90 perfects = $.02 write-up per perfect). This procedure will maintain the standard ratio of standard cost of goods sold to sales income and provide for fair inventory valuation.

By-products and Joint Products

Another important area of control is in the recognition and valuation of by-products and joint products. Production records should show the production of each grade of material from each production process. With standards established for expected quantities of each product or grade, comparisons can be made of actual production and reasons for variances established. If all the products or grades are sold, the valuation usually follows sales prices and presents no particular problems. However, if some of the joint or by-products are used as raw materials, detailed studies must be made to establish proper values. If the material is used as a substitute for another raw material which would be purchased, the fair value of the by-product would be the value of the material it replaces or an arbitrary percentage of that value in order to give both the producing and using product an advantage. If some of the material is used as a substitute material and some is sold, the sales price at which it is sold should not be less than the price at which it is charged to the consuming product. Otherwise, the purchaser may be securing a competitive advantage.

Sometimes a new product is developed to utilize by-product materials for which no use had existed previously. The question then arises as to the value to be placed on the by-product material. If it is taken at no value because it is of a sort which had previously been destroyed and sales prices are set on this basis, it may be that a market will develop which will make it necessary to produce directly the material which previously was a by-product. Then the material which had no value becomes costly and the end product which had been profitable suddenly shows a loss. Close control is needed here. It is probably in order to continue using the by-product at no value until the new consuming product is established. Then, either through cost reduction or sales price increases a residual after profit and other costs can be procured and assigned as a value to the by-product. It is the responsibility of the accounting department to follow all of these possibilities and establish joint and by-product values which will be fair to the consuming and producing end products, maintain a sound competitive price structure, and encourage the utilization of all such materials to the fullest extent.

Salvage of Obsolete Equipment, Scrap, and Trim

A salvage section operates under the general supervision of the purchasing department. It is the responsibility of this section to review all requests for obsolescence of materials and equipment and determine whether or not any market can be found. This section is also informed of all scrap and trim losses, for, in some production, such as stampings from metal plate, there are frames which can be sold as scrap metal. In others there is scrap, such as ends of rolls and frayed edges of burlap which can be sold to nurseries for wrapping materials. Thus, while realizable values of these are too low to reflect in the unit cost of the end products, they do have some salvage value. Through a constant search for buyers, the salvage section is able to find outlets and realize substantial income from and save costs of hauling to the dump of items which otherwise would be destroyed. The accounting department has the responsibility of determining the net income from salvage and of crediting it to the proper operations or products.

Tracing Indirect Costs to Their Source

Inadequate control of material will not only increase the cost of the material component of the finished product but will also result in avoidable indirect costs. If the proper quantities of material are not available, shutdowns or at least expensive machine or production line changes will be experienced. Inadequate testing of incoming raw materials or poor records of tests may permit substandard materials to be used, causing excessive scrap or completely ruining a lot or batch. Improper inspection of finished products and incomplete records of perfect and imperfect production may result in complaints from customers. Inaccurate finished stock records may result in unfilled delivery promises and loss of goodwill. All of these need only be mentioned to bring to mind the possible adverse effects on profits.

Then there is the indirect cost of financing the inventory. With the constant increase in commodity prices, more and more cash must be converted into inventories just to maintain quantities. When the sellers' market passes and balanced stocks must be carried to service the trade, inventory quantities will have to be increased in many companies. The accountant should be able to inform management of the amount of inventory required and carried for each product line and the costs in terms of going interest rates of financing these requirements. The records should provide for the correlation of inventories and sales forecasts so that inventory requirements and the resulting cash requirements can be reflected in the current and long-term cash budgets.

COORDINATING CONTROL

In any large industry there must be a central point at which decisions are made and policies established. In the Armstrong Cork

Company this coordinating function is vested in an operating committee. All departments having responsibilities relating to materials, as well as the sales and general production departments, are represented. A general vice-president is chairman of this committee which meets biweekly. The committee receives reports and recommendations from the staff and operating departments and either approves, disapproves, or sends the recommendation back for further study. Thus, in a matter of approximately two hours every two weeks, all of the material control functions are coordinated and kept in efficient operation. The smaller the company the less formal the procedure and the fewer the participants in the coordinating and also in the control functions.

CONCLUSION

Material is the one inert element of cost. It is completely controllable, but, because it is inert and inarticulate, it does not force itself upon the attention of management. Other problems demand attention and it is assumed that material costs cannot go far out of line. In these days of excessive prices, this is a dangerous assumption. Material is cash in another form. It should have the same care and control as cash.

47. HOW TO MEASURE
MARKETING PERFORMANCE *   Richard A. Feder †

Given the size of advertising and sales promotion expenditures in the modern consumer products company, one would assume that management is supplied information which provides considerable insight into the effect of "marketing dollars" on profits. Such is not the case, with the result that the typical merchandising effort includes many spending inefficiencies which are considered unavoidable "costs of the marketing game." In this article I shall propose a method of identifying and correcting some of these wastes and inefficiencies.

COMMON FAILURES

Though estimates vary, many professional marketing men contend that the average consumer products company spends from 1 percent to 5 percent of its marketing funds at a loss, i.e., in areas where present and future profit potentials do not warrant investment spending. This is usually the result of many different factors, including the following:

> Attempts to achieve too high a share of an unusually competitive market, i.e., the profits generated by the sales responsible for the *last* share points added are less than the cost of the effort which produced them.
> Failure to adjust the level of marketing effort to compensate for local seasonal variations.
> Failure to adjust national spending strategies for local product preferences or for unique local competitive conditions.

Conversely, there are frequently areas which could profitably use more funds than they get. These include secondary markets in which the company and its competitors underspend in order to

* From the *Harvard Business Review* (May-June, 1965). Reprinted by permission of the President and Fellows of Harvard College.
† Richard A. Feder, Assistant Product Manager for Colegate-Palmolive Company. AUTHOR'S NOTE: I am indebted to Anthony Tarallo of Touche, Ross, Bailey & Smart, and Eric Kisch, a doctoral student at the Graduate School of Business of Columbia University, for help in developing this article.

finance heavier efforts elsewhere. In these markets profits are often highly responsive to additional marketing activity.

Accounting's Answer

Failures such as those noted are all examples of the effect of employing an inappropriate level of marketing activity relative to the profit potential or profit responsiveness of a specific area. To be sure, attempts have been made by many companies to identify by area the responsiveness of profits to marketing effort. Typically, however, they use a breakdown of accounting figures, and the value of traditional financial data for this purpose is severely limited. For one thing, the conventions which underlie the accounting system were originally designed for auditing. Accordingly, "generally accepted accounting practices" dictate that marketing expenditures be written off when they are incurred—not when they produce sales. Within this framework certain advertising and promotional activities which create *retail* movement of goods are expensed against unrelated segments of *wholesale* movement.

In many companies market area reports are further distorted by the allocation of unidentified costs and bookkeeping adjustments which are irrelevant from the standpoint of profit responsiveness. Under full costing assumptions, many products in many markets normally show losses. In fact, some of these products are profitable from an incremental standpoint, but the profitable areas are not usually identifiable. Differences in product mix and complicated accounting practices produce a situation in which the amount of allocated fixed costs is not uniform or recognizable by market area. In an effort to avoid taking incorrect action in a profitable area, marketing management is normally reluctant to enact spending changes on the basis of these reports.

To these two complicating factors we must add still another. Traditional accounting periods do not necessarily correspond to the time span during which an advertising campaign produces its full increment of sales. An analysis performed on the basis of the results achieved in any one month would probably exclude a substantial portion of the sales generated by the marketing effort expensed in that period. On the other hand, considerably longer periods (say, a year) probably combine the results of many spending decisions, concealing both overspending and underspending. Here again traditional accounting conventions preclude the measurement of profit responsiveness.

Spending by Intuition

Lacking a tool which measures profit responsiveness by area and faced with the necessity of making a decision, marketing management usually apportions funds geographically on the basis of relative population, previous wholesale movement, and/or the relative size of each retail market. But a decision based purely on population does not take into account the facts that the kinds of people reached and the costs of reaching them are not constant from area to area. Allocations made on the basis of previous wholesale movement tend to perpetuate past mistakes. And spending proportion to the relative size of each retail market ignores important differences among the competitive situations operative in each area.

Since each of these limiting factors has an effect on the rate at which a single company's marketing dollars product profits, product management will not normally allocate funds on the basis of any *one* of the three standards. How does it relate them? Lacking a suitable alternative, it usually does so "intuitively," with the result that spending inefficiencies, as noted earlier, have come to be regarded as unavoidable "costs of the marketing game."

PROPOSED SYSTEM

To improve marketing decisions, I propose that management have a list prepared (by the financial, market research, data processing, and product management functions) which shows optimum *past* marketing expenditures by market area.

When adjusted for the anticipated competitive and seasonal changes appropriate to each area, this list can function as a reasonable standard against which to compare and alter *future* marketing expenses. Of course, this tool is not perfect. However, preliminary testing indicates that it is a better method than those currently available to marketing management for controlling marketing spending.

Realistic Model

Of course, if the optimum levels of past expenditures are to be listed correctly, they must reflect the decision making situation realistically; that is, they must reflect the goal of apportioning advertising and sales promotion funds to produce some ideal *combination* of short- and long-range profits. Reduced to the mechanics of a model, the marketing objective is to invest money in each market area up to the point where an additional dollar would produce greater *immediate* profits if spent elsewhere. The decision to spend beyond this point in an area requires the existence of an amount of *future* potential which justifies the sacrifice of immediate profits. (The future potential referred to could be either sales gains or the avoidance of sales losses.)

To the extent that our model is valid, measuring marketing effectiveness requires two elements: a financial tool which measures the *rate* at which the "last dollar" of marketing effort produced profits in each area, and market research data documenting the *variables* affecting these rates in terms of competitive changes and growth tends.

Controlling spending efficiency requires the early identification of potential problem areas. Naturally, any tool which attempts to report achievement rapidly will of necessity require a degree of compromise. The proposed approach assumes the existence of a discernible and consistent time lag between wholesale and retail movement in each market area. This system also analyzes profit responsiveness in a way which does not take into account every last sale produced by a unit of marketing effort. Because of these necessary expedients, the applied model is definitely *not* accurate enough to discern situations involving relatively small spending inefficiencies. It is designed, instead, to help marketing management anticipate and avoid the extreme spending errors.

By utilizing the necessary compromises described, we place certain limitations on the end use of this data. In particular, this system can be effective only when used by executives with extensive marketing experience. For instance, analysis of the profits achieved in each market area will disclose that many low-yield spending decisions which might appear to be mistakes to nonmarketing executives *are, in fact, either unavoidable or instances of deliberate investment spending*. Both the determination of appropriate past expenses and the adjustment of these expenses to compensate for anticipated competitive changes require a high degree of marketing insight. We should, therefore, regard this system as a tool to be used *by* marketing management, rather than *on* it.

Some executives, marketing and financial, might ask: "Can't we find these past spending inefficiencies by some kind of special analysis; do we need a whole system?" A system is needed because we require knowledge of where to look before we do look. Spot analysis guided even by the best marketing intuition will probably result in substantial oversights. In addition, it is doubtful that such analysis can be completed in time to make the kinds of spending changes to be discussed. When budgets are being drawn up or when advertising commitments are being reviewed, decisions usually have to be made right away on the basis of existing information.

EXPENSES AND REVENUES

Let us begin with the "nuts and bolts" of the new system—the mechanics of accounting for income and outgo. For concreteness, let us take a representative product line in a hypothetical but typical consumer products company, the ABC Corporation.

What would a *traditional* presentation of actual first quarter performance of the product line look like? Such a presentation appears in Part A of Exhibit I. This traditional style of profit-and-loss (P-and-L) statement tells little about marketing effectiveness.

As discussed earlier, a prerequisite of any meaningful financial information is the isolation of *relevant incremental* revenues and expenses. Accordingly, in Part B of Exhibit I the items listed in Part A have been reorganized to differentiate between those which have marketing significance (items listed above the "Net marketing earnings" line) and those which do not. Within this framework, standard profit contribution (SPC) is the gross revenue produced by the marketing effort. We come now to two different groups of figures—one used by *marketing* executives for self-evaluation, the other used by *corporate* management for evaluating the marketing function:

1. Subtraction of the advertising and sales promotion expenses from the SPC gives us gross marketing earnings (GME). This earnings figure is the *internal* focal point of the marketing control system; that is, the responsiveness of profits to marketing effort is measured by marketing management in terms of the effect on GME of changes in the level of advertising and sales promotion expenditures.

2. Commercial production and product management expenses, on the other hand, are the incremental overhead costs of administering marketing funds. These expenses (sales promotion materials, advertising production, product management salaries, market research surveys, etc.) do not directly affect the SPC level in the same sense that media expenditures or trade allowances do. For this reason they are located below the GME line on the P-and-L sheet. Deduction of these overhead costs from the GME gives us net marketing earnings (NME). This amount, representing marketing management's contribution to corporate overhead and corporate profits, is the

external focal point of the marketing control system; in other words, corporate management evaluates the marketing function on the basis of the size of the NME.

VARIETIES OF PROFIT-AND-LOSS STATEMENT FOR A PRODUCT OF THE ABC CORPORATION, JANUARY-MARCH, 1965
(In thousands of dollars)

A. TRADITIONAL VERSION

Sales		$15,000
Standard variable distribution costs	$ 760	
Standard variable manufacturing costs	6,030	
Budgeted fixed distribution expenses	100	
Budgeted fixed manufacturing expenses	870	
Distribution expense variances	14	
Manufacturing expense variances	(12)	
Inventory adjustments	(67)	7,695
Gross profits		$ 7,305
Administrative overhead expenses	$1,300	1,300
Profits before advertising		$ 6,005
Advertising	$2,007	
Sales promotion	1,568	
Commercial production	175	
Product management expenses	210	3,960
Net profits before taxes		$ 2,045

B. NEW VERSION *(Unadjusted)*

Sales		$15,000
Standard variable distribution costs	$ 760	
Standard variable manufacturing costs	6,030	6,790
Standard profit contribution		$ 8,210
Advertising	$2,007	
Sales promotion	1,568	3,575
Gross marketing earnings		$ 4,635
Commercial production	$ 175	
Product management expenses	210	385
Net marketing earnings		$ 4,250
Budgeted fixed distribution expenses	$ 100	
Budgeted fixed manufacturing expenses	870	
Distribution expense variances	14	
Manufacturing expense variances	(12)	
Inventory adjustments	(67)	
Administrative overhead expenses	1,300	2,205
Net profits before taxes		$ 2,045

Exhibit I *(Continued on next page)*

C. NEW VERSION (*Adjusted*)

Sales		$15,000
Standard variable distribution costs	$ 760	
Standard variable manufacturing costs	6,030	6,790
Standard profit contribution		$ 8,210
Advertising	$1,683	
Sales promotion	1,507	3,190
Gross marketing earnings		$ 5,020
Advertising and sales promotion accrual account:		
3/31/65	$ 615	
(Advertising and sales promotion accrual account:		
12/31/64)	(230)	
Commercial production	175	
Product management expenses	210	770
Net marketing earnings		$ 4,250
Nonmarketing expenses	$2,205	2,205
Net profits before taxes		$ 2,045

Exhibit I (*Concluded*)

Other Expenses

We now come to the figures reported below the NME on the P-and-L statement. Because the levels of fixed distribution and fixed manufacturing expenses are independent of volume and outside the area of marketing management control, they have been separated from their variable counterparts and are included after the NME. (By contrast, the manufacturing and distribution cost figures used in the computation of the SPC are produced by the data processing department. Computers multiply the appropriate standard rates for the *variable* portions of these two expenses by the actual sales volume.) Similarly, manufacturing and distribution variances are also reported after marketing profits. This is consistent with the fact that marketing management accepts as "givens"—and makes decisions on the basis of—standard manufacturing and distribution costs. Deviations from the budgeted amounts for either of these items are considered to be the contributions (deductions) of the respective departments to corporate profit.

TIME FACTORS

Having isolated the relevant expenses, it is now necessary to adjust certain of these items in order to evolve financial results which correspond *in time* to the realities of the marketplace. This is the purpose of Part C of Exhibit I. It will be noted that the advertising and sales promotion expenses under SPC differ from those in Part B. This is because these amounts have been adjusted to compensate for the fact that a major portion of the marketing effort is directed specifically toward retail, rather than wholesale, movement of goods. Retail sales deplete retail inventories, creating concomitant adjustments throughout the distribution chain. Eventually, manufacturer sales are increased.

On the adjusted P and L in Part C of Exhibit I, marketing effort aimed at the retail level is matched with the subsequent wholesale movement generated by this inventory depletion. It is thus necessary to determine the approximate time lag between sales to the trade and sales to the consumer by correlating market research estimates of retail movement with factory sales. Let us suppose that, for our product line of the ABC Corporation, studies have shown this lag to be approximately 30 days in all market areas. The adjusted statement for the first quarter, therefore, reports sales and trade allowances for January, February, and March, but uses December, January, and February figures for media expenditures and coupon redemptions. Advertising and sales promotion accrual accounts are used to reconcile the level of marketing expenditure (and the NME) to the amounts reported in Part B. (These entries are mechanically the same as those used in traditional accounting for opening and closing inventories in the computation of cost of goods sold.)

MARKET AREA SUMMARIES

The upper portion of Exhibit II shows part of a series of reports which lists by market area all expenditures for advertising and sales promotion. The production of the full complement of market area summaries is a relatively straightforward programming assignment well within the data processing capabilities of the average large consumer products company. Rather than show all of the individual areas in this exhibit, I have included only those which warrant special consideration. The basis on which these five were selected, and the significance of the financial analysis and market research data in these reports, will be discussed later.

Period of Analysis

As stated earlier, *the purpose of marketing-oriented financial data is to identify areas in which the company overspent or underspent*

MARKET AREA SUMMARIES, JANUARY-MARCH, 1965

(Dollar figures in thousands except where noted.)

	Area A	Area B	Area C	Area D	Area E + F + G . . . n = U.S. Total
STANDARD PROFIT CONTRIBUTION					
Advertising	$360	$770	$620	$850	$680 / $8,210
Sales promotion	42	203	165	290	276 / 1,683
	58	172	130	191	124 / 1,507
GROSS MARKETING EARNINGS	$180	$395	$325	$369	$280 / $5,020
Advertising and sales promotion accrual account: 3/31/65	28	115	110	138	150 / 615
Financial analysis					
Average opportunity rate:					
This period	2.60	1.05	1.10	0.75	0.70 / 1.45
Last period	2.45	0.95	1.45	1.00	1.20 / 1.70
Percent standard profit contribution	4.4%	9.4%	7.6%	10.4%	8.4% / 100.00%
Percent advertising and sales promotion	3.1%	11.5%	9.2%	15.0%	12.4% / 100.00%
Incremental standard profit contribution, this year vs. last year	($53)	($50)	($75)	$115	$25 / $744
Incremental advertising and sales promotion, this year vs. last year	($20)	($85)	$10	$165	$100 / $354
Incremental gross marketing earnings	($33)	$35	($85)	($50)	($75) / $390
Incremental opportunity rate	(1.65)	0.40	(8.50)	(0.30)	(0.75) / 1.10

Market research data

	Area A		Area B		Area C		Area D		Area E + F + G		U.S. Total	
	This Year	Last Year	This Year	Last Year	This Year	Last Year	This Year	Last Year	This Year	Last Year	This Year	Last Year
Total dollar retail market	$1,790	$1,810	$6,150	$6,175	$2,590	$2,680	$7,525	$7,395	$5,900	$4,950	$54,650	$56,000
Percent share of retail market	50.2%	51.9%	35.6%	36.1%	48.6%	50.3%	38.7%	32.4%	42.9%	46.1%	45.8%	44.6%
Percent distribution	88.3%	88.2%	96.2%	96.2%	97.9%	98.1%	98.1%	97.9%	96.4%	96.6%	96.2%	96.2%
Media efficiencies: TV ...: Cost per thousand homes*	$2.02	$2.11	$2.15	$2.12	$3.95	$2.50	$1.75	$1.75	$1.95	$1.96	$1.95	$1.93
Cost per thousand prime prospects*	$3.10	$3.26	$2.65	$2.70	$4.67	$3.10	$1.92	$2.03	$2.15	$2.30	$2.30	$2.27

Exhibit II

* Dollar figures not in thousands.

relative to the immediate profit potential. This requires the determination of the length of the period in which marketing effort generates immediate profits. For activities which produce trade sales
indirectly, such as consumer advertising, this is a difficult matter to
resolve logically. Past studies have indicated that a single unit of
indirect marketing effort usually produces sales at a decreasing rate
over an extended period of time. The type of analysis proposed here
requires identification of the period within which such an effort
produces the *greatest part* of its returns. Analysis which confines
itself to the results achieved within this period, while not yielding
precision, will allow the identification of *extreme instances* of overspending or underspending.

Now let us return to the ABC Corporation case. Suppose our
inquiries disclose the following facts for the product line in question:

> Testing has indicated that the relevant variables respond consis-
> tently when analyzed *quarterly;* i.e., there seems to be a high degree of
> correlation between the behavior of sales, GME, marketing effort, mar-
> ket share, and market size *over a three-month period.* (Where good
> correlations have been absent, there have been obvious explanations.)
> For instance, given substantially increased competitive expenditures
> while the particular company's spending remains unchanged, marketing
> management should expect an increase in the size of the total market,
> a decreased market share for the company, and a smaller amount of
> gross profits (SPC) relative to the amount of marketing effort purchased
> by the company.
>
> Comparisons made between *shorter* periods do *not* evidence such
> behavior. And the use of longer periods does not seem to increase sub-
> stantially the degree of observable consistency.

On the basis of these findings, indicating that a unit of marketing
effort probably produces most of its sales within 90 days, it is
decided that the adjusted P and L and the market area summaries
(Exhibits I-C and II) should be issued at least quarterly, and preferably each month for the ensuing three-month period.

Financial Analysis

In the proposed system the capabilities of the modern computer
are utilized to perform certain basic financial analyses of the market
area results. The purpose of the analysis in Exhibit II is to focus
marketing management attention on those areas which represent
maximum profit improvement opportunities. These figures tell us:

1. *The rate at which the total marketing effort produced profits in each
   area.* Turning to the first line of control figures, for instance, we see

that during the first quarter each dollar invested in advertising and sales promotion in Area D produced a rounded average of $0.75 GME ($369,000 GME $\div$ $290,000 $+$ $191,000 for advertising and sales promotion). Accordingly, 0.75 is referred to as the *average opportunity rate.*

2. *The relative amount of marketing effort used in each area.* In the fourth line of control figures we see that Area E received 12.4 percent of total advertising and sales promotion funds yet produced only 8.4 percent of total SPC. This indicates that funds were diverted from other areas for use in Area E.

3. *The profits produced by changes in the level of marketing effort between comparable periods, and the rate at which these changes generated profits.* From the last four lines of control data we find, for instance, that in Area B SPC was $50,000 lower than during the first quarter last year; advertising and sales promotion were lower by $85,000 over the same period, resulting in GME increase of $35,000; and additional profits were generated by this change at a per dollar rate of 0.40, .ie., $35,000 $\div$ $85,000 $=$ 0.40. Since profits do not normally respond to increases or decreases of marketing effort at the "average opportunity rate," this "incremental opportunity rate," is of major interest to marketing management. (The incremental opportunity rate is assigned a positive or negative value depending on the basis of the direction of the GME change; i.e., spending changes which increase the GME always have positive signs, and vice versa.)

The choice of "this year versus last year" comparisons for deriving an incremental SPC rate is an effort to avoid the effect of seasonality; spending and market-size changes are generally smaller when computed on this basis than they are if calculated for consecutive periods. Of course, the incremental opportunity rate is not a "pure" figure. Since no two periods are identical from the standpoint of the level and mix of activity operative within the marketplace, one cannot assume that the spending changes on a product line are *solely* responsible for its profit differences. However, when considered in light of the changes in marketing conditions also to be documented in this analysis, the incremental opportunity rate can be a most useful tool.

Market Research

In Exhibit II most of the important marketing variables influencing the effectiveness or the desirability of past spending decisions are documented. These include:

1. *Market share.* Ideally, management would like a dossier on all competitive activity, but the practical difficulty of securing this information at a reasonable cost in time for decision making requires a

compromise. Share-of-market estimates, easily available at moderate cost, are therefore included in this report. For instance, during the three-month period, ABC's share of the retail market was 38.7 percent in Area D, up from 32.4 percent a year ago, indicating a probable increased share of total effective marketing effort for the brand in this market area.

2. *Size and trend of the retail market.* During the retail period corresponding to the first quarter of wholesale business, the estimated total retail market for ABC's product was $54,650,000. Comparing this with $56,000,000 for the comparable period last year, we infer that the overall market is declining at a rate of about 2.4 percent per year.

3. *Retail distribution.* The report shows the percent of the total estimated retail grocery volume achieved by stores in which ABC had distribution. During the period under discussion, distribution in Area C was 97.9 percent, down from 98.1 percent during the comparable 1964 period. This is a relatively insignificant movement, indicating that distribution changes probably did not affect changes in the rate at which marketing effort produced profits in this area.

4. *Media efficiencies.* Since television is the primary advertising medium used by the ABC Corporation, the market area summaries include the estimated cost per thousand households and the cost per thousand prime prospect households. (For the ABC product the latter figure represents a division of total TV expenditures by the estimated number of five-member households reached.) The sharp increase in both these indexes for Area C has no doubt affected the level of profits produced.

The fact that these media efficiency rates differ considerably from market area to market area is not necessarily significant, as all competitors using the same media within each area are normally subject to the same relative inefficiencies. Substantial changes within and area between comparable periods, however, would generally call for special attention.

Speed of Reporting

Traditionally the kinds of market research data included in Exhibit II are used in a way which does not have an immediate impact on profits. The function of the data on these reports, however, is to provide a basis on which marketing management can identify undesirable overspending or underspending *in time to take corrective action.* Since there is an obvious and direct relationship between the time it takes to identify spending inefficiencies and the cost in the marketplace of these inefficiencies, the value of the information proposed is directly proportional to the speed with which it can be delivered.

The mechanics of the financial data in Exhibit II are such that they can usually be performed by data processing within two weeks of the end of the accounting period. Since the required market research data document *retail* trends, and because we are relating wholesale profits to the activity of a *prior* retail period, the ABC Corporation has approximately six weeks in which to gather the desired market research data. Not all sources of this information report within six weeks. Data derived from a national consumer panel can be obtained in this time period; however, these data are thought by some to be less accurate than those developed on the basis of a retail store audit, which usually takes considerably longer. Whether or not this is so, the *direction* and *relative magnitude* of the significant *changes* reported by reputable research firms using *either* method are generally the same. Since it is the changes which are of primary importance for the kinds of decision making being discussed, the framework presented here assumes the use of the more rapidly developed information. The possible loss of marginal accuracy is offset by the additional profit opportunities that are produced by the extra lead time.

MANAGEMENT BY EXCEPTION

Having dealt with the mechanics of the system, we can now turn to its use. It will be recalled that the first thing which must be done is to isolate those areas in which past spending involved the sacrifice of immediate profits. While producing a P and L for each market area is not a difficult problem for the modern computer, the digestion of a great number of these statements can be a problem for the product manager. Here the rule of "management by exception" applies. Our desire is to reexamine those areas involving possible inefficiencies. Severe overspending or underspending will normally produce exceptionally high or low average opportunity rates.

Let us suppose that the marketing executives of the ABC Corporation apply the rule of "management by exception" and select five market areas for special attention. These are the areas detailed in Exhibit II. How does the new system help ABC's executives learn from the past? And how can it help them plan better for the future?

Analysis of Past

Since additional marketing effort generally produces profits at a decreasing rate, the optimum level of spending (where marginal cost equals marginal revenue and gross marketing earnings are at a maximum) can be thought of as the point at which the incremental opportunity rate passes from a positive to a negative figure. (It must be kept in mind, however, that this assumes a degree of consistency between periods which does not in fact exist. Without the tempering influence of professional marketing judgment, the incremental opportunity rate can have only limited utility.)

— *Market Area A.* Here we have an instance of an underpromoted area. Management's review might be summarized as follows:

> *Facts.* This relatively small market received a smaller percentage of ABC's marketing effort than it earned. There have been decreases in market share, marketing effort, and GME; a high negative incremental opportunity rate is symptomatic.

> *Analysis.* The unusually acute responsiveness of profits to changes in the level of marketing effort indicates that this area is relatively "underpromoted" by all companies.

> *Judgment.* The past decision to decrease spending in this area was not the best one. It appears that the market might profitably have used an increase of the same magnitude or a spending level of $140,000 (actual first quarter expenditures of $100,000, plus double the decrease of $20,000).

Market Area B. In this territory the situation is quite different from that of Area A:

> *Facts.* ABC's market share in this area is lower than average. There is decreased marketing effort, an increased GME, and a low average opportunity rate but one that improved during the first quarter.

> *Analysis.* During the last quarter of 1964 management reviewed this market, and at that time the facts of low share and low average opportunity rate for a number of consecutive periods suggested that the presence of strong regional competitors made this an expensive market in which to "buy" sales. This led to the decision to seek a lower, more profitable share level in the first quarter.

> *Judgment.* Increased GME during the first quarter tends to confirm the desirability of this decision. However, a further reduction of effort might have been even more profitable. Before testing this hypothesis, management might decide to continue spending at the first quarter level ($375,000) to determine whether there is any residual loss of share inherent in the past spending policy.

Market Area C. Here ABC's managers find strong external influences at work:

> *Facts.* There are decreases in average opportunity rate, market share, and GME; there is an unusually high negative incremental opportunity rate; there are poor media efficiencies relative to the last period; and there is no significant change in the size of the total market.

> *Analysis.* Poor performance in this area is either the result of a sharp increase in competitive activity or of media inefficiencies. The

latter is suggested by the fact that market size did not expand. More-over, discussion with local sales personnel indicates that there was no noticeable change in the level of competitive effort during the period.

Judgment. Media inefficiencies cost ABC $85,000; SPC was down $75,000, and advertising and sales promotion were up $10,000. In the opinion of management, this problem should be corrected within the framework of the first quarter spending level of $295,000.

Market Area D. Questions of investment spending arise here:

Facts. EXHIBIT II shows an increased share (but low relative to the national average), a negative incremental opportunity rate, and a decreased average opportunity rate.

Analysis. This is a highly competitive major market in which management has elected to pursue an investment-spending policy in order to expand the ABC franchise. The degree to which this investment is desirable is a function of its cost (in terms of the amount of imme-diate profits sacrificed) relative to the future profit potential of those additional customers who will try the ABC product during the invest-ment-spending period, be satisfied with it, and thus respond more readily to future ABC marketing efforts.

The immediate cost implicit in this policy is equal to the amount of funds diverted to the area times the rate at which they would have generated additional profits if spent elsewhere. During the first quarter, Area D received 4.6 percent more of total marketing effort than it earned (i.e., it got 15.0 percent of total advertising and sales promotion funds, and contributed 10.4 percent of total SPC). This represents additional funds of approximately $145,000 (i.e., 4.6 percent of total marketing expenses of $3,190,000). Had these funds been invested at the total United States incremental opportunity rate of 1.10, they would have produced about $160,000 additional GME. Instead, the use of these funds in Area D produced GME losses at the incremental rate of 0.30 or losses of $47,500. The cost of this investment-spending decision can therefore be estimated roughly at about $207,000 (a ball-park estimate, not an exact figure).

Dividing ABC's annual SPC in Area D (not shown in this exhibit) by its average share of this market, we obtain an approximate annual gross revenue value of $80,000 for each share point. Since the repur-chase rate after trial of ABC's product by users of competing products is estimated by the market research department to be 15 percent, the future annual value of each share point gained in the short run by investment spending in Area D is probably about $12,000. ABC cor-porate policy dictates a maximum payout period of three years for investment spending. It can, therefore, be inferred that each additional share point in this area justifies a maximum immediate loss of profits of $36,000. Since the share of market increase attributable to invest-ment spending in this area during the first quarter was 6.3 points, man-agement would regard this policy desirable if it cost no more than $225,000 (6.3 $\times$ $36,000).

Judgment. The cost of investment spending in this area during the first quarter was approximately $207,000 or less than its long-range value to the company. However, since marketing management deems it unlikely that further share gains above the 38.7 level can be made profitably during the second quarter, it is decided that the correct level of expenses to be adjusted for the ensuing period is the $316,000 spent in this area during the first quarter of 1963.

Market Area E. Here we have a case where our market area summaries are less useful than in the other cases:

Facts. Sharply increased market size and marketing spending; sharply decreased market share; a negative incremental opportunity rate—these are characteristics appearing in Exhibit II.

Analysis. There was a very heavy amount of competitive activity in this area during the first quarter. This effort, perhaps the result of a competitor adopting a strategy similar to the one used by ABC in Area D, created an environment in which projections made on the basis of the incremental opportunity rate would have no validity. The incremental rate relates changes of the SPC to spending changes. When additional major changes take place in the market (other than distribution or media efficiency changes), the incremental rate is not a realistic basis for analysis. In Area E it would be misleading to assume that the incremental expenditure of $100,000 produced only $25,000 more SPC. Had this additional spending not occurred, it is almost certain that the prior level of SPC would not have been achieved.

Judgment. While the market area summary does not lend itself to systematic analysis and decision making in cases such as this one, it can be a useful adjunct to the professional judgment of the marketing staff. Strategies which management believes will offset these competitive tactics can be evaluated in terms of the value of the "saved" share points as against the immediate profit sacrifice implicit in the diversion of effort. For example, on the basis of this kind of analysis and professional judgment at ABC Corporation, executives might well decide to employ a strategy in the following quarter involving a spending level equal to a seasonal adjustment of $450,000 in the first quarter.

Better Future Decisions

Having made the necessary judgments in the five areas in which spending resulted in an immediate profit sacrifice, the ABC management has developed a list of optimum past marketing expenditures for all its market areas. This list can now be adjusted for the seasonal changes appropriate to the next quarter on the basis of the normal monthly distribution of total retail sales in each area. While total retail sales data are not always a valid tool for apportioning effort between areas, these data are a satisfactory basis for allocating effort *within* an area. The reason for this is that competitive environments—in terms of competition and consumer attitudes toward alternative products—differ less when examined at two different times in the same area than when examined in two separate areas. Again, the basis for adjustment is not perfect, but it is better than available alternatives.

Once adjusted by the market research department for anticipated seasonal changes, these tentative spending levels must then be examined by product management to ascertain whether expected competitive activity necessitates any further alteration. The end product of this process of review and adjustment is a series of decisions on spending (not included here) against which planned and committed expenditures are compared. A list of planned marketing expenses is prepared by the data processing departments of the firm and by its advertising agencies. Individual media commitments and sales promotion plans are supplied to these centers by product management shortly before the close of the preceding quarter. These plans are then broken down by machine and reported by media (or promotion) and by month for each market area.

Differences between planned and recommended expense levels will indicate where second quarter spending inefficiencies are most likely to occur. The degree of change which marketing management can effect will be a function of many factors. While certain types of marketing effort are highly flexible, alteration of other types involves the payment of substantial production premiums and long lead times. It could therefore be assumed that at the time when ABC's managers receive the adjusted expenditure list (about the third week in April, for the first quarter), they would probably be considering changes of the local media expenditures for May. Alternatives such as buying or selling a "cut-in" on a network television show during May might also be arranged with other ABC lines.

With respect to June effort, management could consider altering certain national efforts. Given the extra lead time, it might possibly change network television lineups, buy regional editions of magazines, or exclude certain areas from previously scheduled (but unannounced) trade allowances. The specific changes actually selected will be a function of the adaptability of the product message to alternative marketing mixes and of management's ability to act creatively within these limitations.

Testing

An information system designed to influence a function as expensive and important as marketing must do more than make sense in the abstract. Only some form of projectable test can determine the value of this approach to a specific company.

An individual company can inexpensively approximate the impact
on profits of the proposed system by a process of simulation. Market
area summaries prepared manually from back data for eight quarters
will usually provide an adequate basis for such a process. On the
basis of each back report, marketing management can formulate
spending decisions that it would have made for the following period
if the new system had been used. The laws of coincidence are such
that a certain number of the planned changes will actually have
occurred. The frequency and amount of the incremental profits which
these changes produced can be used as an indication of the profit
potential of the information system had it been available to the
company to guide spending decisions in all market areas.

CONCLUSION

In this article discussion has been confined to the use of the
proposed information system as a guide for apportioning effort among
market areas. The basis on which these decisions are made can also
be used to apportion effort among lines of products and among
varieties within the line. Similarly, this approach is also a valid
framework within which to monitor media mix and product test
markets. In all such cases the marketing objective is the same: to
take funds from that area (or product, or strategy) where profits
will decrease least and to use them in the area where profits will
increase most.

To this end, I have proposed certain changes in the form and use
of the financial data supplied to marketing management. The changes
do not and cannot travel the total distance between imperfect and
perfect information. More realistically, the financial data produced
by this system are similar to the market research estimates with
which they have been designed to coincide; both have a degree of
error inherent in them. In spite of this limitation, both are of value
as background for professional judgment in the making and monitoring of marketing decisions.

This is not a sophisticated system; it is a rough beginning—a
place from which to move toward refinement. The nature of the ultimate refinement cannot be predetermined. Perhaps marketing management will some day have information and techniques which will
lead to an investment of marketing funds by area (and by product)
such that the last dollar spent on each will return an equal amount.
Ideally, this return would equal the company's cost of capital, adjusted

for risk and discounted to compensate for investment spending against future profit potential, but that day is a long way off.

In the meantime, we can advance toward the ideal, allocating funds and effort ever more skillfully, if not perfectly. Any real progress we make will come only as the result of well-directed and well-coordinated effort on the part of the market research, product management, and financial functions. The proposed system provides this direction and allows more profitable decision making as gains are made.

48. COST CONTROL FOR
MARKETING OPERATIONS—
GENERAL CONSIDERATIONS *

INTRODUCTION

The control of marketing costs has received substantially less attention from accountants than has the control of manufacturing costs. Speaking at the N.A.C.A. International Cost Conference in 1948, Howard C. Greer summarized progress from 1928 to 1948 in the following words:

> During this 20 years we have talked a lot, but done very little, to improve the accounting control of distribution activities. We have made considerable progress in the development of techniques, but not much progress in their application. . . .
>
> Today's problem is not primarily the one of learning how to prepare distribution cost analyses but rather one of putting distribution cost information to work in the development of an economical and efficient distribution cost system.[1]

Among the reasons offered to explain this situation are that (1) the nature of marketing operations makes it difficult to apply accounting cost control techniques, (2) management has been preoccupied with production problems during the past decade, and (3) many accountants have not been sufficiently familiar with marketing and the needs which marketing management has for cost control information. Whatever the reasons, it seems evident that in many companies the marketing cost control field offers an opportunity for the industrial accountant to expand his services to management.

There are accounting cost control tools available and the field study disclosed a few companies which use these tools with good effect. The tools are not new—they are chiefly budgets and standards of various types—but success in their application requires an understanding of the characteristics of marketing costs and the needs

---

* From *N.A.C.A. Bulletin, Research Series No. 25* (April, 1954). Reprinted by permission of the National Association of Cost Accountants.

[1] "Accounting as an Aid to a Sound Distribution Program," *N.A.C.A. Conference Proceednigs*, 1948, p. 160.

which marketing management has for cost information. Moreover, the approach to control of costs in the marketing area needs to be somewhat different from that adopted in the factory.

With the above facts in view, the purposes of this study are:

1. To reexamine accounting techniques which may be useful to aid management in the control of marketing costs.
2. To determine how well these techniques do in fact serve their intended purposes.
3. To ascertain how accounting techniques for the control of marketing costs are used in practice.

In this report an analytical approach to the subject was chosen because clear thinking is needed as a guide to the development and application of accounting techniques to aid management in controlling marketing costs. Two additional reports will present applications of marketing cost control methods drawn from current company practice. These reports will appear in future issues of the *N.A.C.A. Bulletin*.

The principal source of material for this report has been a field study in which members of the N.A.C.A. Research Staff visited 42 companies to learn what techniques they use and to discuss these techniques with accounting and marketing management personnel. While this study deals with marketing from the standpoint of a manufacturer, a limited number of merchandising companies in wholesale and retail fields were interviewed because manufacturers perform some of the same functions.

DEFINITION OF TERMS

Marketing Cost

Broadly defined, marketing includes all activities involved in the flow of goods from production to consumption. "Distribution" is also widely used with the same meaning, although some companies limit it to the physical handling of finished goods in storage and transportation. In general, marketing activities consist of finding potential customers, persuading them to buy, and delivering the goods at the place and time wanted by the customer.

An individual company usually does not itself perform all of the operations in marketing its products. Some manufacturers sell their entire output to a single distributor who does the marketing. At the other extreme are manufacturers who sell direct to consumers through retail stores or salesmen. In some industries the manufacturer's salesman customarily sets up displays, keeps stock in order, and does other work in the retail store. A given company is, of course, concerned with controlling only those costs which arise in marketing operations which it performs for itself.

In company organization practice, some functions defined above as marketing are often under the line authority of manufacturing and administrative division heads. For example, in one company warehousing and shipping of finished products are manufacturing responsibilities and office operations such as billing and customer accounting are under the treasurer.

Cost Control

In *The Uses and Classifications of Costs* it was stated that:

> Control presupposes effort directed toward a desired result. It involves not only the predetermination of the desired result but also the action to be taken to achieve a conformity of the actual results with the planned results.[2]

Previous discussions of marketing costs have not always made a clear distinction among the purposes for which costs are wanted. In particular, the analysis of costs for planning future operations has been confused with the measurement of current performance against previously determined objectives for cost control. These two areas have been described as follows by E. W. Kelley:

> Cost control of marketing operations is the measurement of an activity against a goal or a standard. Management has already determined the marketing method. Cost control measures performance in the execution of the prescribed method and indicates appropriate action to correct unfavorable deviations. Analysis of marketing operations is the study of the present method of distribution in comparison with all other possible methods. Such analyses are used to determine the most effective pattern of marketing policy for management to follow.[3]

Cost control is also distinguished from costing for profit determination in that cost control is concerned with charges at the point of origin, while costing for profit determination is concerned with disposition of the charges by assignment to periods, products, etc.

This study is limited to control of marketing costs. An earlier N.A.C.A. research study dealt with cost analysis for planning and

---

[2] *N.A.C.A. Bulletin, Research Series No. 7,* Section 2 (May 15, 1946), p. 947.
[3] "Distribution Cost Control—And Beyond," *N.A.C.A. Bulletin* (April, 1951), p. 907.

the reader is referred to the reports presenting findings from that study for a discussion of cost analysis.[4]

Control of marketing costs is primarily a management function, for management has the authority to decide what is to be done, how it is to be done, and to take actions necessary to see that its plans are carried out.

The accountant, as an accountant, collects, analyzes, and interprets information which enables management at all levels to make better decisions because it has factual information available and need not act on the basis of guesses and unsubstantiated opinions. In many companies, accounting executives are also active participants in management and take part in making and carrying out decisions. The field study showed that the extent to which available cost control techniques are used and actually serve their intended purposes is determined directly by top management's attitude toward the importance of cost control. This attitude is reflected in cost consciousness, or its absence, down the line to supervisors and branch managers. Marketing management has often been less concerned with the need for controlling costs than has factory management.

PLANNING THE ACCOUNTING SYSTEM TO FACILITATE CONTROL OF MARKETING COSTS

In order that an accounting system may have maximum usefulness to aid managerial control over marketing costs, it must be designed to provide the data that will be wanted. Moreover, the desired figures should be produced with a minimum of clerical work in order that they may be available promptly and at a reasonable cost.

E. W. Kelley has listed the following features which are essential in an accounting plan where control of marketing is an objective:

1. A system of responsibility accounting for distribution operations.
2. Statement of functions for each responsibility.
3. Decision as to the size of the operating unit for which accounting is to be made.
4. Provision for the necessary natural accounts to correctly catalog the costs for each function.[5]

---

[4] "Assignment of Nonmanufacturing Costs for Managerial Decisions," "The Assignment of Nonmanufacturing Costs to Products," and "The Assignment of Nonmanufacturing Costs to Territories and Other Segments" *N.A.C.A. Bulletin, Research Series Nos. 19, 20, 21,* Section 4 (May, 1951), Section 4 (August, 1951), Section 3 (December, 1959).

[5] "Distribution Cost Control—And Beyond," *N.A.C.A. Bulletin* (April, 1951), p. 909.

Accounting for Costs by Responsibilities

Success in cost control requires an organization in which clearly defined responsibility for costs is matched with authority to take the actions necessary to effect control. Delegation of authority and placement of responsibility—in other words, the development of an organization—is a management function. The company organization plan then becomes the basic guide which the accountant follows in preparing a chart of accounts. In the words of one company representative interviewed, "the objective in designing our chart of accounts is to focus attention on the people spending the money."

In such an accounting plan, responsibility for controlling costs is the primary basis for cost classification.[6] It is primary because control over costs must be applied at the place and time where costs originate, that is, within the area of authority where the decision to incur the cost is made. Usefulness for control is largely lost after costs from several responsibilities have been merged together in a single account. Initial classification of costs by responsibility for control does not preclude subsequent regrouping of costs by functional classes customarily displayed in the income statement and for allocation to arrive at product costs for pricing. These different bases of cost classification are readily provided for by appropriate coding. . . .

Coordination between marketing organization and chart of accounts is emphasized in several companies interviewed by placing control unit account numbers on organization charts. One company requires each organizational unit to include an organization chart with its preliminary budget. This enables management to review proposed changes in organization at the same time the budget is reviewed and approved. The practice also keeps the accounting department advised of changes in organization which affect responsibility for control of costs and which may call for change in the chart of accounts.

Controllable and Noncontrollable Costs

The distinction between controllable and noncontrollable costs is made from the point of view of the individual responsible. While

---

[6] For purposes of cost control, a responsibility may be defined as "an organizational unit engaged in the performance of a single function or a group of closely related functions having a single head accountable for activities of the unit." "The Analysis of Manufacturing Cost Variances," *N.A.C.A. Bulletin, Research Series No. 22,* Section 2 (August, 1952), p. 1549.

controllable and noncontrollable costs have sometimes been considered synonymous with fixed and variable costs, these classifications are not the same. The timing and method of control differ, but fixed costs as well as variable costs should be assigned to the individuals who possess authority to incur both types of costs.

In marketing, as in manufacturing, there are service departments set up to supply services to other divisions of the organization. Large companies sometimes have numerous specialized service units in their marketing organization. For example, one company interviewed has a marketing service division containing the following departments: (1) marketing research, (2) product planning, (3) advertising and sales promotion services, (4) sales services, (5) product service, (6) marketing administrative service, (7) marketing personnel development. These departments supply advice and information to sales management to aid it in directing the company's sales operations. Smaller companies have simpler organizations, but some marketing service departments are usually present.

The head of a service department has primary responsibility for the costs of his own department. A secondary responsibility for service department costs may rest with heads of other departments, for they often influence service costs through the amount and kind of service demanded. The following examples show how some companies reflect this division of responsibility in their accounting for service department costs in order to gain cooperation of both groups of departmental managers toward controlling service department costs.

1. Marketing service department costs are allocated to product line sales managers. While the bases of allocation were chosen principally to obtain product profit or loss, it was stated that the system creates an awareness of the cost of services received.

2. Another company reasons that district sales managers provide the demand for marketing services and consequently sales managers are charged for usage made of automobiles, trucks, warehouses, and similar facilities. This method causes managers to consider whether or not they need a service and how much they need. Responsibility for operating the service most economically rests with supervisors in charge of the respective service departments. However, sales managers participate on an informal basis because they are interested in reducing the amounts charged to them for services consumed.

3. In a third company, service departments charge operating departments at hourly rates based on direct cost of the services supplied. These interdepartmental charges do not include the fixed portion of service department costs because service departments are established

to implement managerial organization policy. Hence responsibility for the fixed portion of the service department costs rests with top management.

The field study indicates that the nature of the services and the extent to which sales managers can control the kind and amount of services received influences practice in establishing secondary responsibility for service costs. Where the sales managers determine the extent to which they use such facilities as company owned automobiles, warehouse space, and specially prepared statistical tabulations, it is common practice to charge the individual managers for costs of such facilities. On the other hand, where services are established and controlled by top management policy, local sales managers are usually not held responsible for costs of these facilities even though they share the benefits.

Typical examples in the latter class mentioned above are services rendered by product sales specialists, sales personnel and training, market research, and accounting departments. These services are designed to improve the effectiveness of the sales organization, but benefits obtained are likely to appear as a long-run improvement in sales and profits rather than as an immediate sales increase. For this reason, several companies stressed the need to place responsibility for controlling costs of such services with executive management at a level where results can be appraised from a broad and long-range point of view. One of these companies found that an attempt to place this responsibility with district sales managers had led these managers to make decisions which were not in the company's best interests. For example, some district managers attempted to economize by refusing to use services designed to improve selling methods but which did not produce an immediate increase in sales. Other managers believed they were saving money by doing clerical and statistical work in their own offices instead of using centralized service departments, but this usually proved to be false economy because sales management was forced to divert supervision time from salesmen to clerical workers. In addition, information was not always reliable because it was not checked against financial records. . . .

Acquainting Accounting Personnel with Marketing Operations

The accountant needs to be acquainted with marketing operations and with the problems which face marketing management. Otherwise, he does not know what information management can use in controlling costs. In addition, the accountant needs to know how marketing executives work and think in order to present accounting figures in such a manner that their significance is understood. Companies interviewed reported the following methods for helping accounting personnel to become familiar with marketing operations.

1. Accounting representatives participate in weekly meetings of the operating committee which deals with marketing operations. In this company the top-level organization is small and centralized so all concerned know all phases of the business.
2. Accounting employees are sent into the field with sales supervisors and salesmen. The same accountants work with sales management in the home office to learn what information sales executives want.
3. A company training plan provides broad knowledge of all aspects of the business for accountants in responsible positions. Marketing and production executives have also had training in accounting and finance which helps them to understand and to use accounting information.
4. Top accounting men have all had experience in both marketing and production. This is assured by planned movement of men over a period of years.

Discussion in the field study often pointed to the need to explore all feasible methods for building up marketing management's confidence in the reliability and significance of accounting figures. Specific comments by company representatives also stressed the need to emphasize service to management and to deemphasize technical accounting terminology and techniques.

ACCOUNTING TOOLS TO AID MARKETING COST CONTROL

Cost control comprises action at two stages: namely, (1) systematic planning to effect control before the fact, and (2) current action to bring performance back into line with planned goals when deviations from plan occur. Current control also requires revision of previously made plans and bringing original goals up to date when conditions change.

Budgets and Standards

As a basis for control of costs, management's plans and objectives are translated into financial goals expressed in budgets. The budget is then the principal accounting tool which management uses in controlling marketing costs. Standard costs are also used in the control of marketing costs, but standard costs are not used so widely or so successfully in marketing as they are in manufacturing.

A budget is a goal covering a period or a project taken as a whole. Standard costs are similar goals expressed in unit form. The two are related by the fact that where standard costs are available, they serve as building blocks with which the budgets are constructed. As stated by one company, "A budget is a plan of expected achievement based on the most efficient operating standard in effect or in prospect at the time it is established."

Exhibit 1 shows a product line operating statement form in which comparisons between actual and budgeted sales and marketing cost figures appear. This form is typical of those used by companies interviewed in the field study for presenting such information to top management.

Standard manufacturing costs have an important use for charging inventory accounts. Marketing costs are not charged to inventory, but predetermined unit marketing costs are sometimes used to facilitate the processes of accounting for marketing costs. In most instances these predetermined marketing costs are estimates or averages designed to assist in matching costs and sales income in monthly income statements and to simplify cost allocation procedures. While such unit cost figures have some characteristics of standard costs, they are usually not standards with which performance is measured. As an example, one company accounts for outward transportation cost by charging a freight expense account and crediting a freight anticipation account at a standard freight cost based on tariff rates per case for the commodities shipped. The sole reason for using a standard cost is that the actual amount of transportation cost cannot be obtained soon enough to complete periodic profit-and-loss statements by products. In this company the standard costs have no function in controlling transportation costs.

However, a few companies interviewed have standard marketing costs which serve both to help control costs and to facilitate accounting for costs. Standard warehousing costs used by one company illustrate this dual purpose application. Here standard warehousing costs are based on physical standards set by industrial engineers. Warehousing cost accounts are charged with standard cost of the units handled each period and a warehousing cost variance account is credited. Actual warehousing costs are debited to the same variance account. Significantly large balances in the variance account are analyzed to determine source and cause as a guide to management in taking corrective action.

PRODUCT LINE OPERATING STATEMENT

DIVISION.......................... MANAGER........................... MONTH.................... YEAR..................

	CURRENT MONTH			YEAR TO DATE		
	ACTUAL $ %	BUDGET $ %	ACTUAL LAST YEAR $ %	ACTUAL $ %	BUDGET $ %	ACTUAL LAST YEAR $ %
1. Sales						
2. Cost of goods sold						
3. Freight						
4. Cash discount						
5. Sales allowances						
6. Gross profit						
7. Salesmen's salaries						
8. Salesmen's expenses						
9. Territorial salaries						
10. Territorial expenses						
11. Total territorial selling expense						
12. Credit expense						
13. Traffic dept. expense						
14. Warehousing and shipping						
15. General management						
16. Total indirect selling expense						
17. Sales promotion						
18. Advertising						
19. Samples						
20. Total promotion and advertising						
21. Total distribution cost						
22. Net profit						
23. Number of shipments						
24. Average price per shipment $\left(\dfrac{1}{23}\right)$						
25. Order getting cost per shipment $\left(\dfrac{11}{23}\right)$						
26. Order handling cost (12, 13, 14)						
27. Order handling cost per shipment $\left(\dfrac{26}{23}\right)$						

Exhibit 1

Past Performance

In the absence of budgets and standards to indicate what current costs should be, actual costs experienced in prior periods may constitute useful comparison figures. One company representative explained that operations in previous periods had been carefully planned and had produced known results in terms of sales and profits. Consequently, the same results should be repeated if current costs are kept in line with those recorded in the preceding periods. Even where budgets and standard costs are in use, marketing cost reports commonly show actual costs of comparable prior periods. The statement form in Exhibit 1 illustrates this practice. The reason usually given for this practice was that management is interested in trends in sales and costs. However, in some cases it was stated that management had not accepted budgets as significant comparison figures.

At the same time, past performance has distinct weaknesses as a goal for current cost control. First, inefficiencies may be perpetuated rather than brought to light and eliminated. When current efficiency is measured by past costs, it is implicitly assumed that past costs are proper costs or, at best, there is no definite measure of the improvement which should be possible. A second weakness lies in the fact that past costs may not reflect cost changes that can be expected as a consequence of conditions which differ from those under which costs were incurred in earlier periods. While these changes may be recognized, there is no quantitative expression of the amount by which current costs should differ from past costs. Frequent and sometimes extensive changes in marketing methods and circumstances under which goods are marketed may make this shortcoming of past costs an important one.

Other Cost Comparison Figures

An individual company often has a number of sales branches, warehouses, or delivery routes. This makes it possible to compare costs of each organizational unit with those of other like units within the same company. The field study showed that intracompany cost comparisons of this type are widely used. Management's attention is thereby called to any unit which shows a marked deviation from costs reported by other units. Such differences are often an indication that costs of the unit in question need to be reviewed. Some companies follow the practice of ranking branches, salesmen, and other units on the basis of unit cost of their operations.

In a few industries, trade associations collect cost data and make available composite figures representing costs reported by all members of the association. These figures are often classified by geographical area, size of company, and other characteristics. Uniformity in classification of accounts and in items charged to the various accounts is, of course, essential if either intracompany or intercompany cost comparisons are to be significant.

BUDGETING FOR COST CONTROL BEFORE THE FACT

As stated above, the periodic budget is the principal accounting technique used in the planning stage of cost control. Sales income as well as costs are budgeted and the complete budget covers income, costs, and profit. The marketing budget for the company as a whole constitutes a profit plan based upon planned sales income and planned costs for obtaining these sales and filling the orders. As described in one company's standard practice manual:

> (The budget) . . . is simply a form of analytical management which provides:
>> First, a definite and approved plan of operations for a specific period of time in the future. This constitutes the planning phase.
>> Second, the means for measuring performance against that plan. This is the control phase.

Activities of individual functional departments must be coordinated in order to realize the desired overall objective. Consequently, each department, sales division, and other organizational unit has its own budget. These departmental budgets reflect plans for each separate operating responsibility. While budgeting proceeds from the bottom of the organization toward the top, departmental budgets must be in harmony with previously determined broad company objectives.

Once approved, the marketing cost budget provides a large measure of control before the fact. The appropriateness of each expense item can be better judged when viewed in relation to the company's plan as a whole and managerial time is saved subsequently because day-by-day approval is not needed for many expenditures covered by the budget.

Responsibility for Marketing Costs Budget

The field study shows that where the budget is an effective cost control tool, responsibility for planning and control coincide all the way down the line from top management to managers or supervisors of departments and sales branches. This idea is expressed in the following words by one company's budget manual.

> The budget allowance bases are established on the postulate that authority and responsibility go hand in hand, and therefore those responsible for operating according to the standards established have an opportunity to partake in its construction and to approve it. Any revisions to be made in the original budget bases are referred to the persons who originally compiled the specific data, for their consideration, comment, and approval."

Another company manual states that:

> a. Budgets will be prepared by those responsible under that budget.
> b. While the finance division assists in budget preparation, it will not prepare any budget other than its own.
> c. Preparation of his budget and conformance with it are part of every supervisor's job.

The budget or accounting department ordinarily supplies assistance in the form of instructions and information to aid those who prepare budgets. The information covers facts needed or useful to the individual for planning his own operations. Some of this data is drawn from the accounting records (e.g., costs incurred in prior periods), and some data are compiled from other sources (e.g., sales forecasts). In doing this, the accounting department acts in a staff capacity for planning, assembling, and consolidating budget information.[7]

Fixed Budgets for Planning Purposes

Budgets prepared for planning are fixed budgets in the sense that budgeted cost allowances are set for the specific sales volume anticipated and for the budget period. As described by one company, "A fixed budget is the target at which the company is aiming." Contrary to the opinion sometimes encountered, a marketing cost budget should not be a restrictive device which prevents expenditures from being made when they are in the company's best interest. The periodic budget is a plan and like other plans can and should be changed if subsequent circumstances make it evident that spending more or less is desirable. Automatic adjustment may be provided

---

[7] In a few companies interviewed, the marketing cost budget is actually prepared in the accounting department. However, these companies use budgeting only as a device for forecasting profits and to aid the accounting department in computing rates for allocating costs. In these companies it was evident that the budget does not serve as a tool to aid management in controlling marketing costs.

through the use of flexible budgets for costs which fluctuate with volume. For other costs, management can authorize changes in individual budget allowances or the entire budget can be revised. The latter procedure is ordinarily limited to circumstances where substantial changes have occurred in the basic premises underlying the original budget.

The marketing budget period used by companies interviewed is most commonly a year, but some companies find that a shorter period is preferable. For example, one company uses a period of six months because it has two selling seasons in each year. Several other companies budget quarterly because they have found it impossible to forecast sales for more than three months. In most cases, those companies are also characterized by rapid turnover of merchandise.

Influence of Purpose for Which Costs Are Incurred

The procedure followed in budgeting marketing costs is influenced by the nature of the work to be done. For purposes of discussion, two classes of marketing activities may be distinguished. These are:

1. Persuading the customer to buy and getting the order. Typical activities in this class are advertising, sales promotion, and selling.
2. Filling the order. Typical activities include warehousing, shipping, and processing documents related to customers' orders.

Activities in each of these groups have certain characteristics in common which determine how the corresponding costs can best be budgeted. However, in practice, activities of both type are often combined as, for example, where a route salesman makes deliveries.

Budgeting Order Getting Costs

Order getting costs cannot be budgeted by establishing a simple and direct relationship between sales orders and costs. The principal reason for this is that order getting activities are a cause rather than a result of sales and the volume of orders obtained depends to some extent upon the amount spent for advertising, sales promotion, and selling. This contrasts with the manufacturing cost budget where production costs can be budgeted after the volume of goods to be produced has been determined because the volume of production does not depend upon the amount of money spent for materials, labor, and factory overhead.

Changed expenditures for order getting activities may change sales volume, but sales may not change at the same rate as costs.

When competition is strong, substantial increases in expenditure may be necessary merely to hold a company's present volume. The lowest unit cost or total cost is not always the preferred objective in controlling order getting costs because such a cost may fail to yield the most profitable volume which can be attained. Effectiveness with which money is spent in the process of getting orders is more important than the amount of money spent.

As a consequence of these facts, company representatives interviewed emphasized the point that the budget for order getting costs cannot be based solely upon a sales forecast. Rather, it is necessary to give simultaneous consideration to the market potential and to the amount to be spent for getting business.

Management uses certain guides in determining how much to budget for order getting activities. The following were frequently mentioned in field interviews:

1. Past experience represented by ratios of advertising and selling cost to sales and similar historical figures. These figures represent known results obtained in the past and therefore are viewed as important indicators of what can be expected from the same sales program in the future. In addition, an order getting program is often more effective if continuity is maintained over a period of years.

2. Activities of competitors measured by amount of advertising, reports from salesmen as to activity of competitors' salesmen, etc.

3. Specific new objectives such as to introduce a new product, to enter a new market, etc.

4. Results from tests. By varying the amount of advertising or number of salesmen in limited areas, it is sometimes possible to make rough measurements of the return obtained from increments in order getting costs.

5. What the company can afford to spend after considering the amount of cash available and other needs for cash for plant expansion, dividends, and such purposes. This factor ordinarily sets an upper limit on the amount that can be budgeted, but does not indicate how much can be profitably spent.

The amount of money spent and the need to coordinate the sales and advertising budget with all other company activities means that the total budgeted for order getting purposes is usually decided at the top level of management.

While changes may be made during a budget period in both the total amount budgeted and the application of this amount for various order getting purposes, the budgets employed are not flexible budgets in the sense the term is used in controlling manufacturing costs. The reason for this is that changes in the budget follow only from changes in management's plans with respect to amount to be spent and direction of the effort to obtain business. Such changes do not follow automatically from sales volume in the way that variable elements of factory overhead tend to follow factory activity. Instead, order getting costs are budgeted and controlled in a manner more like the fixed components of factory supervision, engineering, maintenance, and similar items.

Budgeting Order Filling Costs

Some order filling costs vary with current volume while other order filling costs vary over longer periods with the capacity provided. The cost of packing material used in the shipping room provides an example of the former type of cost while depreciation and property taxes on a warehouse illustrate the latter. Many order filling costs are semivariable; i.e., they contain both fixed and variable components. For example, warehouse labor cost may have a fixed component representing the minimum crew needed to handle a minimum volume and a variable component representing additional manhours which are controlled with volume above that which can be handled by the minimum crew.

Exhibit 2 shows a warehouse cost comparison report form in which variable and fixed expenses are listed separately. Expense items not included in fixed or variable categories (salaries, handling charges on goods stored outside company warehouses) are controlled separately by this company. Thus salaries are controlled by a budget based upon expected personnel needs for the period and in this respect, they fall in a category between long period fixed expenses and expenses variable with current volume.

In budgeting variable order filling costs, use is made of the fact that the total amount of such a cost is determined by sales volume or some measure of activity related to sales volume. The first step in setting budget allowances is to establish the relationship between the amount of each variable cost component and an appropriate measure of activity. The sales plan or sales forecast then determines the volume of work to be done in each cost center during the coming period and the cost to be budgeted for the period is the product of unit rate times expected volume.

The fixed component of order filling costs is, in part, established by previously made commitments entailing continuing charges for depreciation, property taxes, rentals, etc. Other cost items of a fixed nature arise from plans with respect to number of salaried employees

WAREHOUSE COST COMPARISON						
	CURRENT PERIOD		BUDGET		LAST YEAR	
ACCOUNTS	$	%	$	%	$	%
Merchandise Shipments						
Shipping Material						
Miscellaneous						
Postage						
Stationery and Supplies						
Repairs						
Telephone and Telegraph						
Travel Expense						
Total Variable Expense						
Depreciation						
Insurance						
Rent—Regular						
Rent—Outside Storage						
Repair Amortization						
Taxes						
Total Fixed Expense						
Total Expense						
Shipping Salaries						
Handl'g Chgs.—Outside Stge.						
Office Salaries						
Total Salaries						
Total Warehouse Expense						
Pro-ration—Wholesale						
Pro-ration—Retail						
Control Salaries—Wholesale						
Control Salaries—Retail						
Total Cont. Sal.						
Grand TotalWhse. Expense						
Dealers Served—Mo.—End						
Co. Stores Served						
Control Salaries per Unit						
Frt. %—Incoming Mdse.						
Inventory						

Exhibit 2

and other sources of cost which are planned on a periodic basis but not controlled with ordinary volume fluctuations within the budget period.

It will be observed that order filling costs behave like manufacturing costs and the same methods of budgeting and cost control used in the factory can also be applied to costs of warehousing, shipping, and similar marketing activities. Thus standard costs and flexible budgets are in use by some of the companies interviewed. Where these are present, budget allowances for the coming budget period are set by using the standard unit costs and flexible budgets to determine how much it should cost to handle the volume of work planned.

Where standard costs have not been established, ratios to sales are usually developed to aid in budgeting the various groups of order filling costs. These ratios are sometimes expressed as percentages of the sales dollar and sometimes as an amount of cost per product unit, i.e., per case, per ton, or other unit.

Ratios are based on past experience, but adjusted for expected changes such as an increase in wages and salaries, transportation rates, etc. Volume and mixture of cost influencing factors expected in the coming period should be like that experienced in the past if historical ratios are the yield accurate budget allowances. Some companies budget fixed costs separately as totals and develop ratios only for variable costs in order to avoid the effect which changes in volume have on cost ratios when fixed costs are included. Specific assumptions are sometimes made with respect to other factors affecting the amount of some marketing costs. As an example, one company budgets outgoing transportation costs on the assumption that a standard mix of quantities and destinations will prevail.

CONTROLLING COSTS OF CURRENT OPERATIONS

Discussion of cost control commonly centers around standard costs and flexible budgets because these are the principal tools which the accountant has developed to aid management in maintaining current control over manufacturing costs. Experience of the companies interviewed in this study shows that these tools are also applied successfully in controlling order filling costs. On the other hand, very few of the companies interviewed have applied standard costs and flexible budgets for controlling order getting costs. The explanation for this fact stems from differences in the activities which comprise the two functions of order getting and order filling.

Standard costs are unit costs and therefore require quantitative measurement of production accomplished by the operations being costed. A unit used to measure production and as a base for a standard cost also needs to be highly correlated with the total amount of the cost to be controlled. To illustrate, if a standard cost is being established for an invoice writing operation, number of lines written is a better measure of production than number of invoices when the number of lines on individual invoices differs. Under these conditions, a standard cost based on number of lines will be a good measure of performance while a standard cost based on number of invoices will be a poor measure because it is affected by a factor unrelated to total cost of the operation, i.e., number of items appearing on individual orders.

Accounting Control Tools for Order Getting Costs

Employees who perform order getting functions work largely with ideas and with people rather than with materials and machines. The psychological processes of thinking and influencing people cannot be standardized and standard operation times set by any methods now available. Moreover, the direct product of order getting efforts consists of ideas, attitudes, and information in the minds of prospective customers. Methods for measuring the quantity and quality of such products are also not sufficiently well developed to furnish the basis for standard costs. Therefore it is necessary to find some other way to measure the production of employees who perform order getting functions.

The ultimate purpose of order getting activity is to produce sales orders. Consequently volume of sales orders can be used to measure the effectiveness with which order getting activities have been performed if the relationship between sales orders received and costs of getting these orders can be determined.

However, companies interviewed usually stated that results obtained from attempts to correlate sales orders with order getting costs had yielded results which were not good enough to constitute the basis for standard costs with which to measure individual performance in cost control. In the words of one company representative, "where there is no direct tie-in between sales and a specific marketing activity, we can't measure effectiveness with which our marketing dollars are spent." Three reasons were commonly cited in explanation of this situation.

1. A wide variety of uncontrollable factors affect the results obtained from order getting efforts and these factors change rapidly. Examples of these factors are competitors' attempts to influence customers, general business conditions, and weather. Consequently, it is impossible to separate performance of individuals responsible for order getting functions from the effects of other factors which also influence the volume of sales orders obtained.

2. Results obtained from advertising, sales proportion, and selling do not always appear in the same period in which the cost was incurred or the effort applied. Some advertising is designed to develop brand recognition or to promote long-range expansion of a product's use rather than to produce immediate sales. Similarly, a sales call which does not produce an order may nevertheless help to get orders in the future. An order obtained today may also be the cumulative result of calls made in a number of prevous periods. There may be a long-run relationship between sales volume and expenditures for advertising, sales promotion, and selling and, where these relationships can be discerned, they have value for planning purposes. However, cost control as defined for purposes of this study calls for a short period measure of production because current control requires current figures.

3. Sales orders are often a joint result which flows from a coordinated combination of advertising, sales promotion, and selling. Therefore, it is impossible to determine what part individuals responsible for each of these functions had in producing a given volume of sales orders.

Standard costs for order getting activities are sometimes based upon units which measure effort expended rather than results obtained. For example, a comparison of actual cost per sales call with the corresponding cost per sales call tells whether the calls made have cost more or less than expected. Similarly, advertising cost per reader or per inquiry received may be used to show how the actual cost compares with the expected cost of reaching prospective customers with the company's sales appeal. Such comparisons measure the efficiency with which a planned activity has been carried out, but they do not measure the effectiveness of the sales effort in terms of sales orders obtained. For this reason, standards are more widely used for comparing alternative methods in sales planning than they are for measuring individual performance in controlling costs.

Under favorable circumstances it may be possible to obtain measures of effectiveness which are valuable for selecting advertising and promotional media or for choosing the selling techniques which are most productive. When advertising and sales promotion projects are designed to stimulate immediate sales of specific goods, comparison of budgeted and actual cost of advertising per dollar of sales is used by some companies to measure results obtained in comparison with results expected when the advertising program was planned. Such budget comparisons may be supplemented by share-of-the-market statistics in order to measure the effect of general changes in market conditions. For example, a company's advertising cost per sales dollar may exceed the budget in a given period because sales volume of all companies in the market has been lower than expected when the budget was established. However, if share-of-the-market statistics show that an individual company has maintained or increased its share of the market, management may conclude that its advertising was as effective as could be expected under the circumstances.

While standards such as those described above are helpful where they can be established, they are cost control tools of a very broad type and give only a rough indication of the effectiveness with which order getting work is performed by the individual responsible. None of the companies interviewed had succeeded in developing standards for order getting activities which are comparable in precision and reliability to standards used in manufacturing.

Accounting methods for controlling costs of order getting follow the processes which management uses in planning these activities. The field study showed that such planning usually proceeds by deciding how many salesmen are needed to cover each area, how many product managers are needed to develop merchandising ideas, how much and what kinds of advertising are expected to produce the desired sales volume and mix, and how large a staff of executives, supervisors, and assistants will be needed to direct the company's marketing operations. These plans are then translated into financial terms by preparing a budget for the forthcoming period.

Management plans advertising, sales promotion, selling, and similar activities on a periodic basis. The fixed budget is the principal tool employed for planning costs of the program and for coordinating these costs with other aspects of the company's financial plan for the coming period. Underlying the total amount appropriated for each principal type of order getting activity employed by the company is a series of budget allowances covering the detailed program which has been planned. This is illustrated by the following example drawn from one company's procedure for budgeting advertising expense.

A tentative advertising program for the coming period is prepared. This plan consists of a series of proposed projects, with an estimate of costs broken down in detail. A summary of these projects is prepared to support the request for an appropriation. If the total amount re-quested is not approved, a subsequent revision in detail plans is made. As the period progresses, commitments and actual expenditures are accumulated by projects and compared with amounts appropriated for the respective projects.

Sales promotion and field selling costs are usually budgeted in a similar manner, with the amounts allowed for various cost items based upon planned sales coverage by field representatives.

Once the budget for such costs has been approved, current control over the amount spent is maintained by reporting actual expenditures compared with corresponding budget allowances. Variances tell whether the program has cost more or less than anticipated when the budget was approved, but they do not measure the effectiveness of the sales effort.

Accounting Control Tools for Order Filling Costs

Order filling consists to a large extent of work which is physical and repetitive in nature. Most of the operations performed are concerned with physical handling of goods or with routine processing of papers. Unlike order getting where it is difficult to express production in units which are reliable measures of individual performance, production in order getting operations is measured by quantities of goods handled and numbers of clerical operations performed. The work is essentially the same as that carried on in the factory where detailed standards are effectively used to aid in cost control.

The field study showed that measures of work output can be found and applied successfully to physical operations in marketing. Following are examples reported by companies interviewed.

Operations	Unit for measuring production
Posting customers' ledgers	Number of postings per hour
Receiving merchandise at warehouse	Tonnage per man-hour
Wrapping and packaging merchandise	Number of pieces wrapped per hour
Billing	Number of lines per hour
Warehouse labor	Stock units handled per 100 hours

When the standard production per hour has been established, these physical unit standards are readily translated into standard costs by multiplying standard times by standard hourly employee earning rates. The actual costs of operations such as those listed above are compared with the corresponding standard costs, and variances which arise are used to measure performance of supervisors responsible in each case.

While such marketing functions as advertising, sales promotion, and selling are ordinarily composed of activities which must be controlled with fixed budgets, they may also include routine physical operations to which standards costs and flexible budgets can be applied. As an example, a company which produces for its own use a large volume of printed sales promotion material uses a standard cost system in the department which manufactures this material. Another example is supplied by a retail store which uses a flexible budget based upon number of transactions per day as a tool for controlling salaries and wages of sales personnel. Where selling is largely a matter of order taking, similar methods are sometimes applied to field selling costs.

Marketing cost standards are less precise than manufacturing cost standards because it is necessary to base marketing standards on average conditions rather than on controlled conditions. Large variances may arise because the actual mixture of variables affecting costs differs from the average mixture upon which the standards are predicated. It is difficult to determine what part of these variances measures performance of responsible employees and what part measures the influence which changing outside conditions have had on actual marketing costs. To illustrate, one company sets quarterly budget allowances for transportation cost by multiplying the forecasted volume of shipments by an estimated unit transportation cost. The latter is an average based upon a composite destination to which goods are shipped. Obviously variances from budget can arise because of shifts in relative volumes of shipments to the various destinations as well as from other reasons.

Sometimes it may be possible to isolate the principal causes of cost variations and to adjust the standards accordingly. An example of this is furnished by a company which has a different standard cost per mile for different classes of automobiles and geographical areas in which company automobiles are used.

The conditions described above do not affect costs of all marketing functions with equal force. Working conditions in a company's own warehouse or office can often be controlled by the same methods applied in the factory. Consequently, cost control can be more precise for such operations than is possible for operations performed where less control can be exercised over variables affecting costs.

Coordinating Current Control with Periodic Planning

The goals used for measuring current cost performance are related to but not necessarily the same as those developed in preparing the periodic budget. Differences between periodic and current cost goals arise because the periodic budget is based upon a given set of expectations as to volume of activity and other factors which influence costs, but current performance needs to be measured against goals which represent conditions under which the work is actually done. Methods used to bring the current control goals into harmony with current circumstances are listed below.

1. Revision of budgets.
2. Managerial approval of variances either before (e.g., by authorization of a special allowance) or after the fact.
3. Use of flexible budgets.

With respect to budget revision, two lines of practice were observed in the field study. Companies which follow the first make no changes in budgets during the budget period unless there are important changes in basic premises underlying the entire budget. However, budget variances which arise are analyzed to separate those ascribable to performance from those which result from changed conditions. Companies which follow the second line of practice make changes regularly (e.g., monthly) or whenever necessary in order that budgets may always be current goals for operating management. In some of these companies, the original planning budget is discarded and comparisons made only with the revised budget. In other companies, operating performance is measured by comparison with the latest revised budget while overall financial comparisons are made against the original budget for the period. In justification, it was usually stated that the latter practice gives maximum usefulness of the budgets as tools for both current cost control in individual cost centers and as a measure of progress toward the company's profit goal for the period.

Flexible budgets have limited use in marketing because, as stated previously, only a limited number of marketing costs can be controlled with current volume. Where cost standards have been developed they are first used in preparing the budget for the coming period by multiplying the planned volume of activity by unit standard cost. The same standard costs are also used to determine the amount of cost allowed for current actual volume.

49. ACCOUNTING TECHNIQUES FOR ESTABLISHING A COST DIFFERENTIAL DEFENSE UNDER THE ROBINSON-PATMAN ACT *

O. Wood Moyle, III †

The Robinson-Patman Act is designed to secure effective suppression of price discrimination between customers of the same seller only where such discrimination is not supported by sound economic differences in the costs of serving them. Hence, while Section 2(a) of the Act declares it to be unlawful for any person engaged in interstate commerce to discriminate in price between different purchasers of similar commodities,[1] a statutory defense is incorporated into the Act by the following proviso:

> That nothing herein contained shall prevent differentials which make only due allowance for differences in the cost of manufacture, sale, or delivery resulting from the differing methods or quantities in which such commodities are to such purchasers sold or delivered.[2]

Defenses under this proviso are known as "cost differential defenses" or "cost justifications."[3]

As may be inferred from the wording of the statute the burden of showing cost justification is on the respondent.[4] Furthermore, not only must a cost difference be shown, but the difference must arise from (1) a different method by which an article is sold, (2) a

---

* From the *Notre Dame Lawyer* (December, 1963). Reprinted by permission of the Notre Dame Law School, Notre Dame, Indiana.

† O. Wood Moyle, III, member of the bar in New York and Utah, associated with the law firm of Moyle and Moyle, Salt Lake City, Utah.

[1] 49 Stat. 1526 (1936), 15 U.S.C. § 13(a) (1957).

[2] 49 Stat. 1526 (1936), 15 U.S.C. § 13(a) (1957).

[3] Probably because of the severity of the accounting standards set by the Federal Trade Commission, cost justification has been attempted in only a few instances. Of 239 cease and desist orders up to December 31, 1954, only 91 were based on a 2(a) violation. A full defense under 2(a) was presented in only 39 and in only 18 of the cases would the cost justification have been a valid defense if proved. Edwards, *Cost Justification and the Federal Trade Commission*, 1 ANTITRUST BULL. 563, 566-67 (1956).

The Commission's severe accounting standards are expressed only through findings against the respondents, since, unfortunately, the Commission has not seen fit to issue regulations in this area.

[4] F.T.C. v. Morton Salt Co., 334 U.S. 37, 44 (1948). In prosecutions under § 2(f), however, the burden is upon the Commission to show knowledge of a lack of cost justification. Automatic Canteen Co. v. F.T.C., 346 U.S. 61 (1953).

different method of delivery, or (3) savings in manufacturing, selling or delivering resulting from a difference in quantity sold or delivered.[5]

The typical cost defense involves the justification of customer price brackets. Under the bracketing system customers are charged different amounts for the same item, the amount charged depending upon the number of items purchased. The seller then attempts to justify the price difference by showing that the saving in the cost of serving the customers who pay the lower price is greater than the price difference. As a simple example, assume the following figures:

Price Bracket	Cost	Price
1	$1.50	$2.00
2	1.00	1.75
3	.67	1.50
4	.50	1.40

The cost and price differences, then, are as follows:

Price Brackets Compared	Cost Difference	Price Difference
1 and 2	$ .50	$ .25
2 and 3	.33	.25
3 and 4	.17	.10

This results in an excess of cost difference over price difference among the brackets as follows:

Price Brackets Compared	Excess of Cost Difference over Price Difference
1 and 2	$.25
2 and 3	.08
3 and 4	.07

The following table gives a comparison of each bracket with all higher price brackets:

Price Bracket	Excess of Cost Difference over Price Difference for Brackets		
	1	2	3
1			
2	$.25		
3	.33	$.08	
4	.40	.15	$.07 [6]

---

[5] Sawyer. *Accounting and Statistical Proof in Price Discrimination Cases*, 36 IOWA L. REV. 244, 247 (1951).

[6] Exemplary figures based on Tone. "Product Costing to Support Price Differentials," *N.A.C.A. Bulletin*, Vol. 37 (1955), pp. 38, 39.

In this example, then, each lower price is justified by a cost difference when compared to every higher price. Thus, Section 2(a) is satisfied.

I

SOME FTC CASES IN WHICH COST DIFFERENTIAL DEFENSES WERE ASSERTED

Before examining the accounting problems involved in establishing a cost differential defense, it may be helpful to consider some of the cases before the Commission in which the defense was put forth. In the first of these, *Bird & Son, Inc.*,[7] the respondent was charged with giving preferences to large mail-order customers including Montgomery Ward. The case involved sales of linoleum which constituted about 96 percent of Bird & Son's business. All customers were given 5/10[8] and 4/70 cash discounts but the preferred customers only were given quantity discounts[9] of 13-23 percent in addition. The average discount was 20 percent, which was given in the form of a rebate. The Commission found that the price differential was more than justified, but the case was complicated by an unusual timing situation. Respondent had determined to discontinue direct selling to retailers before the Robinson-Patman Act was passed, thus eliminating the practices of which the Commission complained. The Commission found that the complaint covered only a negligible proportion of Bird & Son's business, direct retail selling having dropped off to about 1 percent of respondent's business in the month before the complaint was issued. It is not clear why, that being the case, the prosecution was pursued, but since the Commission would be naturally reluctant to issue a cease and desist order under such circumstances, the weight given the accounting aspects of this case should not be too great.

The first successful cost study of real magnitude appears in *Minneapolis-Honeywell Regulator Co.*[10] The respondent was indicted for preferential pricing of oil furnace burner control sets consisting of three units: a thermostat, a limit control, and a primary control. Although Minneapolis-Honeywell stated prices separately for each

---

[7] 25 F.T.C. 548 (1937).

[8] Purchaser is allowed to deduct 5 percent of the list price if he pays cash within ten days.

[9] A quantity discount is a reduction in unit price depending upon the size of the individual order. A volume discount depends on the total purchases of the customer during a given time period. See generally Taylor, *Cost Accounting under the Robinson-Patman Act*, 3 ANTITRUST BULL. 188, 193-95 (1958).

[10] 44 F.T.C. 351 (1948).

unit, the case turned on the price of complete sets since one set constituted a minimum effective purchase. The fact that such grouping was allowed considerably simplified respondent's accounting difficulties. Data were considered for the period from 1938 to 1941, but emphasis was placed on 1941, the last normal [11] year that the pricing system was in effect. The respondent attempted to justify price brackets which depended on the expected purchases of customers during the coming year. The brackets and prices, both of which varied from time to time for 1941, were as follows:

Bracket Discount	Unit Volume	Set Volume	Price per Set
	1-149	1-49	$20.25
1	150-1,049	50-349	17.35
2	1,050-2,999	350-999	16.45
3	3,000-7,499	1,000-2,499	15.35
3A	7,500-14,999	2,500-4,999	15.35
4	15,000-22,499	5,000-7,499	14.90
4A	22,500-29,999	7,500-9,999	14.25
5	30,000 and over	10,000 and over	13.75
6	—	—	— [12]

Considerable difficulty was encountered with what are known as "off-scale" sales, i.e., a sale where the purchaser is given the price of a bracket to which his volume of purchases does not entitle him. For example, if a purchaser of 300 sets, who should fall in Bracket 1 and be charged $17.35 per set, were granted the price of Bracket 2, $16.45, that would constitute an off-scale purchase. Here, the respondent carried purchasers in its records under the classification of the price bracket offered. The Commission accountant protested so vigorously to that method that the study was recast with the customers placed in the price brackets to which their purchases would have entitled them.

The Commission took a generally negative view toward this off-scale selling. During 1941 there were approximately 77 off-scale accounts which break down as follows:

1—Erroneously included.
6—Retroactive credit (i.e., purchases exceeded estimates so the purchase was given a credit).
40—Customers who did not live up to expected volume. The company did not consider it practical to increase the billing price at the end of the year.

---

[11] The respondent's operations were greatly distorted by World War II.
[12] Minneapolis-Honeywell Regulator Co., 44 F.T.C. 351, 380 (1948).

4—Dual transactions. Burner manufacturing companies were given credit for the purchases from respondent by furnace manufacturers who purchased the burner companies' burner, but installed their own controls.

2—New customers. Customers whose rate per month would qualify them for a lower price bracket but who did not purchase from respondent until after the beginning of the year.

2—Customers went out of business or into war work, creating the inverse of the situation immediately above.

22—Customers' bracket prices were allegedly lowered to meet competition.[13]

None of the above was accepted as cost justified or acceptable under any other basis by the Commission. This raises two problems. First, the 40 accounts of those not living up to expectations resulted from the respondent's business requirement that prices be set in advance of the calendar year. The only apparent solution would be for Minneapolis-Honeywell to charge the highest likely price and grant rebates at the end of the year, thus increasing the customers' risks and depriving them of capital, both of which might be injurious to respondent's competitive business.

The second problem involves the 22 accounts for which the bracket prices were allegedly lowered to meet competition. Although the Commission in fact rejected the allegation, suppose the Commission had found that these sales were made to meet competition and were, therefore, justified under Section 2(b).[14] What effect would that have on the remaining accounts under the 2(a) defense? Should all costs allocable to those sales justified by 2(b) be removed? It would seem so, but must they? If so, real difficulties could ensue. The Commission has not yet answered this question, but the Commission's accountant testified, in effect, that the allocable costs should be removed, if possible, from the study, intimating that they could be left in if allocation were extremely difficult.[15]

The accountants employed by Minneapolis-Honeywell concluded that the lowest price bracket, 4, 4A, 5, and 6, could not be cost

---

[13] Record, pp. 2660-62, Minneapolis-Honeywell Regulator Co., 44 F.T.C. 351 (1948).

[14] *Provided, however,* that nothing herein contained shall prevent a seller rebutting the prima facie case thus made by showing that his lower price . . . was made in good faith to meet an equally low price of a competitor. . . . 49 Stat. 1526 (1936), 15 U.S.C. § 13(b) (1957).

[15] Q. "[W]hen you make a preferred price in order to meet competition . . . you cannot use the figures applicable?"
A. "No, I wouldn't say that. I would say you would remove it if you could, but you can't always do it. . . ." Record, p. 2518, Minneapolis-Honeywell Regulator Co., 44 F.T.C. 351 (1948).

justified, so only justification of the first five was argued. The results for 1941, in effect accepted by the Commission, were as follows:

Bracket Discount	Price Scale	Distribution Costs	Cost Differentials	Price Differentials
	$20.25	$11.72		
1	17.35	4.12	$7.10	$2.90
2	16.45	1.80	2.32	.90
3	15.90	.91	.89	.55
3A	15.35	.38	.53	.55
4	14.90			.45
4A	14.25	.21	.17	.65
5	13.75			.50 [16]

The cost justifications were as follows:

Discount	Discount	1	2	3
1	$4.20			
2	5.62	$1.42		
3	5.96	1.76	$.34	
3A	5.94	1.74	.32	($.02) [17]

The 2 cents' failure of justification between Brackets 3 and 3A was considered *de minimis* and the latter bracket accepted by the Commission.

In *United States Rubber Co.*,[18] the first of two cases involving the sales of canvas and waterproof footwear, cost studies again were presented in an attempt to justify discount brackets. The brackets were based on quantity, time of order, and type of goods sold as follows:

1. List price. Any size order, any time, sold by a branch office for immediate delivery.
2. Less 3 percent. Sales of advertised brands of less than 144 pairs or less than case lots, sold by branches between January 1 and June 30 for shipment between April 1 and October 25, payment by December 1.
3. Less 5 percent. Case lots 144-479 pairs, dates as in 2, advertised brands.
4. Less 8 percent. Case lots 480 or more pairs, advertised brands, dates as in 2; or any order of 480 or more pairs in case lots (sufficient to allow independent manufacture) provided sufficient time is allowed for orderly manufacture and delivery.[19]

---

[16] TAGGART, COST JUSTIFICATION 264 (1959) [Hereinafter cited as TAGGART] (an excellent presentation of the accounting data of selected cases).
[17] *Ibid.*
[18] 46 F.T.C. 998 (1950).
[19] Such orders are known as "make-up" orders.

5. Less 13 percent. Make-up orders of 480 or more pairs solicited and handled by branch sales personnel.
6. Less 13 percent and 5 percent.[20] Same as 5 for unadvertised brands.
7. Less 18 percent and 5 percent. Any order accepted from a national chain or mail-order company, which is sold by the wholesale division (located at the factory) for private brand unadvertised footwear.[21]

The discount brackets for canvas footwear were substantially the same as for waterproof footwear except that the dates in 2, 3, and 4 were adjusted to the seasonal demands in that type of foorwear.[22]

The Commission found all but a few of the differentials justified. Those not justified were as follows: [23]

	Brackets Compared	Price Differential	Cost Differential	Excess of Price Differential over Cost Differential
Canvas	3 and 5	$0.0800	$0.0361	$0.0439
Canvas	4 and 5	0.0500	0.0050	0.0450
Waterproof	2 and 5	0.1000	0.0936	0.0064
Waterproof	3 and 5	0.0800	0.0376	0.0424
Waterproof	4 and 5	0.0500	0.0020	0.0480
Waterproof	4 and 6	0.0935	0.0888	0.0047

There was also a failure of $0.0092 between Brackets 3 and 4 at the Mishawaka plant.[24] The Commission stated that the three differences of less than $0.0100 would have been *de minimis* but that the other failures necessitated a cease and desist order. The order forbade discrimination of more than 2 percent of the higher price, but provided that due allowance might be proved in any action for alleged violation.[25] It should be noted that only in one instance of failure was Bracket 5 not involved. The compliance report filed by United States Rubber with the Commission merely deleted that bracket,[26] so the defense must be called a success.

The second footwear case, *The B. G. Goodrich Co.*,[27] had a very similar fact situation. Goodrich employed an additional discount bracket in which were classified, roughly, the purchasers who would fall in Bracket 7 in the *United States Rubber Co.* case but who were

---

[20] List price less 13 percent, then the balance less 5 percent which is not the same as 18 percent.
[21] 46 F.T.C. 998, 1008-09 (1950). All figures are exclusive of cash discounts.
[22] Purchases between August 1 and December 31 for shipment between December 1 and April 25, payment by June 1.
[23] 46 F.T.C. 998, 1012 (1950). Differences are per dollar of gross sales. Figures are from the Naugatuck plant.
[24] 46 F.T.C. 998, 1012 (1950).
[25] *Idem.* at 1013.
[26] TAGGART 337.
[27] 50 F.T.C. 622 (1954).

served by the branch offices. Such service incurred a charge of 5 percent so this extra bracket was given a discount of 18 percent plus 5 percent less 5 percent.[28] The complexity of accounting in this type of apparently simple case is shown by the fact that the defense of these eight categories had to be shown with data that concerns some 607 varieties of footwear,[29] the cost of each variety presumably being different.

At the conclusion of the hearing it was stipulated that Goodrich's cost of manufacturing unadvertised brands was at least 2.5 cents per list sales dollar less than that of advertised brands of waterproof footwear. This amount resulted in a cost justification of all differences save those between Bracket 5 and those with greater discount. Since sales in Bracket 5 amounted to less than one half of 1 percent of total sales of waterproof footwear in 1949, the respondent's unopposed motion to dismiss was granted and the Commission dismissed the complaint.[30]

Perhaps the most important cost justification case is *Sylvania Electric Products, Inc.*[31] Sylvania manufactures about 600 types of radio tubes. Tubes used for replacement purposes were distributed through two primary channels, Sylvania distributors and Philco. Philco was given a lower price than the distributors, but apparently the reduction on a given tube was reached in a haphazard manner. Of the 44 tubes, 22 high priced, 22 low priced—stipulated as typical for purposes of analysis—Taggart presents 24 examples wherein the discount rate in 1948 varied from 8.2 to 48.4 percent.[32] Fortunately for the respondent, the Commission allowed the prices to be averaged, even though the ratios of tubes purchased by the distributors and Philco varied from tube to tube.[33] The averaging reduced any possible failure of justification to *de minimis*. The averaging here was in a rather special circumstance since the demand for replacement tubes depends on which older tubes break or wear out. The result is that the type of tube purchased by distributors is more or less out of their control.

---

[28] TAGGART 344.
[29] *Idem.* at 361.
[30] *Idem.* at 364.
[31] 51 F.T.C. 282 (1954).
[32] TAGGART 366.
[33] Note the impact of allowing the averaging. Costing 600 tubes in a production plant would be almost impossible, as would determining other costs per tube. As a practical matter, cost justification would have been impossible. Also, since the average justification was very close, about half of the discounts, which varied greatly, would have failed.

National Lead Co.[34] is an example of simpler attempts at justification. Here the respondent attempted to justify higher prices for less than carload orders of oxides by showing that the difference reflected freight charges only. The data simply did not support the argument. The difference for deliveries in Detroit, for example, was 90 cents per hundredweight while the freight differential was only 2 cents, leaving 88 cents out of 90 unjustified.[35]

Respondent then tried to defend its zone pricing [36] by showing that the average cost of serving customers in a zone equalled the differential for that zone. The Commission did not accept that argument, holding that such a grouping of customers ignored the effect of the zone pricing on customers near the edges of the higher priced zones.[37]

The accepted defenses permitted a one-quarter cent per pound difference on white dry lead orders of 20 tons or more if the order was actually shipped; [38] and a one-quarter cent per pound difference on orders of 500 or more pounds of white lead-in-oil. The latter was found to be ". . . no more than the allowable differences in costs of the containers. . . ." [39]

In the final case, *Thompson Products, Inc.,*[40] the respondent attempted to justify two practices. The first was the giving of nonretroactive volume rebates [41] to distributors. The rebate schedule for 1953 was found cost justified.

---

[34] 49 F.T.C. 791 (1953).

[35] *Idem.* at 864.

[36] Zone pricing is the practice of determining the price charged a particular customer by the geographical area into which it falls, notwithstanding the actual cost of serving that customer.

[37] [T]he fact that the average cost of shipping to customers over an area of a dozen or more states amounts to some arbitrary figure does not justify the discriminations which result in particular transactions with individual customers located in border territories. 49 F.T.C. 791, 868 (1953).

[38] 49 F.T.C. 791, 868 (1953).

[39] 49 F.T.C. 791, 872 (1953).

[40] 55 F.T.C. 1252 (1959).

[41] A discount is retroactive if the rate of the highest bracket applies to all purchases. It is nonretroactive if the rate applies only to the purchasers within the bracket. For example:

Annual Purchase Brackets	Discount Rate	Annual Purchases	Nonretro-active Discount	Retro-active Discount
$ - 999	0%			
1,000-2,999	1	$ 2,000	$ 10	$ 20
3,000-9,999	2	4,000	40	80
10,000 and over	3	12,000	220	360

from Taylor, *Accounting under the Robinson-Patman Act,* 3 ANTITRUST BULL. 188, 195 (1958).

Annual Purchases   Nonretroactive Rates
Connecting Rods, Engine Bearings and Shims

$ 0	to	$ 750	0 %
750		2,000	3½
2,000		5,000	5
5,000		10,000	7½
	Over	10,000	10

All Other Products

$ 0	to	$ 5,000	0%
5,000		7,000	2
7,000		12,000	3
12,000		18,000	4
18,000		24,000	5
24,000		30,000	6
30,000		36,000	7
36,000		48,000	8
48,000		60,000	9
	Over	60,000	10 [42]

An attempt was also made to justify differentials given to original equipment manufacturers such as Ford, General Motors, and Studebaker. Respondent attempted to treat all such manufacturers as a group. Had this been done the discount would have averaged 39.28 percent, while the cost difference would have been 38.15 percent, according to the prosecution's own proposed findings.[43] Had such an average been allowed the complaint may well have been dismissed. The Commission, however, refused to allow the averaging on the grounds that, since parts for individual makes of automobiles are not competitive, each price to manufacturers should be treated separately. This part of the defense then failed and a cease and desist order was issued.

It was in this case that the Commission strongly stated that return on capital is not an allowable cost. Thompson had attempted to show that the capital invested in its distributor organization yielded less return than that invested in other areas of the corporation. The respondent then tried to charge the difference to distributors' costs. The Commission thought that technique to be an attempt to spread savings experienced in sales to the favored customers to those discriminated-against's costs, and wholly outside the cost allowable under 2(a).[44]

---

[42] TAGGART 443.

[43] *Idem.* at 435.

[44] The return rate factor or element here claimed is thus entirely outside the sphere of actual cost differences. . . . 55 F.T.C. 1252, 1276 (1950).

II

PROBLEMS ENCOUNTERED IN ESTABLISHING COST JUSTIFICATIONS

Having examined the backgrounds of several justification attempts it is now possible to proceed to a more detailed treatment of specific problems and the accounting techniques employed to deal with them.

Price

The price justified should be the actual price paid, not the billed price or initially quoted price.[45] There is, however, some uncertainty as to how to treat cash discounts. Three approaches are possible: (1) the prices can be compared before discount, (2) the discounted prices can be compared, or (3) the prices can be discounted to the extent that the discounts are in fact taken.[46] The Commission has accepted justification of prices figured net of discounts,[47] but the Commission's accounting staff has been pressing for a requirement that the prices offered be justified.[48] When the issue was squarely presented in *Sylvania Electric Products, Inc.*, the Commission avoided it by deciding on other grounds.[49] It would seem that where the same discount is offered to both parties, the most equitable result would come from comparing prices after the discount has been taken. The report of the Advisory Committee on Cost Justification so recommends.[50] An exception to this general approach might have to be made in instances where the cash discount is used merely as a device of differentiation, such as when the seller knows the smaller purchasers cannot make cash payments. But such a case can be dealt with when encountered. An indication of the opinion of the Commission in this matter may be found from its regular inclusion of a definition of price in its cease and desist orders as being net of all discounts.[51]

---

[45] Fruitvale Canning Co., 52 F.T.C. 1504 (1956).

[46] These approaches lead to three different amounts. For example, assume billing prices of $1.50 and $2 and a 2/10 cash discount. The discount is taken by all of the $1.50 customers and one half of the $2 customers. If the billed prices are used, 50 cents ($2.00-$1.50) must be justfied. If the discounts actually taken are removed, 51 cents ($1.98-$1.47) must be justified. If discounts offered are used, 49 cents must be justified ($1.96-$1.47).

[47] Bird & Son, Inc., 25 F.T.C. 548 (1937).

[48] Sylvania Electric Products, Inc., 51 F.T.C. 282 (1954). TAGGART, 384.

[49] Sylvania Electric Products, Inc., 51 F.T.C. 282 (1954).

[50] Advisory Committee on Cost Justification, *Report to the Federal Trade Commission* ¶ IIB3 F.T.C. Mimeo (1956).

[51] Fruitvale Canning Co., 52 F.T.C. 1504 (1956); International Salt Co., 49 F.T.C. 138 (1952).

In certain situations, it may be necessary to adjust prices in order to make a fair comparison. These situations are usually encountered when the prices being compared are for goods similar enough to be of like nature and quality but dissimilar in actual production costs. The resultant difference can be justified as a difference in manufacturing cost but such a difference is not technically due to a difference in the manner or quantity of sale. When the difference is really one of quality, such a difference should not have to be justified. In the *B. F. Goodrich Co.* case,[52] the Commission allowed the difference as a cost of manufacture,[53] but, from the standpoint of accounting principles, the situation is better handled by price adjustment.

In adjusting the price, the factory, or manufacturing, cost is first determined. Then the cost of the article sold to the favored customer is compared to the selling price to determine the gross markup. That markup percentage is then applied to the factory cost of the article sold to the disfavored customer to obtain the adjusted price.[54] This is the price which it is expected that the respondent would have charged the favored customer had the products been identical. This price adjustment method, i.e., assuming an identical gross margin percentage, seems a more accurate method of determining the hypothetical price difference than does adding on the cost difference, and this method was found acceptable by the Advisory Committee.[55]

Price averaging has been allowed in several instances. It should be noted that a form of averaging often appears in price bracket justifications. If the brackets are in terms of quantities purchased and goods are sold at slightly different prices, a justification based on units purchased creates an averaging of dollar discounts. Averaging also occurs, in effect, when the Commission considers a pricing system that has had numerous recent price changes.[56]

But the most important averaging is found in *Minneapolis-Honeywell*[57] and *Sylvania*.[58] These cases indicate that when prices for

[52] 50 F.T.C. 622 (1954).

[53] TAGGART 355.

[54] For example, assume the product sold the favored company costs 20 cents at the factory and is sold for 24 cents. The comparable product costs 21 cents and is sold for 30. The preferred customer's markup is four twentieths or 20 percent. The adjusted price would be 21 plus 20 percent of 21 making 25.2. The difference would be 30 less 25.2 or 4.8. The unadjusted price difference would be 6 cents, and if the factory cost differential is allowed 5 cents still must be justified. (Figures are from TAGGART 432.)

[55] Advisory Committee of Cost Justification, *Report to the Federal Trade Commission* ¶ IIB6 F.T.C. Mimeo (1956).

[56] Fruitvale Canning Co., 52 F.T.C. 1504 (1956).

[57] 44 F.T.C. 351 (1948) (Burner control sets of thermostats, limit controls, and primary controls).

[58] 51 F.T.C. 282 (1954) (radio tubes).

individual items are somewhat arbitrary because the items are thought of in a group, or when they are considered part of an assortment by the manufacturer and demand within the product line is rather independent of price, the prices may be averaged. This enables respondent to allow what would otherwise be an overjustification of one item to carry over to another item and aid the second item's justification. This may be very important if management has in fact first determined what the price of the set should be, and then divided the total into individual prices as an afterthought. Allocation of costs is also much simpler, reducing the complexity and expense of the study necessary for justification. Averaging was allowed even though customers bought the members of the sets in different ratios.

Customer Grouping

A strict reading of the statute would not permit any customer grouping. A reasonable interpretation of the statute does permit such grouping, however, and the Commission has permitted it from the first.[59] Such grouping is necessary both for managerial convenience and for simplification of the preparation of reports.

Justifying quantity or volume brackets presents the additional difficulty that there must be an unjustifiable differential between the top customer in one bracket and the bottom customer in the next. The Commission has held that such differences, if the brackets are reasonable, are permissible, provided that there is no showing of actual competitive injury between such borderline cases:

> . . . Any annual quantity system of pricing is vulnerable to this argument and it may be controlling when it has practical aspects. Where it is purely theoretical, however, it does not constitute a satisfactory basis for disallowing the whole effort at cost justification.[60]

One of the tests of such bracketing would be that the brackets be sufficiently small to allow the increments to be of a relatively small dollar amount. In no case has the Commission struck down a bracketing system for having too extensive brackets, but an analogous situation was presented by the zone pricing system which was not accepted in *National Lead*.[61] Some of the zones in that case constituted areas of a dozen or more states.[62]

---

[59] Bird & Son, Inc., 25 F.T.C. 548 (1937).
[60] Record, p. 1339, Minneapolis-Honeywell Regulator Co., 44 F.T.C. 351 (1948).
[61] 49 F.T.C. 791 (1953).
[62] *Idem.* at 868.

If the justification is attempted for sales to different classes of customers care must be taken to assure that the customers within each class are relatively homogeneous. The relative number of purchasers in a class should not matter; in *Sylvania* [63] respondent was allowed to compare the costs of serving approximately 380 distributors with the cost of serving Philco. But a comparison between a large and small group may open the study to criticism for lack of homogeneity. If certain expenses should be allocated more to one member of the class than another the result may be that splitting the class might result in one member's being justified and the other not. This objection was accepted when respondent attempted to compare the costs of serving 485 customers of varying sizes and types with Atlas and Socony.[64] If preferential prices are given to several customers the study must not justify the sale to just one of them without a showing that the one selected is typical.[65] If the preferred customers are grouped it must be shown that they are homogeneous.[66]

Sampling

Cost studies typically cover one year, with the year selected being the last normal business or calender year before the issuance of the complaint.[67] Although the Commission will consider data covering several years before the cost study, emphasis is placed on the year of the study.[68] Consideration of the previous years seems to go primarily to testing whether or not the year studied is a normal year.

Since the year studied is before the issuance of the complaint, data sufficient to make a proper study may not be available. Thus allocation percentages based on time studies may have to be derived from analysis of similar activities on a later date.[69] Some evidence that techniques have not changed between the year studied and

---

[63] 51 F.T.C. 282 (1954).

[64] Such a grouping fails to take into consideration the fact that among the 485 distributors in one of the groups there are those upon whom respondent expended a comparatively small amount of sales effort. Champion Spark Plug Co., 50 F.T.C. 30, 42 (1952).

[65] International Salt Co., 49 F.T.C. 138, 154-55 (1952).

[66] Thompson Products, Inc., 55 F.T.C. 1252 (1959). (Respondent failed in an attempt to group automobile manufacturers because they were purchasing parts that were not interchangeable.)

[67] Sylvania Electric Products, Inc., 51 F.T.C. 282 (1954); B. F. Goodrich Co., F.T.C. 622 (1954).

[68] Because respondent's cost study was based on its price schedule for 1941 and because that is the most recent year covered by the evidence, our consideration has been directed primarily to that schedule. Record, p. 1338, Minneapolis-Honeywell Regulator Co., 44 F.T.C. 351 (1948).

[69] Sylvania Electric Products, Inc., 51 F.T.C. 282 (1954). TAGGART, 370.

the time at which the allocation ratios were determined should be introduced.

It may develop that, in the best judgment of the accountants employed, the normal year studied has some elements which are not normal, and for those elements different periods may be used. Two examples of this occurred in *B. F. Goodrich*.[70] The salesmen's calls studied were those made between July 1, 1948, and June 30, 1949. That period was selected because most of the orders filled during calendar 1949, the time period of the study, were solicited between those dates.[71] The bad debt account was taken on the basis of the 1936 to 1942 average rather than as the amount actually lost in 1949. The accountants felt the immediate postwar period did not give a fair statement of average bad debts.[72]

When compiling data of sales by the home office or of national accounts all of the accounts should be considered. When considering branch offices, sales, or warehouses, however, some sampling techniques are usually applied. In *United States Rubber Co.*,[73] for example, branches in Pittsburgh, Buffalo, and St. Louis were studied. The latter two were included on the recommendation of the Commission staff to assure that the results were typical.[74]

The study in *Goodrich* [75] covered branches in Pittsburgh and Chicago. Since some of the products handled by the company were not processed in those areas, time studies of some product handling in New York and Minneapolis were also included. In *Morton Salt*,[76] invoicing costs were determined from only one area (Chicago), but that area handled about 70 percent of the invoices issued.

Care must be taken that all of the costs incurred by an area office and included in the study are applicable to the area studied. A strong objection in *Morton Salt* [77] was that some of the invoicing expense charged to the Chicago office was actually allocable to Dallas, Kansas City, and San Francisco.

A similar problem is created if costs vary from area to area. If that is the case, the area sampled to determine the costs allocable to

---

[70] 50 F.T.C. 622 (1954).

[71] TAGGART, 345.

[72] *Idem.* at 353.

[73] 46 F.T.C. 998 (1950). See TAGGART, 284-339.

[74] TAGGART, 290.

[75] 50 F.T.C. 622 (1954). See TAGGART, 345.

[76] 39 F.T.C. 35 (1944). See TAGGART, 173.

[77] TAGGART, 182.

the preferred customers should be the same as that sampled to determine the costs of the nonpreferred customers.[78]

Selection of one or more plants as typical in order to simplify proof of manufacturing cost differentials is acceptable. Some attempt should be made, however, to show that there was no bias in the selection of particular plants. The choice should probably be made by some outside body, by a random device, or be based on sound reasoning. Selection by company officials of a single plant as typical without any survey or other basis to support the selection was one of the objections to the study in *Morton Salt*.[79]

Once the marketing areas or plants have been determined even further selection may be employed. The study in *United States Rubber Co.*[80] was for one year. Transportation costs were taken from data for April and September only,[81] however. It also appeared from the study that the time and expense of filling orders were about the same regardless of the size of the order. The expectation was sustained for the Pittsburgh branch by a time study of three salesmen from March until June during the following year.[82]

Salesmen were also time studied in *Goodrich*.[83] Eight salesmen from Pittsburgh and 21 from Chicago were selected. They kept detailed daily reports for a year. The amount of time spent per call was determined by especially detailed reports which were made for an average of 22 days. The accuracy of the reports was verified by having time study men accompany eight of the salesmen for a period of from one to three days.

If certain items are selected for analysis the respondent should make the theory upon which the selection is based clear to the examiner. Failure to do this resulted in confusion in *Niehoff*.[84] Respondent was trying to justify a volume discount schedule by showing, in part, a cost saving in processing and filling orders. Seventeen orders were selected by an industrial engineer and the sales manager as typical of the types of orders received by the company. The orders were

---

[78] Standard Oil Co., 41 F.T.C. 263, 280 (1945).

[79] 39 F.T.C. 35 (1944). There was also an undertone of suspicion on the part of the Commission's staff when it was brought out that certain allocations were made on the recommendations of employees who were not accountants. See TAGGART, 184.

[80] 46 F.T.C. 998 (1950).

[81] One month from the busy season of both canvas and waterproof footwear.

[82] Waterproof footwear only, the canvas footwear sales having been distorted by the war.

[83] 50 F.T.C. 622 (1954). TAGGART, 347.

[84] C. E. Niehoff & Co., 51 F.T.C. 1114 (1955).

then time studied through processing and filling to give the following results:

Number	Sales Order Number	Net Billing	Number of Packages	Number of Items	Processing Cost per Dollar of Net Invoice
1	44524	$ 12.00	2	1	$0.0992
2	44525	37.66	23	6	.0349
3	44576	45.14	29	20	.0431
4	44575	56.51	49	8	.0366
5	45968	125.20	69	33	.0211
6	44572	134.47	116	25	.0233
7	46162	206.79	171	37	.0174
8	44577	208.64	86	36	.0159
9	44573	223.76	163	63	.0211
10	45969	259.80	110	49	.0147
11	45945	305.01	163	56	.0177
12	46161	341.79	236	49	.0130
13	44991	496.98	391	68	.0144
14	45078	523.22	334	81	.0166
15	45301	785.80	623	101	.0136
16	45079	811.57	598	94	.0141
17	44993	846.66	469	89	.0123 [85]

Respondent then plotted on a graph the total net processing costs per order as a function of net billing price. Then the proportion of the price differential cost justified was computed for sample customers. Total net billings of the customer were divided by the number of orders to obtain the average order size. The average order size was used to determine the average cost per order and that was multiplied by the number of orders to obtain total processing and filling costs. Then the same procedure was used to compute what would have been the cost of serving a preferred customer had the preferred customer purchased the same total dollar amount but with average orders of the size that the preferred customer in fact used. The difference of the two resultant figures yields the cost difference. Then from the net amount paid by the injured customer was subtracted the amount that would have been paid by the preferred customer had he purchased the same volume but at the price per item he in fact paid. That yields the price difference. The difference in cost was then divided by the difference in price to obtain the percentage of the price differential that was cost justified by differences in the cost and filling and processing orders.[86]

[85] *Idem.* at 1134.
[86] See Footnote 86 at bottom of p. 710.

The prosecution attacked this approach by presenting the purchase habits of the customers who had placed the 17 sales orders that had been analyzed. The dollar values of the mean purchases of those customers were not related to the dollar values of the orders studied, and purchase sizes of each customer ranged widely:

Customer	Net Billing of the Order Studied	Customer's Average 1949 Purchase	Customer's Purchase Range in 1949	Number of 1949 Shipments
1	$ 12.00	$123	$ 3 -537	22
2	37.66	105	1 -322	17
3	45.14	41	3 -114	38
4	56.51	150	17 -325	4
5	125.20	45	1 -512	90
6	134.47	58	0.22-211	24
7	206.79	13	1 - 36	9
8	208.64	54	2 -160	7
9	223.76	128	87 -218	4
10	259.80	210	1 -847	30
11	305.01	183	17 -311	6
12	341.79	163	2 -648	18
13	496.98	99	1 -772	99
14	523.22	12	12	1
15	785.80	145	4 -660	49
16	811.57	292	1 -3,199	83
17	846.66	178	2 -934	62 [87]

This exhibit suggested to the examiner that the 17 customers were somehow selected as typical and that the orders selected were intended to be representative of the orders placed by those purchasers. That, of course, is not the case. The orders were selected as fair samples of different sizes of orders, and the customers placing the orders were not considered. The reason for the selections should have been made perfectly clear to the examiner.

---

[86]

	Net Billing	Number of Shipments	Billings per Shipment	Cost per Billing Dollar
Greiner Automotive	$11,230	32	$351	$.0152
Wholesalers	1,140	8	142	.0280

Actual cost of filing A. W. orders..............$1,140 × .0280 $31.92
              Cost at Greiner rate.............. 1,140 × .0152 17.33
                    Cost Difference $14.59

Net amount A. W. should have paid (93.1% bracket, $1,266.67 sales at list price)..$1,179.27
Net amount for same volume at Greiner price (82.6% bracket).. 1,046.27
                                   Price difference..$ 133.00

Proportion of price difference justified by savings in *order processing* costs (14.59 divided by 133) 11.0%. TAGGART, 411 (Footnotes omitted).
[87] TAGGART, 418.

The examiner was also concerned with the problem of averaging. There was no evidence offered to demonstrate that respondent's method of computing the cost was accurate. Put in other terms, does the cost of the mean order equal the mean of the costs of the component orders? [88] This latter defect may have been determinative since the examiner did not feel that the burden of averaging the costs of the separate orders would have been too great. [89]

Advertising

Allocation of advertising expense is extremely difficult. The effect of institutional advertising on the sales of particular products is at best conjectural. Since the burden of proof is on the respondent, it cannot expect to be able to show a difference. The normal practice is to include institutional advertising for the sake of study completeness and then to allocate the expense on the basis of dollars of sales, thus providing no cost difference. [90]

Some differences can be proved if the price differential complained of is between trademarked items and private brands. In that case consumer oriented advertising of trademarked items can be charged directly to the trademarked item as a sales expense.

Since respondent in *Sylvania* [91] was allowed to consider all products as a whole, nearly all advertising expenses could be charged directly to Sylvania distributors. The only excepted items were general advertising expenses and trade paper advertising, which were treated as institutional advertising expenses.

It is doubtful that general expenses need be handled quite so conservatively. Advertising expenses in *United States Rubber Co.*,[92] were divided into five categories: three separate types of footwear, institutional advertising, and expenses incurred in administering the other

---

[88] For example, assume a purchaser places five $100 orders and one $700 order. His actual cost would then be

$$5 \times \$3.40 = \$17.00$$
$$1 \times 7.35 = \underline{7.35}$$
$$\$24.35$$

The total orders amount to $1,200 in six orders, a mean of $200 per order. Six orders of $200 each would cost $6 \times \$4.50 = \$27.00$.

Respondent's approach is, then, $2.65 from the actual cost. Computations from the table in C. E. Niehoff, 51 F.T.C. 1114, 1135 (1955).

[89] Respondent's actual records could have shown the exact processing cost of each and all orders from the 17 selected customers . . . but this was not done. C. E. Niehoff, 51 F.T.C. 1114, 1136 (1955).

[90] United States Rubber Co., 46 F.T.C. 998 (1950); Sylvania Electric Products, Inc., 51 F.T.C. 282 (1954).

[91] 54 F.T.C. 282 (1954). TAGGART, 373.

[92] 46 F.T.C. 998 (1950). TAGGART, 310.

four. The last item was distributed to the direct expenses pro rata. Of the four direct charges remaining, one concerned a line of footwear not covered by the pleadings so it was disregarded. The remaining three were then expressed as percentages of the gross sales of the line or lines applicable. The amount chargeable to the preferred or nonpreferred customers was then determined by multiplying the percentage thus obtained by the total gross sales of the appropriate line or lines made to each customer group.

A similar approach was used in *B. F. Goodrich*.[93] Allocation of general advertising overhead between waterproof and canvas footwear was on the basis of advertising space used for each.[94] Allocation to brackets was by list sales.[95]

Any final allocation by other than sales or sales dollars is likely to meet stiff resistance from the Commission.[96] In *Niehoff*[97] the examiner allowed the portion of advertising expense representing catalog costs to be equally divided among the customers regardless of their size. There was some testimony that the smaller customers received as many or more catalogs per customer than the larger customers. The Commission, however, found that evidence equivocal and was much impressed by a showing that some of the larger customers had more than one salesman so would require more than one catalog. The Commission concluded that the burden upon respondent to show the allocation to be proper had not been met and the examiner was overruled.

Salesmen's Salaries

Salesmen's salaries are allocated by the amount of time spent with each class of customer.[98] The Commission staff has argued consistently that the only accurate way to determine the amount of time

---

[93] 50 F.T.C. 622 (1954). TAGGART, 352.

[94] This would be the equivalent of United States Rubber Co., 46 F.T.C. 998 (1950), only if the media expenses per unit of space were constant. Seasonal rate changes might affect the ratio used as might a possible proclivity toward a different size of advertisement during the summer than the winter. Why space purchased rather than money spent to purchase space was used is unclear.

[95] *Accord*, International Salt Co., 49 F.T.C. 138 (1952).

[96] Respondent's president admitted that averaging this total expense on a per customer basis was arbitrary. It can be allocated only on a per dollar of sales basis which, of course, furnishes no cost justification. . . . C. E. Niehoff & Co., 51 F.T.C. 1114, 1137 (1955) (Examiner's report).

[97] 51 F.T.C. 1114 (1955).

[98] An exception would be the "inside salesmen" in Bird & Son, 25 F.T.C. 548 (1937), whose salaries were allocated on the basis of yardage sold.

An alternative method of allocation, often used in accounting for other purposes, would be by sales dollars. The Commission's objection to this approach is that it would be a form of bootstrapping. By that it is meant that preferential price to a customer in part justifies itself: a reduction in sales price reduces the cost of selling, which cost is determined by a percentage of the price.

spent is by time studies.[99] Some accountants have disagreed, however. Respondent's accountant in *Minneapolis-Honeywell*[100] argued that in many instances a person's estimate of his own time allocation can be more accurate than a time study, particularly if the tasks performed are complex and interrelated. Similarly, in *International Salt*,[101] a time study attempt was abandoned. The accountant felt that the salt business was so seasonal that no fair sample could be taken and that a full year's study would be impracticable.

The Commission has allowed other methods of allocating salesmen's salaries when that method has appeared practical and accurate. The method used in *Minneapolis-Honeywell*[102] appears to be the most detailed that has appeared without the use of time studies.[103] The unit respondent decided to work with was cost per call. Once cost per call was determined the cost of selling to any particular customer could be determined because a record of all salesmen's calls had been kept. First the number of calls that would ordinarily be made in a single day on a particular type of customer was determined. That was done by taking a salesman who made calls only on that type of customer, then dividing the number of calls made by that salesman in one year by the number of sales days in the same year. The resultant figure[104]

The bootstrapping argument could be circumvented by allocating the cost on the basis of list price (i.e., price before the preferential discount is taken). This would result, effectually, in a volume allocation of cost for particular items. The objection to list price allocation is that it does not reflect what the salesman does (i.e., how he spends his time) or what he is supposed to do (a salesman is not ordinarily hired to maximize volume).

A third alternative would be to allocate sales costs on the basis of profits. Respondent would argue that the purpose of the sales force is to make sales that will maximize company net income, so that profit ratios are the proper bases for allocation. This approach has not yet been fully argued to the Commission.

Finally salesmen's time could be allocated on the basis of how much time a sale should take, rather than how much time it in fact did take. An efficiency expert would determine how much time a type of sale should ordinarily take and any excess would be termed waste time and would be allocated to general overhead. This general approach to cost accounting was presented by respondent in Minneapolis-Honeywell Regulator Co., 44 F.T.C. 351 (1948), but was not seriously pursued and no findings on the technique were presented by the examiner or the Commission.

[99] I have always contended in previous cases before the Commission that nothing short of time studies of selling activities should be considered as proper support for measuring factors to be used in separating those costs which are closely related to effort expended by the separate employees. . . . Warmack, Federal Trade Commission Accountant. Record, p. 2469, Minneapolis-Honeywell Regulator Co., 44 F.T.C. 351 (1948).

[100] 44 F.T.C. 351 (1948).

[101] 49 F.T.C. 138 (1952).

[102] 44 F.T.C. 351 (1948).

[103] The Second World War had so altered respondent's business that accurate time studies were not possible.

[104] Some adjustments were made to compensate for the type of territory in which the salesman operated. A salesman in a more dense area may have less travel time and thus a higher call per day potentiality.

was then divided into the daily salary of the salesman whose cost per call on that type of customer was being determined. The quotient was the amount of that salesman's salary chargeable to the customers in that bracket per call in determining sales costs.[105] The Commission did not accept the study as completely accurate but found it within a reasonable margin of allowable error.[106]

The easiest simplification of salesmen's salary allocations would be on the basis of the number of calls made by a salesman during the period studied. This approach was used successfully in *Bird & Son*.[107] Allocation by the number of calls requires, however, that the average length of time of the calls on the nonpreferred customers at least equals the duration of the average call on preferred customers.[108]

The Commission will not ordinarily accept the assumption that the time per call is independent of the size of the order taken.[109] Respondent should present clear evidence that such is the case.[110]

In *Niehoff*[111] the opposite assumption was made. Respondent presented convincing testimony that because of the nature of the business salesmen actually spent a longer time with smaller customers

---

[105] To this figure were added pro rata expenses and direct supervision costs. Indirect supervision costs were then added in. They were figured by taking the number of days the zone manager worked, less the number of days he was selling, to determine the number of days he was supervising. The ratio of number of days supervising to number of days working was applied to the zone manager's salary and other costs directly charged to him. The result was divided by the total number of man days of salesmen under him, which was in turn divided by the number of a particular type of call that could be made by the salesman in a day to get the amount chargeable to a particular call. The zone manager's superior was similarly treated. The sum of these charges gave the cost of a particular call. For a specific example see Record, pp. 2406-2417, Minneapolis-Honeywell Regulator Co., 44 F.T.C. 351 (1948).

[106] Cost studies of the sort presented . . . do not afford precise accuracy but must necessarily embrace a number of conjectural factors and allocations. There is inherent in them a reasonable margin of allowable error. Where they are made in good faith and in accordance with sound accounting principles, they should be given a very great weight. . . . We have accordingly accepted the results of the cost study as fairly reflecting respondent's cost differentials within a reasonable margin of error. Record, p. 1338, Minneapolis-Honeywell Regulator Co., 44 F.T.C. 351 (1948).

[107] 25 F.T.C. 548 (1937) ("Outside" salesmen's salaries were distributed in the first instance by the number of calls, then further broken down on the basis of yardage).

[108] This must be the case if the number-of-calls basis is to be in accord with the Commission approved time based allocation.

[109] The orders of preferred customers must be larger in the average instance, allowing the salesmen's costs to be more widely distributed, for respondent to obtain partial cost justification through sales costs.

[110] [T]he allocation of merchandise expenses was made on the assumption that the cost of each call by a salesman was of equal duration regardless of the purchaser. There is no record basis for such an assumption. International Salt Co., 49 F.T.C. 138, 155 (1952).

[111] 51 F.T.C. 1114 (1955).

than with the larger ones.[112] Respondent then proceeded as if the time spent on all customers were equal.[113] Respondent then distributed salesmen's costs equally to all customers, claiming that salesmen called on all classes of customers the same number of times.

The actual records of salesmen's calls had been destroyed so the testimony of the president and sales manager of Niehoff was presented to show that all customers were called with approximately the same frequency. The Commission remained unconvinced, showing that the call record of the only salesman examined was contradictory to the general statement.[114]

The conclusion to be drawn from these cases is that time studies should be made if at all possible. If a time study cannot be undertaken detailed data should be presented to approximate the same result as closely as possible.

Other Sales Expenses

Salaries of private secretaries are allocated in the same manner as are those of their superiors. General overhead, such as light, heat, and rent, should be apportioned among departments on the basis of area used, then allocated as are direct department expenses.

Most items of expense in the sales distribution branches—such as sales accounting, stenographers, operating traveling expenses, etc.— are allocated by the number of invoices and papers or the number of invoice lines.[115] For most of these functions it appears that invoice lines would be a more accurate measurement, since it is not to be assumed that the handling of orders is independent of the number of types of items in the order. If respondent intends to use invoices as an allocation measure, then some evidence should be presented to show that the ratio of invoices to invoice lines is the same for all groups of customers.[116]

Some additional difficulty has been encountered in the allocation of telephone expenses. Time studies of telephone use are extremely difficult so respondents have allocated telephone expenses by the number of invoices and documents.[117] The Commission staff excepts to

---

[112] Smaller purchasers had less efficient inventory control so their needs could not be so easily determined.

[113] The Commission could not except this treatment was injurious to the respondent.

[114] C. E. Niehoff & Co., 51 F.T.C. 1114, 1140 (1955).

[115] Bird & Son, Inc., 25 F.T.C. 548 (1937); United States Rubber Co., 46 F.T.C. 998 (1950).

[116] United States Rubber Co., 46 F.T.C. 998 (1950) (number of orders).

[117] Minneapolis-Honeywell Regulator Co., 44 F.T.C. 351 (1948).

this practice as baseless. The item is so small, however, that there is no Commission ruling on it.

III

Conclusion

It is apparent that a company faced with a price preference prosecution should prepare its cost justification defense with utmost care. The accountants should be prepared to explain the basis for each allocation employed in the study, and questionable items should be either omitted or allocated in a way that does not aid the justification. It should also be noted that respondent's chances for success are far greater, especially at the negotiation stage, if a study is made before governmental inquiry, and the company's discount structure is based on that study.

Hopefully, the Commission will, in the near future, either issue regulations as to permissible accounting techniques, or begin a series of decisions with more specific findings as to techniques used in particular cases. The probable success of a study could then be more accurately predicted and the needless expenditure of money on exhaustive, but unaccepted, studies avoided.

50. CONTROLLING RESEARCH
COSTS WITH A BUDGET *

Adolph G. Lurie †

The budgeting and cost control principles used in effective management of the manufacture and sale of products can also be used by management in controlling the expenditures for research and development.

The establishment of a research and development budget in total is a relatively simple matter. However, the preparation of such a budget for effective cost control is a more comprehensive procedure. The methods which may be followed for both steps will be outlined here.

Budgets for research and development can be established by several different methods depending upon the viewpoint of top management. Suggested methods for determining the amount of dollars to be expended during a given period, usually a year, can be based upon any one of the following considerations, or any combination of them that management may desire to recognize:

1. The total amount of the budget may be based upon the sales for the past period or it may be a fixed percentage of the estimated sales for the ensuing period.
2. It may be desirable to budget a percentage of net profits before taxes.
3. Management may decide to base the budgeted expenditure upon the amount that had been spent previously, modified either upwards or downwards by changes in volume of sales, changes in profits, or similar considerations.
4. The research budget may be dependent upon the operating budget and the amount determined from the forecast of sales or upon budgeted profits before research and development.
5. A general review and study of economic conditions, future prospects, competition, etc. may influence the establishment of the budget.
6. The least scientific method of approaching this problem is to fix the amount by arbitrary determination.

* From *N.A.C.A. Bulletin* (March, 1953). Reprinted by permission of the National Association of Cost Accountants.

† Adolph G. Lurie, associated with the public accounting firm of Alexander Grant & Company.

Thus the total amount of the budget for research and development is established in one or more of these ways and the first major premise for the budgetary and cost control of a research and development department is provided. It is just a starting point for this purpose. Merely establishing a budget does not give the directors of the research department any guide for programming their efforts. Such guidance is invaluable for those who must make decisions, direct the orderly progress of the development program, and intelligently plan and control the work of the department.

A Twofold Budget

The preparation of the budget is a twofold operation, consisting of setting up a budget classified by types of expenditures, to enable the technical director and supervisors to provide for facilities and staff in accordance with the amount of money available (Exhibit 1)

RESEARCH AND DEVELOPMENT DIVISION

Expense Budget

Year Ended December 31, 1953

1. *Payroll*

a. Technical employees	$150,000
b. Nontechnical employees	30,000
c. Service employees	20,000
d. Plant labor	10,000
Subtotal	$210,000

2. *Supplies and materials*

a. Expendable equipment	$ 25,000
b. Operating supplies	15,000
Subtotal	$ 40,000

3. *Other direct costs*

a. Books, dues, subscriptions, etc.	$ 5,000
b. Travel expenses	15,000
c. Technical, engineering, and consulting fees	15,000
d. Taxes, insurance, depreciation	5,000
e. Light, heat, power, etc.	5,000
f. Miscellaneous	5,000
Subtotal	$ 50,000
TOTAL BUDGET	$300,000

Exhibit 1

and also a budget for projects contemplated during the period (Exhibit 2). The order of preparation of these two budgets depends upon management's approach to the problem but both budgets are for the same dollars. These budgets should be a joint project of the research department and the budget or cost accounting department, to insure compliance with techniques established for the accounting of the expenditures. The first of the two arrangements of the budget is relatively easy to prepare and can be fairly definitely fixed. The second, which breaks the total up by projects, should provide for changes throughout the period to allow the technical director and his supervisory staff flexibility in their operations.

THE EXPENSE CLASSIFICATION BUDGET

The budget of expense classifications may be fairly simple in form but, if a comprehensive budget is desired, can also be quite involved. The degree of complexity depends largely upon the size of the department, the amount of money involved, and the amount of information and control desired by those responsible for managing the research department. A basic budget may consist of:

1. *Payrolls*—salaries and wages, including related costs, such as social security taxes, compensation insurance, group insurance, pensions, etc.
2. *Supplies and materials*, such as expendable equipment and operating supplies.
3. *Other direct operating costs.*

Such a grouping, comprising only a few figures, may be adequate for a satisfactory budget and cost control of the expenditures of a small or medium-sized department. A description of the elements entering into each of the above classifications is shown in more detail in the comprehensive budget outline below:

1. The subdivisions under payrolls may be the following:
   a. Salaries of professionally trained personnel.
   b. Salaries and wages of nonprofessional employees, such as laboratory technicians, draftsmen, etc.
   c. Salaries of service employees, usually stenographers, and clerical workers of the department.
   d. Plant labor, consisting of hourly workers borrowed from operating departments for specific work as required.
2. Supplies and materials consist of two major items: namely,
   a. Expendable equipment purchased for specific projects or for general use in the research department, which does not become a part of the basic equipment.
   b. Supplies and materials.

3. Other direct costs can include but need not be limited to the following.

    a. Books, periodicals, dues, subscriptions, and similar items for the department staff or library.

    b. Travel expense.

    c. Fees for outside technical, engineering, and consulting services.

    d. Taxes, depreciation, and insurance on building, permanent fixtures, furniture, and equipment.

    e. Cost of service facilities from the plant, such as light, heat, power, steam, etc.

    f. Miscellaneous.

The largest item in a research department budget is usually the salaries and wages of those employed in the department. It is relatively simple to develop the dollar amounts by totaling the salaries to be paid to the individuals engaged in research work, including payroll taxes, insurance, and the cost of other benefits. An estimate can be made of the plant labor required in the operation of the research and development department, based upon a study of previous experience.

The budget for supplies, materials, and expendable equipment can also be based upon past experience, adjusting for changes in present requirements and the relative cost of these materials. Under present conditions, even though the quantity required may be the same as for the previous year, the cost would rise due to increased prices.

Other direct costs can be readily determined from the factors involved. Dues and subscriptions are relatively fixed. The books to be purchased for the library can be based upon past experience. Travel expense depends upon several factors, such as the number and location of principal meetings of technical societies, the locations of the plants of the organization, the area in which the customers are located, and the general company policy with regard to travel expense. Past experience can be a good guide in determining what the expenses might be in the future.

Technical, engineering, and consulting fees can be ascertained from a review of the projects contemplated during the period. The capabilities of the research personnel and the contemplated changes therein must be considered in arriving at the amount of money that would be spent for outside assistance.

Taxes, insurance, depreciation, light, heat and power, and other similar expenses are usually fixed by the distribution of the total cost to the company and the amount to be allocated to the research and development department would, therefore, be obtained from the budget of the operating divisions.

CREDITS AGAINST RESEARCH AND DEVELOPMENT EXPENDITURES

Consideration may also be given to setting a policy with respect to credits from the operation of the research and development department resulting from:

1. The sale of finished materials produced by the research and development department.
2. The sale of unusable expendable equipment or scrap resulting therefrom.
3. The transfer of expendable equipment or other materials to operating departments.
4. Charges to customers and others for technical services.
5. Any other miscellaneous credits, depending upon the accounting policy of the organization.

In a situation in which sales may be sizable in amount and also regular, it would be advisable to establish a section in the budget for credits. Thus, management can control the situation and see that all possible credits are given to the development department. However, where sales resulting from research and development work are limited in relation to the entire research program, it would be far simpler not to include such items in the budget but to allow the division to dispose of materials as they see fit, providing an incentive to sell unusable equipment and materials, thereby increasing funds for completion of projects.

THE PROJECT BUDGET

We have discussed the establishment of a budget by classes of expenditures. However, the important phase of research budgeting for cost control is the preparation of a budget for each project to be undertaken during the period. This likewise can be relatively simple or quite elaborate, depending upon the degree of management cost control desired. The simplest procedure would be merely to list the projects which will be undertaken, showing the amount of the budget allocated to each. Provisions should be made for additions to the list of projects during the period as new fields of research are entered. The total of the amounts authorized for the several projects must agree with the total of the amount budgeted by classes of expenditures.

A more detailed approach to budgeting research projects might be one in which projects are grouped under several headings. Major classifications could be as follows:

1. Improvement in the manufacture, quality, and usage of present products.
2. Research and development of new products.
3. Projects requested by customers or the sales department.
4. Pure or "blue sky" research, having no commercial value.
5. Service departments, research library, clerical, stenographic, drafting room, etc. This should provide only for that portion of research and development expense not directly allocable to projects.
6. Balance available for projects to be authorized at a later date.

Under the first four of the above classifications, there could be a specific budget authorized for each project, in groups as follows:

1. Completion of projects authorized in prior periods.
2. Projects to be started in current period.

Exhibit 2 is a sample form which could be followed in setting up this portion of the budget. As previously stated, the total of all the items entered on it must agree with the total expense classification budget.

A logical starting point is a determination of the amount necessary to complete projects already in progress. Another portion of the budget easily determinable is the cost of operating the research service departments. These two factors, deducted from the total budget, result in the balance available for new projects. The research directors and supervisors can then determine the portion of this remainder to be allocated towards research relating to products presently being produced, new products, or for pure research. The manner in which the totals for each of these major classifications is determined, depends upon the nature of the business and the direction in which research and development effort is to be expended, based upon the policy of the organization.

Following the determination of the amount for each major classification, the next step is an apportionment to the individual projects being considered for active investigation. In this apportionment, no attempt should be made to show the manner in which funds are to be expended, since the amount of materials, labor, or supplies required for each project cannot be determined readily and must be ascertained as the project progresses. Under the procedure outlined, management authorizes the research and development division to spend a specified sum in its overall operation and also specifies the amount which may be spent for the projects to be undertaken. Efforts to pinpoint the budget to the extent that a figure for the several classifications of expenditure for each project is developed might

RESEARCH AND DEVELOPMENT DIVISION

Project Budget

Year Ended December 31, 1953

	Current Budget	Prior Expenditures	Total Authorized
1. *Present products*			
a. Projects in progress			
(1) Product x improvements ..	$ 5,000	$15,000	$ 20,000
(2) Product y usage	10,000	10,500	20,500
(3) Product z quality	10,000	7,500	17,500
Subtotal	$ 25,000	$33,000	$ 58,000
b. New projects			
(1) Product x new process	$ 25,000		$ 25,000
(2) Product y quality control ..	30,000		30,000
(3) Product z new use	20,000		20,000
Subtotal	$ 75,000		$ 75,000
Total present products	$100,000	$33,000	$133,000
2. *New product research*			
a. Projects in progress			
(1) Product xx	$ 15,000	$12,500	$ 27,500
(2) Product yy	10,000	5,000	15,000
Subtotal	$ 25,000	$17,500	$ 42,500
b. New projects			
(1) Product P	$ 30,000		$ 30,000
(2) Product Q	25,000		25,000
(3) Product R	10,000		10,000
Subtotal	$ 65,000		$ 65,000
Total new products	$ 90,000	$17,500	$107,500
3. *Pure research*			
a. Projects in progress			
(1) Item S	$ 5,000	$ 3,500	$ 8,500
(2) Item T	7,000	3,000	10,000
Subtotal	$ 12,000	$ 6,500	$ 18,500
b. New projects			
(1) Item U	$ 3,000		$ 3,000
(2) Item V	5,000		5,000
Subtotal	$ 8,000		$ 8,000
Total pure research	$ 20,000	$ 6,500	$ 26,500

(Continued on next page)

(Continued from preceding page)

Project Budget

Year Ended December 31, 1953

	Current Budget	Prior Expenditures	Total Autho-rized
4. *Sales department service*			
a. Projects in progress			
(1) Product x	$ 7,000	$ 1,000	$ 8,000
(2) Customer z	3,000	1,500	4,500
Subtotal	$ 10,000	$ 2,500	$ 12,500
b. New projects			
(1) Product y	$ 2,000		$ 2,000
(2) Product q	3,000		3,000
Subtotal	$ 5,000		$ 5,000
Total sales department service	$ 15,000	$ 2,500	$ 17,500
5. *Service departments*			
a. Library	$ 10,000		$ 10,000
b. Drafting room (general)	5,000		5,000
c. Stenographic and clerical	10,000		10,000
	$ 25,000		$ 25,000
6. Balance for unauthorized projects .	$ 50,000		$ 50,000
	$300,000	$59,500	$359,500

Exhibit 2

so limit the research department as to interfere with its smooth operational functioning.

The outlined procedure provides sufficient flexibility so that the directors of research may use their own judgment in shifting the efforts within their division among the various projects. In this connection, it is advisable to revise the budgets periodically by issuing supplementary budgets. Unused balances may be transferred from projects which are completed to "balance for unauthorized projects," to new projects, or to projects in progress.

As shown in Exhibit 2, the project budget, it is desirable to indicate the amount expended before the current period, it being assumed that such amounts plus the budget for the current period will be the total amount authorized to date for each project. The total budget for the individual project is an extremely important guide for management, since control of the total expenditure should be maintained to decide whether a project should be abandoned or continued to its successful conclusion. It should be recognized that a long-range program must be established and provisions should be made so that the full program can be completed without capricious change of policy on the part of financial executives.

Making the Research Budget an Effective Tool

Upon the completion of the expense and project budget, approval by top management is desirable and usually required. A letter of transmittal of the budget, outlining the high spots and indicating the anticipated results of the research effort, is quite helpful for obtaining a prompt approval. In preparing the budget, a realistic and practical approach should have been used, so as to enable management readily to foresee the beneficial results of the proposed efforts. The budget should not be top-heavy on pure research or nonproductive work and, depending upon the nature of the business, should have sufficient stress upon the improvement in present products, either from the production, quality, or use viewpoint, and upon the development of new products. This is desirable to obtain the proper interest, enthusiasm and approval of top management.

The budgeting procedure described here is of value only if actual expenditures are properly recorded in accordance with the budget, and comparisons made between the amounts actually expended and those authorized. Cost records are advisable, as well as monthly or quarterly cost reports in form similar to the budget, so that those responsible for the functioning of the research department can control the expenditures and determine the amount of funds available for subsequent operations. With such budgeting and reporting, the research director can plan for the future, and financial executives can assist in the direction of the research and development division towards the ultimate goal of all concerned, namely, progress for the organization, growth, and additional profits.

51. CONTROLLING RETAIL INVENTORY THROUGH PLANNED OPEN-TO-BUY POSITIONS *

Gardner M. Jones †

A perennial problem in retail store operations is the persistent tendency of inventories to creep upward. Various means have been employed to counter this tendency: frequent inventory taking with sell-off of overage merchandise, periodic across-the-board markdowns, special promotions on slow-moving items, and limits on amounts purchased. In the retail shoe business, a device known as "pairage control" is employed to plan how many shoes to buy and carry. It is helpful but still permits the purchasing and upward accumulation of inventories.

This paper describes an adaptation of retail shoe stock level management which is a combination of economic quantity technique, dollar purchase limitations, and pairage control. The long-run purpose of the procedure is to improve inventory turn through stock reduction and better timing of deliveries for purchases in a way that will not impair the ability to service sales.

The technique, in outline, is this:

1. Estimate month-by-month sales and therefore monthly cost of goods sold.
2. Establish monthly ratios of beginning-of-month inventory to an average inventory, based on the relationship of experienced monthly sales to an average month's sales.
3. Use a target turnover rate, applied to expected cost of goods sold for the year, to establish a desired average inventory level for the year.
4. Establish desired beginning-of-month inventory levels, based on the ratios found in 2, applied to the desired average inventory found in 3.
5. Establish amounts needed to purchase for each month, based on expected monthly cost of goods sold plus or minus the inventory changes needed to accomplish the target beginning-of-month inventory levels.

* From the *N.A.A. Bulletin* (November, 1964). Reprinted by permission of the National Association of Accountants.

† Gardner M. Jones, Professor of Accounting at Michigan State University, East Lansing, Michigan.

6. Based on 5, establish future month "open-to-buy" allowances, which define purchase dollar commitment limits for each future month.
7. Within open-to-buy dollar allowances, establish pairage quotas to guide buyers.
8. Maintain current records of open-to-buy balances, both in dollars and pairs.
9. Provide discretionary purchasing funds outside of the above system for managerial "opportunity purchases."
10. Review the appropriateness of stock balances twice a year, considering both overstocks and out-of-stock conditions.

DETERMINING INVENTORY-TO-SALES RATIOS

Turnover rates vary considerably among retail shoe departments but run typically from two or three for some men's shoe departments to three or three and a half for women's and four for children's shoes. A turnover of four means that the stock turns every three months, or, stated differently, that on the average three months' supply is on hand. By translating desired turnover into months' supply on hand, we obtain a figure which is convenient to work with on a month-to-month basis.

Months' supply on hand can also be stated as the ratio of inventory to a month's cost of goods sold. For working purposes a convenient approximation (for any specific month) is the ratio of beginning-of-the-month inventory to that month's cost of goods sold. This is the planned measure that is used in the proposed procedure to regulate stock levels and, therefore, purchases.

This is a seasonal business. The peaks and valleys of seasonal sales vary uniquely, depending on the type of shoes, outlet, location, and type of clientele. In order to meet peak sales demands without being overloaded with stock in slack periods, we adopt a variable monthly ratio of the beginning-of-the-month stock to the cost of goods sold, which will average out to the desired annual rate. A suitable sliding-scale ratio will cause planned stock levels to be more closely tailored to seasonal peaks and valleys.

Recognition of a basic principle of economic inventory management is then incorporated into the procedure: as expected sales increase, the amount of inventory needed to service those sales increases less than proportionately. A now generally accepted notion is that inventory levels need change only in proportion to the square root of the change in sales.

For example, let us suppose that sales next month were expected to be double the average monthly sales. The inventory level needs to expand only to $\sqrt{2}$ or 1.414 times the average inventory. If expected sales are to be one half the average monthly sales, the needed inventory can be reduced to $\sqrt{\frac{1}{2}}$ or .707 times the normal inventory. Knowing this characteristic of inventory behavior, we are in a position to forecast the amount of beginning-of-month inventory position needed to support each month's expected sales.

AN EXAMPLE

The remainder of the paper contains an example of the application of the ideas suggested to this point.

Department A's net sales forecasts are shown in Exhibit 1, along with the calculated cost of goods sold. The planned markup is 40 percent, but markdowns reduce the effective net margin to 34 percent of sales price; thus cost of goods sold are 66 percent of net sales. Let us suppose that an inventory turn of 3.0 is desired, as an average for the year; thus a stock to cost of goods sold ratio of 4.0 is desired, as average. Average monthly cost of goods sold is $13,160. The average inventory should then be $52,640, but it may vary from around $40,000 to $65,000 for individual months, depending on the sales expectations for particular months.

Exhibit 1 shows the determination of appropriate inventory levels under this approach. The extremes are represented by the months of February and December. For February, sales are 58 percent of an average month. Therefore, the required inventory sinks to about 76 percent of the average inventory. In December, sales run 171 percent of "normal." The needed inventory is, therefore, 131 percent of the average. Under the proposed approach, the purchases peak in the month immediately preceding a selling peak, and the inventories peak at the beginning of peak selling months.

Month by month, a schedule of amounts of allowable purchase commitments is constructed in the manner of Exhibit 2. We also maintain a record for keeping track of purchase commitments made for every month. At the end of each month (or more frequently) all future purchase orders which have been placed are costed out, added in the appropriate month columns, and posted to a cumulative record (Exhibit 3), where they are subtracted from the previously available commitment allowance remaining from the prior month. At each posting, it is immediately possible to see how much remaining "purchasing power" is uncommitted.

Projected Inventory Needs

	January	February	November	December	Total	Average
1) Net sales	17370	11730	21210	34230	239240	19940
2) Cost of goods sold (66% of net sales)	11460	7740	14000	22590	158000	13160
3) Sales as a % of an average month's sales	87.1%	58.3%	106.4%	171.6%		100%
4) Inventory needed as % of average stock level	93.3%	76.4%	103.0%	131.1%		100%
5) B.O.M. inventory (line 4 x ave. inventory level) (a)	49100	41220	54220	69000		(a) 52640

(a) To achieve an annual turnover of 3.0, average stock must equal four times the average monthly cost of goods sold.

EXHIBIT 1

Computation of Monthly Purchasing Requirements

	January	February	September	October	November	December
Needed for:						
This month's sales (cost)	11460	7740	15700	13360	14000	22590
End of month inventory (a)	41220	54700	53170	54220	69000	49100
Total needs	52680	62440	68870	67580	83000	71690
Less: available beginning of this month	49100	41220	57430	53170	54220	69000
Purchases for delivery this month	3580	21220	11440	14410	28780	2690

(a) Same as next month's beginning inventory

EXHIBIT 2

Records may also be kept in the usual way for pairs. However, when a buyer orders he has to not only consider the sizes in stock but he also has to face the "budget" limitations of the dollar-available-to-buy position for the future delivery month.

FLEXIBILITY FOR DEPARTMENTAL MANAGERS

An absolute and intractable application of the above procedure would have a negative psychological effect on the manager and/or buyer. It is tempered with some discretionary buying authority. Not only does the buyer need some discretionary fund for taking quick advantage of merchandise items that catch a sudden public fancy, or for promotional events, but he needs to feel that he still has something to say about purchases, unhampered by the somewhat mechanistic inventory level device we have developed. Thus, as a part of the purchases control package, we provide that each month he may exercise a discretionary purchasing fund *outside* the purchase limitations arrived at here, amounting to an arbitrary percentage (perhaps 10 percent or less) of the month's purchase quota, or $300, whichever is greater. Any unused *discretionary* purchase authority may be carried over for use in succeeding months. However, unused *scheduled* purchase commitment authority for a given month may not be carried over.

	January	February			November	December
Cumulative Open-To-Buy Positions Allowed						
Open position, forward, 1/1/6x ($)	480	720			28780	2690
Orders placed, January	364	780			–	–
Uncommitted balance 2/1	116	(60)			28780	2690
Orders placed, February		20			–	–
Uncommitted balance, 3/1		(80)			28780	2690
Orders placed, March						
Uncommitted balance, 4/1						

EXHIBIT 3

LIMITATIONS

One serious problem in application is the trade practice in manufacturing and shipping of footwear. Orders are placed four to six months in advance of delivery, and manufacturers often ship far in advance of the peak selling seasons to avoid having serious storage problems at their plants. The effect is for the retailer to take delivery

REVISION OF INVENTORY AND PURCHASING SCHEDULES

| | Inventories [a] | | Purchases | |
Month	Actual	As Rescheduled	As Made	As Rescheduled
J	49900	49100	12280	3580
F	55500	41220	15550	21220
M	63340	54700	15470	8580
A	64650	49060	7260	13230
M	60470	50850	2910	12650
J	51080	51200	5760	10400
J	44400	49160	6060	10840
A	39000	48530	22200	20090
S	50000	57430	10200	11440
O	44500	53170	21600	14410
N	52740	54220	18730	28780
D	57470	69000	14270	2690

[a] Beginning-of-month balances

EXHIBIT 4

perhaps two months before he really needs the footwear. So the items show up as August purchases, for instance, when they are really for October selling. The applier of the recommended technique must then adjust his target ratios or provide for a careful identification of purchases by the month for which they are actually intended.

The effects of changing holidays (such as Easter) must also be taken into account when planning the respective month's purchase allowables.

SHIFTING OF PURCHASING PLANS

Exhibit 4 shows the change in purchase commitment patterns that were scheduled as a result of applying the above technique in one retail shoe department, and the changes in beginning-of-month inventory balances. It is noticeable that, as a result of this procedure, inventory balances take the same time pattern as sales, except that inventory fluctuations are dampened and inventories peak just before each sales peak (Exhibit 5).

No attempt was made here to reduce inventories, but merely to hold their level at a point which will ensure a continuation of the existing turnover rate. However, the next step is to apply the procedure further, with a planned increase in the turnover rate by a planned reduction in inventory levels. This is not done suddenly and arbitrarily, but is accomplished gradually. The improved inventory usage policy is thus placed into effect over a period of time and in a systematic manner.

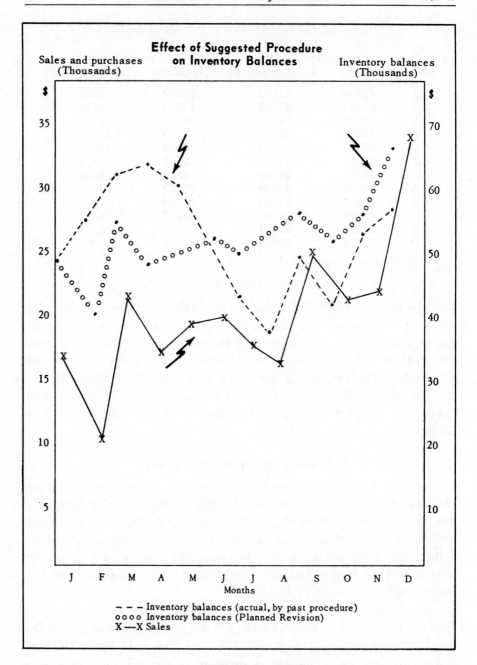

Effect of Suggested Procedure on Inventory Balances

Sales and purchases (Thousands)

Inventory balances (Thousands)

Months

J F M A M J J A S O N D

- - - Inventory balances (actual, by past procedure)
o o o o Inventory balances (Planned Revision)
X —X Sales

EXHIBIT 5

The economic payoff of the method comes only when an average inventory reduction has been achieved to the point where reduced carrying cost of stock (and reduction in markdowns due to excess stock carry-overs) will compensate for the extra clerical work involved. An *immediate* payoff should not be expected; it takes a year or more before the effects of this technique can be observed in economic terms.

52. TECHNIQUES FOR BUDGETING ADMINISTRATIVE AND COMMERCIAL EXPENSES *

Francis C. Reith †

In budgeting administrative and commercial expense there appears to be considerably less standard practice than in most other fields of budgetary control. In many respects, it seems that industry has concentrated its scientific cost control endeavors in the factory. As a result, administrative and commercial expense represents a comparatively new field of budgetary control, one in which there is much opportunity for the development of new techniques. However, as a general rule, the most difficult problems with respect to "A and C" budgets are not those of a procedural nature, i.e., the mechanics of budget preparation, the use of budgets as a means of expense forecasting, and the establishment of reports for the control of actual expenses to approved budgets. These procedural problems ordinarily can be solved by the adaptation of techniques successfully tested and used in other fields of budgetary control and cost analysis.

The real problem and the real challenge in budgeting administrative and commercial expenses lies in the analysis and evaluation of these expenses. Generally speaking, they do not lend themselves to the same type of analysis and control as direct labor and indirect manufacturing expense. Furthermore, within the scope of "A and C" budgets there are many different types of expense, each of which requires a somewhat different technique or approach insofar as its evaluation is concerned. Accordingly, this paper is devoted primarily to the problems of evaluation and analysis rather than to procedural matters.

WHAT EXPENSES ARE INCLUDED?

For convenience, the terms "administrative budgets" and "administrative expenses" will be used throughout the remainder of this

* From *N.A.C.A. Bulletin* (April 1, 1949). Reprinted by permission of the National Association of Cost Accountants.
† Francis C. Reith was Manager, Administrative Budget Department of Ford Motor Company, at the time this article was written.

paper as relating to all expenses of an administrative, selling, and engineering nature. Undoubtedly considerable variation exists among companies with respect to classification of administrative expenses. Nevertheless, the different types of expense listed below are normally considered within the scope of administrative budgets and may be cited as a reasonably comprehensive list:

Executive offices	Industrial relations	Advertising
Public relations	Purchasing	Sales promotion
Legal	Finance	Product service
Engineering	Accounting	Warehousing
Research	Office services	Stock control
		Shipping

The inclusion of industrial relations and purchasing in the above list may raise a question. In most companies these expenses are perhaps considered a part of manufacturing operations and, therefore, included in manufacturing overhead budgets. However, larger companies which have purchasing and industrial relations central staff activities may include the expense of these staff organizations in their administrative budgets. Under such an arrangement, it is also advisable that the company executives responsible for these functions in the central staff develop standards for the cost of their function in decentralized operations and periodically review actual costs against these standards.

Responsibility Must Be Fixed and Acknowledged

In the development of an administrative budget program which is intended primarily as a tool for cost reduction and as an incentive for improved efficiency, the following principles should govern, and be a part of, the budget system:

1. Assign unmistakable organization responsibility for all expenses included in the program.

2. Require each responsible executive to develop an annual operating program.

3. Require each responsible executive to thoroughly analyze all elements of the anticipated cost and personnel requirements of his operating program.

4. Develop expense standards or yardsticks to indicate where savings can be made and to provide an incentive for cost reduction.

5. Require each responsible executive to justify his proposed expenditures before the company's principal operating committee. Insure recognition for accomplishment.

Perhaps the most important requirement in a program for cost reduction is the one given first in the above enumeration and implied in the remaining principles, i.e., that the executives of the company responsible for incurring the expenses be clearly identified and that they recognize and accept responsibility for expense control as an integral part of their respective jobs. In most cases, the chief executive of the company and the budget department can only provide the incentive and the tools for good expense control. In the final analysis, it is primarily the executives responsible for utilization of personnel, for supervising the operations, and determining the policies and practices governing the cost of the operation, who can achieve important economies.

In contrast to manufacturing operations, many of the activities covered by administrative budgets represent jobs which are not routine and continuous, and thus are not measurable on a quantitative basis. As a result, an annual operating program is an important requirement on which to build a good budget. Further, as an aid in ascertaining where savings can be made, the responsible executive should have expense standards or yardsticks, usually developed jointly by his staff and the budget department. If these matters are taken seriously and a program adopted under which the responsible executive is required to justify his proposed expenditures before the company's principal operating committee, the basic ingredients for an aggressive expense reduction program are present.

Four Types of Expense: Four Techniques for Budgetary Analysis

From an analytical point of view, there are several types of expenses and related budgets and, therefore, it is not advisable to use one technique or one method in the evaluation of all types. For purposes of this discussion, all administrative budgets have been arranged in four groups, each of which requires a different type of analytical approach. Following are the groups, with typical examples of each:

Appropriation	Profit and Loss	Expense Standard	Administrative
Advertising	Publications	Sales offices	Industrial relations
Public relations	Printing	Parts warehousing	Purchasing
Engineering	Building services	Loading and ship-	Accounting
Sales promotion	Food services	ping	

The remainder of this paper is devoted to a discussion, with illustrations, of effective means of evaluating the budget amounts for each of these four groups.

Appropriation Type Activities

Definition. Budgets within this group cover activities which do not involve a recurring, administrative type of responsibility but which, in the main, are operated on a program or project basis.

Method. With respect to activities of this type, the following is an effective method of budgetary control:

1. Distribute actual expenses on a project basis.
2. Prepare budgets on basis of projects or programs, including comparisons with previous periods and with expenditures likely to be made beyond the current budget year.
3. Include with the budgets an indication of the results which will be obtained for the amount of money spent on the respective projects.

Illustration.

	Proposed Expenditures in 1949	Expenditures in—		Total Estimated Expenditures for Project
		Previous Periods	Future Periods	
Development of reversible propeller	$165,000	$131,000	$151,000	$447,000

The development of budgets on a project basis for appropriation type of expense has the dual advantage of (1) insuring that the budgeted amounts will be related to the job to be done and (2) providing the reviewing agency with an indication of what is intended to be accomplished with the requested amount of money. Beyond these basic requirements, the budget department should determine additional important bases of evaluation. For example, an indication of the effectiveness of advertising through the use of Starch reports for magazines, Nielson and Hooper studies for radio, etc., provides helpful information in reviewing proposed advertising expenditures.

The budgetary handling of this category of administrative expense may perhaps be made even more concrete by the following examples of special data helpful in evaluating certain of the appropriation type budgets:

Advertising

1. Analyze by (a) media, (b) product, and (c) program.
2. Convert to dollars per unit or percent of sales.
3. Compare with previous periods and with competition.
4. Measure the effectiveness of media, current programs, and themes.

Engineering

1. Analyze by (a) product and (b) project.
2. Convert to dollars per unit.
3. Compare with previous periods and with competition.

Public Relations

1. Analyze by program.
2. Convert to percent of sales.

Profit-and-Loss Type Activities

Definition. Budgets within this group generally cover activities of a service nature and it is usually possible to compare the cost of the operation with an outside competitive price.

Method. For activities of this type, the following method is an effective basis of expense control:

1. Establish operations on a clearly segregated basis.
2. Develop forecasts of requirements for services to be rendered.
3. Assess using activities for services rendered, employing *outside* comparative data as a basis for pricing services.
4. Budget expenses (on a variable basis where possible) to control costs within established service prices.

Illustration. Assuming that a company owns the building housing its administrative offices, the costs of which are reflected in the company's administrative expenses, the annual budget would be developed as shown in Exhibit 1 if the method outlined above is used. This arrangement measures the costs of operating the building

BUILDING OPERATIONS

Proposed Budget

A. *Proposed 1949 Expenses*

Estimated Income from Services Rendered		$525,000
Proposed Operating Expenses:		
Salaries	$155,300	
Materials	63,000	
Maintenance	82,400	
Taxes	46,500	
Depreciation	189,800	537,000
Estimated Net Profit or (Loss)		$(12,000)

B. *Historical Progress*

Period	Total Expenses	Rate per Sq. Foot
1947	$777,000	$5.18
1948	636,000	4.24
1949	537,000	3.58
Objective		3.20

Exhibit 1

against what is, in effect, a standard which represents the cost to the company if the building were being rented. In the event that present costs are in excess of the standard, the budget can be used to measure the progress of the manager of these operations in reaching the objective and, when the objective is achieved, controlling his costs within the standard. Where the volume warrants it, the use of a similar approach (on a variable budget basis where feasible) is particularly beneficial for such operations as print shops, publications, cafeteria and restaurant services, etc.

Administrative Type Activities

Definition. The administrative type covers activities of the company which have a continuing, routine type of operation but where the work, in the main, is not measurable on a quantitative basis and where payroll represents the most important individual item of expense.

Method. The following is an effective method of developing budgets for activities of this type:

1. Develop annual operating plan in terms of functions to be performed and the anticipated level of activity.
2. *Examine functions in light of the possibility of eliminating those that are unnecessary.*
3. Express operating plan in terms of personnel requirements and dollar costs.
4. Compare with previous periods.
5. Apply yardsticks and factors to traveling expenses, long-distance telephone calls, supplies, employees served, etc.

Illustration. See Exhibit 2.

One of the best methods of effecting cost reduction in expenses of administrative type activities is the development of measures designed to persuade and encourage economical efforts on the part of the executives responsible for these operations. Ordinarily the budget department will achieve effective results by the very establishment of procedures and requirements as outlined above. Further, the presentation of the budget in the manner illustrated—after it has been developed and submitted by the activity—will provide the operating executive with a thorough analysis of his budget, pointing up areas which appear out of line and giving him credit for the progress he has made in the preparation of this budget. More important, this analysis provides the reviewing agency with a means of evaluating the budget.

PROPOSED PURCHASING BUDGET

Analysis Summary:

The proposed purchasing budget for 1949 is $1,142,000 and provides for 285 employees as of December 31. This represents a *reduction* in expenses of $110,800 or 8.8 percent and in personnel of 37 or 11.5 percent from 1948 actuals. $62,800 of the saving represents salaries of the 23 employees saved by combining the purchase research and ....

Table 1

Proposed Personnel Strength and Expenses

	Proposed 1949	Actual 1948	(Increase) Decrease
Personnel:			
Salaried	248	278	30
Hourly	37	44	7
Total	285	322	37
Expenses:			
Salaries	$793,600	$889,800	$96,200
Supplies	40,700	37,500	(3,200)
Travel	22,900	16,500	(6,400)
Telephone	18,000	15,300	(2,700)
Services purchased (etc.) .	42,400	65,800	23,400

Exhibit 2

Expense Standard Type Activities

Definition. This type covers those activities incurring administrative expenses with respect to which there are a number of installations performing essentially the same function and where the results of the activities can be measured on a quantitative basis.

Method. Probably the best budget for this type of activity is one based on standards developed through industrial engineering analyses, institution of uniform operations and procedures, time studies, and so forth. While such a budget should be the ultimate goal for expense standard type activities, a period of at least one year will usually be required to effect such a program. Where more immediate results are required, it is frequently possible to develop valuable comparative performance measures and, using data on the most efficient installations, to establish standards for application to all installations. The following method has been found effective under such circumstances:

1. Classify operations and expenses into management areas.
2. Arrange for accumulation of actual expenses on this basis.
3. Prepare comparative analysis of historical data.
4. Develop standard budget allowances, using a variable budget system.

Illustration. Assume that a budget is to be established for the parts merchandising activities of a particular company with six warehouse locations. Analysis indicates that the activity logically falls into, say, four functions: stock handling, stock control, accounting, and administrative and service. For each function, in turn, there are such expense categories as salaries and wages, materials, freight, depreciation, utilities, etc. A standard budget allowance, both nonvariable and variable, should be determined for each of these functions, by expense category.

Taking the salaries and wages expense of the stock handling function as an example (Exhibit 3), plot on a single graph the monthly performance of actual expense against volume of stock handled for each of the six warehouses for the preceding 12 months. A standard can then be selected on the basis of the pattern set by the 72 plottings, using, say, the most efficient one third. This standard should then be reviewed with operating supervision and, after necessary revisions have been made, given to the six warehouse managers as their standard budget allowance.

Standards set in this manner are particularly effective on a variable budget basis where this is practical. As indicated in the above illustration, variable budget standards have the important advantages of:

1. Providing an incentive to the management of the operations which are out of line, and
2. Indicating the high cost installations to central management for its immediate action.

CONTROL OF ADMINISTRATIVE COSTS A PROFITABLE ENDEAVOR

In closing, it might be noted that many companies are now giving more attention to controlling administrative and commercial expenses than they have in the past. Naturally the amount of money and effort expended for such budgeting and cost control must be related to the expected cost savings. It has been my experience, confirmed by others in this field, that wherever such attention and effort have been given, the resulting savings have paid for the cost of the program many times over.

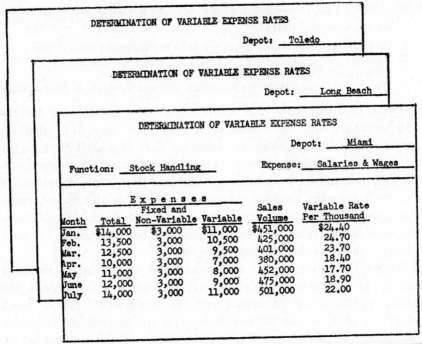

DETERMINATION OF VARIABLE EXPENSE RATES

Depot: Toledo

DETERMINATION OF VARIABLE EXPENSE RATES

Depot: Long Beach

DETERMINATION OF VARIABLE EXPENSE RATES

Depot: Miami

Function: Stock Handling   Expense: Salaries & Wages

| | | Expenses | | | |
Month	Total	Fixed and Non-Variable	Variable	Sales Volume	Variable Rate Per Thousand
Jan.	$14,000	$3,000	$11,000	$451,000	$24.40
Feb.	13,500	3,000	10,500	425,000	24.70
Mar.	12,500	3,000	9,500	401,000	23.70
Apr.	10,000	3,000	7,000	380,000	18.40
May	11,000	3,000	8,000	452,000	17.70
June	12,000	3,000	9,000	475,000	18.90
July	14,000	3,000	11,000	501,000	22.00

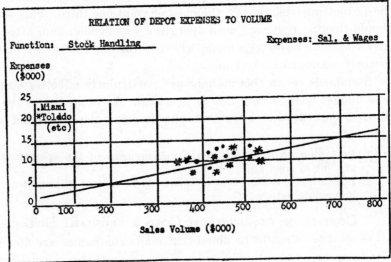

RELATION OF DEPOT EXPENSES TO VOLUME

Function: Stock Handling   Expenses: Sal. & Wages

Expenses ($000)

.Miami
*Toledo
(etc)

Sales Volume ($000)

Exhibit 3

53. REDUCING CLERICAL COSTS THROUGH IMPROVED MANPOWER UTILIZATION *

Charles H. Grady, Jr. †

The cost of clerical services can be reduced when proven supervisory techniques are brought to bear on clerical operations, wherever they occur. Financial executives are concerned, however, because such techniques are not generally understood or used by clerical supervisors. The financial executives naturally seek reversal of the rapid increase in the ratio of clerical to production workers.

The disproportionate increase in office staffs is sometimes interpreted as an unavoidable by-product of modern business complexity. However, to cope with this, the office (as well as the factory) has been provided with much time-saving equipment. Like the factory, the office has had systems modernizations, organizational improvements, programs for simplifying work, streamlining procedures, and measuring work. Still, the trend persists. Why?

Compare the average day of a clerical supervisor with that of his factory counterpart, and some of the reasons for this trend become apparent. While the factoy supervisor spends a large portion of his time in planning and directing the activities of his people, the clerical supervisor busily processes individual work items—usually the most difficult ones. Unfortunately, the clerical supervisor does not see himself as a production planner and overseer of the activities of each person in his operation, but as the person best qualified to answer questions and give technical advice. What he needs is to improve his control of manpower utilization.

NEED FOR IMPROVED MANPOWER UTILIZATION

The factory supervisor ends each day with a review of the day's activities (actual vs. scheduled production) and lays his plans for

---

* From N.A.A. Bulletin—Management Accounting (March, 1965). Reprinted by permission of the National Association of Accountants.
† Charles H. Grady, Jr., Administrative Services Department of Arthur Andersen and Company.

tomorrow's operations. He determines the locations and volumes of the backlogs, their priorities, and develops a plan for making work assignments the following morning.

By way of contrast, the clerical supervisor usually ends his day in much the same manner as his clerks. He puts his work away for the night (after taking care of the last "hot" item of the day) and goes home. The clerical supervisor does no planning for tomorrow, because each clerk follows a regular routine in working on his particular jobs and duties. Incoming items to be processed are routed automatically to the clerks who do those jobs—consequently, the work flows without direct control.

Of course, the office supervisor often wonders why, with this well-established routine, there are so many fires to put out. More often than not, while he is concentrating his efforts on "pushing and pulling" individual work items through the office, some clerks have run out of work or are stretching out the work that is available. Meanwhile, other clerks may have excessive backlogs which are creating bottlenecks. These bottlenecks, in turn, are adding to the problems that the supervisor himself will eventually have to handle.

If the reader concurs with this general comparison of the operational methods of production and clerical supervisors, he must conclude that the clerical supervisor does not control his operation and does not direct the activities of his people as effectively as the factory supervisor. This, then, may be one of the primary reasons for the continued trend toward larger proportions of clerical workers in relation to production workers.

The productivity of any factory or office preparation, and the resultant size of the work force, will depend upon the degree of adherence exercised by supervision and management to three basic operating principles. These are the principles of organization, procedures, and manpower utilization. Since the office operation has generally kept pace with the factory in organizational and procedural advances, it is primarily in the area of better manpower utilization that a reversal of the trend toward larger clerical staffs can best be achieved.

If manpower utilization is not effectively controlled by the supervisor, it is almost always necessary to "play it safe" by staffing with enough people to cover all possibilities of peak loads, vacations, absenteeism, etc. This providing for maximum needs is a natural reaction of a supervisor and will continue until he is provided with tools, and training in their use, that will enable him to effectively control the workload and the activities of the people assigned to him.

Steps to Effective Clerical Cost Reduction

Clerical managers generally agree that techniques used in controlling factory production operations do not apply to clerical activities. However, this does not mean that effective manpower utilization methods cannot be developed and put into use in most paper handling operations. Indeed, forward-looking management in numerous companies has proved the cost reducing ability of methods that have been used to improve manpower utilization. By controlling and scheduling clerical work, the number of people needed to handle the load has been cut.

No manpower utilization program can be entirely successful without the support and overall control of management. After an effective system for scheduling and controlling clerical work has been implemented, management should be able to evaluate cost controls by obtaining periodic performance reports from supervisors. A performance report is an integral part of a manpower utilization system and should be installed on a continuing basis.

To control the flow of work, as well as the number of man-hours used to process work, the supervisor must have the means of determining, and then using, the following information:

1. The volume of work received in the clerical group.
2. The amount of time that it should take to process known volume of work—either expected performance or standard time.
3. The nature of the "peaks and valleys" in the overall work flow, as well as in the workload of each clerk.
4. The amount of time that is actually used to process units of work—actual performance.
5. The overall status of work in the clerical group—backlogs, both as to quantity and age.

The use of each of these items is set forth below and commented upon in ensuing paragraphs, together with illustrations of sample forms that might be used in an effective manpower utilization improvement program. Finally, overall management manpower reports are discussed, to show how control data flows from supervisors to management.

Volumes of Work

There are three factors involved in determining the actual volume of work that is processed in each clerical area. First, the work must be broken down into measurable functions. Second, a way of measuring each function (which is a unit subject to measure) must be developed. Third, the volume of work processed within each work function must be obtained.

The logical first step for determining these factors in a clerical operation is to obtain a general description of each job by interviewing the supervisor. The factors needed to establish work volume for manpower utilization purposes are then detailed.

This listing of work functions is expanded until all functions in the clerical area have been identified, a unit of measure established, and volumes determined. All work of a *fixed* nature, as well as all *variable* volume functions, should be included.

Work Standards

It is necessary to establish a reasonable completion time (standard) for each work function. A means of measuring and determining the attainable performance of clerks is essential to controlling and scheduling work.

There are, however, wide differences of opinion on how to accomplish this essential step. The differences revolve around the two questions: (1) What work activities should be used as units of measure for setting standards? (2) What method should be used to set the standards?

A unit of measure is a complete series of work steps that has a definite beginning and end. In a typical example, an accounts payable operation, an invoice would be matched with a purchase order—the two documents would then be checked against a receiving record—a block stamp for approval and distribution purposes would be affixed—and the package of papers would then be passed on to another clerk. The unit of measure should be such a complete series of steps. If each step were considered a separate unit of measure, the work performance standards developed might be more exact, but would be unwieldy and impractical for most supervisors to use in making work assignments in their day-to-day operations.

In setting clerical standards, the more common methods used are:

Time Study—the measurement of work elements through use of a stop watch.

Predetermined Standard Data—time requirements for certain elemental work steps are measured and cataloged. By reference to the catalog, standards can be built up for various activities.

Log Sheets—employees record all functions performed and the time spent on each function.

Test Batches—the determination of actual performance on a given amount of work during a relatively short period of time.

Observation—actual performance of a function is observed, unknown to the person doing the work.

Supervisor Estimates—primarily applicable to functions which are difficult to test or observe, such as preparation of reports or maintenance of continuing logs or control sheets.

Without going into detail as to the advantages and disadvantages of each method, the writer has found the last three methods to be more satisfactory for the following reasons:

1. They are simple to apply. Test batches can be assigned directly by the supervisor, who records the number of units assigned and time consumed to complete the assignment. When a sufficient number of tests has been recorded, a standard can be determined. As a further check, the supervisor can observe performance on a known quantity of work and record the observation. Finally, on work which is difficult to test or observe, the supervisor can probably estimate a reasonable standard.
2. They are practical standards that can be used in making work assignments with predictable completion times. Since the standards set are based on actual performance, they are attainable.
3. They are more readily accepted by the supervisor and his clerks as being realistic. For this reason, they should be attained more frequently than any arbitrarily set standards.

The most important point to consider in setting clerical standards is that the mere existence of a standard in itself is of no use—its usefulness depends solely on how it will be used to increase clerical productivity.

Work Flow and Volume Fluctuations

After the determination of work volumes and establishment of work standards have been completed, the peaks and valleys in the work load, for each clerk and for the overall clerical operation, should be determined. This is essential in order to allow the supervisor to make timely shifts of people or work to take advantage of any complementary peaking between clerks during the normal work cycle, which may be daily, weekly or monthly.

In Exhibit 1, a preliminary analysis of five clerical positions has been made to determine relative individual loads during a month. This analysis shows that the cashiering positions have a heavy load during the first part of the month, that the reporting clerks are light at this time, and that the payroll clerk has a light day each Monday. Logically, a combination of work between the cashiering and reporting positions seems feasible. Assuming that cashiering receives heavy

Complementary Peaks in Workload

Position	Working Day of Month
	1 2 3 4 5 6 7 8 9 10 11 12 13 14 15 16 17 18 19 20 21
Cashier	Heavy / Normal / Light / Heavy
Asst. Cashier	Heavy / Normal / Light
Reporting Clerk (#1)	Light / 2-day Hvy. / Lgt. / 2-day Hvy. / Normal
Reporting Clerk (#2)	Light / 2-day Hvy. / Normal
Payroll Clerk	Monday light, Tues., Wed. normal, and Thurs., Fri. heavy each week.

EXHIBIT 1

volumes on Mondays, there is also a possibility of another combination with the payroll clerk, who has a light load each Monday. Naturally, further investigation is necessary, but the important first step is to determine where to look for complementary work loads. A simple chart of this type is helpful in making such a determination.

Measurement of Productivity

Successful development of manpower utilization controls rests on the design of working, and practical, tools for the supervisor to use (1) in making work assignments to individual clerks and (2) in comparing the actual performance of each clerk against the expected or standard performance.

The best choice of tool for a supervisor depends upon the nature of the clerical operation to be controlled. Accordingly, the method of assigning work and measuring employee performance must be tailored to fit each clerical operation. Described below are four methods that fit different kinds of circumstances.

Batch Method. A practical method is that of making direct assignments of a quantity of measured work to be completed within a predetermined (standard) period of time. By means of an assignment schedule, as illustrated in Exhibit 2, the supervisor, or a control

Assignment Schedule   Date ____10/14____

Employee	Activity	Assigned	Standard completion time (minutes)	Actual time Start	Stop	Elapsed	Remarks
Jane	A	30	90	9:00	10:50	1:10	Break incl.
Mabel	F	10	60	9:00	10:00	60	
Mary W.	C	65	150	9:00	11:55	1:55	
Mabel	H	22	60	10:15	12:00	1:05	45 min.ov. errors fr. Br. 3twice wk

EXHIBIT 2

Batch Flow Control Ticket

Batch __# 64__   # Items ___30___

Operation #	Date	Start time	Stop time	Elapsed time	Standard time	Item count	Remarks
1	6/2	8:00	9:00	60	60 Min.	30	
2	6/2	9:30	9:55	30	30	29	#36421 to
3	6/3	3:15	4:15	60	40	29	supervisor
4	6/3	4:30			150		
5					20		
6					20		

EXHIBIT 3

clerk, maintains a continuous record of the progress of work through the office. The assignment schedule shows specific work assignments that have been made to individual clerks, including an estimated amount of time to complete (standard completion time). Such a schedule provides the supervisor the data needed to make, at standard completion times, the assignment of more work. The performance of individual clerks can be evaluated by comparing standard to actual completion times.

As shown in Exhibit 2, Jane was assigned 30 units of Activity A work at 9:00 a.m. By referring to the standard time for processing

a unit of that activity, the supervisor determined the total time
that should be taken to process 30 units and entered the standard
completion time of 90 minutes. When Jane has completed the assignment, she reports for another assignment, and so on throughout
the day.

Typical types of clerical operations in which the batch assignment
system is used effectively are in a key punch section, a receivables
posting operation or an order entry department.

Flow Control Method. Another good method is to control the flow
of an operation where the same items move from one desk to another,
with different work steps being performed along the way. In such an
operation, items of work are grouped into batches with a flow control
ticket attached. Each work station posts the time spent on each
batch, with the flow control ticket remaining with the batch through
the entire operation. A typical batch-flow control ticket is illustrated
in Exhibit 3. This type of control enables the supervisor to (1) determine the status of work in process, (2) evaluate individual performance and (3) know the overall processing time (degree of service) of
his operation. A particular operation may be staffed with one or
more clerks.

At least two important items, from the supervisor's standpoint,
can be obtained from an analysis of the work on Batch 64, which is
at Operation 4 in Exhibit 3:

1. A processing delay of about one and one-half days occurred between
   Operations 2 and 3; on the other hand, Operation 4 started working
   on the batch only 15 minutes after receiving it. This situation should
   alert the supervisor to a possible bottleneck situation at Operation 3.
2. Although Operation 2 bettered the standard time slightly, Operation 3 exceeded the standard by 50 percent. The supervisor should
   investigate the reasons for this situation if low employee performance continues.

Typical clerical operations in which the flow control method is
readily used are in accounts payable, billing, and similar functions.

Combination of Assigned and Unassigned Work Method. In certain operations, while some work can be directly assigned, a time
allowance must be allocated to each clerk to perform duties which are
of a fixed or regular nature, or which are impractical for the supervisor to assign directly.

Exhibit 4 illustrates a control which can be used over both types
of functions. The day is divided into three assignment periods.

Processing Department – Daily Assignment Report

Date _____ 10/14

Name –	Mary			June			Helen			Mabel			Index	Prod. hours
Index	8/11	11/2	2/4:30	8/11	11/2	2/4:30	8/11	11/2	2/4:30	8/11	11/2	2/4:30		
Process loans, complete	3			2						3				
Process loans, partial							2							
Closing instructions				1			2							

Processing

Activity	By	Unit	Index
Process loans, complete	Proc.	File	40
Process loans, partial	Proc.	File	15
Closing instructions	Proc.	File	45

EXHIBIT 4

Functions which were not to be directly assigned were measured, and it was determined that in total they required approximately one and one-half hours daily. Work for the balance of the working day (six hours) is directly assigned, two measured hours for each period, at the times of day indicated on the schedule.

To make an assignment for each period, the supervisor (or a control clerk) must refer to the index of standards for the assignable functions. By using the standards, he can assign the equivalent of two hours work. Here, assignments have been made for the first period of the day. This enables him to know how each clerk is performing throughout the day and to compute individual productivity on a continuing basis.

Overall Forecast Method. In operations where most work comes directly to individual clerks (telephone applications or inquiries, walk-in customers, etc.), an indirect method of work assignment can often be designed based on a forecast of work loads expected on certain days of the month or week, and even at different times during the day. In such cases, staffing can be planned based on the forecast.

In conclusion, the main consideration in any type of assignment system is that it should enable the supervisor to match clerical man-hours available with work volumes on a timely basis. A system that simply reports, on an after-the-fact basis, that a certain number of hours were used to process a given volume of work is not a useful tool that permits a supervisor to increase, and then maintain, high productivity in his operation.

Backlog Controls

The last essential step for effective manpower utilization is to provide the supervisor with a method of keeping track of backlogs of work in his operation. To do this, he needs current data on the volumes of new work coming in to the operation, as well as the unit counts of work processed.

Generally speaking, large backlogs result in poor service being provided by the operation; on the other hand, low backlogs may indicate poor utilization of personnel. Using the standards that have been developed for measuring the productivity of the activities in operation, backlogs can be converted into hours of work. The supervisor is then able to balance man-hour requirements against the work backlog.

Shown in Exhibit 5 is a simple and easy to maintain schedule that a supervisor may use in controlling the overall backlog in his department. Daily figures are maintained on incoming items, completed work, and backlogs. In this example of 20 "A" work units received on Monday, 18 were completed. The backlog at the end of the day was 42 units (in this example, a backlog of 40 units was left over from the previous week). The standard completion time for Work Unit A is two units per hour. Production and backlog can be converted into hours of work by multiplying unit volumes by the standard for each volume.

Weekly Volume and Backlog Summary

Week ending 10/14

Work Unit	Monday Units In	Out	Backlog	Backlog in standard hours	Weekly totals Units In	Out	Standards hours In	Out	Backlog
A	20	18	42*	21	91	128	45	64	2
B	175	140	80	10	680	674	85	88	7
C	360	200	420	70	1550	1600	258	266	35
D	17	17	–	–	73	73	18	18	–
E	10	6	4	4	41	41	41	41	–
F	7	8	8	16	43	45	86	90	14
Misc.				10			50	40	10
Total backlog hours				131			583	607	68

* Includes backlog from the previous week.

EXHIBIT 5

Such forms enable the supervisor to control the normal routine of his department on a daily basis by constantly relating individual work assignments to expected completion times. By knowing the status of work backlogs of the operation on a continuing basis, the supervisor does not need to "play it safe" with excess staffing. He can relate actual manpower requirements to actual work volumes and staff his operation accordingly, usually at pronounced cost reduction.

CONTROL BY MANAGEMENT

Management's administration of this system is exercised by means of a regular performance report from the supervisor. Once the control system is implemented and management is convinced that the staffing is correct for the existing volumes of work, the performance report should be used by management for its evaluation of supervisors, as well as the clerical force as a whole. If performance reporting is not maintained on a continuing basis, management has no way of evaluating supervisory controls; much of the time, effort, and expense in implementing the system has been wasted.

Performance reporting is an important aid to the supervisor in maintaining the system. To his people, it demonstrates management's solid backing, to the supervisor it gives the knowledge that management is interested in his operations, that it knows his area is staffed realistically and that his future staffing needs are likely to be reviewed objectively as changing work loads indicate.

The form and frequency of reporting performance should depend on the size and nature of the operation. Essentially, the report should indicate (1) volume processed, (2) number of hours that should have been expended (standard hours), and (3) hours actually used. The *productivity* of the operation is expressed in terms of standard hours compared to actual hours as a percentage. Performance reports must be tailored to the operation; they can include such data as individual productivity, backlogs of work and age of backlogs, etc.

Results of Establishing Control

After installation of such a program designed to strengthen manpower utilization, the supervisor of a clerical operation in any department should be able to assure control of an effective and economical operation: he would have the tools with which to supervise, he would know when and what action should be taken to clear up any trouble areas, his clerks would be receiving an equitable distribution of work, a good worker could be rewarded, a poor worker could be shown how to improve.

Management then knows that the clerical operations are realistically staffed, and is also provided with the means of evaluating supervisors' requests to increase or decrease the staff—based not merely on conjecture, but on actual work load requirements. The management that has the ability to relate available manpower to actual work volume has effective manpower utilization and a confident control over clerical costs.

54. PROFIT PERFORMANCE MEASUREMENT OF DIVISION MANAGERS *

Joel Dean †

I. INTRODUCTION

In introduction we shall touch on (A) the importance, (B) the difficulty, and (C) the role of profit centers in measuring executive performance.

A. Importance

Measuring executive performance is important in five ways:

1. It directs top management's supervision and assistance to where it is most needed and where it will be most productive.
2. It shapes the future executive team by indicating whom to promote, whom to retain, and whom to remove.
3. It directs the activity of executives toward high scores on the aspects of performance on which they are measured and judged.
4. It gives job satisfaction directly by letting the executive know how he is doing.
5. It provides the objective, factual foundation for sound incentive compensation.

B. Difficulty

Measuring executive performance in a big company is difficult. The performance you want to measure is achievement of the company's goals. Measuring the executive's contribution to this achievement is made complex by the fact that the corporation usually has several objectives which overlap and in some degree conflict: profits, growth, market share, and eternal life.

Profits should be the corporation's dominant goal in view of its obligation to stockholders and to a free enterprise society, but other

---

* From *The Controller* (September, 1957). Reprinted by permission of the Controllers Institute of America, Inc.

† Joel Dean, president of Joel Dean Associates, Inc., is an economic and management consultant as well as Professor of Business Economics in the Graduate School of Business, Columbia University.

objectives contribute in diffuse ways to long-run profits and thus cannot be ignored in measuring executive performance. Hence, the main executive performance you want to measure is contribution to the corporation's profits today and tomorrow.

The problem is made more difficult by the fact that facets of executive activity are numerous and contribute to profits in complex ways. There are few profit determining activities that are absolutely good or bad in themselves. To make the most money often requires foregoing a high score in one activity in order to push another (e.g., high quality product vs. low cost of making it).

To combine performance measures to separate activities requires proper weights which are hard to determine and change continuously. For example, a textile mill manager is scored on (1) quality control, (2) cost compared with standards, (3) safety, (4) equipment modernity, (5) production volume, (6) meeting delivery deadlines. How should these facets of performance be weighted?

Thus, responsibility for profits in a big company is in danger of being diffused. This makes measurement hard and cuts economic efficiency of the firm. Decentralization, i.e., setting up profit centers, is a promising way to overcome this diffusion of profit responsibility.

C. Role of Profit Center Decentralization

For measuring performance, executives can be put in two groups: (1) staff specialists, (2) businessmen, i.e., profit center (i.e., division) managers.

Complex problems of measuring and weighting executives' contributions to profits are best solved by dividing the corporation into semiautonomous profit centers whose management is measured by the contributions his center makes to corporation's overhead and profits.

A big, integrated multiple-product company functions best if made into a miniature of the competitive free enterprise economy. You can do this by dividing firms into independent operating units which act like economic entities free to trade outside as well as inside the company.

Powered with the right incentives, each profit center in maximizing its own contribution profits will do what will also maximize the profits of the entire company. It works the same way that selfish profit-seeking by individual firms in a private enterprise society generates the high productivity and automatic economic adjustments of a competitive economy.

II. Requirements for
Profit Center Performance Measurement

To make a profit center system achieve these desired results of stimulating and measuring executive performance, it is necessary to:

A. Mark off profit centers correctly.

B. Establish economically sound intracompany transfer prices and business arrangements.

C. Measure the contribution profits of the profit center correctly.

D. Determine realistic standards of contribution profit performance.

E. Establish incentives in the form of executive compensation and non-monetary rewards that will induce profit center managers to do what will be best for the corporation as a whole.

A. Profit Center Boundaries

The problem of marking off profit center boundaries has two aspects: (1) segregating service functions from profit centers, (2) defining the scope of each profit center.

Service centers comprise staff activities which cannot be satisfactorily measured in terms of profit performance. Profit centers and service centers shade into one another so that each company's solution needs to be different. The contribution of a service center to company profitability may be great but is hard to isolate and measure definitively.

The problem of gearing staff service to profit performance is partly solved by pulverizing staff services and distributing among profit centers, where the activity must be justified economically.

Some services could be sold on a profit center basis but institutional arrangements would be too complicated and burdensome, e.g., engineering. Some services might not be used enough or in the right way if made a profit center, e.g., legal department or economics department.

The second problem is to define the scope of each profit center. A profit center is defined as a semiautonomous group of facilities and functions chosen so that profit performance can be the main guide to evaluation of divisional performance and the main guide by which the division manager makes his critical decisions.

Decisions involve economic choices among mutually exclusive courses of action. Each decision requires balancing of various kinds of costs and revenues. The company's interest lies not in maximizing a particular kind of revenue or minimizing a particular kind of cost in isolation but in maximizing difference between all revenues and all costs. Hence the scope for profit performance measurement should be a major guide in marking off profit center boundaries.

The details of divisional boundaries and institutional arrangements are important. Failures and frustrations of decentralization are often traceable to bad boundaries and rules. Boundary lines determine how well a particular profit center functions in the corporation's interests, i.e., minimize conflicts of interest. Good boundaries make the profit performance of the division manager more meaningful, produce better incentives, supervision, and development guides.

Four economic tests can be applied in marking off profit centers: (1) operational independence, (2) access to sources and markets, (3) separable costs and revenues, and (4) managerial intent.

1. *Operational Independence*

Unless a division has a large measure of independence it will have inadequate scope to reach decisions on a profit-oriented basis and hence delegation will be defeated. The division manager needs discretion over buying, production, scheduling, inventories, product mix, and pricing. This discretion should be exercised under broad rules of the game established centrally.

2. *Access to Sources and Markets*

Independent access to sources and markets is essential if make-or-buy decisions are to be made correctly. It is also essential for make-or-sell decisions, i.e., choice between selling a product at an early stage of the process or later (e.g., cured vs. uncured hams).

Access to outside sources and markets is most useful if outside markets are highly flexible in the long run, i.e., capable of either supplying or absorbing the company's needs without extreme price disturbances. Markets which appear too imperfect in the short run frequently are not over a period of months or years, e.g., major components of an automobile.

3. *Separable Costs and Revenues*

Profit centers should be marked off so as to minimize the necessity for cost and revenue allocations, since these are necessarily arbitrary and contentious.

Contribution profits of the division can be defined so as to exclude central and other costs outside the profit center manager's control. But when these controllable profits are too small a part of the total a profit center does no good.

4. *Managerial Intent*

No division's contribution can be measured solely by its profits but this must be a good measure of performance if the division is to be a profit center.

Top management must be resolved to abide by the behavior and performance and the impersonal guidance of the price system which this measure of divisional performance implies.

B. Economic Transfer Prices

A second underlying requisite of effective profit center controls is competitive intracompany transfer prices negotiated in arm's length bargaining by profit center managers.

Transfer pricing must preserve profit-making autonomy of the division manager so that his divisional profit performance will coincide with the interests of the company. Small differences in unit price of transfer products make big differences in division profits and executive bonuses.

Conflicts of interests can be held at a minimum by transfers at marginal cost, but this prevents meaningful division profit performance and undercuts the main gains of profit center control.

Competitive negotiated transfer prices can be obtained by applying three simple principles:

1. Buyers and sellers completely free to deal outside or inside the company.
2. Prices determined by negotiation between buyers and sellers with a minimum of arbitration.
3. Negotiators have access to data on alternative sources and markets and have facilities for using the markets.

C. Measurement of Profit Contribution

A third requirement is good measurement of the profit contribution of the division. Performance measurement of profit center management must be geared to the multiple and overlapping goals of the corporation.

Performance Areas

Key performance areas can be grouped and labeled in various ways. One pattern is:

1. *Current Profitability*, the dominant measurement, will be discussed later.
2. *Growth* is usually conceived as sales growth, either absolutely or relatively to the industry. Frequently it is best measured in terms

of market share. In whatever way it is measured, growth usually requires the development of a market franchise. This is generally achieved at the expense of some short-run profits. But presumably, it contributes to more distant profits and hence it is a part of the picture of the management's profit performance.

3. *Progress* has many dimensions. Three important ones are
   a. Investment in ideas. Research is at the expense of short-run profits, designed for long-run survival.
   b. Modernity and acceptability of the product. Sometimes this, too, causes short-run profit sacrifice.
   c. Productivity. This can be indicated by output per man-hour and rate of return on facilities investments.

4. *Executive Development:* investment in people for future profits.

The last three factors—growth, progress, and people—though measurable in their components, are hard to weigh and reconcile with current profitability. The key question is whether the right amount of near profits were sacrificed in attaining these various determinants of distant profits. The answer requires high-level judgment and technical familiarity with the kinds of investment in market franchise, in ideas, in facilities, and in people that are entailed.

Measurement of the current profitability of a division entails three kinds of considerations:

   a. The concept of profits.
   b. The form in which that profit concept will be used.
   c. The measurement of profits.

Profit Concepts

As to the concept of profit there are three choices:

   1. Book net profits.
   2. Real net profits.
   3. Contribution profits.

Book net profits tie into the stockholder reports, have a surface acceptability, and are not very fudgible. But they embroil executives in fruitless debates about allocation of corporate overheads over which they have no control and raise moot questions about capital consumption costs of plant acquisitions at widely differing price levels.

Real net profits may settle the latter questions (inflation and depreciation) but do not settle problems of allocation of overhead beyond the division manager's control.

Contribution profits have fewer of these drawbacks being confined to costs and revenues over which the profit center manager has control.

Form of Profits

As to the form in which any of these three profit concepts may be expressed, there are three choices:

1. As dollar amounts.
2. As percentage of sales.
3. As a rate of return on investment.

All three forms are useful in measuring different aspects of executive performance. For best results each needs to be compared with a suitable bogey.

1. Contribution profit dollars aid economic decision making by focusing division management energies on dollars of added profit.
2. Contribution profits as a percent of sales facilitate comparison with past performance and with comparable outside companies. Standing alone and without a bogey this performance measure is misleading.
3. Contribution profits as a return on investment provides the most important guide to top management in evaluation of profit center performance.

Measurement of Profits

Technical problems of profit performance measurement are in practice less formidable than they appear to many newcomers.

A moderately good approximation to contribution profits can be drawn from most accounting systems with few adjustments given correct profit center demarcation and transfer prices. Isolating the book value of investment used by the division is always possible with some rough approximations.

Determination of the economic value of the book investment can be done quite cheaply with a tolerable degree of accuracy, once the concept is accepted. Current assets have book values and real values generally close enough together. Other assets can be adjusted to replacement value or disposal value by sampling and index numbers with adequate accuracy. If the concept of economic investment rather than book investment is unacceptable the defect is not fatal, particularly when the company has grown fast so that most of its assets are at recent price levels.

D. Standards of Profit Performance

Standards of profit performance, our fourth requirement, is a big, complex subject. In this analysis we can only mention four thoughts.

1. Measurement of profit performance of division managers achieves in itself many of the benefits of decentralization. Indeed a good case can be made for not attempting to formalize the standards of profit

performance. Instead, leave this to the informal judgment of top management, which must in any event tailor the standard to the individual division and take many dimensions of longer-term profit performance into account, e.g., growth, progress, and executive development.

2. Lack of standards should not hold up decentralization: rough standards can be used first and refined later.

3. Historical perspective is essential in developing performance standards: back-casting of comparable performance measurements will be needed.

4. Par for the profit center course should also take account of economic climate and competitive conditions in the industry. Sometimes this can be done roughly by comparison with the earnings of independent firms of approximately the same product line.

E. Incentive Compensation

The final requirement for effective profit center operation is incentives which will power the profit center manager to maximize his division's contribution-profits now and in the future. The following basic considerations should underly the development of a balanced plan for incentive compensation of the managers of profit center divisions:

1. Objective measurements of profit performance are in themselves incentives to the kind of man who makes a good division manager. But profit center control will be most effective if powered with incentive compensation which is geared dominantly to the contribution profits of the division.

2. Incentive compensation should fit the organizational environment and personality of the profit center management: (a) independence, (b) economic sophistication, and (c) minimal concern about bureaucratic politics. This means it should be geared to his division's performance.

3. Since incentives are a reward for extraordinary performance the base salary should approximate a competitive level and the ceiling or target bonus should be 40 to 50 percent of this salary though it is hard to find a principle to justify any ceiling.

4. The company's total incentive compensation fund should be based on a maximum percentage of corporate net income which may each year be put into the fund after deducting compensation for capital—a symbol of good faith to the stockholders. (Example, General Motors 12 percent of net income after deducting 5 percent of net capital.)

5. The amount of incentive compensation for any profit center manager should be determined by group judgment preferably at the board level based on multiple measurements of profit performance, compared when feasible with objectively determined standards.

6. Whether the payment should be in cash, in deferred compensation, or in stock options ought to be tailored to the financial personality of the manager rather than determined by uniform formula.

55. MONITORING CAPITAL INVESTMENTS *

L. C. Grant †

Capital investment computer programs have achieved widespread acceptance in a short time as a means of analyzing investments under consideration by financial management. In so doing they have won respect for the augmented investor's method—or discounted cash flow method—which until recently was regarded only in academic environments as the most beneficial of the many tools of financial analysis.

To date, the capital investment program has been used primarily in a static manner, i.e., as a tool for analyzing an investment before the investment is initiated. This article proposes that a dynamic approach be taken. Financial management is obviously just as concerned with the eventual progress of an investment as it is with a preview of what the results are expected to be. This approach to investment analysis would encompass both an initial preview and a convenient means of follow-up. Essentially, it is a Capital Investment Monitoring System, based upon IBM's Capital Investment Programs as they already exist with little or no modification.

For the reader not already familiar with these programs, all of which are nearly identical, it may be well to review the input options, the method, and the results achieved. The user provides the program with the following data:

I. Basic Data—total capital invested, maximum expected service life, and effective income tax rate.

II. Mode Option Data—

A. Depreciation—depreciable portion of total investment. Number of years over which to depreciate. Method of depreciation, whether straight line, declining balance, sum of the years' digits, or other.

* From the *Financial Executive* (April, 1963). Reprinted by permission of the Financial Executives Institute.

† L. C. Grant, IBM District Education Center, International Business Machines, Houston, Texas.

B. Salvage Values—portion of investment subject to salvage. **Value decline.** Number of years over which to reduce salvage value. Method of reducing salvage value, whether straight line, exponential decline, depreciable book value, or other.

C. Earnings or Savings Pattern—whether uniform, straight line decline, rapid decline in later years, or other.

D. Borrowing Factors—percent of invested capital to be borrowed. Method of payment, whether uniform principal and interest, uniform principal only, or other.

E. Probability values to account for possible early obsolescence or deterioration—a factor representing whether deterioration or obsolescence has the greater effect. The average service life expected, or other.

F. Method of Calculating Rate of Return—whether to include reinvestment of cash flow as a particular after tax rate, or not to include it, or other method.

The program analyzes earnings, depreciation, interest, and taxes to arrive at a net cash flow for each year up to the maximum service life. Net cash flow is essentially net profit calculated as follows:

C.F.=Earnings—Tax Rate (Earnings—[Depreciation+Interest])

The program then utilizes a trial and error method of determining what interest rate will serve to make the cash flow through any given year have a present value equal to the initial investment, and still provide a return over the investment of the same rate. This rate, then, will provide for an exact return of the capital invested by the end of the year involved, with this rate of return as well.

The program also calculates a probability for each year that the investment will terminate in that year, because of loss of all economic value as a result of deterioration or obsolescence. After calculating these factors for each year through maximum service life, the program calculates an overall expected rate of return by summing through the project's life the products of the rate of return for each year and the associated probability that the investment will terminate during that year. The format of the program's computer output is shown in Figures 1 throught 1E.

THE NEED FOR ACCURATE INITIAL ESTIMATES

As a means of stressing the importance of the follow-up on an investment program, examine the effect which inaccurate initial estimates have on the rate of return eventually realized. First, let us outline a basic input example and then observe the reaction of its rate of return in response to changes in several factors.

Assume an investment as outlined in Figure 1. This initial investment preview reveals an expected rate of return of 9.32 percent. If a portion of the operating expenses to be netted against the gross earnings were underestimated by $5,000 in each of the 20 years considered, the uniform investment earnings would have been $35,000 each year instead of $40,000. For this situation the program arrives at an expected rate of return near 8 percent, as shown in Figure 1A.

Under conventional methods, how might this variance have been brought to management attention? Most likely, cost accounting reports from the center where this investment is situated would reveal that actual operating costs exceeded the predicted or standard costs

FIGURE 1—BASIC MODEL

Capital—200,000　　　*Inv. Life*—20　　　*Tax Rate*—52

Modes of Operation—2　2　2　2　2　1

Per Cent—90　　　*No. Years For Depreciation*—12

Per Cent—80　　　*No. Years*—15　　　*Min. Val. For Salvage*—12,500

Uniform Earnings—40,000

Per Cent—20　　　*No. Years*—7　　　*Int. Rate For Interest*—525

Obsoles.—50　　　*Av. Life For Probability*—12

Yr.	Depr. Tab.	Salv. Tab.	Earn. Tab.	Int. Tab.	Cash Flow	Prob. Tab.	Earn. Rate	Yr.
1	$15,000	$150,167	$40,000	$2,100	$28,092	0.006	—10.87	1
2	15,000	140,333	40,000	1,844	27,959	0.010	— 0.98	2
3	15,000	130,500	40,000	1,575	27,819	0.014	2.70	3
4	15,000	120,667	40,000	1,291	27,671	0.021	4.70	4
5	15,000	110,833	40,000	993	27,516	0.028	6.01	5
6	15,000	101,000	40,000	679	27,353	0.037	6.95	6
7	15,000	91,167	40,000	348	27,181	0.047	7.69	7
8	15,000	81,333	40,000	0	27,000	0.058	8.30	8
9	15,000	71,500	40,000	0	27,000	0.068	8.83	9
10	15,000	61,667	40,000	0	27,000	0.076	9.29	10
11	15,000	51,833	40,000	0	27,000	0.082	9.71	11
12	15,000	42,000	40,000	0	27,000	0.085	10.08	12
13	0	32,167	40,000	0	19,200	0.085	10.22	13
14	0	22,333	40,000	0	19,200	0.081	10.36	14
15	0	12,500	40,000	0	19,200	0.074	10.51	15
16	0	12,500	40,000	0	19,200	0.066	10.82	16
17	0	12,500	40,000	0	19,200	0.055	11.09	17
18	0	12,500	40,000	0	19,200	0.045	11.32	18
19	0	12,500	40,000	0	19,200	0.035	11.52	19
20	0	12,500	40,000	0	19,200	0.026	11.69	20

Expected rate of return 9.32

by $5,000 for the year. Whether this is a large or small percentage error depends on the magnitude of the amounts involved. The percentage estimating error could have been as low as 1 percent if the cost was estimated at $500,000 and turned out to be $505,000.

Management would probably not be very concerned with such a small error but, in reality, that error has decreased the rate of return from 9.3 percent to 7.7 percent, or 17 percent. Here is a case where budget variance analysis falls far short of what is expected from it— a case where a rate of return analysis after the first year would have appropriately aroused management concern.

What would happen if the residual salvage value of the investment failed to materialize? Figure 1B illustrates that the rate of

FIGURE 1A—EARNINGS DECREASED

Capital—200,000   *Inv. Life*—20   *Tax Rate*—52

Modes of Operation—2   2   2   2   2   1

Per Cent—90   *No. Years For Depreciation*—12

Per Cent—80   *No. Years*—15   *Min. Val. For Salvage*—12,500

Uniform Earnings—35,000

Per Cent—20   *No. Years*—7   *Int. Rate For Interest*—525

Obsoles.—50   *Av. Life For Probability*—12

Yr.	Depr. Tab.	Salv. Tab.	Earn. Tab.	Int. Tab.	Cash Flow	Prob. Tab.	Earn. Rate	Yr.
1	$15,000	$150,167	$35,000	$2,100	$25,692	0.006	—12.07	1
2	15,000	140,333	35,000	1,844	25,559	0.010	— 2.28	2
3	15,000	130,500	35,000	1,575	25,419	0.014	1.35	3
4	15,000	120,667	35,000	1,291	25,271	0.021	3.31	4
5	15,000	110,833	35,000	993	25,116	0.028	4.58	5
6	15,000	101,000	35,000	679	24,953	0.037	5.49	6
7	15,000	91,167	35,000	348	24,781	0.047	6.20	7
8	15,000	81,333	35,000	0	24,600	0.058	6.79	8
9	15,000	71,500	35,000	0	24,600	0.068	7.29	9
10	15,000	61,667	35,000	0	24,600	0.076	7.73	10
11	15,000	51,833	35,000	0	24,600	0.082	8.14	11
12	15,000	42,000	35,000	0	24,600	0.085	8.51	12
13	0	32,167	35,000	0	16,800	0.085	8.61	13
14	0	22,333	35,000	0	16,800	0.081	8.72	14
15	0	12,500	35,000	0	16,800	0.074	8.85	15
16	0	12,500	35,000	0	16,800	0.066	9.18	16
17	0	12,500	35,000	0	16,800	0.055	9.48	17
18	0	12,500	35,000	0	16,800	0.045	9.72	18
19	0	12,500	35,000	0	16,800	0.035	9.93	19
20	0	12,500	35,000	0	16,800	0.026	10.12	20

Expected rate of return 7.76

return would drop from 9.3 percent to 9.0 percent—a 3 percent variance. If the investment proved too immune to deterioration and wholly susceptible to obsolescence, Figure 1C demonstrates the significant effect on the rate of return—a drop from 9.3 percent to 5.6 percent.

Had management been able to begin accounting for this unanticipated risk when it first revealed itself as a possibility, it would have had the option of divesting itself of the investment. Certainly, no accounting tools would have enabled it to consider the effect of a change in obsolescence risk.

If developments after the investment is made reveal the average life of such projects to be more nearly eight years instead of 12 as

FIGURE 1B—SALVAGE VALUE DECREASED

Capital—200,000   Inv. Life—20   Tax Rate—52

Modes of Operation—2   2   2   2   2   1

Per Cent—90   No. Years For Depreciation—12

Per Cent—80   No. Years—15   Min. Val. For Salvage—0

Uniform Earnings—40,000

Per Cent—20   No. Years—7   Int. Rate For Interest—525

Obsoles.—50   Av. Life For Probability—12

Yr.	Depr. Tab.	Salv. Tab.	Earn. Tab.	Int. Tab.	Cash Flow	Prob. Tab.	Earn. Rate	Yr.
1	$15,000	$149,333	$40,000	$2,100	$28,092	0.006	—11.29	1
2	15,000	138,667	40,000	1,844	27,959	0.010	— 1.43	2
3	15,000	128,000	40,000	1,575	27,819	0.014	2.24	3
4	15,000	117,333	40,000	1,291	27,671	0.021	4.25	4
5	15,000	106,667	40,000	993	27,516	0.028	5.56	5
6	15,000	96,000	40,000	679	27,353	0.037	6.53	6
7	15,000	85,333	40,000	348	27,181	0.047	7.28	7
8	15,000	74,667	40,000	0	27,000	0.058	7.91	8
9	15,000	64,000	40,000	0	27,000	0.068	8.45	9
10	15,000	53,333	40,000	0	27,000	0.076	8.93	10
11	15,000	42,667	40,000	0	27,000	0.082	9.37	11
12	15,000	32,000	40,000	0	27,000	0.085	9.77	12
13	0	21,333	40,000	0	19,200	0.085	9.92	13
14	0	10,667	40,000	0	19,200	0.081	10.08	14
15	0	0	40,000	0	19,200	0.074	10.24	15
16	0	0	40,000	0	19,200	0.066	10.60	16
17	0	0	40,000	0	19,200	0.055	10.91	17
18	0	0	40,000	0	19,200	0.045	11.17	18
19	0	0	40,000	0	19,200	0.035	11.38	19
20	0	0	40,000	0	19,200	0.026	11.57	20

Expected rate of return 9.02

originally intended, the effect would again be significant—a drop to 7.8 percent from 9.3 percent as shown in Figure 1D. Again, a capital investment reanalysis would have anticipated this effect where traditional accounting methods would not.

SPECIAL FACTORS CAN CHANGE RATES OF RETURN

Lastly, let us examine the effect of something such as the recent depreciation law changes. Most industries were enabled to write off their capital expenditures in one to five years less than previously allowed. If the law change allowed our model investment to be depreciated over ten years instead of 12 as shown in Figure 1E, the rate of return would increase to 9.96 percent from 9.32 percent. This would be the result of reducing taxes in early years when the

FIGURE 1C—OBSOL. FACTOR INCREASED

Capital—200,000　　　*Inv. Life*—20　　　*Tax Rate*—52

Modes of Operation—2　　2　　2　　2　　2　　1

Per Cent—90　　　*No. Years For Depreciation*—12

Per Cent—80　　　*No. Years*—15　　　*Min. Val. For Salvage*—12,500

Uniform Earnings—40,000

Per Cent—20　　　*No. Years*—7　　　*Int. Rate For Interest*—525

Obsoles.—100　　　*Av. Life For Probability*—12

Yr.	Depr. Tab.	Salv. Tab.	Earn. Tab.	Int. Tab.	Cash Flow	Prob. Tab.	Earn. Rate	Yr.
1	$15,000	$150,167	$40,000	$2,100	$28,092	0.090	—10.87	1
2	15,000	140,333	40,000	1,844	27,959	0.084	— 0.98	2
3	15,000	130,500	40,000	1,575	27,819	0.078	2.70	3
4	15,000	120,667	40,000	1,291	27,671	0.074	4.70	4
5	15,000	110,833	40,000	993	27,516	0.069	6.01	5
6	15,000	101,000	40,000	679	27,353	0.064	6.95	6
7	15,000	91,167	40,000	348	27,181	0.060	7.69	7
8	15,000	81,333	40,000	0	27,000	0.056	8.30	8
9	15,000	71,500	40,000	0	27,000	0.052	8.83	9
10	15,000	61,667	40,000	0	27,000	0.048	9.29	10
11	15,000	51,833	40,000	0	27,000	0.045	9.71	11
12	15,000	42,000	40,000	0	27,000	0.042	10.08	12
13	0	32,167	40,000	0	19,200	0.039	10.22	13
14	0	22,333	40,000	0	19,200	0.036	10.36	14
15	0	12,500	40,000	0	19,200	0.033	10.51	15
16	0	12,500	40,000	0	19,200	0.030	10.82	16
17	0	12,500	40,000	0	19,200	0.028	11.09	17
18	0	12,500	40,000	0	19,200	0.026	11.32	18
19	0	12,500	40,000	0	19,200	0.024	11.52	19
20	0	12,500	40,000	0	19,200	0.022	11.69	20

Expected rate of return 5.63

money has a greater present value, without adversely affecting cash flow, because depreciation is not a cash outlay.

The foregoing examples serve to illustrate two points: first, the factors which influence an investment's rate of return are constantly changing; secondly, traditional accounting procedures fail to reflect the true response of an investment to these changing factors. A continuing rate of return analysis, however, would take the changes into account and reflect their true effect in a meaningful common denominator—the rate of return.

THE MEANS OF MAINTAINING A CONTINUING ANALYSIS

How might such a continuing rate of return analysis be accomplished? Investment proposals initiate in any number of departments

FIGURE 1D—AV. LIFE DECREASED

Capital—200,000   Inv. Life—20   Tax Rate—52

Modes of Operation—2   2   2   2   2   1

Per Cent—90   No. Years For Depreciation—12

Per Cent—80   No. Years—15   Min. Val. For Salvage—12,500

Uniform Earnings—40,000

Per Cent—20   No. Years—7   Int. Rate For Interest—525

Obsoles.—50   Av. Life For Probability—8

Yr.	Depr. Tab.	Salv. Tab.	Earn. Tab.	Int. Tab.	Cash Flow	Prob. Tab.	Earn. Rate	Yr.
1	$15,000	$150,167	$40,000	$2,100	$28,092	0.010	−10.87	1
2	15,000	140,333	40,000	1,844	27,959	0.019	− 0.98	2
3	15,000	130,500	40,000	1,575	27,819	0.032	2.70	3
4	15,000	120,667	40,000	1,291	27,671	0.050	4.70	4
5	15,000	110,833	40,000	993	27,516	0.071	6.01	5
6	15,000	101,000	40,000	679	27,353	0.093	6.95	6
7	15,000	91,167	40,000	348	27,181	0.110	7.69	7
8	15,000	81,333	40,000	0	27,000	0.120	8.30	8
9	15,000	71,500	40,000	0	27,000	0.119	8.83	9
10	15,000	61,667	40,000	0	27,000	0.108	9.29	10
11	15,000	51,833	40,000	0	27,000	0.090	9.71	11
12	15,000	42,000	40,000	0	27,000	0.068	10.08	12
13	0	32,167	40,000	0	19,200	0.047	10.22	13
14	0	22,333	40,000	0	19,200	0.030	10.36	14
15	0	12,500	40,000	0	19,200	0.017	10.51	15
16	0	12,500	40,000	0	19,200	0.009	10.82	16
17	0	12,500	40,000	0	19,200	0.004	11.09	17
18	0	12,500	40,000	0	19,200	0.002	11.32	18
19	0	12,500	40,000	0	19,200	0.001	11.52	19
20	0	12,500	40,000	0	19,200	0.	11.69	20

Expected rate of return 7.87

throughout an organization. They are submitted on standard forms and are reviewed by financial management in order to provide tax rates, allowable depreciation method, and, if needed, loan costs and amount of loan. They then determine the extent to which borrowing might affect the rate of return.

Cards are punched from the forms, and passed against an estimating history on magnetic tape containing a statistical analysis for each estimator in the organization. The computer finds the associated estimator record, and from it applies a factor to the proposal estimates of earnings and salvage values which serve to reduce the estimate if the estimator is normally overly optimistic, or increase the estimate if the estimator is normally overly pessimistic.

FIGURE 1E—DEPREC. LIFE DECREASED

Capital—200,000   *Inv. Life*—20   *Tax Rate*—52

Modes of Operation—2   2   2   2   2   1

Per Cent—90   *No. Years For Depreciation*—10

Per Cent—80   *No. Years*—15   *Min. Val. For Salvage*—12,500

Uniform Earnings—40,000

Per Cent—20   *No. Years*—7   *Int. Rate For Interest*—525

Obsoles.—50   *Av. Life For Probability*—12

Yr.	Depr. Tab.	Salv. Tab.	Earn. Tab.	Int. Tab.	Cash Flow	Prob. Tab.	Earn. Rate	Yr.
1	$18,000	$150,167	$40,000	$2,100	$29,652	0.006	—10.09	1
2	18,000	140,333	40,000	1,844	29,519	0.010	— 0.13	2
3	18,000	130,500	40,000	1,575	29,379	0.014	3.58	3
4	18,000	120,667	40,000	1,291	29,231	0.021	5.61	4
5	18,000	110,833	40,000	993	29,076	0.028	6.93	5
6	18,000	101,000	40,000	679	28,913	0.037	7.90	6
7	18,000	91,167	40,000	348	28,741	0.047	8.66	7
8	18,000	81,333	40,000	0	28,560	0.058	9.28	8
9	18,000	71,500	40,000	0	28,560	0.068	9.81	9
10	18,000	61,667	40,000	0	28,560	0.076	10.28	10
11	0	51,833	40,000	0	19,200	0.082	10.39	11
12	0	42,000	40,000	0	19,200	0.085	10.51	12
13	0	32,167	40,000	0	19,200	0.085	10.64	13
14	0	22,333	40,000	0	19,200	0.081	10.78	14
15	0	12,500	40,000	0	19,200	0.074	10.92	15
16	0	12,500	40,000	0	19,200	0.066	11.24	16
17	0	12,500	40,000	0	19,200	0.055	11.50	17
18	0	12,500	40,000	0	19,200	0.045	11.72	18
19	0	12,500	40,000	0	19,200	0.035	11.92	19
20	0	12,500	40,000	0	19,200	0.026	12.08	20

Expected rate of return 9.96

This factor is one standard deviation from the mean of a distribution of that person's guessing accuracies. A less conservative management might prefer to use one half or one quarter of one standard deviation from the mean. This could be varied automatically based upon the population size of the distribution for a particular estimator, to reflect further the degree of management confidence in his estimating skill. If no previous estimating history for an individual is available, a constant factor might be supplied this program by the manager who knows the estimator's ability.

The estimator history tape is updated by data from the investment, and the distribution statistics are recalculated by a statistical analysis program.

The output of the first pass on the computer is a set of revised estimate cards for each proposal. The cards are used as input to the capital investment program, and a standard report format with the overall expected rate of return is printed. If management approves the proposal a tape record is established, including the report data, on what would be considered an investment inventory tape.

THE FUNCTION OF THE INVESTMENT INVENTORY TAPE

After the investment record is entered on the investment inventory tape, it is subjected to current data quarterly during the first 20 percent of its life, and annually thereafter. The estimate history tape is updated at the same time. Pertinent current data consists of actual earnings, actual salvage values if available, and any additional information which management feels might merit revision of the factors originally established.

The investment inventory tape, being supplied with actual results, is now able to provide a basis for forecasting future investment performance. The active investments for a particular quarter are input to a forecasting run on the computer which utilizes exponential smoothing with trend correction to arrive at forecasted earnings and salvage values.

Since this procedure arrives at a forecast for only the next period, the remaining periods up to maximum life are forecast on the basis of bearing the same relationship to their corresponding estimates as the next period forecast bears to its original estimate. The forecasts are added to the investment inventory tape.

On the same pass, the probability factors originally computed which pertain to periods prior to this quarter are reduced to zero,

INITIAL INVESTMENT
PROPOSAL PROCEDURE

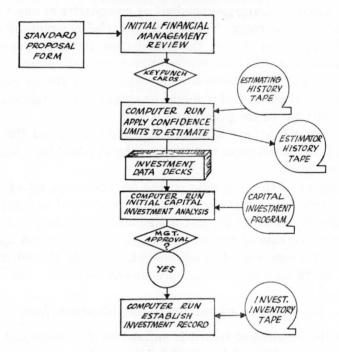

PERIODIC MONITOR RUN

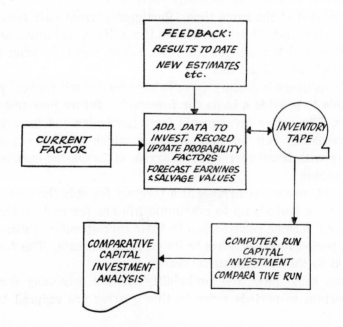

and those original values are added to the probabilities for the next two periods of the investment's life. This procedure gives recognition to the fact that because expected rates of return for each previous period were based on termination of the investment in that period, they should no longer give any weight to the overall expected rate of return for the investment.

At this point there is for each investment a record of the original estimates, a record of actual results to date, and a record of new estimates for the period remaining. This information is all that is needed to run a comparative rate of return analysis with the capital investment program, or a modification of its depending upon the capicibility of the computer available. The result of this run would be a modification of the standard capital investment program output format.

In addition to the standard output, the following columns would be added to the table: actual earnings to date and forecasted earnings to maximum life; actual cash flow to date and computed projection of same to maximum life; actual salvage values to date and projected salvage values to maximum life; actual rates of return to date and computed rate of return based on forecasted factors; and a new probability tabulation which could be simply the corrected tabulation mentioned previously, or a completely recomputed set of probabilities based upon remaining life.

The program would also arrive at a new overall expected rate of return. Here, then, is a report which can communicate to higher management the progress of investments in terms of probability.

Other applications which would be of value in this area include statistical reports on estimating performance, and a multiple correlation run indicating the effect which extrinsic financial variables have upon realized rates of return. Programs are available to accomplish these applications.

The time factors between processing runs are, of course, flexible. An organization which is basically in manufacturing would find that quarter and annual interims would probably be sufficient. A financial institution, however, is in the business of making investments, so a closer degree of control would be appropriate—in this case weekly and monthly or even daily and weekly runs would be made for portfolio analysis.

The value of such a capital investment monitoring system with regard to results cannot be overemphasized. The main portion of the system is built upon IBM applied programs, enabling the user to adapt such a system to his organization with a minimum of expense. The overall result of such a system is management awareness as to the status of investments, thereby enabling them to take corrective action at the earliest possible moment.

Space limitations prevent inclusion of the detailed auxiliary and modification programming which would make such a system complete. It is not a complex task, and the effort would be well spent.

56. ANALYSIS AND CONTROL
OF A CASH FLOW SYSTEM *   Martin N. Kellogg †

In the past few years and to an increasing extent in the recent period due to increasingly tight money supplies, management interest has been focused upon means to better utilize the large amounts of cash which flow through the business process. One very important phase is concerned with increasing the rate at which cash is made available through business operations. For example, a company with monthly receipts of $6 million has the opportunity to recover about $1,000 per year in interest (at 6 percent per year) for every day it can make that cash available for business use.

Recently this problem was studied for a large company with average monthly billings of $60 million. Indications were that, although it is practical to expect receipt of cash within ten days of performance of service, in actual practice it is more likely an average of 30 days. These 20 days of unproductive use of working capital are worth about $200,000 per year in interest (at 6 percent per year). Even at the low rate of 3 percent per year the amount would be about $100,000 per year.

From the above remarks the reason for management interest in this problem and its solution is obvious, and a practical technique will have extensive implications and value. Therefore, the following analysis of the problem and technique of solution have been developed in answer to this need.

THE CASH FLOW PROBLEM

The incoming cash flow cycle can be broken into four processes which are shown at the top of the following page.

The velocity of incoming cash flow can be increased only to the extent that this cycle is shortened in time, but to achieve this, positive control over the above listed dates must be maintained.

* From *The Controller* (October, 1957). Reprinted by permission of the Financial Executives Institute.

† Martin N. Kellogg, Peat, Marwick, Mitchell and Co.

Process	Controlling Dates
1. Performance of Service:	Date service is commenced.
	Date service is completed.
2. Billing:	
	Date bill is issued.
3. Collection:	
	Date bill is collected.
4. Banking:	
	Date cash is deposited.

Investigations disclosed that positive control over the incoming cash flow is not achieved with present systems. However, this was only a subjective evaluation with the exception of one minor sub-process (miscellaneous collections) for which testing disclosed that for 35 percent of the items the elapsed time between completion of service and bill issuance dates was between eight and 24 weeks. The problems in obtaining a quantitative evaluation of the lag in cash flow were:

1. The extremely large volume of items involved (estimated bills originated by collection points were 244,000 per month), which prohibited anything but a small sample.
2. The necessity for first describing the cash flow system in order to determine the exact nature of the problem as to areas of responsibilities and specific problems involved in each area.
3. The necessity for first determining and describing the control devices which are relied upon for regulation of each area.

Upon completion of Items 2 and 3 above, the remaining problem is: *How can this large volume of data be evaluated in order to objectively verify the need for a more efficient control system for cash flow?*

If an objective verification is accomplished and indicates a need for increased controls, then a second problem arises: *How can a positive control system be established?*

Evaluating Cash Flow Veloctiy by Statistical Sampling

A very clear-cut method of evaluating the necessity for increased control of cash flow is to describe for each process of the cycle a time period which is desirable under an efficient and controlled system. This time period would be compared to the time actually realized in current practice, and if the difference were significant, it would be concluded that the current system was not efficiently controlled. Conversely, if the difference were not significant, the current system would be accepted, and further work would be discontinued.

The above reference to a time period does not mean a fixed period. For any such system the time period varies from item to item generating a distribution of time periods. Examples I and II show two distributions. Example I illustrates a desirable cash flow cycle distribution with an average completion period of ten days (weighted by dollar volume). Example II illustrates an undesirable distribution with an average completion period of 30 days.

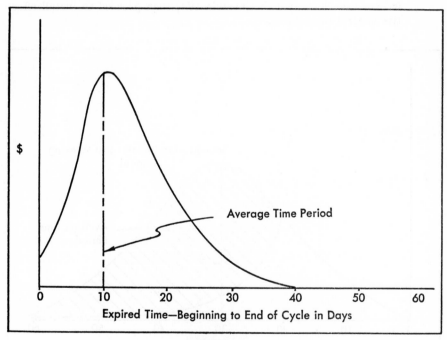

EXAMPLE I
Desirable Distribution of Cash Flow

At present it is not known whether Example I or Example II (or some other distribution not shown) correctly pictures the actual cash flow distribution. The purpose of a sampling analysis is to make a correct discernment between two levels. This program may be simply stated as follows:

1. Establish a statement to be tested (i.e., the average elapsed time of the current system is the same as the desirable average elapsed time as shown in Example I).
2. Determine the risk level (i.e., what chance of an erroneous conclusion is acceptable?). This can be determined by balancing the costs of avoiding an erroneous conclusion against the cost resulting from actions based on erroneous thinking.
3. Determine the required sample size. This would depend on the choice for Item 2 above, but preliminary analysis indicates that a sample of 600 items from any one process would give very reliable results.[1] This would apply to the 244,000 items per month originated by collection points.
4. Accomplish taking of sample group(s).
5. Determine confidence interval around sample mean.
6. Compare confidence interval with desirable time period distribution. If the confidence interval includes the desirable average time (as illustrated in Example III), conclude that the current process is acceptable and no further control devices are needed. If the opposite is true (as illustrated in Example IV), then proceed to install effective control procedures.

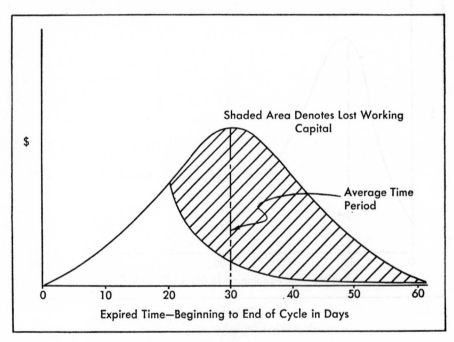

EXAMPLE II
Undesirable Distribution of Cash Flow

---

[1] Further analysis of specific situations very likely would permit significant downward revisions on this figure which is based on the assumption of scant knowledge of the actual process distribution.

In the preceding discussion, it was implied that sampling verification of the general process of billing by collection points will be conducted. It should be further pointed out that verification of many subprocesses will be desirable. This will indicate specific responsibilities and processes which require direct attention.

In all cases, process definitions will have to be clearly specified so that conclusions relate to specific areas of responsibility. This will then provide the necessary basis for a control system.

CONTROL OF CASH FLOW VELOCITY BY STATISTICAL SAMPLING

Assuming that the above test verifies the need for increased controls over the cash flow cycle, it is necessary to develop an efficient means of achieving this.

The situation can be readily analyzed as a problem in statistical quality control; that is, it is a continuous process for which the production is cash receipts. Production of high quality means a high velocity of cash flow (short time period). Production of low quality means a low velocity of cash flow (long time period).

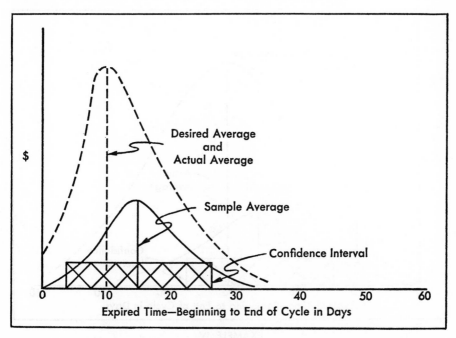

EXAMPLE III
Sample with Confidence Interval Including Desired Average
(Process Is Accepted)

The objective of control is to achieve the highest rate of quality commensurate with economical control costs. This balance may be achieved by statistical analysis and control. The techniques of statistical quality control have long enjoyed practical acceptance, and since this particular situation presents no new technical problems, it is not necessary to provide a lengthy detailed discussion except for the following comments.

The initial verification information will be very useful in the first phases of establishing the control procedure. Specifically it will provide knowledge of the present process average and confidence intervals around which the control limits may be established. These limits will be set at a lower level than the present in order to enforce improvements, but only at a level which will focus attention upon the worst offenses. Tightened control will not be attempted at once, but will be achieved through gradual pressures of stepped reduction in the acceptable time period as indicated in Example V.

Based upon daily sampling inspection of items of the process (sample size of four items), average values will be plotted on a

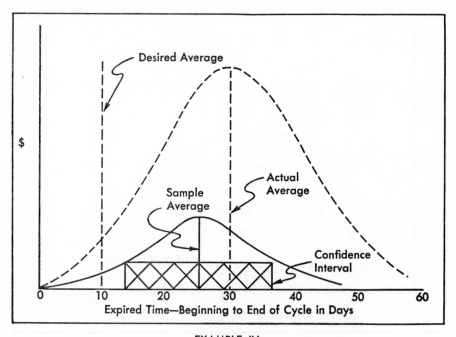

EXAMPLE IV
Sample with Confidence Interval Not Including Desired Average
(Process Is Not Accepted)

control chart. Sample averages which are not within control limits indicate action must be taken. In the case of those samples plotting above the upper control limit, administrative action would be required to reduce the time period. Those plotting below the lower control limit indicate an improvement in the process which is translated into a reduction of the control limits.

Through these pressures and improvements, the time cycle will be reduced to its practical minimum. At this point inspection will continue as a control device to prevent the system going back to its former state, but sampling can be reduced by significant proportions.

ADVANTAGES OF THE STATISTICAL ANALYSIS SOLUTION

The methods which have been described provide a definite objective manner of resolving the problem as discussed.

Verification of the problem is accomplished with minimum data gathering and clearly defined objectives. The method of gaining and maintaining control is both direct and subtle, accomplishing significant results with minimum disturbance to the system.

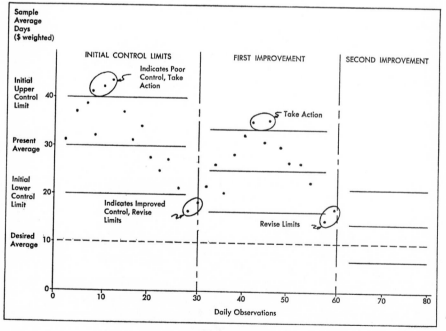

EXAMPLE V
Control Charts: Simulated Cash Flow Control

Another advantage which can be derived from the control system is control of clerical accuracy (e.g., bill preparation and pricing). The same samples used for the one may be used for the other. This can become a significant audit tool.

It should also be noted that this procedure has a great deal of significance to all industries with similar cash flow problems, particularly insurance, transportation, stock brokerage, and investment trust companies to name a few that have the same type of extensive and diverse cash collection points.

PART V

REPORTS FOR MANAGEMENT

The reporting process closes the control cycle. The readings in the preceding sections of the book have been concerned with the other processes in the control cycle. These include the selection of the goals of the enterprise and the development of the subgoal structure. Of particular concern to a student of accounting and budgeting is the quantification of these goals.

Performance takes place and accounting is concerned with measuring that performance in relation to goals which have been set. The reporting of the performance completes the control cycle by carrying to the manager information about the acceptability of the performance. If the goals have been attained he may allow operations to continue without change. If not, he may revise the goals or the instructions on the means of achieving them.

Since the object of the reporting process is to facilitate detection and correction of mistakes, promptness in reporting is important. The first two readings deal with this problem. Appraising the significance of variances from standard is the subject of Readings 61 and 62.

Reporting is a communication process. Successful ways to increase the effectiveness of the communication is to use an operations letter and a chart system.

57. PERT—A DYNAMIC APPROACH
TO SYSTEMS ANALYSIS *

James G. Case †

Recently, an advanced method of management control, known as Project Evaluation and Review Technique (PERT), has been described in many trade and technical publications.

PERT is now a tried and proven technique and has been successful. However, thus far, the emphasis has been placed on its use in engineering and research scheduling. In my opinion, there exists an even more dynamic use for PERT in the field of overall business administration. Management is constantly confronted with problems of scheduling and unraveling the endless red tape of the ever-expanding administrative requirements of business. This is particularly true in the financial and data processing fields, although it is not limited to these areas. PERT, properly used as an analytical method, can accomplish as significant time savings in the administrative fields as it has in the research and engineering fields.

In the financial area, accountants are constantly asked by management for faster and more accurate information. New methods and procedures, and newer, more reliable equipment, are constantly being developed to aid and expedite the movement of information through the administrative maze. The object is to enable management to make better decisions. In most cases, time is of the essence and accuracy must be maintained. The PERT technique, properly used, is an effective answer for reducing time delays and emphasizing efforts to accomplish the overall results desired.

The complex of administrative scheduling has much in common with scheduling major engineering and research projects. Administrative flow is a matter of assembling details into a meaningful summary of the information. As in an engineering or research project, the details must be timed and coordinated if any degree of

* From the *N.A.A. Bulletin* (March, 1963). Reprinted by permission of the National Association of Accountants.
† James G. Case, Speer Carbon Company (Division of Air Reduction Corp.), Niagara Falls, New York.

efficiency is to be maintained. Also, as in the case of a project, the larger and more complex the administrative problem, the greater are the benefits to be derived by the use of the PERT technique.

In the following pages, after explanation of the technique, we will apply the PERT to the example of a cost accounting closing. The example will illustrate how the overall function can be reduced to its critical areas and further cost-time analysis applied to the feasibility of suggested solutions for difficulties in these areas. The example will pursue only a few aspects of the total network to their logical conclusions, for, as one critical part is resolved, other areas and inferences become critical. These, in turn, must be subjected to review.

The principles involved find an excellent application in the example of a cost accounting closing. However, PERT is by no means limited to this application. The same principles can be applied to the availability of cash to meet a budget appropriation, clerical operations, paper flow, sales-order procedures, some types of production control, and to many other business procedures which, by their nature, require planning, coordination, and scheduling.

Developing the Network

To properly develop a PERT network, these four steps or phases must be followed:

1. Organization of events and final objective.
2. Connection of interrelated events with activity lines showing direction of flow.
3. Collection of time factors, or time necessary to accomplish an event.
4. Coding of events for reference.

The primary phase in the development of a PERT technique is the establishment of the overall administrative objective to be accomplished and the identification of all major events that contribute to that objective. An event is defined as a particular job or milestone along the path of progression towards the completion of the function described. This primary phase is accomplished by an analysis of the function itself and the collection, subassembly and assembly of the information necessary to accomplish this function. This analysis may be performed by an individual or a team; however, it must, by necessity, be complete and contain a degree of detail sufficient to appraise the critical path (longest time necessary to complete the entire function) of the network. The first figure on Exhibit 1 illustrates simply a breakdown of events (terms used are suggestive of the cost closing which is to be presented as a more detailed example).

Phase 2 in the development of the network requires the linking together of the various events with activity lines. These lines, showing the direction flow of information, reflect the existing situation. It can be noted that, at this point, the administrative use of the technique differs from the engineering use insofar as the network, i.e., the activities and events, is already established. The approach becomes one of improving and evaluating an existing network, rather than projecting a tentative one. Beyond this phase, the evaluation and review procedures are identical to those now applied to engineering programs. The activity lines are shown in the second figure on Exhibit 1.

Phase 3 requires the user to collect the time factors along the various activity paths. These time factors are normally estimates of average time required to perform and complete a given event. Administrative application needs only one time element, since, in most cases, it deals in real time, historically established. The probability aspects of a PERT network, frequently used in research and engineering applications, require minimum, probable, and maximum time estimates. These have little value to the administrator who has access to the real or normal time to accomplish the event.

The definition of events, activities, and estimates of time used should be made by qualified individuals at the level of responsibility for the activity. The estimates should be precise, not protective. If an individual should provide a cushion of slack time in an estimate and the particular activity should happen to be along the primary or alternative critical paths, the estimate will be subjected to review and justification, as a matter of course. This self-checking feature of a PERT network makes sure that accurate data will be provided for the critical path or alternate paths. The third figure on Exhibit 1 shows activity times as they would appear in a network.

At this point, the network should be coded. This means numbering the events in ascending sequence. The use of the code is necessary if a computer is used to review the network; however, even with a manual operation, coding can be a valuable aid in referencing events. The fourth figure in Exhibit 1 illustrates a completed and coded network.

The completion of these preliminary phases creates a synthesis or mathematical model of the time and coordination schedule for an

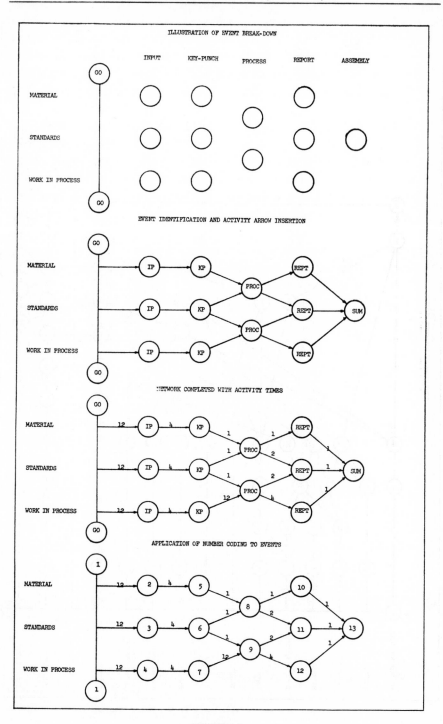

EXHIBIT 1

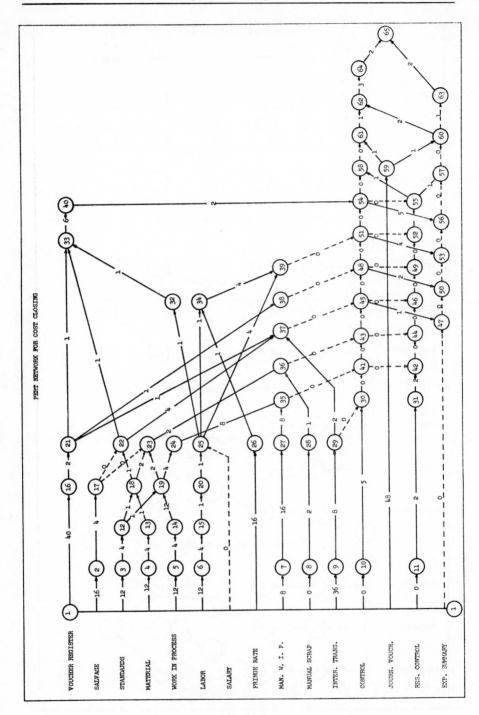

EXHIBIT 2

existing administrative procedure. This synthesis is the keystone of future analysis. Whether it is programmed for a computer or calculated manually, the arrow diagram will indicate the critical path, the alternate critical paths, and the time consumption of activities along these paths. With these guides, management can make a reliable evaluation of the procedure, providing new equipment or methods changes, if desired, and determining, by reconstruction of the model, their effects upon the schedule for accomplishing the entire task.

Application of PERT Technique to a Cost Closing

Using the methods described, a cost closing at plant level will be analyzed by the application of the PERT technique. This closing requires collection, control, and summary of data necessary to produce a plant profit-and-loss statement acceptable for corporate consolidation. It should be pointed out that this application may itself only represent an event in a large network; on the other hand, it could be the master network controlling subsidiary networks related to particulars of data flow. In either case, the network is developed and coded as in Exhibit 2, for the single purpose of controlling and improving the final delivery time of the profit-and-loss statement.

The time factors used are expressed in terms of departmental working hours; this automatically adjusts for calendar deviations or necessary overtime. Also, use of working hours assumes a normal work force. The hours can be lessened if more effort is directed towards a particular event.

Once completed and coded, the network can be programmed for a computer. In this particular example, the input is organized for the IBM 1401 computer using a "less" program (Exhibit 3). It should be noted that three factors are necessary to enable the computer to make up its computations:

I Initial code: The event number preceding the activity.

J Finish code: The event number succeeding the activity.

D Activity time: The length of time necessary to complete a given activity.

All input information must be carefully verified with the arrow diagram of the network before it is loaded into the computer. The computer calculates and reports the data illustrated by Exhibit 4, the column headings of which have the following significance:

Arrow   The activity path described.

ESD   Earliest start time.

LSD   Latest start time.

EFD   Earliest finish time.

LFD   Latest finish time.

TF   Total float or delay time allowed without delaying the final result.

FF   Free float or delay time allowed without delaying the following event.

CRITICAL AND SUBCRITICAL PATHS

The double asterisk against an item in Exhibit 4 identifies it as one of the activities on the critical path, and the last time given in the LFD column indicates the total time length of the critical path. In this case, it is 63 hours. The computer report establishes the critical path, as at the top of Exhibit 5. (This line and the others on the exhibit can be read from Exhibit 2.) It is obvious that the voucher register is critical principally because of the 40 hours input time between Events 1 and 16. Hence, to decrease the overall time of closing, the voucher register input time must be reduced. In considering this, it is helpful to know the next critical path. By substituting zero for the 40 hours in the voucher register input and recomputing the problem, an entirely new critical path can be developed along the interdivisional transfer line, again as appears on Exhibit 5. Interdivisional transfer is presently a subcritical path, and will become critical only when the critical path along the voucher register line is reduced by more than the difference in total hours (five hours). By again applying the method of substitution, i.e., of zero for the 36 hours on the interdivisional transfer input time, a third path is established along the line of journal vouchers. It, too, appears in Exhibit 5. This second subcritical path has a total float time of seven hours when compared with the critical path. Hence, it will become critical only when conditions are altered to the extent of at least seven hours along the critical path and two hours along the first subcritical path.

The conclusion to be drawn from this example is that, if the closing time is to be reduced, the input times of the critical and the two subcritical paths must be reduced to the extent necessary to create another critical path. Hence, the effort to improve the system

EXAMPLE OF INPUT DATA I. B. M. 1401 LESS PROGRAM			
	I. Event	J. Event	D. Hours
Input salvage	0001	0002	016
Input standards	0001	0003	012
Input material	0001	0004	012
Input work in process	0001	0005	012
(Intervening Steps Omitted)			
Key punch material	0004	0013	004
*Key punch work in process	0005	0014	004
Key punch labor	0006	0015	004
Complete manual work in process	0007	0027	016
Complete manual scrap	0008	0028	002
Check out interdivisional transfer	0009	0029	008
Post control	0010	0030	005
Post research control	0011	0031	002
Check out standards for material	0012	0018	001
Check out standards for work in process	0012	0019	001
Extend material	0013	0018	001
*Extend work in process	0014	0019	012
Check out labor	0015	0020	001
Check out voucher register	0016	0021	002
Complete salvage for material	0017	0022	000
Complete salvage for scrap	0017	0023	000
Complete material runs	0018	0022	001
Complete salvage runs	0018	0023	002
Complete rejections	0019	0023	002
*Complete work in process runs	0019	0024	004
Complete labor distribution	0020	0025	001
Voucher register to maintenance	0021	0033	001
Voucher register to inventory summary	0021	0037	001
Complete voucher register distribution	0021	0038	001
Material to maintenance	0022	0033	001
Material to inventory summary	0022	0037	004
Scrap run to summary	0023	0036	002
*Work in process to summary	0024	0035	008
Labor extended for maintenance	0025	0032	001
(Intervening Steps Omitted)			
Check out expense	0060	0062	002
Work variance analysis	0060	0063	001
Total control	0061	0062	001
Prepare cost of sales	0062	0064	003
Finish statement	0063	0065	002
Finish statement	0064	0065	002

* Substitute times for these steps discussed in text

EXHIBIT 3

should be directed along these lines. Improvements of other areas of the system are presently of no value to the schedule. For instance, any improvement of the work in process time will not improve the time schedule of the overall closing. To illustrate this, we can establish the work in process time of the system, apart from the input.

EXAMPLE OF I. B. M. 1401 LESS PROGRAM REPORT

DESCRIPTION	ARROW		ESD	LSD	EFD	LFD	TF	FF
Input salvage	0001	0002	016	000	022	016	038	022	000
Input standards	0001	0003	012	000	022	012	034	022	000

(Intervening Steps Omitted)

Key punch labor	0006	0015	004	012	035	016	039	023	000
**Input voucher register	0001	0016	040	000	000	040	040		
Key punch salvage	0002	0017	004	016	038	020	042	022	000
Check out standards for mat.	0012	0018	001	016	040	017	041	024	000
Extend material	0013	0018	001	016	040	017	041	024	000
Check out stds. for work in proc.	0012	0019	001	016	038	017	039	022	011
Extend work in process	0014	0019	012	016	027	028	039	011	000
Check out labor	0015	0020	001	016	039	017	040	023	000
**Check out voucher register	0016	0021	002	040	040	042	042		
Complete salvage for material	0017	0022	000	020	042	020	042	022	000

(Intervening Steps Omitted)

Labor extended for maintenance	0025	0032	001	018	041	019	042	023	000
**Voucher register to maintenance	0021	0033	001	042	042	043	043		

(Intervening Steps Omitted)

Labor to summary	0025	0039	004	018	047	022	051	029	001
Fringes to summary	0034	0039	004	019	047	023	051	028	000
**Process maintenance run	0033	0040	006	043	043	049	049		
Post control	0030	0041	000	044	051	044	051	007	000

(Intervening Steps Omitted)

Post expense	0050	0053	000	048	056	048	056	008	002
Post labor to expense	0051	0053	004	046	052	050	056	006	000
**Check out maintenance	0040	0054	002	049	049	051	051		
Post control	0051	0054	000	046	051	046	051	005	005
Post research	0052	0055	000	046	055	046	055	009	005
Post maintenance to research	0054	0055	000	051	055	051	055	004	000
Post expense	0053	0056	000	050	056	050	056	006	006
**Post maintenance expense	0054	0056	005	051	051	056	056		
Post research to expense	0055	0057	001	051	055	052	056	004	004
**Post expense	0056	0057	000	056	056	056	056		
Post control	0054	0058	000	051	057	051	057	006	001
Check research	0055	0058	001	051	056	052	057	005	000
Input journal vouchers	0001	0059	048	000	007	048	055	007	000
**Post expense	0057	0060	000	056	056	056	056		
Post journal vouch. to expense	0059	0060	001	048	055	049	056	007	007
Post control	0058	0061	000	052	057	052	057	005	000
Post journal vouch. to control	0059	0061	001	048	056	049	057	008	003
**Check out expense	0060	0062	002	056	056	058	058		
Total control	0061	0062	001	052	057	053	058	005	C05
Work variance analyzation	0060	0063	001	056	060	057	061	004	000
**Prepare cost of sales	0062	0064	003	058	058	061	061		
Finish statement	0063	0065	002	057	061	059	063	004	004
**Finish statement	0064	0065	002	061	061	063	063		

**Steps in critical path

EXHIBIT 4

The procedure for this merely requires the substitution of zero for the time factor of all input time activities (those activities having an initial code of 001). Applied to the work in process line, this would

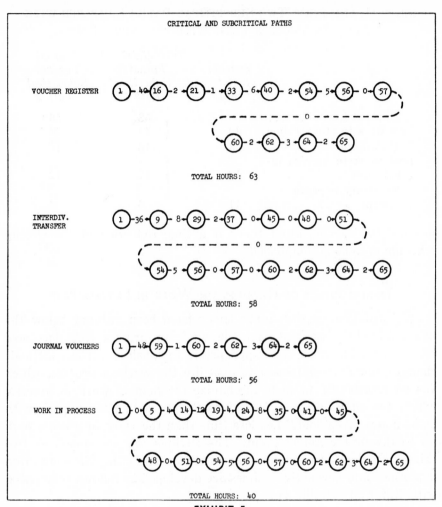

EXHIBIT 5

mean a critical path reduced to 40 hours (except for input time), as indicated against the work in process caption in Exhibit 5. The necessary time improvement to make work in process the critical path can be calculated as shown at the top of page 794.

From this comparison, the areas and amount of improvement needed in input time to make the work in process path critical can readily be established. The voucher register path must be improved by at least 11 hours, the interdivisional transfer path by at least six hours, and the journal vouchers path by at least four hours. It, therefore, becomes necessary to direct effort towards im-

CRITICAL AND FIRST TWO SUBCRITICAL PATHS COMPARED WITH
WORK IN PROCESS PATH WITHOUT INPUT TIME

	Voucher Register Critical Path	*Interdivisional Transfer Subcritical Path 1*	*Journal Voucher Subcritical Path 2*
With input time	63	58	56
Less work in process time	40	40	40
Difference	23	18	16
Less work in process input time	12	12	12
Necessary improvement	11	6	4

proving the various input times if a time reduction of the closing schedule is to be accomplished.

TESTING EFFECT OF CHANGES ON WORK IN PROCESS PATH

We will assume that input times have been reduced below the hours stated above, and that the work in process time has now become critical. If so, it is appropriate to consider various methods changes and new equipment to expedite the work in process, which (as on Exhibit 2) feeds to mechanize the manual work in process, which (as on Exhibit 2) feeds into the work in process path with eight hours "free float," i.e., less time than the work in process path up to the first common event. The savings are envisioned as two thirds of a clerk's time amounting to $233 per month. The suggestion is pursued and new activity times are developed as follows (compared with times on Exhibit 3):

I	J	D
0005	0014	006 hours
0014	0019	014 "
0019	0024	006 "

The procedure of substitution is again followed and the network recomputed. The output report indicates that changing the manual work in process time in this way would result in an overall work in process time of 46 hours as compared to a present work in process time of 40 hours. Hence, the mechanization of the manual work in process would actually delay the closing by six hours. If time is paramount, it will be rejected, at least as a single proposal.

However, further analysis of the data processing time required to produce the tabulation of the work in process indicates that the major critical activity is the calculation of the time required to produce the work in process report. The suggestion is to order new equipment that will calculate approximately four times faster than present equipment. The excess cost of the new equipment is approximately $250 per month more than present equipment. Again, the affected area is studied and new time estimates developed, resulting in the following new activity times:

I	J	D
0005	0014	004 hours
0014	0019	006 "
0019	0024	004 "

Recomputation, using these times, indicates that the work in process time can be reduced to 36 hours by using new equipment, as compared to the present time of 40 hours. This suggests a reduction in the critical path time, if no other path is higher than 36 hours. However, it is realized that the $250 is an added cost. Hence, still another idea is to combine the Suggestions 1 and 2, thus using the cost saving of the first to offset the additional expense of the second.

A restudy of the activity times affected must be made. The new substitutions are as follows:

I	J	D
0005	0014	006 hours
0014	0019	006 "
0019	0024	004 "
0024	0035	014 "

Again, the network is recomputed and reported on. Work in process time is 38 hours. Hence, by obtaining new equipment and mechanizing the manual work in process, the overall work in process time can be reduced by two hours at an additional cost of only $17 (the difference between $250 and $233).

Which course to take is for management to decide. However, it is important to note that PERT has answered what the final effect on the closing will be in each case. Furthermore, this information can be given to management before rather than after the decision is made. Let us assume that the suggestions just discussed are accepted and that the work in process time is reduced to 38 hours. By taking this new time and adding the 12-hour input time of the new critical path, the total time for the cost closing is 50 working hours. The original critical path required 63 working hours. The difference of 13 working hours represents a reduction in time of more than one and one-half days to accomplish the closing.

To realize the major advantages of using the PERT technique, a constant review of the network is necessary. From time to time, new functions, personnel, or equipment may be added which will affect the critical path. Further, the technique should be used regressively, that is, as a method of further analyzing the critical areas of the overall network.

CONVERTING THE NETWORK TO A TIME SCHEDULE

It seems appropriate to turn aside here from our pursuit of the best critical path possible to point out briefly that the PERT network offers materials for a time schedule. By taking the original arrow diagram shown in Exhibit 2 (with its critical path of 63 hours) and converting it to conform with a time base, a projected schedule can be developed as in Exhibit 6. The schedule is based on real time consumption in order to complete certain functions and should show the major events of a given function. At least the Ip (input event), the J (ending event), and the major process routings should be indicated. The amount of detail must be adequate to disclose the coordinating features of each path where delays may occur.

The float times, indicated by dotted lines, allow management to evaluate how much delay can be absorbed along a given line. This is an extremely useful guide to evaluate the use of overtime and to direct effort towards expediting the entire closing.

Further, a schedule of this type can be reviewed and compared with current actual time to give management up-to-date progress reports. In short, it tells management personnel where they stand in relation to the overall results desired.

ADVANTAGES OF PERT

Of the major advantages of PERT, one of the more useful to management is that it shows the entire picture and summarizes in sequence the administrative events necessary to complete an overall function. The summary of events, in itself, becomes an exceedingly useful "tool" for management. Since it depicts all operations, it can be used to indicate shortcuts or suggest other methods to obtain the same results.

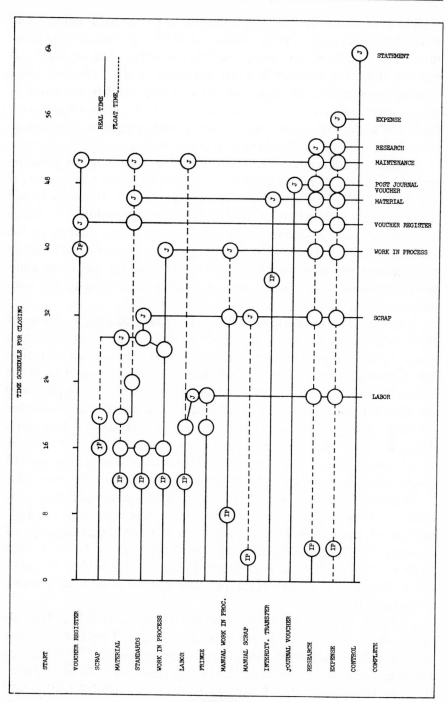

EXHIBIT 6

The analysis of the network indicates a critical path and areas of slack time. The critical path enables management to more effectively direct the man-hours of effort towards expediting the total job. It further indicates areas which do not need to be expedited, thus eliminating costly overtime or even more costly misdirected effort in these noncritical areas. Also, the analysis of the network indicates alternate paths and their costs, guiding management's decisions in cases of breakdown or delays within the system.

Further, PERT creates a mathematical synthesis of an administrative network. Whether performed manually or on a computer, if one is available, this synthesis becomes a guide or standard to aid management's evaluation of new methods or procedures in terms of cost and time savings and the final effect of the change to the overall function. The synthesis also provides a guide with which management can measure the feasibility of new equipment or additional personnel and the cost/time savings contribution to the complete network.

Likewise, the network provides a realistic schedule in terms of the completion of the whole function rather than the completion of a single event that may or may not contribute to the overall objective. The schedule is even more realistic because it is expressed in terms of working units of time, rather than calendar units. In addition to the time schedule factor, the PERT approach effectively establishes the cost of expediting or "crashing" an administrative procedure. Also, the more realistic schedule becomes an excellent control tool. By reviewing actual times against the standards allowed, management can be given a current report of the progress of the total network.

Management, faced with decisions regarding new equipment, personnel, and methods in accomplishing events, has need for a scientific method of evaluation before rather than after the institution of changes. PERT, properly used as a mathematical model, will serve to prove the time/cost savings effect of changes before they are instituted, thus giving management the necessary standard with which to evaluate them.

In short, Project Evaluation and Review Technique is a dynamic approach to administrative analysis, planning, and control. In view of the repetitive nature of administrative processes, cost/time savings resulting from this method can be enjoyed repeatedly. In my opinion, the analytical use of PERT for general business administration will prove even more dynamic than the primary defense contracts scheduling for which it was developed.

58. QUICKER REPORTS THROUGH COST PLANNING AND CONTROL *

Howard C. Greer †

Start with the fact that managements want prompt information about results. Continue with the fact that the manager who cannot get this information quickly from his accountant probably will find some way to get it elsewhere. What can the accountant do about it?

Historically, statement preparation (reporting) has been regarded as necessarily the last in a series of accounting functions normally performed in a specified and immutable order. Characteristically the accountant has considered himself as cast successively in the following roles:

> First, as a recorder (entering transactions)
> Second, as a classifier (posting to accounts)
> Third, as a summarizer (balancing the ledger)
> Fourth, as a reporter (preparing statements)

Asked how quickly he can develop an income statement and balance sheet, an accountant will typically reply, "As soon as we can get the entries made, the journals totaled, the accounts posted, and the trial balance run off." He will consider it heretical to suggest that statements might come first, bookkeeping later. Yet exactly that approach is necessary to develop the necessary information on results as promptly as it is needed, i.e., immediately after the accounting period has ended. Contrast two possible attitudes toward the problem:

Position A: We will do the bookkeeping as rapidly as possible, and present the statements as soon as the bookkeeping has been finished.

Position B: We will prepare the statements as quickly as we can assemble the required data, and complete the bookkeeping later.

My thesis today is that accountants should do an "about face" on their habits and inclinations, and transpose themselves from Position

---

* From *N.A.C.A. Bulletin* (July, 1956), Section 2. Reprinted by permission of the National Association of Cost Accountants.

† H. C. Greer, Vice-President of Finance, The Chemstrand Corporation, Decatur, Alabama.

A to Position B. The "why" is obvious; the "how" is suggested in this paper.

THE "WHAT" AND "WHENCE" OF PRELIMINARY INCOME DETERMINATION

Managerial interest centers on "results"—volume handled, profit realized. Wanted first is a condensed income statement, supplemented by some facts on quantities produced and sold. What components should be identified? Where can information on each be most quickly obtained?

Exhibit 1 lists the principal elements in the computation of profit for a typical manufacturing enterprise. The indicated arrangement may or may not be the one best suited to detailed analysis, but it does suggest a normal buildup sequence for net income determination, when "time is of the essence."

BASIS OF PRELIMINARY INCOME DETERMINATION

Item	Income Component	Source of Information
1	Sales revenues	Billings
2	Cost of goods sold (at standard) ...	"
3	Gross margin (at standard)	1-2
4	Product cost variances	Various (x)
5	Adjusted gross margin	3-4
6	Overhead expenses	Various (Y)
7	Operating profit	5-6
8	Financial expenses	Expirations, accruals
9	Pretax income	7-8
10	Income tax	Computation
11	Net income	9-10

(X) Product Cost Variances

4-a	Production volume	Computation
4-b	Quality and yield	*Output reports
4-c	Labor efficiency	*Output reports, pay rolls
4-d	Maintenance	Stores issues, pay rolls
4-e	Purchase variances	Vouchers
4-f	Inventory variances	Inventory reports

(Y) Overhead Expenses

6-a	Research and development	Vouchers, pay rolls, etc.
6-b	Administration	" " " "
6-c	Marketing	" " " "

* Possibly including special reports on experimental production, training activities, etc.

EXHIBIT 1

There are six basic items in this calculation. The first two (sales revenues and standard cost of goods sold) can be obtained directly from the record of shipments billed (sales journal). A third (financial expense) can be calculated in advance (from journal entries recording expirations and accruals). A fourth (income tax) can be quickly calculated in the course of preparing the statement.

Thus only two of the basic elements in income determination are matters of involved calculation. One of them (overhead expenses) usually requires reference to several primary sources (vouchers, payrolls, expirations, accruals, and perhaps even stores issuances and job order close-outs), but the task is usually neither involved nor time-consuming. The other (product cost variances) is a complex factor, evaluated only with skill and intuition, but notable chiefly as the single "elusive" component in the entire calculation.

What did we earn last month? Well, it was (1) the gross margin at standard on sales invoiced during the period, less (2) the total of outlays made for research, administrative, marketing, and financing expenses, less (3) the excess of actual over standard cost of goods produced, adjusted for (4) the applicable income tax deduction. Measure those items and you have the answer, whether or not the ledger has been posted. Add some facts on quantities shipped and quantities manufactured, by product lines, and you have the story the manager wants to hear.

The trick is to give him the facts so quickly that he has no incentive or inclination to ferret them out for himself. That means having them in his hands before a day has passed. How do we go about it?

SALES REVENUES AND GROSS MARGIN OF STANDARD

Sales volume is the single most important fact in practically every business enterprise. Management must keep track of it constantly, from day to day, in prospect as well as retrospect. To obtain facts on sales, who is going to wait for a bookkeeper to total a journal, post an account, take off a balance, and write up a report? Nobody.

Good reporting of facts about sales includes (1) initial forecasts of orders expected for the coming accounting period (and perhaps several after that), (2) day-by-day summaries of orders received, shipped, and on hand, including cumulative billings for the month to date (3) frequently revised projections of expected billings for the remainder of the current accounting period, and the probable total for the entire period, and (4) an immediate report of the exact total, less returns and allowances, within a few hours after the last shipment has left the plant.

With this sort of continuous follow-up, no one need be long in doubt as to the size of the first item in the income statement. Before noon of the first working day after closing this amount is precisely determinable and immediately available for use in income determination.

Cost of goods sold, figured at standard, can be calculated with almost equal speed. Provision can be readily made for keeping this computation current, from day to day, as sales are recorded, so that a "gross margin at standard" emerges just about as promptly as the "sales revenue" figure to which it is related. Thus the manager can be immediately informed, at any time (1) how much business has been done, and (2) what margin should have been earned had costs been held within "allowed" limits.

Overhead Expenses

Deductions from gross margin at standard include (1) excess of actual over standard costs and (2) expenses deductible as applicable to the "period" rather than the volume transacted. The latter class of charges, being the simpler, may be first considered.

The "overhead expense" burden is normally not too difficult to measure. The expenses in this group (research, development, engineering, administration, selling, delivery, advertising, promotion, financing) usually follow a pattern established by budgets and programs known in advance. The approximate outlays can be predicted with a fair degree of accuracy, and deviation from the prediction can be observed and measured without undue difficulty.

Principal sources of such charges are three: (1) payments to outsiders for supplies furnished or services rendered (vouchers entered); (2) compensation to employees for work performed (salary and wage payrolls); (3) supply and expense prepayment expirations and expense accruals (scheduled journal entries). Occasional charges develop from other sources, but the above are chiefly important.

How much expense from vouchers payable? It is a simple matter to keep a cumulative running total of such charges, taken from the voucher register as often as needed. The important task is to get the vouchers passed and entered promptly. The alert accountant must know not merely what bills have been put through for payment, but what others are "in the mill."

The effective way to handle this is to maintain a record of all purchase orders placed, commitments made, deliveries received, special services performed, recurring charges, and special activities, with the expectable cost of each—this for quick comparison with the voucher register at the month end to see that actual obligations incurred are fully reflected in the accounts. This undertaking deserves far more attention than it commonly receives.

Payroll charges are fairly simple to accumlate. Salary payments are scheduled well ahead of time and are precisely calculable. Wage payments are determinable for all but the final week of the period, which usually can be estimated with no important error. An allowance for "fringe benefits" must be added, usually as a predetermined percentage of compensation paid.

Numerous charges derive from write-offs of expenses prepaid or write-ons of expenses accrued. These calculations are (or can be) made well in advance of the end of the period, and readily incorporated in overhead expense computations. Where usage of inventoriable operating supplies is a factor, summaries of quantities consumed may have to be brought up to a date close to the end of the period (with issuances of the last day or two temporarily ignored), but this is normally an insignificant element in overall results.

Financial expenses, and other nonoperating charges, are most commonly of the expiration accrued type, and are readily calculable in advance. Occasional "extraordinary charges" may require special handling, as noted in a subsequent section, but (with few exceptions) ordinarily cause no serious complications.

PRODUCT COST VARIANCES

This leaves only one unknown in the profit equation—the amount by which actual manufacturing costs have exceeded (or fallen short of) the established standards for such operations. By accounting convention this amount is considered a proper charge against income for the current period, and it must therefore be determined, by some means, before the income statement can be completed.

Measurement of product cost variances by ordinary bookkeeping procedures is apt to be a complex and time-consuming process. For prompt reporting it usually will be found necessary to adopt some alternative method of arriving at the approximate amount to be taken up in the accounts. Since the charge is inherently the product of a somewhat arbitrary and conventional assignment of costs, there is less necessity for precise calculation than in some other segments of the income statement.

The method employed will depend on the nature of the business and the character of its accounting procedures. In some cases a straight input-output inventory calculation may be possible (i.e., total production expenditures, less value of output at standard, adjusted for changes in process inventories, equals excess manufacturing cost). Commonly, however, the valuation of process inventories takes too long to permit using those figures in a "first day" report, and some other approach is required.

Variances from standard are likely to result from three or more circumstances, including the following: (1) differences between actual and expected cost of materials purchased; (2) differences between actual and standard expense of conversion of raw materials into finished goods; (3) differences between actual and assumed (book) value of inventories, reflecting both quantity discrepancies and price adjustments. Each must be separately computed.

The "purchase variance" amount is easily computed. Where the practice is to carry all parts, materials, and supplies at standard valuations, differences between actual and standard costs are calculated at time of purchase, and currently accumulated as an income charge. As soon as the last voucher is put through, the total of this charge is immediately available.

The "production variance" is the product of several factors, of which the following can be readily identified: (1) off-standard facilities usage (volume variance); (2) off-standard labor performance (efficiency variance); (3) off-standard product-materials ratio (yield variance). Each should be the subject of a separate determination.

Cost standards presumably include a fixed expense component for each unit of output, each machine hour, each factory day, or some other facilities usage measure. A cumulative daily output report will disclose the quantities produced, or hours operated, or some similar data, from which the amount of fixed charges "absorbed" can be easily calculated, with the remainder representing the volume variance.

Labor efficiency is a trickier item to figure, and the calculation may be little more than a series of educated guesses. Specific allowance can be made, however, for any known excess costs as those resulting from experimental production, employee training, etc. Output reports will disclose such factors as yields, scrap, degraded product, etc. and will facilitate an accurate estimate of material variances.

Inventory adjustments (reflecting discrepancies disclosed by physical counts and changes in valuations resulting from adoption of new cost standards) can be timed to occur at the beginning (or middle) of an accounting period, and thus need cause no last-minute delays in profit determination. Since the assignment of such adjustments between periods is arbitrary in any case, they may be handled to create a minimum of interference with monthly account closings and periodic reports.

"Problem" Elements in Profit Determination

While the procedures above, sketchily described, will provide a close approximation of profits realized, available within a few hours after the period has ended, there are always a few erratic and unpredictable elements in income computation, requiring special treatment and necessitating sophisticated interpretation. Fortunately, their very character sets them apart from the routine components of profit making activities, and permits their assignment on a reasoned, if somewhat arbitrary, basis.

First in order of importance is the expense of plant and equipment maintenance, frequently occurring in conjunction with additions, improvements, and rehabilitations. Since there are normally somewhat violent spurts and dips in such activities, the outlays are variable and difficult to measure by ordinary accounting devices. A further complication results from the fact that varying portions of such outlays may be expensed or capitalized, leaving the income charge a widely fluctuating and very uncertain amount, hard to calculate quickly when a period ends.

Several solutions are possible. If management's wish is to have the income statement reflect maintenance outlays expensed within the period, an expedited job close-out program must be installed. Shortcuts are permissible (e.g., labor *hours* may be accumulated by jobs and charged out at an average hourly rate, and stores issuances may be priced out as statistically determined group averages). It is not necessary, of course, that charges be assigned by departments for preliminary income determinations—merely that total outlays be known and a distinction between capital and income observed.

Where maintenance is handled seasonally, or concentrated during periods of shutdown (or low volume), management may prefer to see expense charges "equalized" over an extended period. This makes for easy advance determination of the amount chargeable to the current period. Early "cutoff" of maintenance charges (several days before closing) is another alternative that facilitates calculations without impairing the validity of any conclusions likely to be drawn from a preliminary income statement.

Other expenses which may fluctuate erratically are those connected with programs of experimentation and development, special advertising campaigns and sales promotions, legal proceedings and settlements of litigation, tax controversies and settlements, casualty losses, insurance recoveries, etc. Even with a leisurely closing schedule, it is often difficult to decide (1) what the final cost will be and (2) how much should be charged to current period results. The difficulty is intensified when the decision must be made hastily.

The solution, of course, is to search out these possible contingencies well in advance, estimate the potential income charge (or credit), and arrive at a policy decision with respect to the proper accounting treatment. Accrued expense and deferred charge accounts may be liberally used in this connection, with improvement in income measurement methods as well as acceleration of reporting schedules.

Some accountants, valuing orthodoxy in form above realism in interpretation, are disposed to complain that income calculations so developed become "mere estimates" (as supposedly distinguishable from factual computations). The truth is, of course, that all period-by-period assignments of costs such as depreciation, maintenance, advertising, research, process development, product design, and many others, are "estimates," the selection of a proper charge being a purely arbitrary and subjective matter. The monthly write-off gains no higher standing because it has been incorporated in a journal entry and posted to a ledger account.

A properly constructed income statement must be strictly factual and precise as to measurable occurrences (e.g., sales, production, materials consumption, labor utilization, and all other factors directly related thereto), but it is necessarily theoretical and approximative as to pro rata absorption of long-term costs (facilities usage, sales promotion, and the like). If the accountant must theorize and approximate (and he must), then he may well do it quickly and conveniently, rather than slowly and ponderously, since the end result will not be appreciably different.

REPORTING SCHEDULE

The preceding discussion has centered on the development of a condensed summary of results of operations for presentation to management at the earliest possible moment. Essential facts should be made available, at least in rough form, by the afternoon of the first working day. Formal statements should be ready for submittal early the following morning.

It must be expected that the figures reported at that time will be few in number, and bare of comparisons, ratios, and interpretative comment. Detailed analyses, cumulative data, and derived calculations should follow quickly, but need not delay the initial report on "what happened."

Exhibit 2 outlines the possible form and timing of successive presentations of various aspects of results, designed to convey essentials quickly and to provide supplemental explanations at the earliest practical dates. Note the various methods employed.

Since the chief executive is the sole target of the initial presentation, it can be made verbally, in a pencil memo and/or a few simple

---

REPORTING SCHEDULE

Report	Content	Periods Covered	Form	Time
* Results summary	Production, shipments, stocks Gross revenues, net income	All months to date Same period last year	Pencil entries on cumulative record	First day (p. m.)
# Preliminary statements	Income statement Balance sheet	Actual (current mo.) Forecast (coming mo.)	Typed tables	Second day (a. m.)
@ Final statements	Income statement Balance sheet Text comment	Current month Year to date	Mimeo report	Fifth day (p. m.)
x Detailed statements	Revenues, costs, expenses Assets, liabilities, equities Text comment	Current month Year to date	Mimeo report	Sixth day (a. m.)

* Results summary shows bare preliminary data—no derived percentages, unit costs, changes, etc. (to president only—accompanied by verbal explanation from chief accountant)

\# Preliminary statements include breakdown by product lines, but no cumulative or derived data (to president only—passed on verbally to directors at his discretion)

@ Final statements include budget comparisons, ratios, unit cost and margin data, etc. (to president and members of board of directors, as formal presentation)

x Detailed statements include analyses of revenues and margins by products, explanation of cost variances, departmental performance against budgets, consist of cash resources and receivables, inventory status and turnover, additions to plant and equipment, depreciation reserves, etc. (full set to president only, individual schedules to department heads concerned)

EXHIBIT 2

charts. A convenient and practical device is to maintain a continuous, cumulative data sheet, in pencil form, on which the key figures for each month can be written in during the afternoon of the first day, as fast as they become available. There is no delay for typing or duplication; prior period data are already on the sheet; corrections can be made easily if they prove necessary. Line charts, presenting basic data, can be brought up to date at the same time, in the same way.

A more formal presentation—consisting, say, of income statements and balance sheets for three successive periods (last month actual, this month preliminary, next month forecast)—should be ready for review the first thing on the following morning. (If an hour of late afternoon overtime is necessary, who will begrudge it?) If the figures raise questions, the accountant should be ready with verbal explanations (he has had all night to study the results, and by morning should be fortified with all the answers).

With this much impetus, completion of all the formal accounting work should go forward rapidly. Experience in one large company has established that five working days are ample for all the required bookkeeping mechanics, preparation of several hundred detailed cost and financial statements, *and their thoroughgoing review with all levels of supervision except top management.* Final income statements and balance sheets can be submitted at the end of the fifth day; detailed reports for top management, on all aspects of results and position, with explanatory comment, should be ready before noon on the next day following.

The experience of this company proves that this program is not only effective and fruitful, but that it can be carried out almost 100 percent within normal working hours, without extra help or significant extra effort. Possibly 10 percent of the accounting staff find it necessary (or desirable) to put in a few hours outside the normal workday (one evening or one Saturday morning, compensated later by corresponding time off), but the overtime burden has been reduced to practically nil. If there is any extra cost involved it is too small to be measurable.

The secret lies in organization, training, advance preparation, alertness, vigor, and common sense. Strip out the nonessentials, and prompt income determination becomes a practical if not a simple achievement. To repeat: accept the obligation of doing the reporting first and the bookkeeping later, and you will be a purveyor of vital information, not merely a custodian of records on out-of-date events.

59. THE OPERATIONS LETTER AS THE CONTROLLER'S MEDIUM OF EXPRESSION *

Paul L. Smith †

Shortly after the turn of the present century, it became apparent that modern business was assuming a complexity which made imperative for most companies the addition of a new member of the management team. That member was, of course, the controller (or comptroller). The increasing pressure of competition necessitated some means of separating from the maze of mounting figures those weak operational areas which called for management's concentration.

It was also found that balance sheet and profit-and-loss statement by themselves give rise to questions which demanded further explanation of the accounting treatment given such debatable issues as depreciation, renegotiation, provision for federal and local taxes, inventory valuation, possible losses on receivables, contingent liabilities and investments. Thus, although he has been delegated many other responsibilities, there are two functions which are the prime contribution of the controller to the management of a modern business. These are:

1. Interpreting the operational results and financial status of the company.
2. Measuring actual performance against the predetermined blueprint or budget.

In accomplishing these objectives, the controller has had two primary media of expression. Firstly, he could discuss the periodic results with his colleagues verbally. Obviously, this left no permanent record and often resulted in misunderstanding, misquoting and later arguments. Secondly, he could issue a series of statistical reports on various phases of his statements with footnotes and asterisked explanations. This type of presentation usually confused top

* From *The Controller* (November, 1953). Reprinted by permission of the Controllers Institute of America, Inc.
† Paul L. Smith, Comptroller of the Acme Shear Company, Bridgeport, Connecticut.

management by the weight of detail and lack of continuity and was thus often skimmed over superficially.

Consequently, to improve the important field of communications a new manner of presenting this information to top management has been developed, termed here as "operations letter." This one document gives a bird's-eye view of the entire business for the accounting period. Stressing profit and loss results, it nevertheless comments on significant balance sheet items in addition. As a permanent record, it also provides a reference to all phases of the business history, including such items not readily available elsewhere as effect of material price changes on overall costs, date and effect on margin of major selling price revisions, dates and amounts of general wage increases, effect of unusual situations on sales and orders received, and reasons for adding or dropping sales lines.

No better description of an operations letter can be given than to actually present a sample. Accordingly, following is such a letter of the type developed for use in The Acme Shear Company. All figures and situations have, of course, been synthetically developed and do not represent actual results for any period. Attempt has been made to point up what are considered several important aspects of the letter, as follows:

1. Statements should be factual and unbiased.
2. Where an opinion or forecast would add value to the presentation, the responsible division head should be consulted and quoted.
3. Strong use is made of the budget and explanations given of variations of actual results from those budgeted, that is, management by exception.
4. Although addressed to the president, all other officers and members of the board of directors are given copies.

As an aid to understanding the following letter, a few comments on The Acme Shear Company are in order. For many years the world's largest manufacturer of consumer type scissors and shears, it numbers several hundred items in its sales line. Basic materials used are cold forged steel, hot forged steel, and cast iron. Its manufacturing processes include a foundry, forge shop, heavy and light presses, grinding, buffing, plating, drilling, branding, assembling and packing operations. A standard cost system is used in valuing input and output of all inventories, with nearly all direct labor workers paid on a piecework basis. An annual direct labor and expense budget is prepared for all departments, which is used to plan operations and gauge performance for the year.

MAY 15, 1953
SUBJECT: APRIL, 1953, OPERATIONS
MR. H. C. WHEELER, PRESIDENT
THE ACME SHEAR COMPANY

Net sales billed for April amounted to $400,000 and resulted in a net profit after taxes of $14,400. A brief summary of April results compared with March, Year to Date, and Budget 1953 is shown in Exhibit 1.

EXHIBIT 1	APRIL RESULTS						
	APRIL	1953	MARCH	1953	YEAR TO DATE		BUDGET
	AMOUNT	% NSB	AMOUNT	% NSB	AMOUNT	% NSB	1953
Net Sales Billed	$400,000	100.0%	$350,000	100.0%	$1,600,000	100.0%	100.0%
Cost of Sales	310,000	77.5	280,000	80.0	1,248,000	78.0	76.0
Gross Profit on Sales	90,000	22.5	70,000	20.0	352,000	22.0	24.0
Comm'l. & Adm. Expense	48,000	12.0	46,900	13.4	208,000	13.0	12.0
Net Profit from Operations	42,000	10.5	23,100	6.6	144,000	9.0	12.0
Other Income & Deductions	7,600	1.9	7,000	2.0	30,400	1.9	2.0
Net Profit Before Taxes	34,400	8.6	16,100	4.6	113,600	7.1	10.0
Federal and State Taxes	20,000	5.0	8,400	2.4	59,200	3.7	6.0
Net Profit After Taxes	$ 14,400	3.6%	$ 7,700	2.2%	$ 54,400	3.4%	4.0%

Exhibit 1

Net profit before taxes in April was 8.6 percent of net sales billed, compared with 4.6 percent in March. This improvement was primarily due to increased sales volume and a greater profit ratio at standard manufacturing cost. Although net profit before taxes was 1.4 percentage points below that budgeted, unfavorable overhead variance was 2.1 percent of net sales billed and was again the primary cause of failure to realize budgeted profit this year.

NET SALES BILLED AND GROSS PROFIT ON SALES

Gross profit on sales of 22.5 percent in April represented an improvement of 2.5 percentage points over March and 0.5 percentage points over year to date. However, this was still 1.5 percentage points under budget, due primarily to overhead variances and heavy scrap losses.

Hot Forged scissors made in United States again produced a gross loss on sales. As discussed in report sent you under separate cover, it would appear advisable to terminate manufacture of this line and purchase from our Swedish supplier.

Net sales billed were $400,000, or $15,300 less than budgeted. Year to date billing of $1,600,000 was $192,800 less than budgeted.

EXHIBIT 2   DETAILS OF NET SALES BILLED AND GROSS PROFIT ON SALES BY PRODUCT CLASS
NOTE: LIGHT FACE FIGURES ASTERISKED INDICATE "UNFAVORABLE"

PRODUCT CLASS	NET SALES BILLED	STD. COST SHIPMENTS	% PROFIT AT STD.	STANDARD COST VARIANCES	SCRAP & INVENTORY RESERVE	SHIPPING EXPENSE	OTHER COSTS	GROSS PROFIT ON SALES	%
				COST OF SALES					
				APRIL 1953					
Cast	$ 120,000	$ 83,640	30.3%	$ 1,660	$ 3,190	$ 1,800	$ 800	$ 28,910	24.1%
Cold Forged Steel	160,000	113,440	29.1	1,350	3,510	2,400	1,180	38,120	23.8
Hot Forged-U.S.	5,000	4,000	20.0	850	160	70	20	100*	2.0*
Hot Forged-Sweden	9,000	6,480	28.0	—0—	60	140	10	2,310	25.7
Pinking Shears	50,000	30,160	39.7	3,830	4,210	750	870	10,180	20.4
Purchased Goods	9,000	6,930	23.0	—0—	70	130	20	1,850	20.5
Castings	37,000	27,750	25.0	150	1,360	560	50	7,130	19.3
Defense-Forged	10,000	7,600	24.0	160	440	150	50	1,600	16.0
Total	$ 400,000	$ 280,000	30.0%	$ 8,000	$13,000	$ 6,000	$ 3,000	$ 90,000	22.5%
				MARCH 1953					
Cast	$ 116,000	$ 86,880	25.1%	$ 640	$ 3,480	$ 2,050	$ 1,800	$ 21,150	18.2%
Cold Forged Steel	132,000	96,040	27.3	710	2,890	2,360	2,460	27,540	20.9
Hot Forged-U.S.	6,000	4,810	19.8	1,110	240	110	20	290*	4.8*
Hot Forged-Sweden	8,000	5,740	28.3	—0—	60	150	10	2,040	25.5
Pinking Shears	42,000	26,460	37.0	640	1,580	750	1,470	11,100	26.4
Purchased Goods	11,000	8,470	23.0	90	90	200	20	2,220	20.2
Castings	23,000	17,300	24.8	200*	900	450	150	4,400	19.1
Defense-Forged	12,000	9,100	24.2	100	560	230	170	1,840	15.4
Total	$ 350,000	$ 254,800	27.2%	$ 3,000	$ 9,800	$ 6,300	$ 6,100	$ 70,000	20.0%
				YEAR TO DATE					
Cast	$ 450,000	$ 326,250	27.5%	$ 5,900	$12,550	$ 7,100	$ 3,600	$ 94,600	21.0%
Cold Forged Steel	620,000	448,880	27.6	9,730	12,970	9,640	4,840	133,940	21.6
Hot Forged-U.S.	24,000	19,220	19.9	4,270	960	370	70	890*	3.7*
Hot Forged-Sweden	33,000	23,690	28.2	—0—	240	500	30	8,540	25.9
Pinking Shears	240,000	145,920	39.2	6,320	9,710	3,700	2,440	71,910	29.9
Purchased Goods	45,000	34,650	23.0	—0—	350	680	50	9,270	20.6
Castings	102,000	76,190	25.3	150	3,810	1,600	240	20,010	19.6
Defense-Forged	86,000	65,270	24.1	630	3,910	1,310	260	14,620	17.0
Total	$1,600,000	$1,140,070	28.8%	$27,000	$44,500	$24,900	$11,530	$352,000	22.0%

Exhibit 2

By product class, as shown in Exhibit 2, these differences were confined principally to pinking shear sales, where production has been restricted during a period of engineering changes.

Profit at standard manufacturing cost was 30.0 percent of net sales billed compared with 27.2 percent in March. Most significant improvement over the prior month was in the Cast product class, which showed a 5.2 percentage point gain. This resulted from absence of sales in April of the unprofitable 190 line. Discontinuance of this line and substitution of the profitable 179, recommended in November, 1952, was fully accomplished by final clearance of inventories in March. In addition, costs of several low-margin Cold Forged Steel items, commented upon in the February operations letter, were reduced through changes in the method of assembly.

April standard profit was also 1.0 percentage points higher than budgeted. Favorable performance was due to Cold Forged Steel cost reductions and proportionately smaller sales volume of the lower margin Purchased Goods and Defense-Forgings.

STANDARD COST VARIANCES

Standard cost variances (Exhibits 3 and 4) were a charge to operations of $8,000 in April compared with $3,000 in March and

EXHIBIT 3   A SUMMARY OF STANDARD COST VARIANCES BY DIVISION

DIVISION	APRIL 1953	(FAVORABLE) (UNFAVORABLE*) MARCH 1953
Cast Iron	$2,230*	$1,460*
Cold Forged Steel	1,160*	620*
Hot Forged	780*	650*
Foundry	340*	390
Pinking Shear	3,720*	670*
Maintenance	40*	10*
Tool Room	30	10
Material Price	240	10
Total Standard Cost Variances	$8,000*	$3,000*

Exhibit 3

EXHIBIT 4   DETAILS OF STANDARD COST VARIANCES FOR APRIL

DEPARTMENT	MATERIAL USAGE	MATERIAL PRICE	DIRECT LABOR	OVER-HEAD	(FAVORABLE) (UNFAVORABLE*) TOTAL
123 Nickel Plate	$ 60	$	$	$ 20*	$ 40
128 Japan				20*	20*
130 Inspect & Pack	140		30*	60*	50
136 Grind				300*	300*
140 Buff				340*	340*
145 Wash				20*	20*
150 Other Cast	30		230*	1,440*	1,640*
218 Heat Treat				100*	100*
250 Other Cold Forged Steel	40			1,100*	1,060*
350 Foundry	410		110*	640*	340*
451 Forge Shop	20			70*	50*
452 Other Forged				730*	730*
650 Pinking Shear	130*			3,590*	3,720*
956 Maintenance				40*	40*
957 Tool Room				30	30
Material Price		240			240
Total	$570	$240	$370*	$8,440*	$8,000*

Exhibit 4

no variances budgeted. Poorest performance was by the Pinking Shear Division.

Overhead variance for April was an unfavorable $8,440. With the exception of the Pinking Shear Division, the variances were principally of controllable expense. Most significant items are shown in Exhibit 5.

EXHIBIT 5

OVERHEAD VARIANCE

DEPARTMENT	EXPENSE ITEM	UNFAVORABLE VARIANCE
Grind	Jigs, Fixtures	$ 203 (A)
Buff	Shop Supplies	236 (B)
Other Cast	Overtime Premium	268 (C)
	Non-Standard Operations	437 (D)
	Shop Supplies	428 (E)
Other Cold Forged Steel	Maint. & Repair Dies	578 (F)
	Apprentice Loss	307 (G)
Foundry	Sand Mullers	240 (H)
Other Forged	Fixed Expenses	603 (I)
Pinking Shear	Rework	2,528 (J)
	Fixed Expenses	1,760 (L)
		$7,588

(A) Error by Maintenance Department in reading specifications caused scrapping of 10 new grinding fixtures at cost of $198.

(B) Usage rate of rouge almost twice normal experience.

(C) Incurred by direct-labor workers only. With production at budgeted rate, hiring of two additional operators appears indicated.

(D) Principally additional inspection operation temporarily required until new nickel plating process meets quality requirements.

(E) Over standard on small tools $204 and wheels $198.

(F) Inexperienced operators cracked three new trimming dies.

(G) Turnover of personnel has averaged 20% higher for this department in past six months than any other department.

(H) After March reduction in output to match budget, sand muller hired temporarily in January was not laid off as scheduled.

(I) Underliquidation of depreciation, property taxes, etc., due to low direct labor.

(J) Due to engineering changes. See remarks under Production section.

Exhibit 5

Detailed comparisons of actual and standard controllable overhead expense for each department have been given the manager of manufacturing for review with foremen.

Material usage variance for April was a favorable $570. Included was $410 from the Foundry Division. This reduction in cost was accomplished by substitution of a better grade of scrap steel than formerly purchased, which made possible a greater proportion of scrap steel (at $19.50/M lbs.) to pig iron (at $33.00/M lbs.) in the melt. Quality of castings is reported to be unchanged.

Direct labor variance was an unfavorable $370. Other Cast Department incurred $230 of this sum. Substitution of a lower priced screw for the kitchen shear by the Purchasing Department has reduced efficiency of assembly operators to a degree that necessitated wage payments on an overstandard average rate during April. With a cost reduction of only $120 on the quantity of screws used versus the $230 loss in direct labor payments, it would appear advisable to resume purchase from our prior supplier.

Scrap and Inventory Reserve

Reserve for inventory deficits amounted to $11,400 at April 25. Scrap charges during April totaled $10,200. Details are shown in Exhibit 6.

EXHIBIT 6	DETAILS OF SCRAP CHARGES		
PRODUCT CLASS	CHARGES	ACTUAL RATE OF OUTPUT	BUDGETED RATE OF OUTPUT
Cast	$ 2,350	3.0%	3.0%
Cold Forged Steel	2,380	1.8	2.0
Hot Forged—U.S.	120	2.4	4.0
Pinking Shears	3,910	9.9	5.0
Castings	1,080	3.9	4.0
Defense-Forged	360	5.0	5.0
Total	$10,200		

Exhibit 6

Pinking shear scrap was 9.9 percent of output compared with 5.0 percent budgeted. During recent engineering changes, it was found that a substantial portion of shears made by previous methods could not be successfully reworked and were thus scrapped. For this same reason, it is expected that May scrap rate will also be high, although final disposition of all old stocks should be completed in May.

Commercial and Administrative Expense

Commercial and administrative expenses for April were $48,000 compared with $46,900 for March and $50,660 budgeted. Details are shown in Exhibit 7.

Only two items of expense were significantly higher than budget. Traveling and entertaining expense of the Sales Department was $2,560 compared with $1,640 budgeted. Included in April expense was $1,240 for the Sales Manager's annual trip to the West Coast. Samples expense was $710 in excess of budget due to $780 cost of samples given salesmen of the new 584 line.

Commissions and Provision for Salesmen's Bonus were less than budget due primarily to lower sales volume. Salesmen's salaries were $910 less than budget principally because the proposed post of Midwest District Supervisor has not yet been filled.

EXHIBIT 7   COMMERCIAL AND ADMINISTRATIVE EXPENSES

	APRIL (19 DAYS)	MARCH (20 DAYS)	BUDGET APRIL (19 DAYS)
Advertising and Promotion	$ 7,600	$ 8,000	$ 7,600
Selling			
Commissions	8,430	7,560	9,440
Salesmen	4,010	4,010	4,920
Supervision	2,040	2,150	2,180
Clerical	1,930	2,040	2,070
Traveling & Entertaining	2,560	1,330	1,640
Provision For Salesmen's Bonus	620	580	1,000
Samples	1,510	760	800
Provision For Vacations & Holidays	400	430	600
Telephone and Telegraph	640	890	900
Other	1,230	1,370	1,620
Administrative			
Clerical	7,640	7,960	8,070
Supervision	3,420	3,610	3,570
Tabulating Machine Rentals	740	740	740
Supplies	900	1,140	1,030
Depreciation	670	710	670
Traveling & Entertaining	700	930	800
Provision For Vacations & Holidays	580	600	610
Parcel Post	430	560	490
Other	1,950	1,530	1,910
TOTAL	$48,000	$46,900	$50,660
Ratio To Net Sales Billed	12.0%	13.4%	12.2%

Exhibit 7

OTHER INCOME AND DEDUCTIONS

Other income and deductions resulted in a net charge to operations of $7,600 in April compared with $8,300 budgeted. Details are shown in Exhibit 8.

SUMMARY OF UNUSUAL EXPENSES

Current month and year to date charges and credits to operations of an unusual and nonrecurrent nature are summarized in Exhibit 9.

PRODUCTION

Standard direct labor for April amounted to $69,200 compared with $73,860 budgeted for that period. A comparison of April with March by department is shown in Exhibit 10.

Pinking Shear production was 52.7 percent of budget for April. During March, quality control spot-checks disclosed that a recent

EXHIBIT 8   OTHER INCOME AND DEDUCTIONS

	APRIL	BUDGET
Other Income		
Profit on Sale of Equipment	$ 320	$ —0—
Miscellaneous	110	—0—
Total Other Income	$ 430	$ —0—
Other Deductions		
Pensions	$5,200	$5,500
Interest on Funded Debt	920	1,000
Donations	710	800
Other	1,200	1,000
Total Other Deductions	$8,030	$8,300
Net Charge To Operations	$7,600	$8,300

Exhibit 8

EXHIBIT 9   SUMMARY OF UNUSUAL EXPENSES

	PROFIT OR LOSS*	
	APRIL	YEAR TO DATE
Profit on sales of equipment	$ 320	$1,430
Writeoff experimental expense of rejected plastic and cold forged steel scissor	720*	2,880*
Writeoff new 625 pinking shear die never put into production	600*	1,200*
Writeoff scrapped and obsolete equipment	390*	2,640*
Legal expenses in connection with pinking shear patent suit	—0—	1,500*
	$1,390*	$6,790*

Exhibit 9

change in design of the pinking shear caused a substantial percentage of shears to cut poorly. Although the situation was immediately corrected, in process and finished inventories contained approximately 60,000 pairs, which had to be reworked to conform to the revised design and manufacturing methods. Consequently, during April nearly half of the department's labor force was engaged in nonproductive rework. Slow-up of manufacturing also caused drop in standard direct labor in Other Cast and Inspect and Pack Departments, since they also perform operations on the pinking shear.

EXHIBIT 10	STANDARD DIRECT LABOR			
	APRIL (19 DAYS)		MARCH (20 DAYS)	
DEPARTMENT	ACTUAL DIRECT LABOR AT STANDARD	OVER (UNDER*) BUDGET	ACTUAL DIRECT LABOR AT STANDARD	OVER (UNDER*) BUDGET
123 Nickel Plate	$ 2,380	$ 20*	$ 2,540	$ 20
128 Japan	1,020	30	1,030	10*
130 Inspect & Pack	4,810	350*	5,420	10*
136 Grind	2,950	10*	3,100	20*
140 Buff	3,420	30*	3,650	20
145 Wash	1,740	10*	1,860	10
150 Other Cast	17,890	870*	19,710	50*
218 Heat Treat	1,000	30*	1,100	10
250 Other Cold Forged Steel	18,010	700*	19,500	210*
350 Foundry	10,900	200	12,470	1,200
451 Forge Shop	1,970	40*	2,060	60*
452 Other Forged	300	300*	380	250*
650 Pinking Shear	2,810	2,530*	5,430	200*
Total	$69,200	$4,660*	$78,250	$ 450

Exhibit 10

Other Cold Forged Steel and Other Forged Departments were $700 and $300 below budget respectively. In both cases this was due to loss of personnel, although replacements have been secured at this writing.

Foundry Division production was still in excess of budget, resulting in further increases in stocks of castings. However, layoff of one molder late in April reduced the rate of surplus from that in March and assured a break-even level for May.

ORDERS RECEIVED

Orders received in April totaled $428,000. Details by product class of orders received and balance of unfilled orders at the end of April and March are shown in Exhibit 11.

EXHIBIT 11	ORDERS RECEIVED		UNFILLED ORDERS	
PRODUCT CLASS	APRIL	YEAR TO DATE	APRIL 25, 1953	MARCH 28, 1953
Cast	$118,800	$ 428,000	$ 76,800	$ 78,000
Cold Forged Steel	169,000	725,000	275,000	266,000
Hot Forged-U.S.	3,800	17,200	3,500	4,700
Hot Forged-Sweden	9,600	41,000	11,600	11,000
Pinking Shears	69,500	272,000	102,500	83,000
Purchased Goods	8,700	46,000	7,300	7,600
Castings	37,900	104,000	58,900	58,000
Defense-Forged	10,700	85,000	22,700	22,000
Total	$428,000	$1,718,200	$558,300	$530,300

Exhibit 11

Orders received for the current month approximated budget both in total and by product class. Year to date this is also true except for an excess of $110,000 in Cold Forged Steel, representing a seasonal fluctuation which is normally offset by a slack period in the fall.

Unfilled orders at April 25 were equivalent to 1.3 months budgeted sales. Backlog was abnormally inflated in two product classes. Cold Forged Steel orders included $122,000 from school suppliers with instructions not to ship before June 1. Pinking Shear backlog has

EXHIBIT 12	INVENTORIES			
	BALANCE AT		APRIL INCREASE	YEAR TO DATE INCREASE
	APRIL 25, 1953	MARCH 28, 1953	DECREASE*	DECREASE*
FINISHED GOODS				
Cast	$ 61,200	$ 63,100	$ 1,900*	$ 2,400*
Cold Forged Steel	195,600	171,300	24,300	78,400
Hot Forged—U.S.	9,000	7,800	1,200	4,100
Hot Forged—Sweden	3,200	4,600	1,400*	1,900*
Pinking Shears	11,200	21,600	10,400*	30,100*
Purchased Goods	7,200	7,400	200*	300
Total	$ 287,400	$ 275,800	$11,600	$ 48,400
IN PROCESS				
Cast	$ 160,700	$ 159,800	$ 900	$ 300*
Cold Forged Steel	204,300	208,700	4,400*	11,600*
Hot Forged—U.S.	14,000	12,800	1,200	3,600
Pinking Shears	101,200	78,600	22,600	24,700
Castings	7,200	6,900	300	100
Defense-Forged	13,700	13,900	200*	400
Foundry Scissors and Shears	24,600	23,100	1,500	3,200
Total	$ 525,700	$ 503,800	$21,900	$ 20,100
STORES	$ 173,600	$ 171,800	$ 1,800	$ 700
MATERIALS	247,000	211,600	35,400	31,600
TOTAL INVENTORIES	$1,233,700	$1,163,000	$70,700	$100,800

	FINISHED GOODS	IN PROCESS, STORES, MATERIALS
Average Balance—April	$281,600	$916,750
Standard Cost Shipments, Output	280,000	293,200
Turnover At Annual Rate—April	12.9	4.2
March	12.3	4.7
Year To Date	12.8	4.6
Year 1952	13.2	4.8

Exhibit 12

risen in the past two months due to tie-up of stocks unavailable and reworking attendant on design changes.

INVENTORIES

Inventories at standard manufacturing cost increased $70,700 during April. Details are shown in Exhibit 12.

Finished Goods inventories increased $11,600 in April, resulting in an increase of $48,400 for the year to date. Included in these figures were $24,300 and $78,400 respectively for Cold Forged Steel stocks. These inventories have intentionally been built up to provide for seasonally large shipments to school suppliers in June and July.

In Process inventories increased $21,900 in April. This rise was due to restricted output of pinking shears during the period of engineering change rework.

Materials increased $35,400 during the month. Heavy purchases of steel were made during April in anticipation of price increases on this item in the near future.

ACCOUNTS RECEIVABLE

Accounts receivable at April 25 amounted to $376,000 compared with $322,000 at March 28. Increase of $54,000 was primarily due to larger sales volume, as number of days' billing was approximately the same. An aged analysis is shown in Exhibit 13.

EXHIBIT 13	ACCOUNTS RECEIVABLE				
	APRIL 25, 1953		MARCH 28, 1953		
	AMOUNT	%	AMOUNT	%	
Current	$314,340	83.6%	$269,840	83.8%	
Past Due 1 Month	30,460	8.1	25,440	7.9	
Past Due 2 Months	9,020	2.4	7,090	2.2	
Past Due 3 Months	6,020	1.6	5,800	1.8	
Past Due 4 Months	3,010	0.8	2,900	0.9	
Past Due 5 Months	1,500	0.4	10,300	3.2	
Past Due 6 Months and Over	11,650	3.1	630	0.2	
	$376,000	100.0%	$322,000	100.0%	
Number of Days' Billing	17.9		18.4		

Exhibit 13

Past due accounts, six months and over, included $9,803 owed by A. R. Putnam Sons, of Chicago, Illinois. This firm is currently in a short cash position due to heavy inventories. However, with its strong season approaching, it appears that sufficient liquidation of inventories can be effected to satisfy all creditors.

P. L. SMITH, *Comptroller*

PLS:AEP

60. INCREASING PRODUCTIVITY THROUGH CONTROL REPORTS *

William Langenberg †

Productivity is a term which has several meanings. Economists use the term on national and industry levels, whereas industrial engineers have applied it to an individual or a group of workers. Management, however, is interested in productivity on a company level. Cost accountants should be vitally interested in its application to the manufacturing facilities of a company. In the future, greater emphasis will be placed upon methods to increase productivity as a means of remaining competitive. It is my opinion that cost accountants should enter the field of productivity accounting and thus participate in the creation of an additional tool for management.

Identifying "Increased Productivity"—and the Means to It

This article attempts to illustrate methods of increasing productivity and its effect upon company policy making. For this purpose there are needed both a measurement of output and of input, the latter measuring an expenditure of various resources. To some extent, this need is covered in the present author's article, "An Experiment in Productivity Measurement," in the January, 1952, issue of the *N.A.C.A. Bulletin.* In order to illustrate further my concept of the measurement of productivity, I have prepared a chart (Exhibit 1) showing the factors of input. What happens to product cost when the valves which regulate the flow of cash are operated to change the relationship of the various factors of input? To find the effect of such changes on the output of goods is the goal of productivity measurement.

Using the input and output concepts, just what is meant when we refer to an increase in productivity? Going back again to the paper just mentioned, we find that either an increase in output (with the

---

* From *N.A.C.A. Bulletin* (April, 1953). Reprinted by permission of the National Association of Cost Accountants.

† William Langenberg, Manager of the Cost Division of Johnson & Johnson, New Brunswick, N. J.

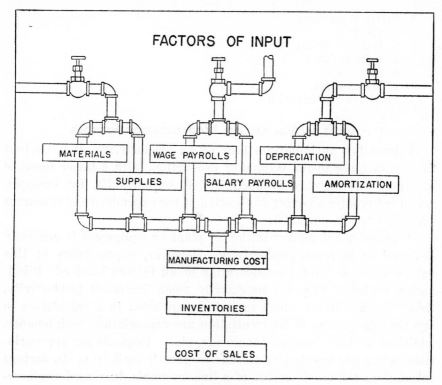

FACTORS OF INPUT

MATERIALS

SUPPLIES

WAGE PAYROLLS

SALARY PAYROLLS

DEPRECIATION

AMORTIZATION

MANUFACTURING COST

INVENTORIES

COST OF SALES

Exhibit 1

same input) or a decrease in the total of the various factors of input (with the same output) results in an increase of productivity. A listing of the major factors of input will bring our problem more into focus.

1. Direct labor hours.
2. Indirect labor hours.
3. Salary hours.
4. Depreciation (equivalent hours).
5. Repairs and maintenance (equivalent hours).
6. Material yield (this may be measured separately).

Since we have already established that a decrease in the ratio of the above factors of input to output is equivalent to an increase in productivity, we are concerned with the ways and means to accomplish this.

There are a good many ways to do this. In the sections of this paper which follow, attention will be given in turn to a number of the more important ones:

1. Volume.
2. Modern facilities.

3. Better supervision
   a. Yield
   b. Machine utilization
   c. Indirect labor
   d. Salaries
   e. Maintenance.
4. Employee participation.

A NOTE ON VOLUME AND MODERNIZATION FACTORS

Volume has an important bearing on productivity. It is obvious that an increase in the volume of production, with a lesser increase in input, will increase productivity. A second shift, for example, would not require an exact duplication of the expenditure of resources necessary to run one shift.

A program for modernization of plant or equipment is generally designed to increase productivity. However, expenditures of this nature warrant careful consideration of all factors involved. Elimination of labor does not necessarily mean increased productivity. Other expense items which need to be included in a calculation to test the advisability of modernization are depreciation, maintenance, additions to salary payroll (engineers, etc.). Requests for appropriations which are based upon savings frequently omit from the savings calculations the requirements of a line mechanic, increased engineering service, and possible changes in material yield.

BETTER SUPERVISION REQUIRES GOOD CONTROL REPORTING

The traditional approach towards the problem of increasing productivity is through more effective supervision and better performance by service departments. The cost accountant can make his most valuable contributions in this area through the issuance of proper reports. The reports must be designed to fit the needs of the individual foreman and the data must be on a quantitative basis. Whereas the effects of increased volume or acquisition of new equipment are generally understood, the importance of the "better supervision" approach merits further consideration.

Here the cost accountant can help most effectively through control reports. However, before going into these, I should like to emphasize that it is assumed that the cost accountant and the production supervisors have learned to work together. To those of us who have cleared this hurdle, the remark may seem to be academic but, where the problem is still in existence, it should be placed at the top of the list of jobs to be done. It is further suggested that the cost accountant familiarize himself with the overall controls which are prepared for guidance of management. If the cost accountant wants to assist in the guidance of others, he must understand financial control guides, such as

1. Financial budgets and forecasts.
2. Return on capital employed.
3. Control of investment
   a. Inventory turnover
   b. Capital expenditure control
   c. Cash requirements.
4. Profit and loss by products.
5. Profit and loss by sales division.

The cost accountant's reporting will be based on recognition of his responsibility, in a manufacturing company, for the following:

1. Budgeting standards of performance.
2. Organizing for control.
3. Measuring performance.

Also accurate product costs will have been established for use in inventory valuations, pricing policies and as control guides furnished to management. The costs should be based upon

1. Effective utilization of labor.
2. Effective usage of machine capacities.
3. Efficient yield of raw materials.

Although top management will operate the various controls on a financial basis, the cost accountant's responsibility for translating the financial data into quantitative controls (yards, pounds, etc.) is a major one and will be of utmost assistance to manufacturing supervisors who are responsible for productivity improvement.

Control reports designed to assist in this task are described in the paragraphs which follow. The sequence of productivity programs and installation of control reports should normally be determined on the basis of the ratio which each element of cost bears to the total product cost. In many cases it will be found that the emphasis has been on direct labor, which may be only a minor part of the total product cost.

CONTROL REPORTS

What shall the parts of the control reporting program be? This question could have a more extended answer than is practicable here. Nevertheless, it is possible to set forth important examples of prin-

cipal control reports needed in this matter of increasing plant productivity. They are dealt with in this section of the article under six
headings.

Yield

Statistics should be prepared which show input and output of raw
materials by mills. Input, in this case, means the value of the raw
materials as they are delivered to the mill. Output should reflect the
value of the raw material in the consumer package. The difference
represents losses and indicates savings potential. Mills or departments which show a low material yield should be examined by process
engineers. Daily reports should then be issued to measure actual
yield against standard.

Daily Material Usage (Exhibit 2) illustrates a report of this type.
The information shown is obtained from an individual Production
Ticket (Exhibit 3). The hypothetical figures have been prepared so
that they may be followed from the individual ticket to the report.
Attention is directed to the column in Exhibit 2 headed "Source," in
which the supplier is indicated by a code letter. It is no surprise to
experience a different yield from various sources of supply. The

---

DAILY MATERIAL USAGE

GAUZE MILL PRIMARY DEPARTMENT

1/14/53

COUNT & WIDTH	GREY YARDS	SLIT OR TENTERED YARDS		LENGTH GAIN OR (LOSS)	WIDTH LOSS	DOLLAR VARIANCE			SOURCE
		ACT.	STD.			LENGTH	WIDTH	TOTAL	
22 x 22—36"	5,000	4,850	4,825	25	1"	$ 1	$(5)	$(4)	C
20 x 20—35"	23,000	21,260	22,375	(1,115)		(30)		(30)	A
36 x 32—36"	296,400	296,400	294,696	1,704		68		68	A
19 x 16—40"	3,000	2,800	2,900	(100)		(3)		(3)	B
56 x 54—38"	70,240	68,000	69,000	(1,000)	1"	(70)	(125)	(195)	A
77 x 72—36"	3,000	2,950	3,000	(50)		(10)		(10)	B
						$(57)	$(145)	$(202)	

In Process
on Floor: Ticket No. 182, 187, 188, 190.

Exhibit 2

```
┌─────────────────────────────────────────────┐
│                            Ticket No.         │
│                   REWIND       164            │
│                                               │
│   Date    1/12        Operator                │
│                       Number    107           │
│                                               │
│   Mill     C          Roll No.  5672          │
│                                               │
│   Count      22x22-36"                        │
│                                               │
│   Mill Yards      5000                        │
│                                               │
│                                               │
│   Hours   1.1                                 │
│                                               │
├─────────────────────────────────────────────┤
│                                               │
│                   TENTER                      │
│                                               │
│   Date    1/13        Operator                │
│                       Number    152           │
│                                               │
│   Tenter Yards     4900                       │
│                                               │
├─────────────────────────────────────────────┤
│                                               │
│              CAMERON SLITTER                  │
│                                               │
│   Date    1/14        Operator                │
│                       Number    222           │
│                                               │
│   Tenter                                      │
│   Number    1                                 │
│                                               │
│                                               │
│   Cuts    12"- 12"- 11"                       │
│                                               │
│   Yield:  Length    4850       Yards          │
│                                               │
│           Width      35"       Inches         │
│                                               │
└─────────────────────────────────────────────┘
```

Exhibit 3

results of an investigation of this nature are shown in the graph in Exhibit 4.

Yields may be further analyzed by operators or machines. Calculations can be made, for example, which show the savings potential for bringing low yield operators up to average of a group. Machines should be studied for required adjustments. Yield losses due to short runs and frequent changeovers should be investigated and identified.

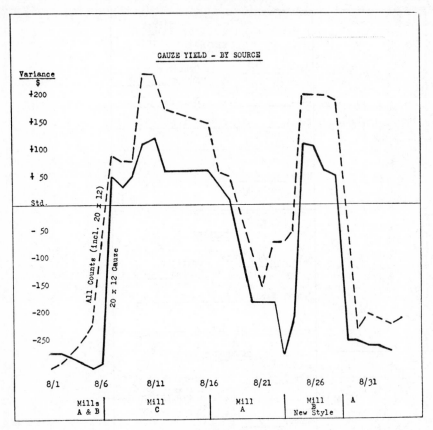

Exhibit 4

Machine Utilization

Whether raw materials or machine cost represents the greater portion of product cost depends upon the industry. However, regardless of its ratio to total product cost, machine expense per hour is probably higher than direct labor per hour in practically every industry. It is important, therefore, to measure the degree of utilization of production equipment. Exhibit 5 represents a section of a Weekly Production Report showing an actual efficiency of machines of 78 percent against a standard of 80 percent. In this case, the standard of 2,976 for Style 1 of Product A, for example, represents the average attainable units per hour, based upon the rated speed of the various machines. Exhibit 6 illustrates the calculation. Checking and comparing machine speeds will reveal the advisability, where it exists, of replacing inefficient units with high-speed equipment.

WEEKLY PRODUCTION REPORT

GAUZE MILL — DEPARTMENT NO. 203

DATE W/E 1/17/53

PRODUCT	MACH. HOURS STD.	MACH. HOURS ACT.	UNITS PER HR. AT STD.	PRODUCTION STANDARD	PRODUCTION ACTUAL	PRODUCTION VARIANCE	EFFICIENCY ACTUAL
PRODUCT A							
Style 1	184.7	187.	2976	556,512	549,556	(6,956)	79%
Style 2	97.5	104.	2250	234,000	219,375	(14,625)	75
Style 3	180.0	240.	3542	850,080	637,560	(212,520)	60
Style 4	220.0	200.	4260	852,000	937,200	85,200	88

PRODUCT	MACH. HOURS STD.	MACH. HOURS ACT.	UNITS PER HR. AT STD.	PRODUCTION STANDARD	PRODUCTION ACTUAL	PRODUCTION VARIANCE	EFFICIENCY ACTUAL
PRODUCT B							
Style 1	135.9	125.	3890	486,250	528,797	42,547	87
Style 2	115.9	103.	2250	231,750	260,719	28,969	90
Style 3	247.6	254.	2970	754,380	735,521	(18,859)	78
Style 4	148.0	160.	3440	550,400	509,120	(41,280)	74
Total	1329.6	1373.					78%
Standard Efficiency							80%

Exhibit 5

MACHINE EFFICIENCY CALCULATION ON THE BASIS OF RATED MACHINE SPEEDS

DEPARTMENT NO. 203

PRODUCT A — STYLE 1

MACHINE NUMBER	RATED SPEED PER MINUTE	PRODUCTION PER HOUR
3202	60	3,600
4421	55	3,300
4154	75	4,500
2784	50	3,000
4422	55	3,300
		28,900
Average Attainable Production per Hour at 100% Efficiency		3,720
Allowance: Personal Fatique, Delay, etc. 20%		644
Standard Production/Hour @ 80% Efficiency		2,976

Exhibit 6

Reports on these comparisons serve as a guide to production scheduling. They are also of considerable value in the formulation of capital expenditure programs.

Indirect Labor

Indirect labor represents an element of cost which is semivariable. An increase in volume does not require an increase in indirect labor to the same degree. This relationship becomes further involved when certain tasks performed by direct labor operators are coded to indirect labor accounts. Examples are cleaning, meetings, classes, etc. It is important to have data available which separate these two elements of indirect labor. Indirect labor performed by regular indirect labor employees varies to some extent with volume, though some tasks are more variable than others. However, charges to indirect labor accounts by direct labor operators are likely to depend upon a number of exceptional factors. One of these factors may be the breakdown of automatic equipment. Labor codes should be set up which furnish this vital information.

As far as productivity increases are concerned, it is not enough to find a downward trend in wage and salary hours charged to manufacturing. These hours must be analyzed further to determine composition of the trend, as shown in Exhibit 7. Another study of importance is the knowledge of minimum indirect labor requirements at various levels of production.

Salaries

The remarks made earlier in connection with indirect labor may be applied to salaries in a general way. It should be mentioned that a plant modernization program and methods improvement usually bring with them a change in the ratio of engineers and maintenance personnel to production workers. The effect of this change must be considered in measuring productivity.

Repairs and Maintenance

Repairs and maintenance expense needs careful evaluation when new equipment is planned and this cost should be considered in computing the prospective savings arising out of the acquistion of modern high-speed machines. A factor of even greater importance than repairs and maintenance expense lies in the elimination of machine

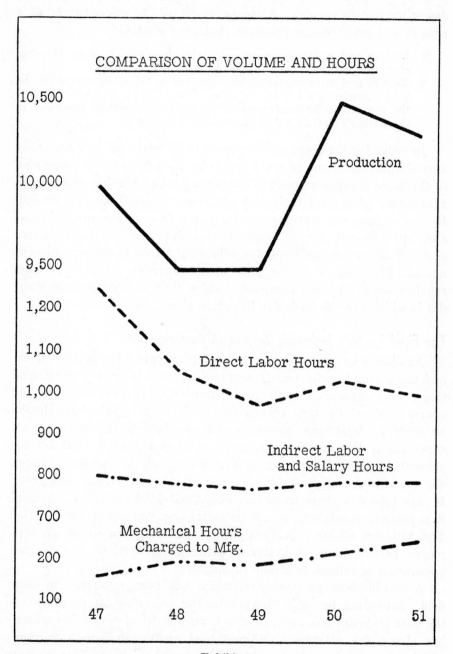

Exhibit 7

downtime due to repairs. A measurement of the effectiveness of a repairs and maintenance program should be twofold:

1. Repairs and maintenance expense related to the trend of idle machine hours due to repairs and maintenance.
2. Repairs and maintenance expense related to the effectiveness of the total manufacturing unit, the latter element being measured through the use of the "measurement of productivity" formula discussed in the author's earlier article previously referred to.

In order for maintenance programs to be effective, it is generally agreed that maintenance work needs to be planned and scheduled in the same manner as production work. Such planning insures the availability of special tools and equipment when they are needed. It also assigns the various crafts to the job at the proper time, assuring a smooth flow of work. It is rather costly to have riggers show up before steam lines and electrical wires have been disconnected. Planning of major jobs should include estimates of time requirements. In some companies, these time studies become standards which are the basis for incentive plans.

The Final Factor: Inducing Employee Participation

Another way of increasing productivity, which is getting more and more attention by management, is through employee participation. Good supervision and good manufacturing practices will increase productivity to a certain level. However, evaluation should be made to determine savings which are beyond the influence of supervision. For example, graph of Savings Potential (Exhibit 8) shows that, through better manufacturing methods and supervision, cost reductions may yield $400,000 during a period of, say, one year. It may take five years to get an additional $100,000. Nevertheless, it is entirely possible to attain potential cost reductions beyond the first $400,000 within a relatively short period of time through employee participation. Employee participation involves a practical application of human relations in industry.

A considerable volume of material has been published in this field. According to some viewpoints, the technological progress of the past 50 years has been, in effect, an industrial revolution which has changed a relatively self-contained craftsman into a worker who has become dependent upon an impersonal machine. This change has had a far-reaching effect upon the self-respect and human spirit of the workers. The same era saw the development of scientific management, based upon Frederick W. Taylor's pioneering in time

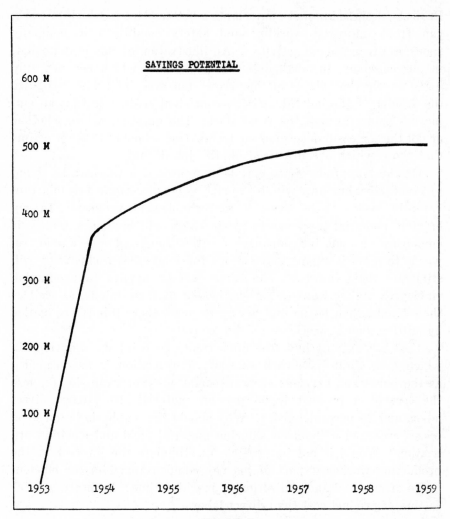

Exhibit 8

and motion studies, in which the emphasis was placed upon increased production and the reward to workers was based upon the number of pieces produced.

Human relations experts are telling us that our industrial revolution has had an adverse effect upon the well-being of man's mind. Frustrations in workers have been related to the technological improvements and the development of automatic manufacturing processes. Hence, industrial relations have become one of the essential tools of management. A growing consciousness of the need of recognizing workers as individuals has developed in recent years.

Projects, designed to make our plants a better place in which to work, run from improved working and safety conditions to company sponsored recreational activities. An illustration of this is the belief, in our company, in small decentralized plants which are not only listed among the "plants of tomorrow" but are planned to recognize the dignity of the individual. One consistent feature is that all employees enter through the front door. The question arises whether or not these measures reverse the trend. One school of thought claims that those which are practiced off the job do not.

On the job, productivity may be increased if a way can be found to create the human "will to work." The piecework formula, apparently, needs to be exposed to technological progress. In my opinion, potential increases in productivity will become a reality if employees are put into business for themselves. For example, rewards to manufacturing supervisors for increased productivity will stimulate their interest. The same concept applies to production employees. If we want to get the benefit of their minds, as well as their hands, then let us find a way to make those minds productive by putting mental processes on the payroll.

Cost accountants have the opportunity to point up situations in which a straight piecework rate of compensation is as outmoded as the horse and carriage in transportation. For example, suppose the cost of a product is 65 percent material, 10 percent direct labor, and 25 percent burden. Why should the emphasis be on good pieces produced without considering material yield and machine utilization? Would it not be possible to stimulate the interest of the production worker if part of his pay compensated him for efficient usage of material and utilization of machine time? Both are greater factors of product cost than direct labor.

CONCLUSION

Many opportunities are available for cost accountants to participate in the various plans for productivity increases and for the measurement of productivity. I am certain that work in this field will further increase the stature of the cost accountant on the management team. It is a broad field. At two points, it requires pioneering action. These are in the measurement process itself and in the matter of worker incentives. It also requires the best in cost reporting that the industrial accountant can bring forth.

61. USE OF CONTROL CHARTS IN COST CONTROL *

Edwin W. Gaynor †

In recent years, significant progress has been made in the application of statistical techniques to the solution of management problems. In this area, statistical quality control has developed some remarkable tools. Of the several which can be considered of value in the field of cost control, the technique of control charts appears to offer promising results. Here is a technique, which, although not a solution to all of our problems, can, if properly used, highlight weak points in a cost structure, not at the end of a month or year but during the actual operation if we so choose. Basically, it is a system of selective sampling. Its fundamental characteristic is the selection and evaluation of a periodic sample selected from the particular population the limits of which we are attempting to control. Its great merit lies in the fact that, by requiring these periodic samples to be taken, the technique reveals variations from a standard which might otherwise remain undetected.

WHAT THE $\overline{X}$ AND R CHARTS ARE

Among the many statistical quality control techniques which have been perfected, the development of the $\overline{X}$ (pronounced either X bar or Bar X) or average and the R (range) charts ranks among the more important. It must be mentioned that this article is not a treatise on statistical methods. It assumes that basic statistical concepts need to be explained here only briefly. Detailed information can be obtained by review of a standard statistical text or consultation with the company's quality control groups. The $\overline{X}$ and R charts measure the deviations from a given standard and offer a technique to determine whether the measurement being analyzed indicates a condition that is either "in control" or "out of control." By *control*,

---

* From *N.A.C.A. Bulletin* (June, 1954). Reprinted by permission of the National Association of Cost Accountants.

† Edwin W. Gaynor, Field Supervisor, Detroit Branch, Navy Cost Inspection Service, Detroit, Michigan.

in this case, we mean *statistical control*; i.e., if the variability of our measurement is due to numerous causes as found in a normal distribution, we are in control. If, on the other hand, the variability is due to large assignable causes, the process is out of control and we begin to investigate the causes for this situation. Each of the two types of charts measures a different type of variability. The $\overline{X}$ chart measures the variability of the averages of the measurements within a given sample, while the R chart measures the variability of the range of the measurements within a given sample.

An Illustration of the Use of $\overline{X}$ and R Charts

Since the proof of any theory lies in its application, a reasonably realistic condition which lends itself to a solution will best serve the present purpose. Assume that, for a specific operation, we have set five minutes as standard time of performance. These five minutes are a measure of time. Time represents money. If time can be controlled, cost can. This standard is considered as an average; that is, it is expected that some operations will be performed in four and three-quarter minutes while, at other times, the operation may take longer than five minutes. However, on a long-range basis, a five-minute average is regarded as satisfactory performance.

Under conventional cost reporting methods periodic variances from the five-minute standard are not discovered until the end of the day or week, or not until production and standard time are compared at the end of a payroll period—or perhaps not at all. Usually, an average for a relatively long period of time is composed of a great many compensating plus and minus variances completely overlooked, simply because they are not apparent. However, with the method under discussion many deviations can be discerned very soon after they take place and immediate steps can be taken to prevent their recurrence.

The first step in establishing a statistical approach to the problem is an orderly and systematic array of factual data upon which a control pattern can be determined. In this case, a period of 15 days was selected and an hourly comparison of acceptable production with performance hours was made. This provides knowledge of the average performance time per unit of good product. (The ideal method to obtain this may be time study on a per unit basis but, under certain circumstances, time study may create additional personnel problems and, therefore, may not be desirable.) It will have been noted that comparison of performance time with good product is specified, since, in the final analysis, all time spent must be related to good product produced. Rework, delays due to breakdown or material shortages, and many other unprovided-for incidents, all add to the cost of the finished product and, therefore, cannot be disregarded. They are the result of some assignable cause and, in turn, affect the cost to be controlled.

The sampling scheme suggested would result in a series of measurements such as those portrayed in Exhibit 1. Each of the measurements represents the time that it took to perform a specified operation at the time the sample was taken. The operation could be of any nature: drilling, boring, cutting, auditing and the processing of invoices, preparing payrolls; or it could be the relationship between an element of cost and a specified unit of measurement of output or volume. In practice, where measurements become burdensome, it is customary to deal only with the deviations or variances from the

OBSERVED STANDARD TIME PER UNIT—FIFTEEN SAMPLES

SAMPLE NUMBER	OBSERVATION WITHIN THE SAMPLE								$\bar{X}$ AVERAGE	$\bar{R}$ RANGE
	1	2	3	4	5	6	7	8		
1	6	5	5	4	5	4	6	5	5.000	2
2	6	6	7	5	7	5	4	5	5.625	3
3	5	5	4	7	6	5	3	5	5.000	4
4	6	6	5	4	7	7	7	5	5.875	3
5	4	6	6	7	8	4	5	5	5.625	4
6	5	4	8	5	3	5	4	5	4.875	5
7	3	5	5	5	6	7	5	6	5.250	4
8	6	6	6	5	5	4	5	5	5.250	2
9	8	7	5	5	6	7	3	6	5.875	5
10	5	5	5	6	7	5	5	5	5.375	2
11	5	6	6	5	7	6	5	5	5.625	2
12	5	6	5	5	7	6	5	3	5.250	4
13	4	5	4	6	5	6	6	5	5.125	2
14	5	4	4	7	6	5	4	5	5.000	3
15	5	5	4	6	6	6	4	5	5.125	2
									79.875	47

Exhibit 1

prescribed standard. Our values are relatively simple, so we shall use the absolute measurements set forth.

After the data have been collected and tabulated in an orderly array, the average and range of each sample are calculated. The average is determined by adding the values of the individual observations and dividing by the number of observations taken. In the case of the sample taken on the third day, the average is calculated as follows:

$$
\begin{array}{rl}
\text{Add:} & 5 \\
& 5 \\
& 4 \\
& 7 \qquad \text{Divide: } 40 \text{ by } 8 \\
& 6 \\
& 5 \qquad \text{Average: } 5 \\
& 3 \\
& \underline{5} \\
\text{Total:} & 40
\end{array}
$$

Since the range is the difference between the highest and lowest measurements within a given sample, its value is determined by subtracting the lesser of the two values from the greater. In the observations taken in the 11th sample, the highest measurement making its appearance is seven and the lowest five. The difference between these values is the range of two. In a similar manner, the averages and the ranges are calculated for each of the 15 samples.

To complete the required mathematical calculations for the solution of the problem there are required the values for the average of the averages $(\overline{\overline{X}})$ and the average of the ranges $(\overline{R})$. These are calculated as follows:

$$\overline{\overline{X}} = 79.875/15 = 5.325$$
$$\overline{R} = 47/15 = 3.13$$

WHAT THE STANDARD DEVIATION IS AND DOES

Beyond this point, there is one more concept to review, namely, standard deviation. In statistics, this is the term applied to the basic measurement of dispersion about the average. In this example, a normal distribution has been used. When charted, the data would follow a pattern very similar to the bell-shaped curve. When a frequency distribution is made of the data presented in Exhibit 1, a curve which reasonably approximates the normal is disclosed. Exhibit 2 is a graphic presentation of this distribution. As more data

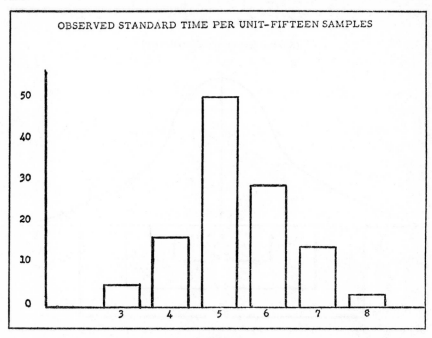

Exhibit 2

become available, it is quite probable that the distribution will approach the normal even more closely. But how does it happen that the standard deviation measures the dispersion of data about the average? In can be proved that, in any normal distribution, there will be the following dispersion of data about the average:

68% of the data will fall within + or − 1 standard deviation
95% of the data will fall within + or − 2 standard deviations
99.7% of the data will fall within + or − 3 standard deviations

The principal value to be derived from the use of this measurement is its ability to disclose where most of the data should fall under normal circumstances. If it is known that the average of a group of measurements is five, and the standard deviation is one, it is then known that 99.7 percent of the measurements should fall within 5 + or − 3 standard deviations, or from two to eight as shown on the following page in Exhibit 3.

Therefore, if we take a sample the average of which is ten, we know that it falls outside these limits. It can be concluded that either distribution is not normal or some condition is causing an abnormal variation. "That is fine," one might say, "but what do we do with it?"

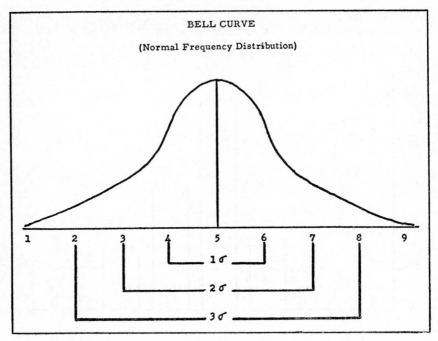

Exhibit 3

Simply this. Through the technique being discussed it is possible to set upper and lower control limits. Any measurements falling within these limits are considered to be normal deviations and, therefore, the operation is in control. Deviations falling outside the control limits are considered to be due to some assignable cause and, therefore, indicate that the operation is out of control. The logical consequence of this conclusion is the investigation of the assignable cause to prevent repetition.

Control Limits and Their Use

We have now reached the point at which it is necessary to determine some values for the control limits already mentioned. Since 99.7 percent of the data will normally fall within three standard deviations, we decide that a set of limits based on this concept will be satisfactory. Determination of these limits is greatly simplified by the use of tables of "Factors for Determining from $\overline{R}$ 3 Sigma Control Limits for $\overline{X}$ and R Charts." These tables, as well as directions for their use, are included in many quality control texts. In our particular situation, the limits for $\overline{X}$ and R are calculated as follows:

Control limits for $\overline{X}$

$\overline{R}$ 3.13
Factor A_2 for sample of 8 from table of factors .... .37
$\overline{X}$ 5.325
Upper control limit 5.325 $+$ .37 $\times$ 3.13 .... 6.48
Lower control limit 5.325 $-$ .37 $\times$ 3.13 .... 4.167

Control limits for R

Factor D_4 for sample size 8 from table of factors 1.86
Upper control limit 1.86 $\times$ 3.13 .... 5.82
Factor D_3 for sample size 8 from table of factors .... .14
Lower control limit .14 $\times$ 3.13 .... .438

With the calculation of the control limits the mathematics of the problem is complete. The remaining task is to chart the data on cross-section paper, indicate the control limits, and observe the results. Exhibit 4 is graphic presentation of the $\overline{X}$, or average, data.

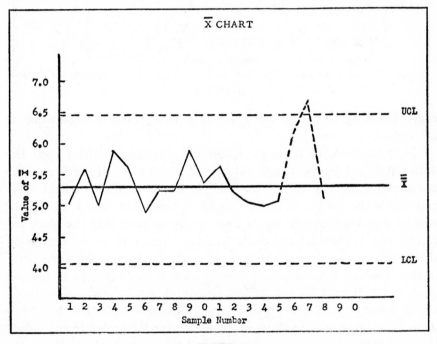

Exhibit 4

The horizontal scale represents the sample number and the vertical represents the values of $\overline{X}$. The calculated values for $\overline{X}$ developed in Exhibit 2 are plotted, as well as the calculated upper and lower control limits. Visual observation discloses that none of the observed measurements falls outside the control limits. Therefore, it can be

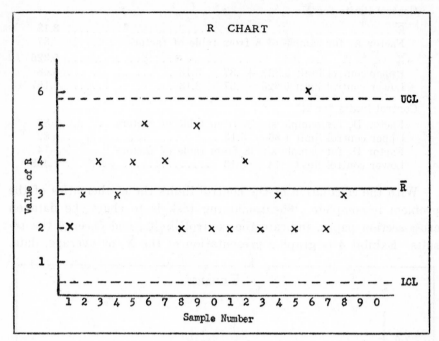

Exhibit 5

concluded that, as far as the average is concerned, the operation is in control.

Now examine the R chart. Exhibit 5 simplifies in chart form the data developed in the range column of Exhibit 1. Here again, the horizontal scale represents the sample number. The vertical scale represents the values of R. As in the $\overline{X}$ chart, the upper and lower control limits are drawn in. It can readily be seen that the observed ranges also fall within the control limits. Again, it can be concluded that, as to range, the operation is in control; that is, the variability of the observed measurements is such that it could be due to normal deviations. It will be noted that no statement is made concerning the acceptability of the operation or procedure. All that has been done is to measure variations from a standard, determine when these variations become significant, and take appropriate action for their correction.

FOLLOWING ON TO IMPROVED COST CONTROL

At this point, we have several tables, a mass of impressive mathematical calculations, and two graphs. But just how do we use this material to assist in controlling costs? The procedure is quite simple.

Take periodic samples or observations every hour, once each day, or whatever period is decided upon as most advantageous and economical, taking care, however, to keep the subsequent observations on the same base as the initial data. After taking the observations, calculate the average and range for each sample and plot on the $\overline{X}$ and R charts. If these new points are within the control limits then, apparently, no significant change has taken place. If they are out of control, investigate the causes.

Suppose that observations for Samples 16, 17, and 18, obtained under the same sampling procedure as used in the collection of data in Exhibit 1, gave the following values:

Sample Number	Observations within the Sample								$\overline{X}$ Average	R Range
	1	2	3	4	5	6	7	8		
16	7	7	7	6	7	2	8	5	6.125	6
17	8	7	6	6	7	7	7	6	6.75	2
18	6	5	4	5	5	7	4	5	5.125	3

Now plot the averages and ranges on the respective charts. It will be noticed that, in Sample 17, the average is out of control while, in Sample 16, the range is out of control.

Being practical about it, you ask, "What does this mean?" In the case of Sample 16, something happened which caused the range to spread from two to eight. Perhaps this does not seem to be very important, since the two periods more or less offset each other. True, but that is precisely where conventional cost analysis may fail. By the end of a week or month, this variation in range could never be detected. Look at it this way. This variation has certainly cost money at the point at which the process went up to a variation from standard to eight. Conversely, although it is a fact that the control limit is set at five, there is a short period of operation at a variation from standard to two. There is always the possibility that investigation along this line can bring to light methods, procedures, machine speeds, personal techniques, or other conditions which will permit reduction of the standard to something less than the currently acceptable five minutes.

In Sample 16 the average remains in control. It is only the range which indicates possible trouble. In Sample 17, however, there is an indication that the entire center has shifted. On the average it is just taking more time to perform this standard function. Why? Perhaps it is due to the weather or to the fact that this is the day before or after a holiday. Whatever the cause, corrective action can be taken. There is awareness of a significant shift in the average.

Conventional analysis would fail to detect a shift in the average for a short period of time.

APPLICABILITY TO WIDE RANGES OF DATA—AND OF COMPANIES

Over the years most industrial accountants have experienced some difficulty in making production people understand cost reports. Here is an opportunity to meet them on their own ground. Statistical quality control techniques are familiar working tools with them and facts presented on this basis will be readily understood. In the final analysis, they are the people who must do the real controlling. Cost analysis presents the facts. It highlights the existence of danger signals which indicate a need for improvement. If this tool is capable of doing a job better, there is little reason to neglect its use.

In the example given here, we chose a simple situation, standard time for a specific operation. However, the usefulness of this technique is not limited to situations involving direct labor. Any significant categories in direct or indirect costs are potential areas for its application. It can be applied either to individual or groups of homogeneous costs related to some common measurement of volume, production, or efficiency. Control of absenteeism, use of stationery and office supplies, incidence of maintenance costs, utilization of operating supplies, application of direct and indirect salaries and wages, and material usage are but a few of the many critical cost situations which come to mind. Many others could be mentioned which might be of varying importance in any given organization. A careful review of the particular operation can bring to light the areas which will respond most readily to this treatment.

Since control charting is essentially a system of sampling rather than of accumulation of a great mass of accounting data, it is admirably suited to organizations desiring some degree of cost control without the attendant increase in overhead cost. It is less costly to take a periodic sample two or three or more times per month than to accumulate all data for a full month, balance it to a control account, and finally arrive at an answer—an answer which is assumed to be correct simply because it is mathematically accurate. It is this aspect of reduced effort in providing cost control, coupled with the characteristic of timeliness, that offers great potentialities in the use of control charts.

The material presented here is certainly not exhaustive. Much more could be said. The approach taken is relatively new to cost control. One can pretty much make one's own rules as one goes along, as long as one does not violate established statistical theory and practice. Perhaps some of the time devoted to conventional cost reporting might be diverted to better advantage on a program such as this. The reports are not quite as attractive and will not necessarily balance out, but they do tend to reveal vulnerable cost situations.

62. CALCULATING CONTROL LIMITS
FOR COST CONTROL DATA *

Carl E. Noble †

The cost accountant is frequently required to answer the question, "How large a variance from standard should be tolerated before considering the variance abnormal?" Variations in cost measurements are expected, even though the factors contributing to these measurements remain unchanged for all practical purposes. The actual measurements are only samples of the basic process producing them. Yet, the standard cost control system fails to furnish an objective technique for dealing with this inherent process variation. It considers an operation satisfactory or unsatisfactory when an actual cost falls on one side or the other of a standard. Occasionally the standard is set in such a manner that a favorable variance is expected and an unfavorable variance indicates that the process is subnormal. Thus, an unfavorable variance is agreed to be a realistic sign for action. This procedure is objectionable on at least three counts: (1) the standard is no longer a measure of expected cost, (2) the deviation of the standard from expected cost is determined largely upon subjective judgment, and (3) the periods during which the operation is better than usual go unnoticed.

This paper recommends that the standard coincide with the expected cost and presents objective methods of calculating control limits for the variances from standard. Past data on established operations usually furnish reliable bases for estimating expected costs and calculating control limits. These control limits serve to flag good as well as poor periods of operation. The importance of investigating a process when the costs are significantly better than standard has been overlooked too long. The discovery of the causes for the improved operations often leads the way to permanent cost reductions.

* From *N.A.C.A. Bulletin* (June, 1954). Reprinted by permission of the National Association of Cost Accountants.
† Carl E. Noble, Chief of the Customer Acceptance Department, Kimberly-Clark Corporation, Neenah, Wisconsin.

CHARTS FOR CONTROL OF RATE OF CARTON PRODUCTION

One method of calculating control limits may be explained with an example involving a machine for converting paperboard into breakfast food cartons. The variance of the actual number of cartons from standard is recorded to the nearest gross for each two hours of operation during the eight-hour working day. Exhibit 1 tabulates the variances for the four two-hour periods during 20

VARIANCES FROM STANDARD IN NUMBER OF BOXES PRODUCED DURING TWO-HOUR PERIODS

		TWO-HOUR PERIODS				
		I	II	III	IV	X	R
	1	— 5	5	14	—14	0	28
	2	16	24	12	7	14.0	17
	3	—15	— 2	—29	— 6	—13.0	27
	4	—16	—17	— 4	—12	—12.3	13
	5	10	13	3	4	7.5	10
D	6	0	—15	— 6	— 7	— 7.0	15
a							
y	7	—10	— 4	— 2	7	— 2.3	17
s							
	8	12	11	— 5	— 4	3.5	17
	9	4	8	—19	—14	— 5.3	27
	10	— 1	1	— 7	— 5	— 3.0	8
	11	— 4	— 9	8	1	— 1.0	17
	12	4	14	8	3	7.3	11
	13	— 1	— 6	3	— 2	— 1.5	9
	14	1	5	— 6	6	1.5	12
	15	0	3	5	— 2	1.5	7
	16	— 9	1	— 1	— 2	— 2.7	10
	17	2	5	3	— 2	2.0	7
	18	6	6	4	— 3	3.3	9
	19	7	— 2	10	0	3.7	12
	20	10	10	— 7	— 2	2.7	17

Exhibit 1

consecutive days. The $\overline{X}$ and R columns show respectively the arithmetic mean and the range of four measurements for each day. The problem is to find the control limits for the $\overline{X}$ and R values plotted on their respective control charts in Exhibit 2.

In calculating these limits, the average $\overline{\overline{X}}$ of the $\overline{X}$'s and the average $\overline{R}$ of the R's are first found:

$$X = \frac{0.4}{-20} = -0.02, \text{ and } \overline{R} = \frac{290}{20} = 14.5.$$

Since it has been assumed that the standard coincides with the expected production level, zero is taken as the center line on the $\overline{X}$ control chart. (If this assumption is incorrect, then one would probably use $\overline{\overline{X}}$ as the center line.) Using zero as the center line, the control limits for the $\overline{X}$ chart are:

$$O \pm A_2 R, \text{ or } O \pm (0.729) \quad (14.5) \text{ or } \pm 10.57,$$

where A_2 depends upon the number of measurements contributing to each $\overline{X}$ (four in this case) and may be found by reference to *American War Standard—Control Chart Method of Controlling Quality during Production*, Z1.3-1942, published by American Standards Association, New York City. The factors D_3, D_4, and d_2 introduced below are also given in this reference.

The center line on the R chart is $\overline{R}$ and the control limits for this chart are:

$$D_3\overline{R} = (O) \ (14.5) = O \text{ and } D_4\overline{R} = (2.114) \ (14.5) = 30.65.$$

It may be observed that, in Exhibit 2, all the points in the R chart are within the control limits but that three of the first four points on the $\overline{X}$ chart are outside these limits. One would suspect that the process was abnormal during the first four days. If investigation reveals that this is true, then all the data for these four days are deleted and new control limits calculated for the remaining 16 days. The following values of $\overline{X}$ and $\overline{R}$ are then obtained:

$$\overline{X} = \frac{2.7}{16} = 0.17, \ \overline{R} = \frac{205}{16} = 12.81.$$

The new control limits are:

$$O \pm (0.729) \ (12.81) = \pm 9.34 \text{ for } \overline{X}, \text{ and}$$
$$D_3\overline{R} = (O) \ (12.81) = O \text{ and } D_4\overline{R} = (2.114) \ (12.81) = 27.09 \text{ for R}.$$

Since all of the last 16 points on both the $\overline{X}$ and R control charts fall within their respective limits, it is reasonable to assume

CONTROL CHARTS FOR VARIANCES IN PRODUCTION OF CARTONS

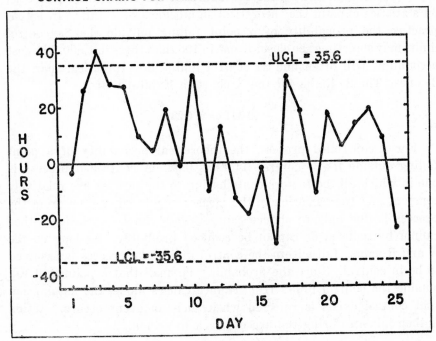

Exhibit 2

that these limits are reliable. Hence, they are projected on the chart to serve as limits for further control of carton production. After additional data have been collected for a month or more, these data should be combined with those in Exhibit 1 and new control limits calculated for the $\overline{X}$ and R control charts. The procedure of removing data taken while the process is abnormal is called rationalization of the data.

Usually, in applications such as this, the total variance for the eight-hour day is plotted, rather than the average variance for two-hour periods. If the total daily variance, $4\overline{X}$, is plotted in Exhibit 2, then the control limits are multiplied by 4. They are:

$$\pm\,4\,(9.34)\ \text{or}\ \pm\,37.36.$$

The control limits described here are called three-standard-deviation or three-sigma (3σ) control limits. If the factors contributing to the production of breakfast food cartons remain constant then, theoretically, one would expect $\overline{X}$ or an R to fall outside the 3σ control limits approximately three times in 1,000, on the average. The terms A_2, D_3, and D_4 are derived in such a manner that they give 3σ

limits when applied as described above. Most elementary textbooks on statistics explain the theoretical significance of σ units. In actual practice the probability of a point falling outside the 3σ control limits may sometimes be closer to one in 100 than three in 1,000. The cost accountant will often find 2σ control limits more practical than the 3σ ones. The 2σ limits for the X chart in Exhibit 2 are:

$$\begin{array}{c}+2\\-3\end{array}(9.34) \text{ or } \pm 6.23$$

For a controlled process, the theoretical probability of a point falling outside its 2σ control limits is 0.05. A controlled process is one in which all the factors contributing to the process are relatively constant and the variation in the measurements emanating from the process is due only to chance causes. This chance variation either cannot be reduced or cannot be reduced profitably. As long as the $\overline{X}$ and R values fall within the control limits, the process is assumed to be in control. Since the probability is small that a point will fall outside the control limits from chance causes alone, the assumption that control exists is rejected when such an event occurs. Action is then taken to bring the process back to normal.

CHART FOR CONTROL OF LABOR VARIANCE

The control of labor variance supplies an example of another common procedure for calculating control limits. It is preferable to secure a number of cost or production measurements during a day (or a shift) and base the limits for day-to-day control upon the variation in these within-day measurements. However, in some cases, it is practical to obtain measurements only at the end of a day. Such is the situation for labor variance in a given department. The variance in hours of the actual labor from standard is given for 25 days in Exhibit 3.

The first step in calculating control limits for these daily measurements is to find the absolute differences, R, between the consecutive variances. These differences or ranges are listed in Exhibit 3. The next step is to find the average of the ranges:

$$\overline{R} = \frac{482}{24} = 20.08$$

The control limits for the R's are calculated in order to measure the degree of control among them. The limits are:

$$D_3\overline{R} = (0)\ (20.08) = 0 \text{ and } D_4\overline{R} = (3.268)\ (20.08) = 65.63,$$

VARIANCES FROM STANDARD HOURS OF DAILY LABOR

Days	X	R	Days	X	R
1	— 4		14	—18	
		30			16
2	26		15	— 2	
		14			27
3	40		16	—29	
		12			61
4	28		17	32	
		1			13
5	27		18	19	
		17			30
6	10		19	—11	
		5			28
7	5		20	17	
		14			11
8	19		21	6	
		20			8
9	— 1		22	14	
		32			5
10	31		23	19	
		41			10
11	—10		24	9	
		23			33
12	13		25	—24	
		26			
13	—13				
		5			

Exhibit 3

where D_3 and D_4 are based upon a sample of Size 2, the number of measurements contributing to each R. It may be observed that all R's lie inside these control limits. In fact, only one R falls outside the 2σ limits, which are

$$0, \text{ and } (2,512) \ (20.08) \text{ or } 50.45.$$

Thus, one may assume that the R's are in good control and that $\overline{R}$ can be used to calculate the standard deviation σ for the daily variances X:

$$\sigma = \frac{\overline{R}}{d_2} = \frac{20.08}{1.128} = 17.80,$$

Assuming the standard variance to be 0, the 2σ control limits for X are

$$0 \pm 2 \ (17.80) \text{ or } \pm 35.6,$$

and the 3σ control limits are

$$0 \pm 3 \ (17.80) \ \text{or} \pm 53.4.$$

The occurrence of one point outside the 2σ control limits in Exhibit 4 should not be disturbing. Approximately one in 20 points are expected to be outside the 2σ limits on the average.

The spread of the control limits, with this method, depends upon the variation between the daily variances. It is assumed that the range between consecutive daily variances is dependent only upon chance causes. However, these ranges obviously are due, to some extent, to real differences in the operation between days. Hence, the ranges tend to be larger and, in turn, the control limits wider than would result from chance causes alone. For this reason, 2σ limits are usually preferred when the control limits are based upon ranges of consecutive daily measurements.

Because real differences in the day-to-day operations are likely to inflate certain ranges of the consecutive daily variances, it is important that a careful job of rationalization be done. Rationalization is applied to remove unusually large R values occurring because of day-to-day changes in the basic cause system. The steps in rationalization involve the calculation of D_4R and the removal of all R values above this limit. A new $\overline{R}$ is then calculated from the remaining R's. These steps are repeated until all values of R are less than $D_4\overline{R}$. If many R's have to be removed in the rationalization process, it is an indication that the basic cause system is varying from day to day, and the data probably are not altogether reliable for setting limits for future control.

APPLICATIONS OF THE CONTROL LIMITS TO COST CONTROL

The common methods of calculating control limits have been described. How, then, do they fit into cost accounting procedure? One application is in the field of presenting cost information to various levels of management. It is usually impractical to plot the voluminous monthly (and weekly) cost data on control charts. Nevertheless, the significant monthly cost deviations should be highlighted. This can be done by first calculating the control limits for the monthly variances. Each variance is then listed on the monthly report in, say, red, black, or green—depending upon whether it is above the upper control limit, within the control limits, or below the lower control limit. Such a procedure is a valuable aid in interpreting the monthly cost data. All too often management spends

CONTROL CHART FOR DAILY LABOR VARIANCE

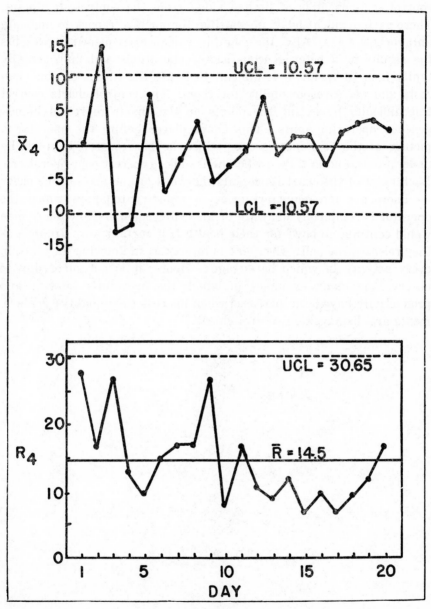

Exhibit 4

time, money, and argument in search of the cause of a variance which may be attributed to chance causes alone.

As an aid to the control of costs on an hourly and daily basis, the control limits through the control chart play a most important role. Even though the monthly report is an integral part of most control systems, it is of limited value from the control standpoint. There is too much delay in waiting for such a report to indicate unfavorable costs. Also, the monthly variance frequently represents the results of a heterogeneous set of operations and may actually typify none of them. It is difficult to locate the causes of abnormal costs and place responsibility for them. The control charts correct this difficulty by letting the points on the charts represent homogeneous operating units. This chart places before the operator a picture of the cost factors over which he has control, in units he understands, and at a time when he is able to correct poor operations. Each point of the chart represents the work of one man or one crew.

There are too many activities in industry today in which the operator is completely unaware of his achievements. How many men would continue to bowl for their health if a curtain were dropped as they released the ball? Everyone is interested in knowing his score in every activity in which he engages. Hence, it is not surprising to observe the many examples in which the operator's interest and productivity have been increased when his cost (and quality) achievements are displayed on control charts.

63. THE DU PONT CHART SYSTEM FOR APPRAISING OPERATING PERFORMANCE *

C. A. Kline, Jr. and
Howard L. Hessler †

I. DESCRIPTION OF THE CHART SYSTEM

By C. A. Kline, Jr.

We are pleased—and somewhat awed—at the interest which our chart system has evoked during the last several years. Until 1949 we had not shown our charts outside of Wilmington to persons who were not members of the du Pont organization, although we had shown them to visitors who expressed a desire to see them. In the fall of that year, Mr. T. C. Davis, our treasurer, was persuaded by friends in the accounting profession to present "the charts" at the American Management Association's Finance Conference which was to be held in December, 1949. The response to that presentation was most gratifying and we have been asked frequently to give repeat performances. In fact, the need of attending to day-to-day business has forced us to decline a number of invitations we would like to have accepted and to restrict our presentations to gatherings which are national in scope.

Function of the Chart System

Any system of financial control, to be of maximum usefulness, should include a forecast of sales and profits, a forecast of working capital requirements and cash resources, and capital-expenditure budgets and working capital standards, together with statements which show the actual operating performance and balance sheet conditions promptly after the close of an accounting period. It is the duty and responsibility of the financial staff to make these data available to executive management, when required and in a form which

* From *N.A.C.A. Bulletin, 1952 Conference Proceedings.* Reprinted by permission of the National Association of Cost Accountants.
† Charles A. Kline, Jr., Assistant Treasurer; Howard L. Hessler, Chart Room Supervisor, Treasury Division, E. I. du Pont de Nemours & Co., Wilmington, Delaware.

will reveal the operating results of each particular product line. You might call this "internal reporting," as contrasted with external reporting to the stockholders, SEC, etc. The complexity of operations and/or the diversity of product lines complicate the accounting problems and clarity in the presentation of operating results without sacrifice of substance should be the objective toward which solutions to specific financial and accounting problems are worked out.

A third of a century ago one of our financial executives at du Pont saw a particular phase of this problem of internal reporting in clear perspective. At that time he conceived and guided the design of what we have come to think of and refer to as our "executive committee charts." This system utilizes charts and tabulations for presenting to the committee data pertinent to the performance of each broad product group, which we term "operating investment." We maintain approximately 350 individual charts, a number of which are presented to the executive committee each month so that, in a year's time, all charts have been reviewed—practically all of them at least four times. Shown here is a *pro forma* set of these charts and tabulations which should give you a clear picture of the chart format and suggest the manner in which the charts are used in actual practice. The use of a series of charts generally similar to those shown is essentially a part of our system of internal reporting which emphasizes visual methods and the minimum of detail.

The du Pont Organization

An essential preliminary to our chart presentation is an understanding of the du Pont organization. To facilitate a brief explanation of the oganization, a basic organization chart is shown as Exhibit 1. There are four permanent committees of the board. However, the two committees which are active in executive management are the finance committee and the executive committee, each of nine members. The finance committee meets twice monthly, and the executive committee meets all day each Wednesday, and at any other time necessity dictates. Absences of executive committee members are arranged in such manner that there is always a quorum present in Wilmington.

The president of the company is chairman of the executive committee and the eight other members of that committee are vice-presidents. The executive committee has charge of the operating end of the company's business. In addition to formulating policy as a

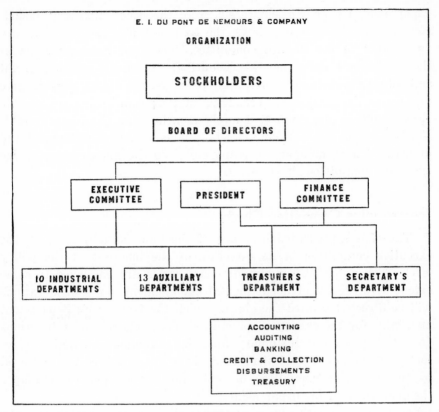

Exhibit 1

committee, its members act individually as advisers in various fields, such as sales, personnel, advertising, etc., but they have no administrative duties in connection with departmental operation and are thus free to devote all their time to policy matters.

There are ten industrial departments, each headed by a general manager who reports to the executive committee. There is also a complement of staff departments, such as legal, purchasing, treasurer's, public relations, etc., servicing the executive committee and the industrial departments. A general manager is responsible, under the executive committee, for the investment and for the manufacture and sale of products assigned to his department in much the same way as though his department were a separate company.

The treasurer's department and the secretary's department may be regarded as auxiliary departments, making 15 auxiliary departments in all. Although the organization chart has been streamlined for this presentation, the treasurer's department and the secretary's

department are shown separately from the other auxiliary departments, since, under our bylaws, the treasurer and the secretary are
responsible to the finance committee. The functional divisions of
the treasurer's department—accounting, auditing, banking, credit
and collection, disbursements, and treasury—are shown also, to give
an idea of the divisional breakdown of the organization responsible
for accounting and finance. I might mention that the treasury division—in which most of our financial analysis work is performed and
of which I am manager—is responsible for the maintenance of the
executive committee chart series.

The Executive Committee Charts

The charts presented here are of the kind actually used by the
executive committee in its direction of the business at the policy
level. Although these or similar chart series are employed to some
extent by all levels of departmental management, our considerations
will be directed toward the charts which the treasurer's department
maintains for the executive committee. These charts and tabulations
do not displace the customary financial statements—whether forecasts, budgets, or historical reports. They are prepared for and used
by the executive committee in reviewing with a general manager
the operations of his department.

Once each month the executive committee reviews charts, the
schedule being so arranged that the charts for each department are
reviewed no less frequently than once every three months. At least
one set or series of charts and tabulations is set up for each department. In some cases the operations of a particular department are
so diverse that it has been found necessary to set up several sets of
charts and tabulations, each set bracketing a portion of the department's activities which it is desired to treat as a separate investment
unit. Thus, for our ten departments, we have 20 separate operating
investment chart series, representing approximately 350 charts. For
each of these series, the results of operations for the current year
are shown against a background of exactly the same data for the ten
preceding years and a forecast for the ensuing 12 months.

Basis of Judgment Is "Return on Investment"

It is our considered opinion, which has been critically reexamined
many times over three decades, that a manufacturing enterprise with

large capital committed to the manufacture and sale of goods can best measure and judge the effectiveness of effort in terms of "return on investment." We, therefore, place primary emphasis upon return on investment and the central theme around which each chart series is built is to bring this end result to the surface and to examine critically the factors which produce return on investment, i.e., *gross profit on sales* and *turnover*. It might be helpful if, at this point, we examine an outline of the formula which is controlling in the chart concept. Such an outline is shown in Exhibit 2. From this formula you will see that we reach the percent return on investment through the factors of earnings as a percent of sales (which is the gross profit margin) and turnover.

The return on investment responds to movement in these two factors. To deemphasize either of them could severely impair the quality of management decisions over a long term. If there has been no change in selling price, an improvement in turnover indicates that capital is being worked harder; i.e., the business is getting increased sales out of the same plant and working capital. Again, if there is no change in selling prices, an improvement in gross profit margin indicates that the cost in proportion to sales dollar is being reduced. In other words, the manager of an operating investment

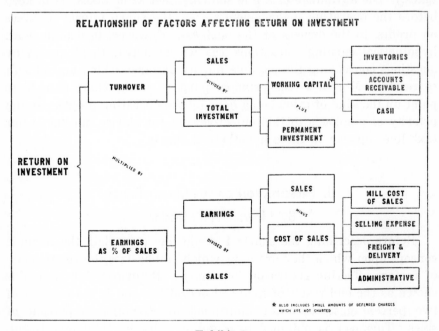

Exhibit 2

can improve his showing by working existing investment harder or by reducing cost, both of which factors or elements are within his control, without encountering the impact of competitive prices, pricing policy or company policy with respect to the use of more capital in a given line.

The figures used in these charts are hypothetical. They do not depict the operating results of any one of du Pont's investments. However, the chart series is complete as to presentment of the basic concept and we have borrowed from actual experiences in deciding upon what trends to present through the medium of these hypothetical figures. We have used our own experience merely as a starting point and, where it was felt that a point could be more forcefully illustrated, have exaggerated the figures in order to accomplish this.

The "% return on investment" and "% profit on sales," which you will see plotted on the charts, were calculated from earnings before the impact of taxes. Where actual situations are involved, it is frequently desirable to add another line which shows the earnings results after taxes. In fact, in the actual use of this chart series in our business, we generally present the earnings picture before and after taxes. (In the current steel wage dispute it has been said with some merit that there is no such thing as corporate profit before taxes.) The advantage of a line showing "net after taxes" is to keep before the operating management's view the sharp impact of taxes on profits, to the owners of the business. However, in dealing with hypothetical earnings situations (as we do here), there are many questions concerning the possible impact of taxes which are difficult to resolve. Moreover, the primary purpose of the chart data is to point up the kind of a job being done by the operating people. Giving priority of emphasis to this objective and for clarity, no "net after tax" lines appear on these hypothetical charts.

II. Presentation of the Chart Series

By Howard L. Hessler

Before describing the charts I would like to explain the formula concept upon which they are built which emphasizes the relationship of factors affecting return on investment. Return on investment is shown as the end result of financial operations and is the product of two percentages: turnover multiplied by earnings as percent of sales. Turnover is obtained by dividing sales by total investment.

Turnover reflects the success or lack of success in working the capital which has been committed to the operation. Earnings as percent of sales, of course, are earnings divided by sales. This percentage reflects the success or lack of success in maintaining cost and selling prices in such relationship as to yield a satisfactory profit margin.

It will be apparent that the usual way of calculating return on investment has not been changed. In these two fractions, sales cancel out, leaving earnings divided by total investment resulting in return on investment. The formula is set up in this manner so that we can single out the effect both of turnover and of earnings as percent of sales, upon return on investment. An analysis of turnover can be made through charts showing sales and total investment. Total investment is broken down into permanent investment and working capital. A further detail of working capital is maintained on charts showing inventories, accounts receivable, and cash. The development of earnings as percent of sales is clearly indicated by the formula. The charts show a breakdown of cost of sales through mill cost of sales, selling expense, freight and delivery, and administrative expenses.

In the use of this formula to bring operating results before the executive committee, we do not build up step-by-step to the ultimate objective of percent return on investment but rather present first the end result and thereafter present the important elements which contribute to this end result. Our first chart, therefore, could well be called the master chart or summary chart of the series because it presents the end result. The three principal percentages, return on investment, turnover, and earnings as percent of sales, which can be used in analyzing the operations of a company or a department, are shown in Chart 1.

Master Chart and Tablulation

Chart 1 shows the end result—percent return on investment and the two important factors contributing to it, percent turnover and percent gross profit margin. Annual data for the ten preceding years are plotted in the left-hand fields by means of a solid black line. The dashed line running across the chart represents the ten years' average.

The current year is also shown in the charts by months in the right-hand fields. The solid black line is "to date" on an annual basis. It must be remembered that our objective is to get a glimpse

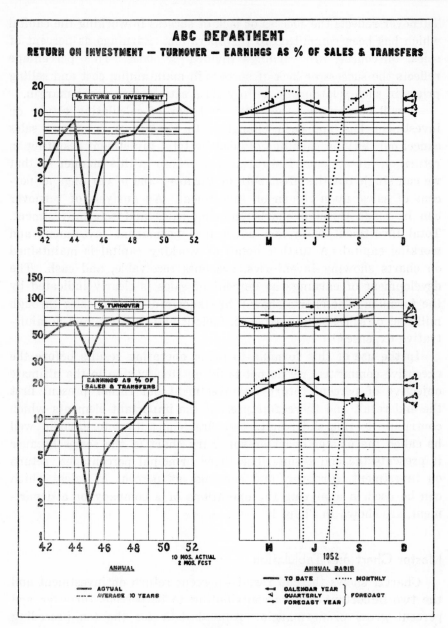

Chart 1

of current performance and anticipated performance, against a background of the past. Therefore, all plottings must be put on an annual basis. The chart, as prepared for illustrative purposes, is based on actual performance for the period from January through October of the year 1952 and, in the upper right-hand field, the end of the solid line on the October ordinate reflects annual percent return on investment based on actual performance to October 31. The dotted line reflects the percent return on investment on an annual basis derived by multiplying each month's actual performance by 12.

The du Pont Company makes four forecasts a year. These are complete forecasts showing sales, cost of sales, earnings and investment, and are disclosed on our charts by means of certain symbols.

The No. 1 forecast is for the period January through December. The anticipated results cast up by this forecast are shown by means of the No. 1 arrow on the December ordinate pointing to the left. The forecast performance for the quarter ended March 31, 1952, put on an annual basis, is indicated by the arrowhead on the March ordinate.

The No. 2 forecast comes out in April for the period from April through March of the following year. The calendar year forecast is now three months actual plus nine months forecast and the new position for this anticipated performance is shown on the December ordinate by means of a No. 2 arrow. The arrowhead on the June ordinate reflects anticipated performance for the six months ended June, 1952, when actual performance for the first quarter plus forecast performance for the quarter ended June 30, 1952, is put on an annual basis. The arrow pointing to the right on the March ordinate presents the forecast performance for the forecast year ended March 31, 1953. This arrow can be placed on the chart immediately after the No. 2 forecast is complete.

The same procedure is followed for our No. 3 and No. 4 forecasts. The No. 3, for the calendar year, consists of six months actual and six months forecast. The No. 4 consists of nine months actual and three months forecast. The arrowhead pointing to the right on the June ordinate reflects the anticipated performance for the 12 months ahead ending June 30, 1953, based on our No. 3 forecast and the arrow on the September ordinate shows anticipated performance per the No. 4 forecast for the forecast year ending September 30, 1953.

Perhaps I should explain the current year ordinate on the ten-year field. This ordinate is placed there primarily for ease in comparing the current year on an annual basis with the ten preceding years. The plotting is also derived from actual plus forecast performance within a calendar year. This chart, prepared shortly after October 31, reflects on the 1952 ordinate ten months actual plus two months most recent forecast and the trend of the latest estimate for the calendar year can be readily compared with that of previous years.

Chart 2 is a typical tabulation of figure data which supports most of the plottings on the previous master line chart (Chart 1). This is the only tabulation shown here, because the figures have no particular significance unless they are shown in connection with the graphic or line chart presentation. In our chart room in Wilmington,

ABC DEPARTMENT
RETURN ON INVESTMENT — TURNOVER — EARNINGS AS % OF SALES & TRANSFERS

TO DATE — ANNUAL BASIS

MOS.	RETURN ON INVESTMENT		TURNOVER		EARNINGS AS % OF SALES & TRANSFERS	
	1951	1952	1951	1952	1951	1952
JAN	9.7	9.6	69.4	66.1	13.9	14.5
FEB	9.8	10.3	70.8	61.7	13.9	16.7
MAR	11.0	11.5	75.5	60.8	14.6	18.9
APR	12.1	13.1	84.5	61.9	14.4	21.1
MAY	12.3	13.8	88.8	62.6	13.8	22.0
JUN	12.1	11.4	85.8	65.1	14.1	17.5
JUL	12.1	10.0	84.2	66.9	14.4	14.9
AUG	12.1	10.0	83.6	68.6	14.4	14.6
SEP	12.3	10.5	85.6	71.4	14.3	14.7
OCT	12.5	11.3	87.5	76.7	14.3	14.7
NOV	12.5		86.0		14.5	
DEC	12.8		83.9		15.2	

ANNUAL

YEARS	RETURN ON INVESTMENT	TURNOVER	EARNINGS AS % OF SALES & TRANSFERS
1942	2.3	46.5	5.0
1943	5.3	58.0	9.1
1944	8.3	65.0	12.7
1945	.7	33.2	2.0
1946	3.4	65.0	5.1
1947	5.5	70.0	7.9
1948	6.0	62.5	9.6
1949	9.8	70.0	14.0
1950	11.9	75.0	15.8
1951	12.8	83.9	15.2
10 YR. AVG.	6 4	62.1	10.3

FORECASTS

FORECAST	RETURN ON INVESTMENT		TURNOVER		EARNINGS AS % OF SALES & TRANSFERS	
	CALENDAR YEAR	FORECAST YEAR	CALENDAR YEAR	FORECAST YEAR	CALENDAR YEAR	FORECAST YEAR
#1	14.2	14.2	72.0	72.0	19.7	19.7
2	14.5	16.3	67.5	75.0	21.5	21.6
3	11.0	13.5	73.0	86.7	15.1	15.8
4	10.8	14.3	73.2	94.8	14.7	15.0

Chart 2

the physical and mechanical arrangement is such that we are able to show a graphic presentation on a right-hand wing and a tabulation of figure data on a left-hand wing at the same time.

Chart of Sales, Transfers—Earnings

Chart 3 shows graphically the basic data for the calculation of earnings as percent of sales shown on the previously displayed mas-

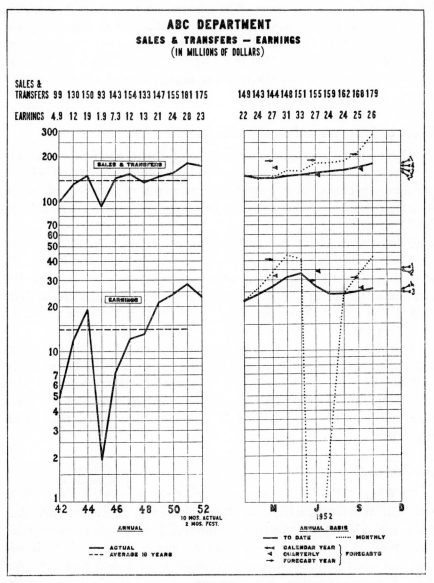

Chart 3

ter line chart and its related tabulation. At the top of Chart 3, sales and earnings are set out in millions of dollars and it is, therefore, unnecessary to present these figures on any other tabulation. Also the basic charting technique is exactly the same as was explained with respect to the master chart. Annual data for the ten preceding years and the latest estimate for the current year are plotted by means of the solid black line. The ten-year average is the dashed line running across the chart. The current year is shown by months. To date on an annual basis is shown by a black line and supported by a tabulation at the top. Each month on an annual basis is presented by means of the dotted line. Notice the calendar year forecast markings, interim quarterly forecast positions, and the forecast 12 months into the future.

Chart of Expenses as Percent of Sales

Chart 4 gives a graphic presentation of the trend of four elements of cost: mill cost, selling expense, freight and delivery, and administrative expenses, each expressed in terms of percent of sales. A summarization of these four elements, when expressed in dollars, would, of course, give cost of sales and the subtraction of cost of sales from sales yields the dollar earnings figures reflected on Chart 3. The trends of expenses as shown on this chart are helpful in analyzing variations in earnings as percent of sales and in the corresponding dollar figures on the sales and earnings chart. The dashed line shows the overall rate of production for each month in order to afford a comparison with mill cost.

It looks as though the production manager of this hypothetical department went wild. First he produced in excess of stated capacity and then he practically shut down the plant. I will try to show later that the production manager was not completely wrong in his planning and that he was justified in following this weird production schedule.

Investment Chart

On Chart 5 the investment position of the particular operation is reflected. When used with Chart 3 showing sales, this chart furnishes the principal factors affecting turnover. The top line shows total investment at cost. Permanent capital consists of plant, both buildings and equipment, land, and any other fixed assets necessary for the particular operation. Working capital consists of allocated cash,

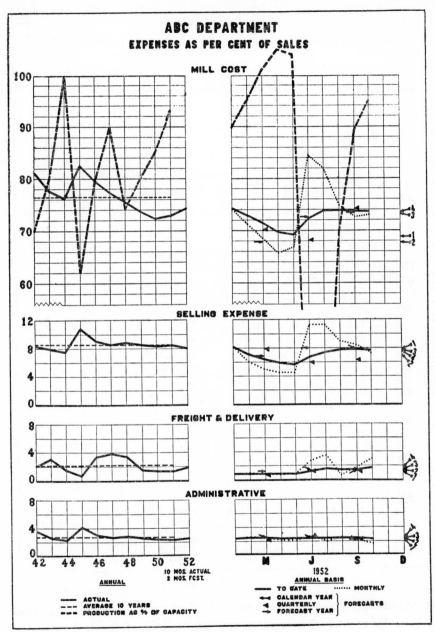

Chart 4

accounts receivable, inventories, and deferred charges. In recent years we have added a dashed line to indicate the dollars of depreciation reserves accumulated against the depreciable permanent investment, because we found it an interesting and helpful factor in think-

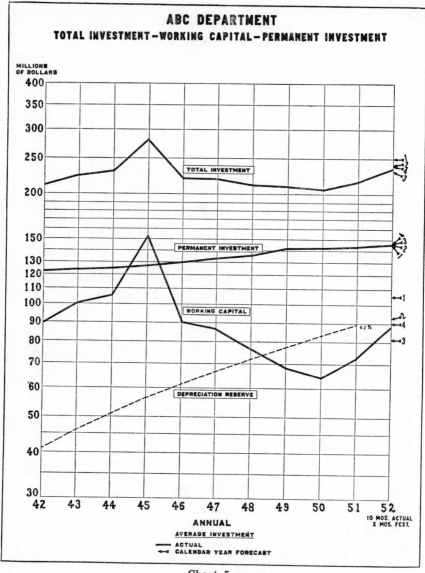

Chart 5

ing about the economic position of a given operation. We also indicate, by means of a small figure at the end of the last calendar year, the ratio of reserve to investment.

Charting Current Assets

An analysis of working capital is shown on the next charts. A change in format takes place in charting working capital on Chart 6.

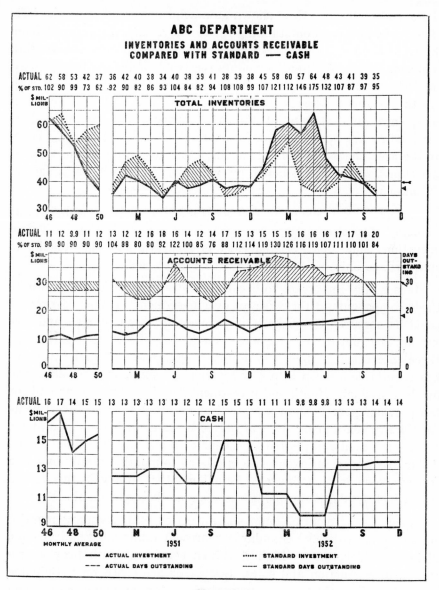

Chart 6

The period charted is contracted to seven years. The solid black line represents actual dollar inventory at the end of the period, supported by tabulation. The dotted line shows what would have been invested in inventory according to inventory standards. On another chart, which deals with the three components of inventory, I will have more to say about inventory standards. Accounts receivable dollar balance at the end of the month is shown as a solid line, read from the left-hand scale, and days outstanding appear as a dashed line, read from the right-hand scale. Accounts receivable standard days outstanding is shown as a dotted line. Accounts receivable standard is expressed as a given number of days' sales outstanding at the end of any month. It reflects terms extended to the trade and our collection experience. In the case of the ABC Department, standard days outstanding are 30. Actual days outstanding under standard, shown by the area shaded by left diagonals, indicates better than expected collections. The area shaded by right diagonals shows a lag in collections.

Another slight change in format is made in plotting cash. In our company, for chart purposes, cash is allocated to the individual operations and this allocated cash is regarded as both actual and standard, so only one line is required to plot cash.

It is highly important to break the inventory position up into its three components. Otherwise an overinvestment in finished product could be obscured by an underinvestment in raw material, and vice versa. The plotting of the actual dollar investment in each of the three categories of inventory is given by Chart 7. Total inventory has been broken down into raw materials, semifinished product, and finished product. Month end investment for the current year and for the previous year is shown, as well as monthly average investments for the five years prior. End of period investment is tabulated at the top of each field and plotted by means of the solid black line. Actual dollar investment in inventories is related to months' supply by using forecast consumption figures. Actual months' supply is the dashed line, which is plotted by using the scale at the right on the chart.

Adequacy of months' supply is measured with standard months' supply as a yardstick. Standards represent minimum requirements, giving consideration to highest return consistent with proper protection to production and sales. Standards are based on anticipated conditions of procurement, transportation, storage, manufacture, and sale, for a year ahead. Allowance is made for adverse conditions not subject to management control but which can reasonably be expected throughout the year. Inventory standards expressed in terms of months' supply represent the number of months' supply of materials that should be invested in inventory at the end of any month in order to provide for estimated consumption based on forecast volume of business. Standard months' supply is shown by means of a dotted

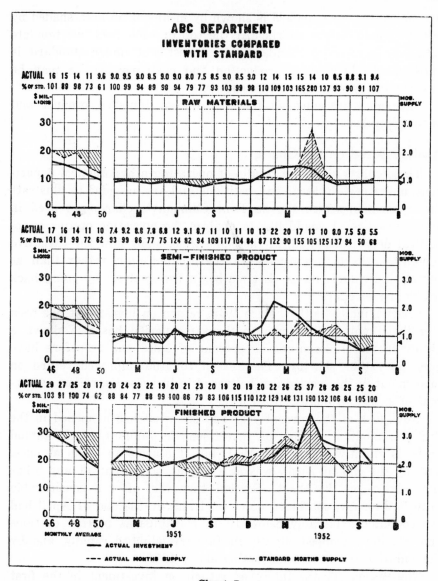

Chart 7

line running across the chart. In the case of the hypothetical ABC Department, standard months' supply is one month for raw materials.

It should be recognized that inventory in excess of standard represents an investment which, to the extent of such excess, decreases turnover and therefore return on investment. There is also the possibility of inventory losses. A condition over standard is shown on the charts by means of an area shaded by right diagonals.

A condition under standard is shown by means of an area shaded by left diagonals on the charts. At the top of each field, we tabulate actual as percent of standard. An investment under standard is undesirable, since plant production and customer service may be interrupted by shortage of inventory.

The same procedure is followed for semifinished product and finished product.

Analysis Based on the Charts

These charts show the results of operating a hypothetical department under certain assumed conditions and are intended to illustrate the manner in which the du Pont Company's charts are used in actual practice. I would like to analyze the operation of this hypothetical department and, at the same time, show how the executive committee charts are used as a coordinated unit, rather than as several individual charts. Let me begin the analysis by going back to the master chart.

Chart 1 indicates that, since 1948, return on investment has been steadily climbing. Turnover in the same period has also shown a steady increase. Earnings as percent of sales and transfers have gone up rather sharply. The reason for the improved return on investment in this period can be traced to increased earnings as percent of sales and increased turnover.

Now, look at the current year and see what has happened in the first few months. Return on investment in January, on an annual basis, is slightly lower than 1951, but it started to climb at once, and, by the end of April, was at a higher point than at any other time shown on the chart. Percent turnover, after a considerable drop in January, continued downward and by the end of April had leveled out considerably below 1951. Earnings as percent of sales and transfers dropped slightly in January, climbed rapidly, and by the end of April were considerably above 1951.

The reason for the improved return on investment in the first four months of 1952 can be traced to increased earnings as percent of sales and transfers, partly offset by decreased turnover. If turnover had not dropped, return on investment would have been even higher than it was in April.

Let us assume that 1951 represents a normal operating year for this department, so we are anxious to determine why the 1952 profit margin is considerably higher than in 1951 and why turnover is lower. We can determine this by referring to the other charts.

Chart 3 shows that sales and transfers in 1951 were $181,000,000. On an annual basis, January was considerably below that level and continued downward over the early months of 1952. By the end of April, sales were about $148,000,000, considerably below 1951. Also, the forecast for the first quarter was missed by a wide margin (the arrowhead pointing to the left on the March ordinate represents the forecast). You will recall from the description of the formula that turnover is the result of sales divided by investment. A tabulation of month end investment, which is not given here, would show that total investment increased during the first four months of 1952. The combination of decreased sales and higher investment results in decreased turnover.

Further analysis of total investment would show that permanent investment has changed very little, and that all of the increase has been in working capital, which is shown on Chart 6. Total inventory increased from $38,000,000 at the beginning of the year to a peak in March, and then dropped off to $57,000,000 in April, at which time it was 146 percent of standard. Accounts receivable, despite reduced sales, increased from about $13,000,000 to about $16,000,000 at which point it was 116 percent of standard. Cash in the same period declined about $5,000,000 but it was not enough to offset the increase in the accounts receivable and inventory.

This completes our analysis of turnover and we conclude that increased working capital and lower sales account for decreased turnover. Now let us determine why earnings as percent of sales increased. Chart 3 shows that in 1951 earnings were $28,000,000. In January, on an annual basis, they showed a decline but then steadily improved and by April they were $31,000,000. By analyzing the cost of sales, we can determine why earnings improved despite a drop in sales volume.

A glance at Chart 4 shows that mill cost as percent of sales declined. The charts show what happened—but they do not tell why. Investigation of lower mill cost revealed it was because of lower unit costs resulting from a high rate of production in the first four months. High production in spite of declining sales is explained by production based on forecast sales which did not materialize. The production manager was justified in his production schedule because he was guided by the sales forecast which called for high volume in the first quarter. Rapidly decreasing selling expense was investigated and it was found that the reasons were a reduction in the sales force and curtailed advertising. We have now determined that the increase in earnings shown on Chart 2 was due to lower mill cost and selling expenses.

Let me summarize the operations of this hypothetical department by referring once more to Exhibit 2. At the end of April, 1952, return on investment was higher than for 1951. This was the result of increased earnings as percent of sales, partly offset by decreased turnover. Decreased turnover was caused by lower sales and higher total investment. Analysis revealed that this was due to higher working capital which, in turn, was caused by increased inventories and accounts receivable. The increase in earnings as percent of sales and transfers was caused by higher earnings which resulted from lower mill cost and selling expense as percent of sales.

The Management Action Stage

It is apparent from the foregoing analysis that the hypothetical ABC Department had a definite inventory problem which might have become serious had current trends continued. Let us assume that the management of this hypothetical department took steps in May to correct the abnormal operating conditions reflected on the charts, that management decided to process as much inventory as possible that month and in June to curtail production to a minimum. You remember how the production-as-percent-of-capacity line showed a sharp downward plunge in June. This shutdown caused an immediate increase in unit mill cost and a sharp drop in earnings. A rapid expansion of sales effort produced added sales volume but increased selling expense. During the period of adjustment, management also brought working capital in line with standards.

I will not in this presentation trace the effects of corrective action in all the charts, but I will point out the changes that took place in the three all-important percentages shown in Chart 1. Earnings as percent of sales declined during the period of adjustment but, by the end of October, they had leveled out to a more normal position in keeping with 1951. Turnover steadily improved with higher sales and decreased working capital to a good position in line with past years. Return on investment, after a decline, started to rise and by the end of October was approaching the more normal 1951 levels.

A True Reflection of Practice

The series of charts presented here is in all respects similar to graphic presentations used by the du Pont executive committee as a tool in the management of the business from the top level. I hope this presentation has been sufficiently clear to let you see how these charts have actually been used and even to suggest some broader use than we have yet developed.

III. Concluding Remarks

By C. A. Kline, Jr.

If you have concluded that there is nothing new in these charts, you are right. Our chart series and tabulations present nothing which cannot be portrayed in a score of ways, and perhaps with even greater clarity. So, not by way of defense but, rather, by way of explanation, I want to call your attention to several points which in our opinion give special merit and appeal to this particular method of presenting the financial results of operations.

First, repeating what I have said before, we are convinced that "% return on investment" is the proper measure of effectiveness of the employment of capital and we believe with equal force that this end result should be presented against a background which emphasizes "turnover" and "gross profit margin."

Second, you will note that the charts do not utilize narrative explanation. There is no opportunity for one reviewing the figures to bog down under the weight of particular words or phrases which may be chosen to explain a given variation in operating results. In the course of presenting the charts to our executive committee, the chart supervisor is always prepared to answer questions or even to propose an answer without question, given the background reasons for sharp variations in current data against the past or against forecasts. However, the primary purpose of reviewing data presented on the charts is to point up the places where further analysis, review, and attention may be desirable or necessary. The charts are intended to show what happened or is anticipated in terms of profit return on investment, and to put the finger on the broad underlying factors which caused the results to be what they were, or are expected to be. This identification of broad factors leading to a particular result enables the executive committee to raise questions with a general manager regarding possible trouble spots and, of course, this frequently leads to further analysis and presentation of underlying facts. The charts stimulate inquiry but do not supply answers, except to indicate cause and effect within the framework of the broad

factors contributing to "% return on investment." This chart series
was inaugurated more than 30 years ago—in 1919, to be exact. We
consider it a tribute to the foresight of those who designed and
installed it that, whereas the format has been changed and perhaps
improved several times, the basic concept which emphasizes return
on investment, supported by the factors contributing to it, has not
given way to any other.

Third, note may be taken of the comparative ease with which the
attention of an entire group can be held to one item at the same
moment. I imagine most of us have had some experience in analyzing
schedules, tabulations, charts, and the like, with a group of men, each
of whom has the data in hand, on a table or elsewhere, and have had
to deal with the perplexing problem presented by the proneness of
each individual comprising the group to pursue his own analysis in
his own way. The manner in which we use these charts minimizes
this problem. You can be pretty well assured that each member of
the group is giving attention to the same item at the same time.

Fourth, more or less rigid rules govern the assembly of data for
the presentation. To the maximum extent possible, the data for all
periods shown on the charts are on a uniform basis and afford common measurements of performance for all investment lines. If we
find that changing conditions require a new approach to presenting
any one or more of the chart series, then all the data for the current
year and the ten preceding years are reset on the new basis. We
all know the loss of confidence in financial presentations that can be
experienced when those using the data are able to allege, and perhaps
to show, that a lack of uniformity or comparability has destroyed
their value. To a very large extent, we avoid that pitfall by keeping
our charts comparable throughout.

Fifth, strict adherence to format is observed until such time as
it becomes clear that a change would substantially improve the
presentation. Then a new format is brought into use, complete at
one time, including a reset for the entire ten-year period. Admittedly, this means slow progress at times in improvement of format,
because a helpful minor change brought to light by experience must
be held on the shelf until an important change or an aggregate
of minor changes makes it worthwhile to modify the whole format.

Sixth, the executive committee, for whose use these charts are
primarily maintained, makes the rules governing the division of
lines of business into chart series and the classification of financial

data into the several items which are set forth in the presentation. To be sure, the executive committee requests and receives the recommendations of the treasurer which are developed in full collaboration with operating people but, in the final analysis, it is the committee's decision which is final, after full consideration of all the pros and cons presented by the treasurer. This approach to data presentation, i.e., by rules decided on by the executive management group—the group by which the data are to be used—serves to remove a potentially wide area for possible disagreement on the classification of the basic data to be presented. Disagreement in these matters dissipates energies and dilutes the value-in-use of internal financial reporting. We are disposed to think our approach to this phase of the problem goes a long way toward getting the maximum value out of presentation of the financial results of our operations.

Calculation of Return on Investment

You will note that in this chart series we calculate the return on investment on the amount invested in plant and working capital rather than on stockholder invested capital. Calculations based on stockholder invested capital would require the deduction of reserves and liabilities from the cost of plant and working capital. The general managers of the company are responsible for the production and sale of the products assigned to them, and for the necessary investment in plant facilities and working capital. The charts are uniform and are designed to afford a comparison of past and current performance for the same operating investment, as well as a comparison with the performance of other operating investments made in corresponding periods.

In this chart series, we are seeking a clear portrayal of the profitableness of the employment of plant property and working capital at the operating level. Funds provided by reserves and liabilities are invested for varying periods of time in different operating properties upon each of which a profit must be earned if a business is to be successful, but these funds are not reflected in stockholder invested capital. A deduction for liabilities and reserves from the amount invested in operating properties would show a fluctuation in operating investment due to growth of reserves and change in amount of liabilities or stockholder capital, which, in turn, would produce such a distortion in the return on investment as to

render meaningless the very figures intended to disclose the profitableness of employment of plant property and working capital.

Said another way, we seek to cast up as clearly as possible the
results produced by operating management. The capital, liability,
and reserve position of an enterprise is largely a reflection of the
philosophy of financial management as to how the business should
be financed. Operating management must turn in a profit on capital
assigned to that management, regardless of how that capital was
raised, if the business is to prosper. Under this concept, capital for
plant is assigned and entrusted to a general manager until formal
authority relieves him from accountability because of sale, dis-
mantlement, or transfer. In a similar manner the assignment of
working capital operates through "standards." It is these "assigned
investments" or the "dollars committed to the particular enterprise,"
against which the profit performance must be judged, in our opinion,
to render "% return on investment" a meaningful and useful management tool.

It is entirely proper, in some instances and under some conditions,
to measure corporate entity profit performance against stockholder
invested capital, and we do it ourselves for many purposes. But it
would not serve our purpose in the chart series. I am sure all must
agree, upon brief reflection, that for all purposes of securing an
indication of the profitableness of dollars devoted to plant and working capital—which dollars must at some time be returned intact to
the corporate entity—the dollar profits made during each and every
period of the use of the property must be related to the total dollars
dedicated to the particular operation.

What about "Economic Profit"?

At this point I might say that we have had under study for some
time the desirability and validity of a supplementary profit measurement calculated on "replacement value of the investment," particularly plant. This would, I think, be called measurement in terms of
"economic profit" in contrast with "monetary profit." We have made
some trial runs but are not yet fully satisfied that the end results
are good enough to stand up against criticism and attack. The difficulties are, as you know:

1. What is a fair estimate of replacement cost or value of plant?
2. What depreciation provision would be proper if plant had been constructed on today's know-how and today's cost?
3. The cost of production in such plant.

4. The price level for our goods in an economy which generally dealt with "economic profit" rather than "monetary profit."
5. The company's tax picture if the whole economy were on an "economic profit" basis.

Construction of the Charts

The charts and tabulations which we show to our executive committee in Wilmington are hand-drawn on cardboard measuring 30 by 40 inches. The letters, numerals, and arrows are purchased from a supplier of such items. They come coated with an adhesive and are pasted on the boards by our chart clerks. Each chart or tabulation is mounted in a metal frame suspended on wheels so that it can be moved from one place to another in the chart room on specially designed and constructed overhead track. The network of track is so arranged that, in a matter of seconds, any series of charts can be brought to the central display point for review.

We are aware that presentation of this type of data is, more and more, being made by means of projection on a screen. The projection method enjoys some flexibility over our method, but we have not yet found that a clear visual presentation of our charts can be obtained by projection in the physical setup presently at our disposal. In addition, we find that the preparation of material for screen projection requires time, skills, and processing equipment which we are not yet prepared to devote to it. There has been some improvement in projection equipment and methods since the end of the war and, no doubt, still further improvements are in the offing. We do not intend to lag behind where progress is being made and it is entirely possible that we shall at some future date abandon the hand-drawn charts conveyed on overhead track in favor of some projection method.

Conclusion

In closing, permit me to say that effective internal reporting is quite as important to a business organization as good external reporting. Therefore, we who are charged with varying degrees of responsibility for the financial and accounting matters of our respective companies must remain alert, must continue in our determination to find and employ the most effective means of presenting financial data to executive management. That is the basic purpose to be served by our use of a chart series. I hope you see something in it of constructive value.